Practical Electrocardiography

SEVENTH EDITION

"For he who'd make his fellow-creatures wise
Should always gild the philosophic pill."

W. S. GILBERT

Practical

SEVENTH EDITION

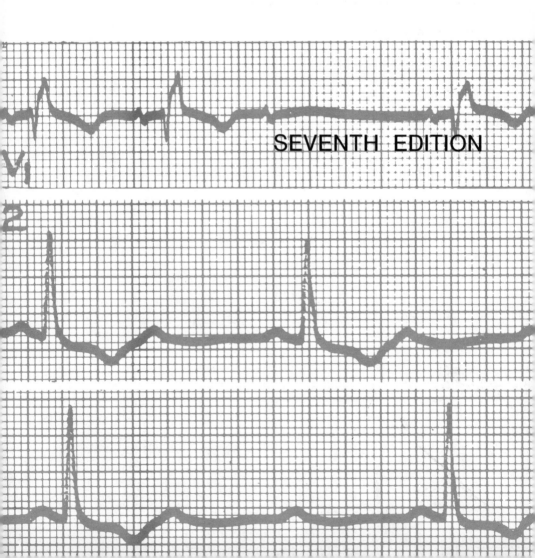

Electrocardiography

Henry J. L. Marriott, M.D.,
F.A.C.P., F.A.C.C.

Director of Clinical Research, Rogers Heart Foundation, St. Petersburg, Florida; Director of Electrocardiograph Department, St. Anthony's Hospital, St. Petersburg, Florida; Clinical Professor of Medicine (Cardiology), Emory University School of Medicine, Atlanta, Georgia; Clinical Professor of Pediatrics (Cardiology), University of Florida, Gainesville, Florida

WILLIAMS & WILKINS
Baltimore • London • Los Angeles • Sydney

Copyright ©, 1983
Williams & Wilkins
428 E. Preston Street
Baltimore, Md. 21202

Made in United States of America

First Edition, 1954

Second Edition, 1957

Third Edition, 1962

Fourth Edition, 1968

Fifth Edition, 1972

Sixth Edition, 1977

Library of Congress Cataloging in Publication Data

Marriott, Henry Joseph Llewellyn, 1917–
  Practical electrocardiography.

  Includes index.
  1. Electrocardiography. I. Title. [DNLM: 1. Electrocardiography. WG 140 M359p]

RC683.5.E5M3 1983   616.1'207547   82-11170
ISBN 0-683-05574-7   AACR2

Composed and printed at the
Waverly Press, Inc.   87 88 89   10 9 8 7 6

TO

Jonni

Who "sat like patience on a monument
Smiling"—and shaping unsubmissive pages!

Preface to the Seventh Edition

At about the time the first edition of this book appeared, electrocardiography as a subject for profitable progress and investigation was widely regarded as "dead." Developments since then indicate that this prophecy of doom represented a gross misjudgment. Far from suffering a decline, electrocardiography has enjoyed robust health and has increasingly flourished.

The advent of various forms of constant or intermittent monitoring (including coronary care, telemetry, Holter and transtelephonic), the development of His-bundle recordings and the great advances made in electrophysiological investigation, the phenomenal progress in the technology of pacemakers and the refinements and experience in exercise testing, each in their several ways, because of their fundamental dependence on electrocardiography, has made a signal contribution to its growing importance.

This edition has been extensively rewritten and expanded. In place of the 21 chapters in the Sixth Edition, there are now 30. The chapters on the hemiblocks, supraventricular tachycardia, preexcitation, escape and dissociation, A-V block (two chapters) and artificial pacemakers have been entirely rewritten and expanded. Also, in this edition, the following topics which were but sections of chapters in the previous edition have been accorded a chapter to themselves: systematic approach to diagnosis of arrhythmias; extrasystoles; supraventricular tachycardia; atrial flutter; atrial fibrillation; ventricular tachycardia; accelerated idioventricular rhythm and parasystole; fusion beats; junctional rhythms; sinus rhythms and the sick sinus; the growing pains of A-V block; and the effects of digitalis and quinidine on the electrocardiogram.

Major additions and revisions have been made in the chapters on bundle-branch block, aberrant ventricular conduction, coronary insufficiency and related matters—including a greatly expanded section on exercise testing.

Other significant additions include material on XYZ leads, the QT interval, U waves, electrical axis, chamber enlargement, Holter monitoring, transtele-phonic monitoring, incidence of arrhythmias and blocks in normal populations, ladder diagrams, sick sinus syndromes, myocardial infarction, coronary mimicry, cor pulmonale, pericardial disease, hypokalemia and hypertrophic cardio-myopathy.

Approximately 500 new references have been included and the illustrations—probably the most important part of any book on electrocardiography—now number almost 500, including more than 150 new ones. As before, review tracings after each of the last 20 chapters serve as a cursory refresher course.

In all of this extensive revision and expansion, I have drawn freely from the text and illustrations of my CME course, *Contemporary Electrocardiography*, published by the Williams & Wilkins Company in 1980.

The index has again received a special measure of tender loving care in this edition. It has been meticulously prepared by Mary Conover (bless her heart!) and all the leading words are NOUNS, since this makes one's search easier, quicker and more logical. For example, you do not have to wonder whether you will find "atrial tachycardia" under "Atrial" or under "Tachycardia" since you know in advance that it will be indexed only under the noun, "Tachycardia."

Aphorisms have always been helpful in teaching and learning because, as Osler picturesquely put it, they are "burrs that stick in the memory." I have therefore again inserted at strategic points in the text several homespun epi-grams that have seemed helpful, and these are appropriately tagged with**.

The aims and scope of this book are unchanged and simplicity remains the central theme. The text is designed to be digestible for beginners, yet it contains a wealth of material of potentially great value to the more sophisticated reader. Once again the publishers have graciously given me a free and unconventional hand in arranging the layout of pages so that I have been able to place illustrations and descriptive text in as convenient proximity as possible.

H.J.L.M.

Preface to the First Edition

Books on electrocardiography seem to possess one or more of several disadvantages for the beginner: the introductory chapters on electrophysiology are so intricate and longwinded that the reader's interest is early drowned in a troubled sea of vectors, axes and gradients; or only certain aspects of the subject are dealt with, for example, the arrhythmias may be entirely omitted; or illustrations are deficient and frequently situated uncomfortably far from the descriptive text.

For several years I have been attempting to introduce fourth year students to the comparatively easy technique of interpreting electrocardiograms. During this period I have been unable to recommend any single text that deals with the subject quickly and simply and yet is sufficiently comprehensive. This book is an attempt to supply such a manual. Its aims are: (1) to emphasize the simplicities rather than the complexities of the electrocardiogram; (2) to give the reader only those electrophysiologic concepts that make everyday interpretation more intelligible without burdening him with unnecessary detail; (3) to cover all diagnostically important electrocardiographic patterns; and (4) to provide adequate illustrations and in every instance to have the illustration conveniently situated to the reader as he reads the descriptive text. To achieve this last desideratum, the publishers have generously waived publishing conventions and given me a free hand in the arrangement and spacing of illustrations and text.

This book is designed for those approaching electrocardiography from the point of view of the clinician. It is hoped that it will enable the beginner to acquire a rapid but thorough grasp of a sophisticated yet simple discipline.

H.J.L.M.

Acknowledgments

It is a great pleasure to acknowledge my indebtedness:

To Mary Conover for again volunteering to prepare the index and doing it with cheerful, accurate zeal.

To Marcie Etheridge Perry and Raymond Rochkind for their excellent line drawings; to Dr. William Schuman for coining the mot juste, electrocardiographogenic; to Dr. Carrol Moody for improving my approach to the electrical axis.

To the following colleagues for graciously providing me with illustrative tracings: Dr. L. E. Bilodeau for figure 22.2, Dr. Harold H. Bix for figure 23.17, Dr. Diego Bognolo for figure 25.15, Dr. Joseph Bowen for figure 22.3, Dr. Richard Cuthbert for figure 24.3, Dr. William Everett for figure 18.14, Dr. Morris Fulton for figure 29.5, Dr. Martin Grais for figure 8.4, Dr. Emory Hollar for figure 23.18, Dr. Leonard Leight for figure 25.13, Dr. Alan Lindsay for figure 8.9, Dr. Robert Mahon for figure 27.10, Dr. Nathan Marcus for figure 28.14, Dr. Pierre Nizet for figure 10.14, Dr. Breffni O'Neill for figure 29.3, Dr. Jack Pyhel for figure 18.16, Dr. Thomas Ross for figure 16.4*A*, Dr. Leo Schamroth for figures 17.19 and 23.15, Dr. Victor Schulze for figure RT-30.1, Dr. Roger Sutton for figure 18.10, and Dr. Edward Swanick for figure 27.9.

To the electrocardiograph departments of the Mercy Hospital in Baltimore, the Tampa General Hospital and St. Anthony's Hospital in St. Petersburg as the sources of most of the remaining tracings; and especially to technicians—past and present—for their interest and zeal in capturing good records of arrhythmias.

To innumerable students and many colleagues and nurses who have stimulated me with encouragement or criticism.

To the publishers, whose gracious cooperation has now been patient and unfailing through seven gestations.

H.J.L.M.

Contents

Introductory Note

Much of electrocardiography is simple, but it does not always provide a clear-cut answer. Our knowledge of the electrocardiogram has definite limitations which must be appreciated. In the arrhythmias and blocks it often gives a clear and irrefutable answer, but with myocardial disease there is much less specificity. Every interpreter, no matter how experienced, encounters tracings he cannot unravel. Not infrequently a tracing is "borderline" or "abnormal but nonspecific" and must be classified as such—an unsatisfying situation for both the interpreter and the patient's physician, yet one which should be frankly and humbly faced.

Profession and laity alike are inclined to lay too much stress on mechanical devices in diagnosis. The electrocardiograph is no exception. A patient with a normal tracing may unexpectedly drop dead of a coronary attack, while another, with a grossly abnormal tracing, may live on without cardiac symptoms for many years.

The electrocardiogram should always be read in the clearest light of clinical observation. All pertinent data should be in the hands of the interpreter. Ideally the clinician in charge of the patient reads his own tracings; failing this he should see to it that his interpreting colleague is furnished with full details, including his own clinical impression, for only so will he and his patient derive maximal benefit from expert interpretation.

As electrocardiographic interpretation and clinical observation are, or should be, inseparable, a few clinical notes of practical diagnostic value are included in this primarily electrocardiographic text.

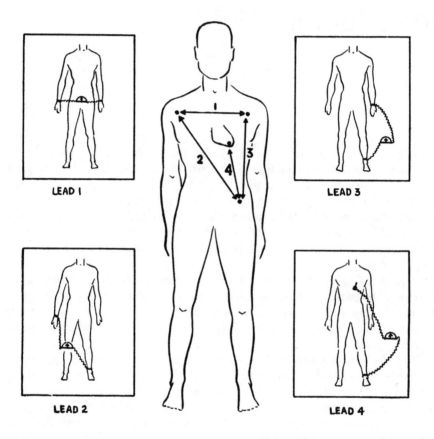

Figure 1.1. The standard limb leads and the original precordial lead. *Caution:* The double-headed arrows in the diagram are not intended to represent Einthoven's triangle.

1

Electrodes and Leads

Contraction of the heart's muscle is the dynamo that powers life; and the spark that initiates that contraction is an infinitesimal electrical current that is generated and discharged by the sinus node. Small as this current is, it can be recorded from the surface of the body as it traverses the cardiac muscle. The machine that records it is the electrocardiograph and the recording is the electrocardiogram (ECG).

To make a recording, it is necessary to complete an electrical circuit between the heart and the electrocardiograph. To this end, electrodes are placed at two (or more) sites on the body and, as the sites vary, so does the "view" of the heart's electrical impulse. Each different "view," derived as it is from the varying placement of the recording electrodes, is known as a "lead."

Standard Limb Leads

These are three in number and have been in use for 80 years. We therefore have had a far longer acquaintance with these than the numerous additional leads more recently introduced. Probably 80 to 90% accuracy in diagnosis can be achieved by inspecting these leads alone. Many arrhythmias and most types of heart block are easily diagnosed from them.

The connections of these leads are illustrated in figure 1.1. Lead 1 connects the two arms; lead 3 connects the left arm with the left leg; and lead 2, the hypotenuse of the triangle, connects the right arm with the left leg. Each lead records the difference in potential between the two connected limbs. Although the electrodes are attached at wrists and ankle, this is purely a matter of convenience—it is easiest to attach bracelets to those parts of the limbs. It is more accurate to think of the potential as derived from the roots of the respective limbs, i.e., from the two shoulders and the left groin. The heart is approximately in the center of the triangle so formed (fig. 1.1).

It is worth noting **Einthoven's law**, which states, in effect, that a complex in lead 2 is equal to the sum of the corresponding complexes in leads 1 and 3 (2 = 1 + 3). This is a helpful rule to remember when the technician has wrongly

1

labelled the leads. For example, if the P wave is seen to be upright in all three leads, you know at a glance that the lead with the tallest P is lead 2.

Precordial Leads

The standard limb leads have two disadvantages: (1) each is derived from *two* points *distant* from the heart and (2) the three electrodes are all in the same plane, i.e., the frontal plane of the body. It is not surprising that we can gain additional information by placing electrodes closer to the heart and moving them round the bend of the thorax to obtain "views" of the heart from different angles. The first precordial or chest lead, introduced in 1932, connected the left leg with the apex beat and was called lead 4 (fig. 1.1). This was a successful innovation and soon a series of precordial points was introduced whose positions are illustrated in figure 1.2. Point 1 is just to the right of the sternum in the fourth interspace; point 2, just to the left of the sternum in the fourth interspace. Point 4 lies in the midclavicular line in the fifth interspace. Point 3 is halfway between 2 and 4. Points 5, 6 and 7 are at the same level as 4 in the anterior, middle and posterior axillary lines, respectively.

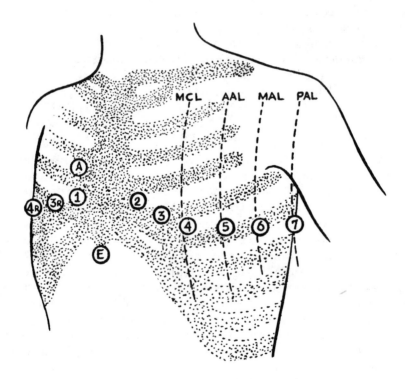

Figure 1.2. Precordial points from which chest leads are derived.

Most cardiologists employ precordial positions from 1 to 6 routinely. Sometimes it is desirable to take additional leads from further points; some of these are also illustrated in figure 1.2. Point E is situated over the ensiform process. The atrial lead point (A) is just to the right of the sternum in the third interspace. The locations of further right precordial points, 3_R, 4_R, etc., correspond with the locations of their opposite numbers on the left side of the chest. Occasionally it is desirable to take leads from the posterior thorax; points 8 and 9 are at the angle of the scapula and over the spine, at the same level as 4, 5, 6 and 7. At times, especially for the purpose of unravelling difficult arrhythmias, it may be useful to obtain a tracing from behind the left atrium by means of an esophageal electrode[2, 5, 8, 9]; or from the cavity of the right atrium by means of a transvenous wire electrode.[11]

In a standard lead the two electrodes are about equally remote from the heart and each is therefore about equally important in its contribution to the tracing. When, however, one electrode is placed in one of the precordial positions while the other electrode is on a limb, it is natural that the closer chest electrode should contribute more to the tracing, and the limb electrode less. The limb attachment of such a lead is therefore called the **indifferent electrode** and the chest electrode is referred to as the **exploring electrode**, since it is moved in an exploratory fashion from point to point across the chest. If the indifferent electrode is attached to the left leg, the connection is designated CF; if to the right arm CR; if to the left arm CL. According to the precordial point employed, a subscribed number is added to the CF, CR, or CL label. Thus, for example, lead CF_5 indicates that the exploring electrode is placed at point 5 in the anterior axillary line while the indifferent electrode is attached to the left ankle. The "MCL" leads, which have become popular for monitoring, are modifications of the CL hookup.

V Leads

Though the exploring electrode exerts a far greater influence on the tracing than the indifferent electrode, the indifferent electrode nevertheless has considerable influence. It was discovered empirically, however, that if all three limb electrodes were connected, through resistances of 5000 ohms each, to form a common **central terminal**, this afforded a more truly indifferent connection—the potential at such a central terminal was practically zero throughout the cardiac cycle. Thus, theoretically at any rate, such a connection leaves the exploring electrode as sole dictator of the pattern. The hookup of the V leads is diagrammatically shown in figure 1.3.

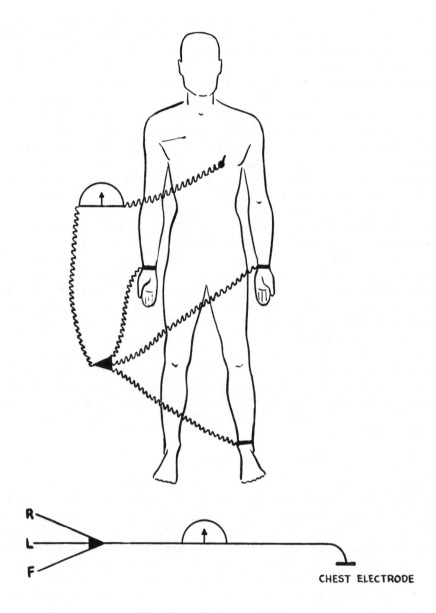

Figure 1.3. The hookup for V leads.

Although theoretically the V lead connections should given the most reliable precordial pattern, in practice it is not so certain that they always do[4]; and at least one authority[6,7] insisted that the CR connection was the most satisfactory. At any rate, it is worth appreciating the expected differences between the various precordial connections. These may best be summarized by stating that the CR leads tend to emphasize positive (upright) deflections, while the CF leads lend emphasis to negative (downward). The pattern of V leads usually lies somewhere in between. It may sometimes be useful to take advantage of the "emphasizing" tendencies of the CR and CF connections, rather than to rely slavishly on the V leads because they are theoretically superior. Such employment of the CR or CF leads may be likened to the use of a magnifying glass to detect otherwise invisible or questionable changes. CL connections found little favor or use until a modified CL ("MCL") hookup came into its own for the constant monitoring of patients in coronary care units (see Chapter 9).

aV Leads

The standard limb leads are strictly **bipolar**, representing as they do the difference in potential between two points. CF, CR and CL leads are also clearly bipolar, in that they too record the difference in potential between two points. In the standard leads the two points involved exert approximately equal influences, whereas in the C leads, as stated above, the precordial point is more influential than the more distant limb connection. With the V leads comes the virtual exclusion of this distant influence because the central terminal shows practically zero potential throughout the heart cycle. They are therefore referred to as **unipolar** precordial leads. From this development it is only a short step to the unipolar *limb* leads. By using the central terminal as the indifferent connection and placing the exploring electrode on one limb, the resulting tracing might well be expected to record the potential at the root of the "explored" limb exclusively. Such leads are labeled VR, VL and VF according to the limb with which the exploring electrode is connected. The connections of VF are diagrammatically shown in figure 1.4*A*. The deflections in such a lead are small; but the amplitude of complexes in such leads can be materially increased by disconnecting the central terminal attachment to the explored limb (fig. 1.4*B*). This device increases the size of the deflections (thus making them more readable) without significantly altering their shape. This *augmentation* of potential is designated by a prefixed "a"—aVR, aVL, aVF.

Relation of Bipolar to Unipolar Limb Leads

In a sense, the unipolar limb leads are the algebraic bricks of which the bipolar leads are built. Lead 1 represents the difference between aVR and aVL; lead 2 the difference between aVR and aVF; and lead 3 between aVL and aVF.

Now, quite arbitrarily, as originally ordained by Einthoven, the polarity of the electrodes is arranged as in figure 1.5 (Einthoven's triangle). F is positive in relation to R in lead 2 and relative to L in lead 3; while in lead 1 L is positive in relation to R. In other words, F is always relatively positive and R is always relatively negative, while L is variable as between leads 1 and 3. The relation-

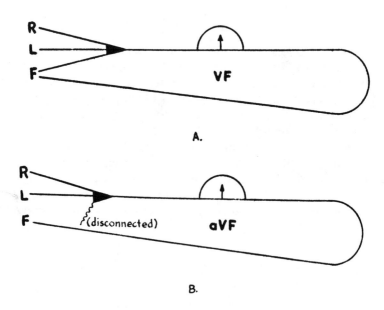

Figure 1.4. (*A*) The hookup for lead VF. (*B*) The hookup for augmented VF (aVF).

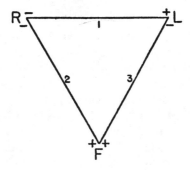

Figure 1.5. Polarity of electrodes in the standard leads.

ships between the bipolar and unipolar limb leads can thus be summarized in the following equations:

$$\text{Lead } 1 = a\text{VL} - a\text{VR}$$
$$\text{Lead } 2 = a\text{VF} - a\text{VR}$$
$$\text{Lead } 3 = a\text{VF} - a\text{VL}$$

The information available from the six limb leads can be deduced from any two of them. In theory, therefore, it is only necessary to take two of the limb leads, but in practice it is valuable to acquire a working knowledge of all six. If only two leads are taken, the most suitable and informative pair are 1 and aVF.[10]

XYZ Leads

With the increased popularity of three-channel ECG machines, leads X, Y and Z are frequently encountered and it is necessary to know their derivation and significance.[1] Lead X has its positive electrode in the left axilla with its negative electrode in the right axilla; it therefore recognizes right-to-left, and left-to-right forces and records them as positive and negative deflections respectively. The scalar mind may think of it as an approximate V_6. Lead Y has its positive electrode on the front of the lower chest and its negative electrode on the neck. It therefore recognizes up-down forces, recording a downward force as a positive and an upward force as a negative deflection; it can be roughly equated to lead aVF. Lead Z uses the anterior chest electrode as its positive with an electrode on the back as the negative pole, and it is therefore the approximate equivalent of an inverted lead V_2.

The XYZ leads are the "orthogonal" (perpendicular to each other) leads from which the vector loop is derived and therefore, theoretically, contain all the information that is contained in the derived loop.

Conclusion

In a routine screening ECG, 12 leads should be employed: the three standard limb leads, the three aV leads and six V leads from 1 to 6 inclusive. For certain purposes, however, this number of leads is inadequate, while for other purposes 12 leads are quite unnecessary. In following the progress of an arrhythmia a single lead, V_1 or 2, is usually ample, whereas in a doubtful case of myocardial infarction it may be expedient to explore additional higher and more lateral areas of the precordium. There should be no rigid routine. While the usual 12 leads are generally adequate and necessary, the number should be freely modified or supplemented by an intelligent understanding of the particular requirements.

REFERENCES

1. Castellanos, A., et al.: XYZ electrocardography. Correlation with conventional 12 lead electro-cardiogram. Cardiovasc. Clin. 1977: **8,** 285.
2. Copeland, G. D., et al.: Clinical evaluation of a new esophageal electrode, with particular reference to the bipolar esophageal electrocardiogram. Am. Heart J. 1959: **57,** 862 and 874.
3. Douglas, A. H., and Cohen, N.: The vector and algebraic relationship of the CF and V chest leads. Am. Heart J. 1954: **48,** 340.
4. Editorial: Are the V leads always superior? Ann. Intern. Med. 1952: **36,** 1548.
5. Enselberg, C. D.: The esophageal electrocardiogram in the study of atrial activity and cardiac arrhythmias. Am. Heart J. 1951: **41,** 382.
6. Evans, W.: *Cardiography,* Ed. 2. Butterworth, London, 1954.
7. Evans, W., and Lloyd-Thomas, H. G.: The infrequent normal electrocardiogram in cardiac pain. Am. Heart J. 1961: **62,** 51.
8. Hammill, S. C., and Pritchett, E. L. C.: Simplified esophageal electrocardiography using bipolar recording leads. Ann. Intern. Med. 1981: **95,** 14.
9. Prystowsky, E. N., et al.: Origin of the atrial electrogram recorded from the esophagus. Circulation 1980: **61,** 1017.
10. Schaffer, A. I., et al.: A new look at electrocardiographic leads. Am. Heart J. 1956: **52,** 704.
11. Vogel, J. H. K., et al.: A simple technique for identifying P waves in complex arrhythmias. Am. Heart J. 1964: **67,** 158.

2

Rhythm and Rate

In every electrocardiogram 10 features should be examined systematically:

1. Rhythm
2. Rate
3. P wave
4. P-R interval
5. QRS interval
6. QRS complex
7. ST segment
8. T wave
9. U wave
10. Q-T duration

A suggested form for recording routine interpretations is given on page 13.

Rhythm

A glance is enough to determine whether the rhythm is regular or irregular. If it is regular, the interpreter should state whether it is sinoatrial (S-A)—as it usually is—A-V junctional, or idioventricular. If it is irregular, a preliminary survey should be made to determine whether there is a definite pattern to the irregularity, e.g., beats grouped in pairs, every fourth beat dropped, etc., or whether the irregularity is erratic, as in atrial fibrillation.

Measuring Intervals

The tracing is inscribed against a background of millimeter squares and every fifth line is thicker than the intervening four. The horizontal span between two consecutive thick lines is ⅕ sec (0.2 sec); the time elapsing between two consecutive thin lines is ¹⁄₂₅ sec (0.04 sec). The basic interval for timing electrocardiographic events is thus 0.04 sec. In practice, if an interval is to be measured, one counts the number of small squares horizontally contained within the interval and multiplies this number by 0.04. It is an easy matter to multiply by 4 and adjust the decimal point. In figure 2.1 about two squares are horizontally contained between the beginning and the end of the QRS complex; the QRS interval interval is therefore 2 × 0.04 = 0.08 sec. The P-R interval (from beginning of the P to the beginning of the QRS) measures 3½ small squares and is therefore 0.14 sec.

Estimating Rate

Most electrocardiographic paper conveniently provides marginal markers at 3-sec intervals. On such records the simplest and quickest method for estimating rate is to count the number of cardiac cycles in 6 sec and multiply by 10.

When such markers are not available, we use the thick lines as points of reference. As there are 300 fifths of a second in a minute (5 × 60), it is only necesary to determine the number of fifths of a second between consecutive beats (if the rhythm is regular) and divide this number into 300. For convenience we select a complex which coincides with a thick line and then count the number of fifths elapsing before the same complex recurs. The QRS complex is usually employed, but it is obvious that any wave will serve provided the rhythm is normal and regular. Should there be only ⅕ sec between consecutive beats the rate would be 300; if ⅖, 150; if ⅗, 100; and so on. Table 2.1 gives the

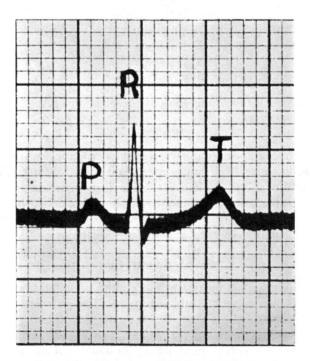

Figure 2.1. Measurement of P-R and QRS intervals.

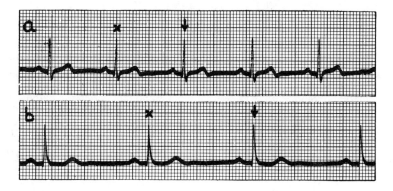

Figure 2.2. Estimation of heart rate (two examples). See text and figure 2.3.

rates prevailing if from 1 to 10 fifths elapse between consecutive beats. For rates between 30 and 100, it is obvious that reasonably accurate approximations can rapidly be made.

In the second example (*b*) in figure 2.2, the QRS marked *x* coincides with a thick line. There are then 6½ fifths of a second (thick lines) before the next QRS is reached. Thus the rate will obviously lie about halfway between 50 and 43 and may be called 46 or 47 with assurance that the approximation is within 1 or 2 beats of the actual rate. This method is obviously quite accurate enough for all practical purposes, and the slower the rate the more accurate the approximation. For even greater accuracy, the intermediate figures provided in

Table 2.1

With This Number of Fifths between Consecutive QRS Complexes	The Rate Is:
1	300
2	150
3	100
4	75
5	60
6	50
7	43
8	37
9	33
10	30

the guide in figure 2.3 may be employed. These figures are obtained by dividing into 1500 (25 × 60) the number of 25ths of a second elapsing between consecutive beats.

When the rate is over 100, the margin of error rapidly increases and, to determine the rate more accurately, it is better to count the number of cardiac cycles occurring in 5, 6 or 10 sec and multiply the number by 12, 10 or 6. This method must also be adopted, regardless of the rate, when the rhythm is irregular. Figure 2.4 illustrates this method for estimating a rapid rate.

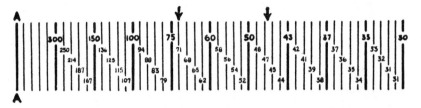

Figure 2.3. Guide for rapid estimation of heart rate. In any tracing select a QRS complex that coincides with a thick line (e.g., those marked *x* in the two examples in fig. 2.2). This thick line is represented by the first thick line, *AA*, in the guide above. Note with which line the next QRS in the tracing coincides (*arrows* in fig. 2.2) and read off the rate from the corresponding line of the guide: first arrow, rate 71 (tracing *a*); second arrow, rate 46 (tracing *b*). *NOTE:* UNLIKE MANY MANUFACTURERS' RULERS, THIS GUIDE IS NOT DRAWN ON THE SAME SCALE AS THE CLINICAL TRACING AND IS OBVIOUSLY NOT INTENDED FOR DIRECT APPLICATION TO IT. IT IS A DIAGRAM *REPRESENTING* THE LINES IN THE TRACING AND IS INTENDED AS AN AID TO MEMORIZING KEY FIGURES.

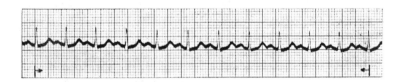

Figure 2.4. Estimation of rapid rates. In the 5 sec between the two markers, there are 11 cardiac cycles. The rate is therefore 11 × 12 = 132 per minute.

SUGGESTED FORM FOR ROUTINE RECORDS

RHYTHM: RATE:

P-R INTERVAL: QRS INTERVAL: Q-T DURATION:

P WAVE: axis:

QRS COMPLEX:
    axis:
    Q waves:

ST SEGMENT:

T WAVE: axis:

U WAVE:

IMPRESSIONS:
    (1)
    (2)
    (3)
    (4)

COMMENT:

3

Complexes and Intervals

When a complex is partly above the baseline and partly below it, it is **diphasic**. When its excursions above and below the line are approximately equal, it is **isodiphasic** or **equiphasic**.

P Wave

This is the first wave of the electrocardiogram and represents the spread of the electrical impulse through the atria (**activation** or **depolarization** of atria). It is normally upright in leads 1 and 2 but is frequently diphasic or inverted in lead 3. It is normally inverted in aVR and upright in aVF and in left chest leads (V_{4-6}). It is variable in the other leads. Its amplitude should not exceed 2 or 3 mm in any lead, and its normal contour is gently rounded—not pointed or notched.

Abnormalities that should be looked for are, therefore:

1. *Inversion* in leads where the P wave is normally upright, or the presence of an upright P wave in aVR (where it should be inverted); such changes are usually found in conditions where the impulse travels through the atria by an unorthodox path—as in ectopic atrial or A-V junctional rhythms (fig. 3.1C).
2. *Increased amplitude*: this usually indicates atrial hypertrophy or dilation and is found especially in A-V valve disease, hypertension, cor pulmonale, and congenital heart disease.
3. *Increased width*: this usually indicates left atrial enlargement or diseased atrial muscle. The normal P wave does not exceed 0.11 sec in duration.
4. *Diphasicity*: an important sign of left atrial enlargement when the second half of the P wave is significantly negative in lead 3 or V_1 (see fig. 30.1B, p. 456).
5. *Notching*: when the left atrium is mainly involved (as in mitral disease) the P wave often becomes wide and notched and is taller in lead 1 than in lead 3—**P-mitrale** (fig. 3.1A). Notching is considered significant when the distance between peaks exceeds 0.04 sec.

14

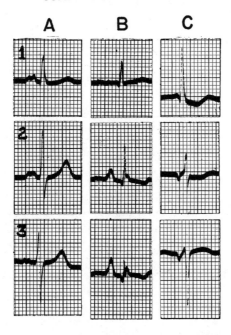

Figure 3.1. Abnormal **P waves**. (*A*) **P-mitrale**; note broad, notched P waves taller in lead 1 than in lead 3. (*B*) **P-pulmonale**; note flat P in lead 1 with tall, pointed P wave in leads 2 and 3. (*C*) **A-V junctional rhythm**; note inverted P in leads 2 and 3 with short P-R interval.

6. *Peaking*: right atrial overload usually produces tall pointed P waves taller in lead 3 than in lead 1—**P-pulmonale** (fig. 3.1*B*).
7. *Absence* of P waves: this occurs in some A-V junctional rhythms and in S-A block.

In summary, P waves are:

        Normally upright in 1, 2, V_{4-6} and aVF
        Normally inverted in aVR
        Variable in 3, aVL and other chest leads.

T_P Wave

This wave, formerly called Ta,[43] represents repolarization of the atria, and is directed opposite to the P wave—if the P wave is upright it is inverted, and vice versa (fig. 3.2C). It is usually invisible because it coincides with the QRS complex. It can best be seen in A-V block, where the P waves are not followed by QRS complexes and there is consequently an opportunity for the T_P wave to show itself (see fig. 23.12, p. 331).

P-R Interval

This is measured from the *beginning* of the P wave to the *beginning* of the QRS complex. It measures the time taken by the impulse to travel all the way from the S-A node to the ventricular muscle fibers, and this is normally from 0.12 to 0.20 sec. It is customary to examine several intervals and record that which appears the longest. The interval varies with heart rate, being shorter at faster rates. Up to a rate of 140 to 150, exercise shortens the P-R interval, mainly through withdrawal of parasympathetic tone.[3] If the conducting system is diseased or affected by digitalis, the P-R may lengthen as the rate increases. Similarly, if the atria are paced artificially the P-R increases as the paced rate quickens.[6] The P-R is proportionately shorter in children, averaging 0.11 sec. at 1 year, 0.13 at 6 and 0.14 at 12 years. An interval prolonged beyond normal limits is regarded as evidence of A-V block (fig. 3.2C).

At relatively slow rates a few apparently normal people, with no evidence of heart disease, have been found to have intervals ranging considerably above 0.20 sec.[45] In a group of over 67,000 apparently healthy airmen, 0.52% were found to have prolonged P-R interals.[5] Most of these prolongations (80%) ranged from 0.21 to 0.24 sec, while in the remaining minority the P-R interval ranged up to 0.39 sec. In another study, 59 of 19,000 healthy aircrew applicants (0.31%) had P-R intervals of 0.24 sec or more.[8] Standing often reduces such prolonged P-R intervals to normal.

P-R prolongation is more likely to be a pointer to othewise latent rheumatic or coronary disease, but one must not brand an individual as a "cardiac" whose only stigma is an unconventionally long P-R interval. Obviously it is a signal for a thorough search to exclude cardiac abnormality, but if none is found, the heart should be acquitted with reservation.

Biological values do not submit to arithmetical laws, and one must bear in mind all the physiological factors that may influence P-R duration. An elephantine man with a correspondingly large heart will generally have a longer interval than a petite woman less than half his size. She may have true block with an interval of only 0.19, while he may well have a normal duration of 0.21 sec. Biological variations too often are lost sight of in attempting to regiment natural values.

The P-R interval is abnormally short when the impulse originates in the A-V node (fig. 3.1C) instead of the S-A node, and also when the passage of the

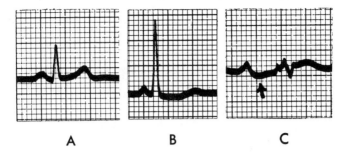

A   **B**   **C**

Figure 3.2. P-R intervals. (*A*) Normal interval of 0.14 sec. (*B*) Short P-R interval of 0.10 sec, from hypertensive patient shortly after an episode of atrial flutter. (*C*) Prolonged P-R interval of 0.30 sec; note shallowly inverted T$_P$ wave (*arrow*) immediately following P wave.

impulse to the ventricle is accelerated as in the Wolff-Parkinson-White syndrome. A short P-R interval is also sometimes seen as a normal variation (fig. 3.2*B*); but this combination (normal P, short P-R and normal QRS) is perhaps not so benign as might be thought, because it is found often in association with hypertension[9] and with the tendency to develop paroxysms of tachycardia.[7]

In summary, the P-R interval is

Prolonged	*Shortened*
(a) In A-V block (p. 322) due to coronary disease, rheumatic disease, etc.	(a) In A-V junctional and low atrial rhythms (p. 290)
(b) In some cases of hyperthyroidism	(b) In Wolff-Parkinson-White syndrome (p 257)
(c) As a are normal variation	(c) In Lown-Ganong-Levine syndrome (p. 272)
	(d) In glycogen storage disease
	(e) In some hypertension patients
	(f) As a normal variation

P-R Segment

This is the baseline between the *end* of the P wave and beginning of QRS. Normally isoelectric, it may be displaced in atrial infarction and in acute pericarditis.

QRS Complex

This complex is the most important in the electrocardiogram, as it represents spread of the impulse through the ventricular muscle (**activation** or **depolarization** of ventricles).

Proper labelling of the component waves of this complex should first be mastered (fig. 3.3):

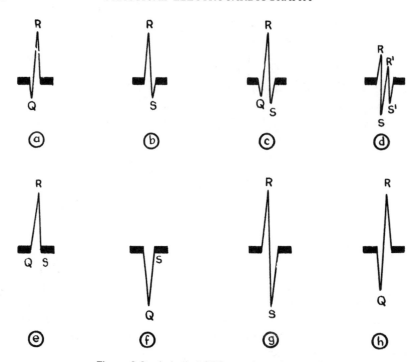

Figure 3.3. Labelled QRS complexes (see text).

1. If the first deflection is downward (negative), it is a **Q wave**.
2. The first upright deflection is an **R wave**, whether or not it is preceded by a Q.
3. A negative deflection following an R wave is an **S wave**.
4. Subsequent excursions above the line are labelled successively R′, r″, etc; similarly later negative excursions are labelled S′, S″, and so on.

If the QRS complex consists exclusively of an R wave, the points at which the complex begins and ends may be labelled Q and S, respectively, though there are no actual Q or S *waves*. When the complex consists exclusively of a Q wave it is described as a QS complex. A word-saving convention is the use of small and large letters to signify the relative sizes of the component waves. Thus, in figure 3.3, (*c*) is conveniently labelled qRs, which is quicker and simpler for the reader's eye than "a small Q, a tall R and a small S wave." In the figure (*a*) would be labelled qR, (*b*) Rs, (*g*) RS, (*h*) QR, and so on. The term "QRS complex" may always be used as a sort of collective noun to describe the ventricular complex no matter what waves actually compose it. Thus all the examples in figure 3.3 may also quite correctly be referred to as QRS complexes.

In interpreting the QRS complexes there are at least seven features that should be routinely inspected:

1. Their *duration* (the QRS interval)
2. Their *amplitude* (or "voltage")
3. The presence of Q *waves* (or equivalents)
4. Their *electrical axis* in the frontal plane (limb leads)
5. The relative prominence of the component waves in the precordial leads, V_1 to V_6, noting the *transitional zone*
6. The timing of the *intrinsicoid deflections* in various unipolar leads
7. The general configuration of the complex, including the presence and location of any slurring or notching.

The *duration* of the normal QRS complex is usually given as 0.05 to 0.10 sec. The QRS interval is measured from the beginning of the QRS to its end, usually in the standard limb leads. The chest leads frequently display a slightly longer QRS spread (0.01 or 0.02 sec longer) than the standard leads; the explanation for this is not clear. A measurement of 0.12 sec or more is indicative of abnormal intraventricular conduction and usually means block of one of the bundle branches or a ventricular arrhythmia.

The *amplitude* of the QRS complexes has wide normal limits. It is generally agreed that, if the total amplitude (above and below the isoelectric line) is 5 mm or less in all three standard leads, it is too low to be healthy; such low voltage is seen in diffuse coronary disease, cardiac failure, pericardial effusion, myxedema, primary amyloidosis and any other conditions producing widespread myocardial damage. It is also found in emphysema, generalized edema and obesity. The minimal normal QRS amplitude in precordial leads waxes and wanes from right to left across the chest, being generally accepted as 5 mm in V_1 and V_6, 7 mm. in V_2 and V_5 and 9 mm in V_3 and V_4. Some define low voltage as an *average* voltage in the limb leads of less than 5 mm with an *average* in the chest leads of less than 10 mm.[12]

It is more difficult to set an arbitrary upper limit to normal voltage. Amplitudes up to 20 or even 30 mm are occasionally seen in lead 2 in normal hearts, while the generally accepted maximum in a precordial lead is 25 to 30 mm.

The amplitude or "voltage" recorded on the tracing is dependent on many factors besides the health of the heart; for example, the distance of the heart from the recording electrode (as determined by size of chest, thickness of chest wall, presence of emphysema, etc.) profoundly affects the size of the recorded deflections. Such factors must receive due consideration before the voltage of any complex is judged too high or too low.

The significance of *Q waves* is one of the most important, and sometimes the most difficult, assessments in the tracing. Size is important, and yet a diminutive Q wave of less than 1 mm. may have real significance, while a QS complex of 10 mm. in certain leads may sometimes be within normal limits. A small narrow Q wave of 1 or 2 mm is a normal finding in leads 1, aVL and aVF, and in chest leads over the left ventricle, e.g., V_5. Indeed, the absence of the expected small Q waves in these leads may be an abnormal sign.[11] On the other hand, deep QS or Qr complexes are a perfectly normal finding in aVR, the Q in aVR being the equivalent of an initial R in other leads—since aVR, for reasons to be explained in Chapter 4, is an "upside down stepchild"; and QS complexes are occasionally found normally in lead 3 and in leads V_1 and V_2. The Q wave should not be more than 0.03 sec in width. To gauge their importance Q waves must be viewed in the light of the overall picture and one must take into account (1) their depth, (2) their width, (3) the leads in which they appear and, most important, (4) the clinical setting.

ST Segment

This segment is that part of the tracing immediately succeeding the QRS complex (fig. 3.4). The point at which it "takes off" from the QRS is called the J (junction) point. Two features of the ST segment should be observed: (1) its *level* relative to the baseline, i.e., whether it is elevated or depressed below the T-P segment, and (2) its *shape*.

Normally it is on the same level as the T-P segment, i.e., it is **isoelectric**, or only slightly above or below it. It is sometimes normally elevated not more than 1 mm in the standard leads, and even 2 mm in some of the chest leads; it is never normally depressed more than half a millimeter or so. An interesting exception is sometimes observed, particularly in healthy young black men[15, 16] where the ST segments may be markedly elevated (sometimes as much as 4 mm) in one or more precordial leads (fig. 3.5), a configuration often described as "early repolarization" (see pp. 414 and 463)."

In shape the ST segment normally curves gently and imperceptibly into the proximal limb of the T wave. It should not form a sharp angle with this limb, nor should it pursue a frankly horizontal course. Horizontality of the ST

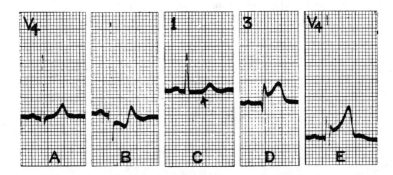

Figure 3.4. ST segments. (*A*) Normal. (*B*) Same lead, same patient as A; 2 min after exercise, showing ST depression. (*C*) ST segment is minimally depressed (certainly less than 0.5 mm) but is horizontal and forms a rather sharp-angled junction with proximal limb of T wave (compare with A). (*D*) ST elevation from myocardial injury (acute infarction). (*E*) ST elevation as a normal variant in a healthy black man.

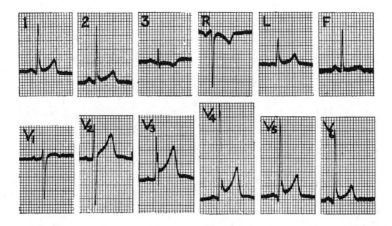

Figure 3.5. From a normal black man of 29 years. Note marked ST elevation in precordial leads,

segment, which is highly suspicious of myocardial ischemia, has also been called "plane depression" (fig. 3.4*C*).

Frank displacement of the ST segment is, of course, the hallmark of myocardial ischemia or injury and is seen with any of the syndromes of coronary artery disease. ST depression in the precordial leads is said to indicate subendocardial, and ST elevation subepicardial or transmural injury or ischemia. Temporary injury, as with DC cardioversion, may produce transient ST elevation.[14]

T Wave

The T wave represents the recovery period of the ventricles, when they recruit their spent electrical forces (**repolarization**). We particularly notice three of its features: (1) its *direction*, (2) its *shape*, and (3) its *height*.

The T wave is normally upright in leads 1 and 2, and in chest leads over the left ventricle (except in infants and very young childen); it is normally inverted in aVR; in all other leads it is variable. Certain general rules govern this variability: (1) The T wave is normally upright in aVL and in aVF if the QRS is more than 5 mm tall, but may be inverted in the company of smaller R waves. (2) In the precordial leads the tendency to inversion of T waves over the left ventricle (V_5 and V_6) rapidly diminishes with increasing age, and in adult males it is generally considered abnormal if the T waves are inverted as far to the left as V_3; in normal women the T wave in V_3 may be shallowly inverted. The T in V_1 may be inverted normally at any age (indeed it is more often inverted than upright); and in V_2 it is also sometimes normally negative. In normal hearts, when the T wave in V_1 is upright, it is almost never as tall as the T wave in V_6.[32]

We may summarize the direction of the normal adult T wave as follows. It is:

Normally upright in 1, 2 and V_3 to V_6
Normally inverted in aVR
Variable in 3, aVL, aVF, V_1 and V_2.

The *shape* of the T waves is normally slightly rounded and slightly asymmetrical. When T waves are sharply pointed or grossly notched,[17] they should be regarded with suspicion, though either of these characteristics may sometimes occur in precordial leads as a normal variant. Notching of the T waves is particularly common in normal children (fig. 3.6); on the other hand, it is sometimes found in pericarditis. A sharply pointed symmetrical T wave (upright or inverted) is suspicious of myocardial infarction (fig. 3.7).

The *height* of the T waves is also important. They are normally not above 5 mm in any standard lead, and not above 10 mm in any precordial lead. Unusually tall T waves (fig. 3.7 *B* and *D*) suggest myocardial infarction or potassium intoxication. Tall T waves are also seen in myocardial ischemia without infarction (fig. 3.7*B*), in certain forms of ventricular overloading (see p. 58), in psychotics and in patients with cerebrovascular accidents. In obesity, the T waves tend to be flattened, regaining their normal amplitude as the excess weight is lost.[17a]

Q-T Duration

This interval, measured from the beginning of the QRS to the end of the T wave, gives the total duration of ventricular systole. It varies with heart rate, sex and age, and its normal values are most conveniently determined by consulting a prepared table based on the calculations of Ashman (table 3.1). A useful rule of thumb is that the Q-T interval should be less than half the preceding R-R interval. This holds good for normal sinus rates. However, as

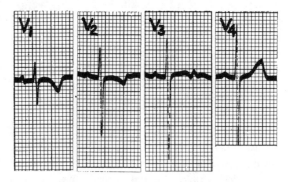

Figure 3.6.   T waves in a normal child. Note marked notching in V_3; this is a common normal transitional form of T wave between the normally inverted T in V_2 and the normally upright T in V_4.

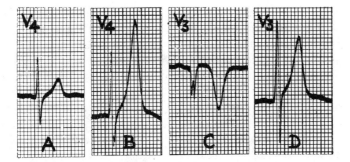

Figure 3.7. T waves. (*A*) Normal T wave. (*B*) Tall T wave of myocardial ischemia in a patient with angina but without infarction. (*C*) Deeply inverted symmetrical T wave of anterior infarction. (*D*) Tall upright symmetrical T wave of inferior infarction.

Table 3.1
Normal Q-T Intervals and the Upper Limits of the Normal[a]

Heart Rate per Minute	Men and Children (sec)	Women (sec)	Upper Limits of the Normal	
			Men and children (sec)	Women (sec)
40.0	0.449	0.461	0.491	0.503
43.0	0.438	0.450	0.479	0.491
46.0	0.426	0.438	0.466	0.478
48.0	0.420	0.432	0.460	0.471
50.0	0.414	0.425	0.453	0.464
52.0	0.407	0.418	0.445	0.456
54.5	0.400	0.411	0.438	0.449
57.0	0.393	0.404	0.430	0.441
60.0	0.386	0.396	0.422	0.432
63.0	0.378	0.388	0.413	0.423
66.5	0.370	0.380	0.404	0.414
70.5	0.361	0.371	0.395	0.405
75.0	0.352	0.362	0.384	0.394
80.0	0.342	0.352	0.374	0.384
86.0	0.332	0.341	0.363	0.372
92.5	0.321	0.330	0.351	0.360
100.0	0.310	0.318	0.338	0.347
109.0	0.297	0.305	0.325	0.333
120.0	0.283	0.291	0.310	0.317
133.0	0.268	0.276	0.294	0.301
150.0	0.252	0.258	0.275	0.282
172.0	0.234	0.240	0.255	0.262

[a] Reproduced with kind permission of the publishers from *Essentials of Electrocardiography* by R. Ashman and E. Hull, The Macmillan Company, New York, 1945.

the rate slows below 65 the maximal normal Q-T duration falls further and further below half the preceding R-R interval; and as the rate increases above 90 the normal Q-T duration gradually exceeds half the preceding R-R. These points will provide a near enough guide for most practical purposes. The diagnostic value of the Q-T duration is seriously limited by the technical difficulties of measuring it exactly.[29]

Q-T prolongation may be idiopathic[33] or acquired. It may accompany congestive heart failure or it may be due to ischemic heart disease,[21] rheumatic fever[19, 20, 28] or other causes of myocarditis[22, 23]; a lengthened Q-T duration may result from cerebrovascular disease,[24] or from electrolyte disturbances.[27, 31] Careful measurement showed that it was not lengthened in hypokalemia unless there was an associated deficit in calcium.[30] Drugs, including quinidine, pro-caine amide and the phenothiazines may cause Q-T prolongation,[26, 27, 36] as may hypothermia[18] or stringent dieting.[25, 35] A prolonged Q-T means that there is delayed repolarization of the ventricular myocardium, and this is associated with an increased predisposition to reentry (see p. 127), thus favoring the development of serious ventricular tachyarrhythmias, syncope and sudden death.[33, 34] It is often prolonged in patients with mitral valve prolapse.[18a] The Q-T is shortened by digitalis, calcium excess and potassium intoxication.

U Wave

This is usually a small wave of low voltage, sometimes seen following the T wave. Its normal polarity is the same as that of the T wave (i.e., when the T wave is upright, it too is upright, and vice versa), and the normal wave is often best discerned in lead V_3. It is rendered more prominent by potassium deficiency (fig. 3.8), and its polarity is often reversed in myocardial ischemia and left ventricular overload secondary to hypertension, or aortic or mitral regurgitation[37a] (fig. 3.8). Negative U waves in the resting ECG are claimed to be a faithful index of significant stenosis of the left main or left anterior descending coronary artery.[37] These are the conditions in which its alterations are of most value in diagnosis, but it is affected by numerous other factors; digitalis, quinidine, epinephrine, hypercalcemia, thyrotoxicosis and exercise all increase its amplitude.[38, 41]

Its source is uncertain; some have postulated that it represents repolarization of the papillary muscles, and others that it represents repolarization of the Purkinje system.[37a] In the cardiac cycle it coincides with the phase of supernormal excitability during ventricular recovery,[40] and in this connection it is interesting to note that most ventricular extrasystoles occur at about the time of the U wave.

Some common artifacts are illustrated in figures 3.9–3.12.

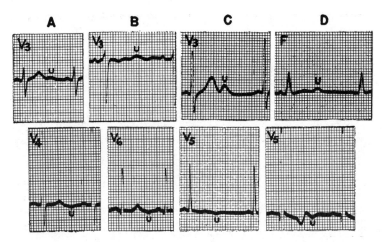

Figure 3.8. U waves. *Upper row*—upright U waves: (*A*) Normal, (*B, C* and *D*) Prominent U waves in hypokalemia. *Lower row*—inverted U waves: (*A*) Tracing from which this was taken showed no abnormalities except for U wave inversion in several leads; this situation is referred to as "isolated U wave inversion." (*B*) From a patient with hypertension whose tracing showed left ventricular strain including inverted U waves. (*C*) From a patient with coronary insufficiency but without hypertension. (*D*) Note marked inversion of T wave as well as U wave; from a hypertensive.

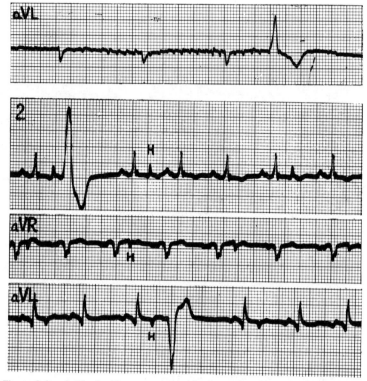

Figure 3.9. Artifacts. The uppermost strip shows the effect of an involuntary muscular tremor affecting the left arm. The lower three strips are from a patient with hiccups; each lead shows the effect of three or four hiccups, one of which is indicated (*H*) in each lead.

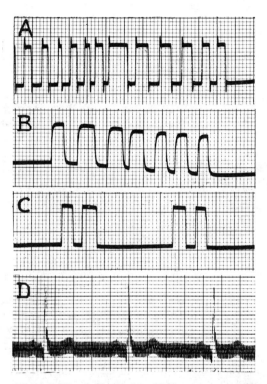

Figure 3.10.   Artifacts. *A* and *B* show common errors in adjustment of the stylus—overshoot (*A*) and over-damping (*B*)—which can significantly distort the QRS complexes. Proper standardization is shown in *C. D* illustrates 60-cycle AC interference.

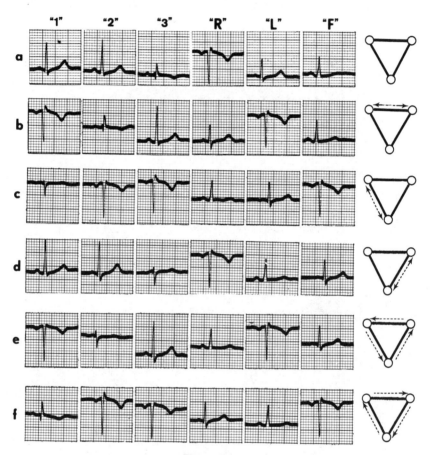

Figure 3.11

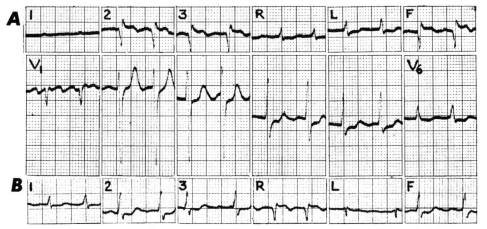

Figure 3.12. (*A*) **Atrial fibrillation** and pseudo-inferior infarction due to **electrode misplacement**. With Q waves and ST elevation in leads 2, 3 and aVF, and with reciprocal depression of the ST segment in aVL and the chest leads, this tracing suggests acute inferior infarction. But lead 1, with virtually no deflections, is the tip-off: the two arm electrodes are on the two legs (and the leg electrodes are on the arms). (*B*) Limb leads with the electrodes attached correctly.

Figure 3.11 (*opposite page*). **Electrodal confusion.**

  a. Electrodes properly placed. Leads are as labelled.

  b. Arm electrodes (lead 1) reversed:

                  "1" is mirror image of 1

                  "2" is 3, "3" is 2

                  "R" is L; "L" is R

  c. Right arm and left leg (lead 2) electrodes reversed:

                  "2" is mirror image of 2

                  "1" is mirror image of 3

                  "3" is mirror image of 1

                  "R" is F; "F" is R

  d. Left arm and left leg (lead 3) electrodes reversed:

                  "3" is mirror image of 3

                  "1" is 2; "2" is 1

                  "L" is F: "F" is L

  e. All three electrodes rotated counterclockwise:

                  "1" is mirror image of 2

                  "2" is mirror image of 3

                  "3" is 1

                  "R" is F; "L" is R; "F" is L

  f. All three electrodes rotated clockwise:

                  "1" is 3

                  "2" is mirror image of 1

                  "3" is mirror image of 2

                  "R" is L; "L" is F; "F" is R

REFERENCES

P Wave

1. Thomas P., and Dejong, D.: The P wave in the electrocardiogram in the diagnosis of heart disease, Br. Heart J. 1954: **16**, 241.

P-R Interval

2. Alimurung, M. M., and Massell, B. F.: The normal P-R interval in infants and children. Circulation 1956: **13**, 257.
3. Atterhog, J.-H., and Loogna, E.: P-R interval in relation to heart rate during exercise and the influence of posture and autonomic tone. J. Electrocardiol. 1977: **10**, 331.
4. Blizzard, J. J., and Rupp, J. J.: Prolongation of the P-R interval as a manifestation of thyrotoxicosis, J.A.M.A. 1960: **173**, 1845.
5. Johnson, R. L., et al.: Electrocardiographic findings in 67,375 asymptomatic individuals, Part VII. A-V block. Am. J. Cardiol. 1960: **6**, 153.
6. Lister, J. W., et al.: Atrioventricular conduction in man: effect of rate, exercise, isoproterenol and atropine on the P-R interval. Am. J. Cardiol. 1965: **16**, 516.
7. Lown, B., Ganong, W. B., and Levine, S. A.: The syndrome of short P-R interval, normal QRS complex and paroxysmal rapid heart action. Circulation 1952: **5**, 693.
8. Manning, G. W., and Sears, G. A.: Postural heart block. Am. J. Cardiol. 1962: **9**, 558.
9. Scherf, D.: Short P-R interval and its occurrence in hypertension. Bull. N.Y. Coll. Med. 1941: **43**, 116.
10. Scherf, D., and Dix, J. H.: The effects of posture on A-V conduction. Am. Heart J. 1952: **43**, 494.

QRS Complex

11. Burch, G. E., and Pasquale, N.: A study at autopsy of the relation of absence of the Q wave in leads I, aVL, V_5 and V_6 to septal fibrosis. Am. Heart J. 1960: **60**, 336.
12. Unverferth, D. V., et al.: Electrocardiographic voltage in pericardial effusion. Chest 1979: **75**, 157.
13. Lepeschkin, E., and Surawicz, B.: The measurement of the duration of the QRS interval. Am. Heart J 1952: **44**, 80.

S-T Segment

14. Chun, P. K. C., et al.: ST-segment elevation with elective direct current cardioversion. Circulation 1981: **63**, 220.
15. Edeiken, J.: Elevation of the RS-T segment, apparent or real, in the right precordial leads as a probable normal variant. Am. Heart J. 1954: **48**, 331.
16. Goldman, M. J.: RS-T segment elevation in mid- and left precordial leads as a normal variant. Am. Heart J. 1953: **46**, 817.

T Waves

17. Dressler, E., Roesler, H., and Lackner, H.: The significance of notched upright T waves. Br. Heart J. 1951: **13**, 496.
17a. Eisenstein, I., et al.: The electrocardiogram in obesity. J. Electrocardiol. 1982: **15**, 115.

Q-T Duration

18. Abildskov, J. A.: The nervous system and cardiac arrhythmias. Circulation 1975: **51** (Supp. III), 111–116.
18a. Bekheit, S. G., et al.: Analysis of QT interval in patients with idiopathic mitral valve prolapse. Chest 1982: **81**, 620.
19. Carmichael, D. B.: The corrected Q-T duration in acute and convalescent rheumatic fever. Am. Heart J. 1955: **50**, 528.
20. Craige, E., et al.: The Q-T interval in rheumatic fever. Circulation 1950: **1**, 1338.
21. Elek, S. R., et al.: The Q-T interval in myocardial infarction and left ventricular hypertrophy. Am. Heart J. 1953: **45**, 80.
22. Fox, T. T., et al.: The Q-T interval in the electrocardiogram of children with tuberculosis. Circulation 1950: **1**, 1184.

23. Gittleman, I. W., Thorner, M. C., and Griffith, G. C.: The Q-T interval of the electrocardiogram in acute myocarditis in adults, with autopsy correlation. Am. Heart J. 1951: 341, 78.
24. Hersch, C.: Electrocardiographic changes in subarachnoid haemorrhage, meningitis and intracranial space-occupying lesions. Br. Heart J. 1964: **26**, 785.
25. Isner, J. M., et al.: Sudden, unexpected death in avid dieters using the liquid-protein-modified-fast diet. Observations in 17 patients and the role of the prolonged Q-T interval. Circulation 1979: **60**, 1401.
26. James, T. N.: QT prolongation and sudden death. Mod. Concepts Cardiovasc. Dis. 1969: **38**, 35.
27. Khan, M. M., et al.: Management of recurrent ventricular tachyarrhythmias associated with Q-T prolongation. Am. J. Cardiol. 1981: **47**, 1301.
28. Kornel, L., and Braun, K.: The Q-T interval in rheumatic heart disease. Br. Heart J. 1956: **18**, 8.
29. Lepeschkin, E., and Surawicz, B.: The measurement of the Q-T duration of the electrocardiogram. Circulation 1952: **6**, 378.
30. Lepeschkin, E., and Surawicz, B.: The duration of the Q-U interval and its components in electrocardiograms of normal persons. Am. Heart J. 1953: **46**, 9.
31. Loeb, H. S., et al.: Paroxysmal ventricular fibrillation in two patients with hypomagnesemia; treatment by transvenous pacing. Circulation 1968: **37**, 210.
32. Meyer, P., and Herr, R.; L'interet du syndrome eléctrocardiographique TV1 > TV6 pour le dépistage précoce de troubles de la repolarisation ventriculaire gauche. Arch. Mal. Coeur 1959: **52**, 753.
33. Moss, A. J., and Schwartz, P. J.: Sudden death and the idiopathic long Q-T syndrome. Am. J. Med. 1979: **66**, 6.
34. Schwartz, . J., et al.: The long Q-T syndrome. Am. Heart J. 1975: **89**, 378.
35. Singh, B. N., et al: Liquid protein diets and torsade de pointes. J.A.M.A. 1978: **240**, 115.
36. Surawicz, B., and Lasseter, K. C.: Effects of drugs on the electrocardiogram. Prog. Cardiovasc. Dis. 1970: **13**, 26.

U Wave

37. Gerson, M. C., and McHenry, P. L.: Resting U wave inversion as a marker of stenosis of the left anterior descending coronary artery. Am. J. Med. 1980: **69**, 545.
37a. Kishida, H., et al.: Negative U wave: A highly specific but poorly understood sign of heart disease. Am. J. Cardiol. 1982: **49**, 2030.
38. Lepeschkin, E.: The U wave of the electrocardiogram. Arch. Intern. Med. 1955: **96**, 600.
39. Lepeschkin, E.: The U wave of the electrocardiogram. Mod. Concepts Cardiovasc. Dis. 1969: **38**, 39.
40. Mack, I., Langendorf, R., and Katz, L. N.: the supernormal phase of recovery of conduction in the human heart. Am. Heart J. 1947: **34**, 374.
41. Palmer, J. H.: Isolated U wave negativity. Circulation 1953: **7**, 205.
42. Symposium: The U wave of the electrocardiogram. Circulation 1957: **15**, 68–110.

General

43. Committee on Electrocardiography, American Heart Association: Recommendations for standardization of electocardiographic and vectorcardiographic leads. Circulation. 1954: **10**, 564.
44. Kossman, C. E.: The normal electrocardiogram. Circulation 1953: **8**, 920.
45. Manning, G. W.: Electrocardiography in the selection of Royal Canadian Air Force aircrew. Circulation 1954: **10**, 401.
46. Packard, J. M., Graettinger, J. S., and Graybiel, A.: Analysis of the electrocardiograms obtained from 100 young healthy aviators. Ten-year follow up. Circulation 1954: **10**, 384.

4

Electrical Axis

The QRS Axis

The orientation of the heart's electrical activity in the frontal plane may be expressed in terms of "axis" or "heart position." The axis may be "normal" or there may be right or left "axis deviation"; and the electrical positions may be "horizontal," "vertical," etc. (see p. 39). But this approach leaves something to be desired. The description, "left axis deviation, horizontal heart," is, like "an elderly old man," both inexact and redundant. Just as we should be precise and say "a 76-year-old man," so we should specify the axis and say, for example, "minus 40°"; this, in a single and relatively accurate figure, combines both "axis" and "position."

The axis can be determined approximately from any two limb leads, but it is most readily and accurately determined if all six limb leads are available for simultaneous inspection. To calculate the numerical axis, one must know the "hexaxial reference system." By taking the three sides of Einthoven's triangle (fig. 4.1A), each of which represents one of the standard limb leads, and rearranging them so that they bisect each other, we obtain a "triaxial reference system" (fig. 4.1B). If we add to this system three further lines to represent the unipolar limb leads (fig. 4.1C), the final figure consists of six bisecting lines, the hexaxial reference system (fig. 4.1D), each line of which represents one of the six limb leads. By convention, the degrees are arranged as shown in fig. 4.1D, with 0° at 3 o'clock and successively greater negative degrees progressing counter-clockwise to −180° at 9 o'clock, and with corresponding positive degrees ranging clockwise.

One further principle: the electrical impulse writes the largest deflection on the lead whose line of derivation is parallel to its path, and it writes the smallest deflection on the lead perpendicular to it. For example, an impulse travelling parallel to lead 1 will produce the maximal deflection on this lead and a minimal deflection on the lead at right angles to it, i.e., aVF.

In general, axes between 0° and +90° correspond with "normal axis." Axes between 0° and −90° represent "left axis deviation," and between +90° and +180° "right axis deviation." This leaves the quadrant between −90° and

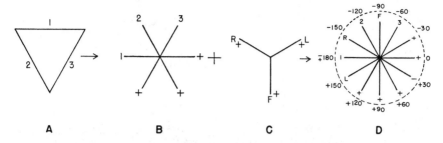

Figure 4.1. Constitution of the hexaxial reference system. (A). Einthoven's triangle, the sides of which represent the three standard limb leads. (B) The triaxial reference system composed of the three sides of Einthoven's triangle rearranged so that they bisect one another. (C) Lines of derivation of the three unipolar (aV) limb leads. (D) The hexaxial reference system composed of the lines of derivation of the six limb leads (B + C) arranged so that they bisect each other.

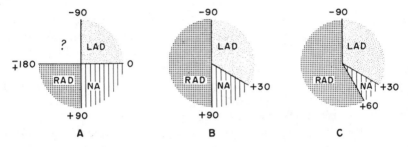

Figure 4.2. Illustrating inconsistencies in the definitions of axis deviations. NA = normal axis. LAD = left axis deviation. RAD = right axis deviation. (A) Convenient and realistic boundaries of axis deviation (adopted in this book). (B) Boundaries recommended by the Criteria Committee of the New York Heart Association. (C) Boundaries described by Sodi-Pallares.

−180° without identity ("no-man's-land"): does it represent extreme right or extreme left axis deviation (fig. 4.2A)? This quandary is resolved by using the precise numerical axis.

A further difficulty arises from the fact that authorities define the bounds of "axis deviations" differently; according to Sodi-Pallares[7] "slight" left axis deviation begins at +30° (fig. 4.2C), whereas most authorities more conveniently place 0° as the rightmost limit of left axis deviation. Similarly, "slight" right axis deviation begins at +60° for Sodi-Pallares, but for others it begins at +90° (fig. 4.2B). The Criteria Committee of the New York Heart Association[4] applies left axis deviation to the segment lying between −90° and +30° and right axis deviation to the area between +90° and −90° (fig. 4.2B). As normal axes range between −30° and +120°, the most realistic boundaries would seem to be those diagrammed in figure 4.2A; this applies "normal axis" to the range between 0° and +90°. "Slight left axis deviation" then applies to the still normal $0°$ to $-30°$ segment, and pathological deviations of the axis to the left ($-30°$ to $-90°$) are referred to as "marked LAD." Similarly, "slight RAD" is applied to axes still within the normal range of $+90°$ to $+120°$, while axes of $+120°$ to $+180°$ are called "marked RAD."

By using the quadrant system illustrated in figure 4.2A, the axis now can be calculated. The two leads that divide the "clockface" into its four quadrants are leads 1 and aVF. In figure 4.3 the positive field of lead 1 is shaded vertically and the positive field of aVF is indicated with horizontal shading; thus, the quadrant assigned to "normal" axis is where the positive fields of both leads overlap. If the QRS is upright in both leads, as shown in figure 4.3b, the axis is "normal." On the other hand, if it is positive in 1 but negative in aVF (fig. 4.3a), it is in the left-axis quadrant. If it is positive in aVF but negative in 1 (fig. 4.3c), it is in the right-axis quadrant; and if it is negative in both leads (fig. 4.3d), the axis is in "no man's land." Using only these two leads, it is easy to place the axis in its appropriate quadrant.

But clearly it is not enough to state that the axis is between $0°$ and $-90°$; one must know whether it is $-30°$, or $-45°$, or $-80°$, and this finer adjustment is achieved by comparing the size of the complexes in the two leads. For example, as shown in figure 4.3b, if the R wave in aVF is about twice the size of the R in 1 (the area enclosed by the complex should be estimated, not just its amplitude), the axis will point twice as close to the positive pole of aVF as it will to the positive pole of 1, i.e., about $+60°$. On the other hand, if the complex (fig. 4.3a) is twice as positive in 1 as it is negative in aVF, the axis will be twice as close to the positive pole of 1 as it is to the negative pole of aVF, that is, about $-30°$. If it is about equally positive in aVF and negative in 1 (fig. 4.3c), the axis will be equidistant from the negative pole of 1 and the positive of aVF, or $+135°$. Finally, if it is almost equally negative in both leads (fig. 4.3d), the axis will be about equidistant from the negative poles of the two leads, or $-135°$. Using just those two leads one can get to within 5 or 10 degrees of the axis in a few seconds. Since the axis may shift more than that with normal respiration, a fairly close approximation is all one can hope to achieve.

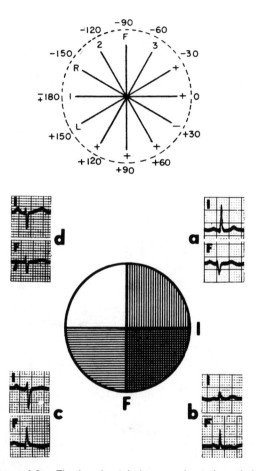

Figure 4.3. The four frontal plane quadrants bounded by leads 1 and aVF. The positive "field" of lead 1 is shaded vertically, the positive "field" of aVF horizontally. Examples of an axis in each quadrant occupy the four corners (leads are from the same tracings as *A*, *B*, *D* and *E* in fig. 4.4).

Another approach complements the 1/aVF method: the smallest deflection shown in any of the six limb leads indicates that the axis is roughly at right angles to that lead in the hexaxial clockface. For example, the tracing in figure 4.4C shows that aVR has the smallest QRS complex. At right angles to aVR is −60° or +120°; but from an initial glance at leads 1 and aVF, it can be seen that the axis is in the left axis quadrant, so the answer is −60°, not +120°. But the QRS is a little more positive than negative in aVR; and so, in search of maximal accuracy, swing the axis a shade towards the positive pole of aVR and call it −70° rather than −60°. With a little practice using this combined approach, it soon becomes a simple matter to place any axis accurately within a few seconds.

In short, the determination of an axis is accomplished in two swift stages: (1) look at leads 1 and aVF and place the axis in its appropriate quadrant; then

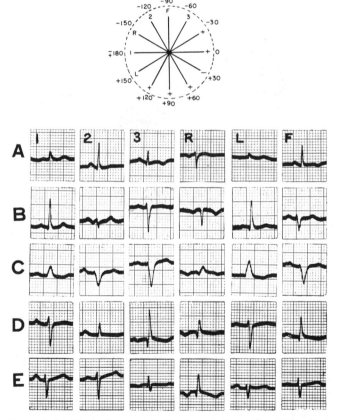

Figure 4.4. Illustrating axes in the frontal plane. The QRS axis in each tracing is as follows: (A) +60°. (B) − 30°. (C) − 70°. (D) +135°. (E) − 135°.

Figure 4.5. A simple triaxial reference figure illustrating the plotting of QRS (minute hand) and T (hour hand) on the clockface of the frontal plane. The axes plotted are those of the tracing in figure 4.4B.

(2) look for the lead with the smallest QRS deflection and place the axis at right angles (perpendicular) to it in the quadrant predetermined in stage 1. This is the best and fastest way to get the frontal plane axis—and it is accurate to within a few degrees.

In some circumstances, a single axis is meaningless. For example, when the QRS is virtually equiphasic in all the limb leads, the axis is usually and lazily described as "indeterminate." But of course no axis is actually indeterminate; and if, in such a case, the axis is really required, it is necessary to find two axes, "initial" for the first half of the QRS and "terminal" for the second half. The same applies when one is determining the axis in right bundle-branch block where the initial and terminal forces are usually widely separated. On the other hand, in left bundle-branch block the initial and terminal forces usually point in much the same direction and a single axis suffices.

These same principles and methods can and should be applied to determine the axis of the T waves, and of the P waves. It is well to plot the QRS and T axes routinely and to symbolize them with a long and a short arrow respectively, as in figure 4.5. These can be conveniently graphed on a simplified axial system, from which unnecessary lines and symbols have been omitted, as is illustrated in figure 4.5. Rubber stamps of both the labelled hexaxial system and the simplified triaxial form are useful toys.

The T wave axis normally points in the same general direction as the QRS axis; if they diverge by more than 50°, a myocardial abnormality (not necessarily structural) is almost always responsible.[3]

One of the advantages of applying the hexaxial reference system is that it teaches us to appreciate the interrelationship of the limb leads and to view the frontal plane record as a whole rather than in fragments. When one grasps this interrelationship it becomes absurd to consider the pattern of a single lead out of its hexaxial context. For example, some writers have stressed the importance of a prominent R wave in aVR in the diagnosis of right ventricular hypertrophy. But, from our knowledge of the mutual interdependence of all the limb leads in the hexaxial reference system, we know that for the QRS in aVR to be mainly positive the mean QRS axis must be *either* further to the right than +120° *or* further to the left than −60°. That is, it may mean either marked right or marked left axis deviation. Obviously it only means *right* ventricular hypertrophy when it is part of a significant *right*ward shift in the axis and says no more than that right axis deviation to more than $+120°$ suggests right ventricular hypertrophy.

During the first 6 months of life, the normally vertical axis moves leftward because the left ventricle grows faster than the right. By the age of 6 months, adult proportions have been reached and the axis then remains stable until, with advancing age in later life, a leftward drift sets in again.[1, 5]

The range of the frontal plane axis in normal adults is wide. Although the great majority of supposedly normal subjects have an axis between $-30°$ and $+110°$, a few supposed normals have axes that lie beyond these limits: in about 10 per thousand the axis is between $-30°$ and $-60°$, with about 3 per thousand between $+110°$ and $+135°$.[2, 8]

This discussion has so far represented the axis in one plane only, the plane of the limb leads, the frontal plane. But the cardiac axis obviously has direction in innumerable other planes, being oriented in three-dimensional space. However, the only other plane that our routine leads at all portray is the horizontal plane, the plane in which the chest leads lie. Unlike the limb leads, which symmetrically encircle the clockface of the frontal plane, the chest leads do not encircle the chest but span only a quarter of its circumference. They are sufficient, however, to determine whether the axis is pointing relatively forward or backward.

When the T-wave axis points anteriorly (TV_1 taller than TV_6) it is often a sign of myocardial abnormality.

Causes of Axis Deviation

The electrical QRS axis may be shifted to the right (beyond $+90°$) or to the left (beyond $0°$) in the following circumstances:

Right	*Left*
Normal variation	Normal variation
Mechanical shifts—inspiration, emphysema	Mechanical shifts—expiration, high diaphragm
Right ventricular hypertrophy	from pregnancy, ascites, abdominal tumors,
Right bundle branch block	etc.
Left posterior hemiblock	Left anterior hemiblock
Dextrocardia	Left bundle branch block
Ventricular ectopic rhythms	Endocardial cushion defects, and several other
Wolff-Parkinson-White syndrome	congenital lesions, both acyanotic and cy-
	anotic
	Wolff-Parkinson-White syndrome
	Emphysema
	Hyperkalemia
	Ventricular ectopic rhythms

In considering mechanical shifts, note that such disturbances as pneumothorax and pleural effusion usually cause a wholesale shift of the mediastinum, heart and all, toward the opposite side, and do not necessarily affect the heart's axis—they push it to one side without necessarily rotating it.

Axis Deviation of P Waves

With axis deviation of the QRS understood, one can see that the pattern of right atrial hypertrophy already referred to (p. 15), with P_1 lower than P_3, is an expression of a tendency toward right axis deviation of the P wave; and similarly the P wave pattern characteristic of mitral stenosis, with P_1 taller than P_3, and P_3 sometimes actually inverted, indicates a shift of the atrial axis toward the left. A P-wave axis to the right of $+60°$ is considered good evidence of chronic lung disease.

Electrical Heart Position

For descriptive purposes, the heart's "electrical position," as determined from leads aVL and aVF, is sometimes referred to. The five generally recognized positions are **horizontal, semi-horizontal, intermediate, semi-vertical** and **vertical**. If the main deflection of the QRS is positive in both leads, the position is called intermediate. If the main deflections are divergent, the heart is horizontal; if convergent, vertical. Semi-horizontal and semi-vertical positions are halfway stations between the intermediate position and the horizontal and vertical extremes.

In other words, horizontal, semi-horizontal, intermediate, semi-vertical and vertical positions respectively represent axes of about $-30°$, $0°$, $+30°$, $+60°$ and $+90°$. Although the use of these five terms to describe electrical position has little to recommend it, there are times when it is convenient to refer to a heart with an axis in the neighborhood of $0°$ to $-30°$ as a horizontal heart, and to one with an axis between $+60°$ and $+90°$ as a vertical heart.

Normal Findings in aV Leads

aVR: All three complexes—P, QRS and T—are inverted. This is to be expected, since the lead is an inverted stepchild in the hexaxial system—its negative pole is flanked by the positive poles of leads 1 and 2 (see fig. 4.1D, p. 33). The inverted QRS complex usually presents an rS pattern, but may be QS or Qr in form.

aVL: All the complexes in this lead are variable; P, QRS and T all may be upright or inverted, according to the heart's electrical position. If the QRS is as much as 6 mm tall, the accompanying T wave should not be inverted. Any pattern of the QRS can be normal, even QS when the voltage is low. However, if the R wave is 6 mm or more, the Q wave should be small by comparison—not more than 1 to 2 mm deep and less than 0.03 sec in duration.

aVF: The complexes in this lead are also variable, depending mainly on the heart's position. The P wave is usually upright but may at times be inverted. Again, as in aVL, if the R wave is 6 mm or more the T wave should be upright and the Q wave should be relatively small—not more than half the amplitude of the R and less than 0.03 sec in duration.

REFERENCES

1. Bachman, S., et al.: Effect of aging on the electrocardiogram. Am. J. Cardiol. 1981: **48**, 513.
2. Ewy, G. C., et al.: Electrocardiographic axis deviation in Navajo and Apache Indians. Chest 1979: **75**, 54.
3. Grant, R. P.: *Clinical Electrocardiography. The Spatial Vector Approach.* McGraw-Hill, New York, 1957.
4. *Nomenclature and Criteria for Diagnosis of Diseases of the Heart and Blood Vessels.* New York Heart Association, New York, 1955.
5. Perloff, J. K., et al.: Left axis deviation; a reassessment. Circulation 1979: **60**, 12.
6. Pryor, R., and Blount, S. G.: The clinical significance of true left axis deviation. Am. Heart J. 1966: **72**, 391.
7. Sodi-Pallares, D.: *New Bases of Electrocardiography.* C. V. Mosby, St. Louis, 1956.
8. Soffer, A.: Range of frontal plane QRS axes. Electrocardiograms of subjects in a multiphasic screening program. Chest 1977: **72**, 477.

Practical Points

Enough variables influence the tracing without introducing unnecessary technical ones. Care should therefore be exercised to ensure that technique is uniform from tracing to tracing and day to day, so that allowances do not have to be made for variations in technique. The following points are of importance.

1. Effective *contact* between electrode and skin is essential. Electrode jelly contains electrolytes and an abrasive; the abrasive is intended to break down the waterproof horny layer of the skin so that the electrolytes of jelly and body may form a continuous conductor. The jelly should therefore be rubbed briskly, not delicately smeared, on the skin before the electrode is applied.

   On the other hand, special jelly is seldom necessary, and Lewes obtained equally good records using a variety of contact substances including handcream, mayonnaise, mustard, ketchup, toothpaste, K-Y jelly and even tap water!

2. *Standardization* should be consistent. It should always, if possible, be full and should be adjusted exactly. When 1 mv is thrown into the circuit, the baseline should deflect exactly 10 mm. If standardization varies from tracing to tracing, it may be difficult to evaluate slight changes. Moreover, the interpreter is given considerable and unnecessary extra work if he has to take note of inconsistencies in standardization and make allowances for them.

3. *Placement of the precordial electrode* is often too casual. Kerwin found that placement by the same technician on the same patient in serial tracings varied by 2 to 3 cm in both vertical and horizontal directions. But placement should be as exact and constant as possible. For this reason only bony landmarks should be used in locating the precordial points (p. 2). Especially in leads close to the transitional zone (p. 46 and fig. 5.4), small displacements of the electrode may produce considerable changes in the pattern.

4. *Position of patient* while the tracing is being taken is of importance. He should be lying uniformly flat. If for some reason he has to be in any other position, a note to this effect should be made. Lying on either side, or sitting up, usually alters the heart's electrical axis and transitional zone; thus serial tracings, if taken in a variety of positions, are difficult to compare.

REFERENCES

Bradlow, B. A.: *How To Produce a Readable Electrocardiogram*. Charles C Thomas, Springfield, Ill., 1964.

Kerwin, A. J., et al.: A method for the accurate placement of chest electrodes in the taking of serial electrocardiographic tracings. Can. Med. Assoc. J. 1960: **82,** 258.

Lewes, D.: Electrode jelly in electrocardiography. Br. Heart J. 1965: **27,** 105.

Schnitzer, K.: *Electrocardiographic Techniques*, Ed. 2. Grune & Stratton, New York, 1960.

5

Genesis of the Precordial Pattern

The Intrinsicoid Deflection

Over the normal heart, the R wave becomes taller and the S wave smaller as the electrode is moved from right to left across the chest. To understand this it is helpful to consider the patterns that result when an electrode is placed at various points along a single strip of stimulated muscle.

In figure 5.1 the muscle strip *ABC* is stimulated at the *arrow* and the wave of activation spreads from left to right to the other end of the strip. If the electrode is placed successively at points 1, 2 and 3 the illustrated patterns are respectively derived: from point 1 an rS complex; from point 2 an RS; and from point 3 an Rs complex. It is easy to deduce from these patterns that as long as the impulse is travelling toward the electrode, a positive deflection (R wave) is produced, while a negative deflection (S wave) is inscribed when the impulse has passed the electrode and is travelling away from it.

A convenient way to rationalize this finding is to think of the impulse as a

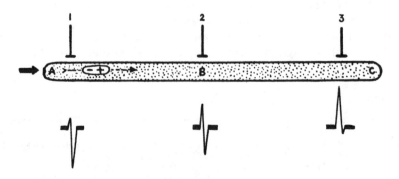

Figure 5.1

moving dipole (or doublet), i.e., a pair of charges, one positive and one negative, travelling together with the positive charge always leading. This is a crude but convenient approximation of what actually occurs when an impulse travels through stimulated tissue. Let us consider in terms of the dipole what happens when the electrode is placed in the middle of the muscle strip (point 2) and the strip is then stimulated. As the dipole travels from left to right, the leading positive charge gets nearer and nearer to the recording electrode; as it approaches it exerts a stronger and stronger influence on the electrode and the tracing becomes more and more positive, until it reaches maximal positivity (peak of R wave) at the moment that the positive charge is immediately under the electrode. A split second later the dipole has moved on and the negative charge is now immediately under the electrode exerting its maximal influence. So the tracing makes a quick swing (the downstroke) from maximal positivity to maximal negativity. Then, as the dipole continues on its journey, its negative tail recedes from the electrode and its influence diminishes. The tracing becomes less and less negative until, when the whole muscle strip has been activated, it regains the isoelectric line.

The downstroke which represents the abrupt swing from maximal positivity to maximal negativity is called the **intrinsic deflection**. It is a deflection of great practical importance, for it tells us the moment that the impulse (dipole) has arrived under the electrode. We know that the start of the upstroke marks the moment that the impulse started from the arrow; we now also know that the start of the downstroke marks the moment that the impulse arrived at *B*. We can thus measure the time it takes for the impulse to travel the distance from the *arrow* to *B*. This, of course, like all timing, is measured horizontally as illustrated in figure 5.2. This simple principle has been used for decades in

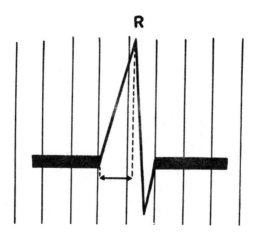

Figure 5.2. Timing of the intrinsic deflection. The time that elapses from the beginning of the QRS complex to the peak of the R wave is measured horizontally.

experimental physiology. Lewis used it to plot the times of impulse arrival at various points in the atria when he was attempting to prove his theory of circus movement; Prinzmetal used it even more extensively in his experiments on the atrial arrhythmias; and modern electrophysiologists today make use of the same principle.

In the light of this let us now examine what happens when electrodes are placed in contact with the myocardium of normally functioning ventricles, either in the experimental animal or in man with the heart surgically exposed. If an electrode is placed in contact with the surface of the right ventricle, a mainly negative (rS) deflection is inscribed; if placed in contact with the left ventricle, a mainly positive (qR) complex is registered. For all practical purposes the patterns are the same as those obtained clinically from precordial points to the right and left, say V_1 and V_5. To appreciate the reason for this one must recall the sequence in which the ventricular muscle is depolarized (fig. 5.3).

The impulse apparently descends the left bundle branch rather more rapidly than the right, with the result that the left septal surface is activated about 0.01 sec before the right septal surface. The net result is that the septum is activated mainly from left to right (*1* in fig. 5.3). Then both ventricular walls are activated simultaneously, but because the right wall is much thinner than the left, the impulse traverses its perpendicular path through the right wall (*2*) and arrives at the epicardium well before impulses on the left have reached the epicardial surface. Then, finally, the left ventricular muscle is "penetrated," first at the apex and then successively toward the base (*3–5*).

Now if an electrode is placed over the thin wall of the right ventricle (*A* in fig. 5.3), the first impulse (dipole) to influence it will be that traversing the septum from left to right (*1*); this is travelling toward the electrode and the deflection produced will therefore be positive. The next impulse (*2*) is also

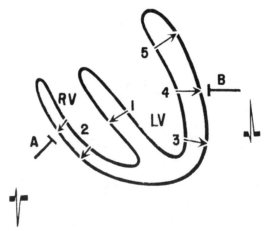

Figure 5.3.   The approximate order of activation of the ventricular myocardium, and the form of ventricular complex derived over each ventricle.

travelling toward *A* and therefore augments the already positive deflection. From this time on, the only dipoles left in the picture are those activating the left ventricle. These are all travelling away from the electrode *A* and therefore cause a negative deflection. The wall is thick and the impulses have a relatively long journey, so the S wave is relatively deep. The composite picture produced is thus an rS complex.

When an electrode is placed over the left ventricle (*B* in fig. 5.3), again the first influence felt is (*1*). This is now travelling away from our electrode and therefore causes a small initial negative deflection (Q wave). From now on the electrode is under the influence of the approaching impulses travelling toward it through the left ventricular wall. Therefore the remainder of the tracing is positive, and the composite picture is a qR complex.

Thus over the right ventricle a deep S wave represents activation of the left ventricle, while over the left ventricle itself its activation is represented by a tall R wave. From both sides of the heart the major deflection represents activation of the major (left) ventricle. As in the single muscle strip, the downstroke from the peak of the R wave is the intrinsic deflection and tells us when the impulse has reached the epicardial surface of the ventricle over which the electrode is placed. As the right ventricle has a much thinner wall, the impulse over this ventricle naturally reaches the surface much earlier than it reaches the surface of the left ventricle; i.e., the peak of the small R wave over the right ventricle is reached earlier than the peak of the tall R wave over the left ventricle.

In clinical practice we obviously cannot take **direct** or **epicardial leads**, and the best we can do is to place the electrode on the chest wall at strategic intervals across the precordium. The resulting series of **semidirect** or **precordial leads** produces patterns very similar to those taken with the electrode in direct epicardial contact. In these clinical leads the downstroke is the analogue of the intrinsic deflection and is therefore called the **intrinsicoid deflection**. This deflection should begin, i.e., the peak of the R wave should be reached, within 0.02 sec in V_1 and within 0.04 sec in V_6. If it takes longer than this for the intrinsicoid deflection to start downward, it means that the impulse is late in reaching the epicardial surface of the ventricle under the electrode, and this indicates either that the wall of the ventricle has become thickened (ventricular hypertrophy) or dilated (so that the conducting paths have been lengthened), or that there is a block in the conducting system to the ventricle concerned (bundle-branch block).

This application of the dipole concept to the complex process of activation of the entire heart is obviously an over-simplification, though a most convenient and practical one. Regardless of what term—impulse, dipole, wavefront, electromotive force or vector—is used in describing the phenomena of myocardial activation, the principles enunciated above are helpful in visualizing the train of electrical events.

"Clockwise" and "Counterclockwise" Rotation

Between the definite "right ventricular" pattern (rS) of V_1 and the definite "left ventricular" pattern (qR) of V_6, there are transitional patterns—the S wave becomes less deep as the electrode is moved toward the left while the R wave becomes progressively taller. The **transitional zone** is the area in which the QRS is equiphasic (an RS complex), and this usually appears in V_3 or V_4 or between them. In figure 5.4 five series of precordial leads from V_1 to V_6 are recorded. The first three show normal transitional zones (T): in *A* lead V_3 shows the equiphasic complex; in *B* lead V_4 shows it; in *C* the actual transitional pattern is not shown, but V_3 presents an rS pattern while V_4 shows an Rs; the transition from one to the other has occurred between the two.

The last two series in the figure show abnormal transitions. In *D* the transition occurs between V_1 and V_2—the Rs pattern is recorded unusually far to the right of the chest. In *E* the transition occurs between V_5 and V_6—an rS pattern is recorded unusually far to the left of the precordium.

In explaining this we picture the heart to have rotated about its longitudinal axis. In describing rotation about this axis we are asked to look *up* at the heart from *under* the diaphragm. Thus if the front of the heart revolves toward the left we have, from our subphrenic viewpoint, **clockwise rotation**. If the front of the heart rotates toward the right we have **counterclockwise rotation**. Clockwise rotation will obviously move the zone between the two ventricles toward the left so that the transitional zone in the precordial tracing shifts to the left (*E* in fig. 5.4), while counterclockwise rotation will shift the transitional zone toward the right (*D* in fig. 5.4). Such rotations are not necessarily abnormal.

Note on Use of Terms "Ventricular Lead" and "Ventricular Pattern"

A precordial record is not derived exclusively from one underlying area of the myocardium. No matter what lead is used, the resulting tracing is always a composite picture, an electrical resultant of all the many simultaneous impulses, or dipoles, that are travelling in various directions through the whole myocardium. It is true that the area of myocardium subjacent to the electrode may make a major contribution to the record—the so-called "local pickup" effect—because an important factor determining recorded voltage is the nearness of the electrode to the electrical force, and therefore a nearby force will exert more influence than a distant one on the pattern produced. As an example, if the electrode is placed at position 6, the impulses travelling through the wall of the left ventricle are appreciably nearer to it than those traversing the right ventricular wall, and the left ventricle therefore exerts a greater influence than the right; but as long as forces continue to be generated in the right ventricular wall, they will be making some contribution to what we have been calling the "left ventricular pattern." The "vector" electrocardiographers (see below) in particular have de-emphasized the "local pickup" effect and rightly point out

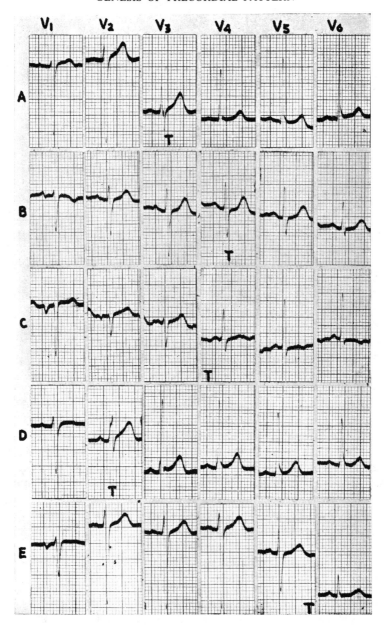

Figure 5.4. Transitional zones (*T*). (*A, B* and *C*) Normal transitions. (*D*) Counterclockwise rotation. (*E*) Clockwise rotation.

that, no matter where the electrode is placed, the resulting pattern is a product of the total electrical forces generated in the myocardium and is not derived from the subjacent area of the heart.

In other words, a right or left ventricular pattern means the type of pattern produced *when the electrode is placed over* the right or left ventricle rather than the pattern produced by the subjacent ventricle. Indeed it is obvious that the so-called right ventricular pattern is mainly derived from left ventricular forces (the deep S wave in V_1 represents *left* ventricular depolarization). Provided one appreciates what is meant by right and left ventricular lead and right and left ventricular pattern, these are useful descriptive terms.

A Word about Vectors

The leads so far described are known as "scalar," and the system employing them is scalar electrocardiography. It seems appropriate to give a word of integration with vector electrocardiography (or vectorcardiography). Students of vector methods have introduced ideas that are helpful and illuminating in our everyday reading of scalar tracings, and the beginner should at least be acquainted with vector terminology and should appreciate the close correlation between scalar and vector methods. The two methods are complementary and should not be thought of as rivals.

Vector is a technical term for force and as applied to electrocardiography obviously means electrical force. As all electrocardiography deals exclusively in electrical forces, all electrocardiography is necessarily vectorial. However, by association and implication, the term has become reserved for that form of electrocardiography in which the heart's forces are represented by arrows and loops, rather than by waves and complexes. *Spatial* vectorcardiography indicates that the arrows or loops are disposed in three-dimensional space—not just two-dimensional symbols on paper like the complexes of the scalar tracing.

Like any other force, a vector has size and direction. Both of these attributes can be conveniently embodied in an arrow whose length is proportional to the size of the force. An instantaneous vector represents the resultant of all the heart's electrical forces at a given moment (any of the thin arrows in fig. 5.5 *A* and *B*). The mean vector is the average or resultant of all the instantaneous vectors (thick arrow in fig. 5.5 *B*). The loop (fig. 5.5 *C*) substitutes for a set of innumerable arrows a single continuous line and is obtained by joining up the heads of all the arrows; conversely the instantaneous vector for any given moment can be derived from the loop by drawing an arrow from the "center" of the loop to a point at its periphery.

There are two methods for deriving a vectorcardiogram:

1. The routine 12-lead electrocardiogram can be translated into the necessary vectors from which the loop is artificially constructed. This is the method that Grant[2] popularized and its advantage is that the only equipment it requires is a standard electrocardiograph and a nimble mind. Its disadvantage is that it derives the vectors from only two planes, the frontal (limb leads) and horizontal (precordial leads), and it obviously can provide no additional information that is not contained in the scalar tracing from which it is derived.

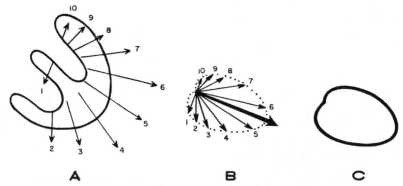

Figure 5.5. The **vector loop**. (*A*) Diagram of successive instantaneous axes (or vectors) as the ventricular muscle mass is depolarized. (*B*) Regrouping of the instantaneous vectors in A as though they all originated from a single "center"; the thick arrow represents the *mean* vector, being the resultant of the 10 instantaneous vectors. If the heads of the vector *arrows* are joined by a continuous line the vector loop is formed (*C*).

2. The loop may be directly written by means of the cathode ray oscillograph. For this purpose electrodes are placed on the torso in such a way that three leads are obtained whose planes are at right angles to each other (orthogonal leads). Thus each of the three planes—frontal, horizontal and sagittal—is equally represented in the resulting vectorcardiogram. As all three planes are represented, this obviously results in additional information in certain cases, and this is the main advantage of the method. Such a vectorcardiogram may be of particular value in distinguishing between right ventricular hypertrophy and right bundle-branch block, and between right ventricular hypertrophy and posterior infarction; and in recognizing atrial abnormalities, lateral ischemia, infarction in the presence of LBBB, and inferior infarction in the presence of left anterior hemiblock.[3] Disadvantages of the method are that the equipment is relatively costly, and that it has little or no place in the diagnosis of arrhythmias.

Two further points are noteworthy: vectorcardiographers cannot agree on the most suitable placement of electrodes for obtaining the most accurate spatial record though most espouse the Frank system; second, the derived loop cannot contain more information than scalar leads recorded with the same electrode positions; and therefore, if one had adequate experience with such leads, one could obtain all the information that the vectorcardiographer can obtain from the loop. Unfortunately scalar leads of this kind have not received the attention and study they probably deserve.

In summary, vectorcardiography is an interesting and valuable research tool, necessarily of rather limited clinical value; limited because it affords only modest additional information over conventional scalar leads, because it cannot take the place of conventional tracings in diagnosing arrhythmias, and because of the more expensive equipment it requires. An interesting survey revealed that established experts in vector interpretation achieved greater diagnostic accuracy from scalar tracings than from the corresponding vectorcardiogram.[7]

REFERENCES

1. Grant, R. P.: The relationship between the anatomic position of the heart and the electrocardiogram. A criticism of "unipolar" electrocardiography. Circulation 1953: **7**, 890.
2. Grant, R. P.: *Clinical Electrocardiography. The Spatial Vector Approach.* McGraw-Hill, New York, 1957.
3. Hoffman, I.: Clinical vectorcardiography in adults. Am. Heart J. 1980: **100**, 239 and 373.
4. Johnston, F. D.: The clinical value of vectorcardiography. Circulation 1961: **23**, 297.
5. Milnor, W. R., Talbot, S. A., and Newman, E. V.: A study of the relationship between unipolar leads and spatial vectorcardiograms, using the panoramic vectorcardiograph. Circulation 1953: **7**, 545.
6. Scherlis, L.: Spatial vectorcardiography: 3-dimensional study of electrical forces in heart. Modern Med. 1957: p. 172 (Feb. 1).
7. Simonson, E., et al: Diagnostic accuracy of the vectorcardiogram and electrocardiogram. Am. J. Cardiol. 1966: **17**, 828.

6

Chamber Enlargement

With the genesis of the normal precordial tracing fresh in mind, the natural pattern to turn attention to is that of ventricular hypertrophy. In so doing, one should keep in mind the discouraging fact that the signs of hypertrophy are not sensitive though reasonably specific (see p. 181).

Left Ventricular Hypertrophy

The pattern of left ventricular hypertrophy (LVH) is what one would predict. If the wall of the left ventricle is thicker than normal, the impulse will take longer to traverse it and arrive at the epicardial surface. Therefore the QRS interval will increase toward or to the upper limit of normal, the intrinsicoid deflection may be somewhat delayed over the left ventricle and the voltage of the QRS complexes will increase—producing deeper S waves over the right ventricle and taller R waves over the left (as in the precordial leads in fig. 6.1).

Many criteria have been proposed for the diagnosis of LVH, and they are all unreliable. Though quite specific, they lack sensitivity; according to Devereux,[10, 29] all the usual electrocardiographic and vectorcardiographic criteria attain a limit of about 60% sensitivity when they approach 95% specificity.

The ancient, honorable and much-quoted criterion for LVH proposed by Sokolow and Lyon[37] simply adds the depth of the S wave in lead V_1 to the height of the R wave in either V_5 or V_6 (whichever is the taller), and if the sum amounts to more than 35 mm LVH is present. This criterion correlates well with the thickness of the left ventricular walls and the diameter of the left ventricular cavity as determined by echocardiography.[39]

One of the most popular formulas so far developed is Estes[13] scoring system: (1) *3 points* if the largest R or S wave in the limb leads is 20 mm or more, *or if* the largest S wave in V_1, V_2 or V_3 is 25 mm or more, *or if* the largest R wave in V_4, V_5 or V_6 is 25 mm or more; (2) *3 points* if there is any type of ST shift opposite in direction to the QRS, provided no digitalis is being taken (if digitalis is being taken, the shift must be of classical "strain" type—see below—and only 1 point is scored); (3) *2 points* if there is left axis deviation to $-15°$ or more; (4) *1 point* if the QRS duration is 0.09 sec or more; (5) *1 point* if the

51

intrinsicoid deflection in V_{5-6} begins at 0.04 sec or later; (6) *3 points* if the "P-terminal force" in V_1 is 0.04 or more. With a maximum of 13 points, 5 indicates LVH and 4 probable LVH. For comparison, the criteria proposed by Scott[32-35] are listed in an adjacent "box." For good exercise, apply these three sets of criteria to figures 6.1 to 6.4, assuming that none of these patients was taking digitalis.

Estes' Scoring System for LVH

1. R or S in limb lead:	20 mm or more	
S in V_1, V_2 or V_3	25 mm or more	3
R in V_4, V_5 or V_6	25 mm or more	
2. Any ST shift (without digitalis)		3
Typical "strain" ST-T (with digitalis)		1
3. LAD: $-15°$ or more		2
4. QRS interval: 0.09 sec or more		1
5. I.D. in V_{5-6}: 0.04 sec or more		1
6. P-terminal force in V_1 more than 0.04		3
Total		13
(5 = LVH; 4 = probable LVH		

Scott's Criteria for LVH[32-35]

Limb leads:

R in 1 + S in 3:	more than 25 mm
R in aVL:	more than 7.5 mm
R in aVF:	more than 20 mm
S in aVR:	more than 14 mm

Chest leads:

S in V_1 or V_2 + R in V_5 or V_6:	more than 35 mm
R in V_5 or V_6:	more than 26 mm
R + S in any V lead:	more than 45 mm

Early in the disease, septal forces (q in leads 1, aVL, V_5 and V_6; r in V_1) tend to increase, but as time goes by and conduction in the left ventricle becomes impaired, they shrink and may disappear (fig. 6.3).[9]

"Strain" is sometimes applied when ST-T-U abnormalities develop. Over the left ventricle (V_5, V_6) the ST segments become depressed with an *upward*

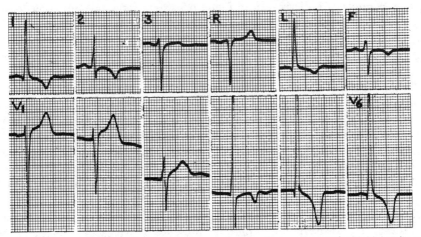

Figure 6.1. Left ventricular hypertrophy and strain. Note: axis $-10°$ with high voltage of QRS complexes in limb and precordial leads; secondary ST-T changes in 1, 2, aVL, aVF and V_{4-6}.

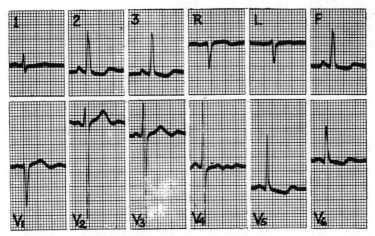

Figure 6.2. Left ventricular hypertrophy and strain. *Note:* Axis of $+80°$ and therefore secondary ST-T changes in 2, 3, aVF and V_{5-6}. Notice QRS amplitude of over 40 mm in V_3 and V_4.

convexity whose final downward curve blends into an inverted T wave (fig. 6.1). The same ST-T changes are usually evident in limb leads having the form (qR) of left ventricular leads. Thus when LVH appears in a heart with left axis deviation, lead 1 and aVL will show ST-T changes (fig. 6.1), whereas in a vertical heart the ST-T changes will appear in lead 3 and aVF (fig. 6.2). If the tracing shows tall R waves in all three standard leads, the ST-T changes may be present in all three. In leads where the QRS is predominantly negative, as in V_1, the ST segment is reciprocally elevated with an *upward concavity*. A further example of LVH is seen in figure 6.3 which shows gigantic precordial QRS voltage, loss of q waves in leads 1, aVL, V_5 and V_6 with loss of r in V_1, and characteristic ST-T displacements.

Not uncommonly, the earliest indication of left ventricular strain is inversion of U waves in left ventricular leads (fig. 6.4).

"Strain" is a useful, non-committal term. The exact mechanism that produces its pattern is not completely settled, but there are several factors believed to contribute to it. It is known to develop in those who have shown the pattern of LVH for some time, and the pattern intensifies when dilation and failure set in; its development correlates well with increasing left ventricular mass as determined by echocardiography.[10a] Myocardial ischemia and slowing of intraventricular conduction are important among the factors which probably contribute to the pattern.

Left axis deviation is not an invariable accompaniment of LVH; indeed, significant left axis deviation implies the presence of myocardial disease in the left ventricle apart from pure hypertrophy.[7, 8]

Along with the left ventricle the left atrium also may suffer; in such cases the stigmata of left atrial enlargement (p. 59) may accompany the pattern of ventricular hypertrophy.

Much the commonest cause of LVH is hypertension. Less frequently the pattern is found in aortic stenosis, aortic insufficiency, coarctation of the aorta, hypertrophic cardiomyopathy and occasionally in other conditions.

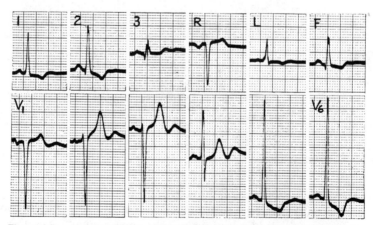

Figure 6.3. Left ventricular hypertrophy. Note huge amplitude of QRS in V_5 and V_6 with high voltage in all chest leads. Axis is $+40°$, and ST-T pattern is typical.

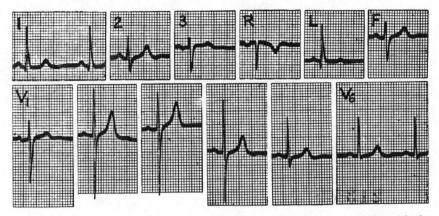

Figure 6.4. From a severely hypertensive patient showing earliest signs of **left ventricular strain**—inverted U waves seen in 1, 2 and V_{4-6}, T wave in aVL abnormally low.

Right Ventricular Hypertrophy

When the left ventricle hypertrophies, the normal dominance of the left ventricle becomes exaggerated and we have seen that the associated electrocardiogram reflects this by exaggerating the normal precordial QRS pattern—tall R waves get taller and deep S waves get deeper. On the other hand, when the right ventricle hypertrophies the normal balance of power is upset and finally reversed, and this is reflected in the electrocardiogram by a reversal of the normal precordial pattern—R waves assume prominence in right precordial leads while deepening S waves develop in left precordial leads.

Most of the criteria for recognizing right ventricular hypertrophy (RVH) center around the QRS pattern in the right chest leads. As the right ventricle hypertrophies, there is an increase in the height of right precordial R waves with concomitant decrease in depth of the S wave and consequent increase in the R:S ratio. If this ratio exceeds 1.0, RVH can usually be diagnosed. There is evidence that V_{4R} is a more useful and reliable lead than V_1, in that it not infrequently reveals an abnormal ratio of more than 1.0 while that in V_1 remains normal.[5] In the fully developed picture of RVH, the precordial pattern is completely reversed so that tall R waves (R, qR or Rs) are written in V_1 with deep S waves (rS) in V_6 (fig. 6.5). An incomplete right bundle-branch block pattern (rSr') in right chest leads may signal RVH; and this pattern seems particularly common in the RVH of mitral stenosis (see fig. 30.1*B*, p. 456). In the limb leads right axis deviation usually develops and at times prominent Q waves, simulating inferior infarction, appear in leads 2, 3, and aVF (fig. 6.6). In children, the $S_1S_2S_3$ pattern (i.e., S wave deeper than R in all three standard leads) is a reliable index of RVH.[24]

A pattern short of RVH is often seen. This consists in rS complexes all across the precordium (clockwise rotation), with right axis deviation in the limb leads. Such a tracing is seen in many cases of emphysema (fig. 6.7).

Right ventricular "strain" manifests itself in ST-T changes similar to those seen in left ventricular but in different leads, namely in those over the right ventricle (V_1, V_2) and in leads 2, 3 and aVF. The changes of well developed RVH are seen in figures 6.5 and 6.6. In infants, after the first day or two of life, an upright T wave in V_1 is good evidence of RVH.[44]

The fully developed pattern of RVH is much less commonly seen than that of LVH, because the causes of right ventricular overloading are less common and because it requires a greater overload to produce the mature pattern. In LVH the left ventricle is already the "major" ventricle and as it hypertrophies its majority becomes accentuated, so that early hypertrophy is fairly readily seen as an exaggeration of the normal pattern. In RVH, on the other hand, the right ventricle, starting as the minor ventricle, has a good deal of overtaking to do before it becomes the major ventricle and materially alters the tracing.

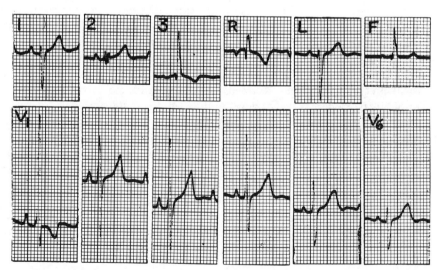

Figure 6.5.   Right ventricular hypertrophy. From a 5-year-old boy with a tetralogy of Fallot. *Note*: Marked right axis deviation (+145°), enormously tall R in V_1 and rS in V_6. The P waves indicate right atrial hypertrophy and are typical for P-congenitale.

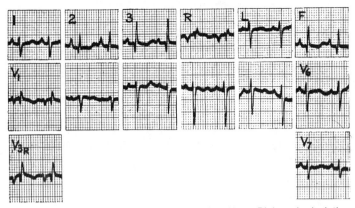

Figure 6.6. **Right ventricular hypertrophy.** *Note:* Right axis deviation (+130°) with prominent R in V₁; in V₃ᵣ the R:S ratio is definitely greater than 1.0, while rS complexes are seen in the remaining V leads.

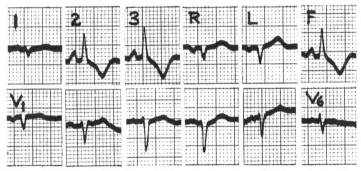

Figure 6.7. From a patient with **emphysema.** *Note:* Right axis deviation (+95°) with rS complexes all across the precordium. The ST-T pattern of right ventricular "strain" is fully developed in leads 2, 3 and aVF. The P-wave pattern suggests P-pulmonale with an axis of +80° and pointed, though not very tall, P waves in 2, 3 and aVF.

In the presence of RVH, the right atrium may also suffer. In such cases the stigmata of right atrial enlargement (p. 58–59) are added to the pattern of ventricular overload. If pure mitral stenosis is the cause of the RVH, the P-mitrale pattern (fig. 30.1*A*, p. 456) may appear.

The main causes of RVH are congenital lesions, such as the tetralogy of Fallot, pulmonic stenosis and transposition of the great vessels; acquired valvular lesions, including mitral stenosis and tricuspid insufficiency; and chronic lung diseases, especially emphysema.

Salient Features of Right Ventricular Hypertrophy
1. Reversal of precordial pattern with tall R over right precordium (V_1, V_2) and deep S over left (V_5, V_6); or rS across precordium
2. QRS interval within normal limits
3. Late intrinsicoid deflection in V_{1-2}
4. Right axis deviation
5. ST segment depression with *upward convexity* and inverted T waves in right precordial leads (V_{1-2}) and in whichever limb leads show tall R waves

Patterns of Systolic and Diastolic Overloading

The patterns of ventricular overload have been subdivided into "systolic overloading" and "diastolic overloading."[3, 4] When the heart has to pump against an obstruction, it is in systole that the strain is felt; when the blood overfills the ventricle, as in aortic regurgitation, the predominant strain is diastolic.

With systolic overloading of the left ventricle, as seen in hypertension and aortic stenosis, the classical pattern of hypertrophy as outlined on pages 51–54 is found, but when the main load is borne in diastole, as in pure aortic regurgitation, mitral regurgitation or in patent ductus, a different pattern appears; this consists of prominent upright T waves as well as tall R waves over the left ventricle (V_{5-6}) as seen in figure 6.8.

With systolic overloading of the right ventricle, as in pulmonic stenosis or pulmonary hypertension, the classical pattern in figure 6.5 is produced; but when the main load is diastolic, as in atrial septal defect, the pattern of complete or incomplete right bundle-branch block (see Chapter 7) results. This pattern apparently does not result from blockade of the right bundle branch but rather results from hypertrophy of the basal portions of the right ventricle.[43]

Combined Ventricular Hypertrophy

Enlargement of both ventricles is suggested if there are voltage criteria for LVH in the chest leads combined with right axis deviation in the limb leads; or if there are criteria for LVH in left chest leads combined with prominent R waves in right chest leads; or if a shallow S wave in V_1 is associated with a strikingly deeper S wave in V_2—the "shallow S-wave syndrome."[35]

Atrial Enlargement

A P-wave axis to the right of +70° ("**P-pulmonale**") suggests right atrial enlargement (RAE) from chronic lung disease; in congenital heart disease with RAE, the axis is usually not so far to the right ("**P-congenitale**"). Both may

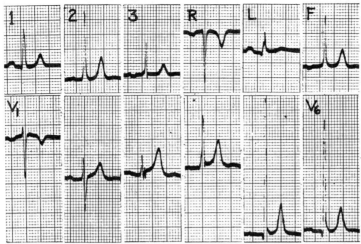

Figure 6.8.   Left ventricular diastolic overloading, from a patient with rheumatic mitral regurgitation. R waves in V_5 and V_6 are unusually tall and are accompanied by tall and pointed T waves. The P waves show P-mitrale pattern, being rather broad and notched with a leftward axis shift to about $-15°$.

show narrow, pointed P waves in limb and right chest leads; but sometimes, when the right auricle enlarges sufficiently to extend toward the left across the front of the heart, the P waves of RAE may be inverted in V_1 and so create the illusion of *left* atrial enlargement (LAE) (see fig. 29.14 on p. 452). In tricuspid disease the P waves may be tall and notched, with first peak taller than second ("**P-tricuspidale**").[14]

Suggestive as these P-wave features are, it is intriguing to realize that QRS criteria are probably better! A qR in V_1 (in the absence of myocardial infarction) correlates best with echocardiographically determined RAE; and the next best criterion is the finding of small QRS voltage in V_1 with abrupt increase (threefold or more) in the QRS voltage in V_2.[28]

In LAE the P wave is often widened to 0.12 sec or more, notched, and its terminal part may be deviated backward and to the left; i.e., it becomes frankly negative in V_1[1] and may become negative in leads 3 and aVF ("**P-mitrale**").[25] The product of width (in seconds) × depth (in millimeters) of the terminal part of PV_1 ("P-terminal force") is used as an index of LAE;[25] if the product is more than 0.04 mm sec, LAE is indicated. The widened P waves are often notched, the interval between peaks being greater than 0.04 sec, in fact fulfilling the criteria for intra-atrial block (see p. 319). Indeed there is good evidence that the pattern of LAE is more often due to a conduction disturbance than to atrial enlargement and it has even been suggested that the term left atrial enlargement be replaced with "intra-atrial conduction defect."[21] In some patients with pure left heart disease, with no reasons for *right* atrial enlargement and every reason for *left*, an unexplained **pseudo-P-pulmonale** pattern may develop.[8]

REFERENCES

1. Arevalo, A. C., et al.: A simple electrocardiographic indication of left atrial enlargement. J.A.M.A. 1963: **185,** 359.
2. Beach, C., et al.: Electrocardiogram of pure left ventricular hypertrophy and its differentiation from lateral ischemia. Br. Heart J. 1981: **46,** 285.
3. Cabrera, E., and Monroy, J. R.: Systolic and diastolic loading of the heart. II. Electrocardiographic data. Am. Heart. J. 1952: **43,** 669.
4. Cabrera, E., and Gaxiola, A.: A critical reevaluation of systolic and diastolic overloading patterns. Prog. Cardiovasc. Dis. 1959: **2,** 219.
5. Camerini, F., et al.: Lead V4R in right ventricular hypertrophy. Br. Heart J. 1956: **18,** 13.
6. Carter, W. A., and Estes, E. H.: Electrocardiographic manifestations of ventricular hypertrophy; a computer study of ECG-anatomic correlations in 319 cases. Am. Heart J. 1964: **68,** 173.
7. Chou, T., et al.: Specificity of the current electrocardiographic criteria in the diagnosis of left ventricular hypertrophy. Am. Heart J. 1960: **60,** 371.
8. Chou, T., and Helm, R. A.: The pseudo P pulmonale. Circulation 1965: **32,** 96.
9. Das, G., et al.: Natural history of electrical interventricular septal force in the course of left ventricular hypertrophy in man. J. Electrocardiol. 1981: **14,** 109.
10. Devereux, R. B., and Reichek, N.: Left ventricular hypertrophy. Cardiovasc. Rev. Rep. 1980: **1,** 55.
10a. Devereux, R. B., and Reichek, N.: Repolarization abnormalities of left ventricular hypertrophy. J. Electrocardiol. 1982: **15,** 47.
11. Davies, H., and Evans, W.: The significance of deep S waves in leads II and III. Br. Heart J. 1960: **22,** 551.
12. Engler, R. L., et al.: The electrocardiogram in asymmetric septal hypertrophy. Chest 1979: **75,** 167.
13. Estes, E. H.: Electrocardiography and vectorcardiography. In *The Heart,* Ch. 21, Ed. 3, edited by J. W. Hurst and R. B. Logue. McGraw-Hill, New York, 1974.
14. Gamboa, R., et al.: The electrocardiogram in tricuspid atresia and pulmonary atresia with intact ventricular septum. Circulation 1966: **34,** 24.
15. Gooch, A. S., et al.: Leftward shift of the terminal P forces in the electrocardiogram associated with left atrial enlargement. Am. Heart J. 1966: **71,** 727.
16. Grant, R. P.: Left axis deviation. Circulation 1956: **14,** 233.
17. Grant, R. P.: Left axis deviation. Mod. Concepts Cardiovasc. Dis. 1958: **27,** 437.
18. Griep, A. H.: Pitfalls in the electrocardiographic diagnosis of left ventricular hypertrophy: a correlative study of 200 autopsied patients. Circulation 1959: **20,** 30.
19. Holt, J. H., et al.: A study of the human heart as a multiple dipole source; IV. Left ventricular hypertrophy in the presence of right bundle branch block. Circulation 1977: **56,** 391.
20. Johnson, J. B., et al.: The relation between electrocardiographic evidence of right ventricular hypertrophy and pulmonary artery pressure in patients with chronic pulmonary disease. Circulation 1950: 31, 536.
21. Josephson, M. E.: Electrocardiographic left atrial enlargement; electrophysiologic, echocardiographic and hemodynamic correlates. Am. J. Cardiol. 1977: **39,** 967.
22. Mazzoleni, A., et al.: Correlation between component cardiac weights and electrocardiographic patterns in 185 cases. Circulation 1964: **30,** 808.
23. McGregor, M.: The genesis of the electrocardiogram of right ventricular hypertrophy. Br. Heart J. 1950: **12,** 351.
24. Moller, J. H., et al.: Significance of the $S_1S_2S_3$ electrocardiographic pattern in children. Am. J. Cardiol. 1965: **16,** 524.
25. Morris, J. J., et al.: P-wave analysis in valvular heart disease. Circulation 1964: **29,** 242.
26. Myers, G. B.: The form of the QRS complex in the normal precordial electrocardiogram and in ventricular hypertrophy. Am. Heart J. 1950: **39,** 637.
27. Parkin, T. W.: Problems in the electrocardiographic diagnosis of ventricular enlargement. Circulation 1962: **26,** 946.
28. Reeves, W. C., et al.: Two-dimensional echocardiographic assessment of electrocardiographic criteria for right atrial enlargement. Circulation 1981: **64,** 387.
29. Reichek, N., and Devereux, R. B.: Left ventricular hypertrophy: relationship of anatomic, echocardiographic and electrocardiographic findings. Circulation 1981: **63,** 1391.
30. Roman, G. T., et al.: Right ventricular hypertrophy. Correlation of electrocardiographic and anatomic findings. Am. J. Cardiol. 1961: **7,** 481.

31. Romhilt, D. W., et al.: A critical appraisal of the electrocardiographic criteria for the diagnosis of left ventricular hypertrophy. Circulation 1969: **40**, 185.
32. Scott, R. C., et al.: Left ventricular hypertrophy. A study of the accuracy of current electrocardiographic criteria when compared with autopsy findings in one hundred cases. Circulation 1955: **11**, 89.
33. Scott, R. C.: The electrocardiographic diagnosis of left ventricular hypertrophy. Am. Heart J. 1960: **59**, 155.
34. Scott, R. C.: The correlation between the electrocardiographic patterns of ventricular hypertrophy and the anatomic findings. Circulation 1960: **21**, 256.
35. Scott, R. C.: Ventricular hypertrophy. Cardiovasc. Clin. 1973: **5(3)**, 220.
36. Scott, R. C.: The electrocardiographic diagnosis of right ventricular hypertrophy; correlation with the anatomic findings. Am. Heart J. 1960, **60**, 659.
37. Sokolow, M., and Lyon, T. P.: The ventricular complex in left ventricular hypertrophy as obtained by unipolar precordial and limb leads. Am. Heart J. 1949: **37**, 161.
38. Soloff, L. A., and Lawrence, J. W.: The electrocardiographic findings in left ventricular hypertrophy and dilatation. Circulation 1962: **26**, 553.
39. Toshima, H., et al.: Correlations between electrocardiographic, vectorcardiographic, and echocardiographic findings in patients with left ventricular overload. Am. Heart J. 1977: **94**, 547.
40. Walker, C. H. M., and Rose, R. L.: Importance of age, sex and body habitus in the diagnosis of left ventricular hypertrophy from the precordial electrocardiogram in childhood and adolescence. Pediatrics 1961: **28**, 705.
41. Walker, I. C., Helm, R. A., and Scott, R. C.: Right ventricular hypertrophy; I. Correlation of isolated right ventricular hypertrophy at autopsy with the electrocardiographic findings. Circulation 1955: **11**, 215.
42. Walker, I. C., Scott, R. C., and Helm, R. A.: Right ventricular hypertrophy; II. Correlation of electrocardiographic right ventricular hypertrophy with the anatomic findings. Circulation 1955: **11**, 223.
43. Walker, W. J., et al.: Electrocardiographic and hemodynamic correlation in atrial septal defect. Am. Heart. J. 1956: **52**, 547.
44. Ziegler, R. F.: The importance of positive T waves in the right precordial electrocardiogram during the first year of life. Am. Heart J. 1956: **52**, 533.

7

Bundle-Branch Block

Of the various forms of intraventricular block, bundle-branch block is most common and best recognized. Other forms result from delayed conduction or block in a subdivision of the left bundle branch (hemiblock—see chapter 8); from diffuse slowing of the impulse throughout the conduction system of one ventricle; or from conduction disturbances in the ventricular wall. In our current state of knowledge, the terms arborization, parietal and periinfarction blocks appear to have outlived their usefulness.[11]

It is appropriate to consider bundle-branch block (BBB) next for two reasons: first, its patterns are in many ways exaggerations of the corresponding ventricular hypertrophy and strain patterns that we have just dealt with; and second, for those whose main interest is the study of arrhythmias and conduction disturbances (for example, coronary care nurses and anesthesiologists), these are the patterns that probably should be mastered first because they provide a morphologic peg on which to hang one's diagnostic hat.

General Principles

If one of the branches of the bundle of His is blocked by disease, the impulse travels down the branch to the other ventricle first. Having activated this ventricle, the impulse spreads through the septum to the ventricle on the side of the block and in turn activates it. In other words, the ventricles will be activated one after the other instead of simultaneously, in series instead of in parallel—as the physicists say.

There are two main situations in which the ventricles are activated successively instead of simultaneously: BBB and ectopic ventricular rhythms. There is, therefore, in these conditions a marked fundamental similarity in the bizarre patterns produced: in each there is prolongation of the QRS interval and the ST segment slopes off in the direction opposite to the main QRS deflection. A premature ventricular beat, a run of ventricular tachycardia and two artificially stimulated ventricular beats are illustrated side by side with bundle-branch block in figure 7.1. The similarity of pattern common to all is evident.

In BBB—since the impulse has to worm its way slowly through the thickness of the septum before the second ventricle can be activated—the QRS interval is prolonged to 0.12 sec or more, and it tends to be more prolonged in left than in right branch block. When the left branch is blocked the impulse reaches the right ventricle punctually but is late in activating the left ventricle. The intrinsicoid deflection over the right ventricle (e.g., in V₁) therefore begins on

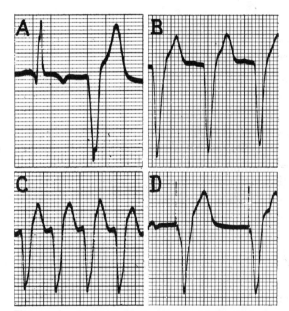

Figure 7.1. Comparison of patterns of (A) **ventricular extrasystole,** (B) **bundle-branch block,** (C) **ventricular tachycardia** and (D) ectopic ventricular rhythm driven by **artificial pacemaker.** Note that each pattern has in common (1) prolonged QRS interval and (2) ST segment sloping off to T wave in direction opposite to main QRS deflection.

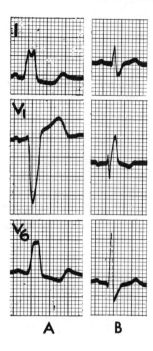

A   **B**

Figure 7.2. Bundle-branch block (A) left and (B) right. The important leads to study in BBB are 1, V₁ and V₆ (see text).

time, whereas over the left ventricle (e.g., in V_6) this deflection is much delayed (fig. 7.2*A*). On the other hand, when it is the right branch that is blocked, just the reverse occurs—the intrinsicoid deflection is on time in left ventricular leads but is late over the right ventricle (fig. 7.2*B*).

Genesis of the Precordial Pattern in BBB

To understand the genesis of the pattern in the V leads, one must visualize the sliced heart (fig. 7.3) as we did for the normal pattern in Chapter 5. In left bundle-branch block (LBBB), the impulse must enter the right ventricle first and so the septum is activated from right to left. These electrical forces are dominant over the weaker free wall forces of the right ventricle and, since they are travelling away from lead V_1 and toward V_6, they write a negative deflection in V_1 and a positive deflection in V_6. That accounts for approximately the first half of the QRS. Once the septal crossing has been completed, the march continues in the same direction as the impulse activates the left ventricle. Thus it is that in LBBB there is a marked tendency toward monophasic complexes— QS in V_1 and monophasic R in V_6. However, in about 30% of LBBB, a small initial r wave is found in V_1—as in figure 7.2; this is generally explained by assuming that, for some reason, perhaps because septal branches of the RBB are diseased, the free wall of the right ventricle is activated momentarily just before the septum.

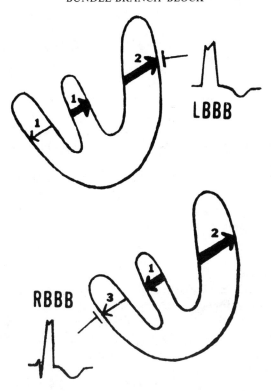

Figure 7.3. Sequence of ventricular activation in BBB. In LBBB (*upper diagram*), the septum is activated (*1*) exclusively from the right side at the same time that the free wall of the right ventricle (*1*) is activated. The meager forces of the free wall are overshadowed by the much stronger septal forces. Once the septum and the right ventricle have been depolarized, the left ventricle alone remains and the direction of its activation (*2*) is similar to that of the septum; hence the complex of LBBB tends to be monophasic and is upright in V_6. In RBBB (*lower diagram*), the septum is first activated, as in the normal heart, from the left side (*1*); a moment later activation begins in the left ventricular free wall (*2*) but, since septal forces are simultaneously spreading in the opposite direction, the free wall deflection (S wave in V_1) is dwarfed. Once the septum and left ventricular free wall have been depolarized, all that is left is the right ventricular free wall. Its feeble forces now have it all their own way and, since they are unopposed, now write the largest deflection of the ventricular complex (R' in V_1).

In right bundle-branch block (RBBB), provided there is no associated delay on the left side, the impulse activates the septum normally on the left and the beginning of the QRS remains normal—r in V_1 and q in V_6. But now, in contrast with the normal state of affairs, there are no opposing forces advancing from the right side to neutralize the left-to-right septal forces and consequently these left-to-right forces are available to oppose those activating the free wall of the left ventricle which normally inscribe a sizeable S wave in V_1. As a result of this opposition, the S wave in V_1 is relatively shrunken and usually measures only 1 to 5 mm in depth (fig. 7.2) as opposed to the usual 7 to 15 mm (fig. 5.4). The height of the R wave in V_6 is not affected to the same extent—probably because of the proximity of the V_6 electrode to the free wall of the left ventricle.

Now comes delayed activation of the right ventricle—the relatively feeble ventricle that normally contributes little to the QRS pattern. But at this point in RBBB, there is nothing left to counteract its feeble forces—the septum and the rest of the left ventricle have already been depolarized—and so it comes into its own with a vengeance and writes the most prominent component of the ventricular complex in V_1: a large, wide R′ wave (fig. 7.2). The corresponding S wave in V_6 is much less prominent, probably for two reasons: *distance*—V_6 is comparatively remote from the right ventricle; and *direction*—spread is much more directly toward V_1 than away from V_6.

Classical 12-lead examples of BBB are illustrated in figures 7.4 and 7.5. In the example of LBBB (fig. 7.4), note the *mono*phasic complex (QS in V_1; monophasic R in V_6); in RBBB (fig. 7.5), note the *tri*phasic complexes—rsR′ in V_1 and qRs in V_6.

We have seen (p. 44) that the septum is normally activated from the left side first. This fact is responsible for a striking difference between the patterns of left and right BBB: when the right bundle branch is blocked, the impulse still travels normally down the left and as usual activates the left side of the septum first. Because of this, the first part of the QRS in pure RBBB remains normal and unchanged. On the other hand, if the left branch is blocked, the normal initial activation of the septum is disturbed and the first part of the QRS is altered. Normal septal activation writes a Q wave in left chest leads (p. 45) which therefore disappears when LBBB supervenes, and one of the hallmarks of uncomplicated LBBB is this absence of normal Q waves in left precordial leads.

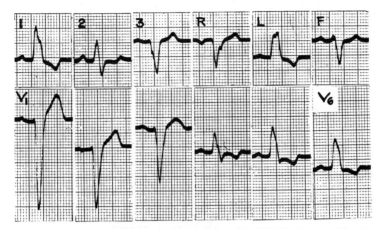

Figure 7.4. **Left bundle-branch block.** Note wide QRS (0.16 sec) with late intrinsicoid deflection in V_{5-6}. There is left axis deviation with the mean QRS axis $-20°$. Note absence of Q waves in lead 1 and V_{5-6}.

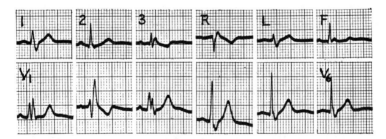

Figure 7.5. **Right bundle-branch block.** Note wide S_1, M-shaped QRS with late intrinsicoid deflection in V_1 and early downstrokes with wide S waves in V_{5-6}.

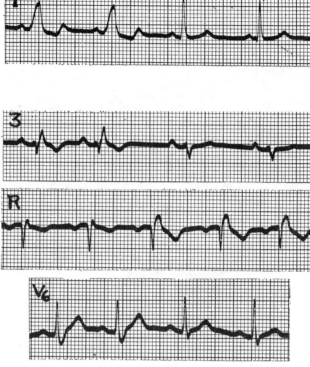

Figure 7.6. Intermittent bundle-branch block. The first strip is lead 1 from one patient; the remaining three leads are from another patient. In the first strip the first two beats show *left* bundle-branch block; the last two are of normal duration and shape. Note that the initial portion of the blocked QRS complexes differs from the initial part of the normal complexes. In the bottom three strips some complexes show *right* bundle-branch block while others show normal conduction; note that the initial deflection is identical in normal and blocked beats.

These features are in the tracings in figure 7.6. In the top strip, two complexes showing *left* BBB precede two showing normal intraventricular conduction. Note that the beginning of the blocked QRS is definitely altered compared with the normal QRS. On the other hand, the bottom three strips show intermittent *right* BBB; note in this case that the initial portion of the QRS complex in each lead is identical in both normally conducted and blocked beats.

Limb Leads in BBB

Characteristic, though somewhat less reliable, changes also develop in the limb leads. Leads 1 and aVL usually have the same general features as V_6—not surprising, since these leads have as their positive pole the nearby left shoulder—showing no Q wave and a monophasic R wave in LBBB (figs. 7.2 and 7.4), and a qRs contour in RBBB (fig. 7.2). LBBB is often associated with left axis deviation (LAD) (fig. 7.4), but there is some evidence that this implies additional disease besides the blocked bundle branch. Certainly it is not uncommon to see a normal axis (fig. 7.7), and it is even possible to have frank right axis deviation (RAD) (fig. 7.8). When LBBB is associated with left axis deviation, the prognosis is less favorable than when the axis remains normal.[8, 10]

The *significance* of LAD complicating LBBB is more evident than its *cause*. When LAD is present, the LBBB is associated with a higher incidence of myocardial dysfunction, more advanced disease of the conduction system and an earlier mortality than is LBBB with a normal axis.[8]

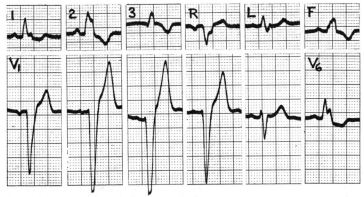

Figure 7.7. Left bundle-branch block. Note wide QRS interval of 0.15 sec with late intrinsicoid deflection in V_6. The mean QRS axis is normal, being about +50°. Note absence of Q waves in leads 1 and V_6.

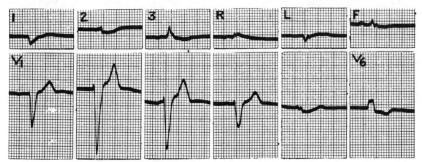

Figure 7.8. Left bundle-branch block. There is *right* axis deviation, but the precordial pattern is typical of *left* bundle-branch block.

Whether LBBB itself produces LAD has been argued for decades. Among 29 men without previous evidence of heart disease, the development of LBBB was associated with a mean leftward shift of the axis of 22 degrees; and the risk of sudden death increased more than 10-fold compared with the control group without LBBB.[31] One explanation for the combination of LBBB with LAD is that the LBBB is incomplete in the presence of anterior hemiblock, though this is probably not the *usual* reason.[39]

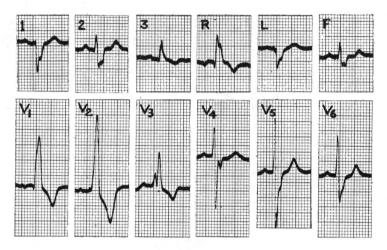

Figure 7.9. Right bundle-branch block with marked right axis deviation—the "uncommon" type of RBBB.

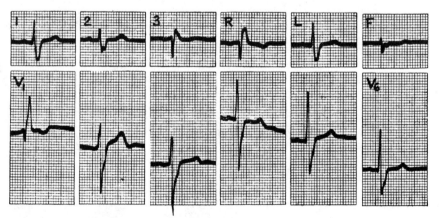

Figure 7.10. The Wilson type of **right bundle-branch block.** Note slender tall R preceding wide S wave in lead 1. Axis of terminal part of QRS is about 180°, while T-wave axis is +15°. QRS-T angle is therefore 165°.

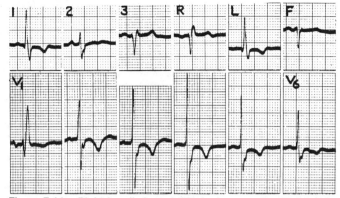

Figure 7.11. Right bundle-branch block. An example with *left* axis deviation. Note the wide S waves in 1 and V$_6$ and the rsR′ pattern with late intrinsicoid deflection in V$_1$. Since the T waves in 1, aVL, and V$_{2-6}$ are in the same direction as the terminal QRS forces, these are *primary* T-wave changes (see p. 72).

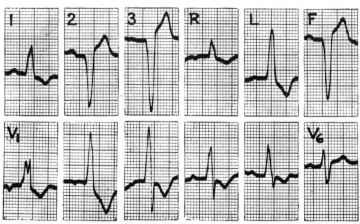

Figure 7.12. Atypical intraventricular block. The limb leads are typical of *left* BBB, while the precordial leads indicate *right* BBB (M-shaped QRS in V$_1$ with late intrinsicoid deflection; wide S waves in V$_6$).

RBBB also can be associated with a normal axis or with right or left axis deviation. If the S wave in lead 1 becomes sufficiently deep, and the QRS complex in lead 3 is upright, frank RAD may be produced (fig. 7.9). The common type (sometimes still called Wilson block) presents a tall, slender R wave in lead 1 which exceeds in amplitude the S wave (figs. 7.10 and 7.11). When frank RAD accompanies the RBBB (the "uncommon" type), or when frank left axis appears (figs. 7.11 and 7.12), the cause is usually to be found in an associated block of one of the divisions of the left bundle branch (see Chapter 8).

An interesting hybrid pattern has been described in which the limb leads suggest *left* BBB while the chest leads indicate *right* BBB (fig. 7.12). Such tracings probably represent RBBB with left anterior hemiblock and are associated with extensive disease of the ventricular myocardium.[41]

ST-T Changes

In BBB the T wave is usually directed opposite to the latter portion of the QRS complex; e.g., in figure 7.4 the T wave in lead 1 is inverted while the latter part of the QRS is upright, and in figure 7.10 the T wave in lead 1 is upright while the latter part of the QRS is negative. This opposite polarity is the natural result of the depolarization-repolarization disturbance produced by the block, and the T-wave changes are therefore known as "secondary"—they are part and parcel of the BBB pattern and mean no more than the block itself. If, on the other hand, the direction of the T wave is similar to that of the terminal part of the QRS (fig. 7.13), this is no longer the natural consequence of the conduction disturbance. Such T-wave changes are called "primary" and they imply myocardial disease in addition to the BBB.

One method of gauging the prognostic severity of T-wave changes in BBB is to measure the angle between the axis of the T wave and that of the terminal part of the QRS complex. Obviously, if the two are oppositely directed (as they are with secondary T-wave changes), the angle between them will be wide and may approach 180°. It is proposed[12] that if this angle is less than 110°, serious organic heart disease is indicated. In figure 7.10 the angle is about 165°, whereas in figure 7.13 it is only a few degrees, each axis being close to 180°.

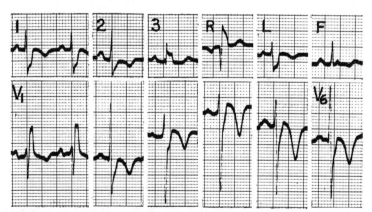

Figure 7.13. **Right bundle-branch block** with primary T-wave changes. The direction of the terminal part of the QRS and that of the T wave are similarly directed in the frontal plane and in V_{2-6}.

Leads	*Salient features of bundle-branch block:* Left Bundle-Branch Block	Right Bundle-Branch Block
V₁	QS or rS	Late intrinsicoid, M-shaped QRS (RSR′ variant); sometimes wide R or qR
V₆	Late intrinsicoid, no Q waves, monophasic R	Early intrinsicoid, wide S wave
1	Monophasic R wave, no Q	Wide S wave

Comparison with Ventricular Hypertrophy

The pattern of BBB in many ways is like an exaggeration of the pattern of ventricular hypertrophy. Compare *A, B* and *C* in figure 7.14. The differences are that the QRS interval is longer in block, the intrinsicoid deflection over the blocked ventricle is correspondingly later, and the secondary ST-T changes are more pronounced. The QRS deflections in block are often of lower voltage and are more likely to show definite notching than in ventricular hypertrophy and strain. One further important detail should be noted: whereas the normal Q waves over the left ventricle may be present or exaggerated in ventricular hypertrophy, in LBBB these normal Q waves are absent. This is because, as the left branch is blocked, the septum is entirely activated from its right side. Figures 7.14 and 7.15 illustrate how LVH sometimes progresses to LBBB.

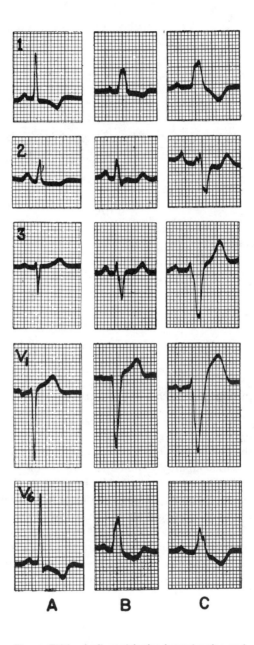

Figure 7.14. Left ventricular hypertrophy and strain (*A*), **incomplete left bundle-branch block** (*B*), and presumably **complete left bundle-branch block** (*C*) compared.

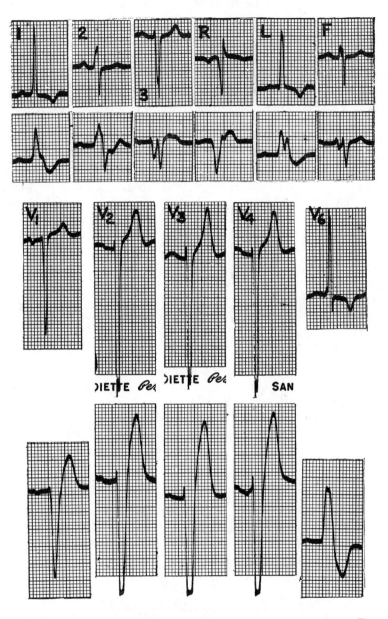

Figure 7.15 Two tracings from the same patient, taken two years apart. First tracing (first and third rows) shows **left ventricular hypertrophy and strain;** because of the initial slurring of R wave and absent Q in leads 1 and V₆ some would call this incomplete LBBB. Second tracing (second and fourth rows) shows fully developed **left bundle-branch block.**

Intermittent and Incomplete BBB

Intermittent bundle-branch block, i.e., prolonged QRS complexes present at times but not at others (fig. 7.6), usually represents a transition stage before permanent block is established.

The designation **incomplete bundle-branch block** has been assigned to those patterns whose QRS intervals place them in the no man's land of 0.10 to 0.11 sec. with a LBBB pattern (fig. 7.14*B*), of 0.09 to 0.10 sec. with RBBB pattern (fig. 7.16).

Sodi-Pallares' criteria[38] for diagnosing incomplete LBBB are initial slurring of the upstroke of the R wave, with or without small preceding Q waves, in left ventricular leads; at a more advanced stage, the Q wave is definitely lost, the slurring is greater and T waves are inverted. All these features are shown in the first tracing in figure 7.15. The incidental finding of the pattern of incomplete RBBB in apparently healthy men carries with it a definite though slight risk that "complete" RBBB will develop.[32]

The problem of secondary R waves (R′) in right precordial leads, in the presence of normal or borderline QRS duration, is sometimes vexing.[24] Are they due to late but physiological activation of the basal region (outflow tract) of the right ventricle, or do they represent abnormal delay in right ventricular activation as a result of incomplete right bundle-branch block or right ventricular hypertrophy? Although there are no foolproof criteria for separating normal from abnormal, the following pointers are helpful[40]:

1. The R′ is probably *normal* if it is present as part of an rSr′ complex in V_1 and/or V_2, but absent in V_{3R} or in a low V_1 taken two interspaces below the conventional V_1 position (fig. 7.17).
2. It is probably *abnormal* if it persists in the lower right precordial leads, or if it is 6 mm. or more tall in V_1 or V_{3R}, or if the R′:S ratio is more than 1.0.

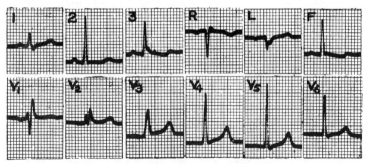

Figure 7.16. Incomplete right bundle-branch block. Note the salient features of the right bundle-branch block pattern—wide S in lead 1 with late intrinsicoid deflection in V_1—but with QRS duration of only 0.10 sec.

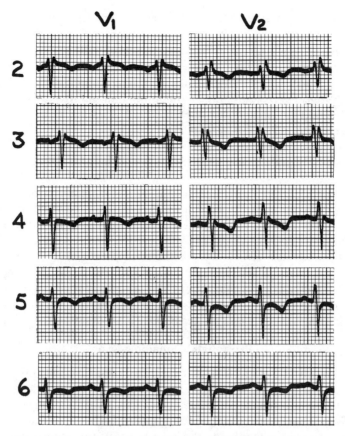

Figure 7.17.   rSr' patterns in right precordial leads. Notice that the r' wave, present in the higher interspaces, decreases in amplitude and disappears in the lower interspaces. (Figures at the left indicate the interspace in which the electrode was placed.)

Incidence and Etiology

It is generally thought that RBBB is considerably more common than LBBB, and that RBBB is more likely to be found without other evidence of heart disease. But in fact they occur with about the same frequency.[35] In the famous Framingham study, at the initial examination of over 5000 participants, there were 17 with LBBB and 16 with RBBB; and in the subsequent 18 years of follow-up, LBBB developed in 55 while RBBB developed in 70. The majority of both had evidence of cardiovascular disease.[35]

On the other hand, both RBBB and LBBB are occasionally seen in apparently normal hearts.[5, 15, 18, 42] Among 122,000 asymptomatic airmen there were 231 with RBBB and 17 with LBBB; in 44,000 under the age of 25, no instance of LBBB was found.[13]

The common causes of BBB in this country are Lenegre's disease, Lev's disease and ischemic heart disease. In other countries where the condition is indigenous, Chagas' disease is a potent cause of RBBB. Other causes are rheumatic disease, syphilis, trauma, tumors, cardiomyopathy and congenital lesions. As many as 14% of patients with *severe* aortic stenosis may have LBBB.[43] Surgical correction of the tetralogy of Fallot or closure of an uncomplicated ventricular septal defect often produces RBBB.[14]

Transient BBB may occur in acute heart failure, acute myocardial infarction, acute coronary insufficiency and acute infections. Transient RBBB is often produced during right heart catheterization and may complicate monitoring with a Swan-Ganz catheter.[2, 22]

Remember that everything that we call "bundle-branch" block is not necessarily due to a lesion in the branch itself. The fibers destined to form each branch may be involved within the His bundle and so result in the pattern of BBB. This assumption is supported by the facts that *left* fascicular block can be produced, along with RBBB, by a catheter in the *right* ventricle[2]; and that bifascicular (RBBB + left anterior hemiblock) aberration can appear and disappear simultaneously[22]—as though the product of a single central lesion. Further, the fact that pacing the distal His bundle can normalize a RBBB pattern[9] indicates that the lesion causing the BBB is proximal to the pacing site.

Prognostic Considerations

LBBB, statistically at any rate, carries with it a less favorable prognosis than RBBB.[16, 25, 37] It is obvious, however, that the ultimate outlook depends not on the conduction disturbance per se but on the disease that is causing it. Therefore, in any given instance of coronary disease causing BBB, the prognosis should be based, not on which bundle the disease process has happened to affect, but one's estimate of the severity of the underlying coronary disturbance. For example, in acute anteroseptal infarction, the development of RBBB carries with it a mortality of 65%[27, 28]; and the development of block in either bundle branch is a potent predictor of late in-hospital death.[21]

On the other hand, the incidental finding of RBBB in apparently healthy men, even when associated with an axis shift presumably indicating an associated left fascicular block, has no adverse effect on long-term prognosis.[32]

Rate-Dependent BBB

At times intermittent BBB is determined by the heart rate. If the rate accelerates, the R-R interval shortens and the descending impulse may find one of the bundle branches still in its refractory period so that block of that bundle is registered for a few beats (fig. 7.18); if the heart then slows, descending impulses may arrive after the refractory period of the branch is over and normal conduction is resumed. The rate at which conduction changes is known as the "critical rate." Knowledge of this phenomenon is of importance because the

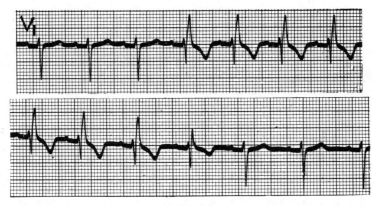

Figure 7.18. Intermittent right BBB—showing "critical rate." As the rate accelerates in the upper strip from 98 to 102, RBBB develops. In the lower strip the RBBB persists as the rate slows to about 90; the first three beats in this strip show presumably complete RBBB, while the fourth shows incomplete RBBB, and then normal conduction resumes. As usual, the critical rate is faster during acceleration than during slowing.

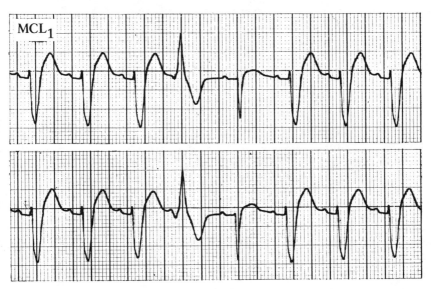

Figure 7.19. Rate-dependent LBBB revealed by the more normal intraventricular conduction at the end of the longer postextrasystolic cycles—the somewhat shorter sinus cycles all end with LBBB.

appearance or disappearance of BBB is often wrongly regarded as evidence of deterioration or improvement when it may be merely the result of a minor rate change. One can also recognize that the BBB is rate-dependent when the longer cycle following an extrasystole permits normal conduction (fig. 7.19).

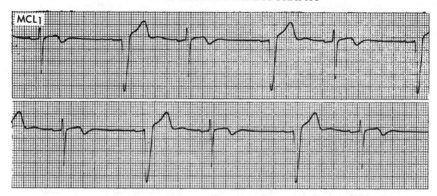

Figure 7.20. Bradycardia-dependent LBBB (paradoxical critical rate). All beats are conducted sinus beats and they are grouped in pairs suggesting 3:2 sinus Wenckebach periods (see p. 325). Those ending the shorter cycles are conducted normally while those ending the *longer* cycles develop LBBB.

Rarely, the intermittent BBB develops only when the cycle lengthens rather than shortens (fig. 7.20); it is then referred to as "paradoxical critical rate" or as "bradycardia-dependent" BBB.[23, 33]

Further discussion of this subject will be found in Chapter 16.

Bilateral Bundle-Branch Block (BBBB)

The patterns of BBBB are varied. If both bundle branches are completely blocked, no impulse can reach the ventricles and the picture is one of complete A-V block. If one branch is completely blocked and the other only partially, the BBB pattern is associated with either a prolonged P-R interval ("first degree A-V block") or dropped beats ("second degree A-V block"). If both bundles are incompletely but equally blocked, only P-R lengthening results with a normal QRS complex. The evidence for BBBB therefore may take five forms:

1. First degree A-V block
2. First degree A-V block + BBB
3. Second degree A-V block + BBB
4. Complete A-V block
5. Sometimes RBBB, sometimes LBBB

Of all of these, only the last is absolute evidence that both bundle branches are involved, since any of the first four manifestations can be produced by blocks other than BBBB.

RSR′ Variants and Dominant R Waves in V$_{1-2}$

This is a good place to summarize the causes of RSR′ patterns and dominant R waves in right precordial leads[24]:

Causes of RSR' variants in V_{1-2}

1. Occurs in 5 per cent of normal young people[7]
2. Frequently associated with pectus or straight back deformities[6]
3. Incomplete RBBB (fig. 7.16)
4. RV hypertrophy (fig. 30.1B)
5. Acute cor pulmonale
6. RV diastolic overloading (fig. 29.7)
7. Wolff-Parkinson-White syndrome
8. Duchenne dystrophy[30]

Causes of dominant R waves in V_{1-2}

1. Occasionally a normal variant
2. RV hypertrophy (fig. 6.5)
3. True posterior (fig. 26.24) or lateral myocardial infarction
4. Wolff-Parkinson-White syndrome (fig. 18.1)
5. Left ventricular diastolic overloading
6. Hypertrophic cardiomyopathy (fig. 29.9)
7. Duchenne dystrophy[30]

REFERENCES

1. Barrett, P. A., et al.: Electrophysiological factors of left bundle-branch block. Br. Med. J. 1981: **45**, 594.
2. Castellanos, A., et al.: Left fascicular blocks during right heart catheterization using the Swan-Ganz catheter. Circulation 1981: **64**, 1271.
3. Chung, K.-Y., et al.: Wolff-Parkinson-White syndrome. Am. Heart J. 1965: **69**, 116.
4. Cokkinos, D. V., et al.: Electrocardiographic criteria of left ventricular hypertrophy in left bundle-branch block. Br. Heart J. 1978: **40**, 320.
5. DeForest, R. E.: Four cases of "benign" left bundle block in the same family. Am. Heart J. 1956: **51**, 398.
6. deLeon, A. C., et al.: The straight back syndrome: clinical cardiovascular manifestations. Circulation 1965: **32**, 193.
7. DePasquale, N. P., and Burch, G. E.: Analysis of the RSR' complex in lead V_1. Circulation 1963: **28**, 362.
8. Dhingra, R. C., et al.: Significance of left axis deviation in patients with chronic left bundle-branch block. Am. J. Cardiol. 1978: **42**, 551.
9. El-Sherif, N., et al.: Normalization of bundle branch block patterns by distal His-bundle pacing. Circulation 1978: **57**, 473.
10. Evans, W., et al.: The significance of deep S waves in leads II and III. Br. Heart J. 1960: **22**, 551.
11. Hecht, H. H.: Atrioventricular and intraventricular conduction: revised nomenclature and concepts. Am. J. Cardiol. 1973: **31**, 232.
12. Henry, E. I., et al.: Significance of the relation of QRS and T waves in bundle branch block: a useful electrocardiographic sign. Am. Heart J. 1957: **54**, 407.
13. Hiss, R. G., and Lamb, L. E.: Electrocardiographic findings in 122,043 individuals. Circulation 1962: **25**, 947.
14. Hobbins, S. M.: Conduction disturbances after surgical correction of ventricular septal defect by the atrial approach. Br. Heart J. 1979: **41**, 289.
15. Johnson, R. L., et al.: Electrocardiographic findings in 67,375 asymptomatic individuals. VI. Right bundle branch block. Am. J. Cardiol. 1960: **6**, 143.

16. Johnson, R. P., et al.: Prognosis in bundle branch block; II. Factors influencing the survival period in left bundle branch block. Am. Heart J. 1951: **41**, 225.
17. Lamb, L. E., et al.: Intermittent right bundle branch block without apparent heart disease. Am. J. Cardiol. 1959: **4**, 302.
18. Lamb, L. E., et al.: Electrocardiographic findings in 67,375 asymptomatic individuals. V. Left bundle branch block. Am. J. Cardiol. 1960: **6**, 130.
19. Lenegre, J.: Etiology and pathology of bilateral bundle branch block in relation to complete heart block. Progr. Cardiovasc. Dis. 1964: **6**, 409.
20. Lepeschkin, E.: The electrocardiographic diagnosis of bilateral bundle branch block in relation to heart block. Progr. Cardiovasc. Dis. 1964: **6**, 445.
21. Lie, K. I., et al.: Early identification of patients developing late in-hospital ventricular fibrillation after discharge from the coronary-care unit; a 5½-year retrospective and prospective study of 1897 patients. Am. J. Cardiol. 1978: **41**, 674.
22. Luck, J. C., and Engel, T. R.: Transient right bundle branch block with Swan-Ganz catheterization. Am. Heart J. 1976: **92**, 263.
23. Massumi, R. A.: Bradycardia-dependent bundle branch block. Circulation 1968: **28**, 1066.
24. Menendez, M. M., and Marriott, H. J. L.: Differential diagnosis of RSR' and dominant R wave patterns in right chest leads. J.A.M.A. 1966: **198**, 843.
25. Messer, A. L., et al.: Prognosis in bundle branch block. III. A comparison of right and left bundle branch block with a note on the relative incidence of each. Am. Heart J. 1951: **41**, 239.
26. Myers, G. B.: The form of the QRS complex in bundle branch block and in anterolateral infarction. Am. Heart J. 1950: **39**, 817.
27. Norris, R. M., and Mercer, C. J.: Significance of idioventricular rhythm in acute myocardial infarction. Prog. Cardiovasc. Dis. 1974: **16**, 455.
28. Norris, R. M., and Sammel, N. L.: Predictors of late hospital deaths in acute myocardial infarction. Prog. Cardiovasc. Dis. 1980: **23**, 129.
29. Papp. C., and Smith, K. S.: The changing electrocardiogram in Wilson block. Circulation 1955: **11**, 53.
30. Perloff, J. K., et al.: The cardiomyopathy of progressive muscular dystrophy. Circulation 1966: **33**, 625.
31. Rabkin, S. W., et al.: Natural history of left bundle-branch block. Br. Heart J. 1980: **43**, 164.
32. Rabkin, S. W., et al.: The natural history of right bundle branch block and frontal plane QRS axis in apparently healthy men. Chest 1981: **80**, 191.
33. Sarachek, N. S.: Bradycardia-dependent bundle branch block. Am. J. Cardiol. 1970: **25**, 727.
34. Scherf, D.: Intraventricular block. Am. J. Cardiol. 1960: **6**, 853.
35. Schneider, J. F., et al.: Comparative features of newly acquired left or right bundle branch block in the general population: the Framingham study. Am. J. Cardiol. 1981: **47**, 931.
36. Scott, R. C.: Left bundle branch block—a clinical assessment. Am. Heart J. 1965: **70**, 535, 691, and 813.
37. Shreenivas et al.: Prognosis in bundle branch block. I. Factors influencing the survival period in right bundle branch block. Am. Heart J. 1950: **40**, 891.
38. Sodi-Pallares, D.: *New Bases of Electrocardiography*, pp. 289–292. C. V. Mosby, St. Louis, 1956.
39. Swiryn, S., et al.: Electrocardiographic determinants of axis during left bundle branch block: Study in patients with intermittent left bundle branch block. Am. J. Cardiol. 1980: **46**, 53.
40. Tapia, F. A., and Proudfit, W. L.: Secondary R waves in right precordial leads in normal persons and in patients with cardiac disease. Circulation 1960: **21**, 28.
41. Unger, P. N., et al.: The concept of "masquerading" bundle-branch block: an electrocardiographic-pathologic correlation. Circulation 1958: **17**, 397.
42. Vazifdar, J. P., and Levine, S. A.: Benign bundle branch block. Arch. Int. Med. 1952: **89**, 568.
43. Wood, P.: Aortic stenosis. Am. J. Cardiol. 1958: **1**, 553.
44. Wu, D., et al.: Bundle branch block. Demonstration of the incomplete nature of some "complete" bundle branch and fascicular blocks by the extrastimulus technique. Am. J. Cardiol. 1974: **33**, 583.
45. Wyndham, C. R. C., et al.: Epicardial activation in patients with left bundle-branch block. Circulation 1980: **61**, 696.

Sensitivity and Specificity

These are current "buzzwords" in medicine and need to be understood in evaluating the accuracy of a test, e.g., the 12-lead ECG in recognizing ventricular hypertrophy or the treadmill test for identifying the presence of ischemic heart disease.

Sensitivity expresses the ability of a test to recognize a disease: if the test recognizes every single case, it has 100% sensitivity; if it recognizes only half the cases, it has 50% sensitivity. It can be represented by a fraction in which the numerator is the number of cases correctly recognized and the denominator is the actual number of cases in the sample tested (including those that were missed the false negatives). To express sensitivity as a percentage, you divide the number of cases recognized by the actual number of cases and multiply by 100:

$$\frac{\text{no. cases correctly recognized by test (true positives)}}{\text{no. cases actually present (true positives + false negatives)}} \times 100 = \%\ \text{sensitivity}$$

Specificity expresses the ability of a test to exclude a disease: if in the test sample, the test is negative in 10 but in fact twice as many should be negative, specificity is only 50%; whereas, if the test were negative in all 20 without the disease, sensitivity would be 100%. Specificity can therefore be represented by a fraction in which the numerator is the number of correct negative tests and the denominator is the number that don't have the disease (including the false positives). To express it as a percentage, you divide the number of individuals without the disease into the number of times the test was negative and multiply by 100:

$$\frac{\text{no. correct negative test results (true negatives)}}{\text{no. persons without the disease (true negatives + false positives)}} \times 100 = \%\ \text{specificity}$$

Thus, one may say that sensitivity is limited by false negatives and specificity by false positives.

8

The Hemiblocks and Trifascicular Block

The development of the concepts of hemiblock and trifasicular block is described by Uhley[37] as "one of the most interesting events in the modern history of cardiology."

The Hemiblocks

In a fascinating series of publications, beginning with a 730-page treatise in Spanish and culminating in a 260-page condensation and update in English,[23-34] Rosenbaum popularized the concept of "hemiblock"—his name for block of one of the two main divisions of the left bundle branch (LBB).

The term is neat, comes trippingly to the tongue, and is undoubtedly here to stay, but there has been considerable debate concerning its propriety. First of all, on analogy with kindred words like hemisphere meaning half-a-sphere, hemiblock ought to mean half-a-block or about the distance that a man with severe angina can walk before his pain comes on, rather than block of half a bundle-branch system. Then again, since most hearts appear to have three major divisions of the left branch rather than two,[8, 9] the lesion represents block of a third rather than a half. And the anatomical purists, because of the spatial relationship of the divisions and the territories they supply, would prefer "anterosuperior" and "posteroinferior" as more accurate descriptive terms than plain "anterior" and "posterior" (fig. 8.1). Because of these several grounds for criticism, a significant conclave of critics would rather we talked of "anterosuperior fascicular block" (instead of anterior hemiblock) and "posteroinferior fascicular block" (instead of posterior hemiblock). In deference to Rosenbaum's work, the fewer syllables and the much more common usage, I shall retain the anatomically less accurate term, hemiblock. Moreover, since, as yet, there are no "right" hemiblocks, I shall omit prefixing "left" and refer simply to anterior and posterior hemiblock.

Genesis of Hemiblock Patterns

Subsequent investigators have made it clear that in many, if not most, hearts there are three significant divisions—anterior, posterior and centriseptal—in the LBB system,[8, 9] as in fact Tawara clearly depicted as early as 1906. But activation of the septum exerts little influence on the frontal plane axis and so, from the point of view of axis shifts, the bifascicular concept remains a useful one electrocardiographically. Others[9] regard the LBB as a fanlike structure in most hearts with no clear-cut subdivisions. Histologically, however, the patterns of hemiblock are associated with diffusely distributed lesions in the LBB system and localization of the pathological lesion cannot in fact be inferred from the ECG.[22, 35]

The anterior (or superior) division of the LBB runs toward the anterior papillary muscle; the posterior (or inferior) division, toward the posterior papillary muscle; and the septal division initiates activation of the midseptum.

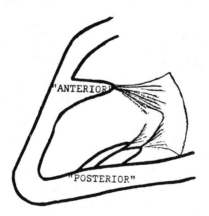

Figure 8.1. The "anterior" papillary muscle of the left ventricle is above, rather than anterior to, the "posterior" papillary muscle.

Figure 8.2 diagrams an approximate frontal view of the left ventricle with the anterior and posterior fascicles of the LBB heading toward their respective papillary muscles. If the anterior division is blocked, as in the left-hand diagram, the initial activation of the myocardium begins at the root of the posterior papillary muscle and travels, from endocardium to epicardium as ventricular activation always proceeds, downward and rightward inscribing, therefore, an r wave in leads whose positive electrode is on the leg (i.e., 2, 3 and aVF) and a q wave in leads whose positive electrode is on the left arm (leads 1 and aVL). Although this q wave is a logical and appropriate element of the anterior hemiblock pattern, it is not absolutely essential to the diagnosis.[12] To activate the rest of the ventricle from this inferior site, the remaining forces must spread upward and to the left; in so doing, they produce a dominant R

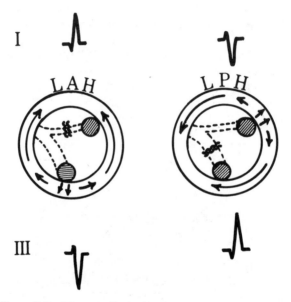

Figure 8.2.   Diagrams illustrating the hemiblock patterns in the limb leads: left anterior hemiblock (LAH) and left posterior hemiblock (LPH). The "anterior" papillary muscle is above and lateral to the "posterior" papillary muscle and the two divisions of the LBB course towards their respective papillary muscles. Thus, if the anterior division is blocked, initial electromotive forces are directed downwards and to the right, inscribing a Q wave in leads 1 and aVL and an R wave in leads 2, 3 and aVF. The subsequent forces are directed mainly upwards and to the left, writing an R wave in 1 and aVL and an S in 2, 3 and aVF, to produce a left axis deviation. In LPH, the initial forces spread upwards and to the left to write an R in 1 and aVL and a Q in 2, 3 and aVF while subsequent forces are directed downwards and to the right to produce right axis deviation.

wave in leads 1 and aVL; a dominant S wave in leads 2, 3 and aVF; and a left axis shift of approximately −60°.

If the posterior fascicle is blocked, the situation is reversed, as depicted in the right-hand diagram. Now initial activation begins at the root of the anterior papillary muscle and first travels upward and to the left, from endocardium to epicardium, inscribing an r wave on leads 1 and aVL and a q wave in leads 2, 3 and aVF. To activate the rest of the left ventricle from this superolateral site, the remaining forces must spread downward and to the right; in so doing, they produce a dominant R wave in leads 2, 3 and aVF; a dominant S wave in leads 1 and aVL; and a right axis shift to about +120°.

In the diagnosis of anterior hemiblock, an additional criterion was added to Rosenbaum's original set by the Mexico school[20]: a delayed intrinsicoid deflection (beyond 0.045 sec) and slurred R wave in aVL. In posterior hemiblock the intrinsicoid deflection is similarly delayed in aVF.

Both hemiblocks, if they are pure, i.e., not complicated by right bundle-branch block (RBBB), will have QRS complexes of normal duration. This is because there is a rich intercommunication between the territories of the fascicles consisting of rapidly conducting Purkinje tissue; and so, although the mean direction of ventricular activation changes dramatically, according to Rosenbaum its duration is little prolonged—at most 0.01 or 0.02 sec, although later work indicates an *average* QRS lengthening of 0.025 sec.[12] From the frontal plane viewpoint, normal ventricular activation spreads simultaneously from two foci (at the roots of the papillary muscles), and many forces are, therefore, travelling in opposite directions and neutralizing each other's influence—the phenomenon of "cancellation." But in the presence of hemiblock, activation of the ventricle proceeds from one site instead of two, and so cancellation is reduced and the amplitude of the ventricular complex increases, sometimes markedly as in Figs. 8.3 and 8.4.

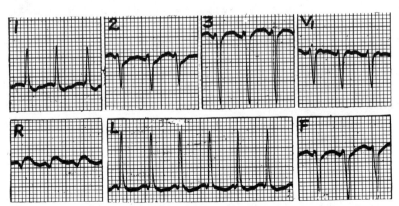

Figure 8.3. Anterior hemiblock: Note q in 1 and aVL with r in 2, 3 and aVF; left axis shift of −60°; normal QRS duration (0.08 sec); large voltage, especially in 3 and aVL, imitating left ventricular enlargement.

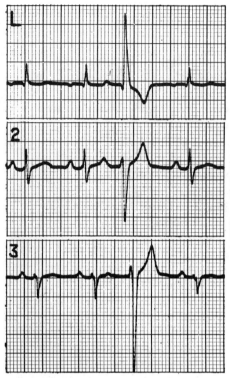

Figure 8.4. Atrial premature beats with ventricular aberration of **anterior hemiblock** type. In the aberrant beats, at the same time that the axis shifts markedly leftward to about −70°, the voltage of the QRS complexes greatly increases so that their pattern simulates that of left ventricular hypertrophy.

Besides being good examples of the increased ventricular voltage occasioned by hemiblock, the tracings in figures 8.3 and 8.4 show typical features of anterior hemiblock. In figure 8.3, note the q waves in leads 1 and aVL; the r waves in leads 2, 3 and aVF; the late intrinsicoid deflection in aVL; and the axis of −60°. In figure 8.4, the first two beats in each lead are sinus beats followed by an atrial premature beat that manifests anterior hemiblock aberration. Apart from the gigantic voltage assumed by the aberrant beat, note the q in aVL and the r in 2 and 3 as well as the superior ("leftward") swing of the aberrant axis.

The cardinal features of pure hemiblock are summarized in the boxes. Note that for left posterior hemiblock (LPH) a special criterion is required: there must be no evidence of or reason for right ventricular hypertrophy. This additional criterion is necessary because right ventricular hypertrophy itself can produce exactly the same pattern in the limb leads as LPH (fig. 29.6, p. 446).

Bifascicular Block

Anterior hemiblock is often and posterior hemiblock is usually accompanied by RBBB, and in either case the resulting duo is a "bifascicular block." In such combinations, of course, the QRS is no longer normally narrow, as it is in the lone hemiblock, but is widened by the associated RBBB. Figures 8.5 and 8.6 present typical examples of RBBB with anterior hemiblock, and figure 8.7

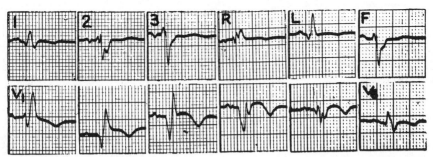

Figure 8.5. Right bundle-branch block + anterior hemiblock against a background of extensive anterior infarction.

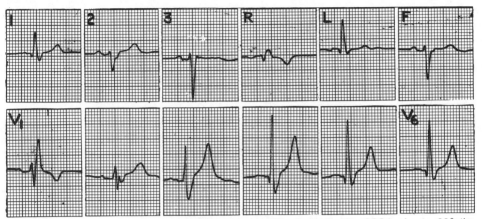

Figure 8.6. Anterior hemiblock with RBBB. The axis of the first half of the QRS is about −60°; the QRS interval is widened to 0.15 sec by the RBBB.

Criteria for Left Anterior Hemiblock

1. LEFT axis deviation (usually −60°)
2. Small Q in lead 1 and aVL, small R in 2, 3 and aVF
3. Normal QRS duration
4. Late intrinsicoid deflection aVL (>0.045)
5. Increased QRS voltage in limb leads

Criteria for Left Posterior Hemiblock

1. RIGHT axis deviation (usually +120°)
2. Small R in lead 1 and aVL, small Q in 2, 3 and aVF
3. Normal QRS duration
4. Late intrinsicoid deflection aVF (>0.045)
5. Increased QRS voltage in limb leads
6. No evidence for right ventricular hypertrophy

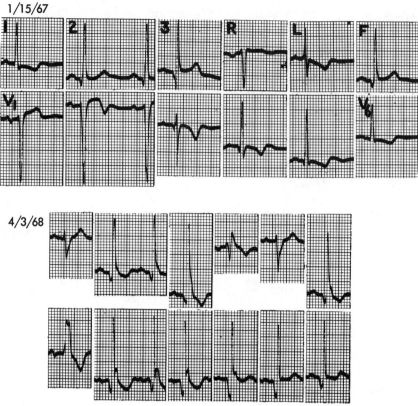

Figure 8.7. Posterior hemiblock. The initial tracing exhibits a normal axis with patholog- ical Q waves in anterior (V$_{3-5}$) and inferior (2, 3 and aVF) leads. The later tracing illustrates widespread development of wide Q waves in the precordial leads with RBBB and marked right axis deviation, presumably due to left posterior hemiblock.

illustrates the combination of RBBB with posterior hemiblock. In determining the axis in the presence of RBBB, remember to use only the first half of the QRS because a hemiblock involves only left ventricular activation and, in the presence of RBBB, the second half of the QRS is, of course, inscribed by delayed right ventricular activation. Another point worth mentioning is that a hemiblock can upset the "rabbit ears" (see Chapter 11) of RBBB. In figure 8.8, both in V$_1$ and in the MCL$_1$ rhythm strip, the left rabbit ear is taller than the right—usually a hallmark of ventricular ectopy. Hemiblock is probably the commonest cause of reversing aberrant rabbit ears and so simulating ectopy.

From time to time, authors have referred to block involving both the right bundle branch and one of the divisions of the left branch as bilateral bundle- branch block (BBBB). But it is better to reserve this term for the situation when the right bundle branch and the main left bundle branch are simultaneously involved; and, when the block on the left side involves only one fascicle of the left branch system, to adhere to the term "bifascicular" block.

Incidence and Prognosis

Anterior hemiblock is much more common than posterior. During the 15 years that Rosenbaum and his colleagues were amassing nearly 900 examples of anterior hemiblock, they encountered only 30 of posterior hemiblock. This degree of preponderance was not found, however, when Kulbertus[14] deliberately induced ventricular aberration: in the course of inducing 116 instances of ventricular aberration by premature atrial stimulation, he produced 38 instances of anterior hemiblock and 22 of posterior hemiblock aberration. Reasons that have been advanced to explain the greater vulnerability of the anterior division include the fact that it is longer and thinner than the posterior fascicle, it is subjected to the stresses and strains of an outflow tract structure, and it has but a single blood supply.

Anterior hemiblock is usually found in people with hearts that are otherwise normal[5] and does not seem to affect longevity. However, there is evidence that men with such axes have a slight but definitely greater risk than average of later developing RBBB.[21] Like BBB, hemiblock may be caused by Lenegre's or

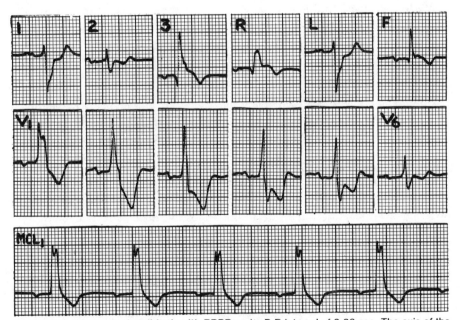

Figure 8.8. Posterior hemiblock with RBBB and a P-R interval of 0.22 sec. The axis of the first half of the QRS is about +120°; the QRS interval is widened to 0.14 sec by the RBBB. Note that the QRS complex peaks early (taller left "rabbit ear") in V_1 and MCL_1 simulating ventricular ectopy.

Lev's disease, aortic valve calcification, cardiomyopathy, or ischemic heart disease. It was found in 17% of 250 consecutive patients with acute myocardial infarction.[18] Temporary hemiblock may result from cardiac catheterization, selective coronary arteriography,[10] or hyperkalemia.[4] Anterior hemiblock may accompany the permanent RBBB that results from surgical correction of the tetralogy of Fallot.[30]

In the past, experts have argued that the development of left bundle branch block (LBBB) does not significantly shift the electrical axis; others have claimed that LBBB can produce significant left axis deviation. Judging by Rosenbaum's study[26] of 98 patients with intermittent LBBB, in which blocked and unblocked complexes could be examined side by side, LBBB often produces a significant left axis shift, sometimes produces even right axis deviation, and leaves the axis unchanged in only a minority.

The combination of LBBB with marked left axis shift is undoubtedly sometimes produced by anterior hemiblock complicating *incomplete* LBBB[26] though, as indicated in the last chapter, this is probably not the usual mechanism.

Miming and Masking

One of the most interesting and important features of the hemiblocks is their ability to both mask and mimic patterns of structural disease. Anterior hemiblock can mask anterior and inferior infarctions,[6, 13] left ventricular hypertrophy, and RBBB[34]; it can imitate anterior[17] and lateral infarctions and left ventricular hypertrophy. Most of these counterfeits are only half-hearted imitations, however, and can often be seen through; but some deceptions may be perfect.

Anterior hemiblock can completely mask inferior infarction by preventing the development of Q waves in leads 2, 3 and aVF. In figure 8.9, the Q waves of inferior infarction are replaced by R waves in the first premature beat in leads 2 and 3 when anterior hemiblock aberration is superimposed on the RBBB. Anterior hemiblock can mask anterior infarction by adding a little r wave to a previous QS complex: If the V_1 or V_2 electrode is placed relatively low, the initial downward forces of anterior hemiblock (fig. 8.2) approach the low-lying electrode and so inscribe an initial positive deflection. The relatively low placement of the chest electrodes in the presence of anterior hemiblock can also mask RBBB[34] which can also be obscured by posterior hemiblock.[16] When RBBB is camouflaged by anterior hemiblock, its presence may be suspected if the QRS interval is wider than expected with hemiblock alone, and confirmed by obtaining high right-sided chest leads which show the typical terminal R'.[34]

Left ventricular hypertrophy can be deprived of one of its salient features when anterior hemiblock lowers the QRS voltage in left chest leads.

Figures 8.3 and 8.4 are excellent examples of the way in which anterior hemiblock can mimic left ventricular hypertrophy in the limb leads. It can imitate anteroseptal infarction by producing a small q wave in front of the

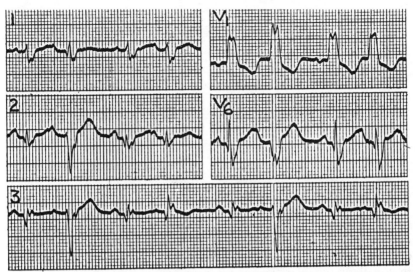

Figure 8.9. Atrial bigeminy with RBBB and inferior infarction. The second beat in each lead, and the sixth beat in lead 3, show **anterior hemiblock** aberration as well. In the limb leads, the development of left anterior hemiblock eliminates the Q waves in leads 2 and 3 and so masks the inferior infarction. (Reproduced from *Hemiblock Lecture Slides*, Tampa Tracings, Oldsmar, Fla., 1971.)

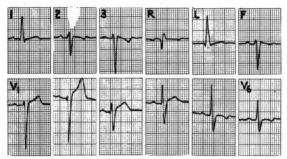

Figure 8.10. Anterior hemiblock, axis −60. The q waves in V_{2-3} are probably secondary to the hemiblock rather than anteroseptal infarction.

normal r wave in V_2 and V_3[17] (fig. 8.10): If the electrode is placed relatively high, the initial downward forces of anterior hemiblock (fig. 8.2) move away from the high electrode and so inscribe an initial negative deflection. Anterior hemiblock imitates lateral infarction only to the extent that it causes a Q wave to appear in leads 1 and aVL and shrinks the R wave in V_{5-6}.

	Miming and Masking by Hemiblocks	
	Can Mimic	*Can Mask*
LAH	Anterior infarction	Anterior infarction
	Lateral infarction	Inferior infarction
	Left ventricular	Left ventricular
	hypertrophy	hypertrophy
		RBBB
LPH	Anterior infarction	Anterior infarction

The diagnosis of anterior hemiblock in the presence of inferior infarction presents problems[2, 3, 11]: both produce left axis deviation (LAD), the hemiblock with S waves, the infarction with Q waves in leads 2, 3 and aVF (fig. 8.11). But if the axis is as far leftward as −60°, the hemiblock is almost certainly present, with or without the infarction, and it is unlikely to be infarction alone.[11] Also in anterior hemiblock, the QRS in lead 2 ends with a deep S wave and never has a terminal r wave; whereas a terminal r or R in aVR is common. These two features are characteristic of hemiblock, whether or not inferior infarction is also present.

The hemiblocks have written a new and exciting chapter in the annals of intraventricular conduction; but there is still much to learn, and it is only fair to point out that in some patients with hemiblock who have come to autopsy, the location of lesions in the LBB system does not always live up to electrocardiographic expectations.[22, 35]

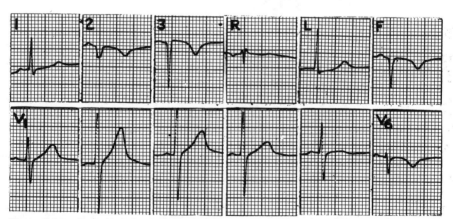

Figure 8.11. Probable **inferolateral infarction** and **anterior hemiblock.** The QS complexes and T-wave inversion in 2, 3 and aVF are diagnostic of inferior infarction, and probable lateral wall involvement is suggested by the shrunken r wave and inverted T wave in V₆. The axis of −60° with terminal r' in aVR and absence of terminal R in 2, 3 and aVF speak for anterior hemiblock.

Trifascicular Block

Semantically, this term can be appropriately applied to simultaneous block, complete or incomplete, in any three of the five ventricular conducting fascicles (His bundle, RBB, LBB, anterior and posterior divisions of the LBB); but it is specifically applied to block simultaneously involving the three peripheral fascicles—the RBB and the two divisions of the LBB. Its manifestations are therefore varied and include all the eight possible combinations of complete and incomplete block in these three fascicles (see table 8.1). If all three fascicles are completely blocked, "complete A-V block" results. If the RBB and the anterior division block completely while the posterior division blocks incompletely, the pattern of RBBB + left anterior hemiblock with "first degree A-V block" appears; and so on.

Table 8.1 lists the eight possible combinations with some of their electrocardiographic expressions. When incomplete block involves two or more fascicles, the number of possible variations is multiplied. For example, combination 8, with incomplete block in all three fascicles, could produce *any* of the expressions of trifascicular block, depending on the *relative* degree of incomplete block in each fascicle.

Notice that this whole concept of trifascicular block ignores the conducting potential of the septal fascicle. The term continues to enjoy common use long since the realization that the ventricular conduction system is usually *quadrifascicular*.

Table 8.1
Manifestations of Trifascicular Block [a]

Combination	RBB	LAD	LPD	ECG Expression
1	C	C	C	complete AVB
2	C	C	I	RBBB + LAH + "AVB"
3	C	I	C	RBBB + LPH + "AVB"
4	I	C	C	LBBB + "AVB"
5	C	I	I	various combinations
6	I	C	I	depending upon relative
7	I	I	C	degrees of incomplete
8	I	I	I	fascicular block

[a] *Key:* C = completely blocked, I = incompletely blocked, and "AVB" = manifestations of first or second degree A-V block.

REFERENCES

1. Anderson, R. H., and Becker, A. E.: Gross morphology and microscopy of the conducting system. In *Cardiac Arrhythmias: Their Mechanisms, Diagnosis and Management*, p. 12, edited by W. J. Mandel. J. B. Lippincott, Philadelphia, 1980.
2. Benchimol, A., et al.: Coexisting left anterior hemiblock and inferior wall myocardial infarction; vectorcardiographic features. Am. J. Cardiol. 1972: **29**, 7.
3. Castellanos, A., et al.: Diagnosis of left anterior hemiblock in the presence of inferior wall myocardial infarction. Chest 1971: **60**, 543.
4. Cohen, H. C., et al.: Disorders of impulse conduction and impulse formation caused by hyperkalemia in man. Am. Heart J. 1975: **89**, 501.

5. Corne, R. A.: Significance of left anterior hemiblock. Br. Heart J. 1978: **40,** 552.
6. Cristal, N., et al.: Left anterior hemiblock masking inferior myocardial infarction. Br. Heart J. 1975: **37,** 543.
7. Das, G.: Left axis deviation; a spectrum of intraventricular conduction block. Circulation 1976: **53,** 917.
8. Demoulin, J. C., and Kulbertus, H. E.: Histopathological examination of concept of left hemiblock. Br. Heart J. 1972: **34,** 807.
9. Durrer D, et al: Total excitation of the human heart. Circulation 1970: **41,** 899.
10. Fernandez, F., et al.: Electrocardiographic study of left intraventricular hemiblock in man during selective coronary arteriography. Am. J. Cardiol. 1970: **26,** 1.
11. Fisher, M. L., et al.: Left anterior fascicular block; electrocardiographic criteria for its recognition in the presence of inferior myocardial infarction. Am. J. Cardiol. 1979: **44,** 645.
12. Jacobson, L. B., et al.: An appraisal of initial QRS forces in left anterior fascicular block. Am. Heart J. 1977: **94,** 407.
13. Kourtesis, P: Incidence and significance of left anterior hemiblock complicating acute inferior wall myocardial infarction. Circulation 1976: **53,** 784.
14. Kulbertus, H. E., et al: Vectorcardiographic study of aberrant conduction. Anterior displacement of QRS: another form of intraventricular block. Br. Heart J. 1976: **38,** 549.
15. Leachman, R. D., et al.: Electrocardiographic signs of infarction masked by coexistent contralateral hemiblock. Chest 1972: **62,** 542.
16. Loperfido, F., et al.: An unusual ECG pattern; left posterior fascicular block obscuring a right ventricular conduction defect. J. Electrocardiol. 1981: **14,** 97.
17. Magram, M., and Lee, Y.-C.: The pseudo-infarction pattern of left anterior hemiblock. Chest 1977: **72,** 771.
18. Marriott, H. J. L., and Hogan, P.: Hemiblock in acute myocardial infarction. Chest 1970: **58,** 342.
19. Massing, G. K., and James, T. N.: Anatomical configuration of the His bundle and bundle branches in the human heart. Circulation 1976: **53,** 609.
20. Medrano, G. A., et al: Clinical electrocardiographic and vectorcardiographic diagnosis of the left anterior subdivision block isolated or associated with right bundle-branch block. Am. Heart J. 1972: **83,** 447.
21. Rabkin, S. W., et al.: Natural history of marked left axis deviation (left anterior hemiblock). Am. J. Cardiol. 1979: **43,** 605.
22. Rizzon P., et al: Left posterior hemiblock in acute myocardial infarction. Br. Heart J. 1975: **37,** 711.
23. Rosenbaum, M. B.: Types of right bundle branch block and their clinical significance. J. Electrocardiol. 1968: **1,** 221.
24. Rosenbaum, M. B.: Types of left bundle branch block and their clinical significance. J. Electrocardiol. 1969: **2,** 197.
25. Rosenbaum, M. B., et al.: Five cases of intermittent left anterior hemiblock. Am. J. Cardiol. 1969: **24,** 1.
26. Rosenbaum, M. B., et al.: The mechanism of bidirectional tachycardia. Am. Heart J. 1969: **78,** 4.
27. Rosenbaum, M. B., et al.: Intraventricular trifascicular blocks. The syndrome of right bundle branch block with intermittent left anterior and posterior hemiblock. Am. Heart J. 1969: **78,** 306.
28. Rosenbaum, M. B., et al.: Intraventricular trifascicular blocks. Review of the literature and classification. Am. Heart J. 1969: **78,** 450.
29. Rosenbaum, M. B.: The hemiblocks: diagnostic criteria and clinical significance. Mod. Concepts Cardiovasc. Dis. 1970: **39,** 141.
30. Rosenbaum, M. B., et al.: Right bundle branch block with left anterior hemiblock surgically induced in tetralogy of Fallot. Am. J. Cardiol. 1970: **26:** 12.
31. Rosenbaum, M. B., et al.: *The Hemiblocks: New Concepts of Intraventricular Conduction Based on Human Anatomical, Physiological, and Clinical Studies.* Tampa Tracings, Oldsmar, Fla., 1970.
32. Rosenbaum, M. B., et al.: Anatomical basis of AV conduction disturbances. Geriatrics 1970: **25,** 132.
33. Rosenbaum, M. B., et al.: Right bundle branch block with left anterior hemiblock surgically

induced in tetralogy of Fallot. Am. J. Cardiol. 1970: **26**, 12.

34. Rosenbaum, M. B., et al.: Left anterior hemiblock obscuring the diagnosis of right bundle branch block. Circulation. 1973: **48**, 298.
35. Rossi, L.: Histopathology of conducting system in left anterior hemiblock. Br. Heart J. 1976: **38**, 1304.
36. Sclarovsky, S., et al.: Left anterior hemiblock obscuring the diagnosis of right bundle branch block in acute myocardial infarction. Circulation 1979: **60**, 26.
37. Uhley, H. N.: The concept of trifascicular intraventricular conduction; historical aspects and influence on contemporary cardiology. Am. J. Cardiol. 1979: **43**, 643.

9

And Now Arrhythmias*

Detection of Arrhythmias

Since the early 1960s, great strides have been made in the detection and identification of arrhythmias. The introduction of coronary care units (May 1962) was a tremendous stimulus and since that time methods have multiplied and been refined. Until then, the "last word" in diagnosis was the "rhythm strip," and popular leads were 2 and V_1. But with the development of special intensive care areas, continuous monitoring became a necessity (for principles governing such monitoring, see Chapter 10).

Dynamic (Holter) Monitoring

At about the same time, a method to monitor the ambulant patient in his workaday environment evolved. This monitoring mode has proved invaluable and has enjoyed numerous improvements and refinements over the past 20 years. The patient is attached, by means of chest electrodes, to a portable tape recorder which records on one or two leads every heart beat during, usually, 24 hours. The patient keeps a diary of his activities so that any symptoms can be correlated with his then rhythm and any disturbance of rhythm can be correlated with his then activity. Thus he is monitored during real life situations—office encounters and pressures, golf or tennis, domestic squabbles, sexual intercourse, driving in traffic, showering, defecating. Its main use is to detect and identify any arrhythmic cause of symptoms such as palpitations, dizziness, syncope or chest pain; or, alternatively, to rule out arrhythmias as the cause of the symptom.

To give some idea of the likely harvest from Holter monitoring: out of 371 monitored patients, 174 (47%) had their symptoms during the 24-hour period of monitoring. Of these 174, the symptoms coincided with a culpable disturbance of rhythm in only 48 (27%), while the remaining 126 patients (73%) experienced their symptoms while their rhythm was entirely normal. Thus, of the original 371 patients, the Holter gave the answer (symptoms due to

---

* See glossary of terms at the end of this chapter.

arrhythmia or not) in approximately half; but in only about 1 in 8 of the original 371 was arrhythmia the cause of the symptoms.[16]

Holter monitoring is also of value in specific cardiac diseases or situations in which information concerning the heart's rhythm is important for prognosis and management—ischemic heart disease, variant angina, mitral valve prolapse, cardiomyopathy, conduction disturbances, evaluation of pacemaker function, Wolff-Parkinson-White syndrome. It may be helpful in the asymptomatic patient in whom an arrhythmia has been detected on routine examination and about which further information is required. And it may be of value in assessing the therapeutic effect of antiarrhythmic drugs and adjusting dosages; but in this context it is important to realize that there may be spontaneous variation in the frequency of arrhythmia from day to day of up to 90%,[6, 8] and therefore there must be a marked and consistent reduction in its incidence before triumphant conclusions are drawn.

Dynamic monitoring has proved an invaluable diagnostic aid, but the limited span of (usually) 24 hours makes it expensively unsuitable for detecting the *infrequent* rhythm disturbance. It has also been of great value in revealing the unexpected frequency of disorders of rhythm in presumably healthy populations of all ages (see below).

Indications for Dynamic (Holter) Monitoring

1. Symptoms suspected to be of cardiac origin (palpitations, dizziness, syncope, chest pain)
2. Specific cardiac disorders (e.g., ischemic heart disease, variant angina, mitral valve prolapse, cardiomyopathy, conduction disturbances, pacemaker evaluation, WPW syndrome)
3. Asymptomatic patient with known arrhythmia
4. As a guide to therapy of arrhythmia
5. Analyzing frequency of arrhythmias in a given population

Transtelephonic Monitoring (TTM)

The unlikelihood of catching the infrequent arrhythmia by Holter monitoring has been largely overcome by TTM,[5, 7] a method in which the patient carries with him a pocket-sized transmitter and, with a few simple instructions, is able to transmit his rhythm over the telephone when symptoms occur. In this way there can be more efficient and economical coverage for days or, if necessary to catch the fugitive arrhythmia, several weeks.

Valuable as this method has also proved, it still leaves the infrequent, *asymptomatic* arrhythmia uncaught.

Indications for Transtelephonic Monitoring

1. To detect the *infrequent* but symptomatic arrhythmia
2. For continued daily monitoring at home of postmyocardial infarction patient recently discharged
3. As an aid in adjusting dosage of antiarrhythmic therapy

His Bundle Recordings

His bundle electrography in man[3, 4, 14] has been an exciting development for those with a special interest in arrhythmias and conduction disturbances. By proper positioning of a multipolar electrode catheter, it is possible to obtain simultaneous recordings of the electrical activity of the A-V node, the bundle of His and the right bundle branch. Thus for the first time we are able to some extent to dissect and partition the P-R interval into two stages: from atrium to bundle of His (A-H interval); and from bundle of His to ventricles (H-V interval). This has proved instructive in elucidating the mechanisms of A-V block.

The main contribution of the technique to date is in confirming assumptions already ingeniously deduced from clinical tracings—it has converted the game of inference into a science.[9] It has confirmed the fact that concealed retrograde conduction follows ectopic ventricular beats; that concealed A-V junctional extrasystoles exist and can mimic A-V block; and that patterns of concealed conduction into the A-V junction account for the irregular ventricular response to atrial fibrillation.

But in addition to its role in confirmation, it has also provided a fresh approach to arrhythmia research; and, when all else fails, it may be the only means of resolving a difficult arrhythmia. For example, a His bundle recording alone may settle the notoriously difficult differentiation between ventricular aberration and ectopy, since ventricular complexes that result from supraventricular impulses must be preceded by His bundle activation, whereas ectopic ventricular complexes are not. Again, by this technique it has been demonstrated that the site of conduction delay during Wenckebach periodicity is usually in the A-V node itself (prolongation of A-H interval) whereas in type II A-V block, the site of block is always infranodal and usually below the

---

Indications for His-Bundle Recordings[14]

1. Determining the level of A-V block
2. Differentiating ventricular ectopy from aberration
3. Identifying concealed junctional extrasystoles
4. Identifying type of SVT
5. Investigating action of drugs

bundle of His (prolongation of H-V interval). Finally, the technique has yielded precise and useful information concerning the action of antiarrhythmic drugs on A-V conduction.

Incidence of Arrhythmias in Normal Populations

Evaluation of cardiac rate and rhythm must take normal data into consideration; and so, before exploring the incidence and intricacies of arrhythmias in subsequent chapters, it is well to be aware of the frequency with which "abnormal" rhythms are found in normal populations—information which the development of dynamic monitoring has enabled us to obtain.

The extent of normal variation in rate and rhythm in normal children is widely unappreciated. Among 134 normal infants monitored for 24 hours during the first 10 days of life, the maximal 9-beat heart rate reached 220/min, while the minimal rate was 42/min. Atrial premature beats were found in 19 (14%). Sinus pauses occurred in 72% of a subgroup of 71 infants, the longest pause reaching 1.8 sec. Of over 2000 infants screened with a standard ECG and a 10-sec rhythm strip, 0.9% had premature beats, many of them ventricular.[12]

Among 92 healthy children aged 7–11 years[13] the fastest rate attained for 9 consecutive beats was 195/min and the lowest rate was 37/min. Junctional escape as a result of sinus slowing occurred in no less than 45%, in one child lasting for 25 min. First degree A-V block was found in 9 children with P-R interval up to 0.28 sec. Three children had Wenckebach periods, one of whom had 53 episodes. Isolated atrial and ventricular extrasystoles were found in 21% and sinus pauses in two thirds of the children monitored.

Among 131 healthy boys aged 10–13 years,[11] waking maximal heart rates ranged between 100 and 200/min with minimal rates between 45 and 80/min. Maximal sleeping rates were between 60 and 100/min with minimal rates between 30 and 70/min. First degree A-V block was found in 8.4% and type I A-V block in 10.7%. Single atrial and single ventricular extrasystoles were found in 13 and 26%, respectively.

Among 50 young women without heart disease aged 22–28 years,[10] the waking maximal heart rate ranged between 122 and 189/min with minimal rates between 40 and 73. Maximal sleeping rates ranged between 71 and 128/min with minimal rates between 37 and 59/min. Atrial premature beats occurred in 64% and ventricular prematures in 54%. One woman had one 3-beat run of ventricular tachycardia and two (4%) had periods of type I A-V block.

Fifty male medical students without apparent heart disease were similarly monitored.[1] Their waking maximal rates ranged from 107 to 180/min with minimal rates between 37 and 65/min. Maximal sleeping rates were between 70 and 115/min with minimal rates of 33 to 55/min. Half of these young men had sinus arrhythmia sufficient to cause 100% change in consecutive cycles, and 28% had sinus pauses of more than 1.75 sec. Atrial extrasystoles were found in 56% and ventricular in 50%. Three students (6%) had periods of type I A-V block.

It is also not widely known that a significant minority of the supposedly healthy work force has arrhythmias that are generally regarded as of serious prognostic significance including multifocal and R-on-T ventricular extrasystoles, ventricular bigeminy, ventricular tachycardia and second degree A-V block.[2]

Among a healthy elderly population (98 subjects aged 60 to 85 years, all with normal maximal treadmill tests), sinus bradycardia was found in 91%, supraventricular premature beats in 88, supraventricular tachycardia in 13 and atrial flutter in one; ventricular arrhythmias included extrasystoles in 78%—many with pairs or multiform beats—and ventricular tachycardia in four per cent.[3a] Even among young athletes extrasystoles are common: all of 20 male long-distance runners aged 19 to 29 years had atrial and 14 (70%) had ventricular premature beats; and 8 of the 20 had periods of type I A-V block.[13a]

Such have been the largely unexpected revelations of dynamic monitoring.

Ladder Diagrams

Ladder diagrams, or "laddergrams" for short, are indispensable for helping one unravel the difficult arrhythmia, for communicating one's interpretation, and in teaching arrhythmias, both simple and complex. We generally use three tiers (fig. 9.1*A*): atrial (A), junctional (A-V) and ventricular (V). One may need to add a sinus node tier (fig. 9.1*B*) or a tier for an ectopic ventricular focus (fig. 9.1*C*), or divide the A-V junction into 2 or 3 layers; but for most purposes the three tiers suffice.

You place the laddergram immediately under the tracing to be graphed and then there are two steps in using it: (1) first you put in *what you can see*, i.e., you put in appropriate lines or bars to represent the visible P waves and QRS complexes; and (2) then, and only then, you work out the conduction pattern and write it in.

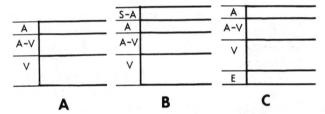

Figure 9.1. The skeletons of laddergrams. For use of each type, see text. (Reproduced with permission from H. J. L. Marriott and R. J. Myerburg: Recognition of arrhythmias and conduction disturbances, in *The Heart*, Ed. 5, pp. 519–556, edited by J. W. Hurst, McGraw-Hill, New York, 1982.)

Various types of beats are represented in figure 9.2. In the *top diagram*, *a* is an ordinary sinus beat; we have a gentle slope indicating the passage of time as the impulse spreads through the atrium; it is slowed in the A-V junction and then it speeds up again in the ventricles. You can put a blob for the point of origin of the impulse, but you do not have to because you can tell which way the impulse is travelling from the slight slope of the line. Then *b* is a sinus beat with first degree block: delay in the A-V junction compared to the normal one. And *c* is an ectopic atrial beat with first degree block and ventricular aberration. This split line is not an accepted symbol but is useful to indicate ventricular aberration.

In the second diagram, *a* represents an A-V junctional beat with activation of the atria before the ventricles; *b* is an A-V junctional beat activating atria after the ventricles; and *c* is an A-V junctional beat with considerable delay back to the atria and normal conduction to the ventricles; the delay back to the atria enables the impulse to spill over into a no-longer-refractory downward tract and we get a reciprocal beat. The *arrowheads*, like the pacemaker blobs, are optional. You do not need them; if you slope the line, it is obvious which way the impulse is going, but the *arrowhead* sometimes helps the eye.

In the third diagram *a* is an ectopic ventricular beat which does not penetrate back into the A-V junction. Then *b* is an ectopic ventricular beat that does penetrate the A-V junction but not to the atria. And *c* is an ectopic ventricular beat with retrograde conduction all the way to the atria.

In the *bottom diagram*, *a* is a dissociated beat—a sinus impulse coming down and meeting an ascending ectopic ventricular impulse in the A-V junction. Then *b* is a ventricular fusion beat—a sinus impulse reaching the ventricles but not occupying the entire ventricular myocardium because an ectopic ventricular impulse has fired and activated part of the ventricles. And *c* is a combination between an ectopic impulse conducted retrogradely to the atria and the sinus impulse; the sinus impulse cannot control the whole of the atria because of the retrograde invasion by the ventricular impulse and now we have an atrial fusion beat.

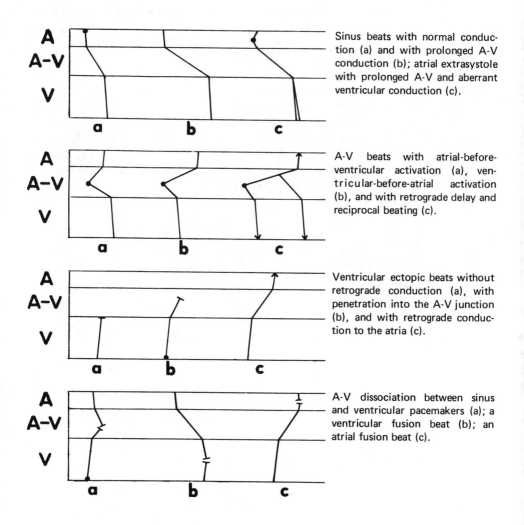

Sinus beats with normal conduction (a) and with prolonged A-V conduction (b); atrial extrasystole with prolonged A-V and aberrant ventricular conduction (c).

A-V beats with atrial-before-ventricular activation (a), ventricular-before-atrial activation (b), and with retrograde delay and reciprocal beating (c).

Ventricular ectopic beats without retrograde conduction (a), with penetration into the A-V junction (b), and with retrograde conduction to the atria (c).

A-V dissociation between sinus and ventricular pacemakers (a); a ventricular fusion beat (b); an atrial fusion beat (c).

Figure 9.2. Laddergrams of various beats.

Now, to get the hang of their use, let us construct a laddergram in the two recommended stages. The tracing in figure 9.3, which is again reproduced in Chapter 11, illustrates a ventricular extrasystole with concealed retrograde conduction prolonging the ensuing P-R interval. The first step is to indicate each of the visible P waves and QRS complexes with an appropriate sloping line. The second step is to indicate conduction of the normally conducted sinus beats by connecting atrial and ventricular lines through the A-V junction. But the sinus beat following the extrasystole is conducted with a prolonged P-R interval, and this requires explanation. Clearly the ventricular extrasystole must have travelled retrogradely into the A-V junction so that the next descending sinus impulse found the junction relatively refractory. We therefore depict the ventricular ectopic impulse travelling backward a certain distance into the A-V junction; and the sinus impulse, conducted normally until it reaches the level to which the ectopic impulse has penetrated, suffering delay below that point.

In subsequent chapters, laddergrams will be freely used as a visual aid to understanding patterns of conduction.

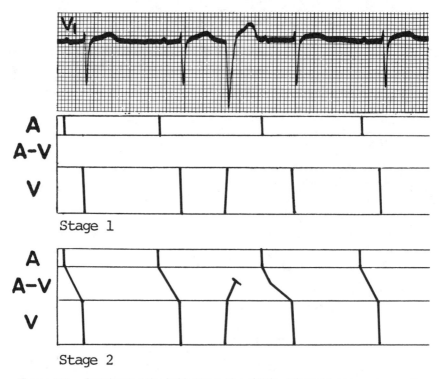

Figure 9.3. Constructing the laddergram of a simple arrhythmia in two stages. For explanation, see text.

Glossary

Aberrant ventricular conduction. The temporarily abnormal intraventricular conduction of a supraventricular impulse, usually associated with a change in cycle length.

Accelerated idionodal rhythm. An automatic A-V rhythm, controlling only the ventricles, at a rate between 60 and 100 beats/min.

Accelerated idioventricular rhythm. An automatic ectopic ventricular rhythm, controlling only the ventricles, at a rate between 50 and 100 beats/min.

Atrial capture. Retrograde conduction to the atria, from A-V junction or ventricles, after a period of A-V dissociation.

Automaticity. The property inherent in all pacemaking cells that enables them to form new impulses spontaneously.

Automatic beat or rhythm. A beat or rhythm arising in a spontaneously beating center, independent of the dominant sinus (or other) rhythm.

A-V dissociation. Independent beating of atria and ventricles.

Block. Pathological delay or interruption of impulse conduction.

Bradycardia. Any heart (or chamber) rhythm having an average rate under 60 beats/min.

Capture(d) beat. A conducted beat following a period of A-V dissociation.

Concealed conduction. Conduction of an impulse within the conduction system, recognizable only by its effect on the subsequent beat or cycle.

Coupling interval. The interval between an extrasystole and the beat preceding it.

Ectopic beat. A beat arising in any focus other than the sinus node.

Ectopy. Ectopic impulse formation.

Escape(d) beat. An automatic beat ending a cycle longer than the dominant cycle and able to appear only because of a slowing or interruption of the dominant rhythm.

Extrasystole. A premature ectopic beat, dependent upon and coupled to the preceding beat.

Fusion beat. A beat resulting from the simultaneous spread of more than one impulse through the same myocardial territory (either ventricles or atria).

Idionodal rhythm. An independent rhythm arising in the A-V junction and controlling only the ventricles.

Idioventricular rhythm. A rhythm arising in and controlling only the ventricles.

Isorhythmic dissociation. A-V dissociation with atria and ventricles beating at the same or almost the same rate.

Parasystole. An automatic ectopic rhythm whose pacemaker is ''protected'' from discharge by the sinus or other circumnavigating impulses so that it is able to maintain its own uninterrupted rhythm in competition with the dominant rhythm.

Pre-excitation. Activation of a ventricle earlier than its activation would be expected via the normal conducting pathways.

Premature beat. An ectopic beat, dependent upon and coupled to the preceding beat, and occurring before the next expected dominant beat; extrasystole.

Tachyarrhythmia. Any disturbance of rhythm resulting in a heart or chamber rate over 100 beats/min.

Tachycardia. Any heart (or chamber) rhythm having an average rate over 100 beats/min.

Ventricular aberration. Aberrant ventricular conduction.

Ventricular capture. Conduction to the ventricles after a period of A-V dissociation.

Wolff-Parkinson-White syndrome. An electrocardiographic "syndrome" consisting of a short P-R interval (<0.12 sec) with widened QRS complex including a delta wave (slurred initial component).

REFERENCES

1. Brodsky, M., et al.: Arrhythmias documented by 24-hour continuous electrocardiographic monitoring in 50 male medical students without apparent heart disease. Am. J. Cardiol. 1977: **39,** 390.
2. Clarke, J. M., et al.: The rhythm of the normal heart. Lancet 1976: **2,** 508.
3. Damato, A. N., and Lau, S. H.: Clinical value of the electrogram of the conduction system. Prog. Cardiovasc. Dis. 1970: **13,** 119.
3a. Fleg, J. L., and Kennedy, H. L.: Cardiac arrhythmias in a healthy elderly population: Detection by 24-hour ambulatory electrocardiography. Chest 1982: **81,** 302.
4. Goldreyer, B. N.: Intracardiac electrocardiography in the analysis and understanding of cardiac arrhythmias. Ann. Intern. Med. 1972: **77,** 117.
5. Grodman, P. S.: Arrhythmia surveillance by transtelephonic monitoring; comparison with Holter monitoring in symptomatic ambulatory patients. Am. Heart J. 1979: **98,** 459.
6. Harrison, D. C.: Contribution of ambulatory electrocardiographic monitoring to antiarrhythmic management. Am. J. Cardiol. 1978: **41,** 996.
7. Judson, P., et al.: Evaluation of outpatient arrhythmias utilizing transtelephonic monitoring. Am. Heart J. 1979: **97,** 759.
8. Michelson, E. L., and Morganroth, J.: Spontaneous variability of complex ventricular arrhythmias detected by long-term electrocardiographic recording. Circulation 1980: **61,** 690.
9. Pick, A.: Mechanisms of cardiac arrhythmias; from hypothesis to physiologic fact. Am. Heart J. 1973: **86,** 249.
10. Sabotka, P. A., et al.: Arrhythmias documented by 24-hour continuous ambulatory electrocardiographic monitoring in young women without apparent heart disease. Am. Heart J. 1981: **101,** 753.
11. Scott, O., et al.: Results of 24-hour ambulatory monitoring of electrocardiogram in 131 healthy boys aged 10 to 13 years. Br. Heart J. 1980: **44,** 304.
12. Southall, D. P., et al.: Study of cardiac rhythm in healthy newborn infants. Br. Heart J. 1980: **43,** 14.
13. Southall, D. P., et al.: A 24-hour electrocardiographic study of heart rate and rhythm patterns in population of healthy children. Br. Heart J. 1981: **45,** 281.
13a. Talan, D. A., et al.: Twenty-four hour continuous ECG recordings in long-distance runners. Chest 1982: **82,** 19.
14. Vadde, P. S., et al.: Indications of His bundle recordings. Cardiovasc. Clin. 1980: **11,** 1.
15. Winkle, R. A.: Ambulatory electrocardiography and the diagnosis, evaluation, and treatment of chronic ventricular arrhythmias Prog. Cardiovasc. Dis. 1980: **23,** 99.
16. Zeldis, S. M., et al.: Cardiovascular complaints; correlation with cardiac arrhythmias on 24-hour electrocardiographic monitoring. Chest 1980: **78,** 456.

10

Systematic Approach to Diagnosis of Arrhythmias

Disturbances of rhythm are most conveniently divided into (1) supraventricular and (2) ventricular. This corresponds with a simple electrocardiographic difference—arrhythmias originating in the atrium or A-V junction (supraventricular), unless complicated by aberrant ventricular conduction (Chapter 16), are characterized by normal QRS complexes, while ventricular arrhythmias produce bizarre QRST complexes with prolonged QRS interval.

Many disturbances of rhythm and conduction are recognizable at first glance. For example, one can usually spot at once atrial flutter with 4:1 conduction, or atrial fibrillation with rapid ventricular response. But there are a significant number of dysrhythmias that defy immediate recognition, and it is for these that we require a systematic attack. The following approach has evolved after analyzing the reasons for the mistakes I have made and those I have repeatedly watched others make; and the system is therefore designed to avoid the common errors of omission and commission. Undoubtedly, we make most mistakes because of failure to apply reason and logic and not because of ignorance.

Before outlining the systematic five-point approach, it is worth making some observations about the principles of monitoring, since in this day of its widespread use anyone concerned with the interpretation of arrhythmias is likely to be involved in continuous monitoring whether in intensive care, on telemetry, on Holter tapes or during stress testing—and much the same principles apply in each context.

Principles of Monitoring (Table 10.1)

Principle 1. **Use a lead containing maximal information.** There is no point in letting available information go down the drain. One never knows when it might be useful; and if one can gather additional data with no additional trouble, why not do so? As an example of lost information that might have been valuable, we are now 20 years into coronary care and do not yet know whether there is any prognostic difference between left and right ventricular extrasystoles. One ongoing study[3] strongly suggests that left ventricular extrasystoles are many times more likely than right ventricular extrasystoles to precipitate ventricular tachycardia or fibrillation. If constant monitoring in its early years had employed a monitoring lead that enabled one to distinguish left

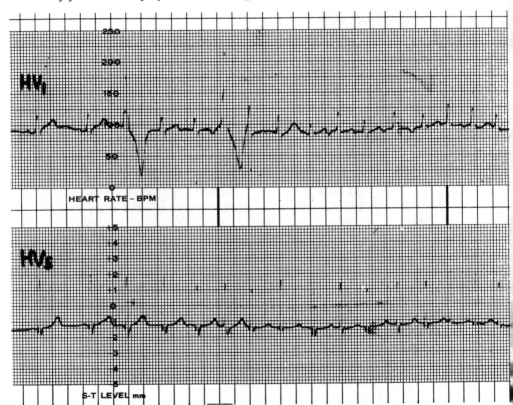

Figure 10.1.   Two simultaneous leads from a Holter recording with precordial electrodes at the V_1 and V_5 positions. Two grossly aberrant beats in V_1 produce an almost imperceptible widening of the S wave in V_6.

ONE LEAD IS NOT ENOUGH

from right ventricular ectopic beats, this information might well be in hand today. But a counterfeit lead 2 was used for many years, and if you turn to figure 15.2 you will see how lead 2 can look identical in all four of the Big-4 to be differentiated: left bundle-branch block (LBBB), right bundle-branch block (RBBB), left ventricular ectopics, and right ventricular ectopics. For this reason, if for no other, lead 2 is one of the least satisfactory leads for constant monitoring.

Principle 2. Another principle of good monitoring is that the system should be as **mechanically convenient** as possible; for most systems a maximum of three wires and electrodes is appropriate, and these should be strategically placed so as not to interfere with physical examination of the heart or with the application of emergency countershock.

Principle 3. But no matter how good the monitoring lead is, **one lead is not enough** for all the time; and there are at least four reasons for this: (1) Two dissimilar complexes can look remarkably similar in a single lead; e.g., in figure 10.1, the clearly bizarre and aberrant beats in V_1 would be almost impossible to spot in V_5. (2) A single lead may not show the insignificant item you are looking for—such as the P wave or pacemaker blip. (3) The morphology of, say, RBBB may not be diagnostic in one lead (e.g., V_1) while confidently diagnosable in another (e.g., V_6). (4) The width of a QRS (or other interval) may not be accurately measurable in a single lead—from one angle it may look considerably narrower than it really is (fig. 10.2).

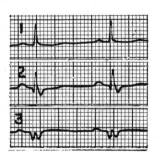

Figure 10.2. From lead 1, no one would think that this patient has intraventricular block with a QRS interval of 0.11 sec as seen in leads 2 and 3. By Einthoven's equation, since the terminal 0.06 sec is a virtually identical negative deflection in leads 2 and 3, that part of the QRS in lead 1 is disarmingly isoelectric.

Table 10.1
Principles of Monitoring

1. Use lead with maximal information
2. Ensure maximal mechanical convenience
3. One lead is not enough
4. Know when to use what other leads

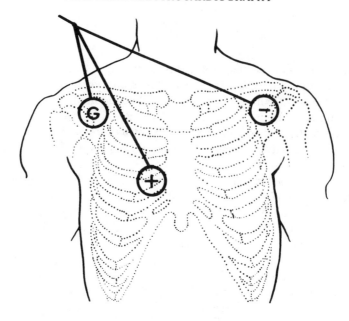

Figure 10.3.   Electrode placement of modified CL₁ (MCL₁).

Principle 4. A direct consequence of Principle 3 is that one must **know when to use what other leads.**

A monitoring lead that satisfactorily fulfills most of the requirements is the modified CL₁ (MCL₁) introduced in 1968[2] (fig. 10.3). The positive electrode is placed at the C_1 (or V_1) position; the negative electrode, at the left shoulder; and the ground (which may be placed anywhere), usually at the right shoulder. This leaves a clear platform for emergency cardioversion and an unencumbered precordium for physical examination. In addition, this lead, since it closely imitates V_1, affords several diagnostic advantages: One can immediately distinguish between left and right ventricular ectopy in most instances; RBBB and LBBB can be recognized with ease; and P waves are sometimes best or only seen in a right precordial lead. Most importantly of all, a right chest lead gives one the best chance of distinguishing between left ventricular ectopy and RBBB aberration.

The only disadvantages of lead MCL₁, which are minor by comparison with its virtues, are that it fails to recognize shifts of axis and is therefore useless for spotting the development of a hemiblock, and that the polarity of the P wave is not as informative as that in lead 2. However, the P wave morphology in a right chest lead is not all that uninformative: whereas the sinus P wave, when it is diphasic, is usually +−, the ectopic or retrograde P wave when diphasic is usually −+ (fig. 10.4).

The MCL hookup possesses considerable flexibility. When MCL_1 fails to provide the answer; it may be helpful to turn to a left chest lead; then it is merely a matter of substituting an electrode at the C_6 position to obtain an MCL_6, which is a reasonable imitation of V_6. Moreover, if the polarity of the retrograde P wave, as familiarly known to us in the limb leads, seems worth recording to document a junctional rhythm, the substituted electrode may be placed low on the left flank below the diaphragm to obtain a reasonable imitation of standard lead 3 (fig. 10.5).

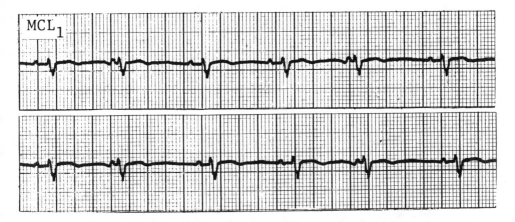

Figure 10.4. Second and fifth beats in each strip are **atrial premature beats.** Note the − + polarity of the ectopic P waves.

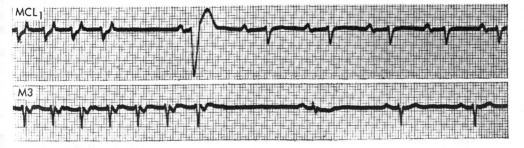

Figure 10.5. Each lead shows the end of a run of **junctional tachycardia** with the retrograde P wave just following the QRS complex. In the second half of each strip, sinus rhythm resumes. Note that the retrograde and sinus P waves are both predominantly positive in MCL_1, whereas in M3 the retrograde P waves show the more familiar inversion characteristic of retroconduction in an inferior lead. On each occasion, after the tachycardia ceases, the returning beat is an escape beat.

A left chest lead (V_6 or MCL_6) is not reliable for distinguishing between left and right ventricular ectopy. In figure 10.6, the first extrasystole probably comes from the left ventricle, whereas the second comes from the right ventricle. But in V_6 they both have a very similar LBBB morphology. Unfortunately, in V_6 both left and right ventricular ectopics may be either positive or negative: In left ventricular ectopy the usual QRS in V_6 is mainly negative (rS or QS), but it may be positive as part of the pattern of concordant positivity. Similarly, in right ventricular ectopy the usual QRS in V_6 is positive, but it may be negative as part of the pattern of concordant negativity.

For examples of the sort of information that can be derived from a right chest lead that is not usually available in lead 2, look at figure 10.7. In figure 10.7*A*, the rSR′ pattern of the sinus beats is typical of RBBB; the qR pattern with early peak in the first extrasystole is typical of ectopy of left ventricular origin; and the rS pattern of the second extrasystole is typical of a right ventricular origin. In figure 10.7*B*, the atrial fibrillation is interrupted by a burst of bizarre beats that are certain to evoke the "lidocaine reflex"; but the telltale shape (rsR′) of the first of these wide beats tells us that it is a run of aberrantly conducted beats rather than a run of ventricular tachycardia.

Stepwise Approach to Diagnosis

If the diagnosis fails to fall into your lap, then the systematic approach is in order (table 10.2). The first step in any medical diagnosis is to **know the causes** of the presenting symptom. For example, if you want to be a "super" headache specialist, the first step is to learn the 50 causes of headache, which are the common ones, which the uncommon, and how to differentiate them; because "you see only what you look for, you recognize only what you know."[6]

As diagnostic challenges, the arrhythmias are no different—the first step is to know the causes of the disturbance of rhythm that confronts you and there

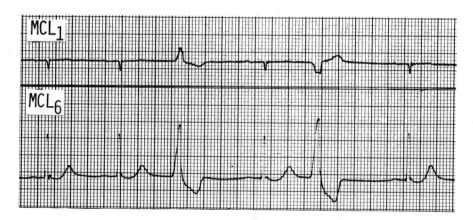

Figure 10.6.   Simultaneous recording of MCL_1 and MCL_6. The third beat is a **left ventricular extrasystole** and the fifth beat a **right ventricular extrasystole**. Note that while the distinction is easy in MCL_1, the "LBBB" morphology of the two beats is strikingly similar in V_6.

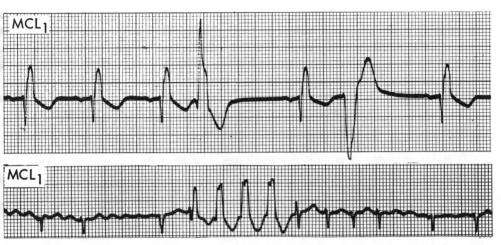

Figure 10.7. The patterns of **RBBB** (sinus beats), **left ventricular ectopy** (fourth beat), and **right ventricular ectopy** (sixth beat) are readily recognized. (*B*) A short run of aberrantly conducted beats during atrial fibrillation; the **aberration** is recognized by the characteristic triphasic (rsR′) contour of the first anomalous beat.

Table 10.2
Approach to Diagnosis

1. Know the causes
2. Milk the QRS
3. Cherchez le P
4. Who's married to whom?
5. Pinpoint the primary

Table 10.3
Eight Basic Rhythm Disturbances

1. Early beats
2. Unexpected pauses
3. Tachycardias
4. Bradycardias
5. Bigeminal rhythms
6. Group beating
7. Total irregularity
8. Regular non-sinus rhythms at normal rates

are only eight basic dysrhythms (table 10.3). "Knowing the causes" of each of these (tables 10.4–10.9) is part of the equipment that you carry around with you—prepared at a moment's notice to use the knowledge when faced with an unidentified arrhythmia.

When a specific arrhythmia confronts you, first **milk the QRS**. There are two reasons for this: first, it is an extension of Willie Sutton's law—Sutton, the bank robber, who robbed banks because that was "where the money was"; and second, because it keeps us in the healthy frame of mind of giving priority to ventricular behavior—in general, it matters comparatively little what the atria are doing so long as the ventricles are behaving themselves.

If the QRS is of normal duration—be sure to check in at least two leads (remember fig. 10.2)—you know that the rhythm is supraventricular and that may tell all you can deduce from such a QRS. But if the QRS is wide and bizarre, you are then faced with the decision whether it is supraventricular with ventricular aberration or is ectopic ventricular; and that is where the fun begins. If you know your morphology, you know what to look for, and you will recognize it if you see it.

During the past decade and a half, the diagnostic morphology of the ventricular complex has come into its own. This began with clinical observation and deductions[1, 5, 7] in which astute coronary care nurses played an important role,[8] and culminated in the confirmatory electrophysiolgical studies of Wellens and his colleagues.[9] Applying the fruits of these labors, Wellens[10] found that inspection of the QRS pattern in the clinical tracing afforded the correct diagnosis in 52 of 56 consecutive wide-QRS tachycardias. Despite the evident

Table 10.4
Causes of Early Beats

1. Extrasystole
2. Parasystole
3. Capture beat, including supernormal conduction during A-V block
4. Reciprocal beat
5. Better (e.g., 3:2) conduction interrupting poorer (e.g., 2:1)
6. Rhythm resumption after inapparent bigeminy

Table 10.5
Causes of Pauses

1. Nonconducted atrial extrasystoles
2. Second degree A-V block
   Type I (Wenckebach, 1899)
   Type II (Wenckebach, 1906; Hay, 1906)
3. Second degree S-A block
   Type I or type II
4. Concealed conduction
5. Concealed A-V extrasystoles

Table 10.6
Causes of Bradycardia[a]

1. Sinus bradycardia
2. Nonconducted atrial bigeminy
3. A-V block; second and third degree
4. S-A block: second and third degree

[a] Note that A-V nodal (idionodal, junctional) and idioventricular rhythms are not *causes* of bradycardia, but *result* from one of the above.

Table 10.7
Causes of Bigeminal Rhythm

1. Extrasystolic
   Ventricular
   Supraventricular
2. Due to 3:2 block
   A-V block, type I and II
   S-A block, type I and II
   Atrial tachycardia or flutter with alternating 2:1 and 4:1 conduction, etc.
3. Nonconducted atrial trigeminy
4. Reciprocal beating
5. Concealed A-V extrasystoles every third beat

Table 10.8
Causes of Chaos

1. Atrial fibrillation
2. Atrial flutter with varying A-V conduction
3. Multifocal atrial tachycardia
4. Shifting (wandering) pacemaker
5. Multifocal ventricular extrasystoles
6. Parasystole
7. Combinations of above

Table 10.9
Regular Rhythms at Normal Rates

1. Normal sinus rhythm
2. Accelerated A-V rhythm
3. Accelerated idioventricular rhythm
4. Atrial flutter with, e.g., 4:1 conduction
5. Sinus or supraventricular tachycardia with (e.g., 2:1) A-V block
6. Ventricular tachycardia with (e.g., 2:1) exit block

availability, simplicity, and accuracy of this method, some authorities persist in ignoring its potential.[4, 11]

If the answer is not afforded by the shape of the QRS complex, the next item to turn to is the P wave—**cherchez le P.** In the past, the P wave, as the key to arrhythmias, has certainly been overemphasized; and a lifelong love affair with P waves has afflicted many an electrocardiographer with the so-called "P-preoccupation syndrome." But there are times when the P wave holds the diagnostic clue and must be accorded the starring role.

In one's search for P waves, there are several clues and caveats to bear in mind. One technique that may be useful is to employ the S_5 lead introduced by French cardiologists 30 years ago. To obtain this lead, the positive electrode is placed at the fifth right interspace close to the sternum (just below the C_1 position), and the negative electrode on the manubrium of the sternum. This will sometimes greatly magnify the P wave, rendering it readily visible when it was virtually indiscernible in other leads. Figure 10.8 illustrates this amplifying

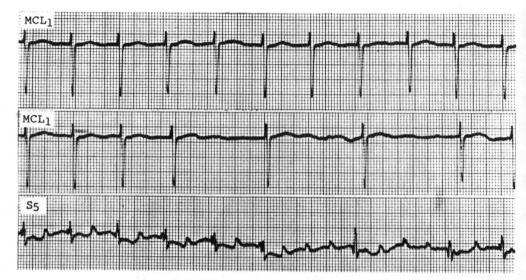

Figure 10.8. The top strip of MCL₁ shows barely perceptible P' waves of an **atrial tachycardia**. The second strip of MCL₁ shows the effect of carotid sinus stimulation: The ventricular rate halves because of increased A-V block, and additional P' waves become barely visible through the artifact. In contrast, the strip of lead S₅ (see text) boasts prominent P waves; the beginning of the strip illustrates the "Bix rule" (see text and also fig. 10.9), and the second half of the strip again shows the effect of carotid sinus stimulation.

effect and makes the diagnosis of atrial tachycardia with 2:1 block immediately apparent. If it succeeds, this technique is a great deal kinder to the patient and safer than passing an atrial wire or an esophageal electrode to corral elusive P waves.

Another clue to the incidence of P waves is contained in the **Bix rule**, after the Baltimore cardiologist Harold Bix, who used to say that whenever the P waves of a supraventricular tachycardia were halfway between the ventricular complexes, you should always suspect that additional P waves were hiding within the QRS complex. In the *top strip* of figure 10.9, the P' wave is midway between the QRS complexes, and one therefore thinks of the "Bix rule." It may be necessary to apply carotid sinus stimulation or other vagal maneuver to bring the alternate P' waves out of hiding; but in this case, the patient obligingly altered his conduction pattern (*middle strip* of fig. 10.9) and spontaneously exposed the skulking P' waves. It is clearly important to know if there are twice as many atrial impulses as are apparent because there is the ever-present danger that the *ventricular* rate may double or almost double, especially if the atrial rate were to slow somewhat. It is better to be forewarned and take steps to prevent such potentially disastrous acceleration.

The **haystack principle** can be of great diagnostic importance when you are searching for difficult-to-find P waves or any other inconspicuous deflection. When you have to find a needle in a haystack, if you value your time and energy you would presumably prefer a small rather than large haystack. Therefore, whenever you are faced with the problem of finding elusive items, always give the lead with the least disturbance of the baseline (the smallest

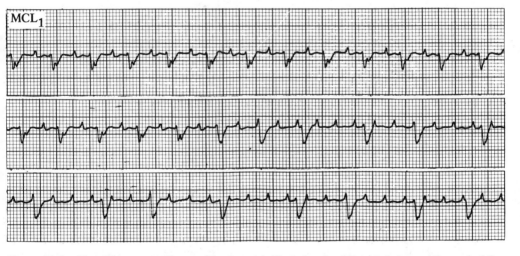

Figure 10.9. The strips are continuous. The *top strip* illustrates the "Bix rule"; toward the end of the *second strip* the conduction ratio changes, and the previously hidden alternate P' waves are brought to light, revealing an **atrial tachycardia** (rate, 212/min).

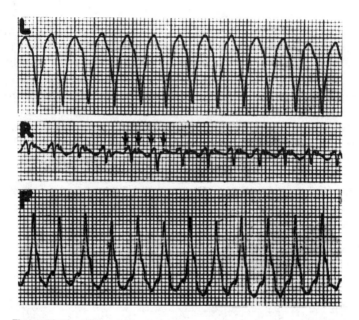

Figure 10.10. The unipolar limb leads from a patient with a **runaway pacemaker**. The pacemaker spikes are not visible in leads aVL and aVF but are plainly seen (*arrows*) in the lead (aVR) with small ventricular complexes.

ventricular complex) a chance to help you. There are some leads that no one would think of looking at to solve an arrhythmia (e.g., aVR), yet the patient illustrated in figure 10.10 died because his attendants did not know or did not apply the haystack principle and make use of aVR. He had a runaway pacemaker at a discharge rate of 440/min with a halved ventricular response at 220/min. Lead aVR was the lead with the smallest ventricular complex, and it was the only lead in which the pacemaker "blips" were plainly visible (*arrows* of fig. 10.10). The patient went into shock and died because none of the attempted therapeutic measures affected the tachycardia, when all that was necessary was to disconnect the wayward pulse generator.

The next caveat is **mind your "Ps."** This means to be wary of things that look like P waves and particularly applies to P-like waves that are adjacent to the QRS complex—they may turn out to be part of the QRS complex. This is a trap for the unwary sufferer from the P-preoccupation syndrome to whom anything that looks like a P wave is a P wave. Many competent interpreters given the strip of lead V_1 or V_2 in figure 10.11 will promptly and confidently diagnose a supraventricular tachycardia for the wrong reasons. In V_1, the QRS seems not to be very wide and appears to be preceded by a small P wave; in V_2, an apparently narrow QRS is followed by an "unmistakable" retrograde P wave. But, in fact, the P-like waves in both these leads are part of the QRS complex. If the QRS duration is measured in V_3, it is found to be 0.14 sec; to attain a QRS of that width in V_1 and V_2, the P-like waves need to be included in the measurement.

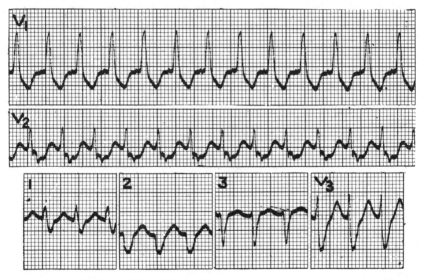

Figure 10.11. The beats in the rhythm strips of leads V_1 and V_2 are readily mistaken for narrow ventricular complexes with constantly related P waves. But the QRS interval, as seen in leads 1 and V_3, clearly measures 0.14 sec. To achieve this width in V_1 and V_2, the P-like waves must be included in the QRS measurement.

Whenever a regular rhythm is difficult to identify, it is always worthwhile to seek and focus on any interruption in the regularity—a process that can be condensed in the three words **dig the break.** It is at a break in the rhythm that you are most likely to find the solution. For example, look at figure 10.12. At the beginning of the strip, where the rhythm is regular at a rate of 200/min, it is impossible to know whether the tachycardia is ectopic atrial or ectopic junctional or a reciprocating tachycardia in the A-V junction; and a fourth possibility is that the little peak is part of the QRS and not a P wave at all (mind your "Ps!"). Further along the strip there is a break in the rhythm in the form of a pause. The commonest cause of a pause is a nonconducted atrial extrasystole, and, sure enough, there at the *arrow* is the culprit—in this situation, a diagnostic ally. As a result of the pause, the mechanism is immediately obvious: When the rhythm resumes, the returning P wave is in front of the first QRS, and the mechanism is evidently an atrial tachycardia.

The next step is to establish relationships or, to put it in more catchy terms, ask yourself **who's married to whom?** This is often the crucial step in arriving at a firm diagnosis. Figure 10.13 illustrates this principle in simplest form. A junctional rhythm is dissociated from sinus bradycardia. On three occasions there are bizarre early beats of a qR configuration that is nondiagnostic. They could be ventricular extrasystoles, but the fact that they are seen *only* when a P wave is emerging beyond the preceding QRS tells us that they are "married to" the preceding P waves and establishes them as conducted (capture) beats with atypical RBBB aberration.

Figure 10.14 illustrates both this principle and the final one, **pinpoint the primary** diagnosis. One must never be content to let the diagnosis rest upon a secondary phenomenon such as A-V dissociation, escape, or aberration—each and all of these are always secondary to some primary disturbance that must be sought out and identified.

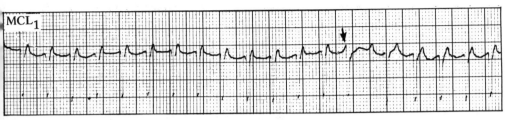

Figure 10.12. The strip begins with an **atrial tachycardia** (rate, 200/min) with 1:1 conduction and a somewhat prolonged P-R interval; this cannot be clearly differentiated from a junctional tachycardia, a reciprocating tachycardia, or even a ventricular tachycardia until the regularity of the rhythm is broken by a nonconducted atrial extrasystole (*arrow*). This break in the rhythm affords the necessary clue since, when the tachycardia resumes, the P′ wave precedes the QRS.

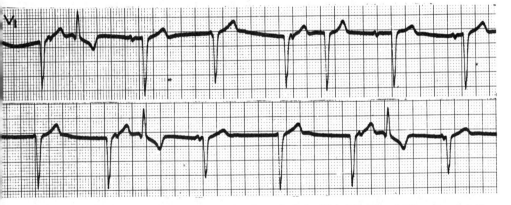

Figure 10.13. **A-V dissociation** between a **sinus bradycardia** (rate, 52/min) and an **A-V junctional rhythm** (rate, 58/min). The early beats are consistently preceded by a sinus P wave just emerging beyond the QRS and are therefore conducted (capture) beats. The strips are continuous.

In figure 10.14, which was obtained from a patient shortly after admission to a coronary care unit on the West Coast, there are a number of wide, bizarre beats that gave the staff concern. One faction, contended that they were ventricular escape beats; the other thought they were conducted, after the longer diastole, with paradoxical critical rate aberration (p. 238). If you ask yourself "Who's married to whom?" it becomes immediately obvious that the beats in question are not related to the P waves. For example, look at the P-R intervals of the last two anomalous beats in the *second strip* and that of the second anomalous beat in the *top strip*. These three intervals are strikingly different measuring 0.31, 0.22, and 0.37 sec, respectively. On the other hand, if you measure the R-R intervals ending with each of these three beats, you find them to be virtually identical; this indicates that the beats in question are

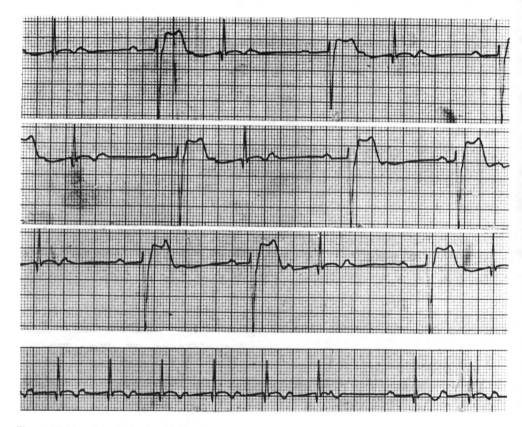

Figure 10.14. "Monitoring lead," identity unknown. The *top three strips* are continuous; the *bottom strip* follows a bolus of lidocaine. The basic disturbance is **type I second degree A-V block.** Following each dropped beat, there is a **ventricular escape beat.** These beats show a variable relationship to the preceding P waves but a constant relationship to the preceding ventricular complexes and are therefore presumably escape beats rather than conducted.

related to the previous QRS rather than to the P wave, which in turn identifies them as escape beats.

In this case, the nurse, regarding them as "PVC's" administered lidocaine and got rid of them (bottom strip). But notice her two mistakes: first, there is nothing "P" about these "VCs"—they are late, not early, beats; and second, one never should treat escape beats—they are rescuing beats, friends in need, and you thank heaven for them. She eliminated them because the lidocaine, as it occasionally will, facilitated A-V conduction, leaving no room or need for escape beats. So by accident she treated the primary disturbance, which was A-V block. What she should have done was apply the fifth principle, "pinpoint the primary," and treat the block with atropine—if indeed the patient required treatment; with an average rate of over 50/min, he may well have been in a satisfactory hemodynamic state and required no immediate therapy.

REFERENCES

1. Marriott, H. J. L.: Differential diagnosis of supraventicular and ventricular tachycardia. Geriatrics 1970: **25**, 91.
2. Marriott, H. J. L., and Fogg, E.: Constant monitoring for cardiac dysrhythmias and blocks. Mod. Concepts Cardiovasc. Dis. 1970: **39**, 103.
3. O'Bryan, C.: Personal communication, 1981.
4. Pietras, R. J., et al.: Chronic recurrent right and left ventricular tachycardia; comparison of clinical, hemodynamic, and angiographic findings. Am. J. Cardiol. 1977: **40**, 32.
5. Sandler, I. A., and Marriott, H. J. L.: The differential morphology of anomalous ventricular complexes of RBBB-type in lead V_1; ventricular ectopy versus aberration. Circulation 1965: **31**, 551.
6. Sosman, M. C.: Quoted by L. Schamroth, in *The Disorders of Cardiac Rhythm*, p. 335. Blackwell, Oxford, 1971.
7. Swanick, E. J., et al.: Morphologic features of right ventricular ectopic beats. Am. J. Cardiol. 1972: **30**, 888.
8. Thorne, D., and Gozensky, C.: Rabbit ears; an aid in distinguishing ventricular ectopy from aberration. Heart Lung 1974: **3**, 634.
9. Wellens, H. J. J., et al.: The value of the electrocardiogram in the differential diagnosis of a tachycardia with a widened QRS complex. Am. J. Med. 1978: **64**, 27.
10. Wellens, H. J. J.: Personal communication, 1981.
11. Zipes, D. P.: Diagnosis of ventricular tachycardia. Drug. Ther. 1979: **9**, 83.

11

The Extrasystoles

Ectopic beats (Gr. *ek* = out of, *topos* = place) are beats that arise from any focus other than the sinus node. Those originating in the ventricles can be grouped into four categories: extrasystolic, parasystolic, escape(d) and unclassified. The extrasystolic, parasystolic and unclassified beats are all premature, i.e., they end cycles shorter than the cycle of the dominant rhythm, whereas escape(d) beats, by definition, end cycles longer than the dominant cycle. The typical extrasystole bears a constant relationship to the preceding beat of the dominant rhythm, parasystolic beats bear a definite mathematical relationship to each other but not to the dominant rhythm; escape beats, like extrasystoles, occur a constant interval after the preceding dominant beat, but unlike extrasystoles are late rather than early; and the unclassified ectopic beats are inconstantly related to the preceding beat and also bear no relationship to each other. Parasystole and escape will be dealt with in later chapters.

Ventricular Extrasystoles*

"Extrasystole" is probably the most appropriate term to use for those ectopic beats that are both premature and constantly related to the previous beat. Because of this constant relationship they are known as "forced" or "dependent" beats. "Extrasystoles," with all its sibilant sounds, is something of a mouthful and it is phonetically easier to refer to them as "premature beats," although this term has been objected to on the grounds that it does not distinguish them from other early beats. However, the two words, premature beat, as a sort of compound noun has by usage taken on the specific connotation of extrasystole. "Beat" is better than "contraction" because it is a shorter word ("short words are best and the old words when short are best of all"—Churchill) and because it is equally applicable to the electrical and mechanical event, whereas "contraction" is purely mechanical. Hence ventricular premature beat (VPB) is preferred to premature ventricular contraction (PVC).

---

* The uninformed sometimes object to "extra-systole" on the grounds that it is not an extra beat. But the word was never meant to indicate an additional systole any more than extramural means an additional painting on the wall! Extrasystole is a Latin-Greek hybrid that means a systole arising outside (L. *extra* = outside) the normal sinus pacemaker, and by usage has come to mean the sort of premature ectopic beat that is accurately coupled to and depends for its existence on the preceding beat.

126

The extrasystole together with its preceding parent beat is a "**couplet**," and the interval between them is the "**coupling interval**." When the interval between ectopic beats and the preceding beats is constant, it is known as "**fixed coupling**."

Mechanism

We do not know for certain how all extrasystoles are generated, and it is probable that several mechanisms can account for both the prematurity and the fixed coupling. By far the most popular theory is the reentry theory which undoubtedly accounts for at least some of the VPBs we encounter. The phenomenon of reentry is important to understand not only in approaching the VPB but also because it is the mechanism believed to account for the great majority of our tachycardias, supraventricular and ventricular.

In order to achieve reentry, there are three prerequisities: an available circuit; a difference in the refractory periods of two limbs in the circuit; and slow enough conduction somewhere in the circuit to allow the rest of the circuit to recover responsiveness. In figure 11.1, the three triangular diagrams represent an available circuit in three different stages of recovery. In circuit 1, the descending impulse forks into two limbs of the circuit and finds both still refractory; in circuit 3, both limbs have recovered. In neither of these circumstances can reentry occur. However, in circuit 2, one limb has recovered while the other remains refractory; the refractory limb prevents passage of the impulse when it is first approached and the wave front travels only down the responsive limb. When this wave front reaches the distal end of the refractory region, the region has had time to recover and so the impulse is transmitted backward through the previously refractory patch and regains the original forking-point. At this point the two pathways available to it have by now also recovered and accept the impulse. Thus, it is as though a fresh impulse originated from the forking-point, but in reality it is still the sinus impulse "starting off on a second journey from a foreign port." If this theory is correct, the extrasystole is not a disturbance of impulse formation but rather the result of a disturbance in conduction. The action of some of our antiarrhythmic drugs can be explained on the basis of this theory—they may work by equalizing refractoriness in the limbs of an accommodating circuit and so make reentry impossible.

It has been long and widely believed that the constancy of the coupling interval confirms reentry as the probable mechanism of extrasystoles. But this is not necessarily so,[28] and serious doubt has been expressed that reentry is the usual or even a likely mechanism.[36]

Figure 11.1. Re-entry: for description, see text.

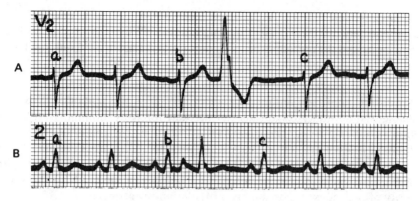

Figure 11.2. Comparison of interval following **ventricular premature beat** (A) and that following an **atrial premature beat** (B); see text.

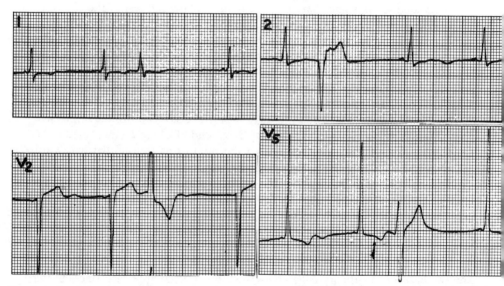

Figure 11.3. The premature beats all have constant coupling intervals and in leads 2, V₂ and V₅ look very different from the conducted sinus beats; however, in lead 1, the VPB bears a striking similarity to the conducted beats.

Diagnosis

The characteristic VPB is wide and bizarre ("sticks out like a sore thumb"), is not preceded by a premature ectopic P wave and is followed by a fully compensatory pause (fig. 11.2, *upper trace*). However, there are exceptions to all of these.

Although the VPB is typically wider than 0.11 sec, it is not always so and probably its most important morphological feature is that it is *different* from the flanking conducted beats. It may only *seem* narrow because part of the complex is isoelectric, and it is striking how often the VPB, in a single lead, can look beguilingly similar to the conducted pattern (fig. 11.3). The moral here, as in so many contexts, is: *when in doubt, take more leads.* On the other hand, it may be a genuinely narrow complex if it arises in one of the ventricular conduction fascicles near its origin (fascicular beat).[34] A rare exception to the typical picture is when an atrial premature beat (APB) or other atrial impulse coincidentally precedes the VPB. The post-extrasystolic cycle may be less than compensatory in several circumstances: when retrograde conduction from the ventricular extrasystole to the atria occurs, discharging the sinus node ahead of its regular schedule (fig. 11.4); when the postectopic cycle ends with an escape beat; and when the VPB interrupts a developing Wenckebach period. To understand these exceptions, it is essential to appreciate the reason for the usual compensatory pause.

If the premature beat does not disturb the sinus rhythm but merely takes the place of a conducted beat (fig. 11.2, *upper trace*), then the interval from the conducted beat before the extrasystole to the conducted beat following the extrasystole will be equal to two sinus cycles—because it *is* two sinus cycles. The compensatory pause is so called because the cycle following the premature beat *compensates* for the prematurity of the extrasystole and the sinus rhythm resumes again on schedule. In figure 11.2 the features of the VPB are contrasted with those of the APB. The sinus rhythm is disturbed by the APB—the sinus node is discharged by the ectopic impulse ahead of schedule—and so its "returning" cycle is also ahead of schedule and the postectopic cycle is less than compensatory. However, at times the atrial impulse discharges and suppresses the sinus node long enough for the returning cycle to be fully compensatory (fig. 11.5). Thus, the compensatory pause is a broken reed as a diagnostic prop and by itself must not be relied upon.

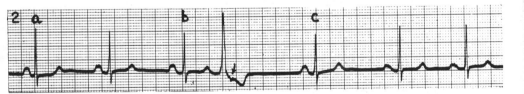

Figure 11.4. Three sinus beats are followed by a VPB with retrograde conduction to the atria (*arrow*). This discharges the sinus pacemaker ahead of schedule and so the returning cycle (*c*) is in turn ahead of schedule, i.e., $b - c$ = less than $a - b$.

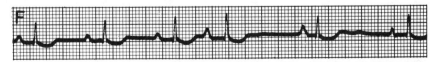

Figure 11.5. Atrial premature beat. The fourth beat is an APB, conducted with a prolonged P-R interval. It suppresses the sinus node with the result that the postextrasystolic cycle is fully compensatory; moreover, the atrial pacemaker is shifted for the last two cycles (atrial escape beats).

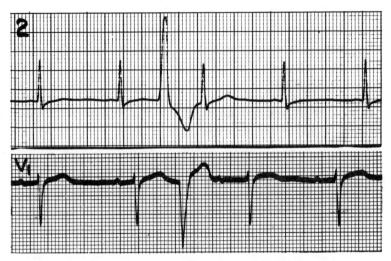

Figure 11.6. *Upper trace* shows a **VPB** sandwiched between two consecutive sinus beats without lengthening their cycle. *Bottom trace* shows another **interpolated VPB** but this one delays the next sinus beat because ("**concealed**") **retrograde conduction** into the A-V junction slows that next descending impulse and prolongs the P-R interval. (See also fig. 11.7.)

Another situation in which the ventricular extrasystole is not followed by a compensatory pause is when it is "interpolated" between two consecutive conducted beats; in such circumstances, the extrasystole is indeed an "extra" beat (fig. 11.6). Interpolated VPBs are often followed by lengthening of the subsequent P-R interval because of retrograde invasion of the A-V junction (concealed retrograde conduction), as in figure 11.6, lower trace. At times an interpolated ventricular bigeminy may progressively lengthen the successive P-R intervals until a beat is dropped and the seeming Wenckebach is completed (fig. 11.7).

Rule of Bigeminy

Simply stated, this "rule" implies that ventricular bigeminy tends to be self-perpetuating because long preceding cycles tend to precipitate a VPB. Once a VPB has materialized, the pause that follows it tends to precipitate another, and so on. In figure 11.8, a right ventricular (RV) extrasystole is followed by the usual lengthened (compensatory) postectopic cycle; this in turn precipitates a left ventricular (LV) extrasystole. The LV extrasystolic mechanism is apparently beholden to the rule of bigeminy and so, once initiated, the bigeminy tends to persist. The importance of the rule is that it acquaints us with the fact that lengthening of the ventricular cycle (slowing the rate) tends to precipitate an extrasystole. Also, by knowing the rule we realize that ventricular bigeminy may not represent such marked myocardial "irritability" as it suggests—preventing only the first extrasystole would prevent them all.

Morphology of Ventricular Ectopic Beats

In figure 11.8, we referred to *right* and *left* VPBs. The ventricle of origin of ectopic beats can best be recognized in lead V_1. If the ectopic ventricular complex in V_1 is predominantly positive, the impulse must be traveling toward the right and therefore coming from the left. Conversely, if the QRS of the ectopic beat is mainly negative in V_1, it must be travelling toward the left and therefore originating on the right. This simple rule of thumb allows one to recognize the ventricular origin of ectopic beats most of the time. This may be of importance in several respects: first, LV premature beats are more often associated with heart disease, whereas RV extrasystoles are commonly seen in normal hearts[18, 34]; then there is some evidence that LV extrasystoles are more likely than RV extrasystoles to precipitate ventricular tachycardia and/or fibrillation in the context of acute myocardial infarction,[31] and it is sometimes useful in confirming which ventricle is being paced by an artificial pacemaker.

Although unfortunately the ventricle of origin cannot always be determined with absolutely certainty from the surface tracing,[11] nevertheless, in a study involving over 1000 consecutive acute myocardial infarctions[31] not one single

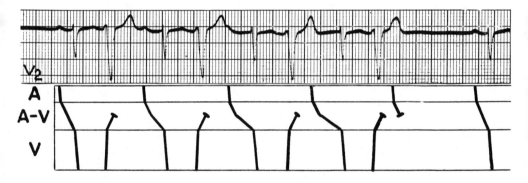

Figure 11.7. The same phenomenon ("**concealed**" **retrograde conduction**) following each of the **bigeminal VPBs**. With each successive VPB, the delaying effect of the retrograde conduction increases until conduction is completely thwarted and a Wenckebach-like sequence is completed.

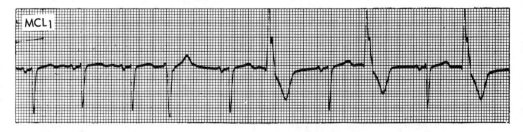

Figure 11.8. The **rule of bigeminy**. The appearance of a right VPB produces a longer (postectopic) cycle and this, by the rule of bigeminy, precipitates a LV bigeminy. In passing, again notice that the left VPBs sport a taller left rabbit ear.

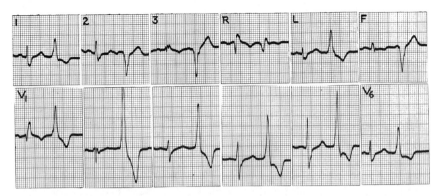

Figure 11.9. A typical pattern of **left ventricular premature beats**. The first beat in each lead is a sinus beat with RBBB; the second beat is a coupled ventricular extrasystole—note that the ectopic complexes are positive in all the chest leads (concordant positivity), and that they manifest a marked left axis deviation in the limb leads.

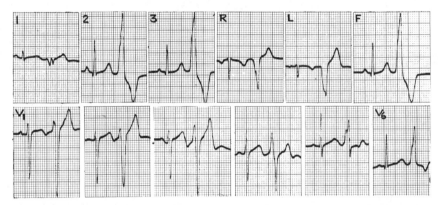

Figure 11.10. A typical pattern of **right ventricular extrasystoles**. In each lead the first beat is a sinus beat and the second a coupled extrasystole having a LBBB pattern in V_6, but wide initial r wave in V_1 and right axis deviation in the frontal plane.

instance of ventricular fibrillation developed among 249 patients who manifested only ectopics with a left bundle-branch block (LBBB) pattern in MCL_1 (presumed *right* ventricular), whereas 82 of 787 (10.4%) that manifested left ventricular ectopics fibrillated. Thus even if the source, as judged by surface morphology, is in doubt, the configuration of the ectopic QRS is helpful in distinguishing potentially malignant from relatively benign ventricular ectopy.

Typical 12-lead patterns of left and right ventricular ectopic beats are illustrated in figures 11.9 and 11.10.

Other morphological features worth noting are: LV ectopics usually produce a monophasic (R) or diphasic (qR) complex in V_1 complemented by a diphasic (rS) or monophasic (QS) complex in V_6 (fig. 11.11). Furthermore, if the upright complex in V_1 has two peaks ("rabbit ears," as coronary care nurses have picturesquely dubbed them),[8] the left ear is often taller than the right (figs. 11.8 and 11.11). RV ectopics, while they may show a typical LBBB pattern in V_6, more often than not have a right axis deviation in the frontal plane and sometimes a wide r ("fat little r wave") greater than 0.04 sec in V_1[34, 40] (fig. 11.12). In artificially paced RV beats, there is almost always a *left* axis deviation with characteristically monophasic complexes in the limb leads (positive in 1

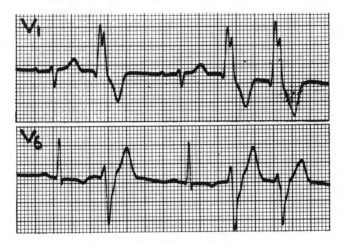

Figure 11.11. Typical morphology of **LV ectopic beats**: qR in V_1 with taller left rabbit-ear, and rS in V_6.

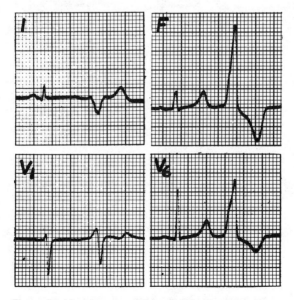

Figure 11.12. A common form of **RV ectopic beats**: a LBBB pattern in V_6, fat initial r wave in V_1 and a right axis deviation in the limb leads.

and aVL, negative in 2, 3 and aVF.)[3, 40] RV ectopics also tend to show a deeper (rS or QS) complex in V_4 than in V_1.[40]

If a ventricular extrasystole follows every sinus beat (fig. 11.13A), the result is bigeminal rhythm (**ventricular bigeminy**). If each sinus beat is followed by two ventricular extrasystoles (fig. 11.13B), the result is **ventricular trigeminy**. This term is also applied (perhaps less correctly) when every third beat (fig. 11.13C) is a VPB. To go beyond threesomes and speak of quadrigeminy, etc., serves no useful purpose. When three consecutive VPBs follow each sinus beat, we already have a better name for it since, by definition, three consecutive VPBs make the shortest definable run of tachycardia; and if every fourth beat is a VPB, no elasticity of terminology can justify implying that the beats are grouped in fours.

In the usual form of bigeminy (fig. 11.13A), in which an extrasystole is substituted for every alternate sinus beat, each extrasystole is followed by a compensatory pause; but it is possible to have interpolated bigeminy producing a form of tachycardia (fig. 11.14) in which, of course, no sinus beats are missing.

When ventricular extrasystoles occur so early that they interrupt the preceding T wave (fig. 11.15A), they carry an ominous significance.[39] A single effective impulse usually elicits a single ventricular response; but at one point in the ventricular cycle—near the apex of the T wave—a single stimulus is likely to evoke repeated responses. This is a dangerous situation, may lead to ventricular

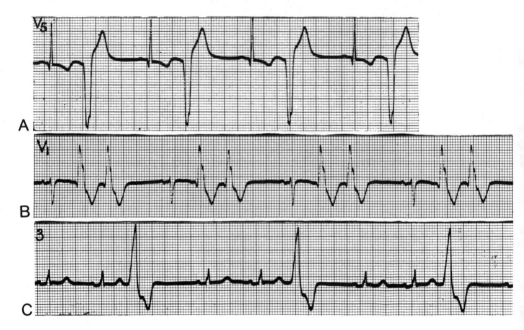

Figure 11.13. (*A*) **Ventricular bigeminy**—every alternate sinus beat is replaced by a VPB. (*B*) **Ventricular trigeminy**—each sinus beat is followed by two VPBs. (*C*) Every third beat is a VPB—another form of **ventricular trigeminy**.

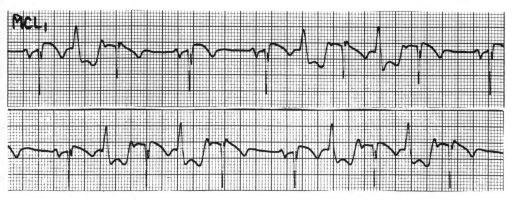

Figure 11.14. On three occasions short runs of tachycardia are produced by VPBs interpolated in two consecutive sinus cycles.

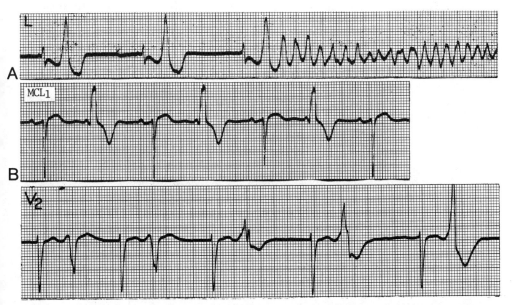

Figure 11.15. (*A*) After two closely coupled (R-on-T) warning ventricular extrasystoles, a third sparks **ventricular fibrillation**. (*B*) At a normal sinus rate (74/min), the ventricular extrasystoles appear after the next sinus P wave and are therefore "**enddiastolic**" extrasystoles. (*C*) **Atrial fibrillation** is interrupted by coupled ventricular extrasystoles of varying morphology—**multiform (or multifocal) VPBs** producing bigeminy.

fibrillation (fig. 11.15*A*) and is therefore called the "vulnerable" phase or period in the ventricular cycle. However, a European study[19] that carefully documented the ventricular extrasystoles that initiated fibrillation in 20 consecutive patients demonstrated that over half of the culpable extrasystoles landed beyond the T wave; and so it is not *only* the early ones that matter! Others have also questioned that the threat of "R-on-T" extrasystoles is supreme. Engel[7] reviewed the situation and decided that the R-on-T phenomenon was not the critical determinant of ventricular tachycardia or fibrillation in acute myocardial infarction. Evidence includes the following data: of 44 bouts of ventricular tachycardia in as many patients, only 6 (14%) were initiated by VPBs that landed on T waves[4]; many runs of ventricular tachycardia began with beats that landed beyond the ensuing sinus P wave[41]; and 78% of repetitive VPBs, defined as two or more consecutive ectopic ventricular complexes at a rate of at least 120/min, began with a "late" extrasystole.[33] Nevertheless, the R-on-T beat has by no means lost its sting and, of a series of 48 patients who developed ventricular fibrillation outside the hospital, the initiating beat was an R-on-T extrasystole in more than two thirds.[1a]

When at a normal sinus rate the ectopic beat is late enough to land after the next sinus P wave (fig. 11.15B), it is often referred to as an **"end-diastolic"** extrasystole.

When ventricular extrasystoles manifest different patterns in the same lead (as in fig. 11.15C), they are assumed to arise from different foci and are often called **multifocal**. It is always possible, however, that variation in shape may result from varying intraventricular conduction rather than from varying sites of origin; in fact, varying patterns of ectopy have been produced from the same artificially stimulated focus.[2a] For this reason, some prefer to use the more cautious term **multiform** rather than multifocal.

Retrograde conduction of ectopic ventricular impulses is common. At times they travel only as far as the A-V junction and then are recognized by lengthening of the ensuing P-R interval—"concealed" retrograde conduction (fig. 11.16A); but they often reach the atria and inscribe a retrograde P wave (fig. 11.16B and C). In fact many years ago Kistin and Landowne[13] detected such P waves, with the help of esophageal electrodes, in nearly half the cases they studied.

Figure 11.16B illustrates VPBs with retrograde conduction to the atria, the retrograde P′ wave negatively deforming the ST segment. Note that this P′ wave is negative in contrast with the sinus P waves and that it occurs before the next sinus P wave is due. These two features are characteristic of retrograde P′ waves from VPBs, and when such conduction can be recognized, the R-P′ interval is usually 0.16 to 0.20 sec (measured from the beginning of the QRS to the beginning of the P′ wave). In abnormal hearts this interval may be considerably increased, indicating retrograde V-A block, as in figure 11.16C in which the R-P′ interval of the first extrasystole is about 0.28 sec.

Prognostic Implications

Ventricular premature beats are ubiquitous. Most people have them more or less frequently and we sometimes find even continuous ventricular bigeminy in apparently normal hearts. They are usually a benign nuisance. During the acute phase of infarction, they appear in 80 to 90% of patients; but they are

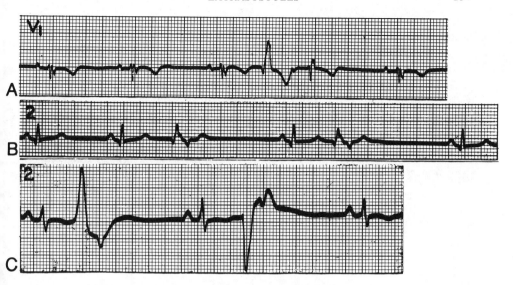

Figure 11.16. (*A*) The fourth beat is an **interpolated VPB**. Notice that it lengthens the P-R interval of the next sinus beat (from 0.16 to 0.22 sec)—evidence of ''**concealed**'' **(retrograde) conduction** into the A-V junction. (*B*) The two **ventricular extrasystoles** are followed by retrograde (inverted) P waves at normal R-P intervals of 0.17 and 0.19 sec. (*C*) Both **VPBs** are followed by retrograde P waves at abnormally prolonged R-P intervals (0.28 and 0.22 sec).

also found in the majority of actively employed middle-aged men.[9] When brought on by exertion they have been considered a sign of myocardial disease, though this is disputed (see Chapter 27). They are more readily provoked by isometric than by dynamic exercise.[1]

Many studies and much effort have been directed to evaluating the prognostic significance of ventricular extrasystoles following myocardial infarction. In patients who have survived myocardial infarction, complex VPBs (multiform, pairs) have been shown to increase the risk of sudden death[29, 35]; but whether similar ectopy increases the risk of sudden death in normal people has evoked divergent opinion. In a 7-year follow-up of 72 asymptomatic subjects with

Table 11.1
Lown's Grading System of Ventricular Ectopy[20, 21]

Grade	Description of Ventricular Extrasystoles
0	None
1	Less than 30/hour
2	30 or more/hour
3	Multiform
4A	Two consecutive
4B	3 or more consecutive
5	R-on-T

frequent and complex ectopy, none died although a number had angiographically proven significant coronary disease.[10]

Lown's grading system[20, 21] for ventricular ectopy (table 11.1) has become a popular frame of reference for gauging the risk of death after myocardial infarction—the risk supposedly increases as the numerical grade advances from 0 to 5. A subsequent study[2] suggests that the system is flawed in that the R-on-T (grade 5), supposedly the bleakest of indices, is less grave than the finding of paired extrasystoles (grade 4A) or ventricular tachycardia (grade 4B).

Moss[30] suggests a simplified two-level grading: low-risk—late cycle, unifocal, having a 2-year mortality of 10%; and high-risk—early cycle and/or multiform with an associated mortality of 20%. In the final analysis, the prognostic significance of VPBs after myocardial infarction is determined by the recency of the infarct—the longer ago the better—and the severity of the myocardial involvement. The presence of frequent and/or complex VPBs is merely an index of severe myocardial disease and therefore companion to a poor prognosis.

Salient Features of Ventricular Premature Beats

1. Bizarre, premature QRST complex, with prolonged QRS interval and ST segment sloping off in direction opposite to main QRS deflection
2. Morphological details sometimes characteristic
3. Usually followed by *fully* compensatory pause (unless interpolated)
4. P wave usually lost (submerged in ventricular complex), sometimes retrograde

---

Atrial Extrasystoles

The usual atrial extrasystole or premature beat (APB) has three features: a premature, ectopic P wave (the *sine qua non* and often labelled P′); a QRS unchanged from that of the conducted sinus beats; and a post-extrasystolic cycle that is less than compensatory. As a rule all of these characteristics are obvious, as in figure 11.17*A*; but no one, by itself, is completely reliable: the P′ wave may be unrecognizable as it sits upon the previous T wave; the QRS may show aberrant ventricular conduction; and the pause following the extrasystole may be fully compensatory because, as has been pointed out years ago, ectopic or retrograde atrial impulses have a way of stunning the sinus node and delaying its next discharge, and this delay may be sufficient to make the resulting cycle fully compensatory. It is extremely rare to have all three of these deceptions conspiring at the same time; therefore, if care is exercised, one usually has no trouble in identifying the APB.

In figure 11.17*A*, B−C is less than A−B; i.e., the postectopic cycle is less than fully compensatory. In figure 11.17*B*, on the other hand, the atrial ectopic impulse suppresses the sinus node long enough to make B−C actually a little

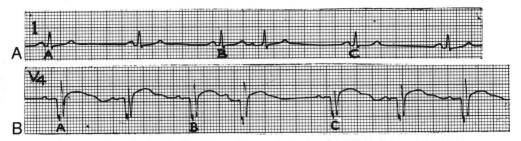

Figure 11.17.   The fourth beat in each strip is an APB. In A, the extrasystole is followed by a less-than-compensatory pause (B−C = less than A−B). In B, the postectopic cycle is fully compensatory (B−C = A−B).

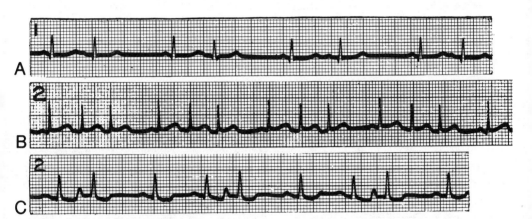

Figure 11.18.   (A) **Atrial bigeminy**—every other beat is an APB. (B) **Atrial trigeminy**—each sinus beat is followed by a pair of APBs. (C) Every third beat is an APB, a sequence also, but less correctly, called **atrial trigeminy**.

longer than A−B; i.e., the postectopic cycle is even more than fully compensatory.

When an atrial extrasystole follows every sinus beat, the result is **atrial bigeminy** (fig. 11.18A). As with ventricular trigeminy, there are two sequences that are called **atrial trigeminy**: this term is more correctly applied when each sinus beat is followed by a pair of APBs (fig. 11.18B), but it is often also used when, as in figure 11.18C, an APB occurs every third beat.

Salient Features of Atrial Premature Beats

1. Abnormal, often inverted, premature P′ wave
2. Normal QRST
3. Ensuing interval about equal to, or slightly longer than, the sinus cycle

Atrial extrasystoles are often nonconducted; in fact much the commonest cause of an unexpected pause is the nonconducted APB (fig. 11.19*A*). It is better to refer to such beats as "nonconducted" rather than "blocked" because, by definition, block implies pathology and many such beats fail to be conducted only because they arise so early in the cycle that the A-V tissues are still *normally* refractory. We should always be at pains to differentiate pathological from physiological nonconduction, especially since failure to do this has led to widespread overdiagnosis and overtreatment of heart block (Chapter 24).

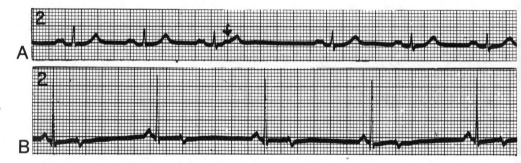

Figure 11.19. (*A*) **Nonconducted APB**: after three sinus beats, an APB (*arrow*) is too early in the cycle to be conducted to the ventricles. (*B*) Each sinus beat is followed by an APB which fails to reach the ventricles—**nonconducted atrial bigeminy**.

** THE COMMONEST CAUSES OF PAUSES ARE NONCONDUCTED ATRIAL PREMATURE BEATS**

Nonconducted atrial bigeminy (fig. 11.19*B*) is quite common and, if the premature P waves are not readily seen, may well be mistaken for sinus bradycardia. Figure 11.20, *A* and *B*, illustrates the development of a much more subtle bigeminy; if the preceding T waves during the regular sinus rhythm were not available for comparison, the slightly deforming P' waves would not be recognizable. Figure 11.20*C* is from a teenager with nonconducted atrial bigeminy that masquerades as sinus bradycardia and was completely undiagnosable from the rhythm strip but was readily enough recognized from the regularly recurring cannon waves in the neck veins after each ventricular contraction.

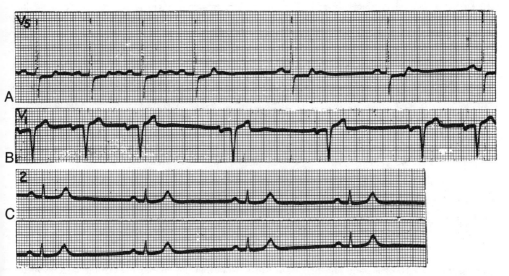

Figure 11.20. (*A*) After four sinus beats in *A* and after three sinus beats in *B*, a run of **nonconducted atrial bigeminy** develops. Note in each strip the subtle deformity of the T wave compared with the preceding T waves, due to superimposed P' waves. In *C*, the T waves look a little too pointed for natural T waves; but when no previous T waves are available for comparison, it is impossible to diagnose the **atrial bigeminy**.

Often the early APB, instead of being nonconducted, is conducted with delay (prolonged P'-R). In figure 11.21*A*, the first APB is conducted with a P'-R shorter even than the sinus beats, whereas the second APB, which occurs earlier in the cycle (shorter R-P'), is conducted with a much prolonged P'-R. In figure 11.21*B*, showing atrial bigeminy, the sinus beats all have normal P-R intervals, and the APBs all have prolonged P'-R intervals. This introduces the important concept of R-P-dependent P-R intervals (the shorter the R-P, the longer the ensuing P-R, and vice versa). This concept is vital to the understanding of type I second degree A-V block and will be taken up in detail in Chapter 23.

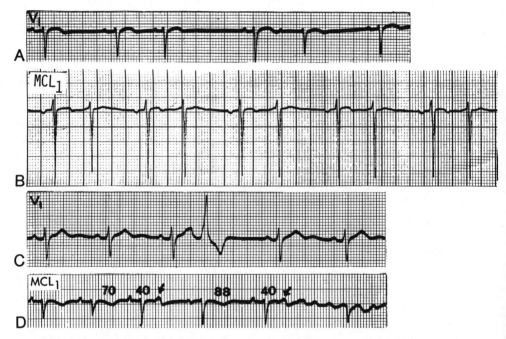

Figure 11.21. (*A*) The third and fifth beats are **APBs**. Note that the shorter R-P' of the second APB is complemented by a much prolonged P'-R interval. (*B*) **Atrial bigeminy** in which the P'-R of the APBs is much prolonged compared with the normal P-R of the sinus beats. (*C*) The fourth beat is an **APB with RBBB aberration**. Note the deformed T wave and the less-than-compensatory postectopic cycle. (*D*) When the APB is premature enough to make the P-P' interval (*40*) less than half the preceding P-P interval (*88*), an atrial tachyarrhythmia is triggered.

The APB may traverse the A-V junction at a normal rate only to find that one of the bundle branches or fascicles thereof is still refractory, and then aberrant ventricular conduction occurs (fig. 11.21C). In such cases the morphology of the QRS may be indistinguishable from ventricular ectopy, but spotting the preceding P′ wave and finding the postectopic cycle less than compensatory will usually establish its atrial origin.

Just as the more premature ventricular extrasystoles are likely to land in the vulnerable phase of the ventricular cycle and initiate ventricular tachycardia or fibrillation, so the earlier APBs may invade the atria in their vulnerable phase and spark tachycardia, flutter or fibrillation. Killip and Gault[12] offer the rule that, when the P-P′ interval is less than 50% of the previous P-P interval, it is quite likely to initiate an atrial tachyarrhythmia (fig. 11.21D).

As a right chest lead (such as MCL_1) is widely used for constant monitoring, it is useful to know that, when sinus beats have diphasic P waves, the positive deflection almost invariably precedes the negative; whereas when ectopic P waves are diphasic, the negative deflection usually precedes the positive (fig. 11.22).

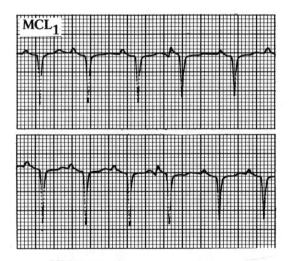

Figure 11.22. The fourth beat in each strip is an **APB**. Note that the diphasic, ectopic P′ wave has a negative/ positive polarity.

A-V Junctional Extrasystoles

Ectopic rhythms arising in the A-V junction may retrogradely activate the atria before, during or after ventricular activation; thus the retrograde P wave may be seen preceding or following the QRS complex, or it may be lost within it. When the P′ wave preceded the QRS complex, the rhythm used to be called "upper nodal"; when the P′ wave followed the QRS, it was called "lower nodal"; and when the P′ wave was lost in the QRS, it was called "midnodal" in accordance with the concept depicted in the *upper diagram* of figure 11.23. We now know, however, that the relationship of P′ to QRS in junctional rhythm is determined more by the rate of propagation in each direction (*lower diagram* in fig. 11.23) than by the level of the initiating pacemaker, and the terms "upper," "lower" and "mid-" have been generally discarded.

The term "nodal," in use for decades, was also partially abandoned several years ago because electrophysiologists reported that there was no evidence of pacemaker activity in the A-V node of animals; as a result, the time-honored "nodal" was largely replaced by "junctional." The question is not yet settled, and there appears to be little harm in retaining "nodal" as the simpler and more traditional term. Scherlag et al.[38] maintain that there are at least two rhythmogenic centers in the A-V junction: the node itself, which has an inherent rate of 45–60/min and responds to atropine by accelerating 20–30 beats/min; and a lower His rhythm with a slower inherent rate (35–45 min) unresponsive to atropine. While adhering to the philosophy that in our present state of

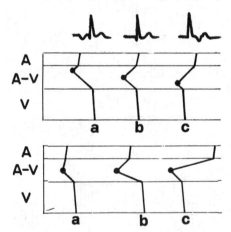

Figure 11.23. The top panel diagrams the concept of "upper," "mid-" and "lower" junctional rhythm. With the impulse travelling at a uniform rate in both directions, the level of origin determines whether atria or ventricles are activated first. In the bottom panel, the relationship of atrial to ventricular activation depends not on the level of the pacemaker, but on the rate of conduction in each direction.

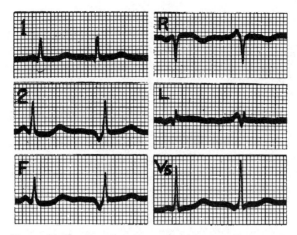

Figure 11.24. Junctional premature beats with antecedent P′ waves. In each lead, the first beat is a sinus beat, and the second, a junctional premature beat with short P′-R interval and typical P-wave polarity.

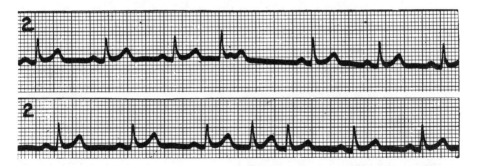

Figure 11.25. Junctional premature beats without retrograde conduction. In the upper strip, the fourth beat is a junctional extrasystole; and in the lower strip, the fourth and fifth beats are a pair of junctional prematures. In neither strip is the regular sinus discharge interrupted by retrograde conduction.

uncertainty it matters little whether we use the traditional or the more recently adopted term, for the sake of consistency we will stick to the current coin, junctional.

Junctional impulses are likely to be conducted retrogradely into the atria, and the usual polarity of the resulting P′ waves is illustrated in the premature beats in figure 11.24: The P′ wave is inverted in leads 2, 3 and aVF and in the left chest leads (V_{5-6}); it is upright in aVR and aVL, almost flat in lead 1 and variable, but often predominantly upright, in V_1.

Figure 11.25 contains junctional premature beats with no sign of retrograde atrial activity. Figure 11.26 shows what are probably junctional premature

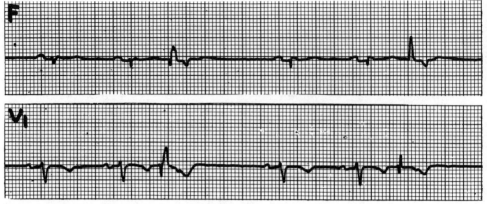

Figure 11.26. The third and last beats in each strip are presumable **junctional premature beats** with aberrant ventricular conduction of the RBBB type and retroconduction to the atria following the aberrant QRS.

beats with differing degrees of right bundle-branch block (RBBB) aberration and retrograde conduction following the QRS. Although the first premature beat in each strip cannot with any degree of certainty be distinguished from ventricular extrasystoles, the fact that the second premature beat manifests a lesser degree of the RBBB pattern is a strong point in favor of aberration rather than ectopy.

A peculiarity of junctional beats is their tendency to develop aberration (usually minor) regardless of whether they are early (extrasystolic) or late (escape). This has been attributed to either (1) "preferential" conduction, which assumes that the impulse arises near the origin of a paraspecific (Mahaim) fiber and is conducted to the ventricles at least partially via this tract and so writes a distorted ventricular complex; or (2) eccentric placement of the junctional pacemaker so that the impulse is distributed asynchronously to the bundle branches and ventricles (see Chapter 16).

REFERENCES

1. Atkins, J. M., et al.: Incidence of arrhythmias induced by isometric and dynamic exercise. Br. Heart J. 1976: **38**, 465.
1a. Adgey, A. A. J., et al.: Initiation of ventricular fibrillation outside hospital in patients with ischemic heart disease. Br. Heart J. 1982: **47**, 55.
2. Bigger, J. T., and Weld, F. M.: Analysis of prognostic significance of ventricular arrhythmias after myocardial infarction. Shortcomings of the Lown grading system. Br. Heart J. 1981: **45**, 717.
2a. Booth, D. C., et al.: Multiformity of induced unifocal ventricular premature beats in human subjects: electrocardiographic and angiographic correlations. Am. J. Cardiol. 1982: **49**, 1643.
3. Castellanos, A., et al.: Unusual QRS complexes produced by pacemaker stimuli. Am. Heart J. 1969: **77**, 732.
4. Chou, T.-C., and Wenzke, F.: The importance of R-on-T phenomenon. Am. Heart J. 1978: **96**, 191.
5. Coronary Drug Project Research Group: The prognostic importance of premature beats following myocardial infarction; experience in the coronary drug project. J.A.M.A. 1973: **223**, 1116.
6. DeBacker, G., et al.: Ventricular premature contractions; a randomized non-drug intervention trial in normal men. Circulation 1979: **59**, 762.
7. Engel, T. R., et al.: The "R-on-T" phenomenon; an update and critical review. Ann. Intern.

Med. 1978: **88**, 221.
8. Gozensky, C., and Thorne, D.: Rabbit ears; an aid in distinguishing ventricular ectopy from aberration. Heart Lung 1974: **3**, 634.
9. Hinkle, L. E., et al.: The frequency of asymptomatic disturbances of cardiac rhythm and conduction in middle-aged men. Am. J. Cardiol. 1969: **24**, 629.
10. Horan, M. J., and Kennedy, H. L.: Characteristics and prognosis of apparently healthy patients with frequent and complex ventricular ectopy; evidence for a relatively benign syndrome with occult myocardial and/or coronary disease. Am. Heart J. 1981: **102**, 809.
11. Kaplinsky, E., et al.: Origin of so-called right and left ventricular arrhythmias in acute myocardial ischemia. Am. J. Cardiol. 1978: **42**, 774.
12. Killip, T., and Gault, J. H.: Mode of onset of atrial fibrillation in man. Am. Heart J. 1965: **70**, 172.
13. Kistin, A., and Landowne, M.: Retrograde conduction from premature ventricular contractions, a common occurrence in the human heart. Circulation 1951: **3**, 738.
14. Kotler, M. N., et al.: Prognostic significance of ventricular ectopic beats with respect to sudden death in the late postinfarction period. Circulation 1973: **47**, 959.
15. Langendorf, R.: Concealed A-V conduction. Am. Heart J. 1948: **35**, 542.
16. Langendorf, R.: Aberrant ventricular conduction. Am. Heart J. 1951: **41**, 700.
17. Langendorf, R., et al.: Mechanisms of intermittent ventricular bigeminy; I. Appearance of ectopic beats dependent upon the length of the ventricular cycle, the "rule of bigeminy." Circulation 1955: **11**, 442.
18. Lewis, S., et al.: Significance of site of origin of premature ventricular contractions. Am. Heart J. 1979: **97**, 159.
19. Lie, K. I., et al.: Observations on patients with primary ventricular fibrillation complicating acute myocardial infarction. Circulation 1975: **52**, 755.
20. Lown, B., and Wolf, M.: Approaches to sudden death from coronary heart disease. Circulation 1971: **48**, 130.
21. Lown, B., and Graboys, T. B.: Management of patients with malignant ventricular arrhythmias. Am. J. Cardiol. 1977: **39**, 910.
22. Marriott, H. J. L., et al.: Ventricular fusion beats. Circulation 1962: **26**, 880.
23. Marriott, H. J. L.: Differential diagnosis of supraventricular and ventricular tachycardia. Geriatrics 1970: **25**, 91.
24. Marriott, H. J. L., and Fogg, E.: Constant monitoring for arrhythmias and blocks. Mod. Concepts Cardiovasc. Dis. 1970: **39**, 103.
25. Marriott, H. J. L., and Myerburg, R. J.: In *The Heart*, Ed. 5, edited by J. W. Hurst. McGraw-Hill, New York, 1982.
26. Marriott, H. J. L., and Thorne, D. C.: Dysrhythmic dilemmas in coronary care. Am. J. Cardiol. 1971: **27**, 327.
27. Massumi, R. A., et al.: Paradoxic phenomenon of premature beats with narrow QRS in the presence of bundle branch block. Circulation 1973: **47**, 543.
28. Michelson, E. L., et al.: Fixed coupling; different mechanisms revealed by exercise-induced changes in cycle length. Circulation 1978: **58**, 1002.
29. Moss, A. J., et al.: Ventricular ectopic beats and their relation to sudden and nonsudden death after myocardial infarction. Circulation 1979: **60**, 998.
30. Moss, A. J.: Clinical significance of ventricular arrhythmias in patients with and without coronary artery disease. Prog. Cardiovasc. Dis. 1980: **23**, 33.
31. O'Bryan, E. C.: Personal communication, 1981.
32. Pick, A., et al.: Depression of cardiac pacemakers by premature impulses. Am. Heart J. 1951: **41**, 49.
33. Roberts, R., et al.: Initiation of repetitive ventricular depolarizations by relatively late premature complexes in patients with acute myocardial infarction. Am. J. Cardiol. 1978: **41**, 678.
34. Rosenbaum, M. B.: Classification of ventricular extrasystoles according to form. J. Electrocardiol. 1969: **2**, 289.
35. Ruberman, W., et al.: Ventricular premature beats and mortality after myocardial infarction. N. Engl. J. Med. 1977: **297**, 750.
36. Schamroth, L.: *The Disorders of Cardiac Rhythm*, Ed. 2, p. 148. Blackwell, Oxford, 1980.
37. Scherf, D., and Schott, A.: *Extrasystoles and Allied Arrhythmias*, Ed. 2. Grune & Stratton, New York, 1973.
38. Scherlag, B. J., et al.: Differentiation of "A-V junctional rhythms." Circulation 1973: **48**, 304.
39. Smirk, F. H., and Palmer, D. G.: A myocardial syndrome, with particular reference to the

occurrence of sudden death and of premature systoles interrupting antecedent T waves. Am. J. Cardiol. 1960: **6,** 620.

40. Swanick, E. J., et al.: Morphologic features of right ventricular ectopic beats. Am. J. Cardiol. 1972: **30,** 888.
41. Tye, K.-H., et al.: R-on-T or R-on-P phenomenon? Relation to the genesis of ventricular tachycardia. Am. J. Cardiol. 1979: **44,** 632.

Review Tracings

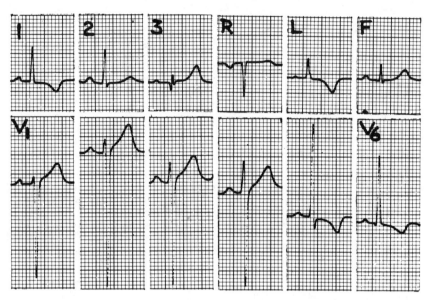

Review Tracing 11.1

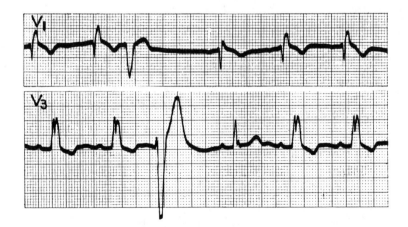

Review Tracing 11.2

For interpretation, see page 482

12

Supraventricular
Tachycardias

Background

For more than half a century, the mechanisms of the atrial tachyarrhythmias have provided a lively forum for discussion and argument, rising at times to the level of acrimony! After the turn of the century, it all began with the jellyfish when Mayer (1908) demonstrated that a ring of its "umbrella" could sustain a continuously circulating excitation wave. Then Mines (1913) and Garrey (1914) in turn showed that a ring of muscle cut from the atrium of fish or the ventricle of a turtle could similarly sustain a "circus movement."

Encouraged by such demonstrations, Lewis[19] claimed to prove that a similar circus movement, negotiating a sweep round the venae cavae, was responsible for both atrial flutter and fibrillation in man. Atrial and "nodal" tachycardia, on the other hand, he believed were due to the rapid repetitive firing of a single atrial or A-V nodal focus. His views held almost undisputed sway for a quarter century.

Scherf et al., in a series of animal experiments and articles between 1942 and 1950, demonstrated that a circus movement was unlikely to be the mechanism of flutter and fibrillation and concluded that all the atrial tachyarrhythmias were caused by rapid discharge of a single focus. Prinzmetal (1950) enlisted the candid eye of the movie camera and came to the same conclusion.[24] But recently, thanks to the development of sophisticated intracardiac recording techniques, the current crop of cardiac physiologists are convinced that the great majority of our supraventricular tachycardias are due to circus movements (reentry, reciprocation). The mechanisms of atrial flutter and fibrillation for the present remain sub judice.

Classification

It is now clear that the overwhelming majority of "supraventricular tachy-cardias" (SVT) are in fact reciprocating tachycardias (RT) due to a circulating

149

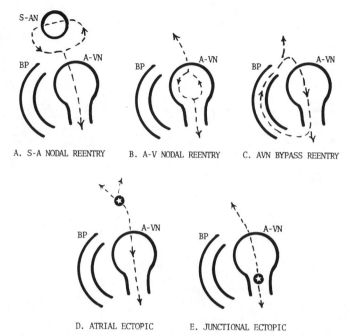

Figure 12.1. Diagrammatic representations of various mechanisms of SVT. S-AN = sinus node; BP = bypass tract; A-VN = A-V node.

wave and not to enhanced automaticity (rapidly firing focus). Such circulating waves have a number of available orbits (fig. 12.1) and, in concert with the rapidly accumulating recent data, SVTs can be reclassified as shown in table 12.1. In fact, such a classification is a bare skeleton, because the number of possible reentry circuits, as Barold says, "staggers the imagination."[2]

To Differentiate or Not to Differentiate

To differentiate the reentry varieties from each other and from their ectopic mimics is often difficult or impossible from the surface tracing and may be achieved only by sophisticated invasive methods. The question naturally arises: Does it matter which mechanism is operative—reentrant or ectopic—from a therapeutic point of view? Indeed, if for no other reason, it is worth making the distinction because, in the intractable case, there is a method tailor-made for the reentry type. For any circulating wave to perpetuate itself, the advancing head must not catch up with the (refractory) tail (fig. 12.2). Thus there must always be a gap of nonrefractory tissue between the head and the tail of the circulating wave. If an extraneous impulse, either natural (premature systole) or artificial (pacemaker stimulus), manages to find the gap between the head and the tail, it will render the gap refractory and the circulating wave will be

Table 12.1
Classification of Supraventricular Tachycardias

A. *Reentry*
   1. S-A nodal (fig. 12.1*A*)
   2. Atrial
   3. A-V junctional (fig. 12.1*B*)
   4. A-V junctional bypass (fig. 12.1*C*)
   5. Kent bundle (WPW)
B. *Ectopic*
   1. Atrial (fig. 12.1*D*)
   2. A-V junctional (fig. 12.1*E*)

Table 12.2
Proportion of SVTs Due to A-V Nodal Reentry (AVNR)

Authors	Total SVTs	AVNR	Percentage
Wellens and Durrer (1975)[31]	54	47	87
Wu et al. (1978)[34]	79	50	63
Farshidi et al. (1978)[9]	60	40	67

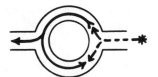

Figure 12.2. A circus movement is interrupted if an extraneous impulse, natural or artificial, "finds the gap" between the head and the tail of the circulating wave.

halted. Thus a temporary pacemaker set to "titrate" the gap is a ready-made method of terminating any circus-movement tachycardia. Furthermore, with more and more victims of intractable tachycardias becoming candidates for surgery, precise definition of the mechanism may be mandatory.

Reentry

For reentry to take place, there are three prerequisites: (1) an available circuit, (2) differing responsiveness in two limbs of the circuit, and (3) conduction slow enough to give the initially unresponsive limb time to recover. In most hearts at normal rates, these conditions are not fulfilled at the time of a normally spreading impulse because all tissues have recovered fully and there are therefore no differences in responsiveness. But an *early* impulse, such as an extrasystole, may find unequal refractoriness since all tissues may not have had

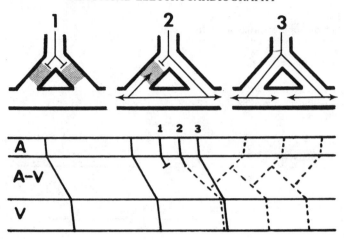

Figure 12.3. The three triangular diagrams represent three stages of recovery in a circuit of conducting tissue. In *1*, both descending limbs of the circuit are refractory; in *2*, one is still refractory, but the other has recovered; and in *3*, both have recovered. Reentry cannot take place at stages 1 or 3; but at the intermediate stage 2, the recovered limb accepts the impulse and, provided conduction is slow enough for the refractory limb to recover, a circus movement is initiated. In the laddergram, the fate of three atrial extrasystoles, 1, 2 and 3, arriving in the A-V junction at the above stages 1, 2 and 3 is diagrammed. Beat 1 is blocked, 3 is conducted normally, and 2 initiates a reciprocating tachycardia in the A-V junction (*dashed lines*).

time to recover fully. Thus most paroxysms of RT are initiated by premature beats. Figure 12.3 illustrates diagrammatically the initiation of RT in the A-V junction by an atrial extrasystole (see the legend to fig. 12.3). The "zone" of prematurity during which an extrasystole can initiate such a tachycardia is known as the "tachycardia-initiating interval." Much the most common mechanism of SVT is A-V junctional reentry (table 12.2).

Although most paroxysms of SVT are initiated by supraventricular extrasystoles, obviously any impulse that reaches an available circuit at a time when it is "ripe" for reentry can initiate RT; and since ectopic ventricular impulses are frequently conducted retrogradely into the junction (and beyond), the SVT may be initiated by ventricular ectopic beats. Figure 12.4 illustrates a reciprocating tachycardia initiated by a single ventricular extrasystole. Figure 12.5 illustrates the initiation of RT by a run of ventricular tachycardia—the first four ectopic impulses are thwarted by the descending sinus impulses; not until the fifth beat of the ventricular tachycardia does the retrograde impulse reach the level of the accommodating circuit (see fig. 12.5, laddergram) and trigger a reentering tachycardia. It then climbs further and activates the atria before the next sinus impulse is due.

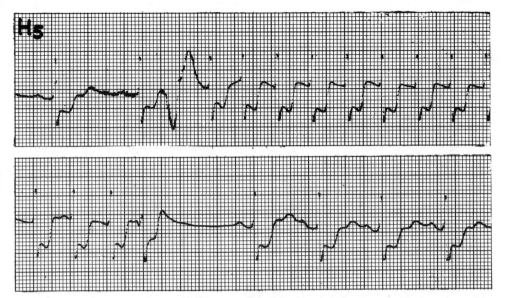

Figure 12.4. Continuous strip from a Holter recording. After two sinus beats, a ventricular extrasystole initiates a **SVT**. Further evidence of its reciprocating nature is that it is also terminated by a premature beat.

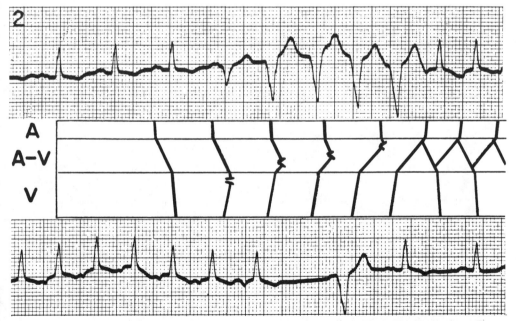

Figure 12.5. After three sinus beats, a run of **ventricular tachycardia** begins with a fusion beat. Three subsequent ectopic ventricular impulses meet the descending sinus impulse progressively higher in the A-V junction (see laddergram). The fifth beat of the tachycardia reaches the atria before the next sinus beat is due and, on the way, finds a "ripe" circuit in the junction and initiates a **reciprocating tachycardia**.

Differentiation between Reentry and Ectopic Tachycardias

There are a number of features in the clinical tracing that may help to distinguish between automatic and reciprocal mechanisms. Some of these aids to identification are dependent upon P-wave detail, and this is frequently obscured because of the inevitable superimposition of the atrial wave upon various parts of the ventricular complex and especially the T wave. Nevertheless, the following points are suggestive of an automatic, ectopic mechanism: (1) the presence of "warm-up" (progressive acceleration for the first few beats); (2) the sameness of all the P' waves, including the first; and (3) a premature stimulus resetting the tachycardia (in much the same way that an atrial premature beat resets the sinus rhythm). On the other hand, in RT, (1) "warm-up" is absent; (2) the initial (ectopic) P' wave differs from the subsequent (retrograde) P' waves; (3) a premature stimulus does not reset, but may terminate the tachycardia (by "finding the gap"): When a tachycardia is terminated by a naturally occurring premature beat (fig. 12.4), it suggests that the extrasystolic stimulus has "found the gap" and therefore favors a reciprocating mechanism; and (4) prolongation of the first P'-R interval is the rule. These differentiating features are illustrated in Figures 12.4, 12.6 and 12.7.

Several other clues point to specific mechanisms: If the P' wave during the paroxysm is similar to the sinus P waves, there is a likelihood of sinus nodal reentry (fig. 12.8). If the P' waves are neither of retrograde form and polarity

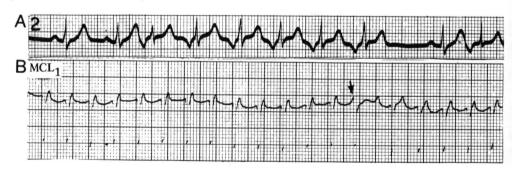

Figure 12.6. (*A*) The P' waves are identical, and there is slight initial "warm-up"; there is no significant P'-R prolongation, and the diagnosis is, most likely, **ectopic atrial** or **junctional tachycardia**. (*B*) At the beginning of the strip, it is impossible to identify the mechanism—it could be ectopic atrial or junctional or reciprocating. Toward the end of the strip, an atrial extrasystole (*arrow*) provides the probable answer: the premature stimulus does not terminate the tachycardia, but it does "reset" the atrial rhythm; i.e., the two atrial cycles embracing the extrasystole equal less than two cycles of the tachycardia, indicating the diagnosis **atrial tachycardia**.

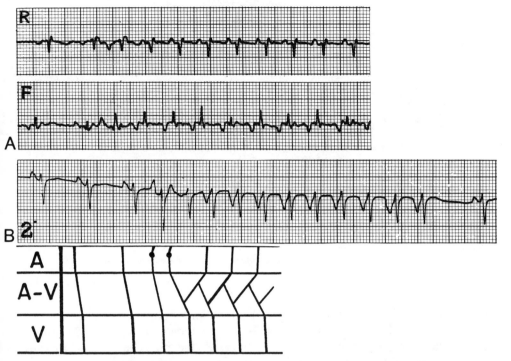

Figure 12.7. (*A*) In each lead, a single atrial extrasystole initiates a run of **reciprocating tachycardia**; note upright retrograde P′ waves in aVR, inverted in aVF. (*B*) It takes "two to tango," and here it took two atrial extrasystoles, the second conducted with delay (long P′-R), to find a "ripe" reentry circuit (see laddergram). The ectopic P′ waves are upright, while the subsequent retrograde P′ waves are sharply inverted.

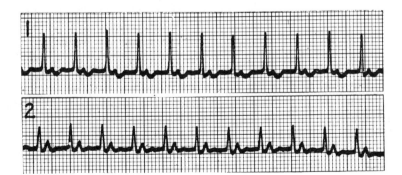

Figure 12.8. **Supraventricular tachycardia**, possibly due to sinus-nodal reentry. Rate 170; upright P waves are clearly discernible immediately following each QRS with P-R intervals of 0.26 sec.

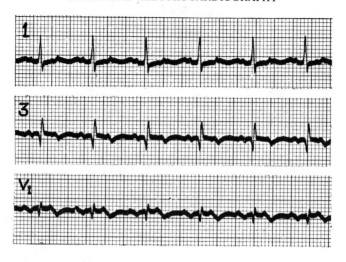

Figure 12.9. An example of probable **ectopic atrial tachycardia** with 2:1 A-V block.

nor like the sinus P waves (fig. 12.9) an ectopic atrial or reentrant atrial tachycardia is likely. The presence of A-V dissociation or A-V block rules out A-V nodal bypass reentry; on the other hand, the presence of ventricular aberration tends to confirm the presence of an A-V nodal bypass; and when the cycle length of the tachycardia increases (rate decreases) with the development of bundle-branch block (BBB), it indicates that the bypass tract is on the same side as the BBB. A negative P' in lead 1 indicates a probably left-sided bypass.[8a]

Additional clues that may lead one to suspect a reentrant tachycardia using a convenient bypass tract are: (1) the "incessant" form of tachycardia (see below); (2) the tachycardia is initiated when the sinus rate accelerates without the intervention of an APB or prolongation of the P-R interval; and (3) the retrograde P' waves are associated with an R-P' shorter than the P'-R.[9]

The relationship of P' to QRS in various RTs is diagrammatically presented in figure 12.10; and the incidence of functioning concealed bypasses found in some carefully investigated series are listed in table 12.3.

Sinus tachycardia may at times be difficult to differentiate from other forms of SVT if the sinus P wave is unrecognizable because it is perched on the T wave (see fig. 12.11). In such cases, vagal stimulation may provide a ready answer.

Accessory Pathways

Patients with accessory pathways are congenitally equipped with the de luxe milieu for the development of RT since they have two parallel pathways between atria and ventricles, with different conduction velocities and different refractory periods. Either route may act as the anterograde or retrograde pathway; if the wave front travels down the normal conduction system and up the accessory bundle, the QRS complex will be normal; but if it travels down the accessory pathway, the QRS will show the characteristics of preexcitation.

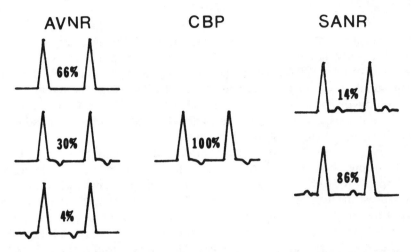

Figure 12.10. Relationship of P to QRS in reentry tachycardias. Series and percentages from Wu et al.[34] Key: AVNR = A-V nodal reentry; CBP = concealed extranodal bypass; SANR = sinus nodal reentry.

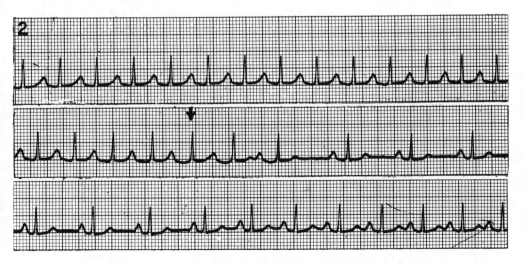

Figure 12.11. In the *top strip*, it is impossible to identify the mechanism of the tachycardia (it could be junctional ectopic, RT, etc.); but carotid sinus stimulation (*arrow*) peels the otherwise unrecognizable P wave off the T wave and makes evident the diagnosis of **sinus tachycardia**.

More and more cases are coming to light in which the accessory pathway is capable of only retrograde conduction (table 12.3). In such patients, the Wolff-Parkinson-White (WPW) pattern fails to show up during sinus rhythm; so a Kent bundle may not be suspected ("concealed WPW"). The importance of recognizing this situation in the intractable tachycardia in whom corrective surgery is being considered is obvious. The RTs complicating preexcitation will be enlarged upon and illustrated in Chapter 18.

In summary, the three most common mechanisms may be suspected from the following observations[34]: A retrograde P wave coincident with the normal QRS (no BBB), with or without evidence of organic heart disease, points to the commonest mechanism of all, **A-V nodal reentry**. A younger subject, a faster rate, BBB during the tachycardia but no organic heart disease indicates a **concealed bypass** in action. P′ waves preceding the normal (no BBB) QRS in the presence of organic disease points to **S-A nodal/atrial reentry**. Based on Wu's series of 66 patients with reentry SVT, the approximate incidence of the above three mechanisms is 76, 14 and 11%.[34]

A Glut of Terms

Apart from the innumerable available circuits, the profusion of descriptive adjectives that have been applied to SVT is nothing short of bewildering; and it is not easy for the clinician to sort out a rational classification. The terms employed fall into two categories: those that apply to clinical behavior—paroxysmal, persistent, permanent, incessant, sustained, nonsustained, chronic, relapsing, repetitive. The second group describe mechanisms—ectopic, automatic, reentrant, reciprocating, circus-movement, slow-fast, fast-slow, orthodromic, antidromic. From this plethora of epithets it is virtually impossible to derive a clear-cut taxonomy.

Paroxysmal retains its traditional meaning—starting and stopping abruptly. Persistent, permanent and incessant appear to be used interchangeably and seem to mean an arrhythmia that is actually neither incessant nor necessarily permanent—as these words were understood before the advent of contemporary electrophysiology—but is definitely persistent in that the tachycardias recur

---

Salient Features of Supraventricular Tachycardia
1. Rapid (100–250), regular, normal QRS complexes
2. Abnormal P waves constantly related to QRS (may not be discernible)
3. ST-T depressions frequently seen

Table 12.3
Proportion of SVTs Using Concealed Bypass (CBP)

Authors	Total SVTs	CBP	Percentage
Wellens and Durrer (1975)[31]	54	5	9
Gillette (1977)[14]	15	10	67
Sung et al. (1977)[27]	46[a]	12	26
Wu et al. (1978)[34]	79	9	11
Farshidi et al. (1978)[9]	60	12	20
Krikler (1978)[17]	20	9	45
	274	57	21

[a] Includes some cases of atrial "flutter-fibrillation."

with annoying perseverance. Here there is overlap with recurrent and repetitive, which mean what they say without a commitment to any particular schedule of recurrence. Clearly there is also overlap with chronic—an arrhythmia that obviously may be recurrent or persistent. Sustained and nonsustained refer to the duration of each bout.

Hence it is evidently possible in the 1980s to have a "chronic, persistent, recurrent, nonsustained, paroxysmal tachycardia"!

On the other side of the ledger, ectopic and automatic are used interchangeably and indicate that the mechanism is a rapidly discharging pacemaking center. Reentrant, reciprocating and circus-movement are all more or less synonymous and mean that the tachycardia concerned is the offspring of a circulating (macro- or micro-) wave. The simple, appealing Anglo-Saxon terms, slow-fast and fast-slow, always apply to reentrant rhythms and inform us which pathway is used for the anterograde (first adjective) and which for the retrograde (second adjective) journey. Orthodromic and antidromic are specifically applied to the reciprocating tachycardias complicating the WPW syndrome and tell us whether the A-V junction was used for the downward anterograde (orthodromic) or upward retrograde (antidromic) journey.

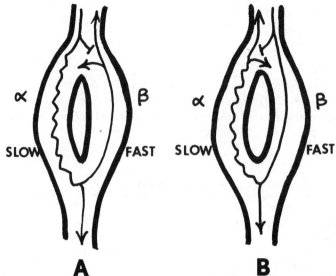

Figure 12.12. Mechanisms of **A-V nodal reentry.** (*A*) Slow-fast: the descending, premature impulse finds the fast (*β*) pathway, with its longer refractory period, still refractory, so travels down the slow (*α*) path producing a prolonged P′-R interval; returning up the now recovered fast pathway it reaches the atria at about the same time that the descending impulse reaches the ventricles, with the result that the P′ wave is lost in the QRS. (*B*) Fast-slow: In the less likely event that the fast pathway recovers before the slow, the descending impulse travels down the fast path and rapidly reaches the ventricles; meanwhile the ascending impulse climbs slowly up the now recovered *α* pathway to produce a long R-P′ interval.

Dual Pathways in the Junction

Investigators have repeatedly demonstrated that the A-V junction may contain two parallel and conductively independent pathways ("longitudinal dissociation"), one characterized by faster conduction but a longer refractory period (beta, *β*); and the other by slower conduction but a shorter refractory period (alpha, *α*).[28] Thanks to such available pathways, two distinct varieties of A-V nodal reentrant tachycardias may dvelop (fig. 12.12): (1) using the fast pathway downward and the slow pathway upward ("fast-slow"), and (2) using the slow path downward and the fast upward ("slow-fast"). These two forms have different manifestations in the clinical tracing (table 12.4).

Fast-Slow Form. This is the less common form and various authors have called it "persistent," "permanent," "incessant" or "repetitive," in honor of its troublesome quality of being almost always present. It is more common in children than in adults and, since its wave front goes down the fast pathway, does not begin with a prolonged P′-R interval; but since it uses the slow pathway for its return to the atria, the R-P′ interval is relatively long. Thus in the clinical tracing it manifests a longer R-P′ than P′-R (fig. 12.13*a*).

Slow-Fast Form. This more common form is usually triggered by an atrial premature beat associated with a prolonged P'-R interval—since the early impulse has found the faster path still refractory and has travelled downward by the slower path. In these cases, the P' wave often coincides with the QRS complex—since it travels up the fast pathway—and is therefore often invisible in the surface ECG (fig. 12.13b).

By no means do all SVTs fit nicely into one of these pigeon-holes. For example, figure 12.7 illustrated two tachycardias initiated by atrial extrasystoles with prolonged P'-R intervals (slow-fast?) in which the R-P' is longer than the complementary P'-R (fast-slow?).

Table 12.4
Dual Pathways of A-V Junction

	Slow-Fast	Fast-Slow
Synonyms	Paroxysmal	Persistent, etc.
Initial P'-R	Prolonged	Normal
Incidence	Usual form in adults	Especially in children
Triggered by	APB	Spontaneous; APB; VPB
P' relations	Coincides with QRS	R-P' > P'-R

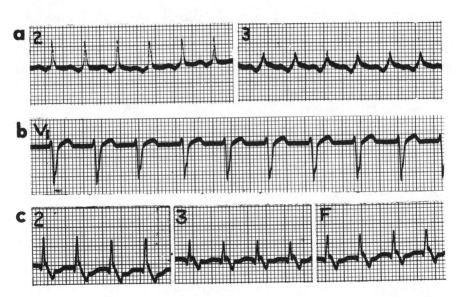

Figure 12.13. Three forms of **junctional tachycardia**. In *a*, the P' waves precede the QRS at a short P'-R interval (R-P' > P'-R = "fast-slow"?). In *b*, the P wave is lost in the QRS—the common "slow-fast" pattern with A-V nodal reentry. In *c*, the P' waves just follow the QRS (R-P' < P'-R = usual pattern of reentry using concealed bypass, or less common "slow-fast" nodal reentry).

Ectopic Tachycardias

With the renewed enthusiasm for circus-movements, the ectopic (automatic) focus tends to be forgotten. But, though the incidence of ectopic atrial and junctional tachycardias is small, they are very real arrhythmias,[16] relatively common in children though rare in adults.[13] It is likely that there are more than one underlying mechanisms: in one series of 52 cases of ectopic atrial tachycardia, most were initiated by late APBs, some began de novo, and a few were ushered in by brief runs of atrial fibrillation.[1]

Two examples of undisputed ectopic atrial tachycardia are the multifocal (or "chaotic") variety (fig. 12.14A), most often associated with chronic lung disease,[20, 26] and the "PAT with block" so often seen as a manifestation of digitalis intoxication (fig. 12.14B). Despite these common associations, it is important to realize that all multifocal tachycardias are not due to lung disease—it may even occur in the newborn[8]; and all "PAT with block" is not caused by digitalis overdosage[23] (fig. 12.15).

Ectopic junctional tachycardia in children may be catastrophic, especially after cardiac surgery.[12]

ST-T Changes

Secondary changes in the ST-T segment may occur. Any tachycardia shortens diastole and therefore curtails coronary blood flow; if the coronaries are already

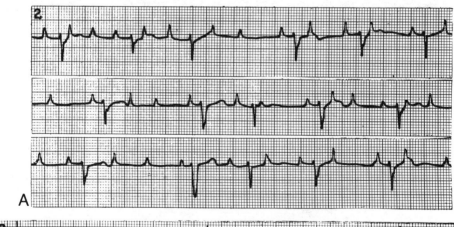

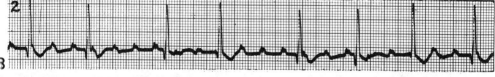

Figure 12.14. (A) **Multifocal atrial tachycardia** in a patient with chronic obstructive lung disease. Note the sharply peaked P-pulmonale even in ectopic P waves, their irregularity in form and rate, and the varying A-V conduction ratio. (B) **Atrial tachycardia** with varying A-V block due to digitalis intoxication.

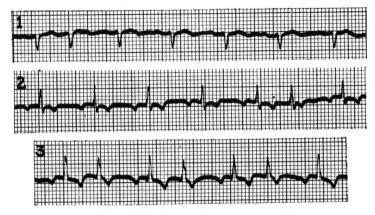

Figure 12.15. Atrial tachycardia with A-V block in a patient *not* receiving digitalis. The P′ waves are barely discernible in lead 1 and are inverted in 2 and 3. The A-V block varies between 2:1 and 3:2. In lead 3 the 3:2 ratio is constant, leaving the ventricular beats grouped in pairs—a common cause of bigeminy (see Chapter 23).

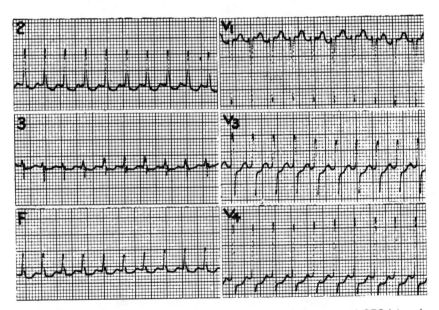

Figure 12.16. Supraventricular tachycardia. Rate 230. Note normal QRS interval and ST depression.

diseased, and sometimes even if they are normal, ST-T changes characteristic of myocardial ischemia may develop. These changes consist of depression of the ST segment with inversion of the T wave and are well shown in figure 12.16. ST and T-wave changes of this sort may persist for hours or days after the paroxysm of tachycardia has ceased, the so-called **post-tachycardia syndrome** (fig. 12.17).

Preexisting BBB

Atrial arrhythmias may be complicated by preexisting intraventricular block (fig. 12.18). In such circumstances the QRS complexes will obviously be prolonged, and this combination may be difficult or impossible to differentiate from ventricular tachycardia.

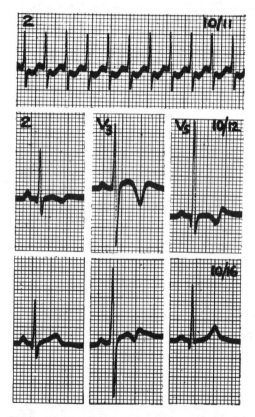

Figure 12.17. Post-tachycardia syndrome. A paroxysm of supraventricular tachycardia is in progress in the upper strip; note associated ST depression. On the following day marked ST-T abnormalities are present; these have disappeared 4 days later. From a 12-year-old boy with a normal heart.

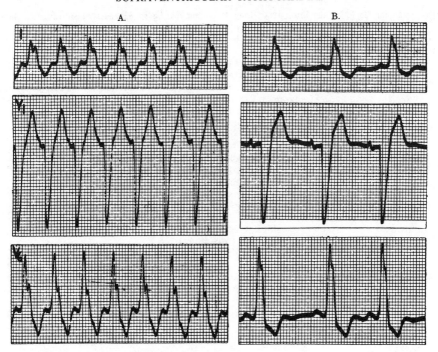

Figure 12.18. **Supraventricular tachycardia** associated with *intraventricular block*. (*A*) This tracing is indistinguishable from ventricular tachycardia. (*B*) When sinus rhythm is later restored the QRST pattern remains virtually unchanged, proving that a supraventricular rhythm was present in *A*.

References

1. Arciniegas, J. G., et al.: Characterization of the onset of ectopic atrial tachycardia with A-V block (abstr.). Am. J. Cardiol. 1981: **47**, 496.
2. Barold, S. S., and Coumel, P.: Mechanisms of atrioventricular junctional tachycardia; role of reentry and concealed accessory bypass tracts. Am. J. Cardiol. 1977: **39**, 97.
3. Brugada, P., et al.: Observations in patients showing A-V junctional echoes with a shorter P-R than R-P interval. Am. J. Cardiol. 1981: **48**, 611.
4. Coumel, P.: Junctional reciprocating tachycardias. The permanent and paroxysmal forms of A-V nodal reciprocating tachycardias. J. Electrocardiol. 1975: **8**, 79.
5. Denes, P., et al.: Multiple reentrant tachycardias due to retrograde conduction of dual atrioventricular bundles with atrioventricular nodal-like properties. Am. J. Cardiol. 1979: **44**, 162.
6. Epstein, M. L., et al.: Incessant atrial tachycardia in childhood; association with rate-dependent conduction in an accessory atrioventricular pathway. Am. J. Cardiol. 1979: **44**, 498.
7. Epstein, M. L., et al.: Long-term evaluation of persistent supraventricular tachycardia in children; clinical and electrocardiographic features. Am. Heart J. 1981: **102**, 80.
8. Farooki, Z. Q., and Green, E. W.: Multifocal atrial tachycardia in two neonates. Br. Heart J. 1977: **39**, 872.
8a. Farre, J., and Wellens, H. J. J.: The value of the electrocardiogram in diagnosing site of origin and mechanism of supraventricular tachycardia, p. 131. In *What's New in Electrocardiography*, edited by H. J. J. Wellens and H. E. Kulbertus. Martinus Nijhoff, Boston, 1981.
9. Farshidi, A., et al.: Electrophysiologic characteristics of concealed bypass tracts: Clinical and electrocardiographic correlates. Am. J. Cardiol. 1978: **41**, 1052.

10. Gallagher, J. J., et al.: Etiology of long R-P′ tachycardia in 33 cases of supraventricular tachycardia. (abstr.). Circulation 1981: **64** (supp. IV), 145.
11. Gallagher, J. J., et al.: Role of Mahaim fibers in cardiac arrhythmias in man. Circulation 1981: **64,** 176.
12. Garson, A., and Gillette, P. C.: Electrophysiologic studies of supraventricular tachycardia in children; I. Clinical-electrophysiologic correlates. Am. Heart J. 1981: **102,** 233.
13. Gillette, P. C., and Garson, A.: Electrophysiologic and pharmacologic characteristics of automatic ectopic atrial tachycardia. Circulation 1977: **56,** 571.
14. Gillette, P. C.: Concealed anomalous cardiac conduction pathways: A frequent cause of supraventricular tachycardia. Am. J. Cardiol. 1977: **40,** 848.
15. Gillette, P. C.: Advances in the diagnosis and treatment of tachydysrhythmias in children. Am. Heart J. 1981: **102,** 111.
16. Goldreyer, B. N., et al.: The electrophysiologic demonstration of atrial ectopic tachycardia in man. Am. Heart J. 1973: **85,** 205.
17. Krikler, D.: Concealed pre-excitation. J. Electrocardiol. 1978: **11,** 209.
18. Langendorf, R.: Aberrrant ventricular conduction. Am. Heart J. 1951: **41,** 700.
19. Lewis, T.: *The Mechanism and Graphic Registration of the Heart Beat*, Ed 3. Shaw, London, 1925.
20. Lipson, M. J., and Naimi, S.: Multifocal atrial tachycardia (chaotic atrial tachycardia). Clinical associations and significance. Circulation 1970: **42,** 397.
21. Lown, B., et al.: Interrelationship of digitalis and potassium in auricular tachycardia with block. Am. Heart J. 1953: **45,** 589.
22. Lown, B., et al.: Paroxysmal atrial tachycardia with block. Circulation 1960: **21,** 129.
23. Morgan, W. L., and Breneman, G. M.: Atrial tachycardia with block treated with digitalis. Circulation 1962: **25,** 787.
24. Prinzmetal, M., et al.: *The Auricular Arrhythmias.* Charles C Thomas, Springfield, Ill., 1952.
25. Ross, D. L., et al.: Spontaneous termination of circus movement tachycardia using an atrioventricular accessory pathway: incidence, site of block and mechanisms. Circulation 1981: **63,** 1129.
26. Shine, K. I., et al.: Multifocal atrial tachycardia. Clinical and electrocardiographic features in 32 patients. N. Engl. J. Med. 1968: **279,** 344.
27. Sung, R. J., et al.: Clinical and electrophysiologic observations in patients with concealed accessory atrioventricular bypass tracts. Am. J. Cardiol. 1977: **40,** 839.
28. Sung, R. J., and Castellanos, A.: Supraventricular tachycardia; mechanisms and treatment. Cardiovasc. Clin. 1980: **11,** 27.
29. Ward, D. E., et al.: Incessant atrioventricular tachycardia involving an accessory pathway; preoperative and intraoperative electrophysiologic studies and surgical correction. Am. J. Cardiol. 1979: **44,** 428.
30. Wellens, H. J. J.: *Electrical Stimulation of the Heart in the Study and Treatment of Tachycardias.* University Park Press, Baltimore, 1971.
31. Wellens, H. J. J., and Durrer, D.: The role of an accessory atrioventricular pathway in reciprocal tachycardia; observations in patients with and without the Wolff-Parkinson-White syndrome. Circulation 1975: **52,** 58.
32. Wolff, G. S., et al.: The fast-slow form of atrioventricular nodal reentrant tachycardia in children. Am. J. Cardiol. 1979: **43,** 1181.
33. Wu, D., and Denes, P.: Mechanisms of paroxysmal supraventricular tachycardia. Arch. Intern. Med. 1975: **135,** 437.
34. Wu, D., et al.: Clinical, electrocardiographic and elecrophysiologic observations in patients with paroxysmal supraventricular tachycardia. Am. J. Cardiol. 1978: **41,** 1045.

Review Tracings

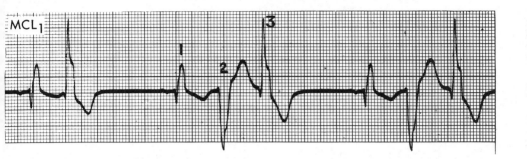

Review Tracing 12.1

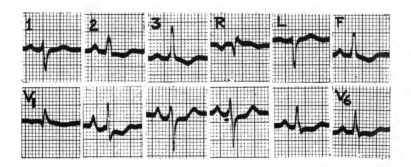

Review Tracing 12.2

For interpretation, see page 482

13

Atrial Flutter

The first ECG of atrial flutter in man was published by Einthoven in 1906; it remained for Jolly and Ritchie in 1911 to draw a clear electrocardiographic distinction between fibrillation and flutter.

Electrophysiological Mechanisms

Although the mechanism mediating atrial flutter is not settled—and indeed, different examples of flutter may have different mechanisms—most recent authorities lean toward some form of reentry.[4, 5, 7, 15]

For a quarter of a century, following the claims of Lewis, a circus-movement around the venae cavae was accepted almost universally as the proven mechanism. Scherf[11] and Prinzmetal,[10] independently, then claimed to have demonstrated that the atrial tachyarrhythmias were due to the repetitive firing of a single focus rather than to a reentry mechanism. More recent work suggests that the likely mechanism in most examples of atrial flutter is either a microreentry or automatic focus low in the atrium.[6, 7, 12–15]

An apparent prerequisite for the development of atrial flutter is delayed conduction within the atria and/or a disturbance in sinus nodal function.[3, 8, 13]

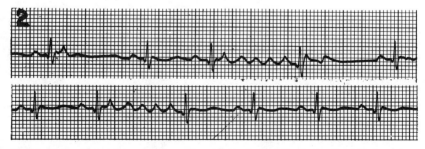

Figure 13.1. The strips are not continuous. Each strip illustrates the initiation of a short, one-second, burst of **atrial flutter**.

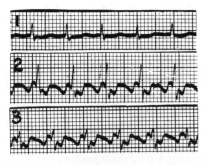

Figure 13.2. **Atrial flutter** with 2:1 A-V conduction. Note that the F waves in leads 2 and 3 are of about equal amplitude and therefore there is no sign of atrial activity in lead 1.

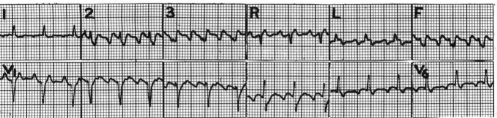

Figure 13.3. **Atrial flutter** in a 12-lead tracing. Note the positive P-like waves in V_1 and negative P-like waves in V_5 and V_6. Evidence of atrial activity, as usual, is minimal in lead 1.

The concomitance of a conduction disturbance itself supports the probability of a reentry mechanism. Further support is afforded by the fact that flutter cannot be converted to sinus rhythm by a single atrial extrastimulus.[7, 15]

Flutter may be precipitated by a single atrial extrasystole arising in the atrial vulnerable period; it may persist for only a few seconds (fig. 13.1), though it usually pursues a more chronic course lasting for weeks, months, or years; patients are on record in whom flutter has lasted for more than two decades.

Electrocardiographic Features

In the ECG atrial flutter is recognized by the constantly undulating or zigzagging baseline that has been likened to the teeth of a saw or to a picket fence. This pattern of flutter waves—conventionally labeled "FF"— is usually best seen in leads 2, 3, and aVF; and because the excursion of the flutter waves is approximately equal in leads 2 and 3, by Einthoven's equation (II = I + III) there is little visible evidence of the flutter in lead 1 (fig. 13.2). In the precordial leads, the flutter wave is usually a discrete positive P-like wave in V_1 (figs. 13.3–13.6) with a correspondingly negative P-like wave in V_{5-6} (fig. 13.3). Occasionally, the flutter waves may be so inconspicuous that they can be seen only in lead Vl or in an esophageal lead (see fig. 13.12).

Since the days of Lewis (1913), atrial flutter is sometimes separated into "common" and "uncommon" forms according to the contour of the atrial waves. The atrial waves of the common form have prominent negative components in the inferior leads (2, 3, and aVF) with impressive positive deflections

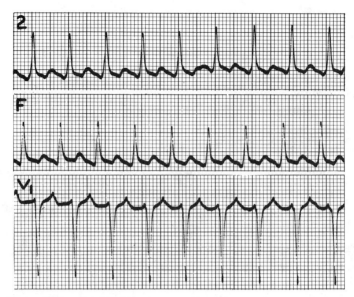

Figure 13.4. Atrial flutter with 2:1 A-V conduction. Alternate F waves coincide with the ventricular complex, and the diagnosis could easily be missed. Note the positive P-like waves in lead V_1.

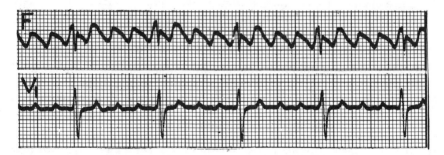

Figure 13.5. Atrial flutter with 4:1 A-V conduction. The zigzag, "saw-tooth" waves are readily recognized in aVF but assume the usual positive P-like form in V_1.

in aVR and aVL; and the undulation of the baseline is continuous. The uncommon form is any other flutter whose waves fail to conform with *both* these features. The common form supposedly originates in the low (caudad) part of one of the atria, while some at least of the uncommon type arise in the high right atrium (cephalad).

The Birmingham school[12] divides flutter into types I and II. Type I has an inherent rate between 240 and 338/min and is readily converted by atrial pacing; whereas type II fails to respond to atrial pacing and has a faster rate (between 340 and 433/min). Type II may represent an intermediate form between classical atrial flutter and atrial fibrillation.

Untreated, the usual A-V conduction ratio is 2:1 (fig. 13.2–13.4), and when this prevails, it may be difficult to recognize either the flutter or the ratio because every other atrial wave will be partially masked and distorted by the QRS-T conglomerate (fig. 13.4). When the conduction ratio increases because of treatment or disease, the recognition becomes easy since consecutive atrial cycles become plainly visible (fig. 13.5).

Conduction ratios of 2:1 and 4:1 are common and are frequently seen in the same tracing (see figs. 13.11 and 13.16), but odd number ratios (1:1, 3:1, etc.) are rare. Figure 13.6 presents an example of 3:1 conduction; and figure 13.7, with a ventricular rate of about 260/min, is presumably due to atrial flutter with 1:1 conduction.

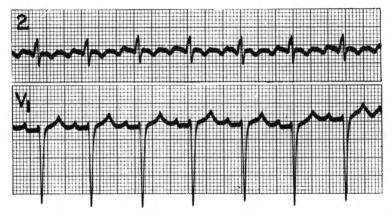

Figure 13.6. **Atrial flutter** at a rate of 306/min with 3:1 A-V conduction—a rare ratio.

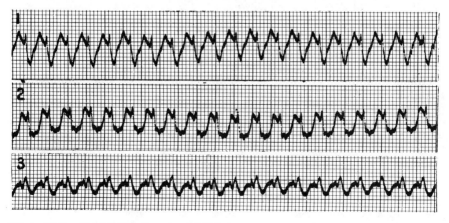

Figure 13.7. **Atrial flutter** at a rate of 256/min with 1:1 A-V conduction and an incomplete right bundle-branch block pattern.

Conduction ratios of 6:1 (fig. 13.8)—and still higher even-number ratios—are sometimes seen. You can tell that there is a stable conduction relationship because the atrial waves retain a constant relationship to the QRS complexes. Compare this with the situation in the two rhythm strips in figure 13.9. In both of these, the relationship of the FF waves to the QRS complexes is constantly changing while the ventricular rhythm is regular; therefore, since the ventricular rate is slow enough, it is reasonable to diagnose atrial flutter with complete A-V block.

There can be considerable variation in the rate of flutter waves (fig. 13.10). Usually between 280 and 320/min, they may be as slow as 200/min and as rapid as over 400/min. The atrial rate may be greatly influenced by drugs. Digitalis tends to accelerate it, whereas quinidine, procainamide, and lidocaine slow the atrial rate. In figure 13.11, the *top strip* was taken while the patient was receiving digitalis alone; quinidine was then started, and 24 hours later, the atrial rate had slowed from 270 to 224/min. In this patient, the drug failed to convert the flutter, and, when it was discontinued, the atrial rate returned to about 275/min.

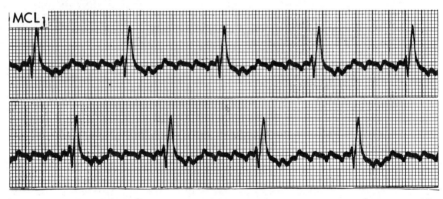

Figure 13.8. The strips are continuous. **Atrial flutter** with 6:1 A-V conduction and right bundle-branch block.

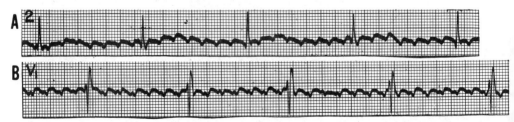

Figure 13.9. Two examples of **atrial flutter** with **complete A-V block**. Note that the relationship of atrial to ventricular complexes is constantly changing, while the ventricular rhythm is independently regular. In *A*, the atrial rate is 310/min, and the junctional escape rate is 42/min. In *B*, the atrial rate is approximatetly 290/min, and the ventricular rate is 44/min. Note the unusual notched morphology of the FF waves.

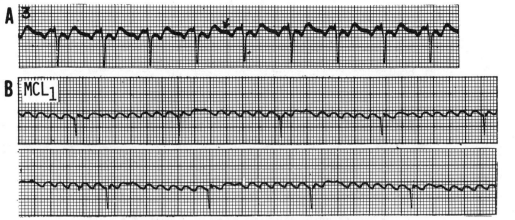

Figure 13.10. (*A*). **Atrial flutter** with the unusually slow atrial rate of 204/min and 2:1 A-V conduction. Note the "isoelectric shelf" between atrial waves (*arrow*). (*B*) Atrial flutter at an unusually rapid rate (about 375/min) with 8:1 A-V conduction.

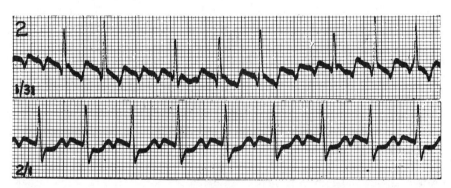

Figure 13.11. **Atrial flutter** before and after quinidine administration. In the *upper strip*, the atrial rate was 270/min with varying 2:1 and 4:1 A-V conduction. After 24-hours' treatment with quinidine (*bottom strip*), the atrial rate is only 224/min with constant 2:1 A-V conduction.

Genesis of Flutter Waves

The genesis of the atrial flutter waves is uncertain. The continuous undulating or zigzag pattern in leads 2 and 3 was one of the points that led Lewis to assume a continuous circulating (circus-movement) wave. But Prinzmetal[10] demonstrated that the continuous zigzag could be "pulled apart" by slowing the atrial rate, leaving an "isoelectric shelf" between consecutive atrial deflections (fig. 13.10*A*). He suggested that the initial negative part of the complex represented depolarization of the atria and the terminal positive part repolarization (Ta or T$_P$ wave).

It is sobering to realize that atrial flutter has yet to be satisfactorily defined. The typical picture is easy to recognize: "saw-tooth" waves in inferior leads at

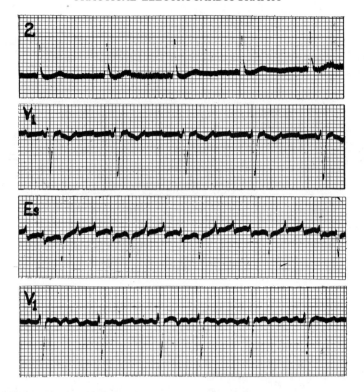

Figure 13.12.   Atrial flutter with 4:1 A-V block. The only routine lead that showed any sign of atrial activity was V₁. The third strip (Es) is an esophageal lead. The fourth strip is V₁ after digitalization, showing **atrial fibrillation**.

a rate of about 300/min. But there is an extensive borderland between flutter and tachycardia, which no one has as yet satisfactorily staked out; and there may, in fact, be no sharply dividing line between the atrial tachyarrhythmias. Prinzmetal claimed decades ago that the typical pattern of atrial tachycardia, produced in the experimental animal by the application of aconitine to the atrial muscle, could be changed, in turn, to the typical pattern of atrial flutter and on to atrial fibrillation merely by increasing the discharge rate of the ectopic focus by warming it. Figure 13.13 illustrates diagrammatically both the development of Ta waves and the shortening of the isoelectric shelf as the rate increases.

To date, although it is now clear that the majority of supraventricular tachycardias are due to reentry, this "unitary concept" of ectopic atrial arrhythmias remains to be conclusively challenged.

Patterns of A-V Conduction

The most interesting feature of the ECG in atrial flutter is the fascinating variety of conduction patterns that may develop because of the interplay at varying levels in the A-V junction.[1] The untreated 2:1 ratio is due to normal refractoriness in the A-V junction and therefore should not be called 2:1 "block"—the junction is playing its normal physiological role as a shield protecting the ventricles from atrial bombardment. The conduction antics in

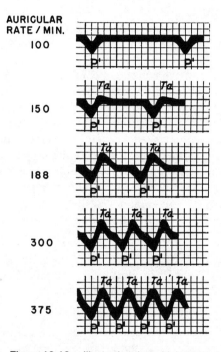

Figure 13.13. Illustrating that with increase in rate (1) the Ta wave assumes greater prominence and (2) the isoelectric shelf becomes shorter. (Reproduced with kind permission of the publishers from *The Auricular Arrhythmias*, by Myron Prinzmetal and others, Charles C Thomas, 1951.)

atrial flutter frequently produce a bigeminal rhythm; two of these bigeminal patterns are illustrated in figures 13.14 and 13.15*B*.

When digitalis or propranolol is administered to reduce the ventricular rate to a normal level, the 2:1 filter continues to operate while the alternate impulses that pass the filter suffer Wenckebach-type conduction delay at a lower level in the junction—perhaps 4:3 conduction at first (fig. 13.16) producing a form of trigeminy, then 3:2 (fig. 13.15*B*), and finally 2:1 conduction. With 2:1 conduction at the higher level and 2:1 conduction now at the lower level as well, the net A-V ratio becomes the desirable 4:1 goal of therapy, with a now normal ventricular rate of about 75/min (fig. 13.15*C*).

Pick and Langendorf[11] long ago pointed out that the A-V conduction time in atrial flutter was considerably prolonged owing to the effect of concealed conduction of the very numerous atrial impulses. They calculated that the usual "F-R" interval during 2:1 conduction (measured from the nadir of the atrial wave to the beginning of the ventricular complex) probably measured between 0.26 and 0.46 sec because of the concealed conduction in the A-V junction of the alternate impulses that failed to reach the ventricles. Thus, although the immediately preceding flutter wave does not represent the atrial impulse that is conducted to the ventricles, its changing relationship to the following QRS alerts one's eye to the developing Wenckebach-type conduction; in figure 13.16, the *square brackets* lying on their backs indicate the progressively lengthening A-V interval, though the actual impulse responsible for the ventricular activation is the preceding one, as indicated in the laddergram.

Atrial flutter is relatively uncommon—its incidence in adults is said to be perhaps one-twentieth that of atrial fibrillation. It is most often found in

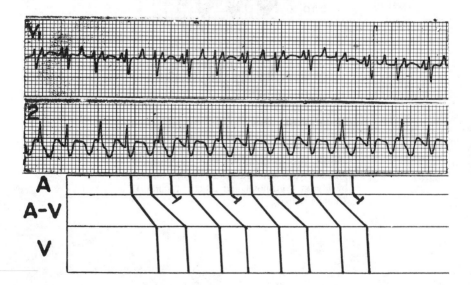

Figure 13.14. **Atrial flutter** at a rate of 268/min with 3:2 Wenckebach periods.

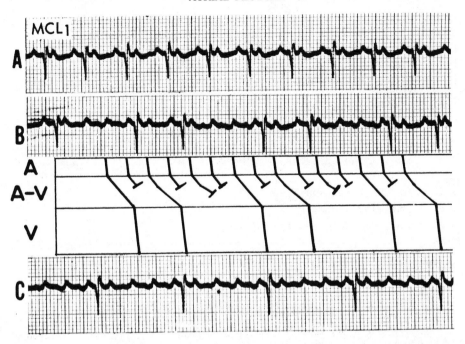

Figure 13.15. Illustrates the effect of propranolol on A-V conduction during **atrial flutter**. (*A*). Before therarpy: Atrial rate is 262/min with 2:1 conduction. (*B*) Less than a minute after 2 mg propranolol had been given intravenously: Atrial rate is unchanged, but the drug has produced 3:2 block of the alternate impulses that have passed the 2:1 filter. This combination of 2:1 filtering at a higher level and 3:2 conduction at a lower level produces alternating 4:1 and 2:1 conduction leaving the ventricular beats in bigeminal rhythm. (*C*) The atrial rate has slowed slightly to 252/min, and the drug has now produced 2:1 block of the alternate impulses so that the net A-V ratio is now 4:1.

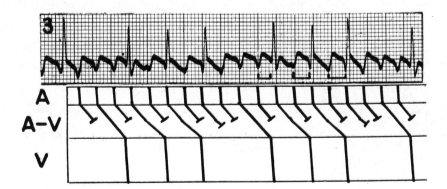

Figure 13.16. **Atrial flutter** at a rate of 306/min with 2:1 filtering at a high level in the junction and 4:3 Wenckebach conduction of the beats that pass the filter. The net result of this is trigeminal grouping of the ventricular beats. The *supine square brackets* highlight the lengthening A-V relationship (see text).

ischemic hearts over the age of 40 years and is strikingly rare in mitral disease compared with atrial fibrillation. It may complicate any form of heart disease, however, and may be precipitated by any acute illness. In the first few years of life, it is much more common than atrial fibrillation, presumably because it requires a greater mass of atrial muscle than the young child possesses to sustain fibrillation.

Salient Features of Atrial Flutter

1. "Saw-tooth" or undulating baseline of "F" waves in inferior leads (2, 3 and aVF)
2. Sharp, P-like waves in V_1
3. Normal QRS complexes in 2:1 to 8:1 A-V ratio
4. T waves may distort the F-wave pattern

References

1. Besoain-Santander, M., Pick, A., and Langendorf, R.: A-V conduction in auricular flutter. Circulation 1950: **2,** 604.
2. Cohen, S. I., et al.: P loops during common and uncommon atrial flutter in man. Br. Heart J. 1977: **39,** 173.
3. Dhingra, R. C., et al.: Clinical significance of prolonged sinoatrial conduction time. Circulation 1977: **55,** 8.
4. Gavrilescu, S. and Cotoi, S.: Monophasic action potential of right human atrium during atrial flutter and after conversion to sinus rhythm: Argument for re-entry theory. Br. Heart J. 1972: **34,** 396.
5. Guiney, T. E., and Lown, B.: Electrical conversion of atrial flutter to atrial fibrillation; flutter mechanism in man. Br. Heart J. 1972: **34,** 1215.
6. Inoue, H., et al.: Clinical and experimental studies of the effects of atrial extrastimulation and rapid pacing on atrial flutter cycle: evidence of macroreentry with an excitable gap. Am. J. Cardiol. 1981: **48,** 623.
7. Josephson, M. E., and Seides, S. F.: *Clinical Cardiac Electrophysiology. Techniques and Interpretations,* pp. 195–202. Lea & Febiger, Philadelphia, 1979.
8. Leier, C. V. et al.: Prolonged atrial conduction. A major predisposing factor for the development of atrial flutter. Circulation 1978: **57,** 213.
9. Neporent, L. M.: Atrial sounds in atrial fibrillation and flutter. Circulation 1964: **30,** 893.
10. Prinzmetal, M., et al.: *The Auricular Arrhythmias.* Charles C Thomas, Springfield, Ill., 1952.
11. Scherf, D., et al.: Mechanism of flutter and fibrillation. Arch. Intern. Med. 1953: **91,** 333.
12. Wells, J. L., et al.: Characterization of atrial flutter; studies in man after open heart surgery using fixed atrial electrodes. Circulation 1979: **60,** 665.
13. Watson, R. M., and Josephson, M. E.: Atrial flutter; I. Electrophysiologic substrates and modes of initiation and termination. Am. J. Cardiol. 1980: **45,** 732.
14. Wellens, H. J. J., et al.: Epicardial excitation of the atria in a patient with atrial flutter. Br. Heart J. 1971: **33,** 233.
15. Wellens, H. J. J.: *Electrical Stimulation of the Heart in the Study and Treatment of Tachycardias,* pp 27–39. University Park Press, Baltimore, 1971.

Review Tracings

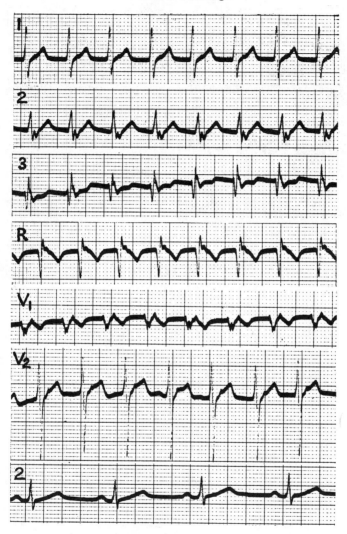

Review Tracing 13.1

For interpretation, see page 482

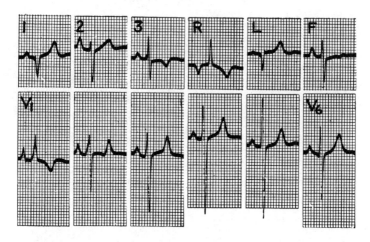

Review Tracing 13.2

For interpretation, see page 482

More Practical Points

Technicians are not expected to learn how to interpret the tracing, but they should be told certain useful points that will make their work more intelligent and more interesting. They should watch the tracing come out of the machine with a trained, alert eye and they should be given the following practical instructions.

Notice carefully the pattern of these four leads:

1. *Lead 1*: If the complexes are all inverted, check your arm electrodes— they are almost certainly reversed (*b* in fig. 3.11, p. 28).

2. *Lead 3*: If the first deflection of the ventricular complex is downward (a Q wave), tell the patient to take a deep breath and hold it for a few heart beats (fig. 26.6, p. 000). This may help to distinguish between important and unimportant Q waves.

3. *Standard limb leads*: If the three main components (P, QRS and T) are virtually invisible in any one of these leads, the probability is that the two electrodes for that lead are attached to the two legs (fig. 3.12)—check your hook-up!

4. *Lead V_6*: If the ventricular complex shows a deep downstroke (S wave) instead of the usual tall upright wave, take a lead further to the left (V_7) to try and get a pattern with the major deflection upward.

14

Atrial Fibrillation

Total irregularity of the arterial pulse, referred to as "delirium cordis," was associated with mitral stenosis in the mid-19th century and was sometimes known as the mitral pulse. Quite independently, a positive systolic wave in the venous pulse was noted in some patients during the latter half of the 19th century and attributed to tricuspid insufficiency. But it was not until Mackenzie (1902) studied such patients with his polygraph that they were both ascribed to a single cause, atrial fibrillation. The first tracings of atrial fibrillation in man were published by Einthoven (1906) and Hering (1908); but it remained for Lewis (1909) to appreciate the significance of the clinical tracing and to introduce the convention of labeling the fibrillatory waves "ff."

Initiation and Mechanism

Just as the ventricles have a vulnerable period, so there is a point in the atrial cycle at which an atrial premature impulse is likely to precipitate an atrial tachyarrhythmia. Killip has formularized the situation as follows: if the P-P′ interval (i.e., the interval from the preceding P wave to the premature P′ wave) is less than half the preceding P-P interval, it is likely to land in the vulnerable period and spark a tachyarrhythmia; but if the P-P′ interval is more than 60% of the preceding P-P interval, it is unlikely to do so[13] (fig. 14.1). Just what the relationship is (if any) between this "vulnerable" period and the "tachycardia-initiating interval" dealt with on page 152 remains to be elucidated.

Sometimes, atrial tachycardia or flutter "degenerates" into atrial fibrillation. Using intra-atrial recordings in patients with acute myocardial infarction, Bennett and Pentacost[3] found that paroxysms of atrial fibrillation always began with a rapid atrial tachycardia showing discrete atrial waves at a rate of about 340/min, and this lasted for up to 30 sec before the fibrillatory pattern took over. Cessation of the arrhythmia was always preceded by reversion to wave form resembling the initiating tachycardia.

The mechanisms of atrial fibrillation are still sub judice.[5] Circus-movement, multiple reentry circuits, and unifocal and multifocal ectopic impulse formation all have their advocates and some supportive evidence.

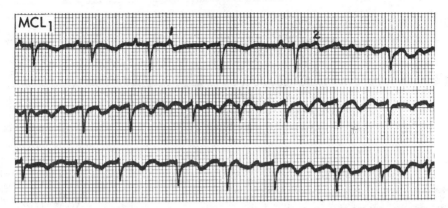

Figure 14.1. **Atrial fibrillation** precipitated by APB (*2*) in *top strip*. The first APB (*1*) ends a cycle more than half the preceding cycle; whereas the second APB (*2*) ends a cycle less than half the preceding P-P interval, therefore lands in the "vulnerable phase" of the atrial cycle and precipitates fibrillation.

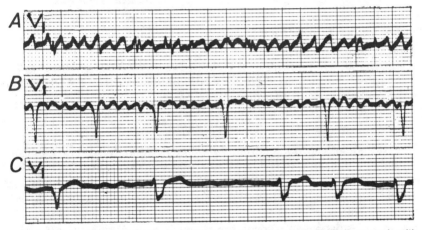

Figure 14.2. Coarse (*A*), medium (*B*), and fine (*C*) **atrial fibrillation**, each with irregular ventricular response.

Electrocardiographic Recognition

In the ECG atrial fibrillation is recognized by irregular undulation of the baseline, usually associated with an irregular ventricular rhythm. The undulations may be gross and distinct (fig. 14.2*A*), they may be barely perceptible (fig. 14.2*C*), or they may be intermediate in form (fig. 14.2*B*); for descriptive purposes these may be called, respectively, coarse, fine, or medium fibrillation. Although the size of the "f" waves seems not to correlate with the size of the atrium or the type of heart disease,[18] large "f" waves are unlikely to be found in the presence of a normal sized left atrium.[1] At times, there may be no recognizable deflection of the baseline, and then the fibrillation may be inferred

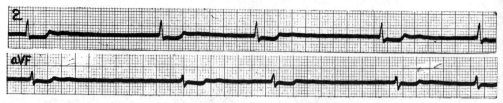

Figure 14.3. "Straight-line" **atrial fibrillation**. There is no discernible undulation of the baseline, but the irregular ventricular response (in the absence of evident atrial activity) makes the presumptive diagnosis of atrial fibrillation.

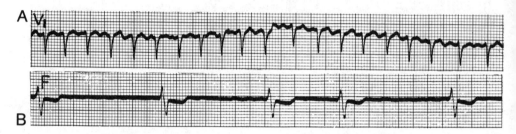

Figure 14.4 (*A*)**Atrial fibrillation** with rapid ventricular response (about 190/min). (*B*) **Atrial fibrillation** with slow ventricular response (about 40/min).

by the irregular ventricular response alone; in this context, the term straight-line fibrillation is sometimes used (fig. 14.3). Fibrillatory (ff) waves are usually best seen in lead V_1 or standard lead 2.

A-V Conduction

The ventricular response to atrial fibrillation is variable. If the A-V junction is normal and unhampered by digitalis or a beta-blocker, rates up to 200/min may develop (fig. 14.4*A*). On the other hand, if the A-V node is diseased or markedly suppressed by drugs, the ventricular response may be markedly reduced (fig. 14.4*B*).

The irregularity of the ventricular response in atrial fibrillation is the result of "concealed conduction" in the A-V junction—the innumerable atrial impulses jostling for penetration get in each other's way, leave the conducting pathways unpredictably refractory and ensure irregular delivery to the ventricles.[14, 15, 17] The same phenomenon also reduces the number of conductible impulses: as in figure 14.5, with a regular supraventricular tachycardia at a rate of 184, all 184 impulses reach the ventricles; but, with the spontaneous onset of atrial fibrillation during the recording of a 12-lead ECG, the number of successful impulses is approximately halved.

When atrial fibrillation complicates the Wolff-Parkinson-White syndrome, the refractory period of the accessory pathway determines the attainable ventricular rate, and rates of well over 200/min, sometimes exceeding 300/min, are found.[4, 23] In this situation, ventricular tachycardia is often erroneously diagnosed (see Chapter 18).

On the other hand, the presence of a regular ventricular rhythm does not exclude the diagnosis of atrial fibrillation. It is not uncommon, as in figure 14.6, *A* and *B*, to have a regular independent ventricular rhythm in the presence of atrial fibrillation because of A-V block. Whenever this is seen, one should consider the possibility of digitalis intoxication.[12] Remember not to call it *complete* A-V block just because there is no conduction—absence of conduction is not necessarily complete block—unless the ventricular rate is slow enough (less than 45/min). Thus in figure 14.6*B*, where the idionodal rate is 36/min, atrial fibrillation with complete A-V block may be diagnosed; but the *upper strip* should be described as atrial fibrillation with some degree of A-V block which, combined with a ventricular (junctional) rate of 51/min, produces complete A-V dissociation.

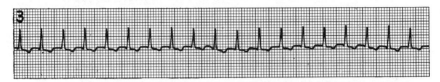

ATRIAL FIBRILLATION BEGAN BETWEEN aVF AND V1

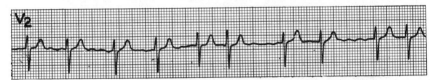

Figure 14.5. **Supraventricular tachycardia** (*top strip*) at rate 184 converting spontaneously to atrial fibrillation (*bottom strip*); during **atrial fibrillation**, the much reduced number of impulses conducted to the ventricles and the ventricular irregularity are accounted for by concealed conduction of innumerable atrial impulses into the A-V junction (average ventricular rate is 100).

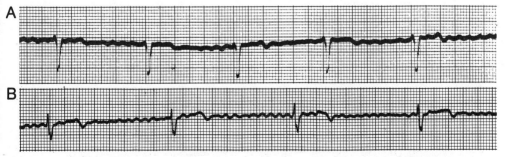

Figure 14.6. Both strips are from lead 3 in different patients. (*A*) **Atrial fibrillation** with independent junctional rhythm (patient had right bundle-branch block with left anterior hemiblock) at a rate of 51/min. (*B*) **Atrial fibrillation** with **complete A-V block** and junctional escape rhythm at a rate of 36/min.

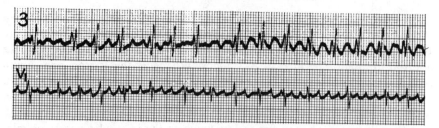

Figure 14.7. Two examples of **atrial flutter-fibrillation**. The atrial waves are too well formed and regular to be called unqualified fibrillation, yet not regular enough to be pure flutter.

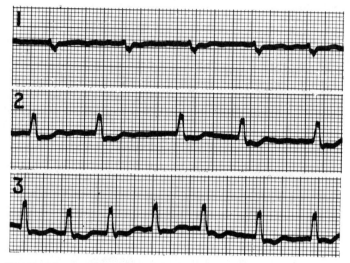

Figure 14.8. **Atrial fibrillation** with right axis deviation; this combination is highly suspicious of mitral stenosis.

Sometimes a mixture of fibrillation with flutter is seen, as in figure 14.7 and may be called **flutter-fibrillation** or **impure flutter**.

A final diagnostic tidbit: The combination of atrial fibrillation with right axis deviation (fig. 14.8) is strongly suggestive of mitral stenosis, especially in the earlier decades.

Salient Features of Atrial Fibrillation

1. Absence of P waves, which are replaced by irregular "f" waves (or no sign at all of atrial activity)
2. Normal QRS complexes, irregular in time and sometimes varying in amplitude

Etiology

Although atrial fibrillation may complicate any cardiac disease and is sometimes seen in the absence of any apparent disease[20] ("lone" fibrillation), the "Big Four" to think of first in causation are mitral disease, ischemic disease, hypertension, and thyrotoxicosis. Advancing age and increased left atrial size are closely related to its development.[11, 21] Chronic atrial fibrillation in the elderly often conceals an underlying sick sinus syndrome, and such patients frequently show the combination of narrowing of the sinus nodal artery, muscle loss in the sinus node, and dilation of the atria, whereas those who develop atrial fibrillation acutely during the last 2 weeks of life as a result of pulmonary embolism or pericarditis usually have atrial dilation without sinus nodal disease.[9]

Chronic atrial fibrillation, once established, usually lasts for life; but occasionally, even when it has persisted 10 or more years after valvotomy for mitral stenosis, it may revert spontaneously to sinus rhythm.[24] Atrial fibrillation developing during the first 72 hours of acute myocardial infarction carries a surprisingly poor prognosis—worse than that of patients resuscitated from major ventricular arrhythmias during the first 24 hours.[8, 10, 16]

Except in myocardial infarction, atrial fibrillation is rare in ischemic heart disease.[19] Whereas in children, atrial flutter is more common than atrial fibrillation, in adult life atrial fibrillation has approximately 20 times the incidence of flutter.[19] Atrial fibrillation is a common complication of chronic constrictive pericarditis though relatively rare in the acute disease.[22] The arrhythmia complicates a significant percentage of all forms of cardiomyopathy[19] and accounts for 20–25% of the tachyarrhythmias associated with the Wolff-Parkinson-White syndrome[6]; it is also fairly common in the Lown-Ganong-Levine syndrome.[2]

References

1. Bartall, H., et al.: Assessment of echocardiographic left atrial enlargement in patients with atrial fibrillation. An electrovectorcardiographic study. J. Electrocardiol. 1978: **11**, 269.
2. Benditt, D. G., et al.: Characteristics of atrioventricular conduction and the spectrum of arrhythmias in Lown-Ganong-Levine syndrome. Circulation 1978: **57**, 454.
3. Bennett, M. A., and Pentacost, B. L.: The pattern of onset and spontaneous cessation of atrial fibrillation in man. Circulation, 1970: **1**, 981.
4. Castellanos, A., et al.: Factors regulating ventricular rates during atrial flutter and fibrillation in preexcitation (Wolff-Parkinson-White) syndrome. Br. Heart J. 1973: **35**, 811.
5. Chung, E. K.: *Principles of Cardiac Arrhythmias*, Ed 2, pp 170–173. Williams & Wilkins, Baltimore, 1977.
6. Chung, E. K.: Tachyarrhythmias in Wolff-Parkinson-White syndrome. J.A.M.A. 1977: **237**, 376.
7. Cohen, S. I., et al.: Concealed conduction during atrial fibrillation. Am. J. Cardiol. 1970: **25**, 416.
8. Cristal, N., et al.: Atrial fibrillation developing in the acute phase of myocardial infarction. Prognostic implications. Chest 1976: **70**, 8.
9. Davies, M. J., and Pomerance, A.: Pathology of atrial fibrillation in man. Br. Heart J. 1972: **34**, 520.

10. Harrison, D. C.: Atrial fibrillation in acute myocardial infarction. Significance and therapeutic implications. Chest 1976: **70**, 3.
11. Henry, W. L., et al.: Relation between echocardiographically determined left atrial size and atrial fibrillation. Circulation 1976: **3**, 273.
12. Kastor, J. A.: Digitalis intoxication in patients with atrial fibrillation. Circulation 1973: **47**, 888.
13. Killip, T., and Gault, J. H.: Mode of onset of atrial fibrillation in man. Am. Heart J. 1965: **70**, 172.
14. Langendorf, R., et al.: Ventricular response in atrial fibrillation; role of concealed conduction in the atrioventricular junction. Circulation 1965: **32**, 69.
15. Lau, S. H., et al.: A study of atrioventricular conduction in atrial fibrillation and flutter in man using His bundle recordings. Circulation 1969: **40**, 71.
16. Lie, K. I., and Durrer, D.: Common arrhythmias in acute myocardial infarction. Cardiovasc. Clin. 1980: **11**, 191.
17. Moore E. N.: Observations on concealed conduction in atrial fibrillation. Circ. Res. 1967: **21**, 201.
18. Morganroth, J., et al.: Relationship of atrial fibrillatory wave amplitude to left atrial size and etiology of heart disease. Am. Heart J. 1979: **97**, 184.
19. Morris, D. C., and Hurst, J. W.: Atrial fibrillation. Curr. Prob. Cardiol. 1980: **5**, 1.
20. Peter, R. H., et al.: A clinical profile of idiopathic atrial fibrillation. Ann. Intern. Med. 1968: **68**, 1296.
21. Probst, P., et al.: Left atrial size and atrial fibrillation in mitral stenosis: Factors influencing their relationship. Circulation 1973: **48**, 1282.
22. Spodick, D. H.: Arrhythmias during acute pericarditis: prospective study of 100 consecutive cases. J.A.M.A. 1976: **235**, 39.
23. Wellens, H. J., and Durrer, D.: Wolff-Parkinson-White syndrome and atrial fibrillation. Am. J. Cardiol. 1974: **34**, 777.
24. Zimmerman, T. L., et al.: Spontaneous return of sinus rhythm in older patients with chronic atrial fibrillation and rheumatic mitral valve disease. Am. Heart J. 1973: **86**, 676.

Review Tracings

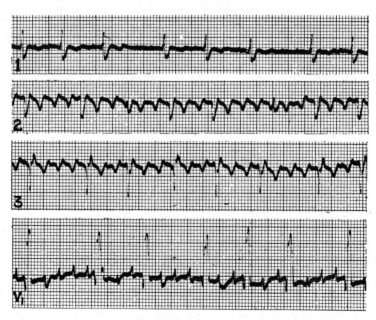

Review Tracing 14.1

For interpretation, see page 482

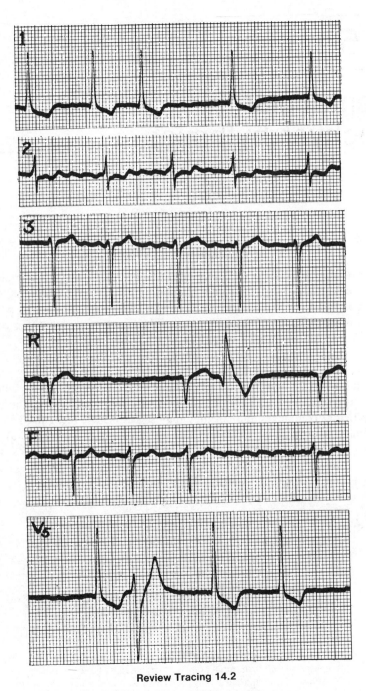

Review Tracing 14.2

For interpretation, see page 482

15

Ventricular Tachyarrhythmias

Ventricular Tachycardia

Ventricular tachycardia (VT) can result from rapid firing by a single focus (enhanced automaticity), or from a circulating wave front using a microscopic Purkinje circuit ("micro-reentry") or a wider sweep using fascicular pathways ("macro-reentry").[1, 2, 11, 74] By definition, VT consists of at least three consecutive, ectopic ventricular QRS complexes recurring at a rapid rate. They are usually regular, despite the widespread doctrine that irregularity helps to identify VT. One of the reasons for this popular belief is that so many examples of atrial fibrillation with Wolff-Parkinson-White (WPW) conduction have been mistakenly published as VT.[31] The P waves are frequently lost in the barrage of ventricular complexes, though they may sometimes be recognized as bumps or notches occurring at a slower rate in no constant relationship to the ventricular complexes (fig. 15.1A). Identification of unrelated P waves is one of the most sought after clues in recognizing VT; yet atrial independence by no means proves a ventricular origin—it just excludes an atrial origin.

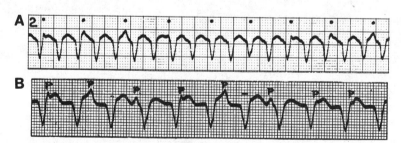

Figure 15.1. Ventricular tachycardia with independent atrial activity. (*A*) Ventricular rate 200/min; atrial activity is indicated by the superposed *dots*. (*B*) Relatively slow ventricular rate (120/min) with independent P waves at slower rate (92/min).

190

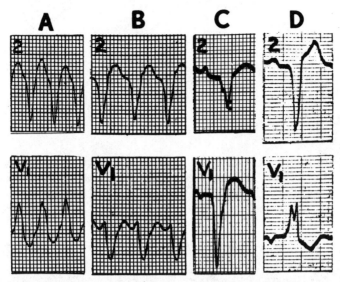

Figure 15.2. Leads 2 and V₁ in (A) LVT, (B) RVT, (C) LBBB and (D) RBBB. Note that lead 2 has a QS configuration in all four conditions and that V₁ contains far greater morphological contrast and therefore diagnostic thrust.

Diagnosis

The diagnosis of VT would be an easy task if it were not for close mimicry by supraventricular tachycardia (SVT) with abnormal intraventricular conduction (synonyms: ventricular aberration or aberrancy; aberrant ventricular conduction). For many years the diagnosis of VT hinged upon such features as independent atrial activity (A-V dissociation), irregularity of the tachyarrhythmia, and fusion beats; and often a single lead, even a lead 2, was regarded as adequate for the diagnosis. In recent years the frailty of these diagnostic props became evident, and there has been greater and greater emphasis on the details of QRS morphology in this important differentiation.[30, 44, 50, 63]

First of all, the inadequacy of a lead 2 can be easily appreciated when one finds that it may look so similar in both left ventricular tachycardia (LVT) and right ventricular tachycardia (RVT) and both left and right bundle-branch block. Figure 15.2 displays a lead 2 in each of these four conditions together with the corresponding V₁; in each case the QRS complex in lead 2 is of QS form, and the greater potential of V₁ for differentiating is immediately obvious. This is one of several reasons a right chest lead (e.g., MCL₁) is superior to lead 2 as a constant monitoring lead in intensive care units.

Second, independent atrial activity, although it rules out the diagnosis of atrial tachycardia and favors VT, does not establish a ventricular origin—it still may be a junctional tachycardia with ventricular aberration and independent atria (fig. 15.3). Because of the frequency of retrograde conduction in VT,[22, 60] it is possible to have either constantly related or independent P waves in VT; and it is also possible to have either with SVT and ventricular aberration.

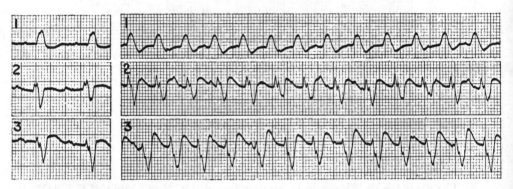

Figure 15.3. Junctional tachycardia with **LBBB** and independent atrial activity. Rhythm strips on right, with their wide QRS complexes and dissociated P waves, suggest ventricular tachycardia; but the identical complexes on the left during conducted sinus rhythm (with prolonged P-R interval) testify to a supraventricular tachycardia.

YOU CANNOT TELL A PACEMAKER BY THE COMPANY SHE DOESN'T KEEP

Third, the truth about irregularity is that all paroxysmal tachycardias, regardless of origin, tend to be as regular as clockwork; yet any of them can be irregular. Therefore, in any given case the presence or absence of regularity or irregularity is inconclusive. One of the chief reasons that VT gained the reputation for irregularity is that many examples of atrial fibrillation with WPW conduction have been mistaken for and published as VT.[31]

Fourth, fusion beats (fig. 15.4) are probably the most secure of the clues so far mentioned,[10] but even these show exceptions, as we have been aware since Kistin[23] demonstrated many years ago that aberrantly conducted junctional impulses could fuse with simultaneous sinus impulses. Thus, the presence of fusion is not conclusive evidence of ventricular ectopy.

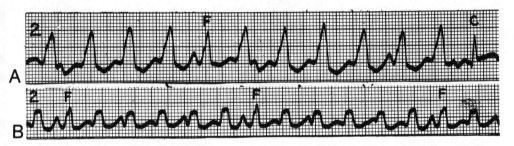

Figure 15.4. (A) **Ventricular tachycardia** (rate, 125) showing independent P waves (A-V dissociation) and capture (C) and fusion (F) beats. (B) **Ventricular tachycardia** (rate, 155) showing independent P waves and fusion (F) beats.

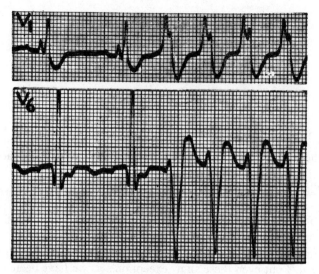

Figure 15.5. Sinus rhythm with **RBBB** interrupted by a run of **left ventricular tachycardia.** Note the "rabbit ears," with left taller than right in V_1, and rS pattern in V_6.

Morphologic Clues. Because of these inherent weaknesses, better clues were sought, and it soon became evident that subtle differences in the shape of the QRS complexes often afforded a reliable indication of their source. In LVT the QRS complex in V_1 is usually either a monophasic R wave or a diphasic qR and only occasionally has a triphasic rsR' pattern. Coronary care nurses[13] were the first to point to the paired peaks—which they soon dubbed "rabbit ears"—in many ectopic beats seen in a right chest lead, such as V_1 or MCL_1, and claim that when the left was taller than the right, it was good evidence for left ventricular (LV) ectopy (figs. 15.5 and 15.6). Note carefully that when the right "ear" is taller than the left, it does not necessarily indicate right bundle-branch block (RBBB) aberration—a misconception that is commonly heard; the truth is that when the right "ear" is taller, the pattern is now in the ball park of aberration, but it remains equally likely to be ectopic ventricular. The sole value of the "rabbit ears" is that when the left is the taller, the odds are heavily in favor of ectopy.

The pattern of LV ectopy most likely to be found in V_6 consists of an rS (present in about 70% of LV ectopy), with conspicuous absence of the normal initial q wave (figs. 15.5 and 15.6*A*). But the rS pattern can be imitated by a combination of RBBB plus left anterior hemiblock; and therefore the rS is not as diagnostic as one would like it to be. A much less common—occurring in about 20% of LV ectopy—but more diagnostic pattern is the QS complex in V_6 (15.6*B*). Notice that this QS pattern may be found complementng the R or

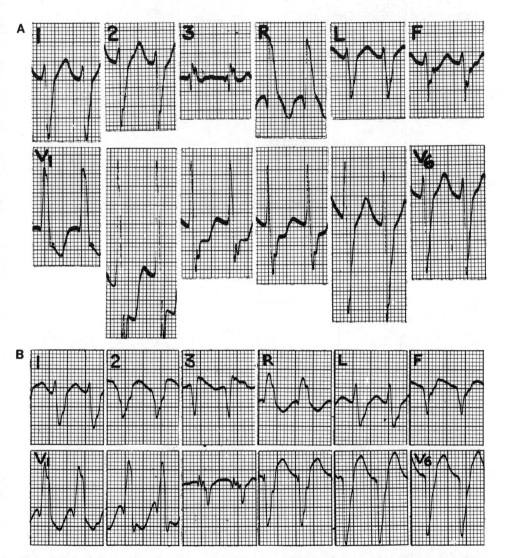

Figure 15.6. (A) **Left ventricular tachycardia** with axis ($-155°$) in no-man's-land, left rabbit ear taller than right in V_1, and rS in V_6. (B) **Left ventricular tachycardia** with axis in no-man's-land ($-135°$), taller left rabbit ear, and QS complex in V_6.

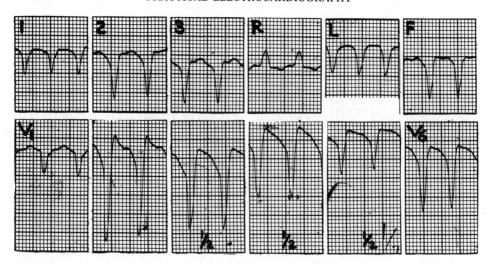

Figure 15.7. Right ventricular tachycardia with axis in no-man's-land and concordant negativity in chest leads.

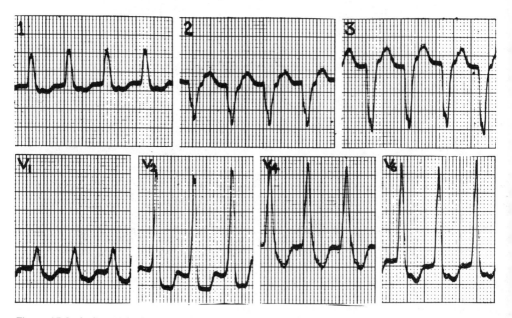

Figure 15.8. Left ventricular tachycardia with marked **left axis deviation**, concordant positivity in chest leads and 1:1 retrograde conduction to the atria—P' waves are seen just after the QRS in leads 1, 2, 3, and V₆.

qR of LV ectopy in V_1; or it may be part of the concordant negativity pattern of right ventricular (RV) ectopy (fig. 15.7).

"Concordance" of the precordial QRS complexes is another useful clue to ectopy: when all the ventricular complexes from V_1 to V_6 are either positive ("concordant positivity") or negative ("concordant negativity"), ventricular ectopy is strongly favored. Concordant positivity (fig. 15.8) indicates LV ectopy but may be mimicked by type A WPW conduction; if this can be excluded, LV ectopy is confirmed. Concordant negativity (fig. 15.7) indicates RV ectopy, and the only potential mimic is left bundle-branch block (LBBB) when leads have not been taken far enough to the left to obtain the usual left-sided monophasic R waves.

Another clue to RV ectopy forms part of the pattern popularized by Rosenbaum[42] more than a decade ago. He described a pattern of RV ectopy that was quite commonly found in healthy athletic youths who were victims of ectopy but had no other sign of heart disease. It consisted of the pattern of LBBB in V_6 but in company with two other features that are foreign to LBBB—right axis deviation (RAD) in the frontal plane and a "fat little r wave" in lead V_1 (fig. 15.9). When monitoring with a single right-sided lead, such as MCL_1, the

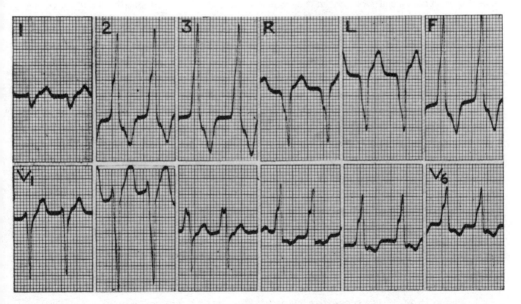

Figure 15.9. Right ventricular tachycardia with **LBBB** configuration in V_6, **right axis deviation** and fat initial r wave in V_1.

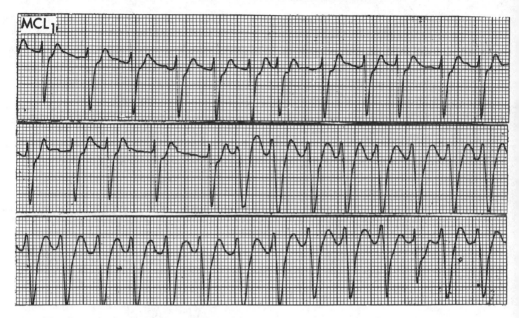

Figure 15.10. In *top strip* and first part of second, there is **atrial fibrillation** with **LBBB**. The abrupt development of a fat initial r wave in the sixth beat in the *second strip* with regularization of the ventricular rhythm signals the development of **right ventricular tachycardia**.

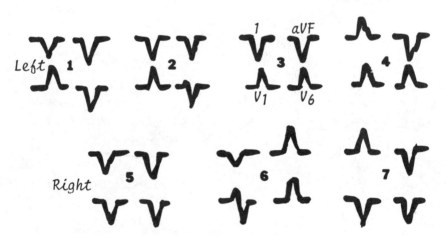

Figure 15.11. Seven **suggestive quartets**: (*1*) axis in no-man's-land, R or qR in V₁, QS in V₆; (*2*) axis in no-man's-land, R or qR in V₁, rS in V₆; (*3*) axis in no-man's-land, concordant positivity; (*4*) marked left axis deviation, concordant positivity; (*5*) axis in no-man's-land, concordant negativity; (*6*) right axis deviation, fat r in V₁, LBBB pattern in V₆; (*7*) marked left axis deviation, concordant negativity.

appearance of fat r waves is, by itself, good evidence in favor of ectopy (fig. 15.10).

A frontal plane axis in the right upper quadrant [between $-90°$ and $-180°$—"no-man's-land" (NML)] is very seldom found in conducted beats (exceptions: some complex congenital heart lesions, hearts with multiple infarctions, etc.) but is not infrequently found in ectopic ventricular rhythms arising from either right or left ventricle (figs. 15.6 and 15.7). Its presence, then, especially when found in conjunction with other suggestive clues, is good evidence in favor of ectopy.

The clues so far described can be gathered together to compile a table of "suggestive quartets" (fig. 15.11). Leads 1 and aVF indicate the axis, while leads V_1 and V_6 document the precordial pattern in right and left chest leads and concordance if it is present.

It is a rather sad comment on our powers of observation and deduction that for 20 years we have been seeing, without apparently registering the significance of, some of these highly diagnostic patterns in indisputably ectopic rhythms, viz., paced rhythms. Surely when one knows that a certain pattern of conduction is produced by pacing from a known ventricular site, it is a logical conclusion that when the same pattern is seen to occur spontaneously, it is likely also to be ectopic ventricular? Quartet number 3 in figure 15.11 is seen repeatedly in LV pacing, while quartet number 5 sometimes characterizes RV pacing.

All of the above clues owe their recognition to clinical observation and deduction and, until recently, had not been confirmed by acceptable scientific experimentation. But now Wellens[60] has compared the features of 70 instances of VT with 70 SVTs with aberrant conduction, later expanded to 100 of each,[63] the origin of all cases in each series being proven by intracardiac recordings. His findings are confirmatory of the following previously suspected features.

1. Irregularity is of little use in distinguishing VT from SVT. VT was completely regular in the majority (55 of 70); SVT, in a larger majority (65 of 70).

2. Fusion and/or capture beats are seldom seen and then only at the less rapid rates (under 160); they found them in only 4 of 33 sustained VTs.

3. Independent atrial activity (A-V dissociation) favors VT; it was present in 32 of the 70 and was not found in any of the SVTs with aberrant conduction.

4. But *absence* of A-V dissociation is not much in favor of SVT since half of the VTs manifested retrograde conduction (cf. fig. 15.8).

The morphological clues and their diagnostic value, as determined in Wellens' studies,[60, 62, 63] are summarized in table 15.1.

The figures in table 15.1 indicate the number of times the specified pattern was encountered, and of that total how many turned out to be ectopic or aberrant. Take, for example, a QR pattern in V_1: the table tells us that they found it 17 times, 16 of which were indeed ectopic. The reason a superior axis and a wide (>0.14 sec) QRS are unhelpful unless the conduction pattern before the tachycardia developed is known is because, in the presence of *preexisting* BBB, SVT is frequently associated with significant left axis deviation and/or a QRS wider than 0.14 sec.

Other Diagnostic Clues. Another pattern almost diagnostic of VT is shown in figures 15.4 and 15.12 where a suspected VT is punctuated by an occasional fusion (Dressler) beat.[10] These are sometimes to be seen when the ventricular rate is relatively slow and indicate that an impulse from the independently beating atria, happening to arrive at an opportune moment, has been partially conducted. To fulfill the necessary criteria, such beats must be on time or slightly early, never late.

Another useful pointer to VT is the presence of early ventricular capture beats that show a more normal QRS contour than the wide beats of the tachycardia (fig. 15.12). Since the capture beat ends a cycle slightly shorter than the cycles ending with the wider beats, it indicates that the wider beats are probably ectopic ventricular. Because, of all the beats, the *most likely* to be aberrant is the beat that ends the shortest cycle. Since this beat is not aberrant, the wide beats are even less likely to be and are therefore wide and bizarre because of ventricular ectopy rather than aberration.

Left versus Right Ventricular Tachycardia. It is widely accepted that one can distinguish between ectopic beats arising in each ventricle by observing the shape of the ventricular complex in lead V_1; and in general this is certainly

Table 15.1
Diagnosis of Ventricular Tachycardia

		Favoring Ectopy			Favoring Aberration	
V_1	Single peak	⋀	15/15	rSR', rsR'	⋀⋀	38/41
	Taller left rabbit ear	⋀	7/7	M-shaped	⋀	19/22
	QR	⋁	16/17			
	RS	⋀⋁	4/4			
V_6	rS	⋁	27/31	qRs	⋀	44/47
	QS	⋁	17/17			
	QR	⋁	8/8			
	Axis −30° to −180°[a]		68/75			
	QRS interval >0.14 sec[a]		59/59			

[a] Of little use if previous tracing not available.

Table 15.2
QRS Morphology/Site of Origin

V₁	LV	RV
$\bigwedge$	22/22	0/22
$\bigvee$	17/17 (sick)	3/3 (well)

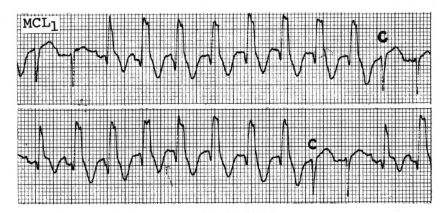

Figure 15.12. Left ventricular tachycardia. The capture beats (c) end cycles that are slightly shorter than the ectopic cycles. Note also: each run of ectopic rhythm begins with a fusion beat and the left "rabbit ear" is taller than the right.

true. However, there are exceptions to every good rule and morphological guidelines are not exempt. Although V₁ is much the best lead for distinguishing between left and right ventricular ectopy, it is not completely reliable in all circumstances. In a series of 39 proven VTs,[17] all of the wide, positive QRS complexes in V₁ were indeed left ventricular; but the wide negative complexes (LBBB pattern) were a different matter (table 15.2). Their origin seemed to vary with the condition of the heart: in normal hearts they represented right ventricular ectopy, but in ischemic hearts the pattern indicated an origin in or near the left septal surface. This LBBB pattern in *left* ventricular rhythms (suggesting a *right* ventricular origin) is attributed to "preferential transseptal activation"[68] resulting in earlier activation of the right ventricle than the left.

Useful as 12-lead QRS morphology is, in the presence of myocardial disease it apparently cannot be relied upon to localize with precision the origin of an ectopic mechanism[68, 73]; this is because the clinical tracing reflects the site of *epi*cardial "breakthrough" which may be many centimeters removed from the *endo*cardial origin of the ectopic impulse.

Nevertheless, the LBBB morphology is of interest and value in another context. In an ongoing study in the Pee Dee area of South Carolina,[37] among over a thousand consecutive patients with acute myocardial infarction, those who have shown *only* the LBBB morphology (usually associated with a right ventricular origin) have never developed ventricular fibrillation and seldom VT; thus, even if they are not in fact right ventricular, they appear to be conspicuously benign.

Varieties of Ventricular Tachycardia

During the past few years, several epithets have been introduced to describe characteristics of VT. It sometimes occurs in short repeated bursts, separated by one or two sinus beats (fig. 15.13), and then is known as **repetitive tachycardia.**[48]

In the term **chronic recurrent ventricular tachycardia**, the meaning of "recurrent" is self-evident, though the distinction from "repetitive" is unclear. At least 3 or 4 discrete, documented episodes are required,[9, 15] and, when "chronic" is added, it is understood that the paroxysms recur over a prolonged period, usually of years, though as little as 1 month is sometimes accepted.[9] Others may require as few as two episodes, but spaced at least a month apart.[39]

It has also become customary to qualify the paroxysms arbitrarily as "sustained" or "nonsustained," depending upon the duration of the individual bursts of tachycardia. The "sustained" variety, usually lasting minutes or hours or days, must last at least longer than 1 min, or require cardioversion before the minute has elapsed.[53] "Nonsustained" is variably defined as lasting less than 10 beats,[15] or less than 60 sec,[53] and ending spontaneously. Frequent isolated VPBs are commonly found between paroxysms.

In patients with chronic recurrent VT, there seem to be striking differences in incidence and prognosis between a RV and LV origin:[39] subjects with LVT tend to be older, male and with diagnosable heart disease; whereas those with RVT tend to be younger, female and without diagnosable heart disease. The

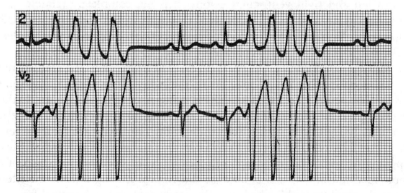

Figure 15.13. Short 4-beat bursts of **ventricular tachycardia.**

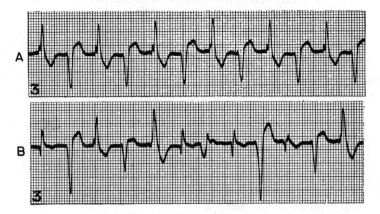

Figure 15.14. Two serious forms of ventricular tachycardia, often presaging ventricular fibrillation. (*A*) **Bidirectional ventricular tachycardia.** (*B*) **Multifocal ventricular tachycardia** (sometimes called **chaotic heart action**).

mechanism of chronic recurrent VT is widely believed to be reentry.[15, 16, 58, 59] However, this is far from certain and Mason[32] gloomily summarizes the status of chronic recurrent VT by reaffirming that the underlying mechanisms are unknown and probably varied. He reiterates the three possibilities, micro-reentry, macro-reentry and automaticity—"with many subdivisions"—and concludes: "Our ignorance is extensive and the result is a disappointing failure to correct or control the arrhythmia in too many patients."

Exercise-induced ventricular tachycardia is almost always provoked by only moderate exertion; it may also be brought on by emotional excitement, upright posture and smoking. It oftens originates in the outflow tract of the right ventricle,[54, 65] and takes the form of rapid, repeated bursts separated by a few sinus beats and perhaps an isolated ventricular extrasystole or two showing the same morphology as the beats of the tachycardia. Its behavior suggests that it arises from a catecholamine-sensitive automatic focus.[65]

The implications of exercise-induced VT are not so grave as they were once thought—the arrhythmia occurs not infrequently in subjects with normal hearts. In one series of 26 people, with exercise-provoked VT, to be sure 16 had ischemic heart disease and 2 had a cardiomyopathy, but the remaining 8 had no evidence of heart disease.[34]

In **bidirectional** tachycardia (fig. 15.14*A*), the wide ventricular complexes alternate in polarity; in **alternating** tachycardia, they merely alternate in amplitude. These two brands are not distinctly separable—often the contour is bidirectional in one lead and alternating in another. The pattern is, however, foreboding and often associated with digitalis toxicity. The mechanisms of these tachycardias are uncertain: some are truly ventricular[6, 7] while others may represent a SVT with RBBB and alternating hemiblock.[7]

Etiology

It is universally known that ventricular extrasystoles can trigger VT. It is much less widely appreciated that single APBs can initiate ventricular ectopic activity, including VT, both in the ischemic and the healthy heart.[35, 61, 66] Figure 15.15 presents two examples of VT precipitated by shortening of the supraventricular cycle.

VT usually affects subjects with organic heart disease, but may on occasion be found in the otherwise normal heart. Lesch was able to collect 34 such cases in 1967[28] and more recently 6 of a series of 17 young patients with VT had no evidence of heart disease.[38] VT may complicate rheumatic disease and was found in 6% of patients with mitral valve prolapse[51]; in some such patients it may assume a "malignant" form.[56]

When VT (or ventricular fibrillation) is found in youth, it is usually associated with one of the following disorders: mitral valve prolapse, cardiomyopathy, myocarditis, hypokalemia (sometimes produced by an energetic slimming program including diuretics), or a long Q-T syndrome.

VT may complicate drug therapy, notably with digitalis, quinidine, procainamide, isopyramide, sympathetic amines and various anesthetics. It may complicate the prolonged QT syndromes and metabolic and electrolyte disorders.

Obviously VT is a major complication of ischemic heart disease, especially with myocardial infarction or cardiac aneurysm. When VT develops within the first 24 hours of acute myocardial infarction, it is probably due to enhanced automaticity[58]; later in the course it is more likely mediated by reentry. In acute myocardial infarction, VT may be precipitated by early ventricular extrasystoles (R-on-T), late extrasystoles and even by *atrial* premature beats.[66] It now seems clear that most VT is precipitated by late beats: of 68 instances, Rothfeld[43]

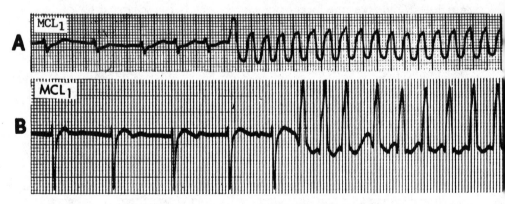

Figure 15.15. Ventricular tachycardia evoked by shortening of the cycle of the supraventricular rhythm. (*A*) In the presence of atrial fibrillation, there is progressive shortening of the conducted cycles until an R-on-T left ventricular extrasystole is provoked. (*B*) An accelerated junctional rhythm is dissociated from the sinus rhythm; the fifth beat, ending a shorter cycle, is a ventricular capture. In this patient, capture beats such as this repeatedly precipitated runs of ventricular tachycardia.

found that 17 (25%) resulted from "R-on-T" beats; 46 (68%) from late extra-systoles; and 5 (7%) from atrial premature beats. And again, in Holtered ambulatory subjects, only 14 of 94 episodes of VT were precipitated by R-on-T extrasystoles.[64]

Other Tachyarrhythmias

Ventricular flutter is the term given by some authorities to a rapid VT giving a modified pattern in the ECG—a regular zigzag—without clearly formed QRS complexes (fig. 15.17*B* and *C*). Little is gained in separating it from VT.

Torsades de pointes (twistings of the points): This special form of ventricular tachyarrhythmia with its "tantalizingly euphonious" French name[24] is uncertain of its place in the taxonomy of dysrhythmias. It is often regarded as an intermediary between VT and ventricular fibrillation, and its mechanism is probably a form of reentry,[14] but its exact nature remains to be elucidated.[47] At times it may be due to bifocal ectopic ventricular activity in mutual competition.[67]

Morphologically, it is characterized by wide QRS complexes whose apices, as its elegant name implies, are sometimes positive and sometimes negative—the points swing back and forth above and below the baseline which originally earned it the simple English sobriquet "the swinging pattern" (fig. 15.16). Now it has gathered a number of ponderous titles including atypical,[4] polymorphous[49] and multiform VT—not to be confused with the chaotic or multifocal type illustrated in figure 15.14*B*. Since morphologically similar tachyarrhythmias may be associated with either prolonged or normal Q-T intervals, and since the distinction has vital therapeutic implications, some authors insist that the term "torsade" be restricted to those polymorphous tachycardias associated with Q-T prolongation.[71]

It is caused by anything that produces or is associated with a prolonged Q-T interval, including drugs (quinidine,[40] procainamide,[49, 71] disopyramide,[36, 55] aprindine,[70] phenothiazines, etc), electrolyte disturbances, insecticide poisoning,[69] subarachnoid hemorrhage[4] and congenital Q-T prolongation. It often develops against a background of bradycardia, especially when due to A-V block[72]; and it has a well established association with Prinzmetal's angina.[27]

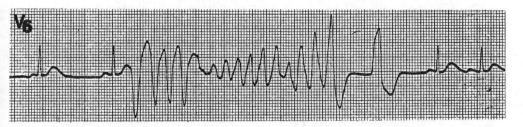

Figure 15.16. Torsades de pointes initiated by an R-on-T ventricular extrasystole.

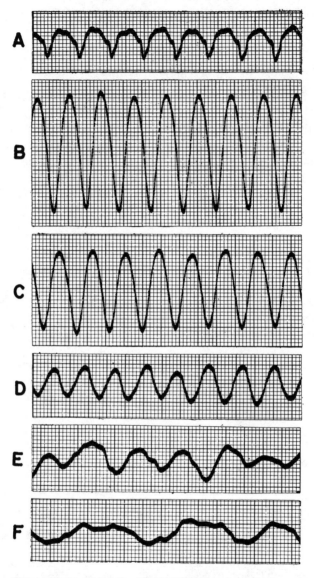

Figure 15.17. The dying heart. Strips from lead 2 taken approximately 1 min apart and illustrating the transitions from ventricular tachycardia through flutter to fibrillation. (*A*) **Ventricular tachycardia.** (*B* and *C*) **Ventricular flutter.** (*D*) Intermediate stage between flutter and fibrillation. (*E* and *F*) **Ventricular fibrillation.**

But its great clinical importance lies in the fact that the usual antiarrhythmic drugs are not only useless but contraindicated since, as causative agents, they make matters worse.

Ventricular fibrillation is usually a terminal, or at a least a catastrophic event; rarely, transient bouts may be responsible for Adams-Stokes attacks. It is easily recognized by the complete absence of properly formed ventricular complexes—the baseline wavers unevenly with no attempt at forming clearcut QRS deflections (fig. 15.17*E* and *F*).

References

1. Akhtar, M., et al: Demonstration of re-entry within the His-Purkinje system in man. Circulation 1974: **50**, 1150.
2. Akhtar, M., et al.: Re-entry within the His-Purkinje system; elucidation of re-entrant circuit using right bundle-branch and His bundle recordings. Circulation 1978: **58**: 295.
3. Atkins, J. M., et al.: Incidence of arrhythmias induced by isometric and dynamic exercise. Br. Heart J. 1976: **38**, 465.
4. Carruth, J. E., and Silverman, M. E.: Torsade de pointes; atypical ventricular tachycardia complicating subarachnoid hemorrhage. Chest 1980: **78**, 886.
5. Cohen, H. C., et al.: Ventricular tachycardia with narrow QRS complexes (left posterior fascicular tachycardia). Circulation 1972: **45**, 1035.
6. Cohen, S. I., et al.: Infra-His bundle origin of bidirectional tachycardia. Circulation 1973: **47**, 1260.
7. Cohen, S. I., and Voukydis, P.: Supraventricular origin of bidirectional tachycardia. Circulation 1974: **50**, 634.
8. Cohn, L. J., et al.: Ventricular tachycardia. Progr. Cardiovasc. Dis. 1966: **9**, 29.
9. Denes, P., et al.: Electrophysiological studies in patients with chronic recurrent ventricular tachycardia. Circulation 1976: **54**, 229.
10. Dressler, W., and Roesler, H.: The occurrence in paroxysmal ventricular tachycardia of ventricular complexes transitional in shape to sinoauricular beats. Am. Heart. J. 1952: **44**, 485.
11. Foster, J. R., and Simpson, R. J.: Initiation of ventricular tachycardia by reentry within the bundle branches. Am. J. Cardiol. 1980: **45**, 895.
12. Goolsby, J. P., and Oliva, P. B.: Electrographic and clinical observations of a recurrent tachyarrhythymia arising from a pacemaker within the distribution of the anterior fascicle. Am. Heart J.: 1974: **88**, 351.
13. Gozensky, C., and Thorne, D.: Rabbit ears; an aid in distinguishing ventricular ectopy from aberration. Heart Lung 1974: **3**, 634
14. Horowitz, L. N.: Torsades de pointes; electrophysiologic studies in patients with transient pharmacologic or metabolic abnormalities. Circulation 1981: **63**, 1120.
15. Josephson, M. E., et al.: Recurrent sustained ventricular tachycardia; 1. Mechanisms. Circulation 1978: **57**, 431.
16. Josephson, M. E., and Seides, S. F.: *Clinical Cardiac Electrophysiology: Techniques and Interpretations.* Lea & Febiger, Philadelphia, 1979.
17. Josephson, M. E., et al.: Sustained ventricular tachycardia: role of the 12-lead electrocardiogram in localizing site of origin. Circulation 1981: **64**, 273.
18. Kastor, J. A., and Goldreyer, B. N.: Ventricular origin of bidirectional tachycardia. Case report of a patient not toxic from digitalis. Circulation 1973: **48**, 897.
19. Keren, A., et al.: Ventricular pacing in atypical ventricular tachycardia. J. Electrocardiol. 1981: **14**, 201.
20. Keren, A., et al.: Etiology, warning signs and therapy of torsade de pointes: A study of 10 patients. Circulation 1981: **64**, 1167.
21. Kistin, A., and Landowne, M.: Retrograde conduction from premature ventricular contractions, a common occurrence in the human heart. Circulation 1951: **3**, 738.

22. Kistin, A. D.: Retrograde conduction to the atria in ventricular tachycardia. Circulation 1961: **24,** 236.
23. Kistin, A. D.: Problems in the differentiation of ventricular arrhythmia from supraventricular arrhythmia with abnormal QRS. Prog. Cardiovasc. Dis. 1966: **9,** 1.
24. Kossmann, C. E.: Torsade de pointes; an addition to the nosography of ventricular tachycardia. Am. J. Cardiol. 1978: **42,** 1054.
25. Koster, R. W., and Wellens, H. J. J.: Quinidine-induced ventricular flutter and fibrillation without digitalis therapy. Am. J. Cardiol. 1976: **38,** 519.
26. Kotler, M. N., et al.: Prognostic significance of ventricular ectopic beats with respect to sudden death in the late postinfarction period. Circulation 1973: **47,** 959.
27. Krikler, D. M., and Curry, P. V. L.: Torsade de pointes, an atypical ventricular tachycardia. Br. Heart J. 1976: **38,** 117.
28. Lesch, M., et al.: Paroxysmal ventricular tachycardia in the absence of organic heart disease; report of a case and review of the literature. Ann. Intern Med. 1967: **66,** 950.
29. Lie, K. I., et al.: Observations on patients with primary ventricular fibrillation complicating acute myocardial infarction. Circulation 1975: **52,** 755.
30. Marriott, H. J. L.: Differential diagnosis of supraventricular and ventricular tachycardia. Geriatrics 1970: **25,** 91.
31. Marriott, H. J. L., and Rogers, H. M.: Mimics of ventricular tachycardia associated with the W-P-W syndrome. J. Electrocardiol. 1969: **2,** 77.
32. Mason, J. W., et al.: Mechanisms of ventricular tachycardia; wide, complex ignorance. Am. Heart J. 1981: **102,** 1083.
33. Meltzer, R. S., et al.: Atypical ventricular tachycardia as a manifestation of disopyramide toxicity. Am. J. Cardiol. 1978: **42,** 1049.
34. Mokotoff, D. M.: Exercise-induced ventricular tachycardia: clinical features, relation to chronic ventricular ectopy, and prognosis. Chest 1980: **77,** 10.
35. Myerburg, R. J., et al.: Ventricular ectopic activity after premature atrial beats in acute myocardial infarction. Br. Heart J. 1977: **39,** 1033.
36. Nicholson, W. J., et al.: Disopyramide-induced ventricular fibrillation. Am. J. Cardiol. 1979: **43,** 1053.
37. O'Bryan, C.: Personal communication, 1981.
38. Pedersen, D. H., et al.: Ventricular tachycardia and ventricular fibrillation in a young population. Circulation 1979: **60,** 988.
39. Pietras, R. J., et al.: Chronic recurrent right and left ventricular tachycardia; comparison of clinical, hemodynamic and angiographic findings. Am. J. Cardiol. 1977: **40,** 32.
40. Reynolds, E. W., and Vander Ark, C. R.: Quinidine syncope and the delayed repolarization syndromes. Mod. Concepts Cardiovasc. Dis. 1976: **45,** 117.
41. Rocchini, A. P.: Ventricular tachycardia in children. Am. J. Cardiol. 1981: **47,** 1091.
42. Rosenbaum, M. B.: Classification of ventricular extrasystoles according to form. J. Electrocardiol. 1969: **2,** 289.
43. Rothfeld, E. L., et al.: Harbingers of paroxysmal ventricular tachycardia in acute myocardial infarction. Chest 1977: **71,** 142.
44. Sandler, I. A., and Marriott, H. J. L.: The differential morphology of anomalous ventricular complexes of RBBB-type in V₁; ventricular ectopy versus aberration. Circulation 1965: **31,** 551.
45. Sclarovsky, S., et al.: Polymorphous ventricular tachycardia; clinical features and treatment. Am. J. Cardiol. 1979: **44,** 339.
46. Smirk, F. H., and Palmer, D. G.: A myocardial syndrome, with particular reference to the occurrence of sudden death and of premature systoles interrupting antecedent T waves. Am. J. Cardiol. 1960: **6,** 620.
47. Smith, W. M., and Gallagher, J. J.: "Les torsades de pointes": An unusual ventricular arrhythmia. Ann. Intern. Med. 1980: **93,** 578.
48. Stock, J. P. P.: Repetitive paroxysmal ventricular tachycardia. Br. Heart J. 1962: **24,** 297.
49. Strasberg, B., et al.: Procainamide-induced polymorphous ventricular tachycardia. Am. J. Cardiol. 1981: **47,** 1309.
50. Swanick, E. J., et al.: Morphologic features of right ventricular ectopic beats. Am. J. Cardiol. 1972: **30,** 888.
51. Swartz, M. H., et al.: Mitral valve prolapse: A review of associated arrhythmias. Am. J. Med. 1977: **62,** 377.
52. Talbot, S., and Greaves, M.: Association of ventricular extrasystoles and ventricular tachycardia with idioventricular rhythm. Br. Heart J. 1976: **38,** 457.

53. Vandepol, C. J., et al.: Incidence and clinical significance of induced ventricular tachycardia. Am. J. Cardiol. 1980: **45**, 725.
54. Vetter, V. L., et al.: Idiopathic recurrent sustained ventricular tachycardia in children and adolescents. Am. J. Cardiol. 1981: **47**, 315.
55. Wald, R. W., et al.: Torsades de pointes tachycardia; a complication of disopyramide shared with quinidine. J. Electrocardiol. 1981: **14**, 301.
56. Wei, J. Y., et al.: Mitral-valve prolapse syndrome and recurrent ventricular tachyarrhythmias: A malignant variant refractory to conventional drug therapy. Ann. Intern Med. 1978: **89**, 6.
57. Wellens, H. J., et al.: Electrical stimulation of the heart in patients with ventricular tachycardia. Circulation 1972: **46**, 216.
58. Wellens, H. J. J.: Pathophysiology of ventricular tachycardia in man. Arch. Intern. Med. 1975: **135**, 473.
59. Wellens, H. J. J., et al.: Observations on mechanisms of ventricular tachycardia in man. Circulation 1976: **54**, 237.
60. Wellens, H. J. J., et al.: The valve of the electrocardiogram in the differential diagnosis of a tachycardia with a widened QRS complex. Am J. Med. 1978: **64**, 27.
61. Wellens, H. J. J., et al.: Initiation and termination of ventricular tachycardia by supraventricular stimuli: Incidence and electrophysiologic determinants as observed during programmed stimulation of the heart. Am. J. Cardiol. 1980: **46**, 576.
62. Wellens, H. J. J.: Personal communication, 1981.
63. Wellens, H. J. J., et al.: Medical treatment of ventricular tachycardia, consideration in the selection of patients for surgical treatment. Am. J. Cardiol. 1982: **49**, 186.
64. Winkle, R. A., et al.: Characteristics of ventricular tachycardia in ambulatory patients. Am. J. Cardiol. 1977: **39**, 487.
65. Wu, D., et al.: Exercise-triggered paroxysmal ventricular tachycardia: A repetitive rhythmic activity possibly related to afterdepolarization. Ann. Intern Med. 1981: **95**, 410.
66. Zipes, D. P., et al.: Atrial induction of ventricular tachycardia; reentry versus triggered automaticity. Am. J. Cardiol. 1979: **44**, 1.
67. D'Alnoncourt, C. N., et al.: "Torsade de pointes" tachycardia: Re-entry or focal activity? Br. Heart J. 1982: **48**, 213.
68. Josephson, M. E., et al.: Relation between site of origin and QRS configuration in ventricular rhythms, p. 200. In *What's New in Electrocardiography*, edited by H. J. J. Wellens and H. E. Kulbertus. Martinus Nijhoff, Boston, 1981.
69. Ludomirsky, A., et al.: Q-T prolongation and polymorphous ("torsade de pointes") ventricular arrhythmias associated with organic insecticide poisoning. Am. J. Cardiol. 1982; **49**, 1655.
70. Scagliotti, D., et al.: Aprinidine-induced polymorphous ventricular tachycardia. Am. J. Cardiol. 1982: **49**, 1297.
71. Soffer, J., et al.: Polymorphous ventricular tachycardia associated with normal and long Q-T intervals. Am. J. Cardiol. 1982: **49**, 2021.
72. Taboul, P.: Torsade de pointes, p. 229. In *What's New in Electrocardiography*, edited by H. J. J. Wellens and H. E. Kulbertus. Martinus Nijhoff, Boston, 1981.
73. Waxman, H. L., and Josephson, M. E.: Ventricular activation during ventricular endocardial pacing. I. Electrocardiographic patterns related to the site of pacing. Am. J. Cardiol. 1982: **50**, 1.
74. Welch, W. J., et al.: Sustained macroreentrant ventricular tachycardia. Am. Heart J. 1982: **104**, 166.

Review Tracings

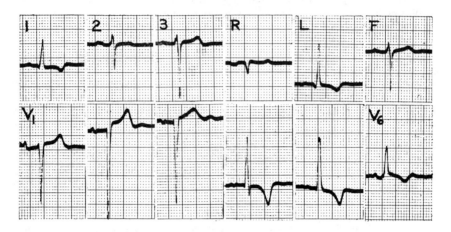

Review Tracing 15.1

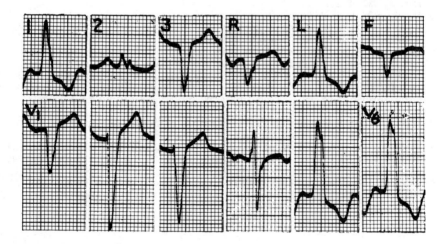

Review Tracing 15.2

For interpretation, see page 482

16

Aberrant Ventricular Conduction and the Diagnosis of Tachycardia

Things are seldom what they seem,
Skim milk masquerades as cream—*Gilbert*

Aberrant ventricular conduction (ventricular aberration or aberrancy) is the temporary, abnormal intraventricular conduction of supraventricular impulses, usually due to a change in cycle length. Its importance rests firmly on two facts: (1) it is common—much more common than many realize and (2) it is often overlooked with the result that supraventricular arrhythmias are frequently misdiagnosed as ventricular and treated as such.

Aberration, then, is not a rare curiosity that can be left for the experts in arrhythmias to worry with. Almost all physicians are occasionally called upon to diagnose and treat paroxysmal tachycardia and atrial fibrillation; and they should, therefore, know the fundamental differentiation between supraventricular and ventricular tachycardias. The dilemma arises in those tachycardias with widened, bizarre QRS complexes, which therefore raise the specter of ventricular tachycardia.

Type A Aberration

The Circumstances

When any responsive tissue reacts to a stimulus, the reaction is followed by a dormant interval, the refractory period, during which it cannot respond to a similar stimulus. This period of rest is necessary for the tissue to recoup its spent forces and return to a state in which it can again react normally to the stimulus. Naturally, any such period has a finite, measurable duration; and if the tissue is asked to respond during its refractory period, the response will be absent or at least subnormal. Characteristics of the refractory period differ with

211

different tissues; e.g., in the heart, the bundle branches usually respond with an "all-or-none" response (i.e., if they respond at all, they respond fully and normally), whereas the A-V node over a relatively long period shows a gradual rather than an abrupt improvement in conduction.

The refractory period of the conducting paths is proportional to the length of the preceding cycle (R-R interval); i.e., the longer the cycle and slower the rate, the longer the ensuing refractory period, and vice versa. Ventricular aberration can therefore result either from shortening of the immediate cycle or from lengthening of the preceding one, or from a combination of both (fig. 16.1).

There are three forms of aberration (table 16.1). The common form is due to fascicular refractoriness (type A). To produce aberration of this type, the obvious ploy is to get an impulse to arrive at the ventricular fascicle before it has recovered from its last activation, i.e., while it is still in its refractory period. Clearly, the simplest way to achieve this is either to have a supraventricular premature beat or to accelerate the sinus rhythm. Figure 16.2 illustrates right bundle-branch block (RBBB) aberration of atrial premature beats—the early impulses have taken the right bundle branch (RBB) "by surprise" (while it is still refractory), and it has been unable to respond and conduct.

RBBB aberration is much more common than left bundle-branch block (LBBB) aberration; in fact it is claimed that 80 to 85% of all aberration is of RBBB type.[7, 26] In a relatively sick population, as in a coronary care facility, LBBB aberration assumes greater prominence and accounts for perhaps a third of the aberrant conduction encountered. And in Kulbertus,[10] experimental

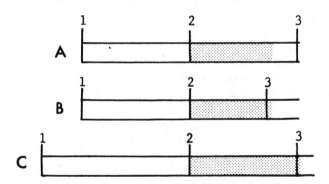

Figure 16.1. In the diagrams, *1, 2,* and *3* are consecutive beats and the *stippled area* represents the refractory period of some part of the conducting system during the second cycle. In *A,* there are two regular cycles with normal conduction. Beat 3 may become aberrant (*lower two diagrams*) if either the first cycle is lengthened or the second cycle is shortened. Shortening of the second cycle (*B*) may bring the beat within the refractory period of part of the conducting system; lengthening of the preceding cycle (*C*) will prolong the refractory period so that the next beat, though no earlier than before, falls within the now longer refractory period.

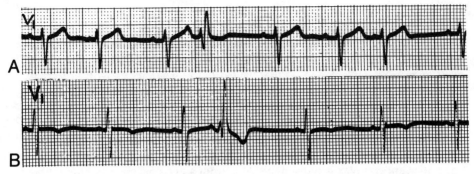

Figure 16.2. In both *A* and *B*, after three normally conducted beats, an **atrial extrasystole** arises, and its impulse arrives at the RBB while it is still refractory; it is therefore conducted with **RBBB aberration.** In *A*, the second and seventh beats are also extrasystoles, but they are less premature and are therefore conducted normally.

Table 16.1
Forms of Ventricular Aberration

Type A	Fascicular refractoriness
Type B	Anomalous supraventricular activation
Type C	Paradoxical critical rate

Table 16.2
Patterns of Induced Aberration[10]

RBBB alone	28	i.e.:
RBBB + LAHB	21	RBBB = 53%
RBBB + LPHB	12	LAHB = 32%
LAHB alone	17	LPHB = 19%
LPHB alone	10	LBBB = 15%
LBBB	10	Uncl = 10%
ILBBB	6	
Unclassified	12	
	116	

study, RBBB accounted for a smaller than expected proportion of the aberrancy produced experimentally. By inducing premature atrial beats in 44 patients, he was able to produce 116 different aberrant configurations (table 16.2), of which RBBB accounted for only 53%.

The Specifics

The first example of ventricular aberration to be published—by Lewis in 1910—showed atrial bigeminy with alternating patterns of aberration. A similar situation is shown in figure 16.3 where the atrial bigeminy is alternately complicated by RBBB and LBBB aberration. Additional points to notice in this tracing are (1) that the increased height of the R wave in lead 1 and the depth of the S wave in V_6 in the RBBB beats presumably indicate an associated left anterior hemiblock and (2) that the earliest indication of RBBB in V_1 may take the form of slurring or notching of the upstroke of the QRS (in fig. 16.3, see first atrial extrasystole in V_1).

The prime importance of aberration is in its mimicry of ventricular ectopy. It is in itself a secondary phenomenon—always the result of some primary disturbance—and never itself requires treatment. At times the morphology of the aberrant complex is indistinguishable from an ectopic pattern; but at other times the aberrant shapes provide broad hints of their supraventricular origin. In the tachyarrhythmias, the most important differentiation is from ventricular tachycardia, though isolated or paired aberrant beats may at times have to be differentiated from ventricular extrasystoles.

The first principle in the diagnosis of aberrancy is: do not diagnose it unless there is *positive* evidence in favor of it. Ectopy is much more common than aberration and, when you hear hoofbeats in this Western World, you do not think first of a zebra: you consider the zebra only if you see its stripes. The positive features in favor of aberration may therefore be called the "stripes" of aberration, and these are listed in table 16.3.

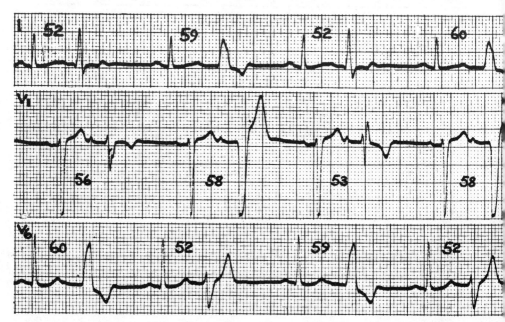

Figure 16.3. Atrial bigeminy with **alternating aberration.** The shorter extrasystolic cycles end with some form of RBBB aberration, whereas the longer cycles end in LBBB aberration. The beats with RBBB, as evidenced by the slightly increased height of the R wave in lead 1 and the rS pattern in V_6, also show **left anterior hemiblock.** In V_1, the first atrial premature beat shows only the earliest sign of RBBB, i.e., notching of the terminal upstroke.

Table 16.3
The "Stripes" of Aberration

1. Triphasic contours
    a. rsR′ variant in V_1
    b. qRs variant in V_6
2. Preceding atrial activity
3. Initial deflection identical with that of conducted beats (if RBBB)
4. Second-in-the-row anomalous beat
5. Alternating BBB patterns separated by single normally conducted beat

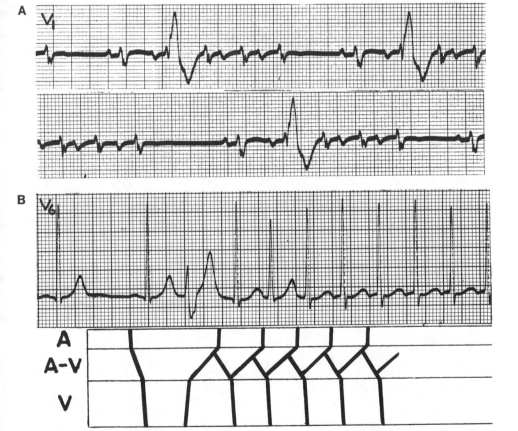

Figure 16.4. (*A*) The strips are continuous. Three short bursts of **supraventricular tachycardia** in which only the first beat (second in the row) develops **ventricular aberration**. (*B*) Here the second in the row of rapid beats is probably a **ventricular extrasystole** initiating a run of reciprocating tachycardia in the A-V junction (see laddergram).

The first four "stripes" are observable in figure 16.4*A* in which the two continuous strips contain three clusters of rapid beats. In each cluster, the second beat alone presents a bizarre appearance, it has a triphasic (rsR′) RBBB pattern, its initial deflection is identical with that of the conducted sinus beats, and it is preceded by a premature ectopic P′ wave. All of these points clinch the recognition of aberration, and we will take each of them up in turn.

Triphasic V_1/V_6 Morphology. The shape of the QRS complex is virtually diagnostic of aberrancy in many cases; the triphasic contours (rsR′ in V_1 and qRs in V_6) favor the diagnosis of aberration with odds of about 10:1. Figure 16.5*A* illustrates a junctional tachycardia—due to digitalis intoxication—with RBBB aberration; the rSR′ pattern is virtually diagnostic of the supraventricular origin of the tachycardia.

On the other hand, figure 16.5*B* presents a pattern in V_1 which is nondiagnostic: it could be a left ventricular tachycardia, or it could be supraventricular with RBBB aberration. But V_6, with its little q wave, tall thin R wave, and terminal s wave, is excellent evidence of its supraventricular origin. This patient also turned out to have a junctional tachycardia.

Figure 16.6 presents an example in which the characteristic morphology is seen in *both* right and left chest leads. The *top strip* shows the narrow complexes of a supraventricular tachycardia in lead MCL₁, with which the patient was admitted. The second strip shows the development of atrial fibrillation during which a lengthened cycle precipitates aberrancy in the following beat ending a

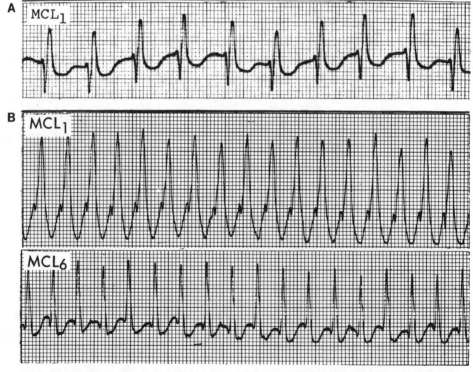

Figure 16.5. (*A*) A tachycardia diagnosable as presumably supraventricular from the triphasic (rSR′) pattern in a right chest lead (MCL₁). (*B*) A tachycardia not identifiable as supraventricular from the right chest lead but readily recognized in a left chest lead (MCL₆) by its triphasic (qRs) contour.

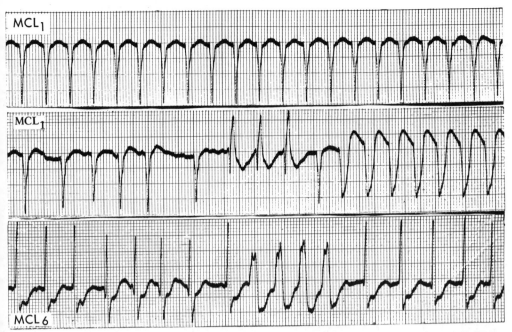

Figure 16.6. *Top strip* shows a regular **supraventricular tachycardia.** In the *middle strip,* **atrial fibrillation** develops and aberration of first **RBBB** and then **LBBB** type appears. In the *bottom strip,* beats 4 to 7 show RBBB aberration, and beats 9 to 12 LBBB aberration. The RBBB aberration is recognizable from its triphasic configuration in both right (rSR') and left (qRS) chest leads.

shorter cycle (Ashman's phenomenon.)[7] The three aberrant beats have the classical rSR' pattern of RBBB. A narrow, more normally conducted beat is then followed by regularization of the rhythm and the appearance of LBBB aberration. Meanwhile, in MCL₆, three of the more normally conducted beats are followed by four beats manifesting RBBB aberration of typical qRS form, followed by a single further more normally conducted beat and then LBBB aberration. This tracing therefore illustrates not only the classical QRS morphology of RBBB aberration in both left and right chest leads, but also the phenomenon of alternating, bilateral aberration.

Despite the availability of morphological clues introduced during the past 15 years,[18, 26] and more recently confirmed,[30, 32, 33] many authors persist in ignoring them[1, 24, 34] and continue to give predominant and undue weight to the presence or absence of independent atrial activity.

Identical Initial Deflection. There is no reason why an ectopic ventricular impluse should write an initial deflection indistinguishable from that of a normally conducted beat. On the other hand, since normal ventricular activation begins on the left side, pure RBBB does not interfere with initial activation, and so the initial deflection remains unchanged. If therefore the anomalous beat in question has a pattern compatible with RBBB and begins with a deflection identical with that of flanking conducted beats, it is a point in favor of aberration.

Preceding Atrial Activity. Sometimes the diagnosis of aberration depends upon the recognition of P waves preceding the abnormal ventricular complex. Figure 16.7 illustrates two bursts of anomalous beats whose shape is not the slightest use in distinguishing between aberration and ectopy. It might well be right ventricular tachycardia or supraventricular tachycardia with LBBB aberration. But careful inspection reveals that each bout of tachycardia is preceded by an accelerating atrial rhythm (P' waves indicated by *arrows*), thus clinching the diagnosis of aberrant conduction. As the atrial cycle shortens, the refractory period of the left bundle branch is encroached upon and the bundle branch fails to conduct.

Figure 16.8 shows another tracing in which the diagnosis of aberration is mainly dependent upon preceding atrial activity. In each of the three strips, the second in a row of rapid beats is anomalous. Is it an aberrant complex because it ends a suddenly shorter cycle? Or is it a ventricular extrasystole initiating a run of reciprocating tachycardia in the A-V junction? The morphology is of no assistance—the right "rabbit ear" is taller than the left so that neither aberration nor ectopy is favored. But if the T wave preceding the anomalous complexes is carefully compared with the T waves of the other sinus beats, it at once becomes plain that something has been added to the pre-anomalous T waves—what else but a superimposed P' wave confirming aberration!

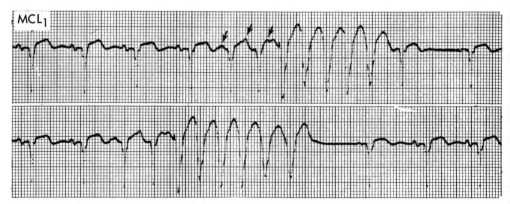

Figure 16.7. Each strip contains a brief run of **atrial tachycardia** with **LBBB aberration**; the telltale antecedent P' waves (*arrows*) clinch the diagnosis. Note the momentary shift of pacemaker following each burst—the returning P wave differs from the sinus P waves.

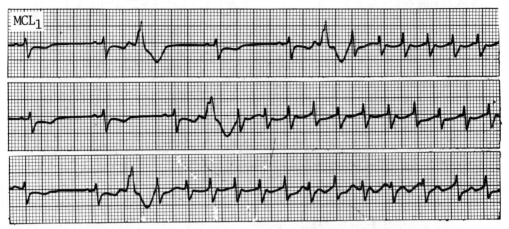

Figure 16.8. Morphologically, the anomalous beats in each strip could be either ectopic ventricular or aberrant. On three occasions, they usher in a run of **supraventricular tachycarda** and so could be aberrant (second in the row) or ventricular extrasystoles initiating runs of reciprocating tachycardia. The differentiation is made by observing the slightly positive deformity (P' waves) preceding each anomalous beat and not seen superimposed on the T waves of the other sinus beats.

Second-in-the-Row Anomaly. The reason only the second in a row of beats tends to be aberrant is because it is the only beat that ends a relatively short cycle preceded by a relatively long one. And since the refractory period of the conduction system is proportional to the preceding ventricular cycle length, the sequence of a long cycle (lengthening the subsequent refractory period) followed by a short cycle provides conditions par excellence for the development of aberration. However, this cycle sequence is not as diagnostic as one would like since the second beat in a row of rapid beats can be a ventricular extrasystole that initiates a run of reciprocating tachycardia in the A-V junction (fig. 16.4*B*).

Alternating BBB Pattern. When a pattern that could be one BBB is separated from a pattern that could be the other BBB by a single normally conducted beat—as in figures 16.6 and 16.10—the presumption is strong that there is bilateral aberration rather than ectopy from alternate ventricles.

Previous Comparative Tracing. It is obvious that if one is lucky enough to have a previous tracing available which shows the same anomalous pattern at a time when it was known to be aberrant, one can then identify the pattern in

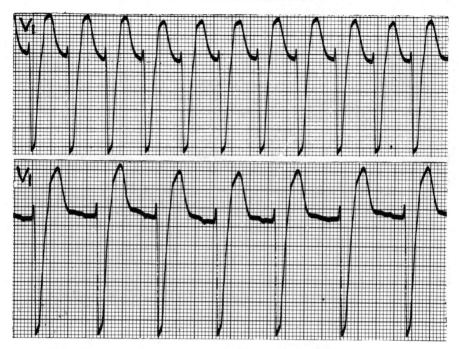

Figure 16.9. *Top strip* during tachycardia shows wide bizarre QRS complexes that could represent right ventricular ectopy or LBBB. *Bottom strip* was taken 1 year earlier and clearly shows a conducted rhythm with the same QRS morphology, thus establishing the supraventricular origin of the later tachycardia.

question. In figure 16.9, the *top strip* shows a tachycardia which could represent a right ventricular tachycardia or a supraventricular tachycardia with LBBB aberration. The *bottom strip* is a tracing from the same patient taken 1 year earlier, and it shows an identical QRS complex during an obviously conducted rhythm. This establishes a supraventricular tachycardia in the top strip.

Ventricular Aberration Complicating Atrial Fibrillation

The common form of ventricular aberration frequently complicates atrial fibrillation. It is probably true to say that when a run of anomalous beats interrupts normal intraventricular conduction during atrial fibrillation, it is more likely due to aberration than to coincidental ventricular tachycardia. Because in the presence of atrial fibrillation one cannot invoke preceding atrial activity as an indication of aberrant conduction, one has to rely more heavily than usual on the morphology of the wide complexes to differentiate aberration from ventricular ectopy. Thus the rsR' pattern in V_1 or MCL_1 (fig. 16.10*B*) or the qRs pattern in V_6 materially assists in establishing the diagnosis of aberrant conduction.

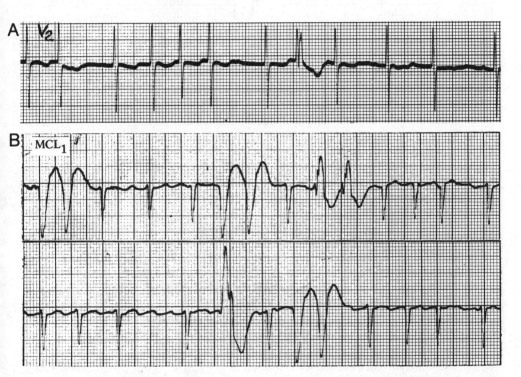

Figure 16.10. (*A*) The eighth beat has an RsR' pattern and is undoubtedly aberrantly conducted; note also that the initial R is virtually identical with the R waves of the flanking conducted RS complexes. (*B*) The strips are continuous. In the top strip, some beats are conducted with **LBBB**, and others with **RBBB aberration.** The RBBB aberration is identified by the rsR' configuration, whereas the LBBB morphology is of no help and could as well be right ventricular ectopic. In the bottom strip, the fifth beat ends in a longer-shorter cycle sequence but is identified as ectopic left ventricular by the taller left "rabbit-ear" configuration.

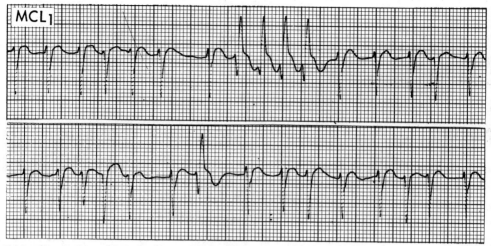

Figure 16.11.   Atrial fibrillation with **ventricular aberration.** The strips are continuous. The run of anomalous beats in the top strip begins with the usual longer-shorter cycle sequence and is identified by the rsR′ pattern (RBBB) as aberrantly conducted. In the bottom strip, a single aberrant beat ends a longer-shorter sequence.

Gouaux and Ashman[7] (1947) first drew attention to the fact that aberrant conduction was likely to complicate atrial fibrillation when a longer cycle was succeeded by a shorter cycle (fig. 16.11); and when a long-short sequence produces aberration, it is sometimes referred to as the **Ashman phenomenon.** But it is important to bear in mind that this cycle sequence cannot be used to differentiate aberration from ectopy because, by the "rule of bigeminy," a lengthened cycle also tends to precipitate a ventricular extrasystole (fig. 16.10*B*). And so, a long-short cycle sequence ending with an anomalous complex is as likely to be a ventricular ectopic as an aberrant beat.

There are several other minor clues that help to differentiate aberration from ectopy in the presence of atrial fibrillation.[16]

Presence of Longer Returning Cycle. Ventricular ectopy tends to be followed by a longer returning cycle. This is because many ectopic ventricular impulses are conducted backward into the A-V junction (concealed retrograde conduction) and, if this happens, the A-V junction is left partially refractory by the retrograde invasion so that the next several fibrillatory impulses are unable to penetrate and reach their ventricular destination.

Absence of Longer Preceding Cycle. As indicated above, a long preceding cycle favors both aberration and ectopy and cannot be used as a differentiating point. On the other hand, absence of a longer preceding cycle is evidence against aberration and therefore favors ectopy (fig. 16.12*A*).

Comparative Cycle Sequences. If an anomalous beat ends a longer-shorter cycle sequence, we have seen that differentiation between aberration and ectopy may be difficult. If in such circumstances an even longer cycle followed by an even shorter cycle ends with a normally conducted beat, the evidence against aberration is strong, and the diagnosis of ectopy is favored (fig. 16.12*B*).

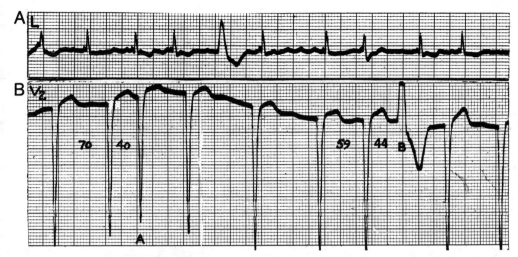

Figure 16.12.   Atrial fibrillation with **ventricular ectopic beats.** (*A*) The anomalous beat ends a shorter-longer cycle sequence, identifying it as probably ectopic ventricular. (*B*) The anomalous beat (B) ends a longer-shorter cycle sequence; but beat A, which is not anomalous, ends an even longer-shorter sequence and is not aberrant. Beat B is therefore even less likely to be aberrant and is ectopic ventricular.

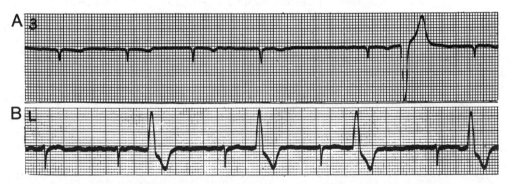

Figure 16.13.   Atrial fibrillation with **ventricular extrasystoles.** (*A*) The anomalous beat ends a cycle markedly shorter than any of the conducted beats and is therefore most likely ectopic ventricular. (*B*) The anomalous beats bear an almost constant relationship to the preceding beats (fixed coupling) and are therefore most likely ectopic ventricular.

Undue Prematurity. When sufficient A-V block is present to ensure that all conducted cycles are relatively long, the sudden appearance of an anomalous beat ending a cycle far shorter than any of the normally conducted beats favors the diagnosis of ectopy (fig. 16.13*A*).

Fixed or Constant Coupling. This clue is obviously applicable only if several anomalous beats are available for comparison. If the interval between the normally conducted beat and the ensuing anomalous beat is constant to within a few hundredths of a second, ectopy is favored (fig. 16.13*B*).

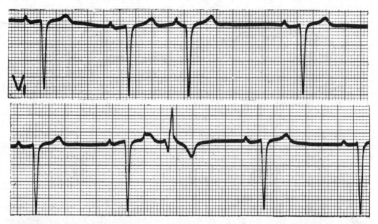

Figure 16.14. Atrial premature beats. The third beat in each strip is an atrial premature beat; in the upper strip the ectopic P wave is clearly visible and is followed by unchanged conduction to the ventricles. In the lower strip the ectopic beat is much more premature (P wave deforms upstroke of T wave) and finds the right bundle branch still refractory, so that **ventricular aberration** of RBBB type occurs. This beat might easily be mistaken for an ectopic *ventricular* beat.

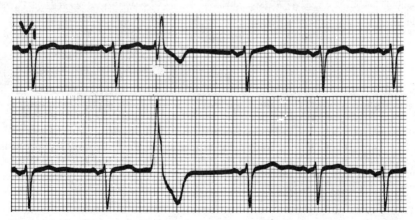

Figure 16.15. Two strips of V₁ from the same patient. The upper strip shows an **atrial premature beat** with **ventricular aberration**; the lower strip, a left **ventricular premature beat**. Note that the aberrant beat has an initial deflection (r) identical with those of flanking sinus beats and a triphasic (rsR′) contour, whereas the ectopic ventricular beat is monophasic (R), reaches an early peak and has a slurred downstroke. (Reproduced from Sandler and Marriott: The differential morphology of anomalous ventricular complexes of RBBB-type in lead V₁. Circulation 1965;31,551.)

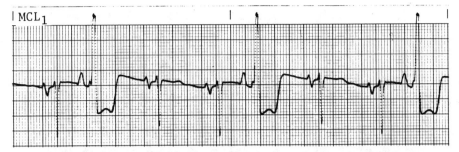

Figure 16.16.   Atrial premature beats. The second, fifth and 8th beats are atrial extrasystoles conducted with a bizarre form of **RBBB aberration**. Note large ectopic premature P waves preceding the aberrant ventricular complexes.

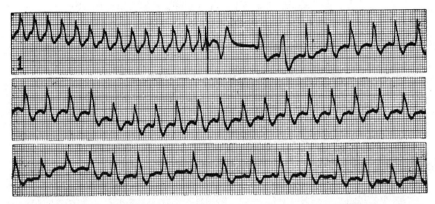

Figure 16.17.   Supraventricular tachycardia with **ventricular aberration.** Continuous strip of lead 1. The record begins with what appears to be a run of ventricular tachycardia. Clinically at rate 245 the first heart sound was constant and there were no irregular cannon waves. After procaine amide the paroxysm gives place to a sinus tachycardia, in which the preceding P waves are well seen at the end of the *bottom strip.* Because the ventricular complexes are identical with those shown during the paroxysmal tachycardia (beginning of *top strip*), there is little doubt that the paroxysm was of supraventricular origin with aberrant ventricular conduction.

For further review, figures 16.14 through 16.23 illustrate aberrant conduction occurring in various supraventricular arrhythmias, and the pertinent points in diagnosis are dealt with in the respective legends. From a study of these examples, it should be evident that confusion can readily occur and that such confusion can have serious consequences.

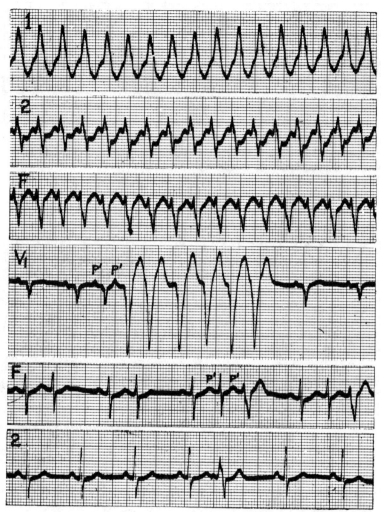

Figure 16.18.   Atrial extrasystoles and **tachycardia** with **LBBB aberration.**
The three upper strips show a pattern suggesting ventricular tachycardia. The
lower three strips demonstrate that the tachycardia is supraventricular with
ventricular aberration; the fourth strip shows the beginning of a paroxysm,
which again looks ventricular but is preceded by the onset of rapid ectopic
atrial activity (P′), indicating that this paroxysm is probably ectopic atrial with
aberrant ventricular conduction. The *bottom two strips* each show telltale
extrasystoles. In lead 2 (*bottom strip*) there is one bizarre premature beat,
which is preceded by an ectopic P wave and followed by a pause that is less
than compensatory. This is then a supraventricular premature beat with aberration, and the aberrant complex is identical with the ventricular complexes
during the paroxysm in the upper lead 2 (*second strip*). In aVF (*fifth strip*) there
are two couplets of atrial bigeminy followed by two triplets of atrial trigeminy. In

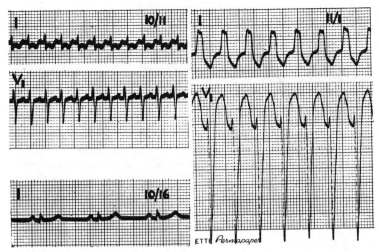

Figure 16.19. Two paroxysms of **tachycardia** in a boy with no demonstrable heart disease. At left the paroxysm is unmistakably supraventricular. At the right, three weeks later, the QRS pattern has altered markedly and now appears to represent ventricular tachycardia at a considerably slower rate. However, the first heart sound was constant and a lead S₅ demonstrated P waves in relation to each QRS complex. Supraventricular tachycardia with aberrant ventricular conduction is therefore the more likely diagnosis (the possible alternative being ventricular tachycardia with 1:1 retrograde conduction to the atria).

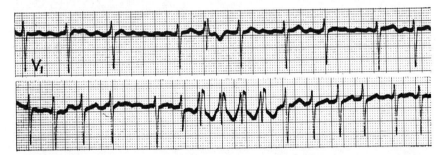

Figure 16.20. **Atrial fibrillation** with **aberrant ventricular conduction.** In the upper strip the fifth beat might well be mistaken for an ectopic ventricular beat; however, it is of RBBB (RSR') form and is more likely an aberrant complex. In the lower strip the fifth beat, which terminates a long diastole, is followed by five aberrant complexes; the first of these shows only minor distortion (slurred upstroke, less deep S wave and frankly inverted T wave) but the following four beats show an RSR' of RBBB, which could readily be mistaken for a short burst of ventricular tachycardia.

these triplets, the second premature beat shows ventricular aberration with bizarre complexes identical with the QRS complexes during the paroxysm in the upper lead aVF (*third strip*). All of this adds up to overwhelming evidence that the "ventricular" tachycardia in the upper three strips is really supraventricular with aberrant ventricular conduction.

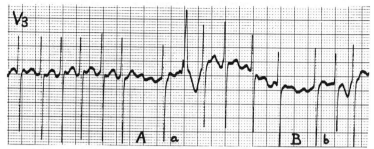

Figure 16.21. **Atrial flutter fibrillation** with **aberrant ventricular conduction,** illustrating the importance of the length of the *preceding* cycle: The rapid ventricular response is interrupted on two occasions by longer than usual diastoles (A and B). These long cycles lengthen the ensuing refractory periods of the conducting tissues. After pause A, therefore, the next short cycle, a, is terminated by a distorted (aberrant) ventricular complex of RBBB form. Pause B is not so long as A and produces less prolongation of the refractory period; the beat terminating the ensuing cycle, b, shows only minor signs of aberration—its T wave is deeply inverted and the QRS has decidedly lower voltage than any of the other beats.

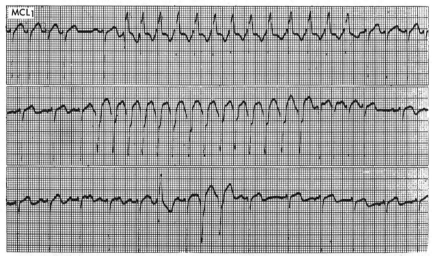

Figure 16.22. Runs of **atrial tachycardia** with aberrant conduction of RBBB type in the *top strip* and of LBBB type in the *second strip.* Both forms are present in *bottom strip.*

Figure 16.23 illustrates aberrancy that led to regrettable mistreatment. The *top strip* shows the patient's rhythm on admission: atrial tachycardia with 2:1 A-V conduction. He was therefore started on digitalis and by the next morning (*second strip*) frequently manifested 4:1 conduction ratios. Because of this "impairment" of conduction, digitalis was discontinued, and quinidine started. The *bottom strip* was taken the following morning and shows the situation that had developed at about midnight and had led to night-long erroneous therapy for ventricular tachycardia. In fact, the *bottom strip* represents atrial tachycardia with 1:1 A-V conduction and RBBB aberration. The quinidine, perhaps partly by its antivagal effect, but certainly through its slowing effect on the atrial rate—from 210 to 192/min—has enabled the A-V junction to conduct *all* of the ectopic atrial impulses. The resulting much-increased ventricular rate— from approximately 90 to 192/min—had produced a dangerous hypotension from which the patient was finally rescued with the combination of a pressor agent and countershock.

In 1958, Rosenblueth documented the effect of atrial rate on normal A-V conduction by pacing the atria of normal dogs. He found that, at an average rate of 257, the animals developed Wenckebach periods and began to drop beats; and, at an average rate of 285, they developed constant 2:1 conduction. Consider what this means in terms of ventricular rate: at an atrial rate of 286, the ventricular rate will be 143; and, if the atrial rate be slowed only 30 beats/ min to 256, the ventricular rate will be 256. In other words, by slowing the atrial rate only 30 beats/min, the ventricular rate has increased 113 beats/min. This is why it can be so dangerous to give an atrial-slowing drug like lidocaine, quinidine or even procainamide in the presence of atrial flutter or fibrillation when the ventricular response is already uncomfortably fast,[20] e.g., if atrial flutter at a rate of 300 is associated with a 2:1 response, producing a ventricular rate of 150, and a drug such as lidocaine is administered, the atrial rate may slow to 250 and A-V conduction may increase to 1:1, producing a dangerous ventricular rate of 250.

From a therapeutic point of view, an extremely important form of aberration may complicate atrial flutter. Uncomplicated and untreated atrial flutter usually manifests an A-V conduction ratio of 2:1. If digitalis or propranolol is then administered, the conduction pattern often changes to alternating 2:1 and 4:1,

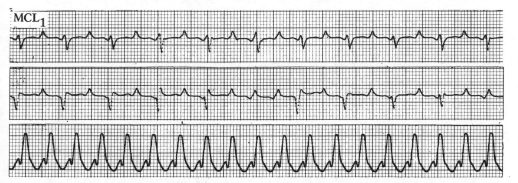

Figure 16.23. The strips are not continuous. Top strip on admission shows **atrial tachycardia with 2:1 A-V conduction.** Middle strip next day shows 2:1 and 4:1 conduction. Bottom strip 24 hours later shows a slower atrial rate with 1:1 conduction and **RBBB aberration**—mistaken for hours and treated as ventricular tachycardia.

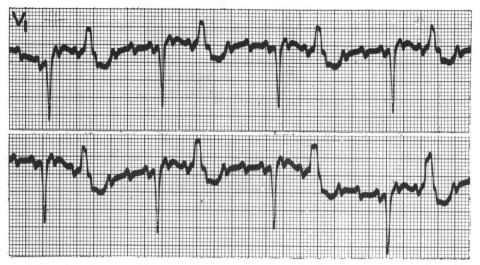

Figure 16.24. **Atrial flutter** with alternating 2:1 and 4:1 conduction and **RBBB aberration** of the beats that end the shorter cycles.

producing alternately longer and shorter cycles; at this stage, the beats that end the shorter cycles may develop aberrant conduction (fig. 16.24). In someone receiving digitalis, this is likely to evoke a diagnosis of ventricular bigeminy and be attributed to digitalis toxicity. Then the still-needed digitalis is wrongfully discontinued, when in fact the situation calls for more digitalis to reduce conduction still further to a constant 4:1 with a then *normal ventricular rate*—always the immediate goal of therapy.

There is a striking tendency, not infrequently seen in aberration complicating tachycardia, for the aberrancy to be bilateral; this is seen in figures 16.10, 16.22 and 16.25. Another intriguing feature shown in these figures is the abrupt switch from one form of aberration to the other—from RBBB to LBBB or vice versa—via a single intervening normally conducted beat. Although unexplained, this phenomenon is sufficiently characteristic to assist in differentiating bilateral aberrancy from bifocal ectopy.

"Critical Rate"

Most of the examples of aberration that we have so far seen have developed because the ventricular cycle, for some reason, suddenly shortened. At times we see the same phenomenon appear as the sinus rhythm *gradually* accelerates. Figure 16.26 presents two examples of slight sinus acceleration in which the cycle gradually shortens until it becomes shorter than the refractory period of one of the bundle branches, whereupon aberrant conduction develops; it will persist until the cycle lengthens enough for normal conduction again to occur. The rate at which the BBB develops is known as the "critical rate," and when such block comes and goes with changes in the heart rate, it is known as "rate-

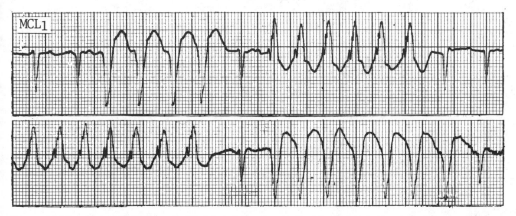

Figure 16.25. **Atrial fibrillation** with **bilateral aberration.** Both strips illustrate the abrupt change from one BBB aberration to the other BBB, with a single intervening normally conducted beat.

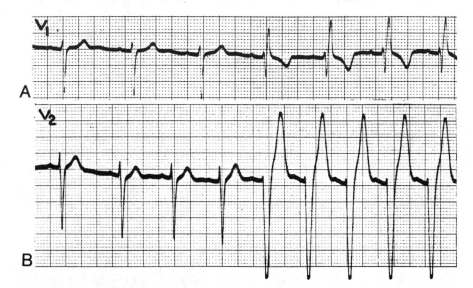

Figure 16.26. **Rate-dependent BBB.** (*A*) From a 19-year-old student nurse: as her sinus rate accelerates and the cycle shortens in response to gentle exercise, progressively increasing degrees of RBBB develop ("critical-rate" or "rate-dependent" RBBB). (*B*) From a 64-year-old man with severe coronary disease; as his sinus rate accelerates and the cycle shortens, LBBB develops at a critical rate of just over 100/min.

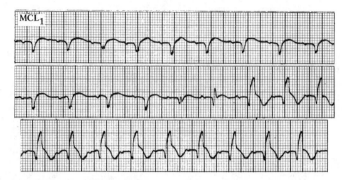

Figure 16.27. Rate-dependent RBBB develops in the *second strip* and continues through the *bottom strip*. As the sinus cycle shortens in the middle of the second strip, increasing degrees of RBBB aberration develop. Note that the P-R remains constant.

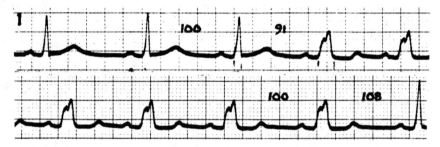

Figure 16.28. Rate-dependent LBBB. Strips are continuous. As the sinus rhythm accelerates, LBBB develops when the rate exceeds 60/min (cycle length <100); but for normal conduction to resume, the rate must fall below 60/min (cycle length > 100).

dependent" BBB. Figure 16.27 presents another example of rate-dependent RBBB.

One of the interesting features of rate-dependent BBB is that the critical rate at which the block develops is different (faster) than the rate at which, once established, the BBB disappears. In figure 16.28, as the sinus rhythm accelerates, normal conduction prevails at a cycle of 100 (= rate of 60/min), and the cycle at which the BBB develops is 91 (= rate of 66/min); but as the rate slows, the BBB persists at a cycle of 100 (= rate of 60/min), and for normal conduction to resume, the cycle must lengthen further to 108 (= rate of 56/min).

The two reasons for this difference in rate requirement during acceleration and deceleration are clear but difficult to describe: (1) Since the refractory period of the ventricular conduction system is proportional to the length of the preceding ventricular cycle, it follows that as the rate accelerates the refractory periods get shorter and shorter; i.e., the potential for conduction progressively

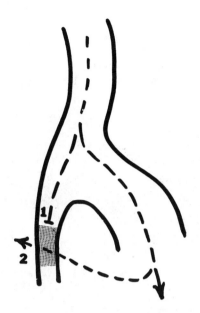

Figure 16.29. Diagram to illustrate one of the two mechanisms responsible for the fact that the "critical rate" is different during acceleration than during deceleration (see text).

improves and therefore there is a tendency to preserve normal conduction. The converse is true as the rate slows. (2) Probably more important is the factor diagrammed in figure 16.29. The *shaded area* in the RBB indicates the refractory segment that precludes conduction when the impulse first arrives (*1*) and so causes RBBB aberration. A moment later, the refractory segment has recovered and, when the transseptal impulse that has meanwhile negotiated the left bundle branch (LBB) approaches it, the RBB is again responsive, and the impulse discharges it (*2*). For the impulse to travel down the LBB and through the septum requires about 0.06 sec; thus the previously refractory RBB is depolarized about 0.06 sec *after the beginning of the QRS complex*. As far as the RBB is concerned, therefore, its cycle begins about 0.06 sec after the beginning of the RBBB QRS complex. When you measure the cycle length conventionally from the beginning of one QRS complex to the beginning of the next, you are not giving the RBB a fair deal since its cycle did not begin until halfway through the first QRS complex. It follows that for normal conduction to resume, the cycle during deceleration (when measured conventionally) must be longer than the "critical" cycle during acceleration by about 0.06 sec. This calculation fits nicely with the observed findings in figure 16.28.

Another way in which the rate dependency of BBB may be revealed is when a sudden lengthening of the ventricular cycle causes the disappearance of a previously present BBB pattern. This is most often seen at the end of the

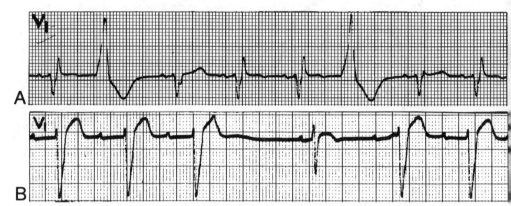

Figure 16.30.   Examples of postextrasystolic revelation of **rate-dependent BBB.** In *A*, after each of the ventricular extrasystoles, the returning sinus beat manifests a lesser degree of RBBB than do the sinus beats ending the normal (shorter) sinus cycles. (*B*) After three sinus beats conducted with first degree A-V block and LBBB, a nonconducted atrial extrasystole results in a prolonged ventricular cycle at the end of which the returning sinus beat is conducted with normal P-R and normal intraventricular conduction, demonstrating that both the A-V delay and the LBBB are rate-dependent.

lengthened cycle following an extrasystole. Figure 16.30 shows two examples of this phenomenon.

The concept of "critical rate" is of greater importance in A-V block than in BBB but has received even less attention. Analogous to the development of BBB at a given "critical rate" is the development of A-V block when the atrial rate reaches a certain critical level and 1:1 conduction gives place to Wenckebach periods and, at a somewhat faster rate, to 2:1 conduction. This is more important than critical-rate BBB because failure to appreciate the role of rate in determining the A-V conduction ratio has often led to unnecessarily aggressive therapy. This whole situation will be dealt with in detail in Chapter 24 on A-V block when the inadequacy of our definitions of the "degrees" of A-V block will be emphasized.

Progressively developing aberration, as in figures 16.26A and 16.27, must be differentiated from progressive degrees of fusion as a ventricular ectopic rhythm takes over. If fusion develops by degrees, the P-R interval must progressively shorten (see figs. 17.2 and 21.7A); whereas, if aberration gradually widens the QRS, the P-R is likely to remain constant throughout the various stages of increasing aberrant conduction—as in figures 16.26A and 16.27.

Type B Aberration

The second form of ventricular aberration, type B (table 16.1), is due to anomalous activation at a supraventricular level, which in turn causes abnormal distribution through the ventricles to produce an aberrant complex. Although not usually included under the heading of ventricular aberration, in the broadest sense of the definition Wolff-Parkinson-White (WPW) conduction is a manifestation of this form of aberration; as a result of anomalous activation and conduction (via a Kent bundle or other bypass tract) above the ventricles, activation of the ventricles themselves is distorted (*1* in fig. 16.31).

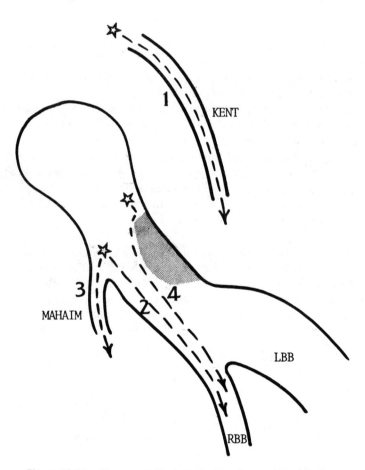

Figure 16.31. Diagram to illustrate the four forms of Type B aberration. (*1*) Kent-bundle (WPW) conduction; (*2*) A-V junctional impulse arising from an eccentrically placed focus spreading preferentially down the ipsilateral bundle branch; (*3*) junctional impulse arising from an eccentrically placed focus spreading preferentially via a Mahaim tract; and (*4*) a junctional impulse arising eccentrically and deflected contralaterally by a patch of diseased tissue.

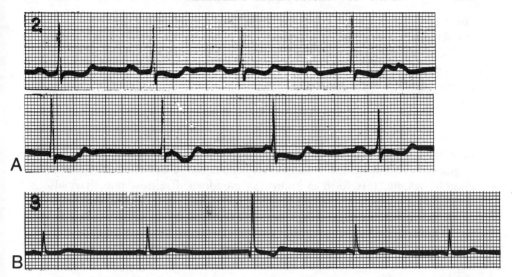

Figure 16.32. Minor **aberration of junctional beats.** (*A*) The two strips are continuous. After three sinus beats showing intraatrial block and first degree A-V block, the fourth sinus impulse is blocked, resulting in four junctional escape beats. Note the slight but definite differences in contour: the junctional beats have small Q waves and taller R waves. (*B*) After two conducted beats, the third beat is exactly on time but without benefit of preceding P wave; its form is obviously changed, but since it is normally narrow, it probably arises in the A-V junction and is conducted with Type B aberration (one obviously cannot absolutely exclude a ventricular septal or fascicular origin.)

A much more common form of aberration of this type is seen with A-V junctional beats. Since there are innumerable potential pacemaker sites in the A-V junction, it follows that most of them cannot be centrally located in the mainstream and are therefore situated off to one side. As most junctional pacemakers are thus eccentrically placed and since longitudinal insulation between parallel fibers in the A-V bundle is effective,[29] it in turn follows that an impulse arising from such a pacemaker tends to be conducted down its side of the junction and the corresponding bundle branch sooner than down the contralateral side and branch (*2* in fig. 16.31); and the QRS complex registers the pattern of more or less conduction delay on the contralateral side. Such a mechanism obviously has nothing to do with cycle length and refractory periods—if the impulse arises eccentrically and spreads asymmetrically, it matters not whether it be an early, punctual or late beat. This is why it is almost the rule for junctional escape beats to show some degree of ventricular aberration. Figure 16.32 presents two examples of minor aberration of junctional escape beats. Although minor aberration is the rule, occasionally it assumes major proportions and can then be mistaken for ventricular ectopy.[9]

A similar form of aberrant conduction can be produced if the eccentrically placed junctional pacemaker, situated near the origin of a Mahaim tract (*3* in fig. 16.31), delivers at least a part of its impulse via the tract and so initiates a distorted QRS complex. Such delivery via "paraspecific" fibers has been called "preferential conduction."[22] A similar form of aberration could result if, owing to disease affecting one side of the junction, the impulse were deflected toward the opposite side (*4* in fig. 16.31) and thus distributed asynchronously via the bundle branches to the ventricles.

Type C Aberration

The third form of aberration, type C (table 16.1), is characterized by the development of abnormal intraventricular conduction only at the end of a *lengthened* cycle; since one would expect conduction to be better after a longer diastolic respite, this form is known as paradoxical critical rate. It is also sometimes referred to as bradycardia-dependent BBB; but this is unsatisfactory as an inclusive term because it is not always necessary to achieve a rate that merits the designation, bradycardia (i.e., under 60/min), for the BBB to develop; e.g., normal conduction may be present at a rate of 82/min, and the BBB may develop only if the cycle length increases to a point equaling a rate of 68/min as in figure 16.33.

So many theories have been advanced to explain this paradoxical phenomenon[6, 21] that it is unlikely that any one of them is universally satisfactory. The currently popular explanation invokes a phase 4 phenomenon. It is well known that as a pacemaking cell spontaneously depolarizes during diastole (phase 4), it becomes less and less responsive to extraneous stimuli. To explain the paradoxical development of BBB after a lengthened cycle, it is assumed that the bundle branch as a whole is functioning as a pacemaker and spontaneously depolarizing. Early in diastole, it will respond to and permit passage of an approaching impulse; but later on, when depolarization has progressed further, it is unresponsive and conduction is therefore impossible. Such an explanation is plausible, but proof is lacking.[6]

At other times, the paradoxical effect appears to be due to vagal influence that both slows the rate and impairs conduction through the bundle branch; this, of course, involves the assumption that the subject is an oddity in whom autonomic innervation extends to the bundle branches. Another possibility in

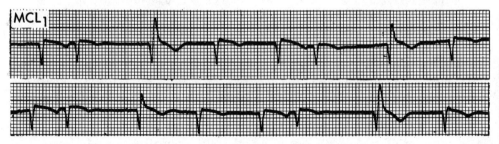

Figure 16.33.   Paradoxical critical rate (Type C aberration). The sinus rhythm is repeatedly interrupted by atrial extrasystoles. The conducted beats ending the lengthened postextrasystolic cycles all show RBBB, whereas the shorter sinus cycles and the even shorter extrasystolic cycles show more normal intraventricular conduction.

some cases postulates a critical level of perfusion to a bundle branch, and that perfusion, which is barely adequate at the end of shorter cycles at faster rates, becomes inadequate by the end of the longer diastoles.

The primary importance of all forms of ventricular aberration is that it may be confused with and must be differentiated from ventricular ectopy—a distinction that becomes especially important when we are faced with a wide-QRS tachycardia.

Differentiation between Supraventricular and Ventricular Tachycardias[18, 23]

With close attention to clinical detail, the bedside diagnosis of regular tachycardia can be surprisingly accurate. First some principles, misconceptions and false doctrines:

1. The proper posture for the diagnostician at the bedside is to apply stethoscope to the precordium and eyes to the neck veins *simultaneously.*
2. Clues to search for are:
   a. Presence or absence of cannon "a" waves or flutter waves in the jugular pulse.
   b. Variation in intensity of the first heart sound.
   c. Splitting of the heart sounds.
3. Splitting of the sounds is due to ventricular *asynchrony,* whereas *irregular* cannon waves in the neck and variation in intensity of the first sound are signs of *dissociation* between atria and ventricles.
4. Signs of dissociation are at times more easily identified at the bedside than in the tracing because the independent P waves are often lost in the barrage of ventricular complexes.
5. *Dissociation does not prove ventricular tachycardia;* but it excludes atrial tachycardia and therefore makes ventricular that much more likely. Dissociation can occur between atrial and A-V pacemakers and, if ventricular aberration is also present, the imitation of ventricular tachycardia may be perfect both clinically and electrocardiographically (see fig. 15.3).
6. *Regular* cannon waves—with every beat—may be seen in atrial tachycardia, A-V tachycardia or ventricular tachycardia with 1:1 retroconduction.

The *electrocardiographic* recognition of typical supraventricular tachycardia is easy; the difficulty arises in separating ventricular tachycardia from a supraventricular tachycardia combined with ventricular aberration. In attempting to make this separation, QRS morphology should receive primary attention. If characteristic features are observed, accuracy and speed are both served; but if morphologic clues are absent or equivocal, one must seek elsewhere.

Although the demonstration of dissociation is of limited diagnostic value, evidence of it should always be sought. If P waves are not recognizable even in V_1, more specialized leads may be informative; a precordial lead known as S_5 may be tried[13]: for this the positive electrode is placed in the 5th right interspace close to the sternal border and the negative electrode over the manubrium (with the conventional patient cable, the LA electrode is placed in the 5th interspace with the RA electrode on the manubrium, and the selector switch is set for standard lead 1). If this fails, an esophageal[4, 9] or intracardiac[31] lead will almost always be successful in displaying P waves. Alternatively, if a tracing is taken during the administration of procainamide[2] or acetylcholine[27] intravenously, the ventricular rate will often slow under their influence, and P waves will become apparent in the now lengthened intervals between ventricular complexes. Such maneuvers, however, are seldom necessary or desirable.

With these many principles in mind, we can formulate a systematic approach to the regular tachycardia:

1. *First look at the neck veins and listen to the first heart sound with the patient holding his breath.* If there are irregular cannon waves in the neck and/or the first heart sound varies in intensity from beat to beat, you have evidence of dissociation, and this suggests a ventricular tachycardia. If the first heart sound is of unvarying intensity and there are either no cannon waves or regular cannon waves in the neck, this is against dissociation and the tachycardia is probably supraventricular (exceptions: (a) ventricular tachycardia with retrograde 1:1 conduction; (b) ventricular tachycardia with concurrent atrial fibrillation).

   If an electrocardiograph is available, do not use carotid sinus or other vagal stimulation until after a tracing has been taken, because if the tachycardia is supraventricular, the vagal maneuver may terminate it, leaving no graphic record to document the paroxysm.

2. *Take an electrocardiogram* and look at the QRS pattern. If it is normal in contour and duration, the tachycardia is supraventricular. If it is widened and bizarre, the tachycardia may be either ventricular or supraventricular with aberrant ventricular conduction. If it is widened, study the V_1/V_6 morphology, observe the frontal plane axis and look for the other morphological clues outlined in Chapters 11 and 15. Try to find a lead in which P waves are identifiable and look for Dressler beats. If previous tracings are available, look for isolated extrasytoles and compare their pattern with that of the tachycardia.

3. If the diagnosis is still in doubt, *try carotid sinus massage, eyeball compression or other vagal stimulation.* If the tachycardia is supraventricular, this may terminate it. In atrial flutter vagal stimulation may temporarily halve the rate by increasing the A-V conduction ratio from 2:1 to 4:1. If the tachycardia is ventricular, it will, with very rare exceptions,[7a] be unaffected.

4. If there is still doubt, take a lead S_5; if this is unrevealing, consider passing an *esophageal* or *intracardiac electrode*; a satisfactory esophageal or intracardiac lead will always reveal P waves when they are unidentifiable in conventional leads. However, in practice, these invasive techniques are

almost never needed and should certainly be avoided whenever possible, especially in patients with acute myocardial infarction.

5. If doubt remains, one may administer *procainamide intravenously* with appropriate precautions. If the tachycardia is ventricular, this will be a correct treatment; if it is supraventricular, the drug may momentarily block A-V conduction and reveal the telltale atrial rhythm between the now more widely spaced ventricular complexes.[2] *Acetylcholine* may have a similar effect.[27]

6. If facilities for recording *His-bundle electrograms* are at hand and the clinical circumstances warrant the procedure, this technique may provide the only certain means of differentiating ventricular aberration from ectopy.[5]

In summary:

Clinically

1. Look for
   a. Wide splitting of heart sounds.
   b. Variation in intensity of first sound.
   c. Cannon waves.
2. Observe effect of carotid sinus stimulation.

Electrocardiographically (in records that look like ventricular tachycardia):

1. Study QRS morphology.
2. Identify P waves.
   a. In conventional leads, especially 2 and V_1.
   b. In lead S_5.
   c. In esophageal or intracardiac lead.
   d. During administration of procaine amide or acetylcholine.
3. Look for Dressler beats.
4. Look for isolated extrasystoles in previous tracings.

REFERENCES

1. Bailey, J. C.: The electrocardiographic differential diagnosis of supraventricular tachycardia with aberrancy versus ventricular tachycardia. Pract. Cardiol. 1980: **6**, 118.
2. Bernstein, L. M., et al.: Intravenous procaine amide as an aid to differentiate flutter with bundle branch block from paroxysmal ventricular tachycardia. Am. Heart J. 1954: **48**, 82.
3. Cohen, S. I., et al.: Variations of aberrant ventricular conduction in man. Circulation 1968: **38**, 899.
4. Copeland, G. D., et al.: Clinical evaluation of a new esophageal electrode, with particular reference to the bipolar esophageal electrocardiogram; II. Observations in cardiac arrhythmias. Am. Heart J. 1959: **57**, 874.
5. Damato, A. N., and Lau, S. H.: Clinical value of the electrogram of the conduction system. Prog. Cardiovasc. Dis. 1970: **13**, 119.
6. Gambetta, M., and Childers, R. W.: Reverse rate related bundle branch block. J. Electrocardiol. 1973: **6**, 153.
7. Gouaux, J. L., and Ashman, R.: Auricular fibrillation with aberration simulating ventricular paroxysmal tachycardia. Am. Heart J. 1947: **34**, 366.

7a. Hess, D. S., et al.: Termination of ventricular tachycardia by carotid sinus massage. Circulation 1982: **65**, 627.
 8. Kistin, A. D.: Retrograde conduction to the atria in ventricular tachycardia. Circulation 1961: **24**, 236.
 9. Kistin, A. D.: Problems in the differentiation of ventricular arrhythmia from supraventricular arrhythmia with abnormal QRS. Prog. Cardiovasc. Dis. 1966: **9**, 1.
10. Kulbertus, H. E., et al.: Vectorcardiographic study of aberrant conduction; anterior displacement of QRS, another form of intraventricular block. Br. Heart J. 1976: **38**, 549.
11. Langendorf, R.: Differential diagnosis of ventricular paroxysmal tachycardia. Exp. Med. Surg. 1950: **8**, 228.
12. Langendorf, R.: Aberrant ventricular conduction. Am. Heart J 1951: **41**, 700.
13. Lian, Cassimatis and Hebert: Intéret de la dérivation précordiale auriculaire S_5 dans le diagnostic des troubles du rythme auriculaire. Arch. Mal. Coeur 1952: **45**, 481.
14. Marriott, H. J. L., and Schamroth, L.: Important dilemmas in cardiac arrhythmias. Md. State Med. J. 1959: **8**, 660.
15. Marriott, H. J. L.: Simulation of ectopic ventricular rhythms by aberrant conduction. J.A.M.A. 1966: **196**, 787.
16. Marriott, H. J. L., and Sandler, I. A.: Criteria, old and new, for differentiating between ectopic ventricular beats and aberrant ventricular conduction in the presence of atrial fibrillation. Prog. Cardiovasc. Dis. 1966: **9**, 18.
17. Marriott, H. J. L., and Menendez, M. M.: A-V dissociation revisited. Prog. Cardiovasc. Dis. 1966: **8**, 522.
18. Marriott, H. J. L.: Differential diagnosis of supraventricular and ventricular tachycardia. Geriatrics 1970: **25**, 91.
19. Marriott, H. J. L., and Thorne, D. C.: Dysrhythmic dilemmas in coronary care. Am. J. Cardiol. 1971: **27**, 327.
20. Marriott, H. J. L., and Bieza, C. F.: Alarming ventricular acceleration after lidocaine administration. Chest 1972: **61**, 682.
21. Massumi, R. A.: Bradycardia-dependent bundle branch block. A critique and proposed criteria. Circulation 1968: **38**, 1066.
22. Pick, A.: Aberrant ventricular conduction of escaped beats: Preferential and accessory pathways in the A-V junction. Circulation 1956: **13**, 702.
23. Pick, A., and Langendorf, R.: Differentiation of supraventricular and ventricular tachycardias. Prog. Cardiovasc. Dis. 1960: **2**, 391.
24. Pietras, R. J., et al.: Chronic recurrent right and left ventricular tachycardia; comparison of clinical, hemodynamic and angiographic findings. Am. J. Cardiol. 1977: **40**, 32.
25. Rubin, I. L., et al.: The esophageal lead in the diagnosis of tachycardias with aberrant ventricular conduction. Am. Heart J. 1959: **57**, 19.
26. Sandler, I. A., and Marriott, H. J. L.: The differential morphology of anomalous ventricular complexes of RBBB-type in lead V_1; ventricular ectopy versus aberration. Circulation 1965: **31**, 551.
27. Schoolman, H. M., et al.: Acetylcholine in differential diagnosis and treatment of paroxysmal tachycardia. Am. Heart J. 1960: **60**, 526.
28. Schrire, V., and Vogelpoel, L.: The clinical and electrocardiographic differentiation of supraventricular and ventricular tachycardias with regular rhythm. Am. Heart J. 1955: **49**, 162.
29. Sherf, L., and James, T. N.: A new electrocardiographic concept: Synchronized sinoventricular conduction. Dis Chest 1969: **55**, 127.
30. Vera, Z., et al.: His bundle electrography for evaluation of criteria in differentiating ventricular ectopy from aberrancy in atrial fibrillation. Circulation 1972: **45** (supp. II), 355.
31. Vogel, J. H. K., et al.: A simple technique for identifying P waves in complex arrhythmias. Am. Heart J. 1964: **67**, 158.
32. Wellens, H. J. J., et al.: The value of the electrocardiogram in the differential diagnosis of a tachycardia with a widened QRS complex. Am. J. Med. 1978: **64**, 27.
33. Wellens, H. J. J., et al.: Medical treatment of ventricular tachycardia; considerations in the selection of patients for surgical treatment. Am. J. Cardiol. 1982: **49**, 187.
34. Zipes, D. P.: Diagnosis of ventricular tachycardia. Drug Ther. 1979: **9**, 83.

Review Tracings

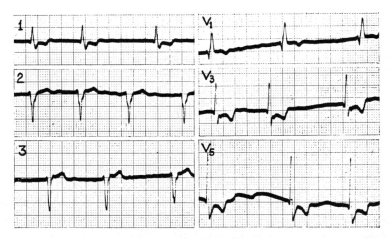

Review Tracing 16.1

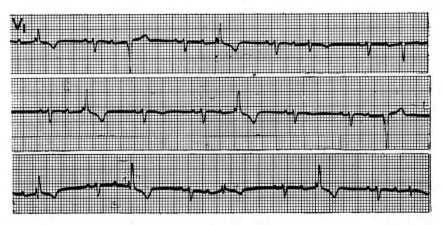

Review Tracing 16.2

For interpretation, see page 482

17

Accelerated Idioventricular Rhythm and Parasystole

Accelerated Idioventricular Rhythm (AIVR)

AIVR achieved popularity with the advent of coronary care (CC)—before constant monitoring it was seldom bruited, although examples had been published as early as 1910 by Thomas Lewis. With the spreading CC vogue, the recognition of AIVR became commonplace, and many unsatisfactory terms such as "nonparoxysmal ventricular tachycardia,"[7] "idioventricular tachycardia,"[8] and "slow tachycardia"[1] were applied to it. To emphasize the fact that the ventricular rate was usually closely similar to the sinus rate, Massumi and Ali[5] suggested the term "accelerated isorhythmic ventricular rhythm"; but this is not universally applicable because the rates of the two dissociated pacemakers, though often similar, need not be so; and because sometimes there is consistent 1:1 retrograde conduction and therefore no dissociation.

AIVR is best defined as an automatic ectopic ventricular rhythm at a rate between 50 and 100/min. Unfortunately, definitions have varied; the lower rate limit has ranged from 40 to 60/min, and the upper limit, from 90 to 125/min, which makes comparisons between the various series invalid. Although it is certainly not the monopoly of myocardial infarction, most reported examples have been culled from CC units where it is seen in about 20% of acute infarctions (the range of reported incidence is 8 to 46%). AIVR usually puts in an appearance during the first day or two of acute infarction, though it may appear at any time. At first it was said to be more commonly associated with acute inferior infarctions, but recent studies have found it to be more evenly shared by anterior and inferior infarctions.

AIVR takes over either because the sinus rhythm slows and permits the ectopic rhythm to escape (fig. 17.1) or because the ectopic pacemaker accelerates and temporarily usurps control from the sinus node (fig. 17.2). In either case, since the two rhythms usually have similar rates, the run of AIVR is often ushered in by one or more fusion beats (figs. 17.1 and 17.2). Besides sinus

244

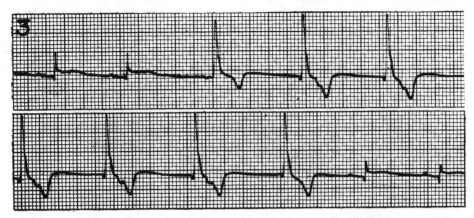

Figure 17.1. Strips are continuous. After two sinus beats, the rhythm abruptly slows and enables an **AIVR** to take over at a rate of 64/min. The third beat in the upper strip is a **fusion beat**. Toward the end of the lower strip, the sinus pacemaker accelerates and recaptures the ventricles.

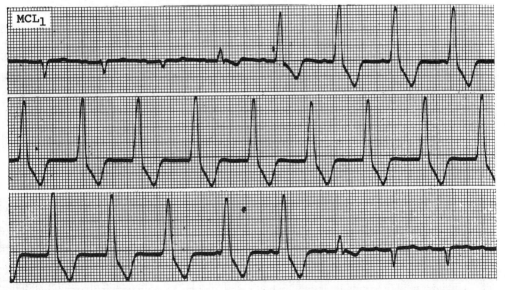

Figure 17.2. Strips are continuous. Sinus rhythm at a rate of 75/min is overtaken by an **AIVR** at a slightly faster rate; the third, fourth and fifth beats are **fusion beats**. In the middle of the bottom strip, the sinus rhythm accelerates and recaptures the ventricles; the sixth beat in this strip is a **fusion beat**.

slowing, other mechanisms that may afford the opportunity for AIVR to escape are A-V block and the postectopic pause following an extrasystole. Occasionally, the run of AIVR begins with a frankly premature beat—a seeming extrasystole—but then settles into a regular automatic rhythm at a modest rate (fig. 17.3). In this situation, one should think of and exclude a parasystolic mechanism (see below). An occasional AIVR may be parasystolic, but the great majority are not.

Once the AIVR gets under way, it usually proceeds as a perfectly regular rhythm, but sometimes it shows progressive acceleration or progressive slowing until it spontaneously ceases (fig. 17.4). Rarely the rhythm may be quite irregular. Usually there is but one accelerated focus, but at times more than one may alternate (fig. 17.5). Sometimes the rate of AIVR is exactly half that of an associated ventricular tachycardia (VT), suggesting that the AIVR may in reality represent VT with a 2:1 exit block.[4]

After a varying number of beats, usually ranging between 3 and 10 but sometimes continuing for 20 or 30 beats, the paroxysm ends. It often stops spontaneously (fig. 17.4), but more often the sinus rhythm accelerates and recaptures the ventricles (figs 17.1 and 17.2). As the rates of the two independent pacemakers again approach each other, one or more farewell fusion beats are common (fig. 17.2). In some instances, instead of dissociation between the two pacemakers, there is retrograde conduction to the atria (fig. 17.6).

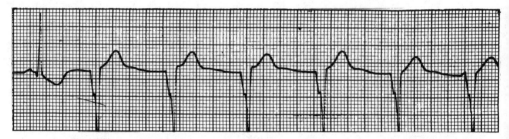

Figure 17.3.   The ectopic rhythm begins with a premature beat and then settles down to a regular **AIVR** at a rate of 70/min. A parasystolic mechanism should be considered.

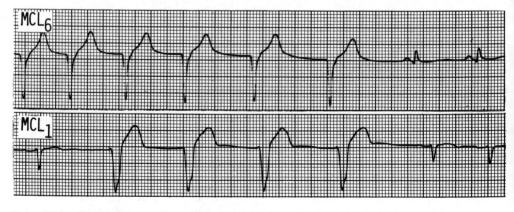

Figure 17.4.   The two strips are from different patients. In each strip, an **AIVR** is seen to slow gradually and then spontaneously stop, whereupon the sinus node awakens and resumes control.

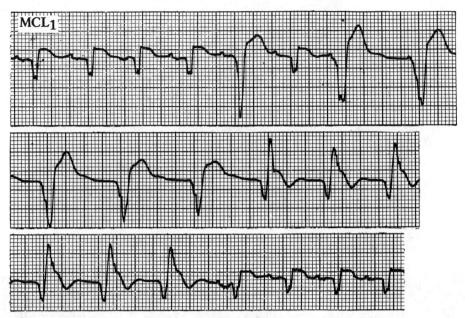

Figure 17.5. The strips are continuous. In the top strip, the sinus rhythm gives place to an irregular **AIVR** from the right ventricle. In the middle of the second strip, control is usurped by a somewhat faster left ventricular **AIVR**.

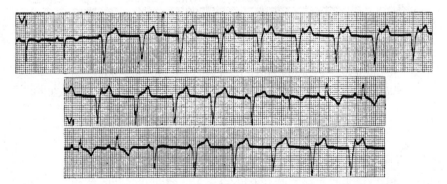

Figure 17.6. Accelerated ventricular rhythm. In *top strip*, the first two beats *appear to be* normally conducted sinus beats. The sinus rhythm then slows and permits an ectopic right ventricular pacemaker to escape at an almost identical rate. The first two ectopic beats are dissociated from the sinus rhythm, but after that retrograde conduction to the atria develops (narrow positive spike deforming early part of ST segments) and continues to end of strip. *Bottom two strips* are continuous and begin with the accelerated ventricular rhythm with retroconduction in its first beat; then come three dissociated beats, then two fusion beats, the second of which looks like a normally conducted sinus beat. Four sinus beats follow with incomplete RBBB and then the accelerated ventricular rhythm returns via a fusion beat with retroconduction again in the two final beats. Now we can recognize the identity of the first two beats in the *top strip* and the sixth beat in the *second strip*—they look like normal beats because they represent fusion between a right ventricular impulse and a sinus impulse in the presence of RBBB (pp. 284–285).

AIVR is usually benign and neither affects the blood pressure nor presages more serious ventricular arrhythmias. However, like every other cause of A-V dissociation, the loss of the atrial "kick" (contribution to ventricular filling) *may* rarely impair the hemodynamics enough to require corrective therapy. Most observers have found no association between AIVR and ventricular tachycardia[10]; but rather surprisingly at variance with general impressions and experience, some authors[2, 4, 9] have documented a high incidence of true (rapid) VT in patients with AIVR. Nevertheless, the prognosis of patients with myocardial infarction complicated by AIVR appears to be just as good as the prognosis of those without AIVR.[6]

AIVR is also found in childhood and is regarded as benign.[3]

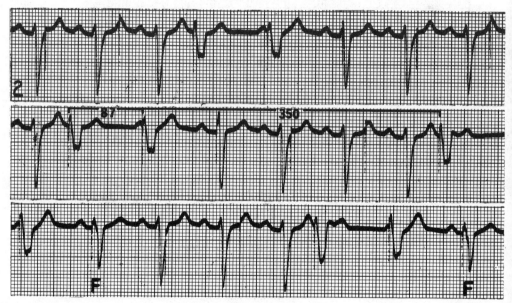

Figure 17.7.   The strips are continuous. **Fixed-rate pacemaker** for comparison with ventricular parasystole. Since the pacemaker cannot be turned off by the sinus impulses, it behaves like parasystole, and all longer interectopic intervals are multiples of the pacemaker's cycle.

Parasystole

Dual rhythm is a comprehensive term that covers all situations in which two separate, competing pacemakers are simultaneously operative. Thus complete A-V block, most other forms of A-V dissociation, and the double tachycardias are all classifiable as dual rhythms. Parasystole (Gr. *para* = alongside; *systole* = contraction) is a special form of dual rhythm in which there is a privileged pacemaker whose rhythm, by virtue of local "protection," cannot be disturbed by its competitor: the parasystolic pacemaker cannot be "turned off" or reset by the competing sinus rhythm. The nature of this "protection" is unknown, but in some cases it may be due to the pacemaker's own rapid discharge rate, which assures its constant refractoriness when sinus impulses approach it; a simultaneous exit block (perhaps 4:1, 6:1 or 8:1) produces a slow manifest rate obscuring the underlying real discharge rate.[12, 13]

Ventricular Parasystole

The fixed-rate artificial pacemaker takes the mystique out of parasystole, and figure 17.7 illustrates the "parasystolic" behavior of such a pacemaker: (1) it is "protected" in the sense that nothing can shut it off; therefore (2) whenever its impulse falls at a time when the ventricles are responsive, a QRS accompanies the pacemaker "blip"; but (3) whenever it falls at a time when the ventricles are refractory, the blip is visible (i.e., the pacer discharges and maintains its uninterrupted schedule), but no ventricular complex results; therefore (4) the longer interectopic intervals are multiples of the shortest interectopic interval (e.g., in the second strip, the long interectopic interval, 350, equals four times the shorter interval, 87); and (5) whenever the artificial discharge coincides with sinus conduction into the ventricles, a fusion beat results (F); (6) because parasystole represents an indepedent rhythm and is not beholden to the preceding beat, it will put in an appearance at varying intervals following the sinus beats (variable "coupling"). These six points are all characteristic of parasystolic behavior.

Diagnosis. Parasystole is first suspected in the clinical tracing if ectopic beats show varying coupling intervals; this inconstancy of the coupling interval indicates an indepedent rhythm but does *not* of itself prove parasystole. To do this, one must demonstrate that the independent rhythm is undisturbable, and

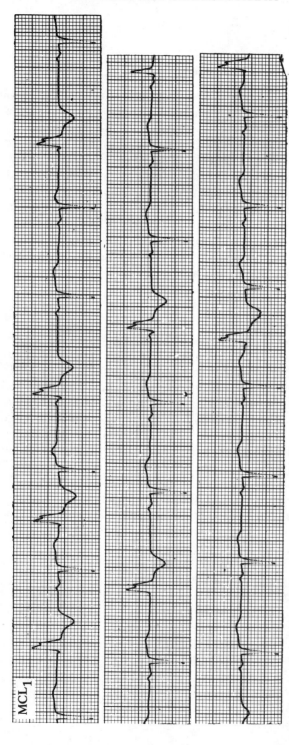

Figure 17.8. **Ventricular parasystole.** Strips are continuous. The intervals between the ectopic beats and the preceding sinus beats obviously vary (varying "coupling" interval), and all interectopic intervals have a common denominator somewhere between 1.43 and 1.56 sec. Thus, consecutive interectopic intervals throughout the three continuous strips measure (in hundredths of a sec) 145, 146, 287 (= 2 × 143.5), 301 (= 2 × 150.5), 302 (= 2 × 151), 294 (= 2 × 147), 441 (= 3 × 147) and 313 (= 2 × 156.5). Note the fusion beat at the end of the *middle strip.*

this is achieved by showing that the interectopic intervals have a common denominator. Thus, in figure 17.8 the first three ectopic beats all bear obviously differing relationships ("coupling" intervals) to their preceding beats, and the interectopic intervals are, respectively, 145 and 146 hundredths of a sec; all subsequent interectopic intervals are multiples of cycles between 143.5 and 145.6 hundredths.

All examples of ventricular parasystole will presumably produce fusion beats eventually if a long enough trace is taken, but such beats are not essential to the diagnosis. In figure 17.8 the last beat in the second strip is a fusion beat— it is upright like the ectopic beats but narrower, and it is preceded by a sinus P wave with a long enough P-R interval for some conduction into the ventricles (P-R interval of sinus beats = 0.19 sec; P-R of fusion beat = 0.16 sec).

A special pattern of fusion occurs if the ectopic ventricular pacemaker is on the side of a BBB, for then both the QRS of the sinus beat and the QRS of the parasystolic (ectopic) beat are wide; but if each activates its respective ventricle simultaneously, the resulting fusion beat may be quite narrow and may indeed look remarkably normal. Figure 17.9 illustrates such a situation. The sinus beats are conducted with *right* BBB, and the ectopic pacemaker is in the *right* ventricle. The third beat in the bottom strip is a fusion beat with a remarkably normal configuration since the sinus impulse is activating the left ventricle

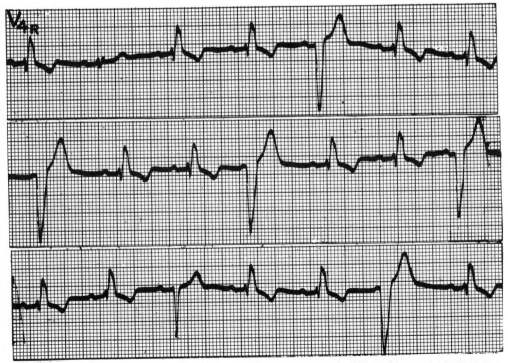

Figure 17.9. The three strips are continuous and show a **right ventricular parasystole** competing with a sinus rhythm with **right bundle-branch block**. The second beat in the *top strip* and the *third* in the *bottom* are fusion beats. There is some variation in the coupling intervals, and the consecutive interectopic intervals measure 249, 242, 240, 238, 237 and 236—the automatic pacemaker is apparently enjoying the phenomenon of "warm-up."

while the ectopic impulse takes care of the right ventricle with precise simultaneity.

In the presence of atrial fibrillation, the diagnosis of fusion is made with less assurance since one never knows exactly when the next fibrillatory impulse is going to be conducted to the ventricles. But in figure 17.10, one can be reasonably certain that the third beat from the end of the second strip (x) is a fusion beat since all preceding interectopic intervals measure 162 to 164 and the interval from the first ectopic beat in the bottom strip to the beat in question (x) measures 328 (= 2 × 164). It is therefore reasonable to conclude that beat x is mainly conducted but contains a small distorting contribution from the ectopic focus.

Since parasystole is an independent, autonomous rhythm that cannot be interrupted, it follows that its impulses must from time to time land on the T waves of the competitive sinus beats. Because of this inevitable R-on-T incidence, parasystole has been declared dangerous, but this is false reasoning. Extrasystoles that alight upon the T wave are admittedly dangerous, but the mechanism of parasystole is quite different from that of the extrasystole, and we have no evidence that (automatic) parasystolic beats on the T wave pose the same threat as (?reentry) extrasystolic beats. Moreover, it is an empirical observation that when a parasystolic discharge coincides with the T wave, it seldom becomes a manifest beat. Parasystole is, in fact, a relatively benign arrhythmia.[11]

Supraventricular Parasystole

All parasystole is not ventricular. Atrial and A-V junctional pacemakers can also assume parasystolic properties. Figure 17.11 shows a continuous tracing from a patient with atrial flutter and varying A-V conduction. Scattered through

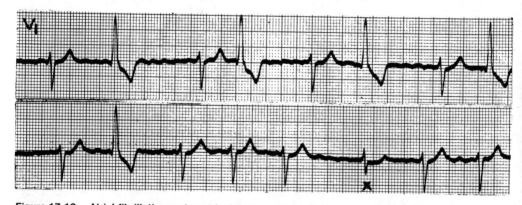

Figure 17.10. Atrial fibrillation and **ventricular parasystole**. Strips are continuous. This picture of atrial fibrillation with irregular A-V conduction is interrupted by regularly recurring anomalous beats that obviously bear no relationship to the preceding conducted beats yet are themselves regularly spaced (interectopic intervals in the top strip are 164, 162 and 163). Clearly they represent a parasystolic rhythm. From the first ectopic beat in the bottom strip to the fusion beat marked x is an interval of 328 (= 2 × 164).

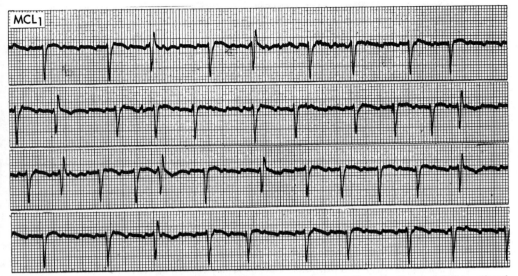

Figure 17.11. The strips are continuous. **Atrial flutter** with varying A-V conduction and **A-V junctional parasystole** with **incomplete RBBB aberration**. Parasystolic measurements: first long interectopic interval (fifth beat in *top strip* to second beat in *second strip*) = 422 = 141 × 3; second long interectopic interval (second beat in second strip to last beat in that strip) = 566 = 141.5 × 4; third long interectopic interval (seventh beat in *third strip* to last beat in that strip) = 278 = 139 × 2; fourth long interectopic interval (last beat in *third strip* to third beat in *bottom strip*) = 272 = 136 × 2.

the tracing are "different" beats that show an rSR′ configuration, and the first thing about these beats that catches the eye is the variation in their intervals from the preceding beats; this immediately makes one suspect an independent pacemaker and suggests parasystole. Then measuring the shortest interectopic intervals, we find that they are almost identical (142, 140, 140, 142). Next we measure the longer intervals and find that they are all approximate multiples (see the legend to fig. 17.11) of the shorter intervals, clinching the diagnosis of parasystole. Since the contour of the parasystolic beats is rSR′, one assumes that they originate in the A-V junction (**junctional parasystole**) and are conducted with incomplete RBBB aberration.

Atrial parasystole is rare. You diagnose it if you can demonstrate (1) that the ectopic P waves vary in their relationship (coupling interval) to the preceding sinus P waves and (2) that the interectopic (P′-P′) intervals all have a common denominator. If sinus and parasystolic impulses simultaneously invade the atrial myocardium, atrial fusion results.

REFERENCES

Accelerated Idioventricular Rhythm

1. Castellanos, A., et al.: Mechanisms of slow ventricular tachycardias in acute myocardial infarction. Chest 1969: **56,** 470.

2. de Soyza, N., et al.: Association of accelerated idioventricular rhythm and paroxysmal ventricular tachycardia in acute myocardial infarction. Am. J. Cardiol. 1974: **34**, 667.
3. Gaum, W. E., et al.: Accelerated ventricular rhythm in childhood. Am. J. Cardiol. 1979: **43**, 162.
4. Lichstein, E., et al.: Incidence and description of accelerated ventricular rhythm complicating acute myocardial infarction. Am. J. Med. 1975: **58**, 192.
5. Massumi, R. A., and Ali, N.: Accelerated isorhythmic ventricular rhythms. Am. J. Cardiol. 1970: **26**, 170.
6. Norris, R. M., et al.: Idioventricular rhythm complicating acute myocardial infarction. Br. Heart J. 1970: **32**, 617.
7. Rothfeld, E. L., et al.: Nonparoxysmal ventricular tachycardia. Circulation 1967: **36** (supp. 2), 227.
8. Schamroth, L.: Idioventricular tachycardia. J. Electrocardiol. 1968: **1**, 205.
9. Talbot, S., and Greaves, M.: Association of ventricular extrasystoles and ventricular tachycardia with idioventricular rhythm. Br. Heart J. 1976: **38**, 457.
10. Yusuf, S., et al.: Heart rate and ectopic prematurity in relation to sustained ventricular arrhythmias. Br. Heart J. 1980: **44**, 233.

Parasystole

11. El-Sherif, N.: The ventricular premature complex: mechanisms and significance. In Mandel, W. J., *Cardiac arrhythmias*, p. 292, edited by W. J. Mandel. J. B. Lippincott, Philadelphia, 1981.
12. Schamroth, L.: Ventricular parasystole with slow manifest ectopic discharge. Br. Heart J. 1962: **24**, 731.
13. Scherf, D., and Bornemann, C.: Parasystole with a rapid ventricular center. Am. Heart J. 1961: **62**, 320.

Review Tracings

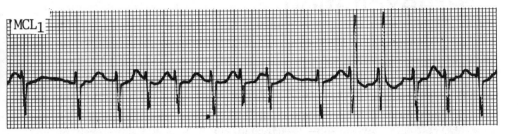

Review Tracing 17.1

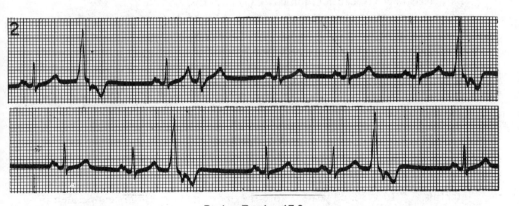

Review Tracing 17.2

For interpretation, see page 483

18

Preexcitation

"Preexcitation," the term introduced by Ohnell in 1944, implies that part of the ventricular myocardium is activated before it would have been by an impulse descending via the normal A-V conduction system. The two main variants of preexcitation are the Wolff-Parkinson-White (WPW) and the Lown-Ganong-Levine (LGL) syndromes; these "syndromes" include the predisposition to supraventricular tachyarrhythmias in persons manifesting one of the characteristic electrocardiographic (ECG) patterns.

The first example of preexcitation was published, but not recognized, by the dean of American electrocardiography, Frank Wilson, in 1915. He naturally thought that the widened QRS complex was the result of some form of bundle-branch block; and it was many years before it was appreciated that the QRS might be widened either because part of the ventricular myocardium was activated late (bundle-branch block) or because part was activated early (preexcitation) (fig. 18.1).

WPW Patterns

Prior to 1930, Wolff and White in Boston and Parkinson in London had collected a number of cases with bizarre ventricular complexes and short P-R intervals.[39, 40] In 1930, 20 years before they personally met, they cooperated in a hands-across-the-sea endeavor and published their combined series of 11 cases, again under the heading: "Bundle Branch Block with Short P-R Interval."

As early as 1893, Kent described muscular connections between atria and ventricles but wrongly assumed that they represented pathways of normal conduction from atria to ventricles. Mines, well ahead of his time, in 1914 suggested that these "bundles of Kent" might mediate reentering tachycardias. But it was not until half a century later that the jigsaw fragments were finally coapted and it was fully appreciated that the accessory pathways (AP), the ECG patterns, and the associated reciprocating tachycardias were interdependent.

256

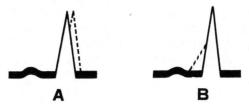

Figure 18.1. (*A*) Bundle-branch block and (*B*) Wolff-Parkinson-White syndrome compared diagrammatically.

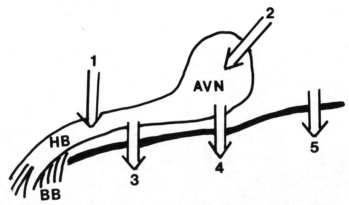

Figure 18.2. The various A-V connections that may mediate preexcitation. *Key*: AVN = atrioventricular node; HB = bundle of His; BB = bundle branches. *1*, atriofascicular connection (James); *2*, intranodal bypass; *3*, fasciculoventricular connection (Mahaim); *4*, nodoventricular connection (Mahaim); and *5*, atrioventricular accessory connection (Kent, Paladino).

The classical WPW pattern consists of a short P-R interval (less than 0.12 sec) and a widened QRS complex with a slurred initial component, the "delta" wave, so named by Segers in 1944. The P-R is short because the descending impulse bypasses the normal delay in conduction that is experienced in the A-V node; the delta wave is caused by slow intramyocardial conduction that results when the impulse, instead of being delivered by the normal Purkinje system, finds itself dumped into ventricular myocardium via an anomalous tract; and the widened QRS is the result of the consequent asynchronous activation of the two ventricles. The various tracts that can mediate preexcitation[2] are diagrammed in figure 18.2.

In most cases, the congenital defect that services this conduction anomaly is an imperfect, porous atrioventricular partition with myocardial bridges ("Kent bundles") traversing the pores. In a few cases, the anomalous A-V connection consists of the partnership of a bypass fiber of James with a Mahaim fiber (fig. 18.2).

In preexcitation, the P-R interval is not always abnormally short (fig. 18.3); in fact, of 589 published cases, 23% had P-R intervals of 0.12 sec or longer, and there is a tendency for the P-R to lengthen with age. Nor is the QRS always abnormally broad—in 23% of 598 cases, the QRS measured less than 0.11 sec[35] (fig. 18.4).

Classifications

Classification of WPW patterns began with Rosenbaum and colleagues in 1945. They divided their patients into two groups on the basis of the direction of the *major deflection* in a right-sided chest lead. Since their classification is still popular but their criteria are often misquoted, their exact words are repeated here:

Depending on the form of QRS in the leads from the right side of the precordium, particularly leads V_1, V_2 and V_E, our cases have been divided into two groups: *Group A*, in which *R is the sole, or by far the largest, deflection in all of these* and *Group B*, in which *S or QS is the chief QRS deflection in at least one of them* [my italics].

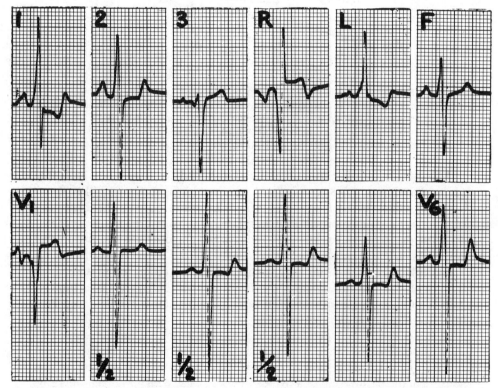

Figure 18.3.   Probable **WPW pattern, type B**. Note the normal P-R interval and the entirely negative QS complex in V_1 with elevated ST segment, which could easily be mistaken for anteroseptal infarction. The slurred initial component of the QRS ("delta" wave) is particularly well seen in aVL and V_1. Leads V_{2-4} are recorded at half-standardization.

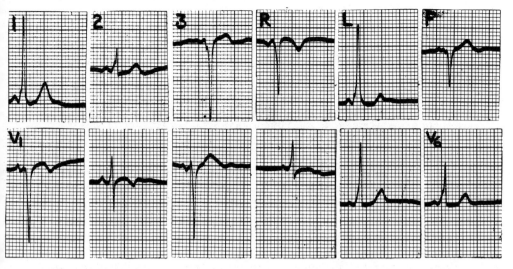

Figure 18.4.   WPW pattern, type B. Note the short P-R interval (0.10 sec) and entirely negative QRS in V₁. Delta waves are well seen in several leads.

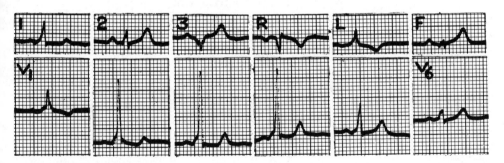

Figure 18.5.   WPW pattern, type A. Note the entirely positive QRS in V₁. The delta waves are well seen in most leads.

It is usually stated that their cases were divided according to the direction of the delta vector, but their own words make plain that this was not so and that the *main deflection* of the QRS provided the differential yardstick. Thus figure 18.5 genuinely belongs to their "Group A"—and everyone else's "type A"—

whereas figure 18.6, despite the positive delta vector in V_1, qualifies for their "Group B."

The simple division into types "A" and "B" is useful in identifying left-sided (type A) versus right-sided (type B) preexcitation. Obviously, right-sided pathways are more accessible to the surgeon than septal or left-sided tracts.

Grant[15] in 1958 pointed out that this differentiation was based on a relatively insignificant shift of the ventricular vector and introduced a new classification based on the axis of the delta wave in the frontal plane: type I—the commonest—had a delta-wave axis in the neighborhood of $-30°$ and so produced Q waves in leads, 2, 3 and aVF simulating inferior infarction (fig. 18.7). Type III—the least common—had a delta-wave axis of about $+105°$ and so produced small wide Q waves in leads 1 and aVL simulating anterior or lateral infarction. Type II had an axis between the other two, at about $+50°$.

Sherf and Neufeld,[35] in their excellent text, prefer a combination of precordial and limb lead patterns so that types A and B are subdivided into those with superior and inferior displacement of the frontal plane axis; thus the main categories in their classification are:

$$AS = \text{type A with superior axis}$$
$$AI = \text{type A with inferior axis}$$
$$BS = \text{type B with superior axis}$$
$$BI = \text{type B with inferior axis}$$

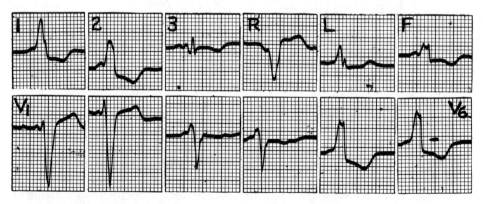

Figure 18.6.   WPW pattern, type B. Note the initially positive but mainly negative QRS complex in V_1. This pattern could well be mistaken for left bundle-branch block, but the P-R interval is only 0.09 sec.

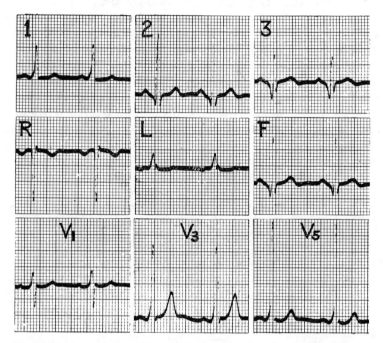

Figure 18.7.   Wolff-Parkinson-White syndrome, showing atypical features: the P-R interval is normal at 0.16 sec, the QRS slightly prolonged at 0.10 to 0.11 sec. Delta waves are clearly seen in leads 1, V_3 and $\dot{V}_5$. The slurred initial component in leads 2, 3 and aVF takes the form of wide Q waves, which may be mistaken for those of inferior myocardial infarction if the overall pattern is not recognized.

These four categories accounted for approximately 90% of their large series of 215 patients, but the remaining 10% required no less than 6 additional subsets. Figure 18.8 presents an example of their type AI.

Thanks to modern investigative and surgical techniques, it has been possible to identify the location of the AP in a large number of patients and correlate it with the clinical 12-lead tracings. In this way, the Duke group have been able to tabulate the tentative ECG findings for 10 locations around the periphery of the A-V rings and in the septum.[11] For example, when the right posterior crux is the site of the preexcitation pathway, an abrupt transition from an isoelectric delta wave with rS pattern in V_1 to a positive delta wave and Rs in V_2 is often found. Or again, if the pathway of preexcitation is at the lateral extremity of the mitral ring, the delta wave is negative in 1 and aVL but positive across the precordium from V_1 to V_6 (fig. 18.8). When the preexcitation conduction was mediated via James and Mahaim fibers, the delta vector was found by Lev and associates to be negative in leads 2, 3, aVF, and V_1 while positive in 1, aVL, and V_{2-3}.[23]

The main function of a classification of WPW patterns is to aid in the localization of the APs. As more and more information is gathered electro-

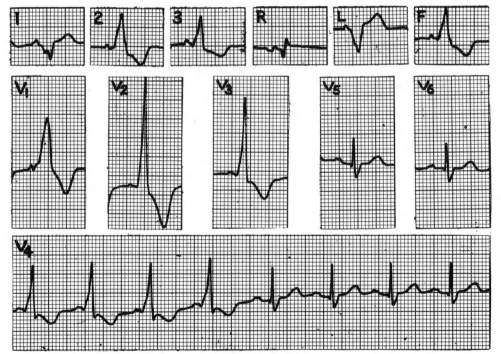

Figure 18.8.   WPW pattern, type AI of Sherf and Neufeld. The negative delta vector in leads 1 and aVL indicates probable left-lateral preexcitation. During the recording of lead V_4, the pattern spontaneously changes from preexcitation with short P-R interval (0.09 sec) to incomplete right bundle-branch block with normal P-R (0.17) sec.

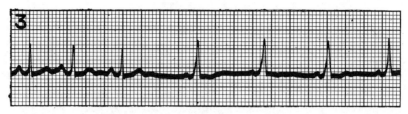

Figure 18.9. After three sinus beats with P-R of 0.13 sec, there is a sinus pause which ends with atrial escape (note change in P-wave contour). The ectopic atrial pacemaker apparently has access to a preexcitation pathway, and the P-R shortens to 0.08 sec as the QRS assumes a delta wave and widens.

physiologically and surgically and localization becomes more and more precisely correlated with the clinical ECG, types "A" and "B" will surely become outmoded. Meanwhile, however, these two types comprise the most used—and most misquoted!—classification.

One of the interesting, and not fully explained, facets of the WPW syndrome is that the pattern of preexcitation may develop only with a change in the atrial pacemaker from sinus to ectopic (fig. 18.9). One possible explanation is that the ectopic atrial focus is situated[44a] in or near the posterior internodal tract which contains fibers that bypass the A-V node.[34]

Determinants of QRS Width

The width of the QRS depends upon the size of the delta wave, which in turn depends on the number of lengths (milliseconds) by which the accessory impulse wins the steeplechase to the ventricles. And this in turn depends on the interplay of several factors[38]: the location of the AP; conduction time from sinus node to A-V node and to AP; conduction time down the AP (whose length may range from 1 to 10 mm); and conduction time over the normal A-V pathways. The result is that the QRS may be anything from normal in duration and barely distorted if the impulse via the A-V junction arrives first, to grossly widened and bizarre if the accessory impulse wins by a wide margin and activation results exclusively from its spread.

Since depolarization is abnormal, repolarization must also be and there are always consequent ST-T abnormalities.

Incidence, Associations and Imitations

If there is any topic in electrocardiography that has received attention in print more in proportion to its fascination than to its prevalence, it is the WPW syndrome. This is understandable since the syndrome not only produces disturbances of rhythm and conduction that attract and hold the fascinated eye, it is also the meeting place of numerous paracardiological disciplines, including anatomy, embryology, physiology, electrophysiology, and pediatrics. During the past decade, apart from more than a thousand papers, several comprehensive reviews,[4, 9–11, 19, 26] each with its own peculiar virtues, and at least one small but comprehensive book[35] on preexcitation have been published. Yet the syndrome is encountered only about 15 times among 10,000 electrocardiograms.

It affects males about twice as often as females and is found in all age groups. In young subjects, it occurs predominantly in those with no other sign of heart disease; however, it is found in a significant number of young patients with hypertrophic cardiomyopathy, and type B WPW occurs in 25% of those with Ebstein's disease.[33] An association has also been claimed with corrected transposition of the great arteries, tricuspid atresia, endocardial fibroelastosis and mitral valve prolapse.[11]

Although the substrate for WPW conduction (accessory pathways) is congenital, evidence of preexcitation may not appear until late in life. It may, for instance, come to light only after a myocardial infarction has impaired conduction through the A-V node, and so give the appearance of being an "acquired" WPW.[12, 14] In others, completion of the "syndrome," i.e., the development of tachycardia, may not occur till late in life. Of the infants who start life with the full-blown syndrome, the great majority happily "outgrow" their predisposition to tachyarrhythmias within a few years.[13]

Patterns of preexcitation may at least partially mimic a number of other entities. Type "A," with the wide positive QRS in V_1, may simulate right bundle-branch block, right ventricular hypertrophy, or a true posterior infarction. Type "B" may be mistaken for left bundle-branch block (figs 18.6 and 18.10), or even left ventricular hypertrophy (fig. 18.4). A negative delta wave, producing Q waves in appropriate leads, may imitate anteroseptal or inferior

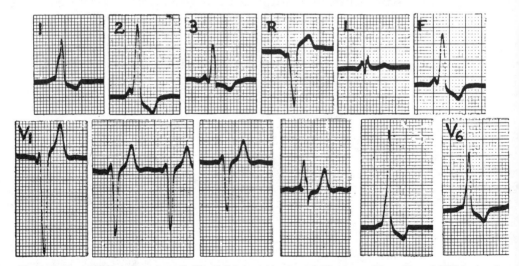

Figure 8.10.   WPW pattern, type B. The P-R interval is about 0.09 sec, and the widened QRS has a slow initial component well seen in several leads. The overall QRS pattern could be mistaken for left bundle-branch block.

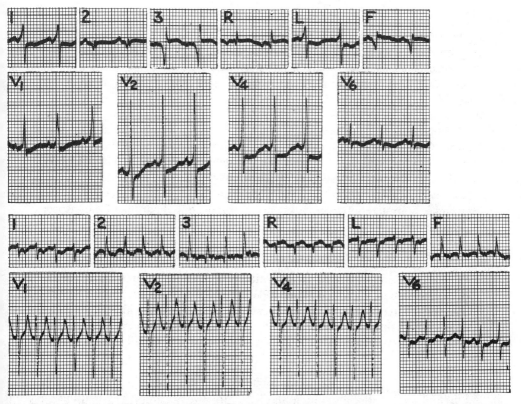

Figure 18.11.   The upper tracing shows **type A WPW** conduction during sinus rhythm in a three-week-old baby. The lower tracing shows SVT with narrow QRS, indicating that the A-V junction serves as the anterograde pathway, and the accessory bundle as the retrograde pathway.

infarction. The QS complex in V_1 in figures 18.3 and 18.4 could easily be mistaken for anteroseptal necrosis. The deep, wide Q wave in lead 3 in figures 18.7 and 18.11 combined with the ST elevation, is certainly highly suggestive of acute inferior infarction, but figure 18.11 is derived from a three-week-old infant with the WPW syndrome.

Ruskin[32] found 31 (70%) of 44 consecutive patients with WPW patterns had delta vectors that produced Q waves mimicking myocardial infarction. One third of the 44 patients were referred to the laboratory with the diagnosis of myocardial infarction. On the other hand, the Q wave of genuine infarction may be masked by a positive delta wave of preexcitation.[14]

In turn, the short P-R and wide QRS of the WPW can be simulated by the dissembling pacemaker catheter.[28, 36] If the catheter becomes looped in the right atrium in the presence of a sinus rhythm faster than the paced rhythm, each atrial contraction may thrust the catheter tip against the ventricular endocardium and produce an ecotpic QRS at a short and constant P-R interval.

Diagnostic Measures

In the patient with a history of tachycardia but whose tracing during sinus rhythm manifests a normal P-R without widening of the QRS, to prove the presence of an accessory pathway it may be necessary to pace the atria at increasing rates or to stimulate the atria at increasingly premature intervals (single atrial-test stimuli). But several noninvasive maneuvers may be successful in making the diagnosis: vagal stimulation,[30] by impairing conduction in the A-V node and so favoring conduction via the AP may reveal a delta wave; intravenous digoxin, by simultaneously inhibiting conduction in the A-V node and facilitating it in the AP, may bring a delta wave to light. On the other hand, drugs that block the accessory pathway (such as procainamide, ajmaline, lidocaine or disopyramide) or that abbreviate conduction in the A-V node (atropine, isoproterenol) may visibly normalize the initial portion of the suspect QRS complex.

Arrhythmias Associated with WPW Syndrome

The clinical importance of preexcitation resides almost entirely in its predisposition to tachyarrhythmias. The WPW heart is custom-made for the accommodation of reentering rhythms because it is equipped with two parallel pathways with differing conductive characteristics. The accessory pathway (AP) usually conducts much faster than the A-V node but usually has a longer

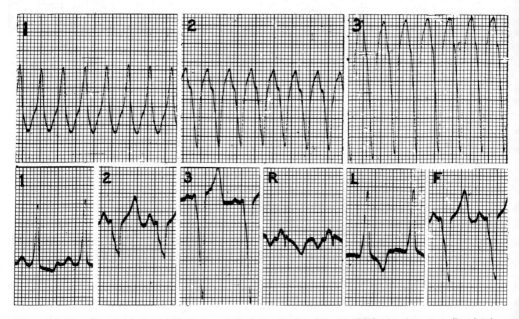

Figure 18.12.   The *upper tracing* shows a regular tachycardia with wide QRS complexes, easily mistaken for ventricular tachycardia. The *lower tracing* shows the patient's limb leads during sinus rhythm and reveals the **W-P-W pattern**. This identifies the tachycardia as RT using the accessory bundle as the anterograde path.

refractory period. With the normal sinus cycle, the descending impulse usually finds both A-V junction and AP responsive and so traverses both avenues to the ventricles, and the dichotomized impulse produces fusion beats within the ventricles. The pattern of fusion obviously depends upon the amount of preexcitation (duration of delta wave), which in turn depends upon the time required for each wave front to reach and spread down its respective path.

Reciprocating Tachycardia

An early beat, on the other hand, such as an atrial extrasystole, may find the AP still refractory after the A-V node has recovered and so its impulse travels only down the orthodox conduction routes; however, by the time it reaches the ventricular end of the AP, that may have recovered and, if the impulse then travels retrogradely through the AP to the atria, the stage is set for reciprocation (reentry, circus-movement). A ventricular ectopic beat may achieve the same success by finding one retrograde pathway receptive while the other remains unresponsive.

Most reciprocating tachycardias have a normal QRS since they travel anterogradely through the junction (fig. 18.11); but in a minority, the AP may have recovered while the A-V node is still refractory and then the impulse travels exclusively down the AP and may complete the circuit in the reverse direction (sometimes called "antidromic," as opposed to "orthodromic," tachycardia). In such cases, the QRS during the tachycardia has the wide, bizarre QRS of the WPW syndrome (fig. 18.12). An occasional patient with a wide-QRS tachycardia enjoys the luxury of two (or more) APs and the circulating wave uses both—one for the downward and one for the upward journey.[11]

Two important diagnostic pitfalls should be appreciated: (1) Just because the patient is known to have preexcitation—as revealed during sinus rhythm—this does not prove that the tachycardia circuit includes the AP. In an important

Table 18.1
Tachyarrhythmias in 161 WPWs

RT[a]	89
RT + AF[a]	32
AF	15
RT + AF + VF[a]	13
AF + VF	5
VF	4
RT + VF	3
Total WPWs	161

[a] RT, reciprocating tachycardia; AF, atrial fibrillation; VT, ventricular fibrillation.

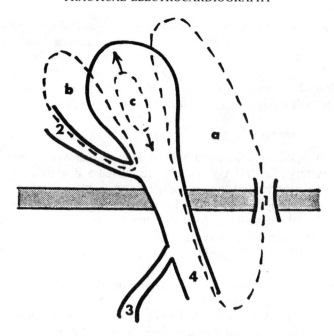

Figure 18.13. Reentry circuits in WPW syndrome. (*1*) Accessory pathway (Kent bundle), (*2*) bypass tract (James fiber), (*3*) Mahaim fiber, (*4*) bundle of His. Circuit *a* consists of a Kent bundle and the normal A-V pathways; circuit *b* consists of a bypass tract and the A-V junction; circuit *c* is confined to the A-V node.

minority—5% in Wellens' series[38]—despite the presence of an AP, the circulating wave gyrates exclusively within the A-V junction (fig. 18.13, circuit "c"), obviously a fact of paramount importance if surgical intervention is contemplated. (2) In some patients, the AP conducts retrogradely but not anterogradely. Thus the patient may sustain a reciprocating tachycardia without ever showing the telltale WPW pattern during sinus rhythm; and since the 12-lead tracing is innocent of delta waves, the mechanism may not be suspected. This situation is referred to as "concealed WPW" and accounts for a significant minority of supraventricular tachycardias.[41, 44, 47] Although subject to misdiagnosed tachycardia, they are protected from frantic ventricular rates if they develop atrial fibrillation by the long refractory period of their AP.

An unusual mode of onset of the tachycardia may afford a clue to the existence of a concealed AP. Gradual, progressive shortening of the sinus cycle with the sudden development of retrograde conduction, without prior lengthening of the P-R interval, may suggest this form of tachycardia.[11]

Atrial Flutter and Fibrillation

Atrial flutter in the WPW syndrome occurs but rarely (fig. 18.14). Atrial fibrillation, on the other hand, is quite common and assumes great importance because of the extremely rapid ventricular rates that may develop. The major determinant of the rate of the ventricular response is the length of the refractory

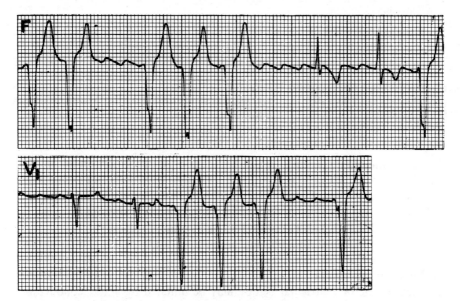

Figure 18.14. **Atrial flutter** in a patient with the **WPW syndrome**. Both normal conduction and preexcitation are evident in each lead. The flutter waves are readily apparent in the longer diastoles.

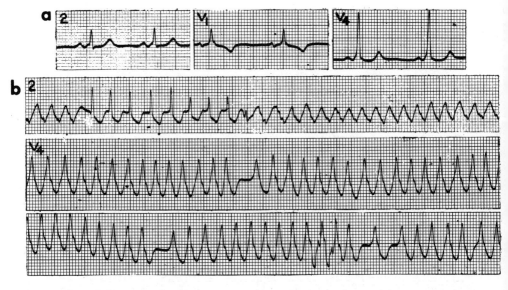

Figure 18.15.   The top panel (*a*) shows the **preexcitation pattern**, while the rhythm strips (*b*) illustrate the typical picture of **atrial fibrillation** during anomalous pathway conduction with a ventricular response at 280/min. Several beats in the first half of lead 2 are evidently conducted via normal pathways at a somewhat slower rate. Note that occasional cycles are more than twice the length of the shortest cycles.

period of the AP.[4, 9] If that refractory period is very short, rates in the neighborhood of 300/min may be achieved (figs 18.15 and 18.16) and then there is serious danger of ventricular fibrillation developing, either because the descending impulse arrives in the vulnerable phase of the ventricular cycle; or because the wild tachycardia evokes serious hypoxia.

It can be extremely difficult, and sometimes impossible, to differentiate ventricular tachycardia from atrial fibrillation with WPW conduction.[25] The QRS morphology can be helpful but one must realize that some of the features so characteristic of ventricular ectopy may be imitated by WPW conduction: the taller left "rabbit-ear" and "concordant positivity" in the chest leads can be simulated by type A WPW, and the "fat" initial r wave in V_1 by type B.

Numerous examples of atrial fibrillation with WPW conduction have been published as irregular ventricular tachycardia[25]; this has earned the undesirable title of "pseudoventricular tachycardia." The true nature of most of these can be suspected at a glance from two characteristic features: (1) the cycle length at times is as short as 0.20 sec, the equivalent of a rate of 300/min; and (2) in other places there are cycles more than twice as long as the shortest cycles. This greater than 100% variation in cycle length would represent a remarkable degree of irregularity in genuine ventricular tachycardia which, in the large majority of cases, is perfectly regular.[49]

Atrial fibrillation may be initiated by an atrial extrasystole arising during the vulnerable phase of the atrial cycle or by a ventricular extrasystole conducted retrogradely to the atria and arriving in their vulnerable phase. The extremely rapid ventricular rate that may develop may precipitate ventricular fibrillation.

Procainamide, quinidine, and lidocaine (fig. 18.16) prolong the refractory period and slow conduction in the AP,[45] whereas digitalis at least in some patients has the unhappy effect of shortening the refractory period, may therefore further increase the already-rapid ventricular rate, and has been repeatedly implicated in the development of ventricular fibrillation.[46]

Ventricular Fibrillation

Although ventricular fibrillation is sometimes the presenting arrhythmia, it usually appears in the wake of atrial fibrillation[4a]; and the patient whose R-R interval during atrial fibrillation drops to or below 0.20 sec is at particular risk of developing ventricular fibrillation.

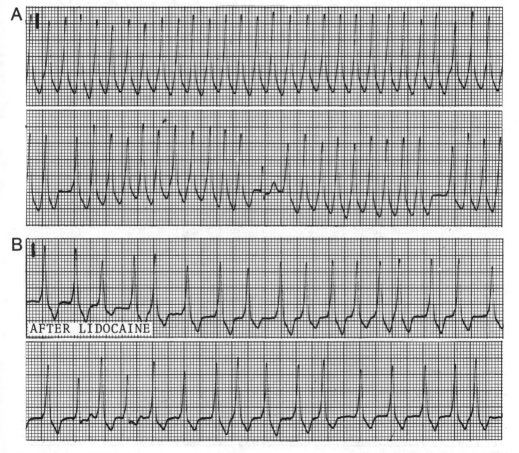

Figure 18.16. (*A*) The strips are continuous. From a young woman with **atrial fibrillation** and the **WPW syndrome**. Note the rate of 290/min, the occasional normal conduction, and the occasional cycle more than twice the length of the shortest cycles. (*B*) The strips are continuous and illustrate the slowing effect of lidocaine (rate, about 165/min).

Incidence

The precise incidence of the various tachycardias complicating the WPW syndrome is not known. Clearly the largest published series are preselected since they consist largely of intractable tachycardias referred to sophisticated centers for investigation. In Wellens' series of 149 patients with WPW arrhythmias,[38] about 70% had supraventricular tachycardia alone, 20% had only atrial fibrillation, and the remainder had both SVT and atrial fibrillation. Campbell found atrial fibrillation in 16 per cent of his WPW patients.[3] In the first 161 patients referred to Duke, the incidence of tachyarrhythmias is shown in table 18.1.

LGL Syndrome

In 1952, Lown, Ganong, and Levine[24] published a series of cases with P-R intervals of 0.12 or 0.13 sec, snapping first heart sounds, and no organic heart disease. Two thirds of the patients were women, and a minority of them suffered from paroxysms of tachycardia. Since that time anything with a short P-R and normal QRS has been called LGL syndrome. Because of the inconsistency of usage and because there is doubt that the described features really represent a clinical entity, Sherf and Neufeld[35] suggest that the term LGL syndrome be dropped entirely and replaced by the noncommittal but accurately descriptive term "short-PR-normal-QRS syndromes," of which figure 18.17 is an example.

The majority of workers have found that the shortened P-R interval is due to less-than-normal delay in the A-V node as manifested by an abbreviated A-H interval in the His-bundle electrogram—?intranodal bypass, see figure 18.2.[20] It is of interest to note that the incidence of short P-R interval and long

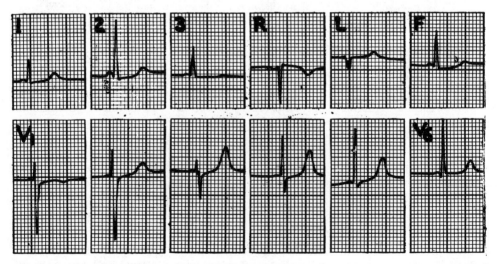

Figure 18.17.   Short-P-R-normal-QRS pattern from a healthy asymptomatic nurse with no history of palpitations or tachycardia. Note the short P-R interval (0.08 sec) with normal QRS complex.

P-R interval is exactly the same—1.3%—in a healthy young population, suggesting that neither is necessarily abnormal and each may represent the extremities of a normal bell-shaped curve of P-R incidence. On the other hand, the short-PR-normal-QRS combination may at times be due to conduction via an extranodal bypass tract but with conduction thereafter via normal His-Purkinje pathways—1 and HB in figure 18.2.

Arrhythmias in Short-PR-Normal-QRS Syndrome

Arrhythmias in the so-called LGL syndrome have not been studied in the same detail as those complicating the WPW syndrome. Although the anatomical substrate for this syndrome at least at times presumably involves an A-V nodal bypass, this bypass apparently played no part in the RTs in a small series studied at Duke.[42] Of 12 patients, 6 had supraventricular tachycardia; 2, atrial fibrillation; and 4, ventricular tachycardia. Four of the RTs were due to reentry in the A-V node, while two used a concealed bypass tract. That the arrhythmias complicating this syndrome may also be life-threatening is indicated by the fact that 3 of the 4 patients with ventricular tachycardia required resuscitation.

REFERENCES

1. Bashore, Th. M., et al.: Ventricular fibrillation in the Wolff-Parkinson-White syndrome. Circulation 1976: **11**, 187.
2. Becker, A. E., et al.: The anatomical substrates of Wolff-Parkinson-White syndrome. Circulation 1978: **57**, 870.
3. Campbell, R. W. F., et al.: Atrial fibrillation in the preexcitation syndrome. Am. J. Cardiol. 1977: **40**, 514.
4a. Cosio, F.G., et al.: Onset of atrial fibrillation during antidromic tachycardia: Association with sudden cardiac arrest and ventricular fibrillation in a patient with Wolff-Parkinson-White syndrome. Am. J. Cardiol. 1982: **50**, 353.
4. Chung, E. K.: Wolff-Parkinson-White syndrome—current views. Am. J. Med. 1977: **62**, 252.
5. Dreifus, L. S., et al.: Ventricular fibrillation: a possible mechanism of sudden death in patients with Wolff-Parkinson-White syndrome. Circulation 1971: **43**, 520.
6. Durrer, D., et al.: Pre-excitation revisited. Am. J. Cardiol. 1970: **25**, 690.
7. Durrer, D., et al.: The role of premature beats in the initiation and the termination of supraventricular tachycardia in the Wolff-Parkinson-White syndrome. Circulation 1967: **36**, 644.
8. Ferrer, M. I.: New concepts relating to the preexcitation syndrome. J.A.M.A. 1967: **201**, 1038.
9. Ferrer, M. I.: Preexcitation. Am. J. Med. 1977: **62**, 715.
10. Gallagher, J. J., et al.: Wolff-Parkinson-White syndrome; the problem, evaluation and surgical correction. Circulation 1975: **51**, 767.
11. Gallagher, J. J., et al.: The preexcitation syndromes. Prog. Cardiovasc. Dis. 1978: **20**, 285.
12. Gavrilescu, S., et al.: Accelerated atrioventricular conduction during acute myocardial infarction. Am. Heart J. 1977: **94**, 21.
13. Giardina, A. C. V., Ehlers, K. H., and Engle, M. A.: Wolff-Parkinson-White syndrome in infants and children: a long term follow up study. Br. Heart J. 1972: **34**, 839.
14. Goel, B. G., and Han, J.: Manifestations of the WPW syndrome after myocardial infarction. Am. Heart J. 1974: **87**, 633.
15. Grant, R. P., et al.: Ventricular activation in the pre-excitation syndrome (Wolff-Parkinson-White). Circulation 1958: **18**, 355.
16. Hejtmancik, M. R., and Herrmann, G. R.: The electrocardiographic syndrome of short P-R interval and broad QRS complexes. A clinical study of 80 cases. Am. Heart J. 1957: **54**, 708.
17. Herrmann, G. R., et al.: Paroxysmal pseudoventricular tachycardia and pseudoventricular fibrillation in patients with accelerated A-V conduction. Am. Heart J. 1957: **53**, 254.

18. James, T. N.: The Wolff-Parkinson-White syndrome. Ann. Intern. Med. 1969: **71**, 399.
19. James, T. N.: The Wolff-Parkinson-White syndrome: evolving concepts of its pathogenesis. Prog. Cardiovasc. Dis. 1970: **13**, 159.
20. Josephson, M. E., and Kastor, J. A.: Supraventricular tachycardia in Lown-Ganong-Levine syndrome; atrionodal versus intranodal reentry. Am. J. Cardiol. 1977: **40**, 521.
21. Kariv, I.: Wolff-Parkinson-White syndrome simulating myocardial infarction. Am. Heart J. 1958: **55**, 406.
22. Lev, M., et al.: Anatomic findings in a case of ventricular pre-excitation (WPW) terminating in complete atrioventricular block. Circulation 1966: **34**, 718.
23. Lev, M., et al.: Mahaim and James fibers as a basis for a unique variety of ventricular preexcitation. Am. J. Cardiol. 1975: **36**, 880.
24. Lown, B., et al.: The syndrome of the short P-R interval, normal QRS complex and paroxysmal rapid heart action. Circulation 1952: **5**, 693.
25. Marriott, H. J. L., and Rogers, H. M.: Mimics of ventricular tachycardia associated with the W-P-W syndrome. J. Electrocardiol., 1969: **2**, 77.
26. Narula, O. S.: Wolff-Parkinson-White syndrome: A review. Circulation 1973: **47**, 872.
27. Newman, B. J., et al.: Arrhythmias in the Wolff-Parkinson-White syndrome. Prog. Cardiovasc. Dis. 1966: **9**, 147.
28. Ohe, T., et al.: Catheter-induced isorhythmic idioventricular rhythm. Chest 1980: **78**, 638.
29. Prinzmetal, M., et al.: Accelerated conduction. In *The Wolff-Parkinson-White Syndrome and Related Conditions*. Grune & Stratton, New York, 1952.
30. Przyblyski, J., et al.: Unmasking of ventricular preexcitation by vagal stimulation or isoproterenol administration. Circulation 1980: **61**, 1030.
31. Rosen, K. M.: A-V nodal reentrance: an unexpected mechanism of paroxysmal tachycardia in a patient with preexcitation. Circulation 1973: **47**, 1267.
32. Ruskin, J. N., et al.: Abnormal Q waves in Wolff-Parkinson-White syndrome: Incidence and clinical significance. J.A.M.A. 1976: **235**, 2727.
33. Schiebler, G. L., et al.: The Wolff-Parkinson-White syndrome in infants and children. Pediatrics 1959: **24**, 585.
34. Sherf, L., and James, T. N.: A new look at some old questions in clinical electrocardiography. Henry Ford Hosp. Med. Bull. 1966: **14**, 265.
35. Sherf, L., and Neufeld, N. H.: *The Pre-excitation Syndrome: Facts and Theories*. Yorke Medical Books, New York, 1978.
36. Voukydis, P. C., and Cohen, S. I.: Catheter-induced arrhythmias. Am. Heart J. 1974: **88**, 588.
37. Wellens, H. J. J., and Durrer, D.: The role of an accessory atrioventricular pathway in reciprocal tachycardia. Circulation 1975: **52**, 58.
38. Wellens, H. J. J., et al.: The Wolff-Parkinson-White syndrome. In *Cardiac Arrhythmias, Their Mechanisms, Diagnosis and Management*, p. 342, edited by W. J. Mandel. J. B. Lippincott, Philadelphia, 1980.
39. Wolff, L.: Syndrome of short P-R interval with abnormal QRS complexes and paroxysmal tachycardia (Wolff-Parkinson-White syndrome). Circulation 1954: **10**, 282.
40. Wolff, L.: Wolff-Parkinson-White syndrome: historical and clinical features. Prog. Cardiovasc. Dis. 1960: **2**, 677.
41. Barold, S. S., and Coumel, P.: Mechanisms of atrioventricular tachycardia: Role of reentry and concealed accessory bypass tracts. Am. J. Cardiol. 1977: **39**, 97.
42. Benditt, D. G., et al.: Characteristics of atrioventricular conduction and the spectrum of arrhythmias in Lown-Ganong-Levine syndrome. Circulation 1978: **57**, 454.
43. Castellanos, A., et al.: Factors regulating ventricular rates during atrial flutter and fibrillation in pre-excitation (Wolff-Parkinson-White) syndrome, Br. Heart J. 1973: **35**, 811.
44. Gillette, P. C.: Concealed anomalous cardiac conduction pathways; a frequent cause of supraventricular tachycardia. Am. J. Cardiol. 1977: **40**, 848.
44a. Kennelly, B.M.: The short PR interval. In *What's New in Electrocardiography* p. 172, edited by H.J.J. Wellens and H.E. Kulbertus. Martinus Nijhoff, Boston, 1981.
45. Sellers, T. D., et al.: Effects of procainamide and quinidine sulfate in the Wolff-Parkinson-White syndrome. Circulation 1977: **55**, 15.
46. Sellers, T. D., et al.: Digitalis in the pre-excitation syndrome. Analysis during atrial fibrillation. Circulation 1977: **56**, 260.
47. Sung, R. J., et al.: Mechanisms of reciprocating tachycardia during sinus rhythm in concealed

Wolff-Parkinson-White syndrome. Circulation 1976: **54,** 338.

48. Wellens, H. J., and Durrer, D.: Wolff-Parkinson-White syndrome and atrial fibrillation: Relation between refractory period of accessory pathway and ventricular rate during atrial fibrillation. Am. J. Cardiol. 1974: **34,** 777.

49. Wellens, H. J. J., et al.: The value of the electrocardiogram in the differential diagnosis of a tachycardia with a widened QRS complex. Am. J. Med. 1978: **64,** 27.

Review Tracings

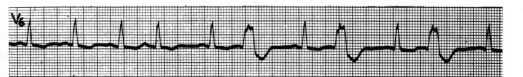

Review Tracing 18.1

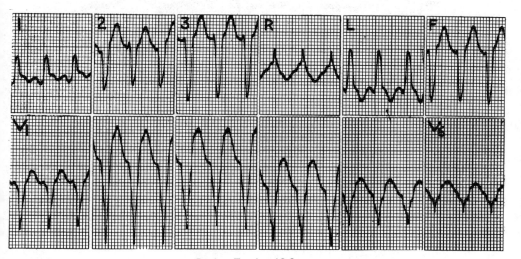

Review Tracing 18.2

For interpretation, see page 483

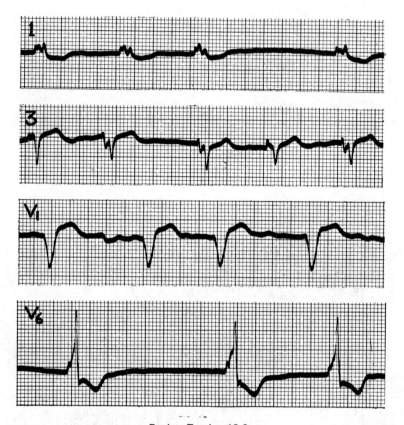

Review Tracing 18.3

For interpretation, see page 483

19

Fusion Beats—
Ventricular and Atrial

The fusion (summation or combination) beat is unrecognizable clinically and is a purely electrocardiographic diagnosis. It is the complex (ventricular or atrial) that results when two (or more) impulses simultaneously activate parts of the same myocardial territory (ventricular or atrial myocardium). The simultaneously spreading impulses, therefore, produce a hybrid complex usually possessing recognizable features of the patterns produced by each alone.

Theoretically, fusion could result from any number of simultaneously spreading impulses, but in practice it is obviously almost always between just two. However, triple fusion has occasionally been recognized in the presence of a WPW syndrome and an ectopic ventricular rhythm.[2, 3]

Ventricular Fusion

The ventricular fusion beat is thought to be of considerable value in recognizing ectopic ventricular rhythms; most authorities believe that the presence of fusion favors ectopy with 85 to 90% odds. The argument runs as follows: if a supraventricular impulse manages to enter the ventricles and merge with a second simultaneously spreading impulse, that second impulse must have arisen within the ventricle itself since—the argument goes—if two supraventricular impulses are heading for the ventricles, the first one to get to the A-V junction will leave the junction refractory and prevent passage of the second; if fusion occurs, therefore, one of the impulses must not be supraventricular and must be ventricular.

By and large, this is probably true; but Kistin[5] demonstrated long ago that it was possible for a descending sinus impulse to fuse with an aberrantly conducted junctional beat. The explanation for this was that the junctional impulse spreads via paraspecific (Mahaim) fibers to the ventricle, leaving the A-V junction clear for the passage of the simultaneous sinus impulse. It is also true that the majority of Wolff-Parkinson-White (WPW) beats represent fusion

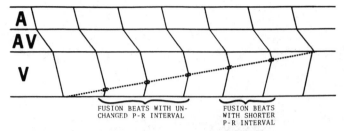

Figure 19.1. Ladder diagram illustrating progressively "higher" levels of fusion within the ventricles. The first beat represents a pure sinus beat; the last beat, a pure ventricular ectopic. Note that at first the P-R intervals remain the same as that of the sinus beat (as long as the sinus impulse invades the ventricles before or no later than the ectopic center fires); but when the ectopic center fires before the sinus impulse has arrived, the P-R becomes shorter than that of the sinus beat.

between the two wave fronts of the dichotomized sinus impulse, some of which spreads normally through the A-V junction and some through the accessory pathway (bundle of Kent). There is no question that it is possible to have fusion between two supraventricular impulses; nevertheless, the usefulness of fusion beats in favoring ventricular ectopy cannot be denied.

Ventricular fusion may result from various pairs of impulses (table 19.1) but is generally seen between a descending sinus and an ectopic ventricular impulse. The ectopic contributor may be an extrasystole, ventricular tachycardia (VT), accelerated idioventricular rhythm (AIVR), parasystole, or an escape or paced beat. Less often, the supraventricular contributor may be an ectopic atrial or junctional impulse. Ventricular fusion can also result from the simultaneous spread of two ectopic ventricular impulses, as when two idioventricular pacemakers, one in each ventricle, are competing for control.

There are three main principles in the diagnosis of ventricular fusion:[6]

1. You must have demonstrable reason to believe that two impulses were due at the moment that fusion is postulated. (This is so obvious that one feels that it should not have to be stated, but it emphatically requires to be stated because fusion beats are plucked out of thin air, without reason, more than any other electrocardiographic item.)
2. The contour of the fusion beat should be intermediate in shape and duration between the QRS contours of the two supposedly fusing impulses. (There are two exceptions to this to be discussed later.)
3. The P-R interval of a fusion beat may be the same as that of the conducted sinus beats, or it may be shorter (fig. 19.1); but if it is shorter, it will not as a rule be more than 0.06 sec shorter than the basic P-R. (In one exceptional circumstance, the P-R may actually be longer; this is when the subject has R-P dependent P-R intervals, i.e., has the potential for varying P-R intervals à la Wenckebach. In such a patient, if the sinus

Table 19.1
Potential Partners in Fusion (Any of the Impulses in A Can Fuse with Any in B)

A	B
Sinus	Ectopic ventricular
Ectopic atrial	Extrasystole
Junctional	Tachycardia
Ectopic ventricular	Accelerated idioventricular
	Parasystole
	Escape
	Pacemaker
	Junctional conducted
	preferentially
	Sinus or ectopic atrial
	conducted by Kent bundle

impulse arises early in diastole, it may be conducted with delay and fuse after a prolonged P-R interval.)

Fusion with Ventricular Extrasystoles

In order for a sinus impulse to fuse with a premature beat, the beat must usually qualify as an "end-diastolic" extrasystole; i.e., at normal sinus rates, the ectopic beat must occur late enough to follow the next sinus P wave. Figure 19.2 shows a ventricular bigeminy in which the coupling intervals are long enough to deposit the extrasystoles after the next sinus P waves. Ventricular fusion beats (labelled 1, 2, 3 and 4) result from the gradually lengthening coupling interval. The first two extrasystoles capture the whole myocardium; but, beginning with the third extrasystole, there is time for the sinus impulse to enter the ventricles before they have been completely activated from the ectopic center. As the coupling interval and with it the P-R interval lengthens, the sinus contribution to the ventricular fusion complex increases (see fig. 19.2, ladder diagram).

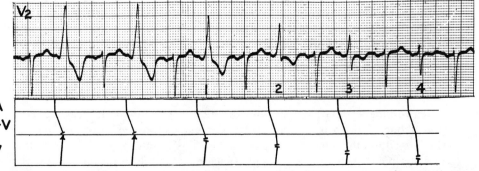

Figure 19.2. "End-diastolic" **ventricular extrasystoles** landing after the next P wave. After the first two extrasystoles, their coupling intervals progressively lengthen so that fusion occurs (beats 1, 2, 3 and 4) at progressively "lower" levels in the ventricles with more and more contribution from the sinus impulse. The P-R interval of beat 4 is as long as that of the sinus beats.

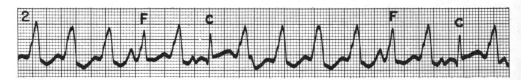

Figure 19.3. Ventricular tachycardia (rate, 126/min) interrupted by two **fusion beats** (F) and two capture beats (C) in a patient with acute inferior infarction.

Occasionally, the coincidence of a more or less simultaneous atrial and ventricular extrasystole produces ventricular fusion.

Fusion during VT

The value of fusion beats in the diagnosis of VT was emphasized by Dressler,[1] and such beats are often referred to as Dressler beats. Their presence is considered excellent evidence in favor of VT, but their value is limited by the fact that they are seldom seen in the faster tachycardias—if the rate is much over 150/min, one is unlikely to find fusion beats. All of the examples published by Dressler had a rate less than 150/min. Figure 19.3 shows an example of fusion beats punctuating VT. Note that the rate of the tachycardia is only about 126/min and that there are capture beats (C) as well as fusion beats (F).

Fusion during AIVR

AIVR is a common source of fusion and for the good reason that its rate is often closely similar to the competing sinus rate. For this same reason, it is not surprising that the championship for consecutive fusion beats has been won by this rhythm! Figure 19.4 is a champion tracing boasting no less than 37 consecutive fusion beats. The beat marked "*x*" in the top strip is the last of the pure ectopic beats, and that marked "*x*" in the bottom strip is the first of the pure sinus beats. Between these 2 beats lie the 37 fusion beats showing contribution by the ectopic and sinus impulses in varying proportions.

Since many examples of AIVR have rates little different from the sinus, it is quite common for short runs of AIVR to begin and end with fusion beats. Figure 19.5 illustrates just such a run of AIVR.

Fusion with Ventricular Parasystole

If two independent rhythms with different rates continue to beat regularly and if one of them is ectopic ventricular and "protected" from (cannot be discharged by) the other, i.e., is parasystolic, it is a mathematical certainty that at some point their discharges will coincide and produce fusion. Ventricular parasystole, therefore, if long enough strips are taken, will always manifest

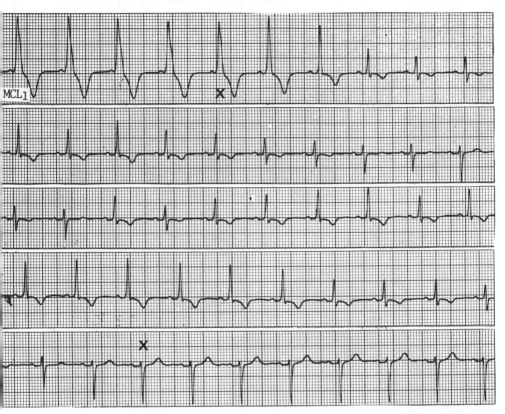

Figure 19.4. Fusion in profusion! In these five continuous strips, there are 37 consecutive fusion beats between the complexes marked "x." The **AIVR** from the left ventricle (seen pure in the first five beats of the top strip) and the sinus rhythm (seen pure in the last eight beats in the bottom strip) have identical rates; slight beat-to-beat fluctuations in the cycle length of one or other pacemaker alters the contribution to the fusion complex by each pacemaker but is not enough to disengage them.

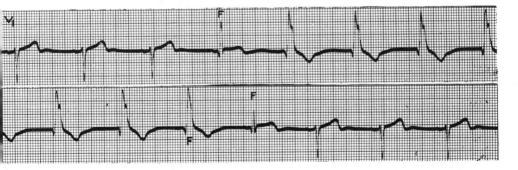

Figure 19.5. The strips are continuous. **AIVR** from the left ventricle (rate, 58/min) taking over from a sinus rhythm with an almost identical rate that slows slightly. The run of AIVR is ushered in and out by **fusion beats (F).**

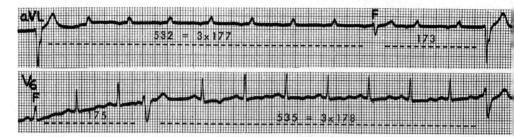

Figure 19.6.   Ventricular parasystole with **fusion beats.** The diagnosis of parasystole is established by the varying "coupling" intervals and the fact that the longer interectopic interval is a multiple of the shorter interectopic interval—from fusion beat (F) to next ectopic beat—in each lead.

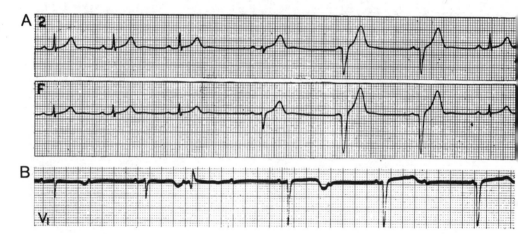

Figure 19.7.   Ventricular escape. A. In each strip, the sinus rhythm slows and allows an idioventricular center to escape for three beats. The first and third of these escapes in each strip form **fusion beats.** B. The strip begins with 2:1 A-V block (note the different P-R intervals of the conducted beats—presumably type I block with R-P dependent P-R intervals); then a ventricular extrasystole is followed by a longer cycle which enables an idioventricular pacemaker to escape. The first of the three escape beats is narrower than the last two, is preceded by a P wave at a conductible interval and is clearly a **fusion beat.**

fusion beats. This is not to say that fusion is necessary for the diagnosis, only that it is an inevitable eventual finding. Figure 19.6 is an example of ventricular parasystole with fusion.

Fusion with Ventricular Escape Beats

This fusion-producing combination is seen, for example, when an AIVR escapes from an even slower sinus rhythm; or when, in the presence of incomplete A-V block, conduction occurs at the same time that an idioventricular pacemaker escapes.

Figure 19.5 illustrated the beginning of a run of AIVR which took over from the sinus rhythm because the sinus rhythm slowed; the AIVR is, therefore, by definition an escape rhythm.

Figure 19.7*A* shows progressive slowing of the sinus rate with consequent escape by an idioventricular pacemaker at a rate of 48/min. The fifth beat in each strip is a full-blown ectopic beat (idioventricular); the fourth and sixth beats are fusion beats.

Figure 19.7*B* begins with 2:1 A-V block and ends with 2 idioventricular beats. The fourth beat in the strip is somewhat narrower than the idioventricular beats, is preceded by a P wave at a conductible interval and is therefore a fusion beat.

Fusion with Paced Beats

The pacemaker is a splendid fusion factory: the demand model is a perfect artificial analog of ventricular escape, and the fixed-rate pacemaker is an equally perfect analog of ventricular parasystole. Both types of pacemaker, therefore, produce fusion beats in exactly the same way as their natural prototypes. Figure 19.8*A* shows a demand pacemaker producing fusion beats as the sinus rhythm accelerates and takes control: as the sinus P wave emerges in front of the pacemaker "blip," partial conduction occurs and fusion (F) results. Figure 19.8*B* illustrates a fixed-rate pacemaker ignoring in its autocratic way the sinus beats in the top strip and finally fusing with one (F) toward the end of the bottom strip.

"Two Wrongs Sometimes Make a Right"

"Two wrongs sometimes make a right" is the picturesque way in which Schamroth indicates that there are circumstances in which two impulses, each

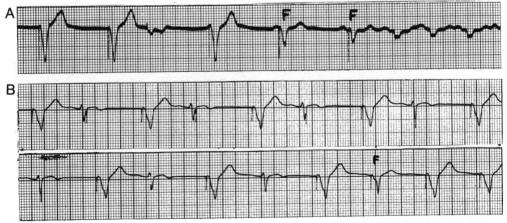

Figure 19.8. Two examples of **fusion** between paced and sinus beats. (*A*) In the second half of the strip, a demand right ventricular pacemaker produces fusion with an accelerating sinus rhythm. (*B*) The two strips are continuous. A fixed-rate right ventricular pacemaker beats relentlessly in competition with the sinus rhythm to produce a form of "escape-capture" bigeminy in the top strip. Toward the end of the bottom strip, it at last achieves fusion (F).

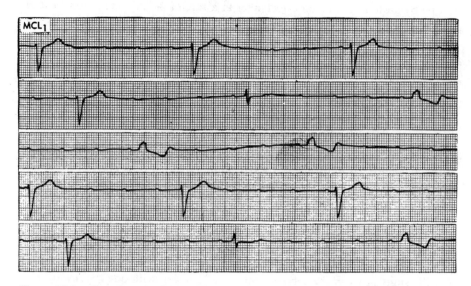

Figure 19.9.   **Complete A-V block** with two competing idioventricular pacemakers, one in each ventricle (right ventricular in *first* and *fourth strips*, left ventricular in *third strip*). In the *second* and *fifth strips*, the middle beats are narrow **fusion beats** thanks to simultaneous activation of the two ventricles.

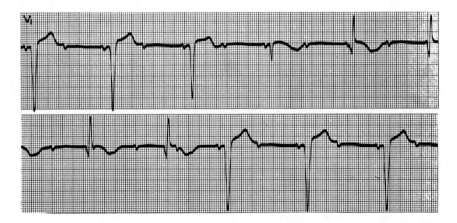

Figure 19.10.   The strips are continuous. The basic rhythm is **2:1 A-V block**, probably type II, with **LBBB** seen at the beginning of the top strip and in the second half of the bottom strip. The last two beats in the *top strip* and the first two in the *bottom strip* represent an idioventricular rhythm from the left ventricle. The third and fourth beats in the *top strip* are **fusion beats**—note the normal appearance of beat 4.

of which on its own produces an abnormal complex, may create a normal-looking complex when they fuse. This may happen when two idioventricular centers, one in each ventricle, are competing for control. Each center by itself would produce a wide ectopic complex; but if they both activate their respective ventricles simultaneously, the resulting fusion complex will be normally narrow and bear no resemblance to either of its "component" complexes (fig. 19.9).

It may also happen if there is an ectopic center on the same side as a BBB. In this case, if the ectopic focus discharges at the same moment that the sinus impulse enters the contralateral ventricle, the resulting fusion complex will be normally narrow (fig. 19.10), though each impulse on its own produces a wide complex.

In both these circumstances, the principle enunciated earlier, that fusion complexes are intermediate in form and width, is violated.

Fusion between Supraventricular Impulses

I pointed out above that fusion, though useful in the diagnosis of ectopy, *could* occur between two supraventricular impulses. In the WPW syndrome, the famous "concertina" effect is due to a progressively changing contribution from each of the two wave fronts of the dichotomized sinus impulse. The first four beats in the bottom strip of figure 19.11 show progressive widening of the QRS, with concomitant shortening of the P-R, as more and more of the QRS is accounted for by accessory-pathway conduction and less and less by orthodox conduction.

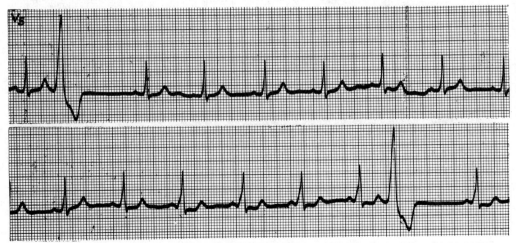

Figure 19.11. The strips are continuous. **WPW syndrome** interrupted by two ventricular extrasystoles. The "concertina" effect is seen at the beginning of the *bottom strip* where the first three or four beats manifest progressive widening of the QRS with corresponding shortening of the P-R.

Fusion between two supraventricular impulses can also occur when an aberrantly conducted junctional impulse fuses with a simultaneously descending sinus impulse.[5] Figure 19.12 illustrates a probable example of this: the independent beats have an incomplete RBBB pattern, whereas the conducted sinus beats have no r′, suggesting that the independent focus is situated leftward in the junction and experiences delay in reaching and traversing the RBB (see Chapter 16). The fourth beat in the top strip and third in the bottom strip are presumable fusion beats between sinus and A-V impulses.

Atrial Fusion

When two impulses simultaneously invade the atria, atrial fusion results. This is most often seen in the presence of a wandering pacemaker when pacemaking is shifting back and forth between sinus node and A-V junction. In such a case, if the junctional pacemaker sends its retrograde impulse into the atrium at the same time that the sinus impulse is also activating atrial muscle, an atrial fusion beat results (fig. 19.13). Atrial fusion may also be seen when an ectopic ventricular pacemaker succeeds in pushing its impulse retrogradely into the atria at a time when the sinus impulse is also on the go (fig. 19.14).

When Kistin[4] demonstrated, with the help of esophageal leads, that retrograde conduction to the atria was a common event with ventricular extrasystoles yet was seldom seen in the clinical tracing, he suggested that their absence could be explained by assuming that they produced relatively isoelectric, and therefore invisible, atrial fusion beats.

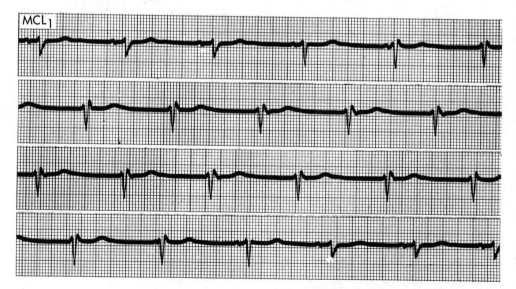

Figure 19.12. The strips are continuous. After three sinus beats, a presumable junctional rhythm escapes because the sinus rhythm slows. The escaping rhythm is characterized by rSr′ configuration suggesting incomplete RBBB, probably because the junctional pacemaker is situated toward the left side. The fourth beat in the *top strip* and the third in the *bottom strip* are **fusion beats**.

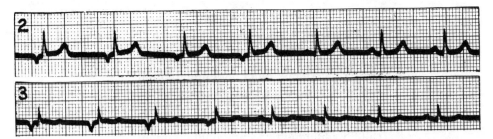

Figure 19.13.   Shifting pacemaker. In each lead, **junctional rhythm** with retrograde conduction shifts to sinus rhythm. In lead 2, the third, fourth and fifth P waves are intermediate in form between retrograde and sinus P's and presumably represent **atrial fusion.** In lead 3, only the fourth P wave is due to fusion.

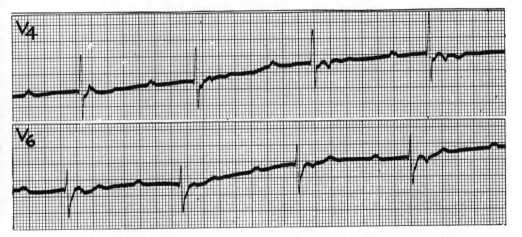

Figure 19.14.   Complete A-V block, yet retrograde V-A conduction occurs after the third and fourth beats in V₄ and after the fourth beat in lead V₆. Following the second QRS in V₄ and following the second and third QRS in V₆, sinus and retrograde P waves coincide to produce **atrial fusion.**

REFERENCES

1. Dressler, W., and Roesler, H.: The occurrence in paroxysmal ventricular tachycardia of ventricular complexes transitional in shape to sinoauricular beats. Am. Heart J. 1952: **44,** 485.
2. Dubb, A., and Schamroth, L.: Ventricular parasystole with the Wolff-Parkinson-White syndrome. Chest 1979: **75,** 607.
3. Kinoshita, S., et al.: Triple ventricular fusion due to intermittent ventricular parasystole in the Wolff-Parkinson-White syndrome. Am. Heart J. 1981: **102,** 290.
4. Kistin, A. D., and Landowne, M.: Retrograde conduction from premature ventricular contractions, a common occurrence in the human heart. Circulation 1951: **3,** 738.
5. Kistin, A. D.: Problems in the differentiation of ventricular arrhythmia from supraventricular arrhythmia with abnormal QRS. Prog. Cardiovasc. Dis. 1966: **9,** 1.
6. Marriott, H. J. L., et al.: Ventricular fusion beats. Circulation 1962: **26,** 880.

Review Tracings

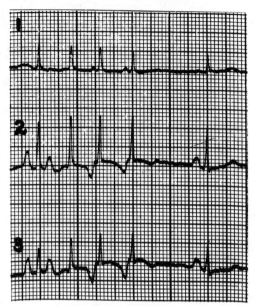

Review Tracing 19.1

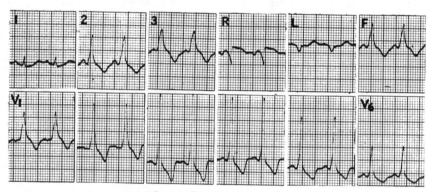

Review Tracing 19.2

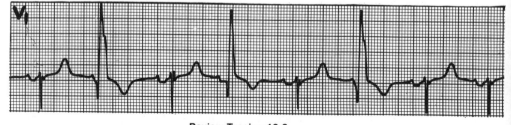

Review Tracing 19.3

For interpretation, see page 483

20

Subsidiary Supraventricular Rhythms

This chapter deals with a number of ectopic rhythms arising in either the atria or the A-V junction. Some are well defined and understood; the identity of others is less secure.

A-V Junctional Rhythms

A-V junctional rhythm was first experimentally produced in the animal by Engelmann in 1903. When Tawara described the A-V node three years later, the rhythm that Engelmann described became "nodal." Zahn then, in 1913, introduced the concept of "upper," "middle," and "lower" nodal rhythm based on the temporal relationship of atrial to ventricular activation; and in the following year, Meek and Eyster described the electrocardiographic features that were generally accepted for decades. Modern methods of investigation, however, have cast doubt on the A-V node as a source of spontaneous impulse formation, on the concept of "upper," "middle," and "lower" junctional rhythms, and on our ability to recognize the source of the atrial impulse from the pattern of the P wave in the surface electrocardiogram.

The A-V junction is divided into four parts[6]: the "approaches" to the A-V node; the A-V node proper; the penetrating portion of the A-V bundle (bundle of His), which enters the central fibrous body and is in danger of strangulation if that body becomes calcified; and the nonpenetrating, nonbranching portion. The branching portion which spawns the bundle branches is regarded as subjunctional.[6] Just where in this junctional conglomerate automatic impulses arise is still a matter of debate. It is widely accepted that the bundle of His possesses pacemaking potential; it is considered probable that the N-H region (junction of node with bundle) also possesses automaticity; and it is widely doubted that the node itself can form impulses. However, Scherlag[17] asserts that there are two forms of junctional rhythm, one that arises in the A-V node proper and one that arises in the His bundle; the characteristics of these two forms are summarized in table 20.1.

Table 20.1
Characteristics of Junctional Rhythms[17]

	Nodal Rhythm	His Rhythm
Intrinsic rate	45–60/min	35–45/min
Atropine effect	Rate increased by 35–45/min	No significant rate change

To avoid terminological controversies, I shall use the noncommittal terms "A-V junctional," "junctional," or just plain "A-V," which has enjoyed uninterrupted usage since 1915.

Junctional Rhythm

In A-V junctional rhythm, the impulse travels anterogradely and retrogradely at the same time, to write a normal QRS-T (unless aberrant) and a retrograde P wave. Depending upon the rate of conduction in each direction, the P wave may be inscribed shortly in front of the ventricular complex, may follow the QRS, or it may be lost within it. An example of junctional rhythm with short P-R interval is illustrated in figure 20.1, and one with the retrograde P waves following the QRS in figure 20.2.

Figure 20.1 also shows the usual retrograde P-wave polarity in the 12-lead tracing: The axis of the P wave is in the neighborhood of −90°—it is nearly isoelectric in lead 1, frankly inverted in leads 2, 3, and aVF, and upright in aVR and aVL; it is usually inverted in left chest leads (V_{5-6}) and at least partly upright in V_1.

Though there is little doubt that the majority of retrograde P waves manifest this polarity, one should know and keep in mind that retrograde conduction can produce positive P waves in leads 2, 3, and aVF[10, 20] and in fact the

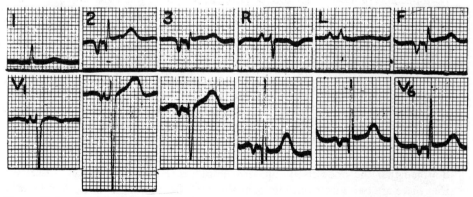

Figure 20.1. **Junctional rhythm** showing the typical polarity of retrograde P waves: flat in lead 1; inverted in 2, 3, aVF, and left chest leads; upright in aVR and aVL; and at least partly upright (often − +) in lead V_1. The P-R interval is about 0.12 sec.

localizing status of human P waves is so uncertain that we can echo the gloomy pronouncement of Waldo and James[21] that neither P-wave polarity nor the P-R interval are dependable guides to the origin of the atrial impulse.

The various rhythms that originate in or occupy the A-V junction are listed in table 20.2. The rhythms "by default" put in an appearance only if the higher pacemaker, the sinus node, fails to maintain control; this may happen if the sinus node itself slows or fails or if block prevents its impulses from reaching the ventricles.

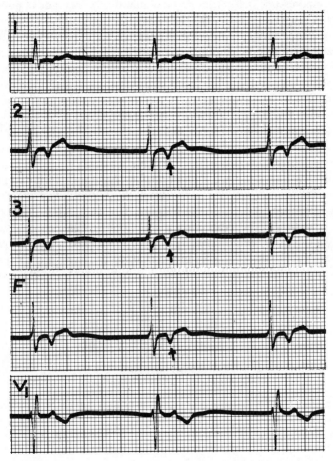

Figure 20.2. A-V rhythm, rate 47. Note the inverted P waves (arrows) following the QRS in 2, 3 and aVF with upright P waves in V₁.

A-V junctional rhythm, therefore, since it is always secondary to failure of the higher mechanism, is never in itself a primary diagnosis; and the same is true of all rhythms by default. When a single junctional beat comes to the rescue after a longer cycle than the dominant cycle, it is an escape beat (fig. 20.3). Junctional escape beats seldom show manifest retrograde conduction to the atria—the escaping junctional QRS stands either isolated or attended by the adjacent, dissociated sinus P wave. In both of the examples in figure 20.3, the absence of retrograde conduction is attributable to the adjacent sinus activity, which obviously precludes retrograde conduction to the atria. But in other instances, where there is no nearby sinus P wave, retrograde P waves are often noticeably absent. In such cases, either there is no retrograde conduction or, alternatively, the retrograde P wave coincides with and is lost within the QRS complex.

When the junction escapes for several consecutive beats without retrograde conduction, a run of "idiojunctional" rhythm results. The prefix "idio-" (as also in idioventricular) implies that the ventricles have their own pacemaker to themselves—not shared with the atria (from the Greek, *idios*, which means "one's own," "private," "personal"). In figure 20.4, after two sinus beats there is a pause, and before the next tardy atrial impulse can be conducted, the junction takes over and retains control of the ventricles for five beats before the sinus node recaptures the ventricles in the next-to-last beat. This then is a run of idiojunctional rhythm dissociated from the concomitant sinus bradycardia.

Salient Features of A-V Rhythms

1. Abnormal P waves closely preceding or following QRS; or absent P waves
2. Normal QRST sequence

Table 20.2
A-V Junctional Rhythms

By Default	By Usurpation
A-V junctional escape	A-V extrasystoles
	Manifest
	Concealed
A-V junctional rhythm	A-V parasystole
Idiojunctional rhythm	Accelerated A-V rhythm
	Accelerated idiojunctional rhythm
	A-V tachycardia
	Reciprocating
	Ectopic

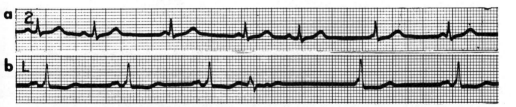

Figure 20.3.   Junctional escape beats. In *a*, the third, fourth, sixth, and seventh beats are junctional escapes owing to the lengthened sinus cycles. In *b*, the fourth beat is a ventricular extrasystole with retrograde conduction; the postextrasystolic pause ends with a junctional escape beat.

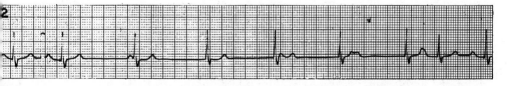

Figure 20.4.   After two sinus beats with first degree A-V block, a sinus pause permits an A-V pacemaker to escape at a rate of about 54/min. The resulting **idiojunctional rhythm** produces a run of A-V dissociation until the sinus pacemaker recaptures the ventricles for the last two beats.

Shifting or Wandering Pacemaker

The terms "shifting" and "wandering" pacemaker often are—but should not be—applied when the P wave changes with usurping ectopic atrial beats. The terms are appropriate when two (usually sinus and junctional) or more competing supraventricular rhythms, having approximately the same rate, vie with one another for control of the heart. Two typical examples are shown in figure 20.5. In lead 1 of figure 20.5*A*, after three sinus beats, an A-V rhythm takes over without measurable change in the atrial rate. In lead 2, the sinus node regains control in the middle of the strip when the A-V pacemaker pauses perceptibly. Often, as is seen in figure 20.5*B*, atrial fusion beats intervene between the pure sinus and pure retrograde P waves.

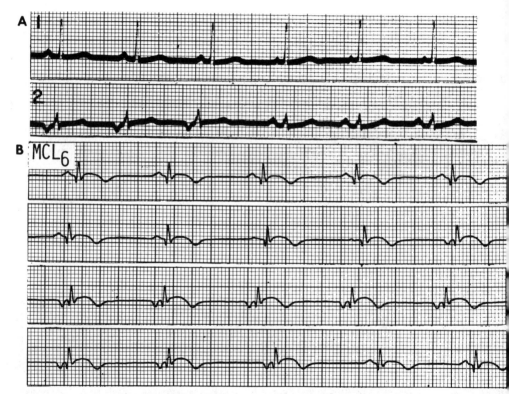

Figure 20.5.   Shifting or **wandering pacemaker.** In *A*, the first three beats in lead 1 are sinus; then without any measurable change in cycle length, pacemaking shifts to the A-V junction. In lead 2, after three junctional beats, the sinus node regains control at the end of a slightly longer cycle. In *B*, the four strips are continuous. The top strip shows only sinus rhythm, and the third strip shows only junctional rhythm. The last three beats in the second strip show atrial fusion. In the bottom strip, after three junctional beats, the sinus node takes over again for the last two beats.

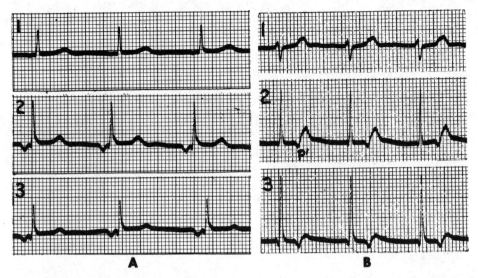

Figure 20.6.   Accelerated junctional rhythm with retrograde conduction. In *A*, the retrograde P waves closely precede the QRS (P-R = 0.12 sec). In *B*, the retrograde P waves follow the QRS at an R-P interval of 0.19 sec.

Accelerated Junctional Rhythm

When the junction seizes control by firing before the next expected beat of the dominant rhythm, it is said to take over "by usurpation." Junctional extrasystoles, junctional parasystole and the junctional tachycardias have been dealt with in previous chapters.

If the junctional rate exceeds 60/min but is less than 100/min, it is usually referred to as an accelerated rhythm. Figure 20.6 presents two examples of accelerated A-V junctional rhythm in which the junctional pacemaker controls both ventricles and atria: in *A*, the retrograde P waves closely precede the QRS complexes with typical retrograde polarity; in *B*, the retrograde P waves follow the QRS at a normal R-P interval.

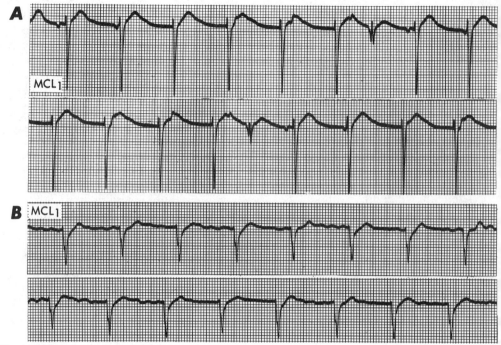

Figure 20.7. Accelerated idiojunctional rhythm with **A-V dissociation.** (A) Strips are continuous; the junctional rhythm at a rate of 76/min is dissociated from the sinus rhythm (rate 72/min). The seventh beat in the *top strip* and the fifth in the *bottom strip* are ventricular capture beats with prolonged P-R intervals and ventricular aberration. (B) Strips are continuous. **Atrial fibrillation** with some degree of A-V block and an accelerated idiojunctional rhythm at a rate of 72/min.

On the other hand, figure 20.7A illustrates an idiojunctional rhythm which usurps control from a slower sinus pacemaker; the two rhythms remain dissociated except for the two ventricular captures by the sinus node. Figure 20.7B illustrates an accelerated idiojunctional rhythm dissociated from fibrillating atria—a combination that should always make one think of the possibility of digitalis intoxication.

Accelerated junctional rhythms are one of the relatively common causes of A-V dissociation, especially seen in acute inferior myocardial infarction, rheumatic fever, and digitalis intoxication.

Ectopic Atrial Rhythms

Left Atrial Rhythms

Our time-honored concepts of A-V rhythm were upset by Mirowski who drew attention to the fact that we have based our diagnosis of junctional activity on the P-wave pattern in the limb leads alone and ignored their morphology in the chest leads.[12] He maintained that many of the rhythms that we call junctional are really of left atrial origin and he suggested that an important criterion for left atrial rhythm was an inverted P wave in V_6, often associated with an upright P wave in V_1. His argument does not explain why "left atrial" rhythms should so often have short P-R intervals, and for the moment the matter must remain unsettled. Meanwhile he has done us a service in focussing attention on the precordial P waves in tracings that show typical "retrograde" P waves in the limb leads.

Probably more helpful in the diagnosis of left atrial rhythm are the rather specific "dome-and-dart" P wave in V_1 (fig. 20.8) and/or the frankly inverted P wave in standard lead 1.[1, 22]

Slow Atrial Rhythm

This is defined[3] as an atrial rhythm at a rate between 50 and 80/min, with P waves different from the sinus P waves and with a normal or slightly longer than normal P-R interval. Thus most examples of "coronary sinus rhythm," as described below, qualify for this category; but slow atrial rhythm does not require P waves of retrograde form, they must merely be *different* from the sinus P wave. This rhythm may be an index of an underlying sick sinus (p. 318).

An alternative and preferable term is **ectopic atrial rhythm**[5]—to be preferred because the changed form of the P wave, presumably due to a shift in the pacemaker, is its characteristic feature rather than an identifying rate which, after all, is in the sinus range; and rates of up to 80/min hardly qualify as "slow."

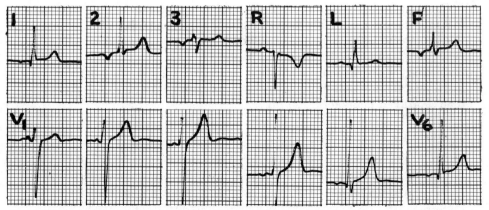

Figure 20.8. Probable **left atrial rhythm.** Note the "dome-and-dart" P wave in V_1 and the slightly inverted P wave in lead 1.

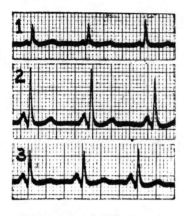

Figure 20.9. An example of a short-PR-normal-QRS "syndrome," often called Lown-Ganong-Levine (LGL) syndrome and formerly sometimes known as coronary nodal rhythm. The P-R interval is only 0.08 sec.

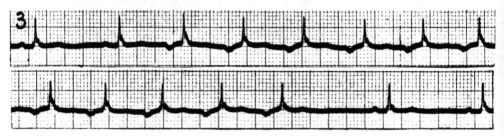

Figure 20.10. Strips are continuous. An example of what has been known as coronary sinus rhythm, but is better called ectopic atrial rhythm. After two sinus beats, the ectopic focus takes over for an 11-beat run, followed by a return to sinus rhythm.

Outmoded Atrial Rhythms

A question is still occasionally asked concerning the nature of the following two terms:

Coronary nodal rhythm was formerly applied by some authorities when the P-R interval was abnormally short (less than 0.12 sec) and followed by a normal QRS complex[2, 8] (fig. 20.9). Others called it the Lown-Ganong-Levine (LGL) syndrome,[9] and this is dealt with in Chapter 18.

Coronary sinus rhythm was the term Scherf[14, 15] applied when the P waves had a typical retrograde morphology but were associated with a normal (rather than short) P-R interval (fig. 20.10).

REFERENCES

1. Bix, H. H.: The electrocardiographic pattern of initial stimulation in the left auricle. Sinai Hosp. J. 1953: **2,** 37.
2. Eyring, E. J., and Spodick, C. H.: Coronary nodal rhythm. Am. J. Cardiol. 1960: **5,** 781.
3. Ferrer, M. I.: Significance of slow atrial rhythm. Am. J. Cardiol. 1980: **46,** 176.
4. Fisch, C., and Knoebel, S. B.: Junctional rhythms. Prog. Cardiovasc. Dis. 1970: **13,** 141.
5. Gaughan, G. L., and Gorfinkel, H. J.: Physiologic and biologic variants of the electrocardiogram. Cardiovasc. Clin. 1977: **8,** 7.

6. Hecht, H. H., et al.: Atrioventricular and intraventricular conduction: revised nomenclature and concepts. Am. J. Cardiol. 1973: **31**, 232.
7. Hoffman, B. F., and Cranefield, P. F.: The physiological basis of cardiac arrhythmias. Am. J. Med. 1964: **37**, 670.
8. Katz, L. N., and Pick, A.: *Clinical Electrocardiography. The Arrhythmias.* Lea & Febiger, Philadelphia, 1956.
9. Lown, B., et al.: The syndrome of the short P-R interval normal QRS complex and paroxysmal rapid heart action. Circulation 1952: **5**, 693.
10. MacLean, W. A. H., et al.: P waves during ectopic atrial rhythms in man. A study utilizing atrial pacing with fixed electrodes. Circulation 1975: **52**, 426.
11. Marriott, H. J. L.: Nodal mechanisms with dependent activation of atria and ventricles. In *Mechanisms and Therapy of Cardiac Arrhythmias*, 14th Hahnemann Symposium, Grune & Stratton, New York, 1966.
12. Mirowski, M.: Left atrial rhythm. Diagnostic criteria and differentiation from nodal arrhythmias. Am. J. Cardiol. 1966: **17**, 203.
13. Pick, A.: Mechanisms of cardiac arrhythmias: from hypothesis to physiologic fact. Am. Heart J. 1973: **86**, 249.
14. Scherf, D., and Gurbuzer, B.: Further studies on coronary sinus rhythm. Am. J. Cardiol. 1958: **16**, 579.
15. Scherf, D., and Harris, R.: Coronary sinus rhythm. Am. Heart J. 1946: **32**, 443.
16. Scherf, D., and Cohen, J.: *The Atrioventricular Node and Selected Cardiac Arrhythmias.* Grune & Stratton, New York, 1964.
17. Scherlag, B. J., et al.: Differentiation of "A-V junctional rhythms." Circulation 1973: **48**, 304.
18. Somlyo, A. P., and Grayzel, J.: Left atrial arrhythmias. Am. Heart J. 1963: **65**, 68.
19. Spodick, D. H., and Colman, R.: Observations on coronary sinus rhythm and its mechanism. Am. J. Cardiol. 1961: **7**, 198.
20. Waldo, A. L., et al.: Sequence of retrograde activation of the human heart. Correlation with P wave polarity. Br. Heart J. 1977: **39**, 634.
21. Waldo, A. L., and James, T. N.: A retrospective look at A-V nodal rhythms. Circulation 1973: **47**, 222.
22. Beder, S.D., et al.: Clinical confirmation of ECG criteria for left atrial rhythm. Am. Heart J. 1982: **103**, 848.

Review Tracings

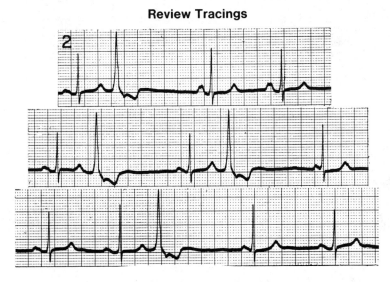

Review Tracing 20.1
For interpretation, see page 483

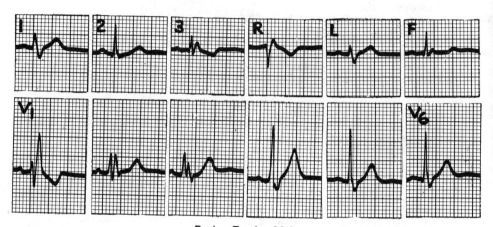

Review Tracing 20.2

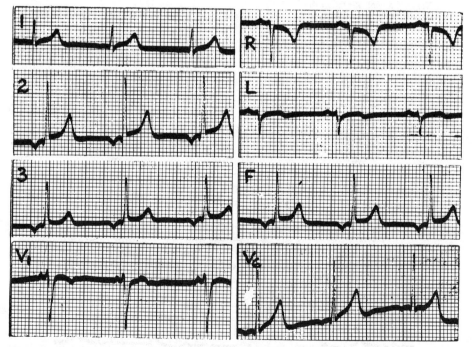

Review Tracing 20.3

For interpretation, see page 483

21

Escape and Dissociation

The dysrhythmic disturbances so far considered have been primary disorders of either impulse formation or conduction. The two phenomena, escape and dissociation, discussed in this chapter, are NOT primary diagnoses—they are, like jaundice or headache, symptomatic of some underlying primary disturbance to which they are secondary.

Escape

The escape(d) beat is an ectopic, automatic beat that ends a cycle longer than the cycle of the dominant rhythm. It is a rescuing beat—a friend in need—and as such, of course, should *never* be treated. The escape beat arises because, for some reason, the higher pacemaker has failed to maintain control and so a pause has been provided that has given the escaping pacemaker time for its slope of diastolic depolarization to reach threshold. Just as the fixed-rate pacemaker is a precise artificial analogue of parasystole, so the demand pacemaker is the analogue of spontaneous escape rhythms. Normally, all potential escape foci are subdued by the faster beating sinus node, and it is only when this hegemony falters that an escaping rhythm (or a demand pacemaker) has the opportunity to assert itself.

Escape can result from three of the four mechanisms that can produce A-V dissociation:

1. Slowing of primary pacemaker
   Sinus bradycardia
2. Block of primary impulses
   Incomplete S-A block
   Incomplete A-V block
   Complete A-V block
3. Pause producers
   Extrasystoles
   Termination of tachycardia

These three mechanisms are illustrated in figure 21.1.

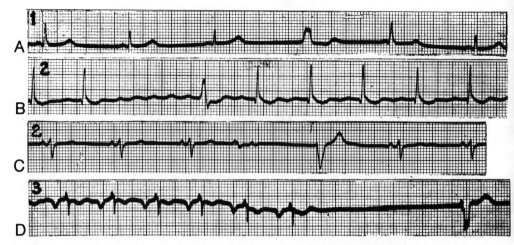

Figure 21.1.   Ventricular escape. (*A*) As a result of sinus slowing, the fourth beat is a ventricular escape, and the fifth a fusion beat. (*B*) An atrial tachyarrhythmia (?flutter) with predominantly 3:1 conduction. After the second beat, several consecutive atrial impulses are blocked, producing a pause that enables a ventricular pacemaker to escape. (*C*) The fourth beat is a VPB; the longer postextrasystolic cycle provides the opportunity for another ectopic ventricular pacemaker to escape. (*D*) The pause following the abrupt cessation of an ectopic atrial rhythm enables a ventricular pacemaker to escape.

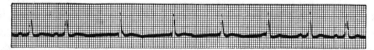

Figure 21.2.   Transient sinus slowing induced by a deep breath. After the second beat, the sinus rhythm slows and junctional escape results for four beats. The sinus node then accelerates and resumes control for the last two beats.

Usually the escaping pacemaker is in the A-V junction (**junctional escape**), but, if this also defaults, a Purkinje focus in the ventricles may take over (**ventricular escape**). **Atrial escape** is not much talked about, yet it is a common finding after ectopic atrial activity.

Junctional Escape

When something goes wrong with the normal formation or conduction of the sinus impulse, the next officer in the pacemaking hierarchy is the A-V junction; so the most common form of escape is junctional. Junctional escapes are recognized by their unchanged or only slightly changed QRS complex ending a cycle longer than the dominant cycle and, for some reason, they are usually *not* associated with retrograde conduction. At times this absence of retroconduction is obviously because the atria have already been activated by the sinus impulse (see fig. 21.2); but even when there is no neighboring sinus activity, there is a conspicuous scarcity of visible retrograde atrial activation in association with single junctional escape beats.

At times junctional escape beats are characterized by marked aberration, and then distinction from ventricular escapes may be difficult and is sometimes impossible. Neither does fusion in such a case clinch the diagnosis of ectopy since Kistin[3] years ago demonstrated that aberrantly conducted junctional beats could fuse with sinus impulses (see Chapter 19).

Ventricular Escape

Ventricular escape is diagnosed when the QRS of the rescuing beat is wide and bizarre. It may be diagnosed with some confidence if the complex manifests a shape characteristic of ventricular ectopy (Chapters 11 and 15); otherwise there is always the possibility that the escaping beat is junctional with type B aberration (p. 237). Figure 21.1 illustrates presumed ventricular escape resulting from each of the three mechanisms listed above.

Atrial Escape

Atrial escape beats are seldom heard of, although they are commonly seen, especially after ectopic atrial activity or retrograde conduction has suppressed the sinus node. They are recognized by the altered P wave that ends a cycle longer than the sinus cycle. Figure 21.3 illustrates atrial escape beats following an APB, following a ventricular extrasystole with retrograde conduction and interrupting a sinus pause.

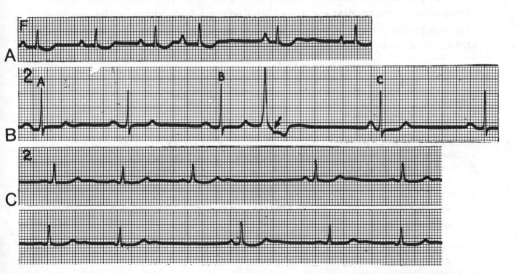

Figure 21.3.   Atrial escape. (A) The fourth beat is an obvious APB followed by a more-than-fully-compensatory cycle. Note that the two returning beats are atrial escapes. (B) After three sinus beats, the VPB with retrograde conduction (*arrow*) discharges the sinus node ahead of schedule so that the returning beat, despite being an atrial escape, is also ahead of schedule; i.e., B − C = less than A − B. (C) In each strip, a sinus pause is interrupted by an atrial escape beat.

A-V Dissociation

A-V dissociation is a much-sinned-against term. The only way to avoid confusion is to define it simply as "the independent beating of atria and ventricles, *period.*" It is important to think of it always as a symptom rather than a diagnosis—it is a secondary phenomenon due to one of four primary mechanisms, and one should no more use A-V dissociation as a diagnosis than jaundice or headache. A-V dissociation is not the same as A-V block (though they have sometimes been used interchangeably), but block is one of the *causes* of dissociation.

There are also three other things to remember about dissociation: (1) it is not the same thing as shifting pacemaker, though there is overlap between the two in the form of atrial fusion beats. (2) Regardless of the mechanism causing it, A-V dissociation deprives its host of his atrial "kick." (3) Fusion beats and A-V dissociation, though usually not thought of as close relatives, are virtually the same thing, both being due to two independently beating pacemakers—the only difference between the two being the site at which their impulses rendezvous. Each of these three items will be taken up in a later paragraph.

A-V dissociation is always secondary to one or more of four mechanisms (table 21.1): sinus bradycardia; blockade of primary impulses (incomplete or complete A-V block, incomplete S-A block); acceleration of subsidiary pacemakers (accelerated idionodal or idioventricular rhythm; junctional or ventricular tachycardia); or a pause producer (extrasystoles, ending of tachycardia).

The atria and ventricles may be dissociated momentarily, as in the ventricular extrasystole or ventricular escape without retrograde conduction; the dissociation may be temporary, as when it is due to sinus bradycardia or to accelerated idioventricular rhythm; or it may be permanent, as in complete heart block.

Table 21.1
Causes of A-V Dissociation

Mechanism	Diagnosis	Other Terms
1. Slowing of sinus node	Sinus bradycardia	
2. Block of sinus impulses	S-A block	Dissociation by "default"
	A-V block	
3. Acceleration of subsidiary pacemaker	Accelerated idiojunctional or idioventricular rhythm	Dissociation by "usurpation"
	Junctional or ventricular tachycardia	
4. Postextrasystolic pause permitting escape	Atrial, junctional or ventricular extrasystole	
5. Combinations of above		

A-V Dissociation due to Sinus Bradycardia

A perfectly healthy athlete may develop dissociation as a result of his physiological bradycardia. Figure 21.4 is from a Japanese wrestler in the pink of condition. He has a normal sinus bradycardia at a rate of about 45/min. But if his sinus rate slows to 44 or 43, his A-V junctional pacemaker is waiting in the wings ready to step on to the stage at 44/min. This is exactly what happens in the top strip: the P waves approach and flirt with the QRS complexes, never quite disappearing within them, until the sinus node slightly accelerates and recaptures the ventricles at the end of the bottom strip. Obviously, a pathological bradycardia, as in a patient with acute inferior infarction (fig. 21.5), can similarly produce dissociation.

When dissociation develops because the sinus rhythm slows, it is sometimes called dissociation *by default*. And when the rates of the two independent pacemakers are virtually identical, as in figure 21.4, French cardiologists coined the term "isorhythmic dissociation."[10]

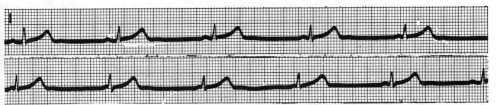

Figure 21.4. Physiological **sinus bradycardia** in an athlete, producing a short run of **isorhythmic A-V dissociation.**

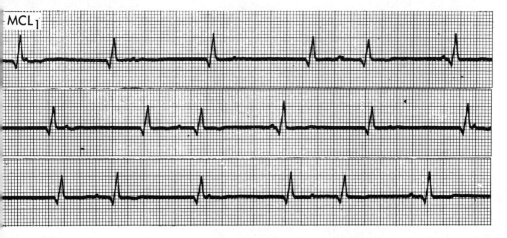

Figure 21.5. The strips are continuous. **Sinus bradycardia** with arrhythmia (rate, about 45/min) in a patient with myocardial infarction and RBBB. Because of the bradycardia, a **junctional escape** rhythm takes over at a slightly faster rate. The early beats seen in each strip—with prolonged P-R intervals when the complementary R-P is relatively short—are capture beats (ventricular captures).

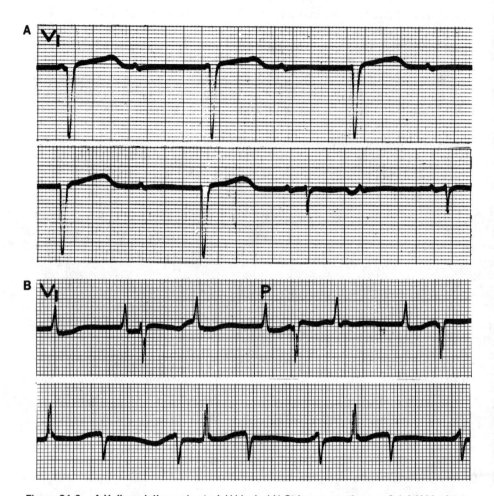

Figure 21.6. **A-V dissociation** owing to A-V block. (*A*) Strips are continuous. **2:1 A-V block,** as evidenced at the end of the second strip, producing dissociation. The idioventricular pacemaker is escaping at a rate of 39/min, slightly faster than the conductible rate of 37/min. (*B*) Strips are continuous. **Complete A-V block** with resulting dissociation in a man of 32 with severe cardiomyopathy. The atrial rate is 78, and the ventricular (junctional) rate is 36/min.

A-V Dissociation due to Block

Incomplete S-A block, by reducing the number of sinus impulses, operates exactly like sinus bradycardia to produce dissociation. Complete S-A block obviously cannot produce dissociation from a sinus rhythm since there are no sinus impulses from which to dissociate. Only if an ectopic atrial or junctional pacemaker escapes, can dissociation develop.

Both incomplete and complete A-V block can result in A-V dissociation. If, because of incomplete A-V block, insufficient impulses reach the ventricle, then a lower pacemaker may take over if its escape rate is faster than the rate of *conductible* impulses. Figure 21.6*A* illustrates a short period of A-V dissociation resulting from incomplete (2:1 at this atrial rate) A-V block. This sort of dissociation is often mistakenly called complete block by those who do not fully understand the roles of the various determinants of conduction (atrial rate, ventricular escape rate, R-P interval, etc.). A-V dissociation due to genuine complete A-V block is shown in figure 21.6*B*.

A-V Dissociation due to Acceleration of Lower Pacemakers

Accelerated A-V junctional (idionodal) rhythm, by snatching control from the slower sinus pacemaker, can lead to dissociation as illustrated in figure 21.7. Clearly, a faster junctional rhythm, junctional tachycardia, can do the same thing with even greater ease. If retrograde conduction is facile, the junctional pacemaker may take charge of both atria and ventricles, and then there is no dissociation.

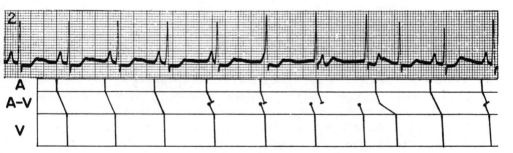

Figure 21.7. A-V dissociation due to usurpation by an **accelerated idionodal rhythm** (rate, about 78/min) from a sinus rhythm with a perfectly normal rate of 74/min. From a girl of 12 years with digitalis intoxication shortly after mitral valvotomy.

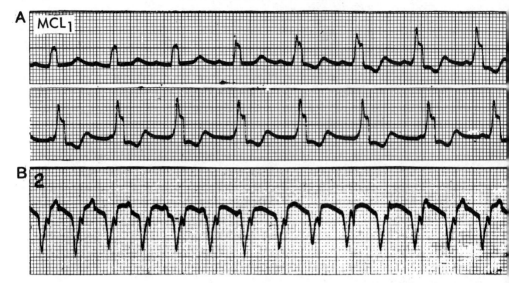

Figure 21.8. (*A*) The strips are continuous. Sinus rhythm (rate, 84/min) with RBBB gives place to a usurping **accelerated idioventricular rhythm** from the left ventricle at a slightly faster rate. Beats 4, 5 and 6 in the top strip are fusion beats. (*B*) A "double tachycardia"—**ventricular tachycardia** (rate, 150/min) dissociated from an **atrial tachycardia** (rate, 136/min).

Exactly the same things can be said of accelerated idioventricular rhythm and ventricular tachycardia. Figure 21.8 illustrates dissociation resulting from each of these rhythms. When a lower pacemaker produces dissociation by beating faster than the normal sinus thythm, it is sometimes known as dissociation by *usurpation.*

A-V Dissociation due to Pause Producers

Anything that produces a cycle longer than the cycle of a potential subsidiary pacemaker offers the opportunity for that pacemaker to escape and maintain its own rate and rhythm independent of the sinus rhythm. Thus the ventricular extrasystole, which often provides a fully compensatory cycle, and even the atrial extrasystole, which lengthens the ensuing cycle by the amount that the ectopic impulse suppresses the sinus node, may give a lurking junctional or ventricular pacemaker, with an intrinsic cycle length shorter than the pause provided, the opportunity it has been waiting for. In figure 21.9, a ventricular extrasystole is followed by a pause long enough to enable a junctional pacemaker to escape, and a short run of A-V dissociation follows.

A-V Dissociation due to Combinations of Above Mechanisms

Sometimes there is a conspiracy of two or more of the above mechanisms, each of which contributes something to the cause of dissociation. For example, in figure 21.10*A* the sinus rhythm slows to bradycrotic range, which enables an enhanced junctional pacemaker (accelerated junctional rhythm) to take over. Figure 21.10*B* shows a combination of A-V block with an accelerated junctional rhythm producing dissociation. Figure 21.10*C* shows the triple combine—all due to digitalis—of sinus bradycardia, some degree of A-V block and a junctional tachycardia all contributing to the A-V dissociation. Figure 21.10*D* shows the combined effect of a nonconducted atrial extrasystole and an accelerated idioventricular rhythm.

A-V DISSOCIATION, LIKE JAUNDICE, IS A SYMPTOM, NOT A DIAGNOSIS

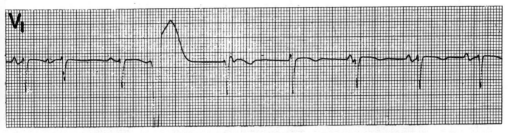

Figure 21.9. The second beat is an atrial premature beat, and the slightly lengthened cycle it engenders precipitates a ventricular extrasystole (rule of bigeminy). As a result of the lengthened postectopic cycle, an **accelerated junctional rhythm** escapes at a rate of 75/min, producing a four-beat run of A-V dissociation.

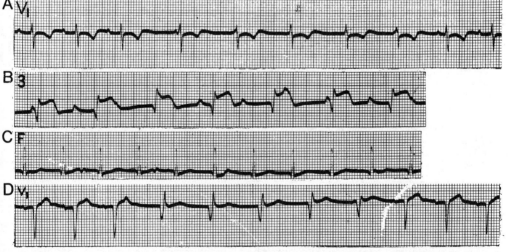

Figure 21.10. **A-V dissociation** due to combinations of factors. (*A*) **Sinus arrhythmia** with the rate dropping low enough (to about 58/min) so that an **accelerated junctional rhythm** takes over at 72 to 75/min. (*B*) **A-V block** of some unknown degree + **accelerated junctional rhythm,** in a patient with acute inferior infarction. (*C*) **Sinus bradycardia** + some degree of A-V block + **junctional tachycardia,** in a patient with digitalis intoxication. (*D*) A **nonconducted atrial premature beat** producing a long enough cycle for an **accelerated idioventricular rhythm** to take over at a rate of 80/min for 5 beats.

Capture(d) Beats

Since many examples of A-V dissociation occur without benefit of A-V block, in such cases, whenever the atrial impulse arrives at the A-V junction at a time when it is not refractory, the impulse is conducted to the ventricles. When a conducted beat interrupts or follows a period of dissociation, it is called a "capture(d) beat." If, as is usually the case, the atrial impulse captures the ventricles, it is called ventricular capture; if, as occasionally happens, an independent ectopic ventricular rhythm sends an impulse back to activate the atria, it is called atrial capture. I emphasize this point because the incorrect epithet is sometimes seen in print; e.g., ventricular capture (when the sinus impulse is capturing the ventricles) is miscalled sinus capture.

Capture beats are recognized by the preceding P wave and the fact that they end a cycle shorter than the dominant cycle, i.e., they are premature; usually they occur singly (fig. 21.11*B*) but sometimes they are seen in pairs (fig. 21.11*A*). If the ventricles are under junctional control, the capture beat has the same configuration as the independent junctional beats (fig. 21.7). The capture

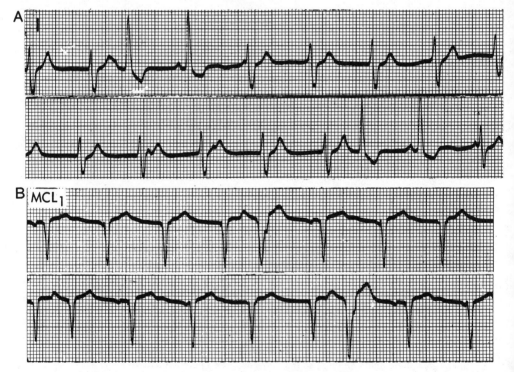

Figure 21.11. (*A*) The strips are continuous. An **accelerated idioventricular rhythm** (rate, 80/min) dissociated from sinus rhythm (rate, 76/min). Paired capture beats are seen in each strip. (*B*) The strips are continuous. An **accelerated junctional rhythm** (rate, 84/min) dissociated from a slightly slower sinus rhythm. One ventricular capture in each strip develops LBBB aberration because of its prematurity.

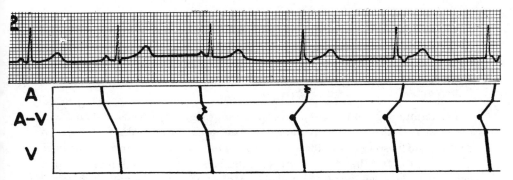

Figure 21.12. An orderly march from sinus rhythm to A-V junctional rhythm via dissociation (beat 3) and atrial fusion (beat 4).

beat will be different from the beats of the independent rhythm if the independent rhythm is ectopic ventricular (fig. 21.11*A*) or if, with a junctional rhythm, the capture beat develops aberration because of its prematurity (fig. 21.11*B*).

A-V Dissociation versus Fusion

Though seldom thought of in the same context, dissociation and fusion have identical causes and are really different expressions of the same thing. Required are two independent pacemakers, e.g., the sinus node and an ectopic ventricular pacemaker as in figure 21.8*A*, each more or less simultaneously delivering its impulse. If the timing is such that the two impulses meet in the A-V junction, the result is A-V dissociation; if the sinus impulse fires ahead of the ectopic ventricular center, they will meet in the ventricular muscle and produce ventricular fusion; if the ventricular center discharges its impulse before the sinus discharge, the ventricular impulse may reach the atrium before the sinus impulse has entirely activated the atrial myocardium, and then an atrial fusion beat results. So the only difference between the three phenomena is the rendezvous they choose for their collision. In fact, a fusion beat can be considered in terms of partial dissociation: an atrial fusion is dissociation between part-of-the-atria and the-rest-of-the-atria-and-the-ventricles; and a ventricular fusion beat is dissociation between part-of-the-ventricles and the-rest-of-the-ventricles-and-the-atria.

Next, the question is often asked of a tracing such as that seen in figure 21.7: "The pacemaker changes from sinus to A-V junction—why isn't that a shifting pacemaker?" The answer is: shifting or wandering pacemaker is used only when the pacemaker for the entire heart changes (see fig. 20.5). In figure 21.7 the ventricles' pacemaker indeed changes from sinus node to A-V junction, but the atria remain independently under sinus control, and so the term does not apply. On the other hand, figure 21.12 presents a genuine shifting pacemaker—control of both atria and ventricles shifts from sinus node to A-V junction.

But there is an overlap between the two in the shape of atrial fusion. Above, I was at pains to point out that fusion was tantamount to partial dissociation.

And in shifting pacemaker there is often intervening atrial fusion between the full-blown sinus control and junctional control; thus partial dissociation (fusion) forms a bridge between the two shifting rhythms, and therefore the terms "dissociation" and "shifting pacemaker" are certainly not mutually exclusive.

"Interference"

The terminology of this subject has been unnecessarily confused. The use of the term A-V dissociation as though it were a *diagnosis* is the first point of confusion. The second is in the application of the term interference. Sometimes it refers to the fact that one pacemaker interferes with the rhythm of a second pacemaker. This was the sense implied by Mobitz when he originally introduced the term **interference-dissociation**, and by Scherf when he later modified the term to **dissociation with interference.** Other authorities[2] ignore this use of the term and employ it in an entirely different sense, though a sense no less correct in the terminology of electrophysics. Their "interference" refers to the meeting of two opposing impulses with resulting extinction of both; such interference is seen in fusion beats (p. 277 ff.) and obviously must occur in A-V dissociation as the independent atrial and ventricular impulses meet, presumably within the A-V junction, and extinguish each other. Thus the "interference" (capture) beat of the first school is the only beat that shows no "interference" of the second type! This paradox is naturally perplexing to the uninitiated, and as neither school ever refers to the perfectly acceptable usage of the other, the confusion is further confounded. Until the terminology of both schools has been grasped, much confusion can be avoided by eschewing the term interference and referring to the conducted beats as capture beats or ventricular captures. The term interference-dissociation has been appropriately shelved as a "functional misnomer and superfluous term."[1]

Conclusion

A-V dissociation is an education in the arrhythmias. We have seen that it can be caused by sinus bradycardia; by accelerated junctional rhythm and junctional tachycardia; by accelerated idioventricular rhythm and ventricular tachycardia; by incomplete S-A block and incomplete and complete A-V block; and by the pause producers—the extrasystoles and the sign-off of any ectopic tachycardia. Moreover, one cannot delve deeply into the mechanisms of dissociation or witness many examples of it without encountering and studying related phenomena like escape beats and rhythms, including A-V junctional rhythm and idioventricular rhythm; atrial and ventricular fusion; and reciprocal beats and rhythm. And what else is there?

The whole subject of A-V dissociation has been fully and repeatedly reviewed[4, 5, 8, 9] and readers who wish to pursue its ramifications and entanglements further are referred to these articles.

REFERENCES

1. Hecht, H. H., et al.: Atrioventricular and intraventricular conduction: revised nomenclature and concepts. Am. J. Cardiol. 1973: **31**, 232.
2. Katz, L. N., and Pick, A.: *Clinical Electrocardiography. The Arrhythmias.* Lea & Febiger, Philadelphia, 1956.
3. Kistin, A. D.: Problems in the differentiation of ventricular arrhythmia from supraventricular arrhythmia with abnormal QRS Prog. Cardiovasc. Dis. 1966: **9**, 1.
4. Mariott, H. J. L., et al.: A-V dissociation: a re-appraisal. Am. J. Cardiol. 1958: **2**, 586.
5. Menendez, M. M., and Marriott, H. J. L.: A-V dissociation revisited. Prog. Cardiovasc. Dis. 1966: **8**, 522.
6. Pick, A.: Aberrant ventricular conduction of escaped beats. Preferential and accessory pathways in the A-V junction. Circulation 1956: **13**, 702.
7. Pick, A., and Dominguez, P.: Nonparoxysmal A-V nodal tachycardia. Circulation 1957: **16**, 1022.
8. Pick, A.: A-V dissociation. A proposal for a comprehensive classification and consistent terminology. Am. Heart J. 1963: **66**, 147.
9. Schott, A.: Atrioventricular dissociation with and without interference. Prog. Cardiovasc. Dis. 1959: **2**, 444.
10. Schubart, A. F., et al.: Isorhythmic dissociation: atrioventricular dissociation with synchronization. Am. J. Med. 1958: **24**, 209.

Review Tracings

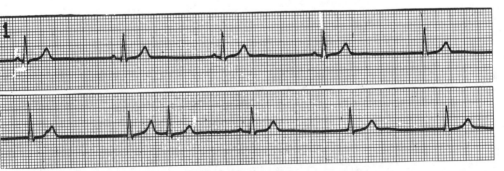

Review Tracing 21.1

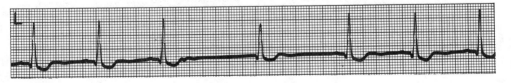

Review Tracing 21.2

For interpretation, see page 483

Review Tracing

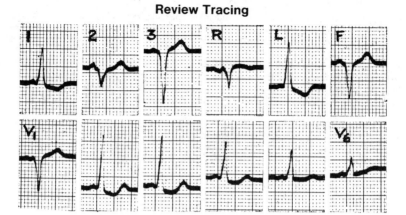

Review Tracing 21.3
For interpretation, see page 483

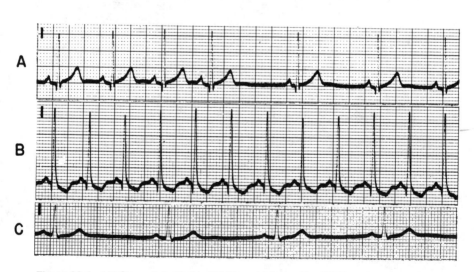

Figure 22.1 (*A*) Sinus arrhythmia. (*B*) Sinus tachycardia. (*C*) Sinus bradycardia.

22

Sinus Rhythms, the Sick Sinus and Intra-Atrial Block

Sinus Rhythms

The normal rate of impulse formation by the sinus node is generally accepted as 60 to 100/min. Above 100 the rhythm is called **sinus tachycardia** (fig. 22.1*B*); below 60, **sinus bradycardia** (fig. 22.1*C*). Sinus tachycardia results from exercise, eating, emotion, pain, hemorrhage, shock, fever, thyrotoxicosis and infections; it is a common reaction to heart disease, including myocardial infarction and heart failure per se, and may be caused by many drugs, such as caffeine, nicotine, adrenaline, atropine, amyl nitrite and quinidine. Sinus bradycardia is seen as a normal variation, especially in well-trained athletes, whose heart rates may be in the thirties at rest—and often not much more with moderate exertion; it is a physiological reaction to sleep, fright, carotid sinus massage or ocular pressure, and it may also result from disease processes, such as obstructive jaundice (effect of bile salts on sinus node), sliding hiatal hernia,[12] glaucoma (oculocardiac reflex), carotid sinus sensitivity and increased intracranial pressure; it is often seen in convalescence and as a result of digitalis therapy. It may be the first, or only, manifestation of the so-called "sick sinus syndrome" (see below). Sinus bradycardia is associated with a significant percentage of acute inferior wall infarctions; provided it is not severe enough to cause hemodynamic deterioration, it seems to be a favorable prognostic sign.[5, 14]

When the sinus node forms impulses irregularly, we have **sinus arrhythmia** (fig. 22.1*A*). This is of two varieties: one that waxes and wanes with the phases of respiration, the heart accelerating with inspiration and slowing with expiration; and a less common type in which the changes of rate bear no relationship to the phases of respiration. Sinus arrhythmia is a perfectly normal finding, but it may on occasion produce such marked irregularity that it can be confused clinically with other more important arrhythmias.

315

When the heart actually drops a beat, it means either that the S-A node has failed to release the impulse (S-A block) or, much more likely, that the impulse after traversing the atria has been unable to get through the A-V conducting tissues (A-V block). Both these types of block may be recognized in any lead in which P waves are clearly formed.

S-A Block

The hallmark of S-A block is a missing P wave, but there are no less than four reasons why P waves may be absent: (1) failure of the sinus node to form impulses (generator failure); (2) failure of the impulse to emerge from the sinus node (exit block); (3) failure of the emerging impulse to activate the atria (inadequate stimulus); and (4) failure of the atria to respond to the impulse (atrial paralysis). Strictly speaking, only the second of these is true S-A block, but it is often impossible to determine which mechanism is responsible for the missing P wave(s) and S-A "block" is too often loosely and erroneously diagnosed. It should be diagnosed only when a mathematical relationship between the longer and shorter sinus cycles can be demonstrated; or when the sinus cycles show the characteristic sequence of a Wenckebach period (see p. 325).

S-A block may be incomplete or complete:

1. **Incomplete S-A block** consists in the more or less infrequent failure of the impulse to emerge from the S-A node, with the result that occasional beats are completely dropped. This is recognized in the tracing by the occasional absence of the entire P-QRS-T sequence (figs. 22.2 and 22.3) and its type and "degree" are recognized by establishing a mathematical relationship between the longer and shorter atrial (P-P) cycles. When no such relationship can be established, **sinus pause** is a useful and appropriate term for the abnormally long cycle, qualified by a statement of its duration, e.g., "a 4.5 second sinus pause."

2. **Complete S-A block** exists when no impulses emerge from the S-A node and therefore no P waves are inscribed. Other terms that are sometimes applied when P waves are absent are: sinus arrest, sinus or atrial standstill and atrial paralysis. In general, these are better avoided because they are often loosely used and only vaguely defined. Atrial paralysis is of course the appropriate

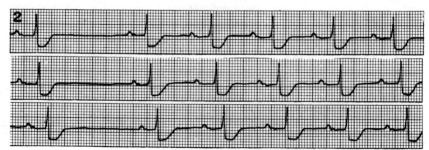

Figure 22.2. Incomplete S-A block. The strips are continuous. The long cycle at the beginning of each strip is due to a dropped sinus beat—an entire P-QRS-T sequence is missing.

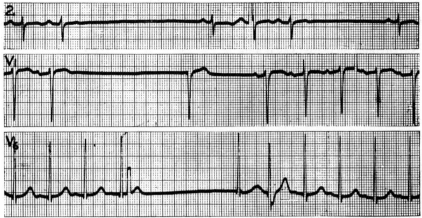

Figure 22.3. Runs of sinus rhythm at a rate of about 100 are punctuated by periods of **S-A block.** Two such periods occur in lead 2. In V_1 the period of atrial standstill is interrupted by an **A-V junctional escape** beat. In V_6 a similar pause is terminated by an escape beat which is followed by a run of sinus rhythm, the first beat of which shows **ventricular aberration** of RBBB form.

term when potassium intoxication is known to be responsible for disappearance of the P waves.

In the absence of S-A leadership, one of two things can happen: either (a) a lower pacemaker, usually in the A-V junction but sometimes in the ventricles, comes to the rescue and takes over the job of pacemaking, or (b) asystole persists and the patient dies. If (a) occurs and the ventricles proceed to beat independently, **junctional** or **ventricular escape** is said to have occurred and the heart's rhythm is called **idiojunctional** or **idioventricular**. Complete S-A block is thus one of the mechanisms leading to the development of idioventricular rhythm.

Complete S-A block is recognized in the electrocardiogram by the complete absence of the entire P-QRS-T sequence, i.e., by a straight and unadorned baseline; this continues until, if the patient is fortunate, independent QRST complexes appear at a slow rate while P waves remain absent.

Salient Features of S-A Block

1. *Incomplete: occasional absence of P-QRS-T sequence*
2. *Complete:*
    a. *P waves absent*
    b. *QRST sequence at slow rate*
    c. *QRS interval normal or prolonged, depending on site of ventricular pacemaker*

S-A block is rather rare, but it can be produced by a wide variety of causes: *drugs,* such as digitalis, quinidine and salicylates; *diseases,* such as coronary disease and acute infections; *physiological* disturbances, such as carotid sinus sensitivity and increased vagal tone.

Sick Sinus Syndrome

This catchy alliterative title was first used to characterize the situation when the sinus node failed to wake up following cardioversion of atrial fibrillation.[11] Most authorities now include any form of sinus nodal depression including marked sinus bradycardia, prolonged sinus pauses (sinus arrest), and sinoatrial block.[7] It is particularly applied to the **tachycardia-bradycardia syndrome**[13]— although its use is this context is inappropriate[9]—in which bursts of an atrial tachyarrhythmia, often atrial fibrillation, alternate with prolonged periods of sinus nodal and junctional inertia (fig. 22.4). Apart from these florid manifestations, the "syndrome" may initially present as paroxysmal atrial fibrillation; as failure of the sinus rhythm to accelerate appropriately in response to fever or exercise; or as "lone" atrial fibrillation.

Although the sick sinus predominantly affects the elderly, no age is immune and the disease has been recognized as early as the first day of life.[4]

Temporary and reversible manifestations of the syndrome can be caused by digitalis, quinidine, beta-blockers, or aerosol propellants. The chronic progressive syndrome is particularly associated with ischemic disease but may result from inflammatory diseases, cardiomyopathy, especially amyloidosis,[6] collagen disease, metastatic disease, surgical injury, etc. In many cases no cause is evident and they are classified as idiopathic; in these it may be part of a sclerodegenerative process also affecting the lower reaches of the cardiac conduction system, especially the A-V node (binodal disease).

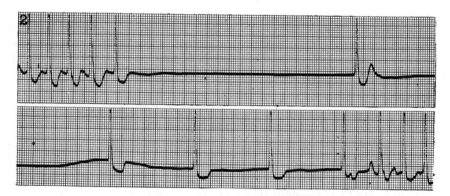

Figure 22.4. "Sick sinus syndrome," better called **tachycardia-bradycardia** ("tachy-brady") syndrome. Irregular atrial tachycardia followed by a prolonged sinus pause punctuated by all too few, badly needed A-V escape beats.

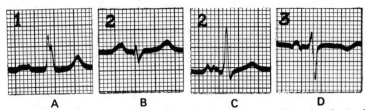

Figure 22.5.   Intra-atrial block. Four samples from four different patients. *A* and *B* show widening of P wave without significant notching; *C* and *D* show marked notching with wide peak interval (more than 0.04 sec).

The diagnosis can usually be made from the standard ECG or a 24-hour Holter recording, always of course carefully correlated with the clinical history. In some cases additional more sophisticated tests may be required, of which the best is the sinus node recovery time after rapid atrial pacing.[3, 8]

Sinus node disorders probably account for half the permanent pacemakers implanted in the United States today.[10]

Intra-atrial Block

If the impulse takes longer than normal to activate the atria, i.e., if the P wave is widened, intra-atrial block is said to be present. The upper normal limit of P-wave duration is not universally agreed upon, but the most satisfactory limit is probably 0.11 sec. The criterion, therefore, for diagnosing intra-atrial block is a P wave with a duration of 0.12 sec or more (fig. 22.5). Further evidence of block is to be found in deep notching of the P wave with a distance between peaks ("peak interval") of more than 0.04 sec (fig. 22.5*C*).

Intra-atrial block is not uncommon and is most often seen in coronary disease, mitral disease and in association with left ventricular hypertrophy.[2] It probably often represents left atrial enlargement rather than true block.

REFERENCES

1. Bower, P. J.: Sick sinus syndrome. Arch. Intern. Med. 1978: **138,** 133.
2. Bradley, S. M., and Marriott, H. J. L.: Intra-atrial block. Circulation 1956: **14,** 1073.
3. Chung, E. K. : Sick sinus syndrome; current views. Mod. Concepts Cardiovasc. Dis. 1980: **49,** 61 and 67.
4. Ector, H., et al.: Sick sinus syndrome in childhood. Br. Heart J. 1980: **44,** 684.
5. Epstein, S. E., et al: The early phase of acute myocardial infarction; pharmacologic aspects of therapy. Ann. Intern. Med. 1973: **78,** 918.
6. Evans, R., and Shaw, D. B.: Pathological studies in sinoatrial disorder (sick sinus syndrome). Br. Heart J. 1977: **39,** 778.
7. Ferrer, M. I.: *The Sick Sinus Syndrome.* Futura Publishing, Mt. Kisco, N.Y., 1974.
8. Gann, D., et al.: Electrophysiologic evaluation of elderly patients with sinus bradycardia. Ann. Intern. Med. 1979: **90,** 24.
9. Kaplan, B. M., et al.: Tachycardia-bradycardia syndrome (so-called "sick sinus syndrome"). Am. J. Cardiol. 1973: **31,** 497.
10. Kaplan, B. M.: Editorial: Sick sinus syndrome. Arch. Intern. Med. 1978: **138,** 28.
11. Lown, B.: Electrical reversion of atrial fibrillation. Br. Heart J. 1967: **29,** 469.

12. Marks, P., and Thurston, J. G. B.: Sinus bradycardia with hiatus hernia. Am. Heart J. 1977: **93,** 30.
13. Moss, A. J., and Davis, R. J.: Brady-tachy syndrome. Prog. Cardiovasc. Dis. 1974: **16,** 439.
14. Norris, R. M., et al.: Sinus rate in acute myocardial infarction. Br. Heart J. 1972: **34,** 901.
15. Shaw, D. B., et al.: Survival in sinoatrial disorder (sick sinus syndrome). Br. Med. J. 1980: **1,** 139.

Review Tracing

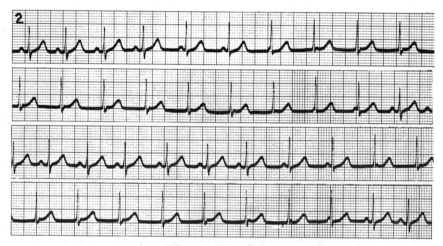

Review Tracing 22.1

For interpretation, see page 483

Review Tracings

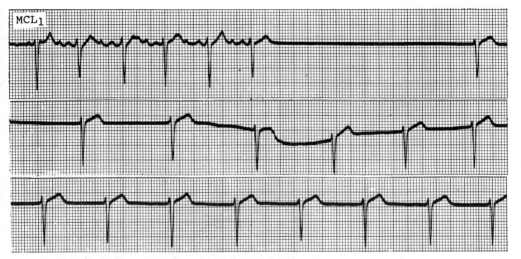

Review Tracing 22.2

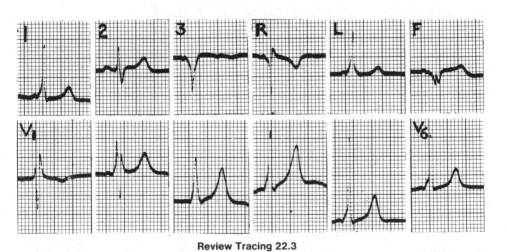

Review Tracing 22.3

For interpretation, see page 483

23

Atrioventricular Block: Conventional Approach

To do justice to this important and much mishandled subject, it will be expedient to divide this account into two parts: This chapter treats the subject in time-honored, conventional terms and, without introducing inaccuracies, avoids the inconsistencies and misconceptions that have plagued the diagnostic criteria for A-V block and which are tackled in the following chapter.

It is conventional to divide atrioventricular (A-V) block into three grades or "degrees." First and second degree block are incomplete whereas third degree is synonymous with complete block.

"First Degree" A-V Block

The "normal" P-R interval measures between 0.12 and 0.20 sec. First "degree" A-V block is generally defined as a prolongation of A-V conduction time (P-R interval) to 0.21 sec or more. In the analysis of records from supposedly normal young people, the incidence of a prolonged P-R interval is between 0.5%[7] and 1.6%.[26] Whether such otherwise normal subjects should be considered to have a "degree" of block is a moot point. Figure 23.1 illustrates two examples of first degree block: the first minor, with a P-R of 0.24 sec; the second shows a P-R lengthening of a higher order.

"Second Degree" A-V Block

By definition, second degree block is present when one or more, but not all, atrial impulses fail to reach the ventricles *because of impaired conduction*. Such failure may occur at any level of the ventricular conduction system.

Wenckebach, in Vienna in 1899, described the dropped beat after progressive lengthening of the previous conduction times; and then in 1906, he in Austria and Hay in Scotland described a second form of block in which the conduction time remained constant before the beat was unexpectedly dropped. Both of these astute observers made their discoveries without benefit of electrocardiograph by studying the waves in the jugular pulse and noting the interval between the "a" and "c" waves as a measure of A-V conduction time. It

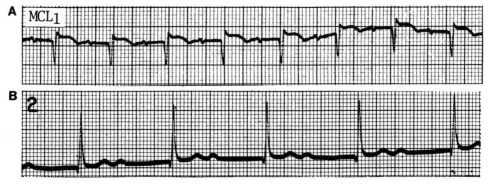

Figure 23.1. Two examples of **first degree A-V block**. *A* is from a patient with acute myocardial infarction and minor P-R prolongation to 0.24 sec. *B* shows marked prolongation to 0.57 to 0.60 sec.

remained for Mobitz in 1924, equipped with electrocardiograph, to suggest that the two forms of block be called, respectively, type I and type II. Classical examples of type I are presented in figures 23.2 and 23.7 and of type II in figure 23.10.

And so it is perfectly correct to refer to these two forms of A-V block as Mobitz type I and Mobitz type II; or, as is less commonly done,[11] Wenckebach type I and Wenckebach type II. What is historically incorrect—a mistake made in many places including the 4th edition of this text—is to call type I "Wenckebach-type" block and type II "Mobitz-type" block. It seems far best to call them simply type I and type II and drop the eponyms except in reference to the "Wenckebach phenomenon" or "Wenckebach period" to describe the distinctive features of progressive delay in conduction culminating in a "dropped beat."

Type I A-V Block

Type I A-V block is relatively benign. The block usually occurs in the A-V node[4, 17] and is usually associated with acute reversible conditions, such as acute inferior myocardial infarction, rheumatic fever, digitalis or propranolol effect. Generally a transient disturbance, it seldom progresses to complete A-V block, although of one series of 16 children manifesting Wenckebach periods, 7 went on to complete block.[28] Chronic type I second degree A-V block may be found in many conditions including chronic ischemic heart disease, aortic valve disease, mitral valve prolapse, atrial septal defect, amyloidosis, Reiter's syndrome, and mesothelioma of the A-V node. In healthy trained athletes, the incidence of both "first" and "second degree" block is surprisingly high.[24, 27] In one series, of 35 endurance athletes, prolongation of the P-R interval was found in 13 (37%) compared with a 15% incidence in as many controls; and "second degree" block was found in 8 (23%) of the athletes compared with 6% in the control subjects.

The most classical form of type I block is the **Wenckebach phenomenon** in which the P-R interval may begin within normal limits but is usually somewhat prolonged; then with each successive beat the P-R interval gradually lengthens until finally an impulse fails to reach the ventricles and a beat is dropped. Following the dropped beat the P-R interval reverts to normal, or near normal, and the sequence is repeated. At times the P-R interval may stretch to surprising lengths, rarely even to 0.80 or 0.90 sec; intervals of 0.50 or 0.60 are not uncommon.

Progressive lengthening of the P-R interval occurs because each successive beat arrives earlier and earlier in the relative refractory period of the A-V node and therefore takes longer and longer to penetrate it and reach the ventricles. In tachycardias it may be a physiological mechanism, but at normal rates it implies definite impairment of A-V conduction although it is occasionally reported in apparently normal hearts.[2] The progressive lengthening usually follows a predictable pattern: the maximal increment of one P-R over its predecessor develops between the first and second cycles and in subsequent cycles the increment is less and less. This in turn leaves its mark on the rhythm of the ventricles: following the pause of the dropped beat, the R-R intervals tend to shorten (fig. 23.2); and the long cycle (containing the dropped beat) is less than two of the shorter cycles—because it contains the shortest P-R interval. Recognition of this pattern enables one to spot the phenomenon in action even when there are no P-R intervals available to measure, as when there is a Wenckebach out of the sinus node (see p. 335).

"Footprints" of the Wenckebach

1. Small groups of beats, especially pairs, trios, etc.
2. Progressive shortening of the cycle of the receiving chambers (ventricles or atria).
3. The longest cycle (of the dropped beat) less than twice the shortest cycle.

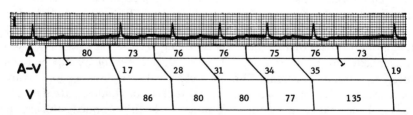

Figure 23.2.   Wenckebach phenomenon. Figures indicate intervals in hundredths of a second. The P-R intervals progressively lengthen until a beat is dropped. Note that the biggest increment (11) is in the second P-R (28) over the first (17) and that there is a tendency for the increments to become less and less (11-3-3-1). The effect of this is to cause progressive shortening of the ventricular cycles (86-80-80-77).

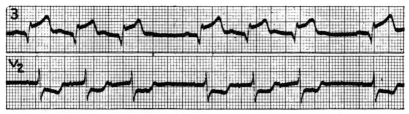

Figure 23.3. Sinus tachycardia with 4:3 **Wenckebach periods** which result in the beats being grouped in threes (trigeminy).

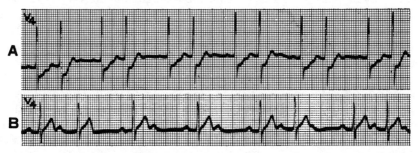

Figure 23.4. (a) Sinus tachycardia with 3:2 **Wenckebach periods** which result in the beats being grouped in pairs (bigeminy). B. Sinus tachycardia with 3:2 **Wenckebach periods** separated by an intervening run of 2:1 A-V block.

"Footprints" of the Wenckebach. The characteristic cycle-sequences that result from this form of conduction can be figuratively referred to as the "footprints" of the Wenckebach. These are three in number: (1) the beats tend to cluster in small groups and particularly in pairs (this is because 3:2 Wenckebachs are more common than 4:3, which in turn are more common than 5:4, and so on). (2) In each group of beats, the first cycle is longer than the second cycle, and indeed, there is a tendency for progressive shortening to occur in succeeding cycles. At first, this seems like a paradox—that as the P-R lengthens, the ventricular cycle shortens—but it will become clear later with a look at the diagram in figure 23.6. (3) The longest cycle—that of the dropped beat—is less than twice the shortest cycle.

The clue that often alerts one to an underlying Wenckebach mechanism, especially during tachycardia, is the presence of pairs or small groups of beats (figs. 23.3 and 23.4*A*); this is thanks to the common occurrence of short (3:2, 4:3, etc.) Wenckebach periods, which also often alternate with 2:1 conduction (fig. 23.4*B*).

ALL THAT'S BIGEMINAL ISN'T EXTRASYSTOLIC

When you look at figure 23.5, you immediately see the "footprints," and although P waves and therefore P-R intervals are obscure, you know that there is a Wenckebach at work: the beats are grouped in pairs and trios; in three out of the four trios, the first cycle is longer than the second cycle; and the longest cycles separating the groups are less than twice the shortest cycles. Since the first beat of each group is preceded by a P wave at a constant, prolonged P-R interval, you know that it is an A-V Wenckebach, even though you cannot see the succeeding P-R intervals.

The reason for the second and third "footprints" becomes apparent with a little study of figure 23.6. This is an idealized diagram of an A-V Wenckebach, highlighting the classical features of its structure; namely, (1) the largest increase in the P-R is in the second over the first—it jumps from 22 to 22 + 12 = 34 (all intervals are expressed in hundredths of a second); after that, the increase in each P-R over its predecessor is progressively smaller. Thus, although the P-R gets longer and longer, it is lengthening by less and less. Since the R-R (ventricular) cycle is composed of the sinus cycle plus the increment of the P-R and the increment is shrinking, the R-R interval will correspondingly shrink (92 to 85 to 83).

When it comes to the double cycle of the dropped beat, 140 is less than twice the shortest cycle (83); and this is because this double cycle, instead of containing an increment, contains a P-R decrement—the P-R drops from 42 to 22, a decrease of 20. The long cycle, therefore, equals 80 + 80 − 20 = 140.

Now let us look at an actual Wenckebach and compare its structure with the idealized one in figure 23.6. In figure 23.7, the sinus cycle is a constant 75 to 76; the second P-R jumps by 10 over the first, from 21 to 31, and the third then increases by only 4 to 35. RESULT: the ventricular cycle shortens from 85 (75 + 10) to 79 (75 + 4). And when it comes to dropping a beat, the P-R shrinks back toward normal and becomes only 23; so the cycle of the dropped beat is 76 + 75 = 151 minus the *decrement* (35 − 23 = 12), and 151 − 12 = 139.

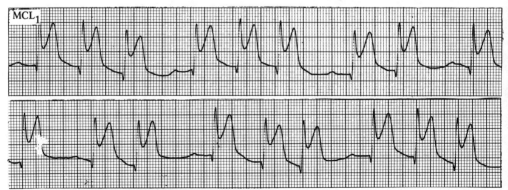

Figure 23.5. The strips are continuous and illustrate the **"footprints" of the Wenckebach** in a patient with an **acute anteroseptal infarction**. The grouping of beats in pairs and trios and the cycle sequences (see text) identify the presence of Wenckebach-type conduction.

A		80		80		80		80		80		80		80		
A-V				22		22	12		34	5		39	3			22
V		140			92			85			83			140		

Figure 23.6. Idealized schema of an A-V Wenckebach—measurements are in hundredths of a second. Note the following: even the first P-R is prolonged (22); the largest P-R increment is in the second P-R (34) over the first (22); the cycles of the receiving chambers (ventricles) progressively shorten; and the cycle of the dropped beat (140) is less than twice the shortest cycle (83).

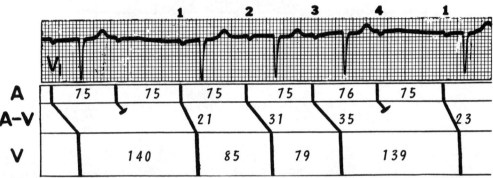

A	75	75	75	75	76	75
A-V		21	31	35		23
V	140	85	79	139		

Figure 23.7. **Type I second degree A-V block** showing a classical 4:3 Wenckebach period. Note the following typical features: (1) even the shortest P-R is longer than normal; (2) the QRS is of normal duration; (3) the larger P-R increment is in the second (31) over the first (21); (4) the first cycle (85) in the group of three beats is longer than the second (79); and (5) the longest cycle (139) is less than twice the shortest (79).

Those then are the features of a classical Wenckebach period; but do not expect all of them to be classical or you will be disappointed. In fact the majority of all Wenckebach periods contain some deviation from the classical structure[5, 18]; but, if you are conversant with the typical features and with the likely deviations from them, virtually all Wenckebachs are readily recognized. Likely divergences from the "norm" include the following: the first increment may not be the largest; every P-R may not lengthen over the previous one; the last increment may be larger than the preceding one; and the last increment may be the largest.[5]

R-P/P-R Reciprocity. I have indicated that the earlier the impulse arrives in the A-V node's refractory period, the longer it takes to get through to the ventricles; and the later it arrives, the less time it takes. Although we cannot tell from the surface ECG when the impulse reaches the junction, we have a rough but excellent guide in the relationship of the P wave to the preceding QRS complex—the R-P interval, measured from the beginning of the QRS to the beginning of the ensuing P wave. And if you look at the tracings of typical Wenckebachs (figs. 23.2 and 23.7) you can easily see that the P-R progressively lengthens *as the P wave retreats toward the preceding QRS.* This is diagrammatically expressed in figure 23.8, and we can articulate this relationship as

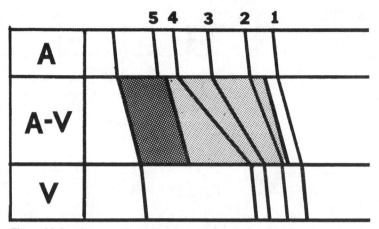

Figure 23.8.   Diagram illustrating the effect on A-V conduction as successive atrial impulses (*1–5*) arrive in the A-V junction earlier and earlier in its refractory period. *Dark stippling* = absolute refractory period; *light stippling* = relative refractory period.

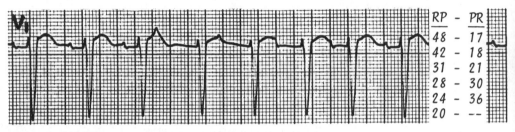

RP	–	PR
48	–	17
42	–	18
31	–	21
28	–	30
24	–	36
20	–	––

Figure 23.9.   This short strip illustrates the reciprocal relationship that exists between the R-P and P-R intervals in subjects with type I conduction delay (see text).

"R-P/P-R reciprocity"; and we can state that the hallmark of type I block in the surface tracing is "R-P dependent P-R intervals." This dependence is elegantly demonstrated in figure 23.9, where there are P-R intervals ranging from a normal 0.17 sec to more than twice that length, and the variation is secondary to the varying R-P interval. After three sinus beats that are normally conducted with a P-R of 0.17 sec, there is a single atrial premature beat that either is conducted with a much prolonged P-R interval of about 0.49 sec or is not conducted and permits an accelerated junctional pacemaker to escape at a cycle length of 0.67 sec. The next, slightly delayed sinus P wave lands on the T wave of this beat and is conducted with a P-R of 0.36 (R-P/P-R = 24/36). The next three sinus P waves land at slightly but progressively longer R-P intervals and are consequently conducted with slightly but progressively shorter P-R intervals (see inset table). In the last four beats, you see exactly what happens in a Wenckebach period but in reverse—the P-R intervals get shorter and shorter because the R-P gets longer and longer; whereas in the Wenckebach period, the P-R intervals get longer and longer because the R-P intervals get shorter and shorter. In each case, the dependence of the P-R on its antecedent R-P is evident.

Type II A-V Block

This much less common form of second degree block is also much more serious. It is usually associated with a BBB pattern and the site of the block is usually below the bundle of His; i.e., in the presence of BBB, the dropped beats are due to intermittent block in the other bundle branch.[4, 17] Type II block is therefore usually a form of bilateral BBB and progresses to complete A-V block with Adams-Stokes seizures. It is recognized when at least two regular and *consecutive* atrial impulses are conducted with the same P-R interval before the dropped beat (fig. 23.10). In this form of block, in contrast with type I block, the P-R interval is independent of its associated R-P. In figure 23.10 the P-R labelled "*1*", after a long R-P, is exactly the same (0.18 sec) as is the P-R (labelled "*2*") that complements a much shorter R-P. Figure 23.11*A* is another

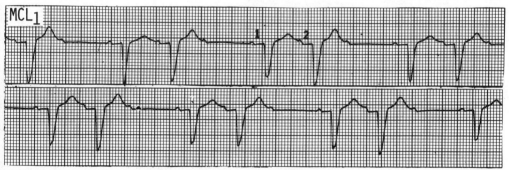

Figure 23.10. The strips are continuous and show **type II second degree A-V block** with 3:2 conduction. Note the following typical features: (*1*) the P-R interval is constant and of normal duration (0.18 sec); and (*2*) **LBBB** is present.

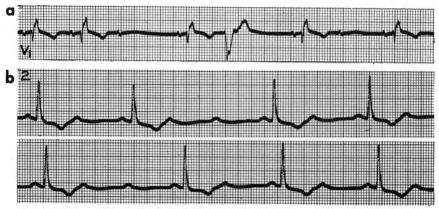

Figure 23.11. (a) **Second degree A-V block, type II.** Two consecutive P-R intervals are unchanged before the dropped beat. The conducted beats have a normal P-R interval and show RBBB; the 4th beat is a right ventricular premature beat. (B) **High grade A-V block.** Sinus rhythm with 2:1 and 3:1 A-V block.

example of type II block; note that the P-R remains unchanged (and normal) despite longer and shorter R-P intervals, i.e., there is no R-P/P-R reciprocity.

High Grade (or Advanced) Second Degree A-V Block

High grade block may be diagnosed when, at *reasonable atrial rates* (not, for example, at a frantic 300/min, as in atrial flutter), two or more consecutive atrial impulses fail to be conducted *because of the block itself*—and not because of interference by an escaping subsidiary pacemaker. In figure 23.11B, on two occasions there are two consecutive atrial impulses that fail to reach the ventricles; and that failure is in the presence of a normal atrial rate (about 85) and is entirely due to the block itself since there is no intruding escape rhythm. Another example of high grade block is illustrated in figure 23.12.

Ideal Criteria for Diagnosing High Grade Block

1. Two, or more than two, consecutive atrial impulses blocked.
2. A reasonable atrial rate (?under 135/min).
3. No escaping pacemaker preventing conduction.

Complete ("Third Degree") A-V Block

When *no* impulses can pass the A-V barrier, complete A-V block has developed. Bilateral bundle-branch block, or trifascicular block, rather than blockade at the A-V node or in the main bundle, is usually the cause of complete A-V block.[13, 14, 21, 23] Lev's and Lenegre's diseases, by producing bilateral bundle-branch block, are probably the commonest causes of complete "A-V" block.

As with the less common complete S-A block, two possibilities now exist: Either the ventricles remain inactive (**ventricular asystole**) and the patient dies, or more likely the A-V node (or a lower pacemaker) takes over and controls the ventricles (**junctional** or **ventricular escape**). In this event the atria continue to beat in their own time, and the ventricles beat in a slower tempo, **idiojunctional** or **idioventricular rhythm**. For example, the atria may continue to beat at a sinus rate of 96, while the ventricles perform at 28 (fig. 23.13). This independence is readily recognized in the tracing by the lack of relationship between the slow ventricular complexes and the more frequent P waves. Each maintains its own rhythm without regard for the other, except that in about 20% of

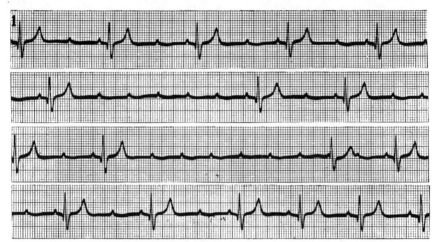

Figure 23.12. **High grade A-V block** (the four strips are continuous). A 3:1 block is present in the *top strip*. The *second strip* contains a 7:1 period. A slightly longer period of ventricular standstill in the *third strip* is terminated by a junctional escape beat. In the *bottom strip* there is 3:1 and 2:1 block. Shallow T$_P$ waves are clearly visible following each of the non-conducted P waves.

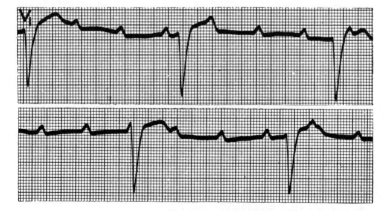

Figure 23.13. **Complete A-V block.** The two strips form a continuous record. P waves and QRS complexes are independent, at ventricular rate of 28, and atrial of 96.

331

complete A-V blocks, although anterograde conduction is impossible, retrograde conduction to the atria can occur[9, 25] (fig. 23.14).

If the escaping rhythm is initiated in the A-V junction, the QRS interval and complex will be normal (unless there is concomitant BBB) and the term **idiojunctional** may be applied to the rhythm. If the rescuing pacemaker is in the ventricular muscle itself, then the QRST complex is bizarre with prolonged QRS interval and has the form of an ectopic ventricular beat (figs. 23.13 and 23.14).

It is perhaps worth clarifying the difference between *idio*junctional and just plain junctional rhythm. The prefix idio- is from the Greek *idios*, meaning private, and idiojunctional (or idioventricular) implies that the ventricles have their own private pacemaker all to themselves and are beating independently of the atria: the atria are beating in their own rhythm, or fibrillating, or they are inactive. Junctional rhythm, on the other hand, means that both the ventricles and the atria are under A-V control—the junction is the pacemaker of the whole heart.

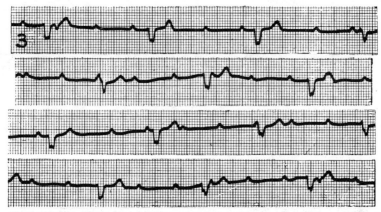

Figure 23.14.   Complete A-V block with idioventricular rate of 36, and atrial of 104. The four strips are continuous. Atrial and ventricular activities are independent except for the first and last ventricular beats—each of these is conducted retrogradely to the atria (note inverted P waves deforming the ST segments of these beats).

Ideal Criteria for Diagnosing Complete Block

1. Complete absence of A-V conduction (P waves and QRS complexes entirely independent and the ventricles beating regularly).
2. A slow ventricular rate (?under 45/min).
3. Plenty of P waves (deployed across all phases of the ventricular cycle).

Pseudo-A-V Block

This term is sometimes applied to the masquerade perpetrated by concealed junctional impulses (fig. 23.15): first degree A-V block, second degree type I and type II and "high grade" A-V block can all be imitated by concealed junctional extrasystoles or parasystole.[3, 6, 16] The importance of this is that, although the presence of such A-V ectopy probably indicates significant junctional disease,[17] accurate differentiation from true A-V block is clearly desirable.

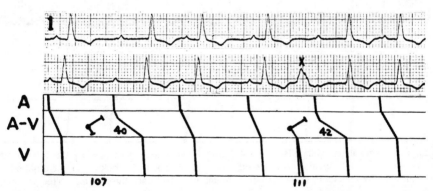

Figure 23.15.   Concealed junctional extrasystoles. The premature beat (*x*) toward the end of the *second strip* has the appearance of an interpolated ventricular extrasystole with concealed retrograde conduction into the A-V junction lengthening the ensuing P-R. But the pauses in the *top strip* and at the beginning of the second strip contain the same lengthened P-R without evidence of the extrasystole. The supposed "ventricular" extrasystole must therefore be a (concealed) junctional beat with LBBB aberration (see laddergram).

Wenckebach Phenomenon at Large

A context in which the Wenckebach phenomenon is commonly seen, though perhaps not always recognized, is when the conduction ratio in atrial flutter is satisfactorily reduced—by digitalis, propranolol or verapamil—from 2:1 to 4:1. Often there is an intermediate stage when 2:1 and 4:1 conduction alternate (producing bigeminal grouping) caused by the development of 3:2 Wenckebach conduction of the impulses that have succeeded in passing the 2:1 filter higher up (fig. 23.16).

All Wenckebachs are not atrioventricular, and all A-V Wenckebachs are not anterograde; and therefore you cannot recognize all of them by lengthening P-R intervals—you recognize them by spotting the "footprints" described earlier in this chapter. The phenomenon can develop anywhere that conduction occurs: out of the sinus node,[22] out of an ectopic focus, between pacing stimulus and ventricular myocardium,[10, 19] in a bundle branch,[20] in the junction below a

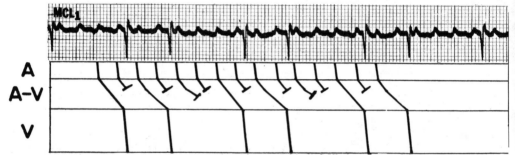

Figure 23.16. Atrial flutter with alternating 4:1 and 2:1 conduction caused by the administration of propranolol. Half the atrial impulses are "filtered"—we should not say "blocked" at this atrial rate—at an upper level in the A-V juncation, while the alternate impulses that pass through the "filter" develop a 3:2 Wenckebach.

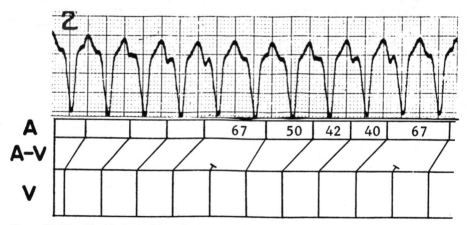

Figure 23.17. Ventricular tachycardia (rate, 150/min) with **retrograde 5:4 Wenckebach** period.

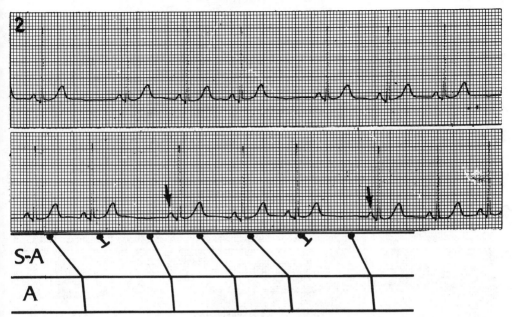

Figure 23.18. The strips are continuous and illustrate group beating due to 4:3 and 3:2 **sinus Wencke-bachs**. One 4:3 period in the bottom strip is diagrammed.

junctional pacemaker, etc. In the two examples here illustrated, the characteristic footprints are detected in the spacing of the P waves. Figure 23.17 shows a ventricular tachycardia with retrograde Wenckebach conduction to the atria in a ratio of 5:4 (see laddergram).

The next example parades its P waves but shows no sign of lengthening P-R intervals. Figure 23.18 is from an eight-year-old boy with streptococcal tonsillitis, and his beats are grouped in threes, always with the first cycle longer than the second; and the shortest cycle is more than half the longest cycles. In this case, the first complexes to manifest the typical grouping are the P waves (the QRS's just follow the P waves obediently), and so the "receiving" chambers are the atria, which means that the Wenckebach must be occurring proximal to the atria, i.e., in the sinus node. This is, therefore, type I 4:3 exit block out of the sinus node.

To diagram this sort of block, first draw in a bar in the atrial tier to represent each P wave; then measure the total Wenckebach period, i.e., from the first P wave of one group to the first P wave of the next group (*arrows*) = 252; then divide this total period by the number of cycles, not forgetting to count the dropped beat: 252/4 = 63. Then with your dividers set for a cycle of 63, mark out pacemaker "blobs" at the top of the S-A tier, beginning at some reasonable interval in front of the first P-wave bar; finally, connect blobs to bars—as in the figure 23.18 laddergram.

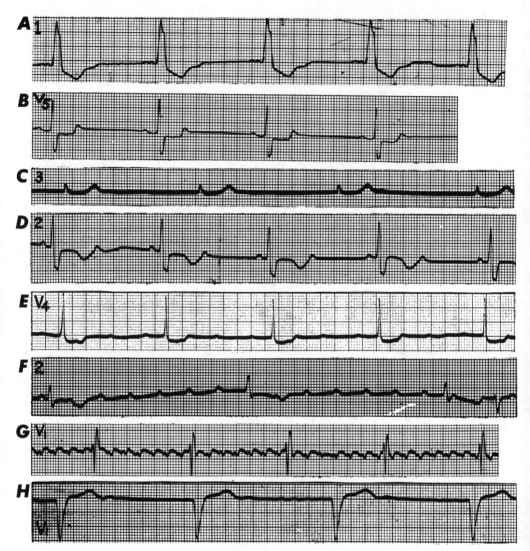

Figure 23.19. (A) **Sinus bradycardia,** rate 40/min. (B) **Nonconducted atrial bigeminy,** with incomplete RBBB; ventricular rate 38/min. (C) Probable **complete S-A block** with junctional escape at 30/min. (D) **2:1 A-V block,** probably type II (normal P-R + RBBB); ventricular rate 38/min. (E) Sinus tachycardia with **3:1 A-V block;** ventricular rate 39/min. (F) Sinus tachycardia with **complete A-V block** and idiojunctional rhythm at rate 21/min. (G) Atrial flutter with **complete A-V block** and idiojunctional rhythm with incomplete RBBB at rate 42/min. (H) Atrial fibrillation with **complete A-V block** and idioventricular rhythm (or idiojunctional with LBBB) at rate 30/min.

Marked Bradycardia

As complete A-V block is the last cause of bradycardia we shall encounter in this adventure through electrocardiography, it is appropriate to recapitulate its several causes. When the ventricular rate is under 45/min, the mechanism may be:

1. Sinus bradycardia (fig. 23.19A)
2. Nonconducted atrial bigeminy (fig. 23.19B)
3. S-A block, incomplete or complete (fig. 23.19C)
4. A-V block, incomplete or complete, e.g.:
   a. Sinus rhythm with 2:1 block (fig. 23.19D)
   b. Sinus tachycardia with 3:1 block (fig. 23.19E)
   c. Sinus rhythm or tachycardia with complete block (fig. 23.19F)
   d. Atrial flutter with complete block (fig. 23.19G)
   e. Atrial fibrillation with complete block (fig. 23.19H)

Prolonged QRS Interval

We are now also in a position to summarize the conditions associated with prolonged intraventricular conduction:

1. Ectopic ventricular mechanisms:
   a. Ventricular premature beats (extrasystoles)
   b. Ventricular escape beats
   c. Ventricular tachycardia
   d. Idioventricular rhythm
   e. Accelerated idioventricular rhythm
   f. Ventricular parasystole
   g. Paced ventricular rhythm
2. Slowed intraventricular conduction
   a. Intraventricular block (BBB)
   b. Aberrant ventricular conduction
3. Conduction to one ventricle accelerated:
   a. Wolff-Parkinson-White syndrome

REFERENCES

1. Barold, S. S., and Friedberg, H. D.: Second degree atrioventricular block: A matter of definition. Am. J. Cardiol. 1974: **33**, 311.
2. Brodsky, M., et al.: Twenty-four hour continuous electrocardiographic monitoring in fifty male medical students without apparent heart disease. Am. J. Cardiol. 1977: **39**, 390.
3. Castellanos, A., et al.: Pseudo AV block produced by concealed extrasystoles arising below the bifurcation of the His bundle. Br. Heart J. 1974: **36**, 457.
4. Damato, A. N., and Lau, S. H.: Clinical value of the electrogram of the conduction system. Prog. Cardiovasc. Dis. 1970: **13**, 119.
5. Denes, P., et al.: The incidence of typical and atypical atrioventricular Wenckebach periodicity. Am. Heart J. 1975: **89**, 26.
6. Fisch, C., et al.: Electrocardiographic manifestations of concealed junctional ectopic impulses. Circulation 1976: **53**, 217.

7. Johnson, R. L., et al.: Electrocardiographic findings in 67,375 asymptomatic individuals. VII. A-V block. Am. J. Cardiol. 1960: **6**, 153.
8. Katz, L. N., and Pick, A.: *Clinical Electrocardiography. The Arrhythmias.* Lea & Febiger, Philadelphia, 1956.
9. Khalilullah, M., et al.: Unidirectional complete heart block. Am. Heart J. 1979: **97**, 608.
10. Klein, H. O., et al.: The Wenckebach phenomenon between electric pacemaker and ventricle. Br. Heart. 1976: **38**, 961.
11. Knoebel, S. B., et al.: The role of transvenous pacing in acute myocardial infarction. Heart Lung 1972: **1**, 56.
12. Langendorf, R., and Pick, A.: Atrioventricular block, type II (Mobitz)—its nature and clinical significance. Circulation 1968: **38**, 819.
13. Lenegre, J.: Etiology and pathology of bilateral bundle branch block in relation to complete heart block. Prog. Cardiovasc. Dis. 1964: **6**, 409.
14. Lepeschkin, E.: The electrocardiographic diagnosis of bilateral bundle branch block in relation to heart block. Prog. Cardiovasc. Dis. 1964: **6**, 445.
15. Levy, M. N., et al.: The AV nodal Wenckebach phenomenon as a possible feedback mechanism. Prog. Cardiovasc. Dis. 1974: **16**, 601.
16. Lindsay, A. E., and Schamroth, L.: Atrioventricular junctional parasystole with concealed conduction simulating second degree AV block. Am. J. Cardiol. 1973: **31**, 397.
17. Narula, O. S.: Wenckebach type I and type II atrioventricular block (revisited). Cardiovasc. Clin. 1974: **6**, 138.
18. Narula, O. S.: *His Bundle Electrocardiography and Clinical Electrophysiology,* pp. 146–160. F. A. Davis, Philadelphia, 1975.
19. Peter, T., et al.: Wenckebach phenomenon in the exit area from a transvenous pacing electrode. Br. Heart J. 1976: **38**, 201.
20. Rosenbaum, M. B., et al.: Wenckebach periods in the bundle branches. Circulation 1969: **40**, 79.
21. Rosenbaum, M. B., et al.: Anatomical basis of AV conduction disturbances. Geriatrics 1970: **25**, 132.
22. Schamroth, L., and Dove, E.: The Wenckebach phenomenon in sinoatrial block. Br. Heart J. 1966: **28**, 350.
23. Steiner, C., et al.: Electrophysiological documentation of trifascicular block as the common cause of complete heart block. Am. J. Cardiol. 1971: **28**, 436.
24. Strasberg, B., et al.: Natural history of chronic second-degree atrioventricular nodal block. Circulation 1981: **63**, 1043.
25. Taboul, P., et al.: Retrograde conduction in complete A-V block. Br. Heart J. 1976: **38**, 706.
26. Van Hemel, N. M., and Robles de Medina, E. O.: Electrocardiographic findings in 791 males between the ages of 15 and 23 years; I. Arrhythmias and conduction disorders (Dutch). Cardiovasc. Dis. Cardiovasc. Surg. 1975: **23**, abs. 91.
27. Viitasalo, M. T., et al.: Ambulatory electrocardiographic recording in endurance athletes. Br. Heart J. 1982: **47**, 213.
28. Young, D., et al.: Wenckebach atrioventricular block (Mobitz type I) in children and adolescents. Am. J. Cardiol. 1977: **40**, 393.
29. Zipes, D. P., et al.: Artificial atrial and ventricular pacing in the treatment of arrhythmias. Ann. Intern. Med. 1969: **70**, 885.

Review Tracings

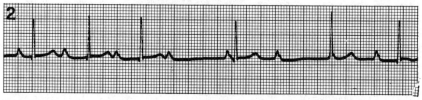

Review Tracing 23.1
For interpretation, see page 483

Review Tracings

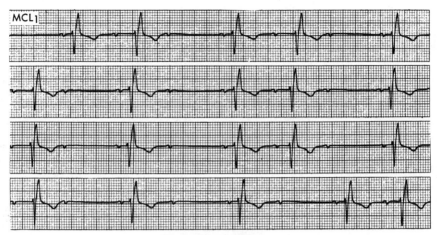

Review Tracing 23.2

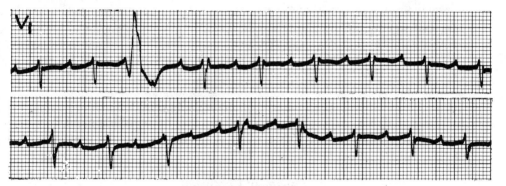

Review Tracing 23.3

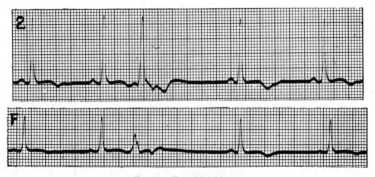

Review Tracing 23.4

For interpretation, see page 484

24

A-V Block: Growing Pains

Chapter 23 presented a conventional but oversimplified approach to A-V block. In it I was careful not to include any of its several aspects that have led to misconception and controversy. But now the time has come.

Up to a quarter of a century ago, there was no consistently effective therapy for heart block and therefore the finer points of classification in relation to prognosis were academic and relatively unimportant. But then the artificial pacemaker made the scene and revolutionized therapy. At last there was a really efficient and reliable way to stimulate the reluctant heart. And so we have since stumbled through an era of extremely effective and sophisticated therapy unaccompanied by needed refinements in diagnosis and prognosis.

One of the first steps in understanding the vagaries of A-V conduction is to appreciate that there are several determinants of A-V conduction besides the state of the conducting system (table 24.1); and of these the atrial and ventricular *rates* are paramount, as I shall repeatedly emphasize in the next few pages.

Causes of Confusion

There are three main reasons (table 24.2) the approach to A-V block remains confused.

1. Defective Definitions

Almost without exception, authors who write about complete and other serious grades of A-V block fail to define their terms and to state precisely what they are discussing. Take complete A-V block for example. Since it is not defined, presumably it is tacitly assumed that everyone knows how everyone else uses the term; but this is far from true. Consider the three situations depicted in figure 24.1. When the strip in figure 24.1*A* was circularized to cardiology departments, over half of the 550 respondents called it complete block, and many similar tracings have been published as such.[2, 11, 12, 17, 23] Others have alluded to tracings like that in figure 24.1*C* as complete block.[10, 14] Whereas figure 24.1*B* is the only one of the three that fulfills the criteria for complete A-V block outlined in the previous chapter.

Table 24.1
Main Determinants of A-V Conduction

1. State of A-V junction and bundle branches
   a. Physiologic refractoriness
   b. Pathologic refractoriness
2. Autonomic influences
3. Atrial rate
4. R/P relationships
5. Ventricular rate
6. Level of ventricular pacemaker

Table 24.2
Reasons for Confusion and Controversy

1. Authors seldom if ever define their terms
2. "Degrees" do not necessarily tally with severity of block
3. Several misconceptions lead to overdiagnosis and overtreatment

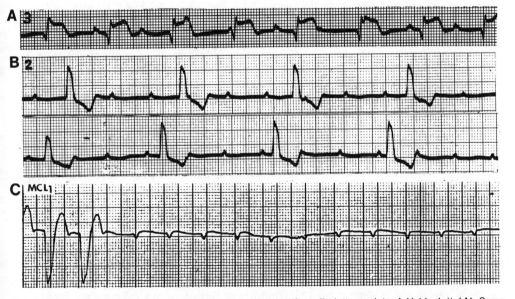

Figure 24.1. Three dissimilar situations that are frequently called "complete A-V block." (*A*) *Some* (undetermined) degree of A-V block combining with an accelerated junctional rhythm to produce complete A-V dissociation; conveniently called **"block-acceleration dissociation."** Acute inferior infarction; prognosis excellent. (*B*) Genuine **complete A-V block** with idioventricular rhythm, rate 37/min. (*C*) Abrupt cessation of A-V conduction with no rescuing (escaping) pacemaker; conveniently distinguished from A and B by calling it **"spontaneous ventricular asystole"** initiated by A-V block. Prognosis: dismal.

Thus, when authors report on a series of patients with (undefined) "complete A-V block," the reader has no idea what "mix" of conduction disturbances is being included. Yet when prognostic implications are being considered and therapeutic recommendations made, it is vital to separate the three manifestations of block seen in figure 24.1, both from each other and from other forms of A-V conduction disturbance. When the worst manifestation of A-V block during acute infarction is that represented by *A* in figure 24.1, the mortality is less than 10%; whereas the mortality associated with the situation depicted in *C* is over 90%, and the mortality of *B* is somewhere in between. It is clearly unrealistic to gather three such disparate entities under one heading.

Similar strictures apply to use of the terms "high grade," "advanced," and "type II" block.

2. The Non-degrees of Block

"Degrees," as we use the term, do not necessarily represent grades of severity—as they presumably should. For example, a patient with first degree block at a rate of 60 may have worse block than a patient with 2:1 block at a rate of 100. This is because the first patient may develop 2:1 block if his rate increases from 60 to 75, whereas the second patient may achieve 1:1 conduction with only first degree block if his rate slows from 100 to 80. Obviously a person with 2:1 block at 75 has worse block than one with 1:1 conduction at 80.

Consider the *bottom strips* in figures 24.2 and 24.3: 24.2 has 2:1 block and 24.3 has none. But if you look at their respective *top strips*, you see that in fact 24.3 has worse block than 24.2: because 24.2 is able to maintain 1:1 conduction at an atrial rate of 100, whereas 24.3 develops 2:1 block at a rate of only 84. As long as our "degrees" are mainly predicated upon conduction *ratio* to the neglect of the more important *rate*, chaos will continue to reign.

Table 24.3
Misconceptions about A-V Conduction

1. That 2:1 A-V block is type II
2. That 2:1 A-V block is high grade
3. That when most of the atrial impulses are not conducted, the block is high grade
4. That when none of the atrial impulses is conducted, the block is complete

3. Common Misconceptions

Several misconceptions (table 24.3) have further fostered confusion. **Misconception 1:** *That 2:1 block is high-grade block.* Many respected authorities[4, 9, 26] describe 2:1 block as "high grade" or "advanced." Yet it is quite illogical to base the grade of block on the conduction ratio without taking rate into consideration. Because it is obvious that 2:1 conduction can be anything from a disaster to a blessing: at an atrial rate of 65, 2:1 block is indeed a disaster and deserves the title "high grade"; but, at an atrial rate of 125, 2:1 conduction may well be a blessing. Clearly blocks should not be branded by ratio alone.

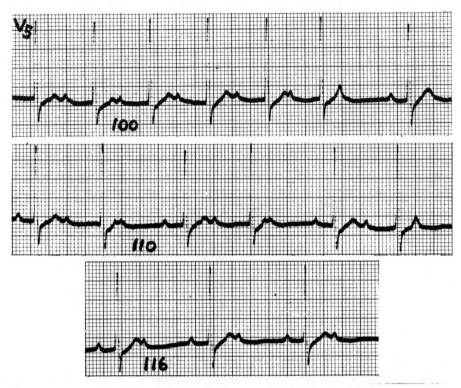

Figure 24.2.   Illustrating the effect of atrial rate on the A-V conduction ratio: at a rate of 100/min, 1:1 conduction with prolonged P-R interval; at 110, 3:2 Wenckebach periods; at 116, 2:1 conduction.

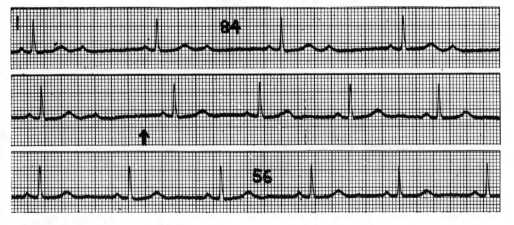

Figure 24.3.   Also illustrating the influence of atrial rate on the A-V conduction ratio. At a sinus rate of 84/min (*top strip*), there is 2:1 conduction. At the *arrow*, carotid sinus stimulation slows the sinus rate to 56/min. and 1:1 conduction results. Strips are continuous.

Misconception 2: *That 2:1 A-V block is necessarily type II.* Although 2:1 block, especially in the acute setting of myocardial infarction, is much more often type I than type II, many authorities automatically assign it to type II, apparently because the P-R intervals of the conducted beats are constant. This indicates both a misunderstanding of the constant P-R criterion and failure to understand the nature and nuances of type I block. The misapprehension is further promoted by such inadequate descriptions of type II block as "constant P-R intervals for conducted sinus beats irrespective of the ratio of atrial to ventricular depolarizations,"[25] and "A-V block with constant P-R intervals."[7] Even the definition ". . . failure of a ventricular response, without antecedent progressive lengthening of A-V conduction time"[10] omits the crucial point that the lack of progressive P-R lengthening must characterize the conduction of *consecutive* atrial impulses and leaves a loophole through which 2:1 block can squeeze.

In order to apply the constant P-R criterion for type II block, it is essential that *consecutive* atrial impulses be conducted with identical P-R intervals before the dropped beat; and that the P-R, when conduction resumes after the dropped beat, remains the same. This implies that the P-R remains unchanged regardless of its associated R-P—in contrast with type I in which the P-R and the R-P are reciprocally related. In type I block with 2:1 conduction, provided the sinus

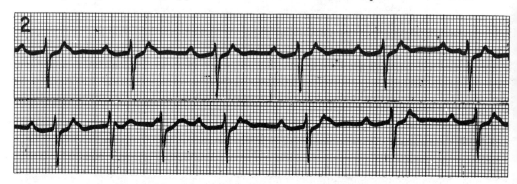

Figure 24.4. Strips are continuous. **Sinus tachycardia,** rate 116/min. with **2:1 A-V block** in the *top strip; bottom strip* begins with a **4:3 Wenckebach period.** The long P-R and absence of BBB, in the top strip alone, strongly suggest that the block is type I.

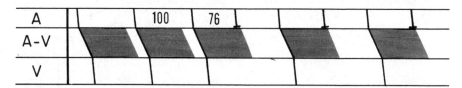

Figure 24.5. Ladder diagram, illustrating how an increase in atrial rate, without change in the refractory period (degree of block), can alter the conduction ratio from 1:1 to 2:1. First two cycles represent a rate of 60/min, last five cycles, a rate of 78/min—numbers are hundredths of a second. *Shaded area* represents an unchanging refractory period.

rhythm is regular, the R-P interval will be constant and so the P-R will be constant because, you will remember, the P-R in type I block is "R-P dependent."

Figure 24.4 presents an example of type I 2:1 A-V block in which the P-R intervals are constant at 0.32 sec until the ratio changes to a classical 4:3 Wenckebach at the beginning of the *second strip*; thus the 2:1 block is associated with all the typical findings of pure type I block: prolonged P-R, no BBB and a nearby Wenckebach period. It should be obvious that when the classical form of Wenckebach conduction alternates with 2:1 conduction, as in figure 24.4, the *type* of block has not changed. When the conduction ratio in Wenckebach periods changes from, say, 5:4 to 4:3, or from 4:3 to 3:2, there is no doubt in anyone's mind that the *type* of block is unchanged; why, when it goes one stage further and becomes 2:1, should there be an immediate diagnostic urge to switch the type and with it the prognostic significance?

When the conduction ratio changes because of an increase in atrial rate from, say, 1:1 with first degree block to 2:1, it is often described as a change for the worse in the *degree of block*,[6] when in reality the grade of block itself has not changed. Let us drive this point home with a fictitious laddergram.

In figure 24.5, the shaded area represents the refractory period (or degree of block) which remains unchanged throughout. But if the atrial rate accelerates so that the cycle shortens from 100 to 76, 2:1 conduction develops: the conduction ratio has changed to 2:1 from 1:1, but the grade of block has advanced not at all. The primary change is the atrial rate and the secondary change is the conduction ratio. It should be clear that we cannot assess the severity, or the change in severity, of any block from a conduction ratio *alone*.

Misconception 3: *That when most of the atrial impulses are not conducted, the block is high grade or advanced.* Loose definitions often imply that high grade (advanced) block is present when the conduction ratio is 3 or more to 1; or when "most" or "more than half" of the atrial impulses are not conducted. But, as with 2:1 block, the seriousness of a 3 or more to 1 ratio is also dependent on the atrial rate at which it develops; and when less than half the atrial impulses are conducted, the seriousness of the situation depends on the reasons for nonconduction. It is possible for even mild block to so conspire with atrial and ventricular rates that almost no conduction occurs (fig. 24.6). Therefore, to make the diagnosis of high grade block, it is necessary to demonstrate that the absence of conduction is due to the block itself and is not the result of an escape rhythm interfering with conduction. In figure 24.6, the block is evident but the opportunism of the ventricular pacemaker makes an important contribution to the prevailing nonconduction; and the fact that conduction can occur with prolonged P-R when the R-P interval reaches 0.60 sec (fifth beat in top strip) indicates that the patient is capable of 1:1 conduction with only first degree block at a rate of 64—hardly high grade block! *Moral:* If *any* beats are conducted, they are the ones that should receive attention, for they contain more information about the patient's conduction capabilities than any or all of the nonconducted beats. And if you calculate the rate represented by the cycle of the captured beat, this gives you the rate at which the patient is capable of 1:1 conduction and which can conveniently be called the "1:1 conduction equivalent."

Figure 24.7 consists of another example of partial A-V block which many would call "high grade" because only one out of every five atrial impulses is conducted—altogether there are 39 atrial impulses and only 8 are conducted. But both the atrial and ventricular rates are largely contributing to the nonconduction, and not just once but on eight occasions the patient is informing us that when the R-P reaches 0.54 sec he is perfectly capable of conducting with a slightly prolonged P-R interval—another way of telling us that if we could give him an atrial rate of 78 instead of 109/min, he would conduct every beat with a little first degree block! Again, hardly high grade block, but similar tracings are often published as such.[2, 8, 21, 22]

Misconception 4: *That when none of the atrial impulses is conducted, the block is complete.* Complete temporary absence of conduction (as in fig. 24.1A) is often accepted as evidence of complete A-V block; and this is again because the importance of rate is not appreciated. To repeat: when associated with appropriate atrial and ventricular rates, just mild block may prevent most or all conduction. Evidence that such a situation may represent the mildest of blocks

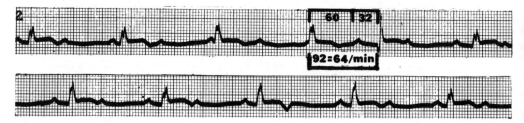

Figure 24.6. Strips are continuous. Out of 21 atrial impulses, only one is conducted to the ventricles (capture beat). That beat informs us that with an R-P of 60, conduction can take place with a prolonged P-R of 32; the cycle length of 92 represents a rate of 64/min which tells us that it would be reasonable to expect 1:1 conduction (with only first degree block) at that atrial rate.

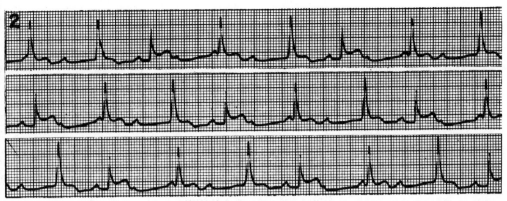

Figure 24.7. The strips are continuous, from another patient with acute inferior infarction. He has sinus tachycardia (rate, 109/min) with some (undetermined) degree of A-V block and a junctional escape rhythm at 60/min. There are 39 atrial impulses, of which only 8 are conducted with prolonged P-R intervals (0.24 sec).

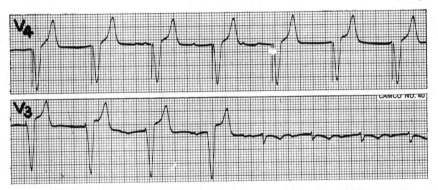

Figure 24.8. **Artificial pacemaker** pacing right ventricle at rate 62 with resumption of sinus rhythm at end of *second strip*. Note that none of the sinus impulses in the *top strip* is conducted, but this is not because of complete A-V block as conduction in the *second strip* testifies. Conduction in the *top strip* fails because of a conspiracy between *some* degree of A-V block, a ventricular (escape) rate of 62, and probably retrograde conduction into the A-V junction from the paced beats. Yet 1:1 conduction with mere **first degree A-V block** is possible at a sinus rate of 78—as evidenced in the second strip.

is afforded by the sequences depicted in figure 24.8. Here the pattern in lead V_4 is similar to that in figure 24.1*A* except that the ventricular rhythm is paced and its rate is only 62/min. In the course of this lead, the P wave emerges in front of the QRS, moves successively back towards the T wave, without conduction occurring, i.e., there is A-V dissociation. But in lead V_3, when the atrial impulse arrives at the critically "right" moment (i.e., when the R-P is exactly right), it is conducted with a prolonged P-R and narrow QRS complex and conduction continues through the rest of the strip. Far from warranting a diagnosis of complete block, impairment of conduction in the A-V junction is obviously minor. And it is this minor degree of block with which the attendant atrial and ventricular rates team up to produce A-V dissociation. The block in figure 24.1*A* may be just as minor as the block in figure 24.8 fortuitously proved itself to be.

There is no neat existing term to describe this situation accurately; to do it justice, some such recital as the following must be used to describe the situation in figure 24.1*A*: "some (undetermined) degree of block which, combined with an atrial rate of 90 and an accelerated junctional rhythm at rate 68, produces complete A-V dissociation." To characterize this dysrhythmia—where absence of conduction is due to two main causes, A-V block and accelerated subsidiary pacemaker—I have suggested the term "block/acceleration dissociation."[13]

Behavior versus Anatomy

And now we come to a knotty problem indeed. I have talked of type I and type II block in the way the terms are generally used, connoting behavior.[1, 10, 19, 27] We have seen that type I behavior (progressive lengthening of conduction times when impulses arrive earlier and earlier in a pathologically prolonged refractory period) is characteristic of the A-V node; and type II behavior ("all-or-none" conduction) is characteristic of infranodal sites (His-Purkinje system). Although type II behavior never occurs in the A-V node, type I behavior can, and occasionally does, occur anywhere in the conduction system. Thus with block in the His bundle, if it manifests type I behavior, the surface ECG will be indistinguishable from a Wenckebach occurring in the A-V node (except that the increments will tend to be smaller); and if it manifests type II behavior, type II block may be seen without BBB. The His bundle therefore may be responsible both for imitating A-V nodal block and for concealing infranodal block.

From the point of view of significance and prognosis, the anatomical level of the block is more important than its behavior; and so it would be ideal if, from the clinical tracing, we could infallibly distinguish between nodal (and call it type I) and infranodal (and call it type II) block. Unfortunately this cannot be done and the only sure way of localizing the level of the block is with intracardiac recordings—which are often neither available nor desirable. However, with a knowledge of the attributes and associations of both types of block (table 24.4), one can usually make an intelligent and correct inference from the clinical setting and the surface ECG.[27]

Moreover, it is also claimed that, in the presence of a narrow QRS (i.e., no BBB), A-V nodal block can be differentiated from infranodal block in most cases by observing the effects of atropine and carotid sinus massage. Atropine "improves" nodal block (shortens the P-R interval and/or increases the proportion of conducted beats) and "worsens" (decreases the proportion of beats conducted) infranodal block; whereas carotid sinus massage "worsens" nodal block (decreases proportion of beats conducted) and "improves" infranodal block (increases proportion of beats conducted).[12a]

Steps in the Right Direction

The difficulties that beset block are not easily resolved, but there are some remedial steps that can be taken:

1. The simple division into three degrees is too simple; clearly *additional categories are needed.* Take for example the category of ventricular asystole, exemplified by figure 24.1*C*, which has never been cleanly separated from complete block. But there are at least two other forms of ventricular asystole that in turn deserve separation from the spontaneous form (fig. 24.1*C*), namely that which results from a lengthening of the atrial cycle (attributed to a phase 4 phenomenon)[5] (fig. 24.9*A*) and that due to vagotonia, as from vomiting (fig. 24.9*B*). Undoubtedly these three forms of block-cum-asystole have differing

Table 24.4
Established Associations of Type I and Type II Block

Characteristic	Type I	Type II
Clinical	Usually acute	Usually chronic
	Inferior infarction	Anteroseptal infarction
	Rheumatic fever	Lenegre's disease
	Digitalis	Lev's disease
	Propranolol	Cardiomyopathy
Anatomical	Usually A-V nodal—sometimes His bundle	Always subnodal—usually bundle branches
Electrophysiologic	Relative refractory period	No relative refractory period
	Decremental conduction	All-or-none conduction
Electrocardiographic	R-P/P-R reciprocity	Stable P-R
	Prolonged P-R	Normal P-R
	Normal QRS duration	Bundle-branch block

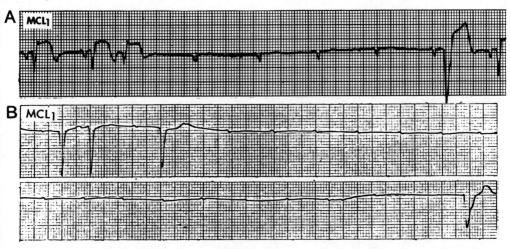

Figure 24.9. Two more examples of **transient ventricular asystole.** In *A*, the asystole is precipitated by an atrial premature beat that suppresses the sinus node and thus lengthens the sinus cycle. In *B*, the asystole is vagally induced—the patient vomited.

mechanisms and prognoses and require different therapeutic approaches; and each, therefore, deserves a category to itself. As a tentative improvement on the outworn three-degree classification, I have suggested the outline presented in table 24.5.[15]

2. Since the "degrees" of block, as presently defined—or not defined!—have created more confusion than they have contributed precision, *degrees should be de-emphasized*, perhaps even abandoned. Note that the term "degree" is not included in table 24.5.

3. In veiw of the major role that both atrial and ventricular rates play in determining the frequency and ratio of A-V conduction, *rates should be included* in all definitions and diagnostic categorizations of A-V block. Rates should be emphasized at the expense of ratios, instead of ratios at the expense of rates.

If these three suggestions were implemented, perfection would not be achieved but it would represent three sizeable steps in the right direction.

Table 24.5
Categories of A-V Conduction Disturbance

1. Prolonged P-R interval
2. Block/acceleration dissociation
3. Occasional "dropped" beats
    a. Type I (Wenckebach periodicity)
    b. Type II
4. 2:1 A-V Block
    a. Type I
    b. Type II
5. High grade block
    a. Type I
    b. Type II
6. Complete block
    a. Junctional escape
    b. Ventricular escape
7. Transient ventricular asystole
    a. Spontaneous
    b. Phase 4 (?)
    c. Vagal

REFERENCES

1. Barold, S. S., and Friedberg, H. D.: Second degree atrioventricular block; a matter of definition. Am. J. Cardiol. 1974: **33**, 311.
2. Beregovich, J., et al.: Management of acute myocardial infarction complicated by advanced atrioventricular block. Am. J. Cardiol. 1969: **23**, 54.
3. Chung, E. K.: *Principles of Cardiac Arrhythmias*, p. 271. Williams & Wilkins, Baltimore, 1971.
4. Chung, E. K.: How to approach cardiac arrhythmias. Heart Lung 1972: **1**, 523.
5. Corrado, G., et al.: Paroxysmal atrioventricular block related to phase 4 bilateral bundle branch block. Am. J. Cardiol. 1974: **33**, 553.
6. Danzig, R., et al.: The significance of atrial rate in patients with atrioventricular conduction abnormalities complicating acute myocardial infarction. Am. J. Cardiol. 1969: **24**, 707.
7. DePasquale, N. P.: The electrocardiogram in complicated acute myocardial infarction. Prog. Cardiovasc. Dis. 1970: **13**, 72.

8. Hart, H. H., and Schamroth, L.: A study in A-V block. Heart Lung 1976: **5:** 633.
9. Josephson, M. E., and Seides, S. F.: *Clinical Cardiac Electrophysiology. Techniques and Interpretations*, p. 80. Lea & Febiger, Philadelphia, 1979.
10. Langendorf, R., and Pick, A.: Editorial: Atrioventricular block, type II (Mobitz)—its nature and clinical significance. Circulation 1968: **38**, 819.
11. Lie, K. I., et al.: Mechanism and significance of widened QRS complexes during complete atrioventricular block in acute inferior myocardial infarction. Am. J. Cardiol. 1974: **33**, 833.
12. Lie, K. I., et al.: Incidence, prognostic significance and therapeutic implications of arrhythmias in acute myocardial infarction. Hart Bull. 1974: **5**, 17.
12a. Mangiardi, L. M., et al.: Bedside evaluation of AV block with narrow QRS complexes: usefulness of carotid sinus massage and atropine administration. Am. J. Cardiol. 1982: **49**, 1136.
13. Marriott, H. J. L.: AV block; an overdue overhaul. Emerg. Med. 1981: **30**, 85.
14. Marriott, H. J. L.: Second-degree AV block. Prim. Cardiol. 1981: Oct., p. 33.
15. Marriott, H. J. L., and Myerburg, R. J.: Recognition of arrhythmias and conduction abnormalities. In *The Heart*, p. 544, edited by J. W. Hurst. McGraw-Hill, New York, 1982.
16. McNally, E. M., and Benchimol, A.: Medical and physiological considerations in the use of artificial cardiac pacing. Part I. Am. Heart J. 1968: **75**, 380.
17. Narula, O. S., et al.: Analysis of the A-V conduction defect in complete heart block utilizing His bundle electrograms. Circulation 1970: **41**, 437.
18. Narula, O. S.: *His Bundle Electrocardiography and Clinical Electrophysiology*, pp. 146–161. F. A. Davis, Philadelphia, 1975.
19. Pick, A., and Langendorf, R.: *Interpretation of Complex Arrhythmias*, pp. 217–223. Lea & Febiger, Philadelphia, 1979.
20. Rosen, K. M., et al.: Mobitz type II block with narrow QRS complex and Stokes-Adams attacks. Arch. Intern. Med. 1973: **132**, 595.
21. Schamroth, L.: *The disorders of Cardiac Rhythm*, p. 536. Blackwell Scientific Publications, Oxford, 1971.
22. Scheinman, M., and Brenman, B.: Clinical and anatomic implications of intraventricular conduction blocks in acute myocardial infarction. Circulation 1972: **46**, 753.
23. Scherf, D., and Dix, J. H.: The effects of posture on A-V conduction. Am. Heart J. 1952: **43**, 494.
24. Singh, S., and Fletcher, R. D.: The site of myocardial infarction: Effect on presentation and management. Pract. Cardiol. 1980: **6**, 35.
25. Stock, R. J., and Macken, D. L.: Observations on heart block during continuous electrocardiographic monitoring in myocardial infarction. Circulation 1968: **38**, 993.
26. WHO/ISC Task Force: Definition of terms related to cardiac rhythm. Am. Heart J. 1978: **95**, 796.
27. Zipes, D. P.: Second-degree atrioventricular block. Circulation 1979: **60**, 465.

Review Tracing

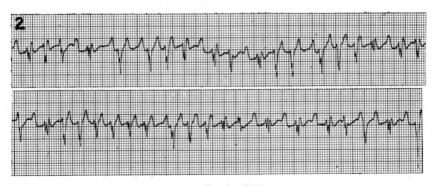

Review Tracing 24.1

For interpretation, see page 484

Review Tracings

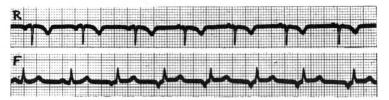

Review Tracing 24.2

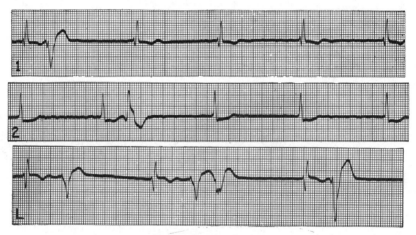

Review Tracing 24.3

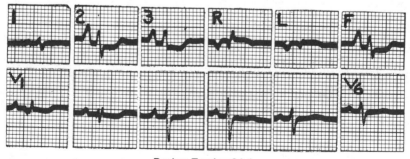

Review Tracing 24.4

For interpretation, see page 484

25

Artificial Pacemakers

The introduction of artificial pacemakers opened a new chapter in arrhythmias, both by producing their own new crop[6] and by shedding new light on long recognized mechanisms.[7] But the wonder machines of medicine are not without their own peculiar problems, and the artificial pacemaker is no exception. It may sometimes snatch the moribund from the jaws of death or restore a near-normal life-style to the cardiac cripple; but it can also spark fatal arrhythmias, induce hiccups, infection or thrombophlebitis, interfere with the golfer's swing, perforate the myocardium, and perpetrate numerous deceptions in the electrocardiogram.

The pacemaker's relationship to the cardiac arrhythmias has many and varied points of contact: It has aided in unraveling the mechanisms of several arrhythmias,[8] including those associated with the Wolff-Parkinson-White syndrome[10]; it has imitated time-honored patterns of arrhythmia; and it has produced its own vintage. As the state of the pacemaker art has progressed, the pacemaker has evolved its own set of pranks and created its own booby traps for the diagnostician.

The 1970s saw a revolution in pacemaker technology so that the field sprouted with more complex models: A-V sequential, automatic antitachycardia, multiprogrammable, etc. By 1978, more than a third of all implanted pacemakers in the United States were programmable; and the advantages of programmability indicate that, in the foreseeable future, all or most pacemakers implanted will be of this genre.[1] Since models have proliferated and many pacemakers can alter their signatures at the will of their programmers, the electrocardiography of pacemakers has become so diverse and complex that it is often impossible to attempt interpretation without a foreknowledge of the model concerned and how it is programmed. Now rate, sensitivity, output and refractory period are all noninvasively programmable, and pacemaking sophistication has reached such a pitch that nothing less than a multichaptered book can possibly do it justice; fortunately such a book is now available.[1a]

For convenience in terminology, one must be familiar with the three-letter code introduced in 1974 and presented in Table 25.1. Thus, for example, a "VVI" model is the common demand pacemaker that paces the ventricle, senses ventricular activity and is inhibited by such sensing.

Types of Pacemakers

There are four *basic* types of artificial pacemakers[2]:

1. Fixed-rate—recognized in the electrocardiogram by the fact that pacemaker "blips" occur with relentless regularity, their rhythm unaffected by the intervention of naturally occurring beats (fig. 25.1).

2. Demand (ventricular-inhibited)—recognized by the fact that, when a natural beat occurs, the regular rhythm of the pacemaker blips is interrupted (fig. 25.2); then, after a predetermined "escape" interval, the pacemaker fires again unless another natural beat anticipates it.

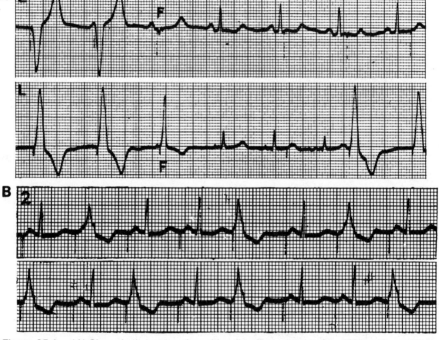

Figure 25.1. (*A*) Sinus rhythm competing with a **fixed-rate pacemaker (VOO)** with resulting fusion beats (*F*). Note that regular rhythm of pacemaker blips is not disturbed by the natural beats. (*B*) **Fixed-rate atrial pacemaker (AOO):** each P wave is immediately preceded by a pacemaker "blip." The paced rhythm is interrupted by frequent ventricular premature beats which happen to coincide with the next expected P waves so that they look like paced ventricular beats.

Table 25.1
Types of Pacemakers[a]

	Paced	Sensed	Response
Fixed-rate ventricular	V	0	0
P-triggered ventricular	V	A	T
QRS-triggered ventricular	V	V	T
QRS-inhibited ventricular (demand)	V	V	I
Fixed-rate atrial	A	0	0
Demand A-V sequential	D	V	I
Fixed-rate A-V sequential	D	0	0
Fixed-rate A-V simultaneous	D	0	0
Atrial synchronous, ventricular demand	V	D	D
Universal, fully automatic	D	D	D

[a] Key: V = ventricle, A = atrium, D = both ventricle and atrium, 0 = neither chamber; T = triggered, I = inhibited.

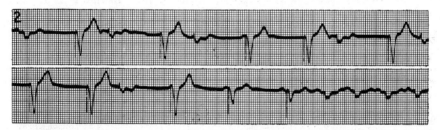

Figure 25.2. Demand pacemaker (VVI). Note that when a natural beat occurs, the pacemaker shuts off. The sinus beats are conducted with intraventricular block and the fifth and sixth beats in the *bottom strip* are fusion beats. In the *top strip*, the first and fourth paced beats are followed by retrograde P waves which in turn are followed by probable reciprocal beats.

3. Atrial-triggered—recognized by the fact that the ventricular blips always follow a P wave at a fixed interval (fig. 25.3).

4. Ventricular-triggered—this seldom seen pacemaker is recognized by the fact that the blip is in, not immediately before, the QRS complex of natural beats.

Notes: (a) If there are no natural beats (fig. 25.4), you cannot distinguish between a fixed rate and demand pacemaker; because the demand pacemaker, if it is not interrupted by natural beats, will continue to fire regularly. (b) The demand pacemaker operates exactly like a ventricular escape rhythm, whereas the fixed rate pacemaker functions like ventricular parasystole. Both are therefore potent manufacturers of fusion beats. (c) Both atrial-triggered and ventricular-triggered pacemakers become demand pacemakers when there are no natural complexes to trigger them.

Dysrhythms Produced by Pacemakers

Early Beats

In several situations, the pacemaker may create early beats. Figure 25.5*A* illustrates a fixed-rate pacemaker which, since it is not turned off by the sinus beats, produces three early beats. A demand pacemaker which fails to sense obviously amounts to a fixed-rate pacemaker and similarly produces early beats when its effective stimulus interrupts the basic rhythm. In figure 25.5*B*, the non-sensing demand pacemaker begins its short three-beat tenure with an early beat.

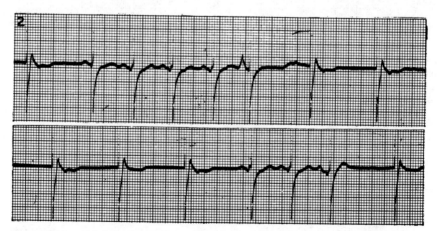

Figure 25.3. Atrial-triggered pacemaker (VAT). Note that all the P waves are followed, at a fixed interval, by a pacemaker "blip." When no P waves appear in time to trigger the pacemaker, it escapes like a demand pacemaker.

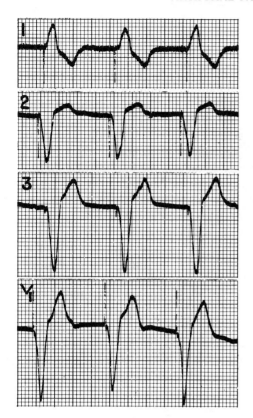

Figure 25.4. Ectopic ventricular rhythm driven by **artificial pacemaker**—note pacemaker ''blip'' immediately preceding each QRS. Since the QRS shows marked left axis deviation and an LBBB pattern, the pacemaker is situated in the right ventricle (transvenous pacemaker).

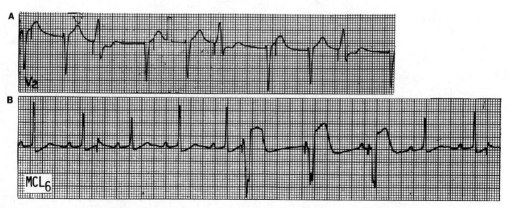

Figure 25.5. (A) **Fixed-rate pacemaker** which, since it is not shut off by the sinus beats, produces early (parasystolic) paced beats. B. **Demand pacemaker** which intermittently fails to sense—see spikes after second, fifth and last beats. The stimulus following the fifth sinus beat is slightly later than the other two and therefore produces a ventricular response and retains control for three consecutive beats.

At times, a failing, ineffective pacemaker retains the capability to pace only at a point early in the ventricular cycle. In figure 25.6, there is complete A-V block with an escaping idioventricular rhythm at a rate of about 36/min. The pacemaker (implanted epicardially in the left ventricle) consistently fails to pace except when its stimulus happens to land at the end of the idioventricular T wave. On the two occasions when it lands there (third beat in top strip and fourth beat in bottom strip), it effectively stimulates the left ventricle. When excitability is better earlier than later in the ventricular cycle, it is credited to "supernormal" excitability. This is, however, a misnomer because the excitability is not better than *normal*, as the term implies, but it is better than expected, judging from the evident lack of excitability later in the cycle.

Another form of "supernormality" produces a special form of ventricular capture. In the presence of anterograde A-V block, the ventricular pacemaker initiates retrograde conduction into the A-V junction and there sets up a refractory period containing a "supernormal" phase during which anterograde conduction becomes possible. In figure 25.7, only when the P wave lands on the T wave is the impulse conducted, and it is conducted with a perfectly normal P-R interval (as is often seen with type II A-V block), whereas P waves landing elsewhere in the ventricular cycle are invariably blocked. Thus, when P waves land at the summit of the T wave, conduction is better than expected and therefore qualifies as "supernormal."

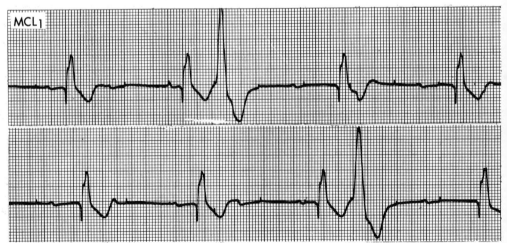

Figure 25.6.   Complete A-V block with idioventricular escape at a rate of 36/min. Pacemaker stimuli are entirely ineffective except when they fall at a critical time following an idioventricular beat—presumably in the "supernormal" phase of excitability.

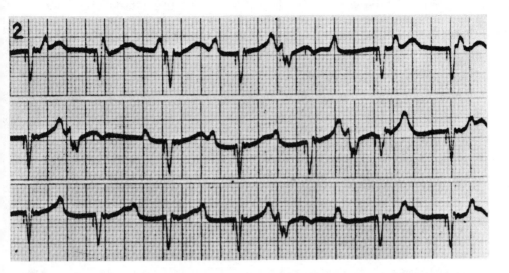

Figure 25.7. **Fixed-rate pacemaker** in the presence of A-V block. Conduction of the sinus impulse occurs only when the P wave lands on the summit of the T wave. Since sinus impulses later in the ventricular cycle are not conducted, conduction earlier in the cycle is unexpected and is therefore probably due to a "**supernormal**" **phase** set up by retrograde conduction into the A-V junction from the previous paced beat.

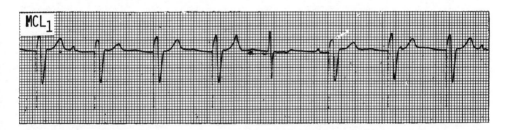

Figure 25.8. The right ventricular paced rhythm (rate, 70/min) is dissociated from the sinus rhythm (rate, 50/min) except for the fifth beat, which is slightly early and is a **capture beat** conducted with a long P-R interval. Note that the ventricular capture is the only beat that is *not* paced.

It is a pity that "capture" has crept into the pacemaker vernacular to connote successful pacing. Semantically, this is acceptable enough; but on grounds of legitimate priority, the "capture(d)" beat has for decades been a conducted beat interrupting any form of A-V dissociation; and the pity in the pacemaker context is that the only beat that by priority of nomenclature has the right to be called "captured" is the one beat that is not paced (fig. 25.8)!

Bigeminal Rhythm

There are several ways in which pacemakers can produce bigeminal grouping, and some of these are illustrated in figures 25.9 to 25.11. A relatively common mechanism is the escape-capture sequence. In this, the longer cycles end with a paced (escape) beat, and the subsequent shorter cycles end with a conducted beat (fig. 25.9). For this to happen, it is necessary for the spontaneous sinus discharge rate to be considerably slower than that of the noncompetitive pacemaker's escape rate or that of the competitive pacemaker's fixed rate.

Retrograde conduction into the A-V junction and often into the atria is common in any form of ectopic ventricular rhythm, and paced ventricular rhythms are no exception. If retrograde conduction is sufficiently delayed and the ascending impulse finds a circuit in the A-V junction ripe for reentry, the impulse may be reflected back to the ventricles to produce a reciprocal beat or ventricular "echo." If this happens after every paced beat, as in figure 25.10, the result is reciprocal bigeminy.

Yet another form of bigeminy will result if the failing pacemaker succeeds in pacing only twice out of every three attempts. Figure 25.11 illustrates such a pacemaker implanted on the left ventricle; firing at a rate of 80/min, it paces successfully twice and then records a dismal failure with every third discharge.

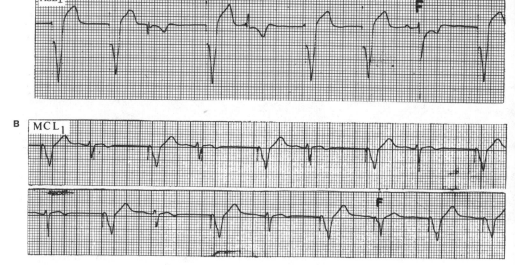

Figure 25.9. Bigeminal rhythm due to escape-capture sequences. In *A*, the **demand pacemaker** has a rate of 70/min, and the competing sinus rhythm is irregular at a rate of 44 to 50/min; as a result, two pairs of beats appear, each pair consisting of a paced beat followed by a conducted (capture) beat. The eighth beat (*F*) is a fusion beat. In *B*, the **fixed-rate pacemaker** has a rate of 72/min, while the sinus discharge rate is only 34/min. The *top strip* consists entirely of escape-capture sequences; the seventh beat (*F*) in the *bottom strip* is a fusion beat.

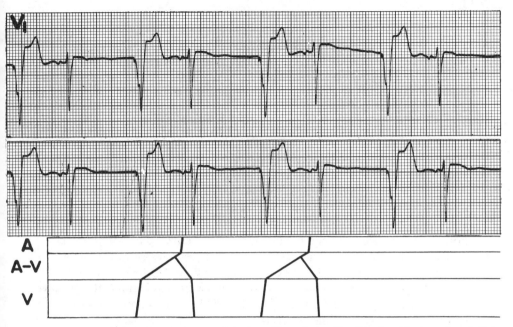

Figure 25.10. Bigeminal rhythm due to paced rhythm with **reciprocal beating** (ventricular echoes). Note that the retrograde P waves, as usual in V₁, have a negative-positive contour.

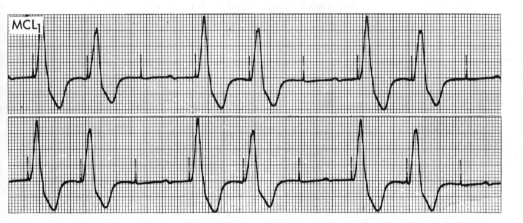

Figure 25.11. Bigeminal rhythm due to the failure of every third pacing stimulus to activate the ventricles.

Tachyarrhythmias

It is painfully well known that artificial pacemaker stimuli, when they land in the vulnerable period of the ventricles, can precipitate ventricular tachycardia or fibrillation. Pacing stimuli can be and frequently are used to deliberately produce supraventricular or ventricular tachycardia for the purpose of diagnosis and to evaulate the efficacy of drugs in their control.

Three other ways in which the pacemaker can produce a dangerous tachycardia are illustrated in figures 25.12 to 25.15. If a fixed-rate (or failing demand) pacemaker at a rate of, say, 70 intersperses its stimuli midway between the competing sinus beats which also enjoy a rate of about 70, the result will be a series of interpolated paced beats producing in effect a tachycardia at a rate of 140. Interpolated tachycardia, at a somewhat slower rate, is illustrated in figure 25.12.

A malfunctioning pacemaker may go berserk and fire at several hundred times a minute ("runaway pacemaker"), sometimes driving the ventricles in a wild tachycardia. The pacemaker in figure 25.13 is firing at a rate of 440/min with a 2:1 exit block between the pacemaker electrode and the responsive myocardium, so that the resulting ventricular tachycardia has a rate of 220/min. Unfortunately, the cause of this patient's predicament was not recognized, and instead of isolating the offending pulse generator, he was treated with drugs and cardioversion with the unhappy result that he died within the hour.

His tracing illustrates another important point, the so-called "haystack principle": If you have to find a needle, would you rather have a large or little haystack? As with the haystack, so with the electrocardiogram: If you have difficulty finding something that is inconspicuous—like small P waves, pacer spikes, etc.—always give the lead with the smallest disturbance of the base line a chance to help you. If only the attendants of this unfortunate patient had looked at aVR, the runaway blips would have sprung immediately to sight. But who would think of using aVR in search of an arrhythmic diagnosis?

Like other electrocardiographic manifestations of electrical activity, the pacemaker spike has magnitude and direction and, though easily seen in most

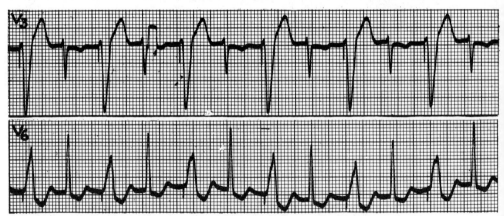

Figure 25.12.   Tachycardia due to interpolated paced beats from a **fixed-rate pacemaker**: Both sinus and paced rhythms have a rate of 62/min, producing an interpolated tachycardia at a rate of 124/min.

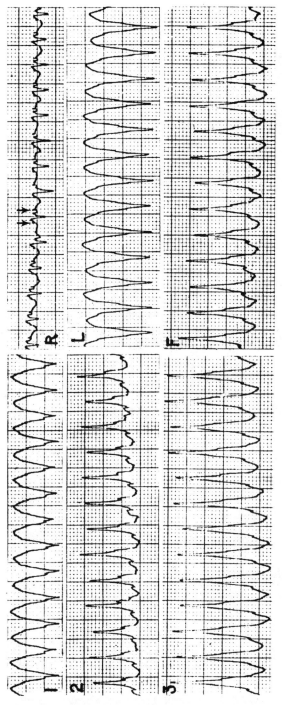

Figure 25.13. Runaway pacemaker producing fatal ventricular tachycardia. The pacemaker "blips" are not well seen except in aVR where there are two for every QRS complex (*arrows*).

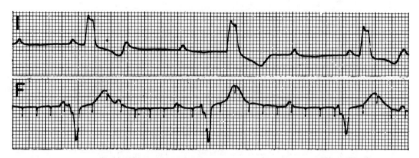

Figure 25.14. Complete A-V block with ineffective **runaway pacemaker.** "Blips" are visible at rate 350 in aVF; note that there is no sign of pacemaker activity in lead 1.

leads, may be inconspicuous or quite invisible in others (fig. 25.14)—a potential source of frustration and misdiagnosis (see below).

The introduction of a dual chamber pacemaker is equivalent to implanting an accessory pathway and is therefore an invitation to reentry. As retrograde conduction is common in any ectopic ventricular rhythm—a fact at first overlooked or underestimated by pacemaker innovators—atrial sensing sets the stage for a reentering tachycardia. The sequence of events following a ventricular premature beat is diagrammed in figure 25.15*A* and illustrated in figure 25.15*B*—the vicious circle of an "endless loop" tachycardia.[4a]

A

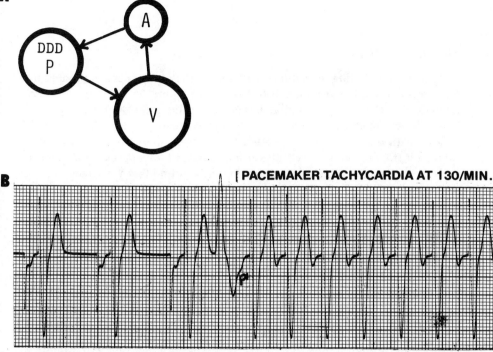

B

[**PACEMAKER TACHYCARDIA AT 130/MIN.**

C

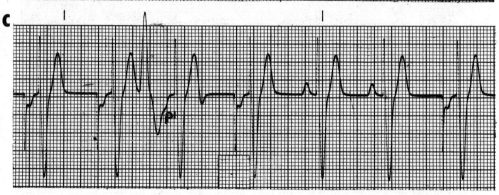

Figure 25.15. (A) Diagram of the sequence of events in "endless loop" tachycardia. (A = atrium; V = ventricle; P = pacemaker.) (B) **Fully automatic (DDD) pacemaker** producing **endless loop tachycardia** in response to a ventricular premature beat. At beginning of strip, pacer is operating in the A-V sequential mode. The fourth beat is a ventricular extrasystole with retrograde conduction (P'); the retrograde P' wave is sensed and, after the preset A-V delay of about 0.16 sec, the ventricle is paced. This beat in turn conducts retrogradely and the vicious circle continues. (C) The programmable atrial refractory period has been lengthened so that a similar premature beat fails to initiate a tachycardia because the retrograde P' now arrives during the atrial refractory period and is therefore not sensed. The sixth and seventh beats in this strip show this versatile pacemaker in the ventriclar mode, i.e., natural P waves are sensed and the ventricles paced after the preset A-V delay.

Miscellaneous Deceptions

Apart from imitating the natural arrhythmias, the pacemaker can produce its own peculiar crop of rhythm disturbances. In figure 25.16, there are two families of cycles, a longer and a shorter, suggesting a faulty pacemaker; the longer cycles are all equal, and the shorter cycles are also equal. Whenever one is faced with this situation, one should measure the short cycle carefully and subtract it from the longer cycle measuring backward *from the end of the longer cycle.* In this tracing (fig. 25.16), if you do this, you find that you exactly reach the summit of the T wave, and this immediately gives us the answer: The pacemaker is intermittently sensing the T waves—and enthusiastic sensing is no crime!

The escaping interval of a demand pacemaker may be longer or shorter than expected.[3] Some models have had "hysteresis" (Gr. *hysteros* = later) built into them; i.e., after being shut off by a natural beat, the first returning beat is *later*

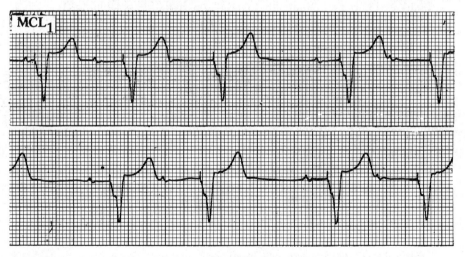

Figure 25.16. A normally functioning **demand pacemaker** deceived by T waves. The pacemaker cycle is 0.96 sec, and the longer cycles of 1.38 sec result when the pacemaker senses the preceding T wave.

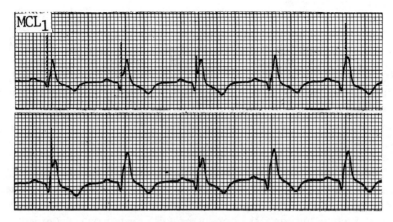

Figure 25.17. Sinus rhythm with RBBB and a normally functioning, right ventricular **demand pacemaker.** Pacemaker artifacts are superimposed on the ventricular complexes as much as 0.08 sec after beginning of the QRS because of the circuitous path taken by the sinus impulse to reach the sensing electrode.

than the set rate of the pulse generator would lead one to expect. On the other side of the coin, "partial sensing" may produce an ensuing cycle that is shorter than the full escape cycle of the pacer. It is important to be aware of these phenomena so as not to be too hasty in condemning the pacemaker as faulty.

Tracings such as that in figure 25.17 are often misinterpreted as indicating faulty sensing because in many beats the QRS complex contains the pacemaker spike indicating that the demand mode failed to sense the natural depolarization. But it is a question of geography[9]: The pacemaker's electrodes are situated within the *right* ventricle, and the conducted beats show a *right* bundle-branch block (RBBB) pattern. This means that, for the conducted impulse to reach the sensing electrode, it must travel down the left branch and work its way through the septum; depending on the exact location of the electrode, this journey may take up to about 0.08 sec.[4] Thus, in the presence of RBBB and a right ventricular demand pacemaker, the pacemaker spike may be found within the QRS as late as 0.08 sec after the beginning of the complex without implying faulty sensing.

Figure 25.18 illustrates another form of deception. Throughout lead 1 and the first three beats in lead 2, one would diagnose a ventricular-triggered pacemaker since the ventricular complex contains the pacing spike within it. But the last beat in lead 2 belies this diagnosis since the premature complex does not trigger the pacemaker but is *followed by* its spike. The spike is therefore constantly related not to the QRS but to the P wave, which it follows at the fixed preset interval of 0.20 sec. The sequence of events was as follows: The patient had an atrial-triggered pacemaker implanted because of high grade type II A-V block. With the regular paced rhythm and consequent better perfusion, conduction was restored, and as is usual with type II block, the P-R interval was normal (0.16 sec) and shorter than the preset P-to-spike interval; therefore, when conduction resumed, the conducted QRS began before the spike was evoked by the P wave.

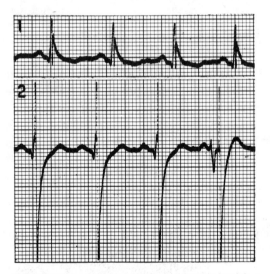

Figure 25.18.   In all except the last beat in lead 2, a pacemaker artifact interrupts the ventricular complex suggesting a ventricular-triggered pacemaker. However, the last beat in lead 2 is premature, does not elicit a pacemaker response, and so argues that it is not a ventricular-triggered model. The stimulus artifact is, however, constantly related to the P wave (P-to-blip interval = 0.20 sec) indicating an **atrial-triggered pacemaker.**

In figure 25.19, a supposedly atrial-triggered pacemaker is, in fact, ignoring the atrial stimulus and responding to the ventricular. The pacer spike is accurately coupled to the QRS (at 0.17 sec) instead of to the P wave. Because the atrial impulse is inherently too feeble or because the atrial electrode has been displaced, the pulse generator is responding to the more remote though stronger ventricular stimulus. It does not respond to *every* ventricular beat, however, because of the built-in 2:1 block that automatically develops when the atrial rate exceeds 110/min.

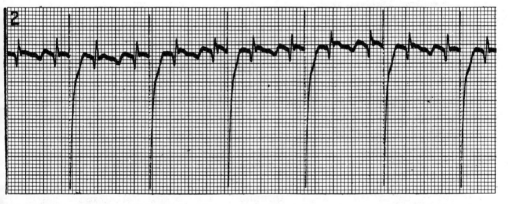

Figure 25.19. This **unipolar pacemaker** artifact follows every alternate QRS at a constant interval. This is an atrial-triggered model that is being triggered not by the atrial impulse but by every alternate ventricular impulse.

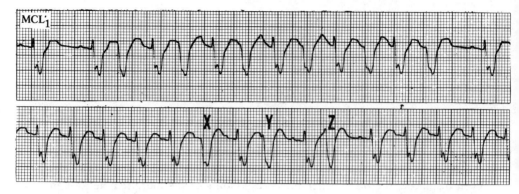

Figure 25.20. A **demand pacer** on standby, whose stimuli are invisible in this monitoring lead, intermittently failing to sense. *Top strip*: tachycardia produced by interpolated pacer beats in which the "blips" are invisible. *Bottom strip*: The coupling interval of consecutive paced beats (*X, Y, Z*) varies, but the interectopic interval is constant—like a bona fide parasystole.

Figure 25.20 recapitulates several of the points already made and illustrates how an innocent pacemaker can perpetrate a double deception. The patient was admitted with an acute anterior infarction. Shortly after admission, he developed sinus tachycardia with 2:1 conduction and left bundle-branch block. Because of these blocks, his cardiologist put in a temporary demand pacemaker on standby. A few hours later, he developed runs of interpolated ventricular bigeminy producing, in effect, a significant tachycardia with a ventricular rate of 138/min (fig. 25.20, *top strip*). These runs of interpolated tachycardia recurred despite the use of lidocaine in increasing dosage and supplemented with procainamide. It was then noticed that the coupling intervals showed variation (as in fig. 25.20, *X, Y,* and *Z* in *bottom strip*), and what was worse, they were consecutively shortening for three beats until the third beat (*Z*) bisected the T wave. After a while, one of the attendants spotted the fact that though the coupling intervals varied, the interectopic intervals were constant— and this suggested *parasystole*. At this point, it did not take long to recall that a fixed-rate pacemaker is parasystolic and that perhaps the troublesome and unresponsive ectopy was due to the pacemaker. With the pacemaker turned off completely, the ectopy immediately stopped, and it was then realized that the pacemaker was guilty of an almost unbelievable double deception: Its demand mode was intermittently failing, and the pacemaker spikes were invisible in the monitoring lead!

REFERENCES

1. Barold, S. S., et al.: The third decade of cardiac pacing; multiprogrammable pulse generators. Br. Heart J. 1981: **45**, 357.
1a. Bognolo, D.: *Practical Approach to Physiologic Cardiac Pacing.* Tampa Tracings, Tarpon Springs, 1983.
2. Castellanos, A., and Lemberg, L.: *Electrophysiology of Pacing and Cardioversion.* Appleton-Century-Crofts, New York, 1969.

3. Castellanos, A., and Lemberg, L.: Pacemaker arrhythmias and electrocardiographic recognition of pacemakers. Circulation 1973: **47,** 1382.

4. Castellanos, A., et al.: A study of arrival of excitation at selected ventricular sites during human bundle branch block using close bipolar catheter electrodes. Chest 1973: **63,** 208.

4a. Furman, S., and Fisher, J. D.: Endless loop tachycardia in an AV universal (DDD) pacemaker. PACE 1982: **5,** 486.

5. Kastor, J. A., and DeSanctis, R. W.: Reciprocal beating from artificial ventricular pacemaker; report of a case. Circulation 1967: **35,** 1170.

6. Kastor, J. A., and Leinbach, R. C.: Pacemakers and their arrhythmias. Prog. Cardiovasc. Dis. 1970: **13,** 240.

7. Katz, A. M., and Pick, A.: The transseptal conduction time in the human heart. Circulation 1963: **27,** 1061.

8. Langendorf, R., and Pick, A.: Artificial pacing of the human heart; its contribution to the understanding of arrhythmias. Am. J. Cardiol. 1971: **28,** 516.

9. Vera, Z., et al.: Lack of sensing by demand pacemakers due to intraventricular conduction defects. Circulation 1975: **51,** 815.

10. Wellens, H. J. J.: Contribution of cardiac pacing to our understanding of the Wolff-Parkinson-White syndrome. Br. Heart. J. 1975: **37,** 231.

Review Tracings

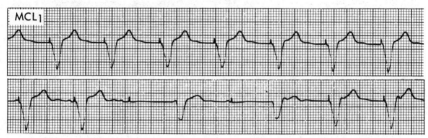

Review Tracing 25.1

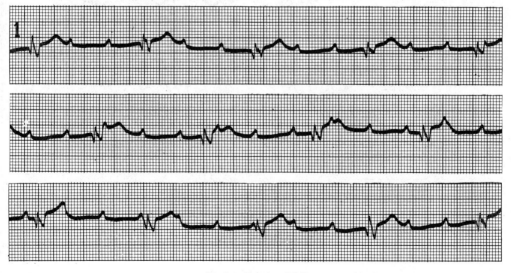

Review Tracing 25.2

For interpretation, see page 484

Review Tracings

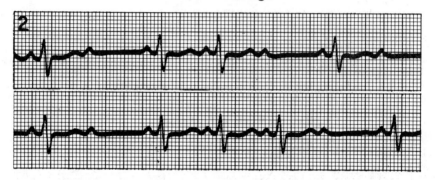

Review Tracing 25.3

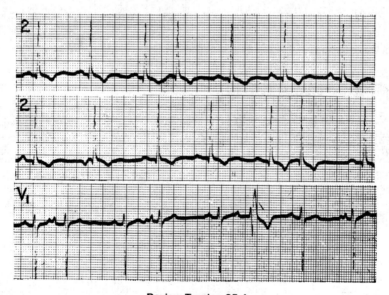

Review Tracing 25.4

For interpretation, see page 484

26

Myocardial Infarction

Experimental Considerations

If a branch of a dog's coronary is tied and an electrode is placed on an area of myocardium supplied by the occluded vessel, the T waves in the derived tracing soon become inverted. If the ligature is then removed and the flow of blood to the muscle re-established, the inverted T waves soon return to normal. The T-wave inversion is therefore clearly the result of simple ischemia. Inverted T waves form the basis of the **pattern of ischemia** in the clinical tracing.

If when T inversion occurs the ligature is allowed to remain in place, a dramatic change in the pattern shortly develops: within a minute or two the ST segment becomes strikingly elevated, dragging up with it and obliterating the inverted T wave. If at this stage the tie is removed, the tracing, gradually passing back through the inverted T stage, again reverts to normal. ST elevation, representing a stage beyond ischemia but still reversible, is known as the **pattern of injury.**

If when the pattern of injury is fully developed the tie is left in place, a further striking change eventually occurs. The entire QRS complex becomes inverted to produce a QS complex, while the ST segment comes back to the isoelectric line and the T wave once more assumes an upright contour. If this pattern is allowed to persist for long before the ligature is removed, it is found to be irreversible—no matter how long you wait, a QS pattern will continue to be recorded from the damaged area. Irreversible structural changes have occurred, and the new pattern is called the **pattern of necrosis.**

The reason necrosis produces Q waves is as follows: If a segment of myocardium is knocked out, electromotive forces cease to traverse it. There is thus a loss of forces directed toward the electrode placed over the inert muscle, and this results in a negative deflection (Q wave). By the same token there will be a relative gain in forces directed away from the inert area, and this may be indicated by increase in the size of the positive deflection (R wave) in leads taken from other surfaces of the heart. This concept is helpful in explaining some of the less classical patterns of infarction encountered.

The explanation for ST-segment elevation is less secure but it is believed that the major cause is a loss of resting membrane potential which depresses the baseline (T-Q segment), leaving the ST segment relatively elevated.[65]

Clinical Infarction

The two main types of infarction used to be called anterior and posterior. But because the term "posterior" is anatomically inaccurate, as it was applied to the surface of the heart resting on the diaphragm, it has become more common to use the terms "inferior" or "diaphragmatic" when referring to lesions of this wall.

If you hold a heart in your hand, it is at once obvious that there are no clearcut surfaces or boundaries; any "walls" defined are at best rough approximations. The four walls usually referred to in discussions of infarction are anterior, lateral, inferior and true posterior (to distinguish it from the false posterior of the older terminology).

The three changes observed in the experimental heart—T-wave inversion, ST elevation and the appearance of Q waves—form the basis of infarction patterns as we see them clinically. Around any patch of infarcted muscle there is a less damaged zone which produces the pattern of injury; and outside this an even less affected area which produces the pattern of ischemia. In the experimental heart these zones can be "tapped" individually with small electrodes placed directly on the epicardium (**direct leads**). Clinically the nearest one can get is several centimeters from the myocardium on the outside of the chest (**semidirect leads**). A natural result of this is that the precordial pattern is usually a composite picture combining the patterns of ischemia, injury and necrosis all in one QRST sequence—the relatively distant electrode is influenced by all three zones instead of only one.

The first step, then, in diagnosing infarction from the electrocardiogram is to know what changes to look for. Those changes are (1) the **fresh appearance of Q waves or the increased prominence of pre-existing ones,** (2) **ST-segment elevations** and (3) **T-wave inversions.** Only Q-wave changes are diagnostic of infarction (necrosis), but changes in the ST segments and T waves may provide strong presumptive evidence. The Q, ST and T changes all have special characteristics: The Q wave is often wide as well as deep; any Q measuring 0.03 sec or more in width is highly suspicious of infarction. The deviated ST segments typically show an upward convexity. The fully developed T waves are pointed and consist of two symmetrical limbs, well likened to an arrowhead. These three changes are summarized in figure 26.1. Note that these changes are registered in **leads that face the area of damage,** and it is convenient to refer to them collectively as "indicative" changes. Opposite, or "reciprocal," changes (i.e., no Q wave with perhaps some increase in height of R wave, depressed ST segments and tall upright T waves) meanwhile appear in leads facing the diametrically opposed surface of the heart. Fortified with a little imagination

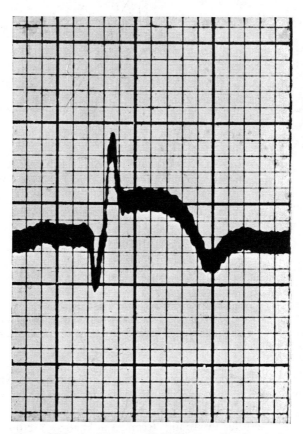

Figure 26.1   Acute myocardial infarction. The three indicative changes–Q wave, ST elevation and T inversion.

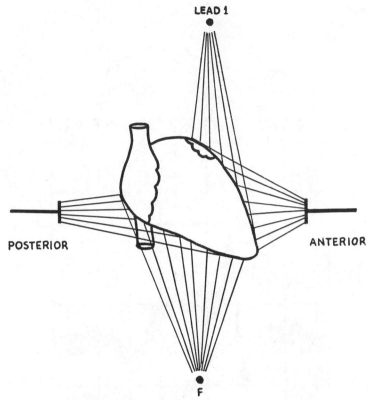

Figure 26.2. Illustrating how the anterior chest leads and lead 1 both face the same "anterior" (really anterosuperior) surface of the heart, while the posterior chest leads and the positive pole (*F*) of leads 2, 3 and aVF face the inferior (diaphragmatic) surface.

and with a glance at figure 26.2, it is relatively simple to decide what changes will occur in which leads when various surfaces of the heart are involved. Leads whose positive poles face the inferior surface (2, 3 and aVF) are most important in the diagnosis of **inferior** infarction. Reciprocal changes are usually seen in leads 1, aVL and some of the precordial leads. In **anterior** infarction indicative changes occur in precordial leads and in leads 1 and aVL, while reciprocal changes develop in leads 2, 3 and aVF. In **lateral** wall infarction leads 1, aVL and V_5 and V_6 are most likely to show indicative changes, and reciprocal changes may sometimes develop in leads taken farthest to the right (V_1, V_{3R}, etc.). None of the routine 12 leads faces the **posterior** surface of the heart, and so infarction of this wall must be inferred from reciprocal changes occurring in anterior leads, especially V_1 and V_2.

The limb lead patterns associated with the two main types of infarction, anterior and inferior, are perhaps worth summarizing first and separately. Anterior infarction produces indicative changes in lead 1 and for this reason is sometimes called Q_1T_1 type infarction. Inferior infarction produces indicative changes in lead 3 and is therefore called Q_3T_3 type infarction. In anterior infarction indicative changes are also seen in aVL and reciprocal changes appear in 2, 3 and aVF. In inferior infarction indicative changes are also found in 2 and aVF, while reciprocal changes develop in 1 and aVL. These changes are summarized in figure 26.3. Remember, however, that the characteristic changes of infarction may appear *only* in the precordial leads, the limb leads remaining normal or near normal.

Salient Features of Acute Myocardial Infarction

	Anterior	Inferior
1. Indicative changes (Q, ST elevation, T inversion) in leads:	1, aVL, anterior chest	2, 3, aVF, posterior chest
2. Reciprocal changes in leads:	2, 3, aVF, posterior chest	1, aVL, anterior chest
3. Progressive changes in pattern from day to day		

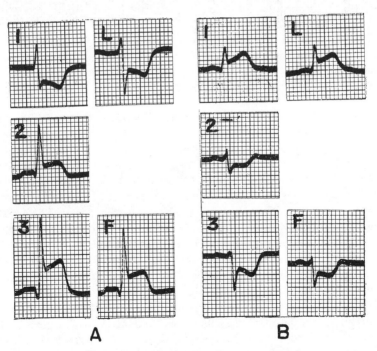

A   B

Figure 26.3. Characteristic early changes of acute infarction in the limb leads. (*A*) Inferior infarction. (*B*) Anterior infarction.

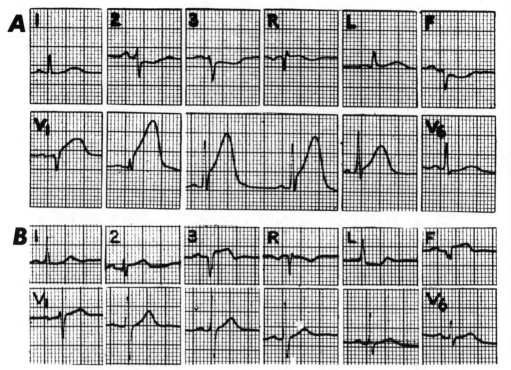

Figure 26.4. (*A*) Early **acute anterior infarction.** ST elevation, with loss of its normal concavity, is evident in four of the five chest leads, with minor reciprocal depression in leads 2, 3 and aVF. (*B*) Early **acute inferior infarction.** There are Q waves in leads 3 and aVF, indicative ST elevation in leads, 2, 3 and aVF and reciprocal depression in leads 1 and aVL, but no such depression in the V leads.

Figure 26.4 illustrates the typical changes of early acute myocardial infarction, anterior (*A*) and inferior (*B*). Note that the ST elevation of anterior infarction (fig. 26.4*A*) is much more pronounced in the chest leads than in the standard limb leads, while reciprocal depression of the ST segment is definite but relatively minor in leads 2, 3 and aVF. In figure 26.4*B* there is ST elevation in leads 2, 3 and aVF with reciprocal depression in leads 1 and aVL; notice that there is no reciprocal ST depression in the precordial leads. The idealized patterns of evolution of both anterior and inferior infarctions are presented in figure 26.5. The reciprocal ST-T changes diagrammed in V_3 with inferior infarction may represent more than mere reciprocity; for it is said that ST-segment depression in anterior leads (V_{1-4}) in the presence of acute transmural inferior infarction usually indicates additional significant ischemia elsewhere[22, 58, 60]: some authors claim further myocardial damage in the posterolateral region,[22] while others find that such "reciprocal" ST depression indicates serious involvement of the anterior descending artery and foretells a stormy course.[58, 60] Depression only in leads 1 and/or aVL, on the other hand, is not indicative of additional involvement and represents a pure "reciprocal" change.[58] However, the issue of reciprocal changes in chest leads is not settled and others express the opinion that precordial ST depression frequently occurs *early* in acute inferior infarction, is not generally caused by significant anterior ischemia, nor associated with more left ventricular dysfunction than is found in patients without such ST depression.[72]

Additional "improved" criteria for the diagnosis of acute inferior infarction, requiring the simultaneous recording of the three standard limb leads, have been proposed.[76]

Evaluation of Q_3

As a prominent Q wave in lead 3 is one of the hallmarks of inferior infarction but is also sometimes a normal finding, its evaluation is often difficult.[68] It is more likely to be abnormal if it is wide (more than 0.03 sec), if it is associated with Q waves also in 2 and aVF, and if it is followed by a slurred upstroke into the R wave.

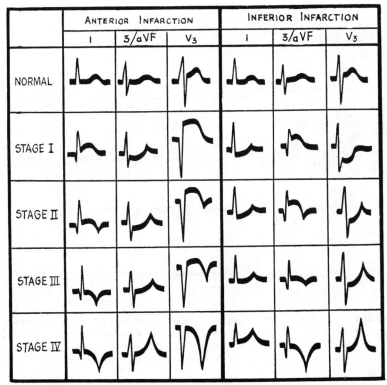

Figure 26.5. Acute myocardial infarction. Stages of evolution in the patterns of anterior and inferior infarctions.

A simple test is sometimes helpful: deep inspiration will usually cause an innocuous (positional) Q_3 to disappear or materially decrease; whereas the Q_3 of infarction is relatively unaffected by this simple maneuver[18] (fig. 26.6, *A–D*). However, the test is not always reliable,[36] to which strip *E* in figure 26.6 bears testimony.

At times, but by no means invariably, it is helpful to refer the decision to the aV leads,[46] for lead 3, connecting left arm and left leg, represents the difference between aVF and aVL (3 = aVF − aVL). If the initial deflection of the QRS in aVF is less positive (or more negative) than the corresponding deflection in aVL, there will be an initial negative (Q) wave in 3. And so if there is no Q wave in either aVL or aVF but the R wave in aVF is not so tall as the R in aVL (fig. 26.7*A*), there will be a Q wave in 3. This will clearly not be a pathological Q wave, as it results simply from difference in the height of normal R waves. In such a situation the aV leads give an immediate favorable answer. If on the other hand there is a Q wave in aVF (fig. 26.7*B*), one has merely transferred the burden of proof to aVF and it then has to be decided whether the Q there is of abnormal significance or not.

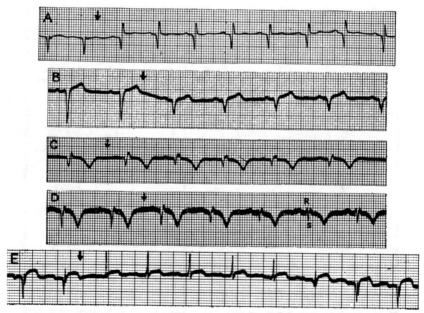

Figure 26.6. Effect of deep inspiration on Q_3 in patients with inferior infarction. Inspiration began at the arrow in each strip. Note that there is relatively little effect on the negative wave in *A*, *B*, *C* and *D*. In *D* the Q wave is replaced by a small initial R wave, but an appreciable negative (S) wave persists. In *E*, however, the pathological Q wave is entirely drawn up.

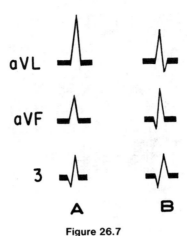

Figure 26.7

Localization of Infarction

Localization of the infarct from the ECG is far from precise.[55, 62] It is however usually possible to identify the main area of involvement and to some extent gauge the infarct's size. Localization is mainly based on the previously stated principle that indicative changes (those epitomized in fig. 26.1, p. 375) occur in leads facing the damaged surface of the heart. Thus if indicative changes are seen in all the precordial leads from V_1 to V_6, we diagnose an **extensive anterior** or **anterolateral infarction**[38] (Figs. 26.8 to 26.11). If such changes occur in only one or more of leads V_1 to V_4, the infarct is labelled **anteroseptal**[37] (fig. 26.12, p. 384). If the limb leads indicate an inferior infarction, but indicative changes are present also in leads V_5 and V_6, we would call it an inferior infarction with lateral extension or an **inferolateral infarction**[41] (figs. 26.13 to 26.15). If the only changes seen are in 1 and aVL, it would suggest **lateral infarction**,[42] and so on.

Subendocardial infarction[9, 30, 35, 49, 50, 70] is diagnosed if (1) the clinical picture justifies the diagnosis of infarction and (2) several of the limb and precordial leads show ST depression and T wave inversions (fig. 26.16) that persist. The subendocardial layer of myocardium is particularly vulnerable because, being close to the ventricular cavity, it is subjected to particularly high pressure during systole and is therefore the earliest zone to "feel the pinch" when coronary adequacy falters.

Right ventricular infarction: significant ST elevation in lead V_4R in patients with inferior wall infarction is said to be diagnostic of a right ventricular infarct[6, 17]; indeed, ST elevation of 1 mm or more in any of the leads V_4R to V_6R is claimed to have 90 per cent sensitivity and specificity.[73]

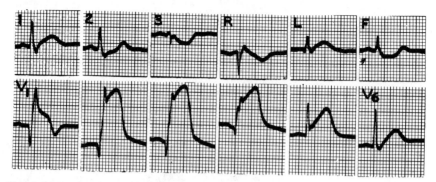

Figure 26.8 Acute anterior myocardial infarction. Note ST elevation in V_{1-5}, and loss of the normal upward concavity of the ST segment in 1, aVL and V_{2-6}, with reciprocal changes in 2, 3 and aVF. Q waves have developed in the right chest leads, and the pattern of RBBB has appeared, indicating septal involvement.

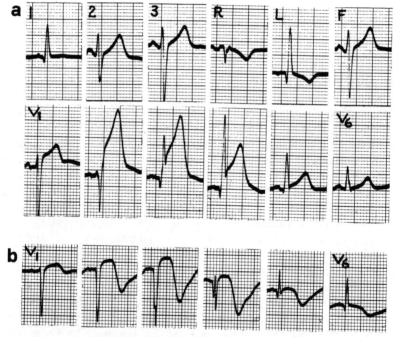

Figure 26.9. Acute extensive anterior myocardial infarction. In *a*, note probable left anterior hemiblock in the limb leads with high ST take-off and tall T waves in precordial leads; in *b*, 2 days later, "coving" of ST segments with deep inversion of T and U waves, while simultaneously R waves have dwindled in V_{1-2}, a QS complex has appeared in V_3, and Q waves have developed or deepened in V_{4-6}.

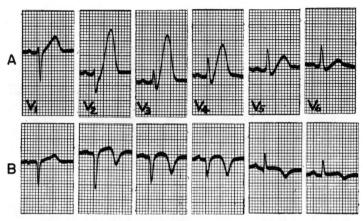

Figure 26.10.   Acute anterior infarction. Note unusual early stage in *A*, with tall T waves and *depressed ST* take-off. *B*, taken a few days later, shows typical evolution of anterior infarction.

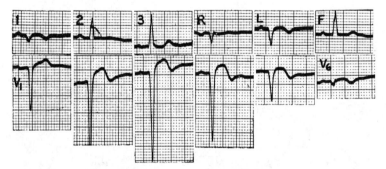

Figure 26.11. Old **anterior myocardial infarction** with persistent ST elevation in precordial leads 3 years after the infarction. A ventricular aneurysm was demonstrated.

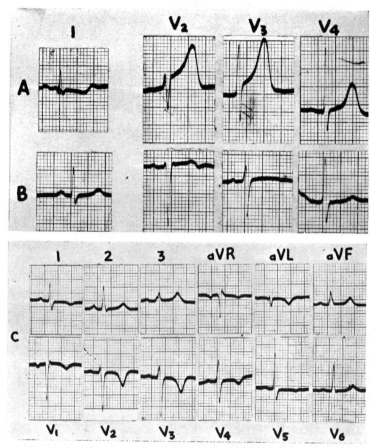

Figure 26.12. (*A*) **Acute anteroseptal myocardial infarction.** Note the tall T waves in V_{2-4}, where they will later be deeply inverted. (*B*) Taken just a few hours later; note striking changes in T waves; tracing is now remarkably normal. (*C*) Taken 6 days later; shows fully developed pattern of anteroseptal infarction. Note that no pathological Q waves have developed, but the infarction can be diagnosed with certainty from the striking evolution in the ST-T pattern.

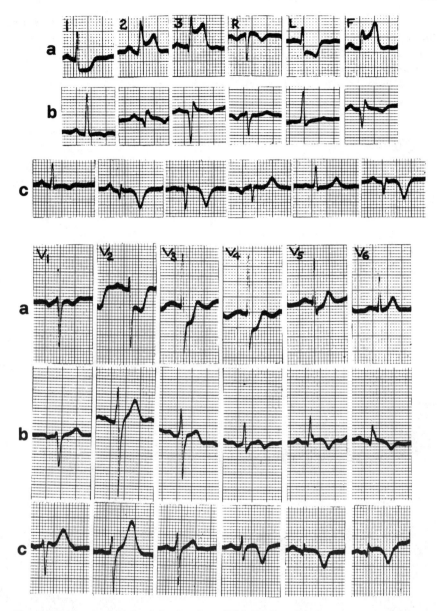

Figure 26.13. Acute inferolateral myocardial infarction. Tracing *a* was taken 3 days before *b*, and *b* 6 days before *c*. Note in *a* indicative changes in 2, 3 and aVF with reciprocal changes in 1, aVL and the chest leads V_{2-5}. Subsequent evolution demonstrates indicative changes in the left chest leads as well, so that the infarction is inferolateral. Note also that the QRS axis shifts from about $+60°$ to $-30°$ (thanks to the development of infarction Q waves, not to left anterior hemiblock) and that the R waves in left chest leads have shrunk away.

Atrial infarction also usually complicates the inferior wall infarct. It must be suspected when, in the presence of ventricular infarction, an atrial arrhythmia develops. Other clues include abnormal P-wave contour and any significant P-R segment displacement (see fig. 26.25), especially widespread P-R segment depression in the presence of an atrial arrhythmia, elevation of the P-R segment in left chest leads with reciprocal depression in right chest leads, or elevation in lead 1 with reciprocal depression in lead 3.[33]

Complex Patterns

Frequently the pattern observed is not so "pure" as the ones so far described. If the anterior and inferior walls of the left ventricle are both involved in the process, **antero-inferior infarction** (fig. 26.17 and 26.18), varying combinations

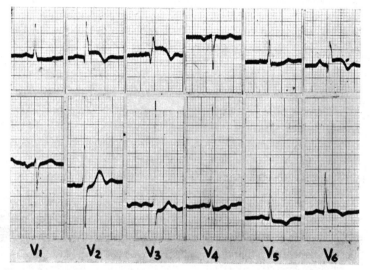

Figure 26.14. Acute inferolateral infarction. Note indicative changes in 2, 3 and aVF. The ST-T changes in V₆ suggest lateral wall involvement as well.

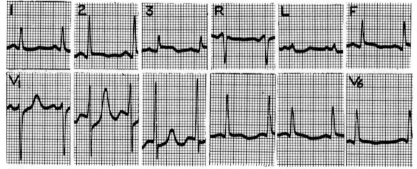

Figure 26.15. Acute inferolateral infarction. There is ST elevation in 2, 3, aVF and V₄₋₆, with classical reciprocal changes in V₁₋₃.

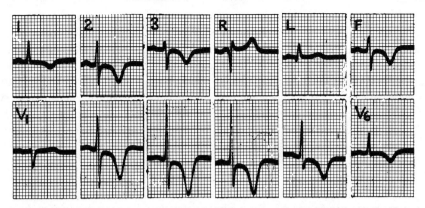

Figure 26.16. Probable **acute subendocardial infarction.** From a patient with the clinical picture of infarction; note widespread ST-T depression in limb and chest leads, but no associated Q waves.

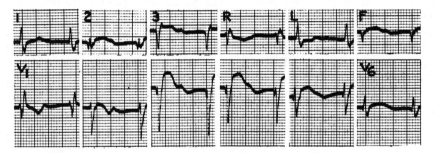

Figure 26.17. Antero-inferior myocardial infarction. Note that indicative changes are evident in both anterior (V$_{2-6}$) and inferior (2, 3, and aVF) leads; RBBB has also developed, indicating septal involvement. There is also marked prolongation of the P-R interval to about 0.40 sec.

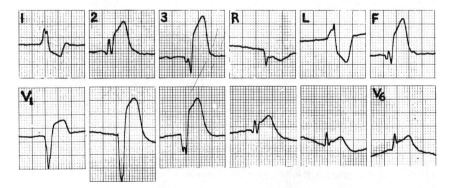

Figure 26.18. Acute antero-inferior infarction. Note the diagnostic "indicative" ST elevation across the precordium (V$_{1-6}$) and in the "inferior" leads (2, 3 and aVF) as well with reciprocal changes in the lateral leads (1 and aVL). There is also a **LBBB** pattern.

of the changes typical of each may occur.[39] Sometimes an inferior infarction develops in a heart that has suffered a previous anterior infarction, or vice versa; in such circumstances the current infarction, producing changes opposite (or reciprocal) to the changes of the previous infarction, may tend to "normalize" the tracing so that it looks "better" than it did before the second occlusion. Some patients may have two transmural infarctions, one recent and one old, and consequently have a poor prognosis yet have no sign of a Q wave.

Bundle-branch block, producing as it does bizarre QRS, ST and T changes of its own, may mask the changes of a superimposed infarction. A sometimes difficult diagnosis is that of infarction in the presence of left bundle-branch block.[4, 12] If a previous tracing is available showing the uncomplicated block pattern, then the appearance of fresh Q waves (especially over the left ventricle, where they are not found in uncomplicated left bundle-branch block) is good evidence of acute infarction. Q waves in 1, aVL or V_6 in the presence of left bundle-branch block (fig. 26.19) are strongly suspicious of anteroseptal infarction,[26, 53] as are notched S waves in V_3 or V_4.[74] A decrease in amplitude of R waves over the left ventricle,[29] is a clue suspicious of acute infarction. At times, the diagnosis may be disarmingly easy if the primary ST-T changes of acute injury replace the secondary changes of the LBBB (figs. 26.18 and 26.19). Similarly, the diagnostic ST-T changes of acute infarction may show through the bizarre pattern of ventricular pacing[44] and other forms of ventricular ectopy.

Right bundle-branch block is less likely to cause confusion.[13] Both anterior and inferior infarction patterns can be seen superimposed on the block pattern

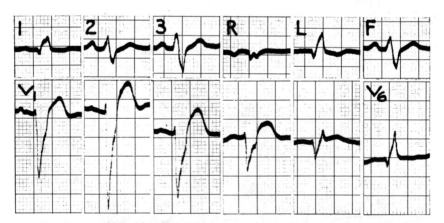

Figure 26.19.   Anteroseptal infarction. The QRS pattern is characteristic of LBBB except that there are unexpected Q waves in 1, aVL and V6. The rSr' in V_5 suggests the possibility of ventricular aneurysm.[16] Note characteristic *upward convexity* of elevated ST segments V_{2-4}.

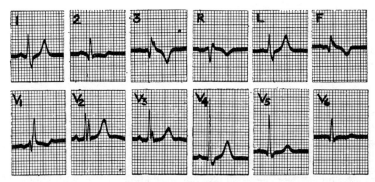

Figure 26.20. **Acute inferior infarction** with **right bundle-branch block.** Q and T changes are evident in 2, 3 and aVF, with reciprocal T-wave changes in V_{2-4}.

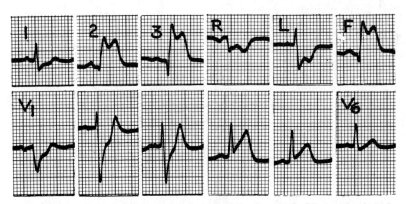

Figure 26.21. Acute **infero-apical** myocardial infarction. Note ST elevation in 2, 3, aVF, V_4 and V_5 with reciprocal depression in other leads. Q waves are developing in 2, 3 and aVF.

(figs. 26.8, 26.17 and 26.20). The block may have preceded the infarction or may have resulted from it; indeed, the presence of bundle-branch block may be considered an integral part of the pattern of **septal infarction.**[46]

A less thoroughgoing involvement of both anterior and inferior walls is presented in figure 26.21 where indicative changes are confined to only V_4 and V_5 in the chest series: an **infero-apical infarction.**

Along with the inferior wall, there may be involvement of the posterobasal region of the left ventricle; this directly posterior involvement is recognized by reciprocal changes in anterior leads (V_1, V_2) including an increase in height and width of their normally small R waves. Figure 26.22 illustrates such an **inferoposterior infarction** with classical indicative changes in the inferior leads and increased prominence of the R waves in V_1 and V_2.

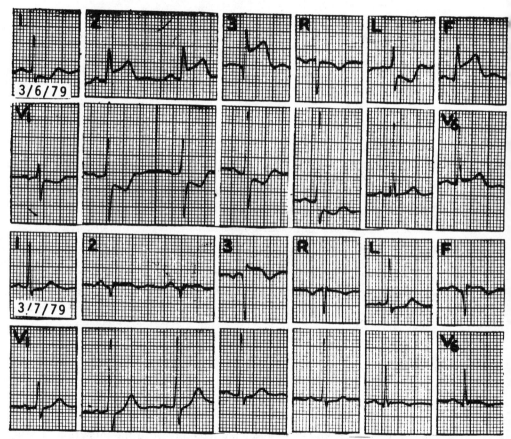

Figure 26.22.   Acute inferoposterior infarction. Two 12-lead tracings taken 24 hours apart and showing evolution both in the indicative changes in leads 2, 3 and aVF and in the reciprocal changes in anterior leads V_1 and V_2. Note the virtually complete loss of R waves in the inferior leads as the Q waves develop, and the abnormally prominent R waves in V_1 and V_2 which double in size by the second day. Judging by the ST-T changes in V_5 and V_6, there is probably also involvement of the lateral wall as well.

Further Observations

Some important general points:

1. *Time relationships* are important. Rarely, no changes develop in the tracing for several days or even for 2 or 3 weeks. Usually, however, they begin to make their appearance within the first few hours. ST-segment changes appear early and progress. At this stage the T waves, later to become inverted, actually become taller and appear as an upward extension of the rising ST segments[2] (figs. 26.9, 26.10 and 26.12). This early tall T wave may be mistaken for the later tall T wave of reciprocal leads, and an early anterior infarction may thus be wrongly labelled as inferior. Sometimes this tall T wave is associated with striking depression of the ST segment,[10] and then of course the reciprocal pattern of an inferior infarction is even more closely simulated (fig. 26.10*A*). To add to the confusion similar tall T waves are occasionally seen as an early stage of inferior infarction[66]; in such cases this may well represent a premonitory stage of diaphragmatic wall ischemia before actual infarction has occurred. Similar but persistent tall T waves are a not uncommon finding in patients with angina[20] (see Chapter 27, fig. 27.4).

Q waves may appear early or may not develop for several days. Whenever the various changes appear they tend to evolve in a fairly typical sequence (fig. 26.5). In the indicative leads the ST segments rise higher and higher and then begin to return to the baseline, while the T waves develop progressively deeper inversion; finally, after weeks or months, the T waves may become shallower and finally return to normal. Thus ST changes are usually the most transitory; the T changes are more lasting; but the Q waves are the most likely to remain as a permanent record of the myocardial scar. Even well established Q waves, however, may at times completely disappear; in fact, diagnostic Q waves are lost within three years in approximately 14 per cent of patients with myocardial infarction.[77] Persistent ST segment elevation[15] (fig. 26.11) the explanation for which is quite uncertain,[54] or the presence of an rsR' pattern in V_5 or V_6[16] suggests the possibility of ventricular aneurysm.

The model sequence of changes depicted diagrammatically in figure 26.5 is not invariable, but there is always some "evolution" of the pattern along similar lines, and to diagnose an *acute* infarction such evolution must be in evidence. For there is no means of being certain, in a single tracing, whether the typical changes of infarction are due to an acute process or are the remnants of an old one. ST segment deviations are least likely to represent an old process, but even they may sometimes endure for a long time and rarely are permanent. Progressive changes from day to day are the conclusive evidence of an active, acute process.

2. The electrocardiogram should be considered *confirmatory* of the clinical impression, and should not supersede it. If the patient is suspected clinically of having sustained a myocardial infarct, he should be treated accordingly even if his tracing is completely normal. The looked-for changes may be late to appear

or, rarely, they may never appear in the routine leads although the infarction is a clinical certainty. For factors favoring missed diagnoses, see page 395.

3. The Q waves of infarction may be better revealed in ectopic ventricular beats than in the conducted sinus beats[3,5] (fig. 26.23).

4. A T-wave pattern of some importance is the T_1-lower-than-T_3 pattern. T_1 is often found normally lower than T_3 in vertical hearts, i.e., when the QRS axis is in the neighborhood of $+90°$. It is also abnormally present in early left ventricular overload, before frank inversion of T_1 has occurred. If both vertical heart and left ventricular overload can be excluded such a pattern is extremely suspicious of an anterior infarction, either old or recent.[11]

5. Apart from the changes specific for acute infarction, other abnormalities frequently appear. The tracing sometimes shows low voltage and this is associated with a doubled mortality rate.[56] The QT duration is frequently prolonged, reaching its maximum in the second week. Any arrhythmia or block may develop, and continuously monitored series indicate that some form of rhythm disturbance occurs in 75 to 95% of all patients. In order of frequency, the commonest to develop are ventricular premature beats, supraventricular premature beats, atrial fibrillation, ventricular tachycardia, accelerated idioventricular rhythms and supraventricular tachycardia. Sinus bradycardia, first degree A-V block, type I A-V block, and complete A-V block with narrow escaping ventricular QRS complexes (idiojunctional rhythm) characteristically complicate acute inferior infarction; whereas BBB, type II A-V block, and complete A-V block with wide QRS complexes (idioventricular rhythm) more often result from anterior infarction.

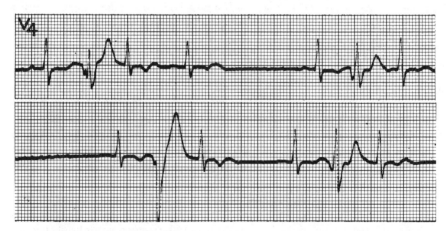

Figure 26.23. Anterior infarction, the indicative Q waves of which are obvious in the ventricular extrasystoles and absent in the conducted beats. (From a 52-year-old physician who had an anterior infarction 2 years previously.)

Infarction without Q Waves

Q waves have come to be regarded as the hallowed hallmark of infarction. But there is nothing sacred about Q waves as such. Their importance is that they represent the replacement of electrical forces directed toward the electrode by oppositely directed forces, i.e., replacement of impulses (dipoles) travelling toward the electrode by impulses travelling away from it. This being so, loss of R wave with or without gain in depth of S wave might well carry the same significance as a Q wave. Indeed, in some circumstances this is true. Loss of QRS amplitude over the left ventricle has already been mentioned as a clue to infarction in the presence of left bundle-branch block.

Furthermore, Q waves have been regarded for decades as an index of transmural (through-and-through; full-thickness) infarction and therefore as a discriminator between transmural and subendocardial infarction. Yet long ago Prinzmetal's team demonstrated that the subendocardium was *not* electrocardiographically silent; and so the mistaken significance of Q waves could have been corrected a quarter century ago. But established traditions die hard and slowly, and still the belief lingers that Q waves are the monopoly of transmural infarcts. The truth is that, although statistically Q waves are more commonly seen in transmural than in nontransmural (subendocardial) infarction, both brands of infarcts are seen both with and without Q waves. These waves are, therefore, in themselves useless in discriminating between them.[28,48,52,55,59,62]

Again, reversal of the normal trend toward heightening of R waves in the first three or four precordial leads may be a helpful sign. In these leads we have seen that the height of the R wave normally increases from right to left. If, however, these R waves dwindle progressively from right to left, it is suspicious of anteroseptal infarction; but it is important to remember that both "poor" and "reversed" progression of the precordial R wave may also be seen in ventricular hypertrophy, left or right, and even in some normal subjects. And even complete loss of R waves (i.e., QS complexes) in V_1 through V_3 is not necessarily evidence of anterior infarction and is seen in left ventricular hypertrophy and other situations (see below).

In true posterior or inferoposterior infarction the only changes may be reciprocal ones observed in the anterior chest leads. At times in true posterior or in lateral infarction[31,70] the sole or chief change may be an increase in the

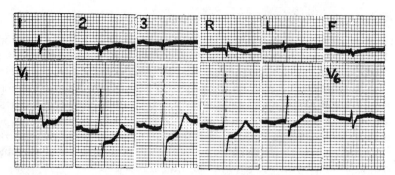

Figure 26.24. Probable **acute posterior infarction.** Note prominent and wide R waves in V₁ and V₂ accompanied by reciprocal ST-T changes in the same leads; these features in anterior leads suggest an acute infarction of the opposite, i.e., posterior, wall.

height of R waves over the right precordium (V_{3R}, V_1, V_2). Similarly, an increased width of the R wave to 0.04 sec or more in V_1 and V_2 may be diagnostic of true posterior infarction[23] (fig. 26.24).

Another infarction pattern, of which the most striking feature is *left axis deviation*, was described by Grant.[24] Its characteristics are (1) an initial wide R wave (0.04 sec or more) followed by a deep S wave in aVF, and (2) marked left axis deviation of more than −30°. A careful study with autopsy correlation showed that many patients with this pattern had infarction of the anterolateral wall. He attributed the axis shift to "peri-infarction block," but subsequent work[7] indicates that this pattern is more often found with LVH or diffuse scarring of the left ventricle than with a discrete infarction. Its probable anatomic basis is left anterior hemiblock (see p. 86). Left anterior hemiblock can also eliminate the Q waves of inferior infarction by substituting r waves for them in 2, 3 and aVF (fig. 26.25). Thus the diagnosis of inferior infarction in the presence of anterior hemiblock presents a special problem, since they both produce significant left axis deviation—the infarction with Q waves, the hemiblock with S waves.

Grant also pointed out that *right axis deviation* may sometimes result from infarction of the diaphragmatic wall[23]; the probable explanation for this is left posterior hemiblock.

In a few patients with anteroseptal infarction and intermittent RBBB, the initial q wave of infarction may appear in V_1 only in association with the RBBB and be replaced by an initial r wave during normal conduction.[75]

Q Waves without Infarction

Just as the absence of Q waves does not exclude, so their presence does not prove, infarction. One of the commonest errors of over interpretation is in the reading of anteroseptal infarction from QS complexes in V_1 and V_2—a pattern much more often produced by left ventricular hypertrophy alone. The following conditions can produce pathological Q waves that simulate those of myocardial infarction:

1. Ventricular hypertrophy, left or right[43, 63]
2. Diffuse myocardial disease[45, 47, 64]
3. Hypertrophic cardiomyopathy
4. Anterior and posterior hemiblock
5. Focal septal block[21]
6. Localized myocardial replacement
7. Acute extracardiac catastrophes, e.g., pancreatitis,[19] pulmonary embolism, pneumonia,[34] etc.
8. Ventricular preexcitation[67]

In addition, significant Q waves may occur as a transient manifestation of myocardial ischemia[57]; and they are rarely seen in apparently normal youths.[32]

Concluding Notes on Diagnosis

The electrocardiogram is not infallible in the diagnosis of infarction. It has been estimated that with 12 routine leads only 80 to 90% of cases are diagnosable. Factors to bear in mind as probable causes of missed diagnoses are:

1. Failure to take serial tracings.
2. Failure to take additional exploratory chest leads in doubtful cases
3. Presence of bundle-branch block
4. Digitalis action tending to neutralize ST elevations
5. Simultaneous infarcts neutralizing each other's patterns
6. Masking by hemiblock

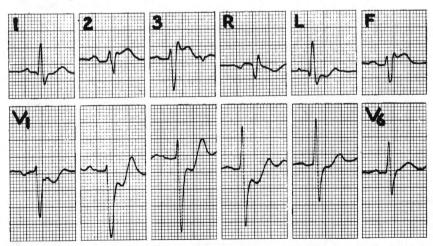

Figure 26.25. Acute inferior infarction with **left anterior hemiblock** and incomplete **RBBB**. The Q waves of inferior infarction are kept at bay by the r waves of the hemiblock in 2, 3 and aVF, but the ST elevation in those leads with reciprocal depression in 1, aVL and V$_{1-5}$ are diagnostic. Depression of the P-R segment, best seen in leads 2 and aVF, bespeak an **atrial infarction** as well.

REFERENCES

1. Abbott, J. A., and Scheinman, M. M.: Nondiagnostic electrocardiogram in patients with acute myocardial infarction: clinical and anatomic correlations. Am. J. Med. 1973: **55**, 608.
2. Bayley, R. H., et al.: Electrocardiographic changes (local ventricular ischemia and injury) produced in the dog by temporary occlusion of a coronary artery, showing a new stage in the evolution of a myocardial infarction. Am. Heart J. 1944: **27**, 164.
3. Benchimol, A., et al.: The ventricular premature contraction. Its place in the diagnosis of ischemic heart disease. Am. Heart J. 1963: **65**, 334.
4. Besoain-Santander, M., and Gomez-Ebensperguer, G.: Electrocardiographic diagnosis of myocardial infarction in cases of complete left bundle branch block. Am. Heart J. 1960: **60**, 886.
5. Bisteni, A., et al.: Ventricular premature beats in the diagnosis of myocardial infarction. Br. Heart J. 1961: **23**, 521.
6. Braat, S., et al.: The value of right precordial leads in detection of right ventricular infarction; a comparison with ^{99m} Tc-pyrophosphate scintigraphy (abstr.). Circulation 1981: **64** (supp. IV), 86.
7. Castle, C. H., and Keane, W. M.: Electrocardiographic "peri-infarction block." A clinical and pathologic correlation. Circulation 1965: **31**, 403.
8. Class, R. N., et al.: Diphtheritic myocarditis simulating myocardial infarction. Am. J. Cardiol. 1965: **16**, 580.
9. Cook, R. W., et al.: Electrocardiographic changes in acute subendocardial infarction. I. Large subendocardial and nontransmural infarcts. Circulation 1958: **18**, 603. II. Small subendocardial infarcts. Ibid.: 613.
10. Dressler, W., and Roesler, H.: High T waves in the earliest stage of myocardial infarction. Am. Heart J. 1947: **34**, 627.
11. Dressler, W., and Roesler, H.: The diagnostic value of the pattern T_1 lower than T_3 ($T_1 < T_3$) compared with the information yielded by multiple chest leads in myocardial infarction. Am. Heart J. 1948: **36**, 115.
12. Dressler, W., et al.: The electrocardiographic signs of myocardial infarction in the presence of bundle branch block. I. Myocardial infarction with left bundle branch block. Am. Heart J. 1950: **39**, 217.
13. Dressler, W., et al.: The electrocardiographic signs of myocardial infarction in the presence of bundle branch block. II. Myocardial infarction with right bundle branch block. Am. Heart J. 1950: **39**, 544.
14. Dunn, W. J., et al.: The electrocardiogram in infarction of the lateral wall of the left ventricle: a clinicopathologic study. Circulation 1956: **14**, 540.
15. East, T., and Oram, S.: The cardiogram in ventricular aneurysm following cardiac infarction. Br. Heart J. 1952: **14**, 125.
16. El-Sherif, N.: The rsR' pattern in left surface leads in ventricular aneurysm. Br. Heart J. 1970: **32**, 440.
17. Erhardt, L. R., et al.: Single right-sided precordial lead in the diagnosis of right ventricular involvement in myocardial infarction. Am. Heart J. 1976: **91**, 571.
18. Evans, W.: The effect of deep inbreathing on lead III of the electrocardiogram. Br. Heart J. 1951: **13**, 457.
19. Fulton, M. C., and Marriott, H. J. L.: Acute pancreatitis simulating myocardial infarction in the electrocardiogram. Ann. Intern. Med. 1963: **59**, 730.
20. Freundlich, J.: The diagnostic significance of tall upright T wave in the chest leads. Am. Heart J. 1956: **52**, 749.
21. Gambetta, M., and Childers, R. W.: Rate-dependent right precordial Q waves: "septal focal block." Am. J. Cardiol. 1973: **32**, 196.
22. Goldberg, H. L., et al.: Anterior S-T segment depression in acute inferior myocardial infarction: Indicator of posterolateral infarction. Am. J. Cardiol. 1981: **48**, 1009.
23. Grant, R. P., and Murray R. H.: QRS complex deformity of myocardial infarction in the human subject. Am. J. Med. 1954: **17**, 587.
24. Grant, R. P.: Left axis deviation. An electrocardiographic-pathologic correlation study. Circulation 1956: **14**, 233.
25. Grant, R. P.: Peri-infarction block. Prog. Cardiovasc. Dis. 1959: **2**, 237.
26. Horan, L., et al.: The significance of diagnostic Q waves in the presence of bundle branch block. Chest 1970: **58**, 214.

27. Hurd, H. P., et al.: Comparative accuracy of electrocardiographic and vectorcardiographic criteria for inferior myocardial infarction. Circulation 1981: **63**, 1025.
28. Ideker, R. E., et al.: Q waves and transmural infarcts; the terms are not the same (abstr.). Am. J. Cardiol. 1981: **47**, 463.
29. Kennamer, R., and Prinzmetal, M.: Myocardial infarction complicated by left bundle branch block. Am. Heart J. 1956: **51**, 78.
30. Levine, H. D., and Ford, R. V.: Subendocardial infarction: report of six cases and critical survey of the literature. Circulation 1950: **1**, 246.
31. Levy, L., et al.:Prominent R wave and shallow S wave in lead V_1 as a result of lateral myocardial infarction. Am. Heart J. 1950; **40**, 447.
32. Likoff, W., et al.: Myocardial infarction patterns in young subjects with normal coronary arteriograms. Circulation 1962: **26**, 373.
33. Liu, C. K.: Atrial infarction of the heart. Circulation 1961: **23**, 331.
34. Mamlin, J. J., et al.: Electrocardiographic pattern of massive myocardial infarction without pathologic confirmation. Circulation 1964: **30**, 539.
35. Massumi, R. A., et al.: Studies on the mechanism of ventricular activity. XVI. Activation of the human ventricle. Am. J. Med. 1955: **19**, 832.
36. Mimbs, J. W., et al.: The effect of respiration on normal and abnormal Q waves: an electrocardiographic and vectorcardiographic analysis. Am. Heart J. 1977: **94**, 579.
37. Myers, G. B., et al.: Correlation of electrocardiographic and pathologic findings in anteroseptal infarction. Am. Heart J. 1948: **36**, 535.
38. Myers, G. B., et al.: Carrelation of electrocardiographic and pathologic findings in large anterolateral infarcts. Am. Heart J. 1948: **36**, 838.
39. Myers, G. B., et al.: Correlation of electrocardiographic and pathologic findings in anteroposterior infarction. Am. Heart J. 1949: **37**, 205.
40. Myers, G. B., et al.: Correlation of electrocardiographic and pathologic findings in posterior infarction. Am. Heart J. 1949: **38**, 547.
41. Myers, G. B., et al.: Correlation of electrocardiographic and pathologic findings in posterolateral infarction. Am. Heart J. 1949: **38**, 837.
42. Myers, G. B., et al.: Correlation of electrocardiographic and pathologic findings in lateral infarction. Am. Heart J. 1949: **37**, 3.
43. Myers, G. B.: QRS-T patterns in multiple precordial leads that may be mistaken for myocardial infarction. Circulation 1950: **1**, 844 and 860.
44. Niremberg, V., et al.: Primary ST changes; diagnostic aid in paced patients with acute myocardial infarction. Br. Heart J. 1977: **39**, 502.
45. Oram, S., and Stokes, W.: The heart in scleroderma. Br. Heart J. 1961: **23**, 243.
46. Osher, H. L., and Wolff, L.: The diagnosis of infarction of the interventricular septum. Am. Heart J. 1953: **45**, 429.
47. Perez-Trevino, C., et al.: Glycogen storage disease of the heart. Am. J. Cardiol. 1965: **16**, 137.
48. Pipberger, H. V., and Lopez, E. A.: "Silent" subendocardial infarcts; fact or fiction? Am. Heart J. 1980: **100**, 597.
49. Prinzmetal, M., et al. Studies on the mechanism of ventricular activity; VI. The depolarization complex in pure subendocardial infarction; role of the subendocardial region in the normal electrocardiogram. Am. J. Med. 1954: **16**, 469.
50. Pruitt, R. D., et al.: Certain clinical states and pathologic changes associated with deeply inverted T waves in the precordial electrocardiogram. Circulation 1955: **11**, 517.
51. Pruitt, R. D., et al.: Simulation of electrocardiogram of apicolateral myocardial destructive lesions of obscure etiology (myocardiopathy). Circulation 1962: **25**, 506.
52. Raunio, H., et al.: Changes in the QRS complex and ST segment in transmural and subendocardial myocardial infarctions. Am. Heart J. 1979: **98**, 176.
53. Rhoads, D. V., et al.: The electrocardiogram in the presence of myocardial infarction and intraventricular block of the left bundle-branch block type. Am. Heart J. 1961: **62**, 78.
54. Richter, S., et al.: Functional significance of electrocardiographic changes after left ventricular aneurysmectomy. J. Electrocardiol. 1978: **11**, 247.
55. Roberts, W. C., and Gardin, J. M.: Locations of myocardial infarcts: A confusion of terms and definitions. Am. J. Cardiol. 1978: **42**, 868.
56. Rotmensch, H. H., et al.: Incidence and significance of the low-voltage electrocardiogram in acute myocardial infarction. Chest 1977: **71**, 708.
57. Rubin, I. L., et al.: Transient abnormal Q waves during coronary insufficiency. Am. Heart J. 1966: **71**, 254.

58. Salcedo, J. R., et al.: Significance of reciprocal S-T segment depression in anterior precordial leads in acute inferior myocardial infarction; concomitant left anterior descending coronary artery disease? Am. J. Cardiol. 1981: **48,** 1003.
59. Savage, R. M., et al.: Correlation of postmortem anatomic findings with electrocardiographic changes in patients with typical anterior and posterior infarcts. Circulation 1977: **55,** 279.
60. Shah, P. K., and Berman, D. S.: Implications of precordial S-T segment depression in acute inferior myocardial infarction. Am. J. Cardiol. 1981: **48,** 1167.
61. Sokolow, M.: The clinical value of the unipolar extremity (aV) leads. Ann. Intern. Med. 1951: **34,** 921.
62. Sullivan, W., et al.: Correlation of electrocardiographic and pathologic findings in healed myocardial infarction. Am. J. Cardiol. 1978: **42,** 724.
63. Surawicz, B., et al.: QS- and QR-pattern in leads V_3 and V_4 in absence of myocardial infarction: electrocardiographic and vectorcardiographic study. Circulation 1956: **12,** 391.
64. Tavel, M. E., and Fisch, C.: Abnormal Q waves simulating myocardial infarction in diffuse myocardial diseases. Am. Heart J. 1964: **68,** 534.
65. Vincent, G. M., et al.: Mechanisms of ischemic ST-segment displacement: evaluation by direct current recordings. Circulation 1977: **56,** 552.
66. Wachtel, F. W., and Teich, E. M.: Tall precordial T waves as the earliest sign of diaphragmatic wall infarction. Am. Heart J. 1956: **51,** 91.
67. Wasserburger, R. H., et al.: Noninfarctional $QS_{2, 3, aVF}$ complexes as seen in the Wolff-Parkinson-White syndrome and left bundle branch block. Am. Heart J. 1962: **64,** 617.
68. Weisbart, M. H., and Simonson, E.: The diagnostic accuracy of Q_3 and related electrocardiographic items for the detection of patients with posterior wall myocardial infarction. Am. Heart J. 1955: **50,** 62.
69. Yu, P. N. G., and Blake, T. M.: The significance of QaVF in the diagnosis of posterior infarction. Am. Heart J. 1950: **40,** 545.
70. Yu, P. N. G., and Stewart, J. M.: Subendocardial myocardial infarction with special reference to the electrocardiographic change. Am. Heart J. 1950: **39,** 862.
71. Zema, M. J., et al.: Electrocardiographic poor R-wave progression; correlation with postmortem findings. Chest 1981: **79,** 195.
72. Croft, C. H., et al.: Clinical implications of anterior ST segment depression in patients with acute inferior myocardial infarction. Am. J. Cardiol. 1982: **50,** 428.
73. Croft, C. H., et al.: Detection of acute right ventricular infarction by right precordial electrocardiography. Am. J. Cardiol. 1982: **50,** 421.
74. Havelda, C. J., et al.: The pathologic correlates of the electrocardiogram: complete left bundle branch block. Circulation 1982: **65,** 445.
75. Rosenbaum, M. B., et al.: Abnormal Q waves in right sided chest leads provoked by onset of right bundle-branch block in patients with anteroseptal infarction. Br. Heart J. 1982: **47,** 227.
76. Warner, R., et al.: Improved electrocardiographic criteria for the diagnosis of inferior myocardial infarction. Circulation 1982: **66,** 422.
77. Wasserman, A. G., et al.: Prognostic implications of diagnostic Q waves after myocardial infarction. Circulation 1982: **65,** 1451.

Review Tracings

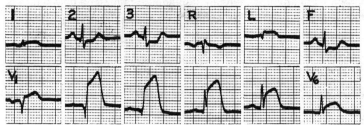

Review Tracing 26.1

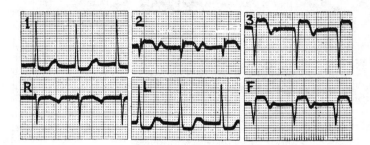

Review Tracing 26.2

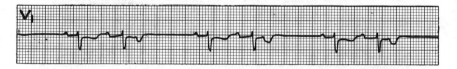

Review Tracing 26.3

For interpretation, see page 484

Review Tracing

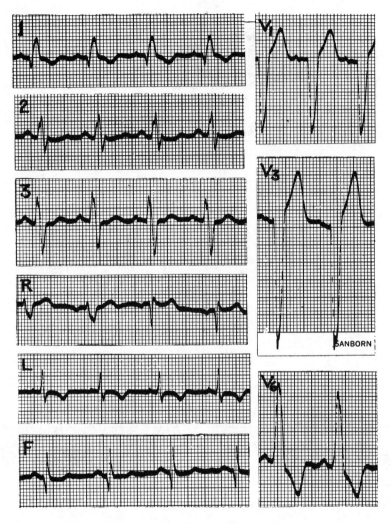

Review Tracing 26.4

For interpretation, see page 484

Some Electrocardiographic Milestones

1858 Kolliker and Muller in Germany demonstrated that contraction of heart muscle was accompanied by electrical activity.

1887 Waller in England recorded the first electrocardiogram in man using a capillary electrometer.

1903 Einthoven in Holland introduced the string galvanometer electrocardiograph and employed the classical standard limb leads in human electrocardiography.

1914 Lewis in England introduced a two-string electrocardiograph. Our knowledge of the sequence of myocardial activation is based on his studies with this machine. Lewis also introduced the concept of the "intrinsic deflection."

1927 Craib introduced the doublet (dipole) concept.

1932 Wolferth and Wood in America demonstrated the value of precordial leads.

1934 Wilson in America introduced the central terminal and with it the unipolar or V leads.

1935 Wilson in America demonstrated the superiority of multiple precordial leads over one such lead.

1938 Schellong in Germany and Wilson and Johnston in America described techniques for recording the frontal plane electrocardiogram as a vector figure using the cathode-ray oscillograph.

1969 Scherlag in America developed the technique for His-bundle electrography.

27

Coronary Insufficiency and Related Matters

Coronary insufficiency may be suspected when ST segments are significantly depressed below the baseline formed by the T-P segment (figs. 27.1 and 27.2). But a number of other conditions cause ST-T changes which may readily be confused with those of coronary disease. These will be dealt with later in this chapter.

An ST-T pattern particularly suggestive of coronary insufficiency is a horizontal ST segment (also known as "plane" depression[33]) making a sharp angle with the proximal shoulder of the still upright T wave (figs. 27.1 and 27.2). Normally the ST segment and T wave should merge smoothly and imperceptibly.

At times the most striking or only evidence of coronary insufficiency is inverted U waves (fig. 27.3). At other times pathologically tall precordial T waves are the sole manifestation of myocardial ischemia (fig. 27.4).

Another sometimes helpful sign of coronary insufficiency is a post-extrasystolic T-wave change.[64, 73] The T wave of the sinus beat following the premature beat changes form and often polarity; sometimes this is accompanied by abnormal lengthening of the Q-T interval (fig. 27.5). Levine called this the

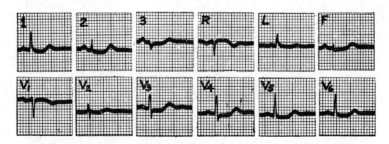

Figure 27.1. Coronary insufficiency. Note horizontally depressed ST segments in many leads.

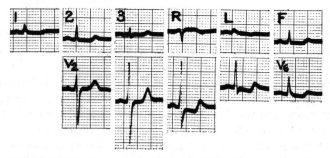

Figure 27.2. Coronary insufficiency. ST depression in many leads with sharp-angled ST-T junctions.

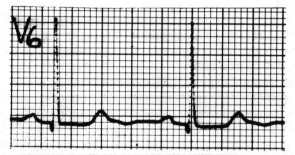

Figure 27.3. Coronary insufficiency—three subtle signs: horizontality of ST segments, sharp-angled ST-T junctions, U-wave inversion.

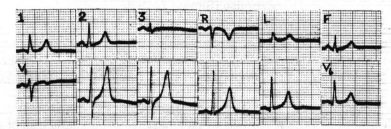

Figure 27.4. Coronary insufficiency. Abnormally tall precordial T waves are the only electrocardiographic sign of myocardial ischemia in this patient with typical angina.

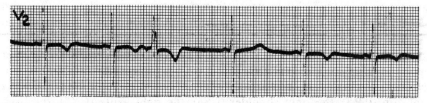

Figure 27.5. Post-extrasystolic T-wave change. After two sinus beats comes a supraventricular premature beat with ventricular aberration. The sinus beat *following* the extrasystole shows a complete change in polarity of the T wave with prolongation of the Q-T interval.

"poor man's exercise test" since the change is included in the initial tracing and so obviates the need and expense of a subsequent exercise test. Useful as this change may be in drawing attention to the possibility of myocardial disease, there is little doubt that it is also often seen in normal hearts.[32, 35, 61] Engel found postextrasystolic T-wave changes in 13 of 19 (68%) subjects with normal hearts compared with 29 of 36 (81%) of patients with proven coronary disease.[32]

Another minor sign which may direct attention to the presence of coronary disease is the TV_1-taller-than-TV_6 pattern. In most normal hearts the T wave in V_6 is taller than the T wave in V_1, which indeed is often inverted. If TV_1 is not only upright but taller than TV_6, it suggests an abnormality of the left ventricular myocardium and is seen in left ventricular overloading as well as coronary disease.[89]

In some patients with coronary insufficiency, diagnostic ST-T changes develop only during an attack of anginal pain (fig. 27.6). Conversely, since ECG abnormalities develop in 97% of patients with unstable angina,[98] absence of ST segment shifts during pain virtually rules out the diagnosis of unstable angina. In the "variant" form of angina,[101] ST *elevation* develops.

Finally, the presence of coronary disease is *not excluded* by a normal tracing.[84] Of 37 patients having multivessel disease and markedly positive exercise tests (3 mm or more ST depression), 30 (81%) had normal resting ECGs.[140] Figure 27.7 is the tracing from a 42-year-old man who had a proved myocardial infarction two years previously and who has suffered from angina of effort since then. The ECG is within normal limits.

Exercise (Stress) Testing

Sometimes the presence of coronary disease can be demonstrated only when the ventricular myocardium is stressed and its oxygen requirement thus increased. The most commonly applied stress is exercise, and the most commonly used form of exercise is the treadmill[4, 83, 107]; the original Master's two-step test, bicycle ergometry and other tests are less frequently employed. Since the previous edition of this book, a veritable spate of articles on stress testing has flooded the cardiological journals as more and more criteria and more and more lead systems have been introduced in an effort to enhance its diagnostic accuracy. In consequence, this chapter has been greatly expanded; but, despite the multiplicity of methods, expansion of criteria and deluge of words, results continue to be plagued by an unsatisfactory proportion of false-positives and false-negatives. For details, beyond the scope of this text, you are referred to excellent reviews.[2, 31, 54, 87, 145]

Recording techniques during exercise have varied considerably. While most bipolar leads place the exploring (positive) electrode at C5, the indifferent (negative) electrode has been variously placed on the manubrium (CM5), the right arm (CR5), the right shoulder (CS5), the right axilla (CX5), the back (CB5), or even the head (CH5). Other systems employ multiple leads and, although approximately 90% of abnormal responses are detected by a C5 lead,

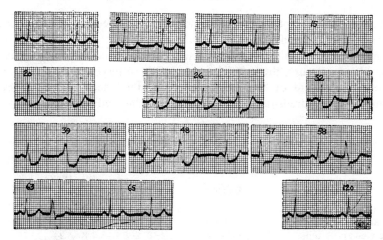

Figure 27.6. Coronary insufficiency. Lead 2 taken during an attack of chest pain which lasted less than a minute. Top left corner strip taken shortly before pain began spontaneously; figures on subsequent strips represent number of seconds after onset of pain. Notice marked progressive ST-T depression and appearance of frequent ectopic ventricular beats. At the end of 2 min, pattern has returned to normal.

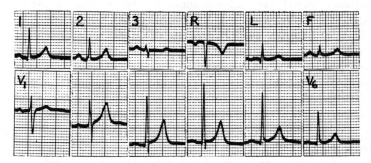

Figure 27.7. Normal tracing in a patient with previous myocardial infarction and subsequent angina of effort.

the more leads used the greater the potential for a positive yield. Therefore more and more investigators are employing multiple leads.

Normal Responses to Exercise

Before attempting to recognize the abnormal, one must be thoroughly familiar with the normal responses to exercise. In the ECG, these include increased P-wave amplitude, shortened P-R interval, decreased R wave amplitude, a rightward axis shift, depression of the early part of the ST segment so that it becomes upsloping to a T wave diminished in amplitude; in some leads the T wave may become taller while it inverts in others. Extrasystoles frequently develop at the height of an exercise test; they may be considered an integral part of an abnormal response, but in themselves are not necessarily an indication of heart disease[59]—see below.

Normal hemodynamic responses include tachycardia and an increase in systolic blood pressure; the normal ranges of these responses to submaximal exercise (achievement of 85% of predicted maximal heart rate for age), as encountered in hundreds of healthy men,[141] are tabulated in table 27.1.

Table 27.1
Normal Responses to Exercise in Healthy Men[141]

	Baseline	Submaximal Response	Recovery at	
			2 Min	5 Min
Heart rate	52–82	158–190	102–138	88–116
Systolic blood pressure	110–140	160–208	140–194	120–158
Diastolic blood pressure	70–90	60–90	60–90	60–86

ST Segment Criteria

The "graded" exercise test aims at standardizing the load on the coronary circulation (which, after all, is what is being tested) rather than that on the skeletal muscles; and uses as its end point 85% of the age-predicted maximal heart rate.[114] Regardless of the form of exercise/stress test, the electrocardiographic endpoint for a positive result is the same. The time-honored criterion for a positive test is a 1- to 2-mm **depression of the ST segment** 0.08 sec beyond the J point (figs. 27.8 and 27.9). Horizontal or downsloping depression of ST segments have been considered most significant and upsloping segments relatively benign; but more recent investigation suggests that significant depression associated with upsloping ST segments is hardly less abnormal.[126] An upsloping ST that still remains 1 mm or more below the baseline 0.08 sec after the J point[103]; or a depression of the J point of more than 2 mm with upsloping ST still 2 mm below the isoelectric line 0.08 sec later[55] are cited as positive criteria.

Not only are the depth and shape of the ST depression important, the rate at which the abnormal changes develop is a reliable index of the presence and severity of the coronary disease.[85] Nearly 90% of patients with left main coronary artery disease have a markedly positive test with 2 mm or more depression of the ST segment, a positive ST response as early as stage I, need to terminate the test during the first few minutes, or exertional hypotension.[152]

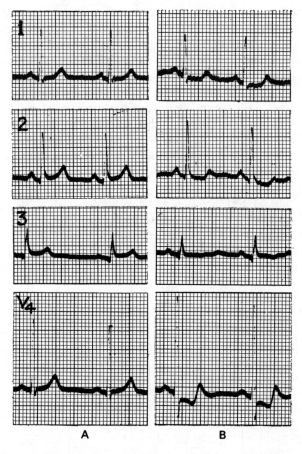

Figure 27.8. Positive exercise test. (*A*) Control tracing before exercise: within normal limits. (*B*) Two minutes after exercise: striking downsloping ST depression and increased height of R wave in V$_4$ with lesser ST-T changes in 1 and 2.

A sequential pattern of ST depression is said to exclude false-positive results and to be predictive of the severer grades of coronary disease[17]; this "evolutionary" pattern ideally consists of the following sequence: J-point depression with upsloping ST→horizontal ST→downsloping ST→inversion of first part of T wave→complete T-wave inversion→gradual return to baseline.

Instead of the classical depression of the ST segment, exercise may produce **ST elevation**[19] (fig. 27.10*A*). This was found in 47 of 720 patients (6.5%)[137] and in another series, in 29 of 840 subjects (3.5%)[10]; of the 21 who had coronary arteriography, 19 had 75% or greater narrowing of the left anterior descending artery and 18 manifested left ventricular dyskinesia. ST elevation is undoubtedly correlated with the more severe grades of myocardial ischemia[142] and is most often seen in patients with previous myocardial infarction. In such patients, the immediate cause of this response to exercise appears to be "depressed left ventricular function"[124] or "abnormal wall motion."[123] In those who have neither previous infarction nor ventricular aneurysm, including those with variant angina, ST elevation is probably the result of coronary spasm.[120, 121, 137]

Exercise-induced ST elevation is an accurate localizer of the underlying myocardial mischief and implies critical stenosis of the artery supplying subjacent myocardium. ST elevation in anterior chest leads or aVL often indicates proximal left anterior descending obstruction.[28, 70] When the sole abnormal finding in patients with previous infarction is ST elevation, it suggests the

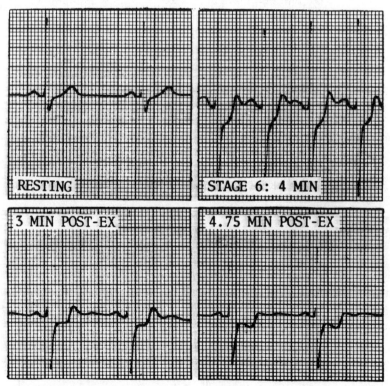

Figure 27.9.   Positive treadmill test showing in succession upsloping, horizontal and downsloping ST segments.

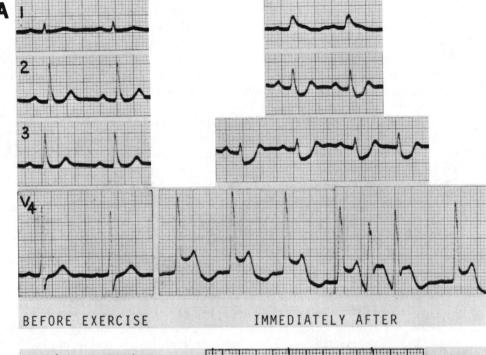

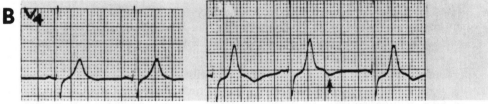

Figure 27.10. (*A*) Positive exercise test showing ST elevation immediately after exercise in leads 1 and V$_4$ with reciprocal depression in leads 2 and 3. Note the pair of ectopic beats in lead V$_4$. (*B*) There is slight upsloping ST depression and minor inversion of U waves in the control tracing before exercise; after exercise there is further depression of the J-point, but the most striking change is the deep inversion of the U wave (*arrow*).

involvement of only one vessel; but if concomitant ST depression is found in other leads it is said to suggest that other vessels are also involved.[22]

In patients with ventricular aneurysm, the ST elevation accurately indicates its site.[123] The location of coronary artery spasm is often accurately reflected: ST elevation in V$_2$ and V$_3$ indicates spasm of the left anterior descending artery, whereas elevation in lead 3 or aVF suggests spasm in either the right coronary or the circumflex artery. Elevation in V$_1$ signals spasm of the left anterior descending or the right coronary artery.[71] When ST depression during exercise is followed by anginal pain and ST elevation in the recovery period, it may predict imminent myocardial infarction in the indicated territory.[58]

Additional Criteria

Since dependence on ST-T changes alone produces a crop of false-positive and false-negative tests, considerable attention has been focussed on other variables. Many investigators have advocated that multiple criteria be simultaneously employed—the so-called "multivariate" approach—to enhance the diagnostic reliability of treadmill testing. The many parameters that have been variously invoked are listed in table 27.2.

Changes in **QRS amplitude** may be diagnostically helpful. Since in the normal person the RS amplitude responds to exercise by shrinking,[15, 133, 141] some observers have said that if it decreases you can rule out coronary disease.[143] In the presence of ischemic disease, the amplitude of the R wave often increases with exercise and, if this signal is read in conjunction with ST-T responses, the sensitivity of the exercise stress test is claimed by some to be significantly enhanced[12, 15, 132]; and, especially in women, analysis of R-wave changes is said to be a useful adjunct to ST criteria.[150] Changes in QRS amplitude may be especially helpful in situations where the repolarization moiety has been rendered less useful by preexisting abnormality as, for instance, the presence of digitalis effect[12] or bundle-branch block.[132]

According to Berman,[12] one of the most sensitive indices of coronary disease is an increase in R-wave amplitude in multiple leads taken in conjunction with ST shifts of 1 mm or more. He recommends continuous monitoring with a single lead supplemented by 12-lead tracings every three minutes during exercise and at 1, 3, 5 and 8 min during recovery. Using this method, a positive test requires 1 mm or more ST shift—down or up—at 0.08 sec after the J point *plus* an increase in the sum of QRS amplitudes (R in aVL, aVF, V_3, V_4, V_5, and V_6 + S in V_1 and V_2).

The small **septal q wave** normally increases with exercise and thus may help to identify false-positive ST changes[92]; failure to increase indicates abnormal septal activation because of ischemia. The development of anterior hemiblock along with QS complexes in V_1 to V_3 has been reported as a sign of exercise-induced septal ischemia.[147]

The helpfulness of QRS changes is disputed by others[8, 38, 133]; indeed some assert that most patients with severe coronary disease safely exercise to high levels and enjoy a reduction in their R-wave amplitude and others regard the R wave changes as so unpredictable as to be useless in the diagnosis of coronary heart disease.[148]

T-wave changes alone are not enough to make the diagnosis of coronary heart disease. For a long time it was thought that exercise differentiated between normal and abnormal T-wave inversion—that it left the abnormal T inverted or exaggerated the abnormality, but "normalized" the normally inverted T

Table 27.2
Multivariate Approach in Diagnosis

Observed Items	Foreboding Responses
ST depression	>2 mm
	Downsloping > horizontal > upsloping
	Early onset (stage I)
	Persistence of change
	Presence in 5 or more leads
ST elevation	Development of
RS amplitude	Increase[12, 15, 46, 132]
Septal q	Failure to increase[92]
U wave	Inversion[42]
VPBs	Repetitive
Peak heart rate	<120/min[87]
Peak blood pressure	<130 mm Hg
Time tolerated	<6 min
Angina	Development of
Standing or hyperventilation	Inappropriate increase in heart rate response[47]

wave. But recent studies demonstrated that, although normally inverted T waves are twice as likely to be "normalized" by exercise, no less than 27% of inverted ischemic T waves are also normalized.[3] This effect is not altogether surprising since spontaneous bouts of clinical ischemia are also at times associated with an "improved" T-wave pattern.[95]

In some patients, abnormal **U-wave inversion** (fig. 27.10B) may be the most diagnostic feature; it suggests significant ischemic disease and especially signals a lesion in the proximal left anterior descending.[42]

It used to be thought that when exercise precipitated **ventricular extrasystoles** it was a sign of coronary artery disease; but it is now known that exercise often produces VPBs in the fit and healthy. In a group of 345 regularly exercising normal men and women, VPBs were provoked by exercise in 35% of the men and in 14% of the women.[29] The tendency to ectopy increased with increasing heart rate and its incidence was similar to that in a cohort of patients who had had myocardial infarctions. Another study suggests that if the axis of the extrasystolic QRS is superiorly directed (left axis deviation or "no man's land"), it may be a specific index of coronary artery disease.[75]

Further efforts to improve the accuracy of treadmill testing for ischemic disease have included the following suggestions: precordial surface mapping with 16 leads[37]; maximal (as opposed to submaximal) testing combined with consideration of clinical symptoms and hemodynamic changes, plus a knowledge of reasons for falsely positive or negative tests[145]; a treadmill exercise score (TES) combining the following numerous parameters: Depth of J-point depression, horizontal or downsloping ST segment, promptness of onset of ST depression, development of ST depression at low heart rates, persistence of ST depression after exercise stops, and inadequate heart-rate response.[52]

Misleading Responses

Many factors besides coronary artery disease influence the interpretation of the electrocardiographic response to exercise. These include heart disease (other than ischemic), preexisting abnormality in the resting ECG, the number and location of the leads available for scrutiny, electrolyte disturbances and drug therapy.[18, 31, 36, 118]

The effect of digitalis is disputed: Some investigators claim that the influence of digitalis promotes falsely positive tests[67, 131] whereas earlier studies[6, 113] led to the conclusion that the administration of digitalis would not. A more recent study[119] determined that indeed digoxin caused a positive test in 25% of healthy men, especially over the age of 60 years; and that the ST-T changes so produced were indistinguishable from the genuine earmarks of ischemic disease. On the other hand, the positive test provoked by digitalis may serve to unmask latent coronary disease.[119] The effect of digoxin on the response to exercise is attenuated by propranolol.[67]

Among the numerous causes of falsely positive tests are the Wolff-Parkinson-White syndrome,[125] hyperventilation,[53, 60] and the prolapsing mitral valve.[39] Women are notorious for producing false-positive tests in as many as half to two-thirds of those tested.[30] ST-T changes in the presence of LBBB are not reliable indices of coronary disease[96] and, in patients with RBBB, ST depression confined to leads V_{1-3} may represent falsely positive tests whereas changes in leftward leads (V_{4-6}) may be more diagnostic.[128]

One must be cautious in interpreting the post-exercise tracing of hypertensive patients receiving thiazides. These drugs may reduce the patient's potassium stores without altering the ECG; in such a situation, exercise may bring to light the latent pattern of hypokalemia[41] whose ST depression may be mistaken for myocardial ischemia. ST-T changes may result solely from the upright posture and these must not be mistaken for displacement indicating ischemia.[56]

Although post-exercise changes are helpfully diagnostic of ischemic disease in the clinical suspect, they are not specific, since patterns indistinguishable from those typical of ischemia develop after exercise in other forms of heart disease.[51] It is therefore better to say that the typical changes indicate myocardial *disease*, often but not necessarily ischemic. Thus the term "false-positive" may at times be a misnomer: It is the myocardium that produces the tracing and therefore the test result; and the fact of angiographically clean coronary vessels does not exonerate the heart muscle[30]—which may be the seat of noncoronary disease, such as cardiomyopathy or rheumatic disease, giving it abundant right to protest appropriately, not falsely, to unwanted stress.

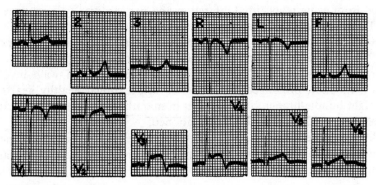

Figure 27.11. From a normal Negro man of 24 years. Note marked ST elevation and T-wave inversion in V_3 and V_4.

On the other side of the coin, falsely negative tests may be found in the presence of severe coronary artery disease: In one study, 15 of 26 critical stenoses of the left coronary artery were associated with negative stress tests.[130] Although a negative test can therefore not be relied upon to exclude significant coronary disease, according to some investigators it virtually excludes the existence of significant left main disease.[94]

The exercise test has its uses but must be regarded as a test of limited value because (a) a negative test fails to rule out significant disease and (b) a positive test, in the presence of atypical chest pain, is difficult to interpret since falsely positive tests are rife.[25]

Electrocardiographogenic Disease

Abnormalities in the ECG do not necessarily indicate cardiac disease, much less coronary disease.[65, 76, 82] When deviations from the normal, especially those affecting the ST segments and T waves, are encountered in the middle-aged and elderly, they are much too glibly interpreted as "coronary insufficiency." Statistically such inferences are no doubt often right, but the habit is bad practice and is scientifically unsound; too many people are limping their ways through life maimed by the unkind cuts of electrocardiographic interpretation.[99] Remember the following facts before attaching the "cardiac" or "coronary" label:

1. The range of normal is wide and its limits cannot be satisfactorily defined.[116] Changes well outside the accepted range are undoubtedly at times normal variants. Examples of this are the persistent "juvenile" precordial pattern particularly seen in healthy young Negroes[48, 68, 102] (fig. 27.11), unusual S-T elevation (fig. 27.12), also especially common in Negroes (fig. 27.11)[129] and often referred to as "early repolarization"—a misnomer![151] It must be differentiated from acute myocardial infarction and pericarditis,[122, 149] see page 463. The ST elevation of "early repolarization" may be restored to the baseline with exercise or isoproterenol.[1, 91, 144] Apparent ST depression due to carryover of T_P wave[136] may suggest myocardial ischemia. Other potential mimics include: ST-T depression in "suspended" hearts[34] (fig. 27.13), precordial T-wave inversion during pregnancy, prolonged P-R intervals in occasional healthy hearts[74, 110] and a right bundle-branch block pattern in marathon runners,[9] whose cardiovascular competence can hardly be questioned.

Striking T-wave inversion, ominously reminiscent of myocardial ischemia, and sometimes leading to unnecessary hospitalization, is found in well-trained, top-ranking athletes, such as professional bicyclists and marathon

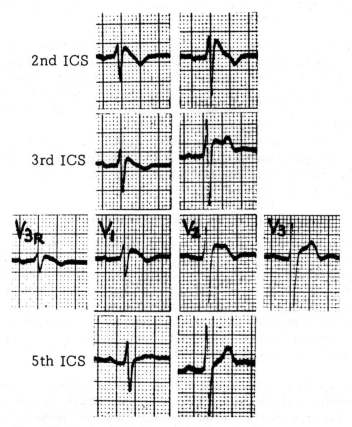

Figure 27.12. Saddle-shaped, step-like and plateau elevations of precordial ST segments from a healthy dentist of 32 years. Notice the variation from interspace to interspace; thus misplacement of the electrode from day to day may trap the unwary into thinking that "evolution" is occurring.

runners.[49, 50, 93, 144] ST and T-wave changes, simulating those of ischemic heart disease, have been reported in normal men with normal coronary arteriograms[127]; and about one third of normal men show 1 mm ST depression and/or labile T-wave inversion of up to 3 mm during ambulatory monitoring.[146] In normal youths, suspicious T-wave changes may be the result of increased sympatho-adrenal activity.[5]

2. Numerous extracardiac factors can produce patterns similar to those seen in myocardial disease. Without necessarily impairing cardiac competence, many factors can cause changes in the repolarization processes of the ventricles which are reflected in the ECG in T-wave or ST-segment alterations. The T wave and to a lesser extent the ST segment are unstable members that are easily upset by a great variety of major and minor provocations. Among the many stimuli that can affect them are eating,[105, 112, 136] drinking ice water,[26] posture,[110] hyperventilation[135]; emotional disturbances such as the startle reaction, fear or anxiety[72, 90] and neurocirculatory asthenia[115]; numerous drugs, including digitalis, quinidine, procainamide, adrenaline, isuprel, insulin; extracardiac diseases such as electrolyte imbalances, the acute abdomen, shock, hiatal hernia, gallbladder disease, cerebrovascular accidents,[16] psychosis and endocrine and metabolic disturbances.

3. Cardiovascular disease other than coronary may counterfeit the changes of ischemic heart disease. Such mimics include myocarditis,[97] cardiomyopathy, hypertension and other diseases producing ventricular hypertrophy.

4. Finally the heart may be the victim of a disease that is not primarily cardiac, let alone coronary. Pulmonary embolism, anemia, hypothyroidism, myocarditis[23] from infections (e.g., pneumonia, infectious mononucleosis), sarcoidosis, hemochromatosis, primary amyloidosis, beriberi, scleroderma, disseminated lupus, Friedreich's ataxia, progressive muscular dystrophy and myasthenia gravis all may produce changes in the tracing indicative of myocardial

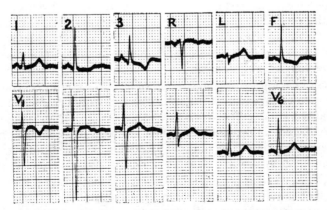

Figure 27.13. Abnormal ST-T pattern in leads 2, 3 and aVF in a young woman with a "suspended" heart but no cardiac disease.

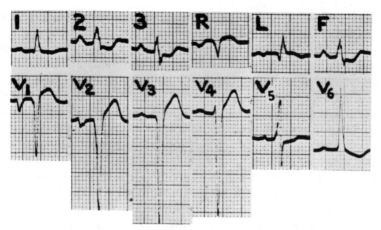

Figure 27.14. **Left ventricular hypertrophy** and **incomplete LBBB**. From a patient with severe aortic stenosis and no sign of anterior infarction at autopsy.

Table 27.3
Mimics of Anteroseptal Infarction

1. Left ventricular hypertrophy
2. Incomplete left bundle-branch block
3. Hemiblock, anterior or posterior
4. Myocardial replacement (neoplasm, sarcoid, etc.)
5. Cardiomyopathy
6. Wolff-Parkinson-White syndrome

involvement and quite indistinguishable from some of the alterations resulting from coronary disease.

Numerous conditions can produce Q waves that may be mistaken for those of myocardial infarction; most of these are listed in table 27.3. Among the more common Q-wave producers is ventricular hypertrophy: Left ventricular hypertrophy, with or without the coexistence of incomplete LBBB, can produce QS complexes in V_{1-2} and even in V_3 (fig. 27.14), often erroneously mistaken for evidence of anteroseptal infarction—probably the single most common mistake made in everyday ECG interpretation.

In a carefully autopsied Japanese series of 63 patients with QS complexes in one or more anterior precordial leads, correlation with anteroseptal infarction was as indicated in table 27.4.

Hypertrophic cardiomyopathy can often be suspected from the presence of gross Q waves that simply do not look like the Q waves of infarction; and a further helpful detail in this connection is the fact that the T waves are discordant,[45] i.e., whereas in myocardial infarction the T wave is inverted in the leads that show significant Q waves, the T waves in hypertrophic cardiomyopathy are upright in the leads that sport Q waves (see figs. 29.9 and 30.23). Transient Q waves may develop with the coronary spasm of variant angina and even in occasional cases of acute pericarditis,[88] hypoglycemia, hyperkalemia, shock, acute pancreatitis and phosphorus poisoning.

Therefore in assessing the tracing that does not conform with our accepted standards we should remember the whole array of common and uncommon possibilities and we should ask ourselves three questions: (1) Could this be a normal variant? (2) Could these abnormalities be due to extracardiac factors, physiological or pathological? and (3) Could these changes be due to heart disease other than coronary?

The danger of attributing changes of the first and second category to heart disease is that the patient is branded as a cardiac. The danger of labelling the third group as "coronary" is that the physician in charge of the case may be thereby blinded to the true nature of the cardiac involvement and of the underlying primary disease. We should often be content to state that the pattern is abnormal but nonspecific. We should also certainly be at pains to spread the gospel that AN "ABNORMAL" TRACING DOES NOT NECESSARILY MEAN AN ABNORMAL HEART.

In many ways this is the most important section of this book. For if the lesson that it attempts to teach is well learned, it may save many from cardiac invalidism. The whole subject of "coronary mimicry" in the ECG was reviewed elsewhere[76] with detailed discussion and a full bibliography and has also formed the subject of an excellent monograph.[45]

Table 27.4
Correlation of QS Complexes with Anteroseptal Infarction

Leads Showing QS Complexes	No.	Anteroseptal Infarction	
		No.	Percent
V₁, V₂, V₃, V₄	3	3	100
V₁, V₂, V₃	9	6	66
V₁, V₂	15	3	20
V₂	8	1	12
V₁	25	1	4
V₂, V₃	2	0	0
V₃	1	0	0

REFERENCES

1. Alimurung, B.: The influence of early repolarization variant on the exercise electrocardiogram; a correlation with coronary arteriograms. Am. Heart J. 1980: **99**, 739.
2. Amsterdam, E. A., et al.: Toward improved interpretation of the exercise test. Cardiology 1980: **66**, 236.
3. Aravindakshan, V., et al.: Electrocardiographic exercise test in patients with abnormal T waves at rest. Am. Heart J. 1977: **93**, 706.
4. Aronow, W. S.: Thirty-month follow-up of maximal treadmill stress test and double Master's test in normal subjects. Circulation 1973: **47**, 287.
5. Atterhog, J.-H., et al.: Sympathoadrenal and cardiovascular responses to mental stress, isometric handgrip and cold pressor test in asymptomatic young men with primary T wave abnormalities in the electrocardiogram. Br. Heart J. 1981: **46**, 311.

6. Bartel, A. G., et al.: Graded exercise stress tests in angiographically documented coronary artery disease. Circulation 1974: **49**, 348.
7. Baron, D. W., et al.: R wave amplitude during exercise. Relation to left ventricular function and coronary artery disease. Br. Heart J. 1980: **44**, 512.
8. Battler, A., et al.: Relationship of QRS amplitude changes during exercise to left ventricular function, volumes, and the diagnosis of coronary artery disease. Circulation 1979: **60**, 1004.
9. Beckner, G. L., and Winsor, T.: Cardiovascular adaptations to prolonged physical effort. Circulation 1954: **9**, 835.
10. Belic, N., and Gardin, J. M.: ECG manifestations of myocardial ischemia. Arch. Intern. Med. 1980: **140**, 1162.
11. Bellet, S., et al.: Radioelectrocardiography during exercise in patients with angina pectoris. Comparison with the postexercise electrocardiogram. Circulation 1962: **25**, 5.
12. Berman, J. L., et al.: Multiple-lead QRS changes with exercise testing: diagnostic value and hemodynamic implications. Circulation 1980: **61**, 53.
13. Blackburn, H., and Katigbak, R.: What electrocardiographic leads to take after exercise? Am. Heart J. 1964: **67**, 184.
14. Blackburn, H., et al.: The exercise ECG test. At what intervals to record after exercise. Am. Heart J. 1964: **67**, 186.
15. Bonoris, P. E., et al. Evaluation of R wave amplitude changes versus ST-segment depression in stress testing. Circulation 1978: **57**, 904.
16. Burch, G. E., et al.: A new electrocardiographic pattern observed in cerebrovascular accidents. Circulation 1954: **9**, 719.
17. Chahine, R. A., et al.: The evolutionary pattern of exercise-induced ST segment depression. J. Electrocardiol. 1979: **12**, 235.
18. Chaitman, B. R., et al.: Improved efficiency of treadmill exercise testing using a multiple lead electrocardiographic system and basic hemodynamic exercise response. Circulation 1978: **57**, 71.
19. Chaitman, B. R., et al.: S-T segment elevation and coronary spasm in response to exercise. Am. J. Cardiol. 1981: **47**, 1350.
20. Chun, P. K. C., et al.: ST-segment elevation with elective DC cardioversion. Circulation 1981: **63**, 220.
21. Coulshed, N.: The anoxia test for myocardial ischaemia. Br. Heart J. 1960: **22**, 79.
22. deFeyter, P. J., et al.: Clinical significance of exercise induced ST segment elevation. Correlative angiographic study in patients with ischaemic heart disease. Br. Heart J. 1981: **46**, 84.
23. de la Chapelle, C. E., and Kossmann, C. E.: Myocarditis. Circulation 1954: **10**, 747.
24. Demoulin, J. C., et al.: Prognostic significance of electrocardiographic findings in angina at rest. Therapeutic implications. Br. Heart J. 1981: **46**, 320.
25. Detry, J.-M. R., et al.: Diagnostic value of history and maximum exercise electrocardiography in men and women suspected of coronary heart disease. Circulation 1977: **56**, 756.
26. Dowling, C. V., and Hellerstein, H. K.: Factors influencing the T wave of the electrocardiogram. II. Effects of drinking ice water. Am. Heart J. 1951: **41**, 58.
27. Dunn, R. F., et al.: Exercise-induced ST-segment elevation; correlation of thalium-201 myocardial perfusion scanning and coronary arteriography. Circulation 1980: **61**, 989.
28. Dunn, R. F., et al.: Exercise-induced ST-segment elevation in leads V_1 or aVL; a predictor of anterior myocardial ischemia and left anterior descending coronary artery disease. Circulation 1981: **63**, 1357.
29. Ekblom, B., et al.: Occurrence and reproducibility of exercise-induced ventricular ectopy in normal subjects. Am. J. Cardiol. 1979: **43**, 35.
30. Ellestad, M. H., et al.: The false positive stress test. Am. J. Cardiol. 1977: **40**, 681.
31. Ellestad, M. H., et al.: Stress testing; clinical application and predictive capacity. Prog. Cardiovasc. Dis. 1979: **21**, 431.
32. Engel, T. R.: Postextrasystolic T wave changes and angiographic coronary disease. Br. Heart J. 1977: **39**, 371.
33. Evans, W., and McRae, C.: The lesser electrocardiographic signs of cardiac pain. Br. Heart J. 1952: **14**, 429.
34. Evans, W., and Lloyd-Thomas, H. G.: The syndrome of the suspended heart. Br. Heart J. 1957: **19**, 153.
35. Fagin, I. D., and Guidot, J. M.: Post-extrasystolic T wave changes. Am. J. Cardiol. 1958: **1**, 597.

36. Fortuin, N. J., and Weiss, J. L.: Exercise stress testing. Circulation 1977: **56**, 699.
37. Fox, K., et al.: Precordial electrocardiographic mapping after exercise in the diagnosis of coronary artery disease. Am. J. Cardiol. 1979: **43**, 541.
38. Froelicher, V. F., et al.: Variations in normal electrocardiographic response to treadmill testing. Am. J. Cardiol. 1981: **47**, 1161.
39. Gardin, J. M., et al.: Pseudoischemic "false positive" S-T segment changes induced by hyperventilation in patients with mitral valve prolapse. Am. J. Cardiol. 1980: **45**, 952.
40. Gazes, P. C., et al.: The diagnosis of angina pectoris. Am. Heart J. 1964: **67**, 830.
41. Georgopoulos, A. J., et al.: Effect of exercise on electrocardiogram of patients with low serum potassium. Circulation 1961: **23**, 567.
42. Gerson, M. C., et al.: Exercise-induced U-wave inversion as a marker of stenosis of the left anterior descending coronary artery. Circulation 1979: **60**, 1014.
43. Gerson, M. C., et al.: Relation of exercise-induced physiologic S-T segment depression to R wave amplitude in normal subjects. Am. J. Cardiol. 1980: **46**, 778.
44. Goldberger, A. L.: Q wave T wave vector discordance in hypertrophic cardiomyopathy: Septal hypertrophy and strain pattern. Br. Heart J. 1979: **42**, 201.
45. Goldberger, A. L.: *Myocardial Infarction: Electrocardiographic Differential Diagnosis*, Ed. 2. C. V. Mosby, St. Louis, 1979.
46. Greenberg, P. S., et al.: Predictive accuracy of Q-X/Q-T ratio, Q-Tc interval, S-T depression, and R wave amplitude during stress testing. Am. J. Cardiol. 1979: **44**, 18.
47. Greenberg, P. S., et al.: Use of heart rate responses to standing and hyperventilation at rest to detect coronary artery disease: correlation with the S-T response to exercise. J. Electrocardiol. 1980: **13**, 373.
48. Grusin, H.: Peculiarities of the African's electrocardiogram and the changes observed in serial studies. Circulation 1954: **9**, 860.
49. Hall, R. J., and Gibson, R. V.: Anterior T wave changes in the ECG of an athlete. Br. Med. J. 1978: **2**, 738.
50. Hanne-Paparo, N., et al.: T-wave abnormalities in the electrocardiograms of top-ranking athletes without demonstrable organic heart disease. Am. Heart J. 1971: **81**, 743.
51. Hellerstein, H. K., et al.: Two step exercise test as a test of cardiac function in chronic rheumatic heart disease and in arteriosclerotic heart disease with old myocardial infarction. Am. J. Cardiol. 1961: **7**, 234.
52. Hollenberg, M., et al.: Treadmill score quantifies electrocardiographic response to exercise and improves test accuracy and reproducibility. Circulation 1980: **61**, 276.
53. Kemp, G. L., and Ellestad, M. H.: The significance of hyperventilation and orthostatic T wave changes on the electrocardiogram. Arch. Intern. Med. 1968: **121**, 518.
54. Koppes, G., et al.: Treadmill exercise testing. Curr. Probl. Cardiol. 1977: **7**, Nos. 8 and 9.
55. Kurita, A., et al.: Significance of exercise-induced junctional S-T depression in evaluation of coronary artery disease. Am. J. Cardiol. 1977: **40**, 492.
56. Lachman, A. B., et al.: Postural ST-T wave changes in the radioelectrocardiogram simulating myocardial ischemia. Circulation 1965: **31**, 557.
57. Lahiri, A., et al.: Exercise-induced S-T segment elevation in variant angina. Am. J. Cardiol. 1980: **45**, 887.
58. Lahiri, A., et al.: Exercise-induced ST segment elevation. Electrocardiographic, angiographic and scintigraphic evaluation. Br. Heart J. 1980: **43**, 582.
59. Lamb, L. E., and Hiss, R. G.: Influence of exercise on premature contractions. Am. J. Cardiol. 1962: **10**, 209.
60. Lary, D., and Goldschlager, N.: Electrocardiographic changes during hyperventilation resembling myocardial ischemia in patients with normal coronary arteriograms. Am. Heart J. 1974: **87**, 383.
61. Leachman, D. R., et al.: Evaluation of postextrasystolic T wave alterations in identification of patients with coronary artery disease or left ventricular dysfunction. Am. Heart J. 1981: **102**, 658.
62. Lepeschkin, E., and Surawicz, B.: Characteristics of true-positive and false-positive results of ECG Master two step exercise tests. N. Engl. J. Med. 1958: **258**, 511.
63. Lepeschkin, E.: Exercise tests in the diagnosis of coronary heart disease. Circulation 1960: **22**, 986.
64. Levine, H. D., et al.: The clinical significance of postextrasystolic T wave changes. Circulation 1952: **6**, 538.

65. Levine, H. D.: Non-specificity of the electrocardiogram associated with coronary artery disease. Am. J. Med. 1953: **15**, 344.
66. Levine, H. J.: Mimics of coronary heart disease. Postgrad. Med. 1978: **64**, 58.
67. LeWinter, M. M., et al.: The effect of oral propranolol, digoxin and combination therapy on the resting and exercise electrocardiogram. Am. Heart J. 1977: **93**, 202.
68. Littmann, D.: Persistence of the juvenile pattern in the precordial leads of healthy adult Negroes, with report of electrocardiographic survey on three hundred Negro and two hundred white subjects. Am. Heart J. 1946: **32**, 370.
69. Lloyd-Thomas, H. G.: The effect of exercise on the electrocardiogram in healthy subjects. Br. Heart J. 1961: **23**, 260.
70. Longhurst, J. C., and Kraus, W. L.: Exercise-induced ST elevation in patients with myocardial infarction. Circulation 1979: **60**, 616.
71. MacAlpin, R. N.: Correlation of the location of coronary arterial spasm with the lead distribution of ST segment elevation during variant angina. Am. Heart J. 1980: **99**, 555.
72. Magendantz, H., and Shortsleeve, J.: Electrocardiographic abnormalities in patients exhibiting anxiety. Am. Heart J. 1951: **42**, 849.
73. Mann, R. H., and Burchell, H. B.: The sign of T-wave inversion in sinus beats following ventricular extrasystoles. Am. Heart J. 1954: **47**, 504.
74. Manning, G. W.: Electrocardiography in the selection of Royal Canadian Air Force Aircrew. Circulation 1954: **10**, 401.
75. Mardelli, T. J., et al.: Superior QRS axis of ventricular premature complexes: An additional criterion to enhance the sensitivity of exercise stress testing. Am. J. Cardiol. 1980: **45**, 236.
76. Marriott, H. J. L.: Coronary mimicry: normal variants, and physiologic, pharmacologic and pathologic influences that simulate coronary patterns in the electrocardiogram. Ann. Int. Med. 1960: **52**, 411.
77. Marriott, H. J. L.: Electrocardiographogenic suicide and lesser crimes. J. Florida Med. Assoc. 1963: **50**, 440.
78. Marriott, H. J. L.: Normal electrocardiographic variants simulating ischemic heart disease. J.A.M.A. 1967: **199**, 103.
79. Marriott, H. J. L., and Nizet, P. M.: Physiologic stimuli simulating ischemic heart disease. J.A.M.A. 1967: **200**, 715.
80. Marriott, H. J. L., and Menendez, M. M.: Noncoronary disease simulating myocardial ischemia or infarction. J.A.M.A. 1967: **201**, 53.
81. Marriott, H. J. L.: Dangers in overinterpretation of the electrocardiogram. Heart Bull. 1967: **18**, 61.
82. Marriott, H. J. L., and Slonim, R.: False patterns of myocardial infarction. Heart Bull. 1967: **16**, 71.
83. Martin, C. M., and McConahay, D. R.: Maximal treadmill exercise electrocardiography. Circulation 1972: **46**, 956
84. Martinez-Rios, M. A., et al.: Normal electrocardiogram in the presence of severe coronary artery disease. Am. J. Cardiol. 1970: **25**, 320.
85. Mary, D. A. S. G., et al.: Use of submaximal ST segment/heart rate relation during maximal exercise testing to predict severity of coronary artery disease (abstr.). Br. Heart J. 1981: **45**, 342.
86. Master, A. M. and Rosenfeld, I.: Two-step exercise test: current status after twenty-five years. Mod. Concepts Cardiovasc. Dis. 1967: **36**, 19.
87. McNeer, J. F., et al.: The role of the exercise test in the evaluation of patients for ischemic heart disease. Circulation 1978: **57**, 64.
88. Meller, J., et al.: Transient Q waves in Prinzmetal's angina. Am. J. Cardiol. 1975: **35**, 691.
89. Meyer, P., and Herr, R.: L'intéret du syndrome électrocardiographique TV1 > TV6 pour le dépistage précoce de troubles de la repolarisation ventriculaire gauche. Arch. Mal. Coeur 1959: **52**, 753.
90. Mitchell, J. H., and Shapiro, A. P.: The relationship of adrenalin and T wave changes in the anxiety state. Am. Heart J. 1954: **48**, 323.
91. Morace, G.: Effect of isoproterenol on the "early repolarization" syndrome. Am. Heart J. 1979: **97**, 343.
92. Morales-Ballejo, H., et al.: Septal Q wave in exercise testing: Angiographic correlation. Am. J. Cardiol. 1981: **48**, 247.
93. Nishimura, T., et al.: Noninvasive assessment of T-wave abnormalities on precordial electrocardiograms in middle-aged professional bicyclists. J. Electrocardiol. 1981: **14**, 357.

94. Nixon, J. V., et al.: Exercise testing in men with significant left main coronary disease. Br. Heart J. 1979: **42**, 410.
95. Noble, J., et al.: Normalization of abnormal T waves in ischemia. Arch. Intern. Med. 1976: **136**, 391.
96. Orzan, F., et al.: Is the treadmill exercise test useful for evaluating coronary artery disease in patients with complete left bundle branch block? Am. J. Cardiol. 1978: **42**, 36.
97. Palank, E. A., et al.: Fatal acute bacterial myocarditis after dentoalveolar abscess. Am. J. Cardiol. 1979: **43**, 1238.
98. Papapietro, S. E., et al.: Transient electrocardiographic changes in patients with unstable angina: Relation to coronary arterial anatomy. Am. J. Cardiol. 1980: **46**, 28.
99. Prinzmetal, M., et al.: Clinical implications of errors in electrocardiographic interpretations: heart disease of electrocardiographic origin. J.A.M.A. 1956: **161**, 138.
100. Prinzmetal, M., et al.: A variant form of angina pectoris. Am. J. Med. 1959: **27**, 375.
101. Prinzmetal, M., et al.: Variant form of angina pectoris: previously undelineated syndrome. J.A.M.A. 1960: **174**, 1794.
102. Reiley, M. A., et al.: Racial and sexual differences in the standard electrocardiogram of black versus white adolescents. Chest 1979: **75**, 474.
103. Rijneki, R. D., et al.: Clinical significance of upsloping ST segments in exercise electrocardiography. Circulation 1980: **61**, 671.
104. Robb, G. P., and Marks, H. H.: Latent coronary artery disease. Determination of its presence and severity by the exercise electrocardiogram. Am. J. Cardiol. 1964: **13**, 603.
105. Rochlin, I., and Edwards, W. L. J.: The misinterpretation of electrocardiograms with postprandial T-wave inversion. Circulation 1954: **10**, 843.
106. Roesler, H.: An electrocardiographic study of high takeoff of R (R')-T segment in right precordial leads. Altered repolarization. Am. J. Cardiol. 1960: **6**, 920.
107. Roitman, D., et al.: Comparison of submaximal exercise test with coronary cineangiocardiogram. Ann. Intern. Med. 1970: **72**, 641.
108. Roman, L., and Bellet, S.: Significance of the QX/QT ratio and the QT ratio (QTr) in the exercise electrocardiogram. Circulation 1965: **32**, 435.
109. Scherf, D.: Development of the electrocardiographic exercise test. Standardized versus nonstandardized test. Am. J. Cardiol. 1960: **5**, 433.
110. Scherf, D., and Dix, J. H.: The effects of posture on A-V conduction. Am. Heart J. 1952: **43**, 494.
111. Scherf, D., and Schaffer, A. I.: The electrocardiographic exercise test. Am. Heart J. 1952: **43**, 927.
112. Sears, G. A., and Manning, G. W.: Routine electrocardiography: postprandial T-wave changes. Am. Heart J. 1958: **56**, 591.
113. Senat, I., et al.: Effects of digoxin on the S-T segment during treadmill exercise testing (abstr.). Circulation 1974: **50**, (suppl. III), 245.
114. Sheffield, L. T., et al.: Exercise graded by heart rate in electrocardiographic testing for angina pectoris. Circulation 1965: **32**, 622.
115. Silverman, J. J., and Goodman, R. D.: Extraordinary alteration of P-R interval in neurocirculatory asthenia. Am. Heart J. 1951: **41**, 155.
116. Simonson, E.: Editorial: Principles for determination of electrocardiographic normal standards. Am. Heart J. 1956: **52**, 163.
117. Simonson, E., and Keys, A.: The effect of an ordinary meal on the electrocardiogram. Normal standards in middle aged men and women. Circulation 1950: **1**, 1000.
118. Sketch, M. H., et al.: Reliability of single lead and multiple lead electrocardiography during and after exercise. Chest 1978: **74**, 394.
119. Sketch, M. H., et al.: Digoxin-induced positive exercise tests: Their clinical and prognostic significance. Am. J. Cardiol. 1981: **48**, 655.
120. Specchia, G., et al.: Coronary arterial spasm as a cause of exercise-induced ST-segment elevation in patients with variant angina. Circulation 1979: **59**, 948.
121. Specchia, G., et al.: Significance of exercise-induced ST-segment elevation in patients without myocardial infarction. Circulation 1981: **63**, 46.
122. Spodick, D. H.: Differential characteristics of the electrocardiogram in early repolarization and acute pericarditis. N. Engl. J. Med. 1976: **295**, 523.
123. Sriwattanakomen, S., et al.: S-T segment elevation during exercise: Electrocardiographic and arteriographic correlation in 38 patients. Am. J. Cardiol. 1980: **45**, 762.
124. Stiles, G. L., et al.: Clinical relevance of exercise-induced S-T segment elevation. Am. J. Cardiol. 1980: **46**, 931.

125. Strasberg, B., et al.: Treadmill exercise testing in the Wolff-Parkinson-White syndrome. Am. J. Cardiol. 1980: **45**, 742.

126. Stuart, R. J., and Ellestad, M. H.: Upsloping S-T segments in exercise stress testing. Am. J. Cardiol. 1976: **37**, 19.

127. Taggart, P., et al.: Electrocardiographic changes resembling myocardial ischaemia in asymptomatic men with normal coronary arteriograms. Br. Heart J. 1979: **41**, 214.

128. Tanaka, T., et al.: Diagnostic value of exercise-induced S-T depression in patients with right bundle branch block. Am. J. Cardiol. 1978: **41**, 670.

129. Thomas, J., et al.: Observations on the T wave and S-T segment changes in the precordial electrocardiogram of 320 young Negro adults. Am. J. Cardiol. 1960: **5**, 468.

130. Timmis, G. G., et al.: The diagnostic inadequacy of exercise testing in critical left coronary artery disease. J. Electrocardiol. 1977: **10**, 321.

131. Tonkon, M. J., et al.: Effect of digitalis on the exercise electrocardiogram in normal adult subjects. Chest 1977: **72**, 714.

132. Uhl, G. S., and Hopkirk, A. C.: Analysis of exercise-induced R wave amplitude changes in detection of coronary artery disease in asymptomatic men with left bundle branch block. Am. J. Cardiol. 1979: **44**, 1247.

133. Wagner, S., et al.: Unreliability of exercise-induced R wave changes as indexes of coronary artery disease. Am. J. Cardiol. 1979: **44**, 1241.

134. Wasserburger, R. H., and Alt, W. J.: The normal RS-T segment elevation variant. Am. J. Cardiol. 1961: **8**, 184.

135. Wasserburger, R. H., et al.: The effect of hyperventilation on the normal adult electrocardiogram. Circulation 1956: **13**, 850.

136. Wasserburger, R. H., et al.: The T-a wave of the adult electrocardiogram: an expression of pulmonary emphysema. Am. Heart J. 1957: **54**, 875.

137. Waters, D. D., et al.: Clinical and angiographic correlates of exercise-induced ST-segment elevation; increased detection with multiple electrocardiographic leads. Circulation 1980: **61**, 286.

138. Weiner, D. A.: Exercise testing for the diagnosis and severity of coronary disease. J. Cardiac Rehabil. 1981: **1**, 438.

139. Weiner, D. A., et al.: Identification of patients with left main and three vessel coronary disease with clinical and exercise test variables. Am. J. Cardiol. 1980: **46**, 21.

140. Williams, D. O., and Most, A. S.: Clinical, angiographic and hemodynamic characteristics of patients with a strongly positive exercise test. Am. Heart J. 1980: **66**, 241.

141. Wolthuis, R. A., et al.: The response of healthy men to treadmill exercise. Circulation 1977: **55**, 153.

142. Yasui, H.: Comparison of coronary arteriographic findings during angina pectoris associated with ST elevation or depression. Am. J. Cardiol. 1981: **47**, 539.

143. Yiannikas, J., et al. Analysis of exercise-induced changes in R wave amplitude in asymptomatic men with electrocardiographic ST-T changes at rest. Am. J. Cardiol. 1981: **47**, 238.

144. Zeppilli, P., et al.: T wave abnormalities in top-ranking athletes: Effects of isoproterenol, atropine, and physical exercise. Am. Heart J. 1980: **100**, 213.

145. Zohman, L. R., and Kattus, A. A.: Exercise testing in the diagnosis of coronary heart disease; a perspective. Am. J. Cardiol. 1977: **40**, 243.

146. Armstrong, W. F., et al.: Prevalence and magnitude of S-T segment and T wave abnormalities in normal men during continuous ambulatory monitoring. Am. J. Cardiol. 1982: **49**, 1638

147. Bateman, T., et al.: Transient appearance of Q waves in coronary disease during exercise electrocardiography. Am. Heart J. 1982: **104**, 182.

148. Fox, K., et al: Inability of exercise-induced R wave changes to predict coronary artery disease. Am. J. Cardiol. 1982: **49**, 674.

149. Ginzton, L. E., and Laks, M. M.: The differential diagnosis of acute pericarditis from the normal variant: new electrocardiographic criteria. Circulation 1982: **65**, 1004.

150. Ilsley, C., et al.: Influence of R wave analysis upon diagnostic accuracy of exercise testing in women. Br. Heart J. 1982: **48**, 161.

151. Mirvis, D.: Evaluation of normal variations in S-T segment patterns by body surface isopotential mapping: S-T segment elevation in absence of heart disease. Am. J. Cardiol. 1982: **50**, 122.

152. Stone, P. H., et al.: Patterns of exercise treadmill test performance in patients with left main coronary artery disease. Am. Heart J. 1982: **104**, 13.

Review Tracings

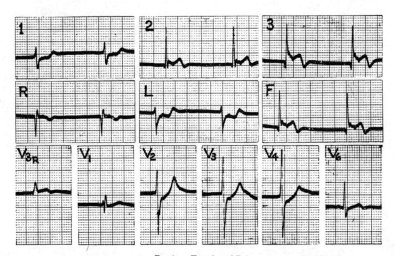

Review Tracing 27.1

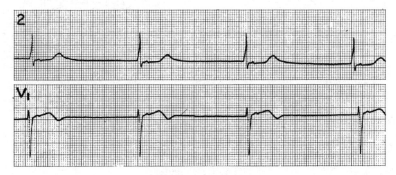

Review Tracing 27.2

For interpretation, see page 485

Review Tracings

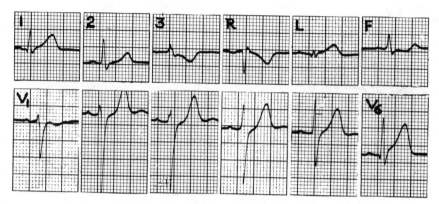

Review Tracing 27.3

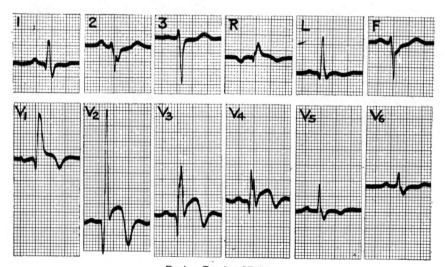

Review Tracing 27.4

For interpretation, see page 485

28

Drug Effects: Digitalis and Quinidine

Digitalis is to the electrocardiogram what syphilis was to medicine—the great imitator. It can mimic heart disease and it can cause almost all manner of blocks and arrhythmias.

Digitalis Effect

1. *ST-T changes:* digitalis causes depression of the ST segments with flattening and inversion of T waves. At the same time the relative Q-T duration is shortened in contrast to quinidine effect (see below). The shape of the depressed segment is often characteristic—sagging, with its concavity upward—and has been said to look as though a finger had been hooked over it to drag it down (figs. 28.1 and 28.2); sometimes it is more like a reversed

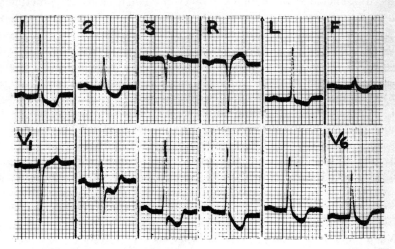

Figure 28.1. Digitalis effect. Note sagging ST segments in most leads, with short Q-T interval.

check mark, as in figure 28.8. These are not indications of digitalis *intoxication* but rather of simple digitalis *effect*, unless they occur in leads with predominantly negative QRS deflections (see below). They may be anticipated in most patients who are approaching adequate digitalization and are not an indication for reducing dosage. These changes occur in animals with approximately 25% of the lethal dose.

ST depression and inversion of T waves usually occur only in those leads with tall R waves. It is claimed that such displacement of ST segments and T waves in the direction opposite to the main QRS deflection means a uniform therapeutic action on the myocardium; but that depression of ST and inversion of T in leads with mainly negative QRS complexes (fig. 28.2) indicates that the drug is causing relative ischemia in the subendocardial muscle layers, and is therefore an indication to reduce the dose.

2. The *P-R interval* lengthens; modest prolongation is regarded as effect rather than toxicity and is likely due to the vagal effect exerted by the glycosides.

Digitalis Intoxication

Digitalis intoxication is always a clinical diagnosis, never a purely electrocardiographic one. There are no rhythmic or conductive disturbances that are peculiar to digitalis toxicity. Of course, there are circumstances in which the electrocardiographer may *suspect* the diagnosis, as when one of the disturbances especially typical of digitalis overdosage (e.g., ventricular bigeminy, accelerated junctional rhythm or type I A-V block) is seen in the presence of typical sagging ST-T changes. But it remains only a suspicion, and it is left to the clinician, weighing all the evidence, to establish the diagnosis.

A Bostonian wag has been credited with the observation that "lanatoside has replaced homicide as the nation's number one killer." Certainly, the intent of this remark has been true; many in the past have been intoxicated with a too large maintenance dose of digitoxin or by the too enthusiastic use of potassium-depleting diuretics in patients receiving a digitalis preparation. But more recently, the trend seems to have reversed itself to some extent, probably because of the present vogue of treating congestive heart failure with diuretics and vasodilators to the exclusion of digitalis.

It is impossible to determine accurately the comparative frequency of the various disturbances that result from digitalis intoxication. This is because it depends how far the toxicity is allowed to run riot. If a series of intoxications is based on fatal cases, the incidence of the more serious effects, such as complete A-V block or ventricular tachycardia will be exaggerated; whereas, if the series involves patients in whom the drug was discontinued at the earliest sign of intoxication,[4] the incidence of complete block and ventricular tachycardia will be minimized.

When digitalis is given in excess or when its toxic effects are felt because of a lowered potassium, the dysrhythmic manifestations can be divided into two

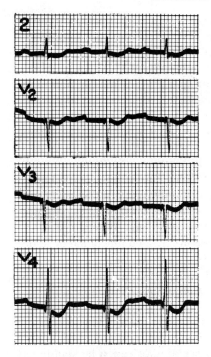

Figure 28.2. Digitalis effect. Note sagging ST segments, even in leads that have negative QRS complexes; also short Q-T interval and first degree A-V block (P-R = 0.26 sec).

Table 28.1
Main Excitant Disturbances

Ventricular extrasystoles—especially bigeminal and multiform
Atrial tachycardia
A-V junctional tachycardia
Accelerated junctional rhythm
Ventricular tachycardia
Bidirectional tachycardia
Ventricular fibrillation

categories: the excitant (table 28.1) and the suppressant effects (table 28.2). Often, there is a combination of excitant and suppressant effects (table 28.3).

Excitant Effects

Except in children, in whom supraventricular disturbances are more common, ventricular extrasystoles are the most frequently seen cardiac manifestations of digitalis overdosage. However, they are of course common in both health and disease of any kind and are in no sense diagnostic of digitalis intoxication. Furthermore, although it is not widely realized, digitalis is often an effective drug for reducing or eliminating ventricular extrasystoles that are not caused by the drug.[9, 14] When they are caused by digitalis, they tend to be bigeminal and, according to Scherf,[13] will always show variation in morphology if long enough strips are taken. Sometimes the bigeminy due to digitalis may be "concealed;" i.e., bigeminal runs may not be seen, but all interectopic intervals will contain only odd numbers of sinus beats.[12] Ventricular extrasystoles will be illustrated in the later section on "Combined Effects."

Atrial tachycardia caused by digitalis tends to possess P' waves of normal sinus polarity but of smaller than average amplitude; they may be somewhat irregular in time and variable in shape ("multifocal atrial tachycardia"). The arrhythmia is often associated with varying ratios of A-V conduction ("PAT with block") and will also be illustrated in the later section on "Combined Effects."

A-V junctional tachycardia is another fairly common manifestation of digitalis intoxication. Whereas the drug usually slows sinus nodal pacemakers, it tends to enhance the automaticity of junctional pacemakers. Sometimes it produces a genuine tachycardia, as in figure 28.3; but at other times it induces a more modest enhancement to a rate between 60 and 100/min, and the disturbance is then most appropriately termed accelerated junctional or idionodal rhythm (AINR), illustrated in figure 28.4.

Figure 28.3*A* illustrates an A-V junctional tachycardia caused by digitalis in the presence of atrial fibrillation. The junctional discharge is almost precisely regular at a rate of 140/min.

The patient who authored figure 28.3*B* was a man who was being relentlessly nudged toward his death by repeated intravenous doses of digoxin. His RBBB was present on admission, and the first evidence of intoxication he manifested was the junctional tachycardia. In the second strip, the junctional tachycardia gives place to a second excitant manifestation of toxicity, ventricular tachycardia

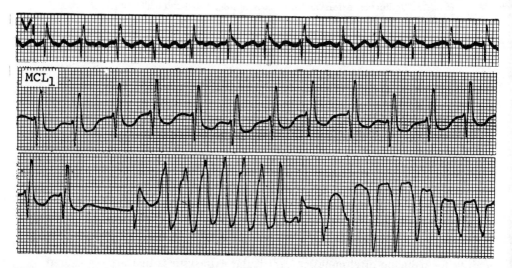

Figure 28.3. (*A*) **A-V junctional tachycardia** (rate, 140/min) with incomplete RBBB in the presence of atrial fibrillation. (*B*) The strips are continuous. Two excitant manifestations of digitalis intoxication: **A-V junctional tachycardia** (rate, 125/min) with RBBB in the *top strip*; in the *lower strip*, the A-V tachycardia suddenly pauses (?exit block), and the lengthened cycle precipitates **ventricular tachycardia** of the "swinging" variety.

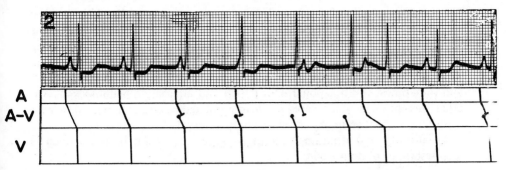

Figure 28.4.   Digitalis intoxication: Accelerated junctional rhythm (rate, 78/min) usurps control from a sinus rhythm (rate, 70 to 75/min). The seventh beat is a capture beat conducted with prolonged P-R interval.

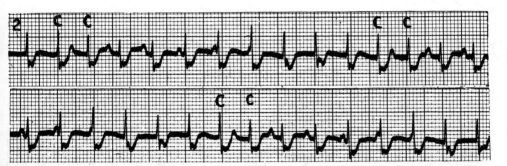

Figure 28.5.   Digitalis intoxication. Strips are continuous. Simultaneous but independent **atrial tachycardia** (rate, 172/min) and **junctional tachycardia** (rate, 154/min). Pairs of captured beats (*CC*) are recognized by the slight shortening of the ventricular cycles.

of the "swinging" variety (torsades de pointes); i.e., the polarity of the QRS swings between positive and negative.

The patient in figure 28.4 is a girl of 12 who required a mitral commissurotomy. After successful surgery her digitalis dosage was not reduced, and she soon developed signs of intoxication. Her earliest sign of cardiotoxicity was the AINR illustrated, a rhythm that frequently leads to A-V dissociation—as in figure 28.4—by usurping control from the somewhat slower sinus rhythm.

Digitalis toxicity is much the most common cause of "double tachycardia,"[3] i.e., the simultaneous existence of two rapidly firing but independent foci, such as the simultaneous atrial and junctional tachycardia in figure 28.5. Figure 28.6

presents an example of the so-called bidirectional tachycardia. This is not a specific term—it is purely descriptive, indicating just what you see in the rhythm strip and implying no particular mechanism. Whatever the underlying dysrhythmic mechanism, the pattern is frequently seen in digitalis intoxication. The mechanism is sometimes bifocal (or at least biform!) ectopic ventricular[5, 10] and sometimes A-V junctional with RBBB and alternating hemiblocks.[11] Another possibility in some cases is an interpolated ventricular bigeminy with fortuitously equal coupling and postectopic intervals.[6]

Atrial flutter and atrial fibrillation have only occasionally been described as manifestations of digitoxicity.[1, 4]

Suppressant Effects

Digitalis has a suppressant effect both on impulse formation in the sinus node and on conduction out of the node. Figure 28.7A shows both sinus bradycardia and a simultaneous 5:4 Wenckebach out of the sinus node (see ladder diagram).

When digitalis impairs conduction in the A-V junction, its effect is on the A-V node itself and therefore the pattern of conduction disturbance is of the "type I" variety. Figure 28.7B presents a 6:5 Wenckebach period in a patient with mild digitalis toxicity.

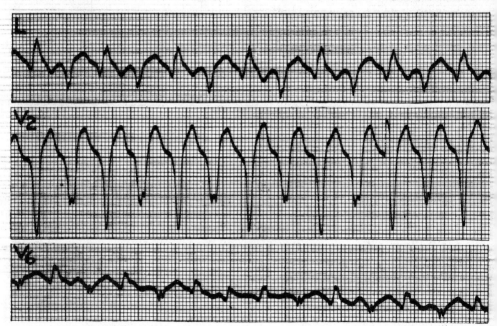

Figure 28.6. Bidirectional tachycardia. In aVL and V₆, there is a tendency for the ventricular complexes to be alternately positive and negative. In V₂, the QRS amplitude alternates ("alternating tachycardia").

Table 28.2
Main Suppressant Disturbances

Sinus bradycardia
S-A block
Type I A-V block
Complete A-V block

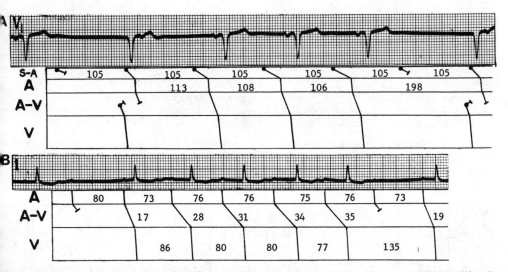

Figure 28.7. **Digitalis intoxication.** (*A*) Sinus bradycardia complicated by a **sinus exit block of Wenck-ebach type**. The second and last beats are junctional escape beats (see laddergram). Wenckebach-type conduction is inferred from the progressive shortening of the atrial (P-P) interval (113, 108, 106)—"footprints" of the Wenckebach. (*B*) **Second degree A-V block, type I:** The typical Wenckebach period shows progressive lengthening of the P-R interval until the sixth beat is dropped (6:5 A-V block)—see laddergram.

Figure 28.8 is from a young man who swallowed an unknown number of digoxin tablets in a suicide attempt; as usual in the normal heart, there is disturbance of conduction without provocation of ectopy.[16]

It is doubtful if digitalis ever produces type II A-V block or bundle-branch block (BBB). However, in advanced stages of intoxication in severely diseased hearts, it is possible that digitalis may impair conduction in the ventricular expressways. This may indeed be the underlying mechanism in some patterns of bidirectional tachycardia.

Combined Effects

One of the commonest combinations of excitant and suppressant effects is the partnership of atrial tachycardia with A-V block—glibly known as "PAT with block." This is a sinister combination carrying a high mortality if the offending drug is not immediately discontinued. It is said to be more likely to

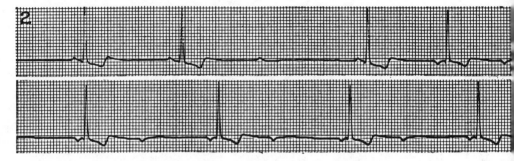

Figure 28.8.   Digitalis intoxication. Strips are continuous. From a young man who swallowed an unknown number of digoxin tablets in a suicide attempt. The sinus rhythm has been slowed to slightly under 50/min. Toward the end of the *top strip*, an ectopic atrial or junctional pacemaker takes over. Note that there is impressive **A-V block—2:1** in *bottom strip*—yet no prolongation of the P-R interval.

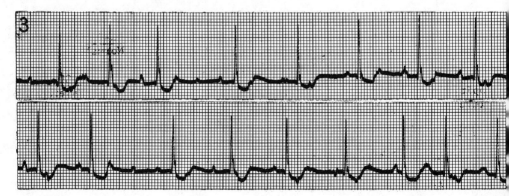

Figure 28.9.   Digitalis intoxication. The strips are continuous. **Multifocal atrial tachycardia** with **varying A-V block**. Note the variable P-wave morphology, irregular atrial rhythm, changing A-V conduction ratio and the sagging ST segments characteristic of **digitalis effect**.

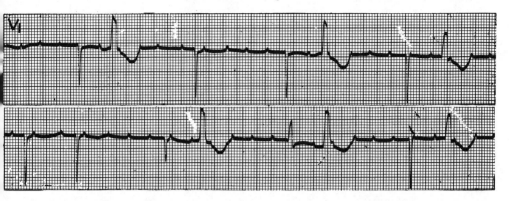

Figure 28.10. **Digitalis intoxication.** Strips are continuous. **Atrial tachycardia** with **varying A-V block** and numerous **ventricular extrasystoles** tending to bigeminy. Note irregularity of the atrial rhythm. From a 30-year-old black woman with postpartum cardiomyopathy who was mistakenly given an overdose of intravenous digoxin.

develop in patients with cor pulmonale and hypoxia.[2] Figure 28.9 is a classical example of this combine: The P′ waves are variable in shape, irregular in rhythm and of normal polarity for the most part; and the A-V conduction ratio, though mostly 2:1, is variable. The sagging ST segments are characteristic of digitalis effect. Figure 28.10 also shows this combination but, in addition, contains ventricular extrasystoles. The tracing is from a 30-year-old black woman with postpartum cardiomyopathy who was mistakenly given 2 mg digoxin intravenously. Not surprisingly, she manifests atrial tachycardia with varying block interspersed with ventricular extrasystoles tending to occur in bigeminal rhythm.

Table 28.3
Combined Disturbances

Atrial tachycardia with A-V block ("PAT with block")
Sinus bradycardia with A-V junctional tachycardia
Regular accelerated junctional rhythm in presence of atrial fibrillation
Double tachycardias, atrial and A-V junctional
Etc

Figure 28.11 presents a third example of "PAT with block" in which you can compare the P' waves of the toxic tachycardia with the patient's sinus P waves.

Figure 28.12*A* illustrates another threefold effect of digitalis overdosage: sinus bradycardia, a minor degree of A-V block and junctional tachycardia.

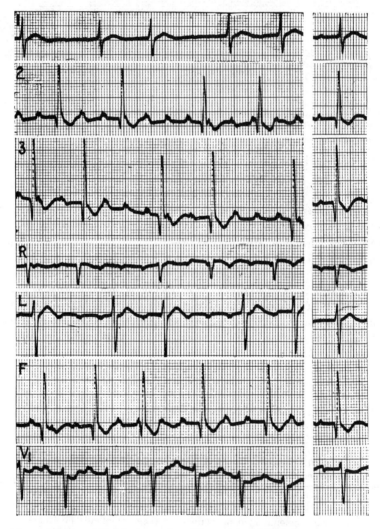

Figure 28.11.   Atrial tachycardia with varying A-V block as a result of **digitalis intoxication.** Note that the P waves are almost normally directed (axis +90°), that the A-V conduction ratio varies and that the atrial rhythm is not precisely regular. The single column of complexes on the right is to show for comparison the form and direction of P waves (axis +60°) when sinus rhythm was restored.

Figure 28.12*B* illustrates a patient with atrial fibrillation in whom the digitalis has produced some degree of A-V block and an accelerated junctional rhythm, the combination of which has caused complete A-V dissociation.

Figure 28.13 is from a patient with atrial fibrillation, true posterior infarction and digitalis intoxication. Lead V_3 shows the accelerated A-V junctional rhythm resulting from the toxicity. Leads V_2 and V_4 show the same accelerated rhythm but with Wenckebach periods out of (exit block) or below the A-V pacemaker; V_2 shows 5:4 and 4:3 Wenckebachs, while V_4 shows the even more common 3:2 ratio producing bigeminal grouping (see laddergram).

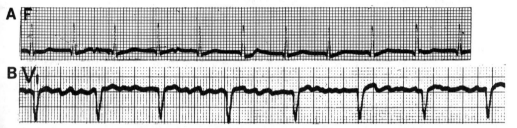

Figure 28.12. Digitalis intoxication. (*A*) **Sinus bradycardia** (rate, 55/min) with some degree of **A-V block** and **junctional tachycardia**—all due to digitalis. The third and fifth beats end slightly shorter cycles and are presumably conducted with prolonged P-R intervals; elsewhere the two rhythms are dissociated. (*B*) **Atrial fibrillation** with some degree of **A-V block** and independent **accelerated idionodal rhythm** (rate, 70/min). The degree of block and enhancement of A-V automaticity necessary to produce the dissociation are both due to digitalis.

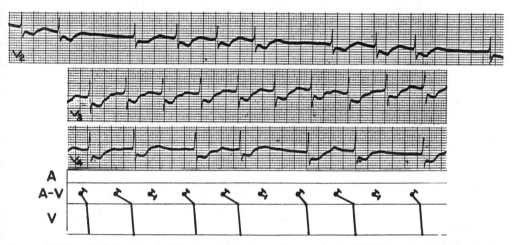

Figure 28.13. Digitalis intoxication. Lead V_3 shows the **accelerated A-V junctional rhythm** (rate, 98/min) resulting from digitalis toxicity. Leads V_2 and V_4 show the same accelerated junctional rhythm complicated by **Wenckebach periods** out of (exit block) or below the A-V pacemaker—V_2 shows 5:4 and 4:3 Wenckebachs, while V_4 shows the even more common 3:2 ratio producing bigeminal grouping (laddergram).

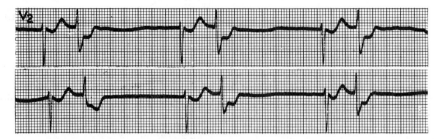

Figure 28.14.   Digitalis intoxication. Note (1) **atrial fibrillation** with regular independent idionodal rhythm, (2) **ventricular bigeminy** with multiform ectopic QRS complexes and (3) ST sagging in a lead with negative QRS complexes.

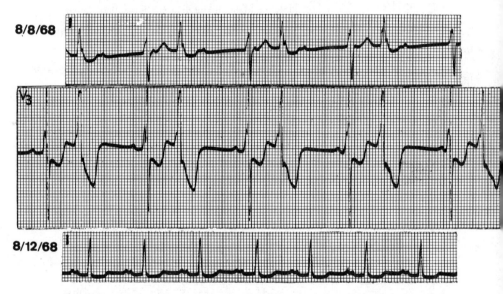

Figure 28.15.   Digitalis intoxication. From a 10-year-old black boy who was mistakenly maintained on a double dose of digitalis preparations after mitral valve surgery. On 8/8/68, he had developed an **accelerated idioventricular rhythm** (rate, 64/min) with **ventricular bigeminy** dissociated from his sinus rhythm (rate, 90/min). There is also some degree of **A-V block**—note the P waves in lead 1 landing beyond the T waves which should be conducted but are not. Both digitalis preparations were discontinued, and by 8/12/68 he reverted to sinus rhythm (rate, 80/min) with first degree A-V block. Note the P-mitrale in lead 1 on both days.

Figure 28.14 is from a patient with atrial fibrillation and severe digitalis intoxication. First of all, there is at least high-grade and probably complete A-V block with resultant escaping idionodal rhythm at the slow rate of about 40/min. There is ventricular bigeminy and, as is always the case,[13] the extrasystolic complexes vary in shape ("variform" or "multiform" rather than "multifocal"). Another (nondysrhythmic) sign referred to on page 426 and said to be diagnostic of digitalis intoxication is the sagging of the ST segment in leads *in which the QRS is predominantly negative*[8]: In the supraventricular beats the QRS is dominated by its S wave, while the ST segment has the typical, scooped-out, sagging aspect so characteristic of digitalis.

Figure 28.15 is from a 10-year-old black boy who, after mitral valve surgery, was mistakenly maintained on a double dose of digitalis. On 8/8/68, he had developed an accelerated idioventricular rhythm, dissociated from his sinus rhythm, with ventricular bigeminy. There is also some degree of block since the atrial impulses in lead 1 land beyond the T wave and yet are not conducted. Four days later, after discontinuing the digitalis, he had reverted to sinus rhythm uncomplicated except for residual first degree A-V block.

Finally, figure 28.16 is from the same patient as figure 28.3*B*—in a later stage of intoxication. He shows a combination of the same A-V junctional tachycardia with RBBB, now with intermittent A-V block below the level of the A-V pacemaker and, in the *middle strip*, the development of a right ventricular tachycardia at a modest rate. The fusion beats (*F*) in the middle of the *bottom strip* are a nice example of the "normalization" that results when BBB is present and a ventricular impulse, arising on the same side as the BBB, fuses with a simultaneous supraventricular impulse (see p. 285).

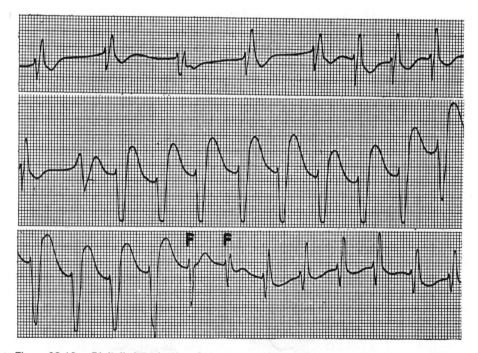

Figure 28.16. Digitalis intoxication. Strips are continuous. The *top strip* begins with **junctional tachycardia** at first with probable 2:1 exit block or block below the A-V pacemaker; the strip ends with 1:1 conduction. After another blocked beat at the beginning of the *second strip*, a right **ventricular tachycardia** takes over (rate, 112/min). In the *bottom strip*, there are two "normalized" **fusion beats** (*F*) between the impulses of the two tachycardias.

Quinidine Effect and Toxicity

Compared with digitalis, quinidine causes qualitatively and quantitatively different changes in the tracing. It regularly lengthens the QT interval in contrast to digitalis effect. It is less likely to cause lengthening of the P-R interval but much more likely to prolong the QRS. Its influences may be summarized as follows:

1. *ST-T changes.* T waves become depressed, widened, notched and finally inverted. Meanwhile the Q-T interval lengthens (fig. 28.17). The ST segment is less likely to become depressed than with digitalis administration.

2. *Blocks* of all types can occur. S-A block may produce fatal atrial asystole. Prolongation of the QRS is frequently seen and is important to the

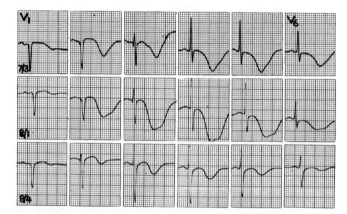

Figure 28.17.   Quinidine effect. From a patient with extensive anterior infarction who was receiving quinidine. Between 7/31 and 8/1 the quinidine effect increases—the broad T-U complex widens still further. On 8/1 quinidine was discontinued and by 8/4 the quinidine effect has largely disappeared.

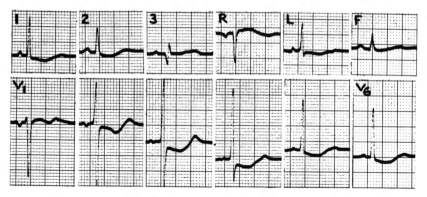

Figure 28.18.   Digitalis plus quinidine effects producing a pattern indistinguishable from that of hypokalemia (see p. 467).

therapist: if this interval increases during treatment by 25 to 50%, it is an indication to discontinue the drug.

3. *Ventricular ectopic rhythms* are occasionally produced.

The combined effects of digitalis and quinidine (fig. 28.18) can closely mimic the pattern of hypokalemia[15] (see also figs. 30.13 and 30.14).

REFERENCES

1. Agarwal, B. L., et al.: Atrial flutter; a rare manifestation of digitalis intoxication. Br. Heart J. 1972: **34**, 330.
2. Agarwal, B. L., and Agarwal, B. V.: Digitalis-induced paroxysmal atrial tachycardia with AV block. Br. Heart J. 1972: **34**, 330.
3. Castellanos, A., et al.: Digitalis-induced arrhythmias; recognition and therapy. Cardiovasc. Clin. 1969: **1** (No. 3), 108.
4. Church, G., et al.: Deliberate digitalis intoxication; a comparison of the toxic effects of four glycoside preparations. Ann. Intern. Med. 1962: **57**, 946.
5. Cohen, S. I., et al.: Infra-His origin of bidirectional tachycardia. Circulation 1973: **47**, 1260.
6. Gavrilescu, S., and Luca, C.: His bundle electrogram during bidirectional tachycardia. Br. Heart J. 1975: **37**, 1198.
7. Kastor, J. A.: Digitalis intoxication in patients with atrial fibrillation. Circulation 1973: **47**, 888.
8. Lepeschkin, E.: *Modern Electrocardiography*, pp. 297–299. Williams & Wilkins, Baltimore, 1951.
9. Lown, B., et al.: Effect of a digitalis drug on ventricular premature beats. N. Engl. J. Med. 1977: **296**, 301.
10. Morris, S. N., and Zipes, D. P.: His bundle electrocardiography during bidirectional tachycardia. Circulation 1973: **48**, 32.
11. Rosenbaum, M. B., et al.: The mechanism of bidirectional tachycardia. Am. Heart J. 1969: **78**, 4.
12. Schamroth, L., and Marriott, H. J. L.: Concealed ventricular extrasystoles. Circulation 1963: **27**, 1043.
13. Scherf, D., and Schott, A.: *Extrasystoles and Allied Arrhythmias*, Ed. 2, p. 586. Heinemann, London, 1973.
14. Scherf, D., and Schott, A.: *Extrasystoles and Allied Arrhythmias*, Ed. 2, pp. 592, 990, 993. Heinemann, London, 1973.
15. Surawicz, B.: Electrolytes and the electrocardiogram. Am. J. Cardiol. 1963: **12**, 656.
16. Vanagt, E. J., and Wellens, H. J. J.: The electrocardiogram in digitalis intoxication, p. 315. In *What's New in Electrocardiography*, edited by H. J. J. Wellens and H. E. Kulbertus. Martinus Nijhoff, Boston, 1981.

Review Tracings

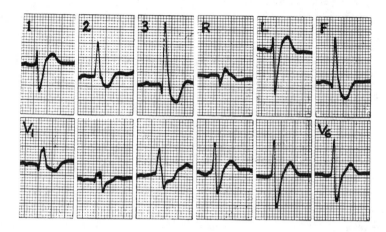

Review Tracing 28.1

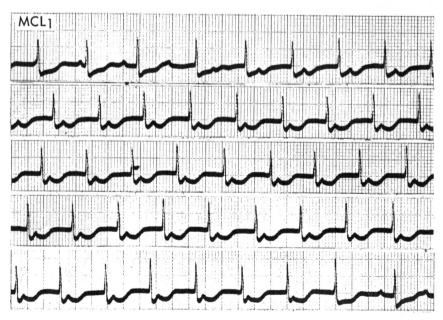

Review Tracing 28.2

For interpretation, see page 485

Review Tracings

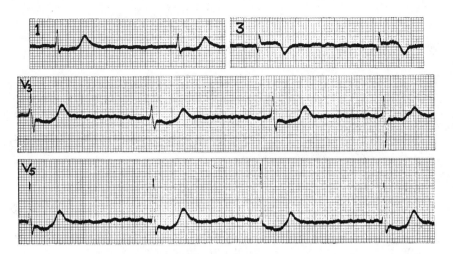

Review Tracing 28.3

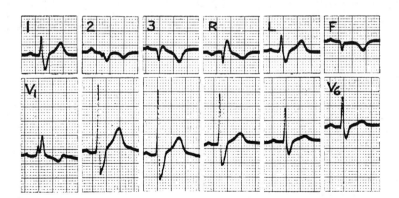

Review Tracing 28.4

For interpretation, see page 485

29

The Heart in Childhood and Congenital Lesions

Several points are of importance in interpreting the electrocardiogram in chidren. First and foremost, variations in the normal are more diverse than they are in adult tracings, so that one should be even more careful in declaring a youthful tracing abnormal than that of an adult. The rate is relatively faster, and the P-R and QRS intervals relatively shorter in childhood.

At birth the right ventricular wall is almost as thick as the left, and this leads to a different balance of power. Apart from the common occurrence of right axis deviation, tall R waves are frequently seen in precordial leads to the right of the precordium with deep S waves in left chest leads. Thus a pattern resembling right ventricular hypertrophy in the adult may be a perfectly normal finding in the child.

A further important point to remember is that T waves may be normally inverted further to the left of the precordium in the child. The percentage incidence of T-wave inversion in the first four chest leads is as follows[22, 28]:

	V_1	V_2	V_3	V_4
6–12 mo	100	91	57	4.3
1–3 yr	96	77	38	4
8–12 yr	82	13.2	4.45	0

Congenital Heart Disease

Many congenital lesions may be associated with a normal electrocardiogram. Normal tracings are more often seen in lesions that place primary stress on the left ventricle, such as aortic stenosis, coarctation of the aorta, ventricular septal defect and patent ductus; they are less often seen in association with lesions that stress the right ventricle, such as pulmonic stenosis and atrial septal defect. Complex defects are only rarely associated with a normal tracing. A normal tracing, therefore, by no means excludes a congenital lesion.

442

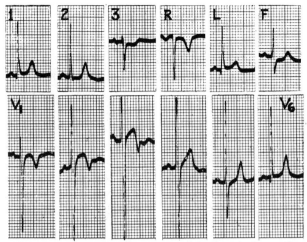

Figure 29.1. From a patient with **patent ductus arteriosus**, showing left ventricular diastolic overloading. Note high voltage of QRS complexes, with tall upright T waves in V_{5-6}. U waves are inverted in 1, 2 and V_6.

Again, there may be great differences between the tracings from different patients with the same deformity; for example, in mild patent ductus or ventricular septal defect the tracing will probably be normal. Later the pattern of left ventricular diastolic overloading may develop (fig. 29.1). When pulmonary hypertension becomes significant, right ventricular hypertrophy will be added to the left ventricular overloading pattern. Finally, when pulmonic hypertension is marked, the pattern may become that of right ventricular hypertrophy alone.

In congenital heart disease few patterns are diagnostic and those that are are associated with the rarer malformations: for example, when the left coronary arises from the pulmonary artery (anomalous left coronary artery), the electrocardiographic pattern is usually diagnostic—Q waves, ST elevation and T-wave inversion are present in leads 1, aVL and the left chest leads, giving a pattern identical with that of lateral infarction.[13] The electrocardiogram of dextrocardia with situs inversus is also almost specific, and those of the ostium primum/common A-V canal group and Ebstein's disease are relatively so (see below). Although the tracing is seldom truly diagnostic, it often serves as a helpful guidepost and it is convenient to gather the most useful pointers under the headings of the four main components of the tracing:

P waves

1. In isolated dextrocardia the P wave in lead 1 is normally upright, whereas in dextrocardia with situs inversus it is inverted (left-sided venous atrium and vena cava); indeed all complexes in lead 1 are inverted (fig. 29.2).

2. **P-congenitale** consists of tall and peaked P waves in leads 1 and 2, with tall, mainly positive P waves in right chest leads (fig. 29.3). The frontal plane axis is generally between +30° and +45°, in contrast with one to the right of +60° in P-pulmonale. P-congenitale is found mainly in cyanotic forms of congenital disease but also in pure pulmonic stenosis. The tallest P waves occur in tricuspid disease (stenosis or atresia) and in Ebstein's disease (fig. 29.4).

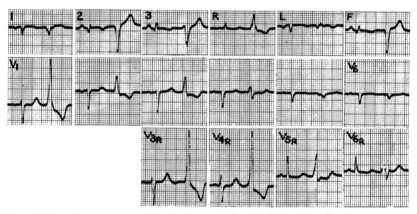

Figure 29.2. From a patient with **situs inversus**, acute inferior infarction and ventricular bigeminy. Note inverted P and QRS in lead 1 and dwindling S wave across left precordium. When precordial leads are taken to the right (V$_{3R}$-V$_{6R}$), the normal transition from rS to R occurs.

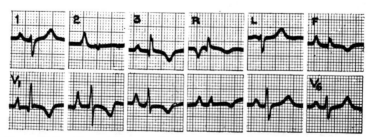

Figure 29.3. From a 44-year-old patient with **pulmonic stenosis**. Tracing shows right ventricular hypertrophy and strain (systolic overloading). Note P-congenitale, indicating right atrial enlargement, with prominent R waves in right precordial leads, marked right axis deviation (+150°) and relatively low equiphasic complexes in V$_{5-6}$.

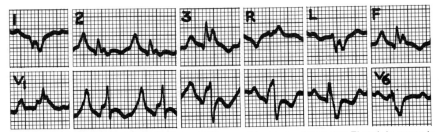

Figure 29.4. **Ebstein's anomaly.** From a 36-year-old woman with severe Ebstein's anomaly. Note low voltage, atypical RBBB and enormous P waves.

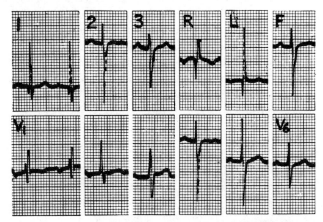

Figure 29.5. From a 13-year-old boy with an **ostium primum** atrial septal defect, cleft mitral valve and small ventricular septal defect (incomplete **A-V communis**); note the almost diagnostic combination of marked left axis deviation of the early portion of the QRS with incomplete RBBB.

QRS Complex

1. Determination of the **mean QRS axis** may provide a helpful initial clue to diagnosis. Diagrams illustrating the distribution of congenital malformations in the various segments of the hexaxial reference system have been published, and these may profitably be consulted.[10, 15, 23] When **left axis deviation** is seen in a patient with cyanotic disease, the most likely diagnosis is tricuspid atresia; but other possibilities include transposition of the great vessels, single ventricle and a number of other anomalies.[20] When the initial portion of the QRS complex shows marked left axis deviation while the terminal part shows a right bundle-branch block, the overwhelming probability is a lesion of the ostium primum/A-V communis group (endocardial cushion defect) (fig. 29.5). Such a pattern is unfortunately also sometimes seen in secundum defects.[14]

2. The patterns of **ventricular hypertrophy** are obviously of considerable diagnostic importance; right ventricular hypertrophy is seen in pure pulmonic stenosis (fig. 29.3), atrial septal defect and most of the cyanotic lesions. In the tetralogy of Fallot, the dominant R wave in V_1 of right ventricular hypertrophy usually changes to RS or rS by V_2 (fig. 29.6) whereas in pure pulmonic stenosis the R wave usually remains dominant in the first 3 or 4 chest leads (fig. 29.3).

Left hypertrophy is seen in aortic stenosis, coarctation of the aorta, ventricular septal defect and patent ductus. In aortic stenosis, an R/T ratio of more than 10 in V_5 or V_6 indicates severe obstruction.[11] Note that ventricular hypertrophy and axis deviation do not necessarily go hand in hand. Indeed, left axis deviation is seen in less than 25% of cases showing left ventricular hypertrophy, and right axis deviation is present in less than 66% of those showing right ventricular hypertrophy.

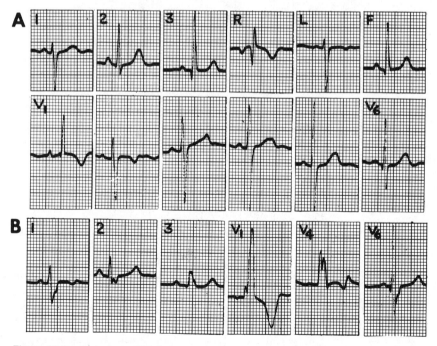

Figure 29.6.   **Tetralogy of Fallot.** (*A*) Note marked right axis deviation (+120°), tall R in V_1 and deep S waves through V_6; also that S waves become dominant at V_2 while T waves are upright at V_3 (compare pattern of pure pulmonic stenosis, fig. 29.3). (*B*) Development of RBBB following surgical correction.

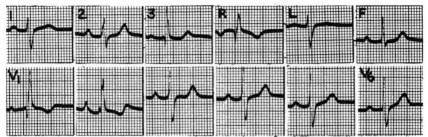

Figure 29.7. Atrial septal defect. Typical RBBB pattern of right ventricular diastolic overloading. Note also 1st degree A-V block and pointed right precordial P waves suggesting right atrial hypertrophy.

3. **Bundle-branch block.** The pattern of right bundle-branch block is commonly seen as a hemodynamic expression of right ventricular diastolic overloading (fig. 29.7). The classic example is atrial septal defect, and up to 90% of patients with this lesion manifest right bundle-branch block. RBBB is also frequently seen in the hemodynamically similar total anomalous pulmonary venous return and turns up occasionally in a variety of other lesions. It is a well-recognized complication of surgery for ventricular septal defect (fig. 29.6). In Ebstein's disease right bundle-branch block is the rule, but in this condition the QRS complexes of the right precordial leads are typically of quite low voltage (fig. 29.4). Left bundle-branch block is rare but is occasionally seen in aortic stenosis and in other lesions placing predominant strain on the left ventricle. It regularly occurs following surgery for septal hypertrophy.

4. **Pre-excitation.** The WPW syndrome has been described in a variety of congenital lesions, but much its commonest associations are Ebstein's anomaly and primary cardiomyopathy.[17, 24]

5. The **Katz-Wachtel phenomenon** consists of equiphasic complexes in two or more limb leads, often with similar equiphasicity in the midprecordial leads. This is seen in many congenital lesions, but is perhaps most common in ventricular septal defect (fig. 29.8).

6. Prominent **Q waves** in the right precordial leads are evidence of right *atrial* hypertrophy; prominent Q waves in left chest leads, or in 2, 3, and aVF, sometimes reaching a depth of 10 mm, are most suspicious of ventricular septal defect (fig. 29.8). Prominent Q waves in limb and left chest leads are also typical of hypertrophic cardiomyopathy (fig. 29.9).

T Waves

In differentiating Fallot's tetralogy from the trilogy (pulmonic stenosis, atrial septal defect and right ventricular hypertrophy) or from pure pulmonic stenosis, T-wave behavior may be helpful. In the tetralogy precordial T waves are usually inverted only in leads taken to the right of the sternum (fig. 29.10), whereas in the trilogy or pure pulmonic stenosis they are frequently inverted as far to the left as V_4 or V_5 (fig. 29.3).

U Waves

These have been largely neglected in descriptions of the electrocardiogram in congenital heart disease; but inverted U waves are a common finding in left chest leads as an early sign of left ventricular overloading, systolic or diastolic.

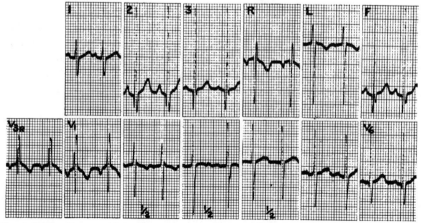

Figure 29.8.   From a child with **ventricular septal defect**. Note deep Q waves in 2, 3 and aVF, incomplete RBBB pattern and equiphasic RS pattern in midprecordial leads.

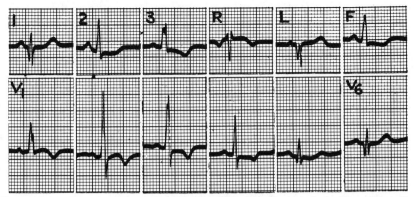

Figure 29.9.   Hypertrophic cardiomyopathy. Note deep Q waves in 1, aVL and V₆, with reciprocal tall R in right chest leads, indicating septal hypertrophy.

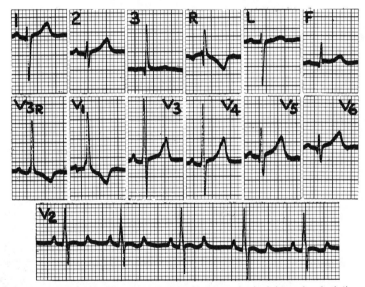

Figure 29.10.   Tetralogy of Fallot. Note marked right axis deviation (+150°) with right ventricular hypertrophy. T waves become upright in V₂ (compare with persistent inversion through V₄ in pure pulmonic stenosis—fig. 29.3).

Individual Defects

The cardinal features of the electrocardiogram in the commoner congenital lesions and in those with distinctive features are as follows:

Ventricular Septal Defect (VSD) (fig. 29.8)

Prominent Q waves in left chest leads or in 2, 3 and aVF. High voltage equiphasic QRS complex in midprecordial leads in 50 to 75%.

Pattern of RBBB, complete or more often incomplete, in 20 to 30%.
Depending on severity and stage, may be normal, or show LVH, combined ventricular hypertrophy or RVH; LVH is often of diastolic overloading type.

Patent Ductus Arteriosus (figs. 29.1 and 29.11)

Similar to VSD; but left atrial enlargement and 1st degree A-V block are more common and RBBB patterns less common than in VSD.

Atrial Septal Defect (fig. 29.7)

Patterns of RBBB in majority—up to 90% in some series.
P-congenitale in some.
First degree A-V block and atrial arrhythmias in a few.

Aortic Stenosis

Normal in at least 25% of those with significant obstruction.
Varying stages of LVH in most of remainder.
LBBB in a few.

Hypertrophic Cardiomyopathy (HCM) (fig. 29.9)

Axis usually normal.
Delta waves are common; occasional WPW.
Prominent Q waves, especially in leads 2, 3, aVF, V_{5-6}, with tall R waves in right chest leads (evidence of septal hypertrophy). Progression from this to LVH.

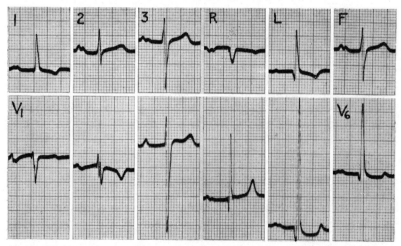

Figure 29.11. From a 24-year-old patient with **patent ductus arteriosus**. Note wide notched P waves (intra-atrial block, evidence of left atrial enlargement), first degree A-V block (P-R = 0.30 sec) and high voltage QRS complexes with ST-T changes indicating left ventricular hypertrophy and strain.

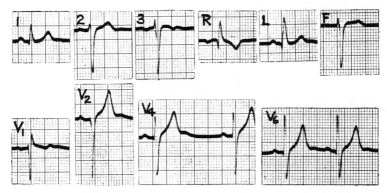

Figure 29.12. From a 15-year-old boy with **coarctation of the aorta**. Note unusually marked left axis deviation (−75°), presumably due to left anterior hemiblock.

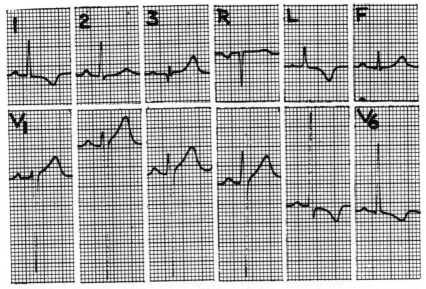

Figure 29.13. From a 32-year-old man with **coarctation of the aorta**. Tracing shows typical pattern of left ventricular hypertrophy and strain (systolic overload).

Coarctation (figs. 29.12 and 29.13)

Normal or LVH.

Pulmonic Stenosis (PS) (fig. 29.3)

RVH with rR or qR in V_1 when RV pressure is equal to or higher than LV pressure; Rs or rS in V_1 when RV pressure is less than LV pressure.
P-congenitale.
In severe PS, R waves dominant and T waves inverted V_1 to V_3 or V_4.

Tetralogy of Fallot (figs. 29.6 and 29.10)

RVH with dominant R and inverted T in V_1; abrupt change to rS with upright
T in V_2 or V_3 (cf. pulmonic stenosis).
P-congenitale.

Transposition of Great Vessels

RVH with a) qR in V_1 suggests intact ventricular septum; b) rsR' in V_1 suggests
VSD.
P-congenitale.
T waves taller in right than left chest leads.

Corrected Transposition (Inversion of Ventricles) (fig. 29.14)

qR in V_1 with no q and RS in V_6.
P-congenitale.
Some degree of A-V block.

Endocardial Cushion Defect (fig. 29.5)

Left axis deviation of initial portion of QRS with incomplete RBBB pattern.
Occasional first degree A-V block.

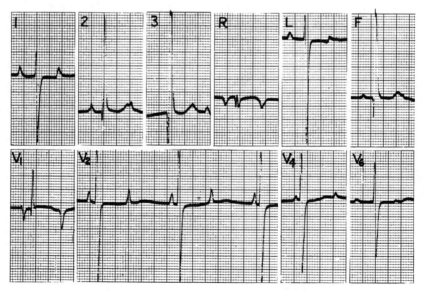

Figure 29.14.   Corrected transposition of the great vessels. Note the left ventricular
(qR) pattern in V_1 with absent Q and deep S in V_6—typical of **ventricular inversion**; also
the P-congenitale type of right atrial enlargement and the high grade (probably complete)
A-V block. (Reproduced from H. J. L. Marriott: *Bedside Diagnosis of Heart Disease.*
Tampa Tracings, 1967.)

Ebstein's Anomaly (fig. 29.4)

Right atrial enlargement without RVH.
Low amplitude, atypical RBBB pattern.
WPW syndrome (type B) in 10%.
First degree A-V block in 15 to 20%.
Arrhythmias, especially atrial tachycardia.

Tricuspid Atresia

LVH, or at least left axis deviation, in 80 to 90%.
Right atrial overload.

REFERENCES

1. Beregovich, J., et al.: The vectorcardiogram and electrocardiogram in persistent common atrioventricular canal. Circulation 1960: **21**, 63.
2. Beregovich, J., et al.: The vectorcardiogram and electrocardiogram in ventricular septal defect. Br. Heart J. 1960: **22**, 205.
3. Braudo, M., et al.: A distinctive electrocardiogram in muscular subaortic stenosis due to septal hypertrophy. Am. J. Cardiol. 1964: **14**, 599.
4. Braunwald, E., et al.: Idiopathic hypertrophic subaortic stenosis. I. A description of the disease based upon an analysis of 64 patients. Circulation 1964: **30**, Supp. IV-3.
5. Brink, A. J., and Neill, C. A.: The electrocardiogram in congenital heart disease: with special reference to left axis deviation. Circulation 1955: **12**, 604.
6. Brumlik, J. V.: Principles of electrocardiographic interpretation in congenital heart disease. In *Advances in Electrocardiography*, p. 203. Grune & Stratton, New York, 1958.
7. Burchell, H. B., et al.: The electrocardiogram of patients with atrioventricular cushion defects (defects of the atrioventricular canal). Am. J. Cardiol. 1960: **6**, 575.
8. Dack, S.: The electrocardiogram and vectorcardiogram in ventricular septal defect. Am. J. Cardiol. 1960: **5**, 199.
9. de Oliviera, J. M., and Zimmerman, H. A.: The electrocardiogram in interatrial septal defects and its correlation with hemodynamics. Am. Heart J. 1958: **55**, 369.
10. de Oliviera, J. M., et al.: The mean ventricular axis in congenital heart disease: a study considering the natural incidence of the malformations. Am. Heart J. 1959: **57**, 820.
11. Fowler, R. S.: Ventricular repolarization in congenital aortic stenosis. Am. Heart J. 1965: **70**, 603.
12. Grant, R. P., et al.: Symposium on diagnostic methods in the study of left-to-right shunts. Circulation 1957: **16**, 791.
13. Kuzman, W. J., et al.: Anomalous left coronary artery arising from the pulmonary artery. Am. Heart J. 1959: **57**, 36.
14. Harrison, D. C., and Morrow, A. G.: Electrocardiographic evidence of left-axis deviation in patients with defects of the atrial septum of the secundum type. N. Engl. J. Med. 1963: **269**, 743.
15. Landero, C. A., et al.: The mean manifest electrical axes of ventricular activation and repolarization processes ($\hat{A}$QRS and $\hat{A}$T) in congenital heart disease; frontal and horizontal planes. Am. Heart J. 1959: **58**, 889.
16. Pryor, R., et al.: Electrocardiographic changes in atrial septal defects: ostium secundum defect versus ostium primum (endocardial cushion) defect. Am. Heart J. 1959: **58**, 689.
17. Schiebler, G. L., et al.: The Wolff-Parkinson-White syndrome in infants and children. Pediatrics 1959: **24**, 585.
18. Scott, R. C.: The electrocardiogram in atrial septal defects and atrioventricular cushion defects. Am. Heart J. 1961: **62**, 712.
19. Scott, R. C.: The electrocardiogram in ventricular septal defects. Am. Heart J. 1961: **62**, 842.

20. Shaher, R. M.: Left ventricular preponderance and left axis deviation in cyanotic congenital heart disease. Br. Heart J. 1963: **25**, 726.

21. Sodi-Pallares, D., and Marsico, F.: The importance of electrocardiographic patterns in congenital heart disease. Am. Heart J. 1955: **49**, 202.

22. Sodi-Pallares, D., et al.: Electrocardiography in infants and children. Pediatr. Clin. North Am. 1958: **5**, 871.

23. Sodi-Pallares, D., et al.: The mean manifest electrical axis of the ventricular activation process (ÂQRS) in congenital heart disease: a new approach in electrocardiographic diagnosis. Am. Heart J. 1958: **55**, 681.

24. Swiderski, J., et al.: The Wolff-Parkinson-White syndrome in infancy and childhood. Br. Heart J. 1962: **24**, 561.

25. Toscano-Barboza, E. M., et al.: Atrial septal defect. The electrocardiogram and its hemodynamic correlation in 100 proved cases. Am. J. Cardiol. 1958: **2**, 698.

26. Toscano-Barboza, E. M., and DuShane, J. W.: Ventricular septal defect. Correlation of electrocardiographic and hemodynamic findings in 60 proved cases. Am. J. Cardiol. 1959: **3**, 721.

27. Wigle, E. D., and Baron, R. H.: The electrocardiogram in muscular subaortic stenosis. Circulation 1966: **34**, 585.

28. Ziegler, R. R.: *Electrocardiographic Studies in Normal Infants and Children.* Charles C Thomas, Springfield, Ill., 1951.

Review Tracing

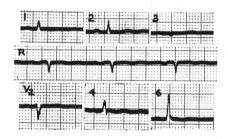

Review Tracing 29.1

For interpretation, see page 485

Review Tracings

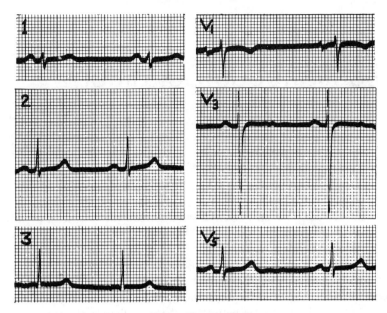

Review Tracing 29.2

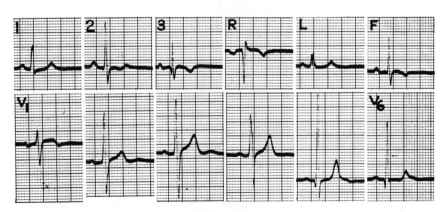

Review Tracing 29.3

For interpretation, see page 485

30

Miscellaneous Conditions

Valvular Lesions

The electrocardiogram plays only a small part in the diagnosis of valvular lesions. Mitral stenosis is the only one which may claim anything like a specific pattern.[21] The **P-mitrale** pattern, consisting of wide, notched P waves in leads 1 and 2, with flat, diphasic or inverted P waves in 3, is frequently found (fig. 30.1). P-wave notching is sometimes best seen in midprecordial leads (e.g., V_3). The combination of right axis deviation (with or without right ventricular hypertrophy) and the P-mitrale pattern or atrial fibrillation is strongly sugges-

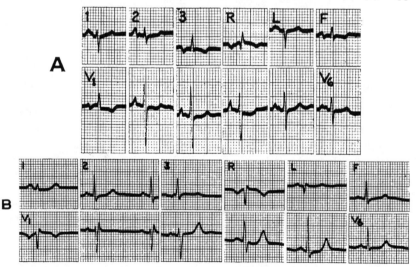

Figure 30.1. (A) From a patient with severe **mitral disease**, showing evidence of left atrial and right ventricular enlargement. Note P-mitrale with wide notched P waves, marked right axis deviation ($+150°$) with prominent R in V_1 and equiphasic complexes in left chest leads. (B) From a 31-year-old woman with pure mitral stenosis. Note P-mitrale, low voltage QRS in lead 1 (P and R about same height) and rSr' pattern of RVH in V_{1-2}. (Reproduced from H.J.L. Marriott: *Bedside Diagnosis of Heart Disease.* Tampa Tracings, 1967.)

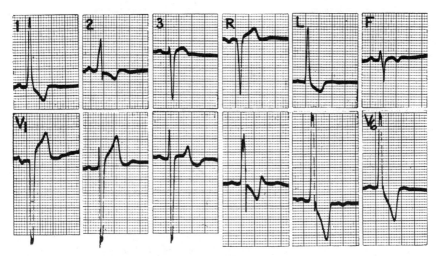

Figure 30.2. From a patient with severe **syphilitic aortic insufficiency**, showing classical pattern of marked left ventricular hypertrophy and strain.

tive of mitral stenosis. The combination of right axis deviation with atrial fibrillation (see fig. 14.8, p. 186) in a patient under 40 is practically diagnostic of mitral stenosis; but it is occasionally found in thyrotoxicosis and in atrial septal defect. When upright, the QRS in lead 1 is often strikingly low and may be rivalled by the height of the P wave (fig. 30.1*B*).

The effect of other valvular lesions can be predicted from the known mechanical effects on the heart. Aortic or mitral regurgitation predominantly affects the left ventricle and initially produces a pattern of left ventricular diastolic overloading; later they, like aortic stenosis, produce the typical pattern of left ventricular hypertrophy and strain (fig. 30.2). Signs of left atrial overload are common in mitral regurgitation.[39, 40]

In 50 subjects with pure severe aortic stenosis at autopsy, the electrocardiograms taken within two months of death showed left axis deviation in only 12; LBBB in 4 and left ventricular hypertrophy in 44 of the remaining 46, with left atrial overload in 15; ventricular extrasystoles and prolonged P-R intervals in 7 each, and atrial fibrillation in 5.[69]

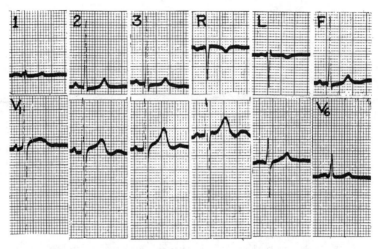

Figure 30.3. From a patient with combined **mitral** and **aortic disease**. Tracing suggests biventricular hypertrophy: the high QRS voltage in 2, 3, aVF and V_{1-4} indicates left ventricular enlargement, to which the inverted U waves in 2, 3 and aVF lend supporting evidence; whereas the prominent R waves in V_{1-2}, together with the axis, which approaches $+90°$, are evidence of right ventricular hypertrophy. The flat, wide and notched P waves in 1 and V_{5-6} indicate left atrial enlargement as well.

Combined mitral and aortic lesions often produce patterns suggesting enlargement of both ventricles (fig. 30.3). Tricuspid stenosis is suggested when right atrial enlargement is associated with a prolonged P-R interval without preponderance of either ventricle; lead V_1 not infrequently shows a low voltage rsr' complex. Pulmonic stenosis was dealt with in Chapter 29.

Acute Cor Pulmonale

The pattern of acute cor pulmonale develops within a few minutes of a massive pulmonary embolism[15, 37] or may develop in the course of other conditions producing acute cor pulmonale.[29] Its greatest importance diagnostically is that its pattern somewhat resembles that of inferior myocardial infarction, and as the clinical picture also may well be confused with myocardial infarction, the distinction may be a difficult one. In the typical case, a Q wave develops in lead 3 and the ST segment becomes elevated with shallow inversion of the T wave. Meanwhile lead 1 has developed somewhat "reciprocal" changes: an S wave appears (indicating a not surprising tendency to develop right axis deviation); the ST segment is depressed while the T remains upright. All these changes are compatible with inferior infarction. Lead 2, however, tends to follow lead 1 and shows no Q wave, but an S wave, a slightly depressed ST segment and an upright T wave; whereas in inferior infarction lead 2 tends to follow lead 3 with a Q, an elevated ST and inverted T.

In the precordial leads, elevated ST segments and inverted T waves are sometimes seen over the right ventricle, while S waves may become more

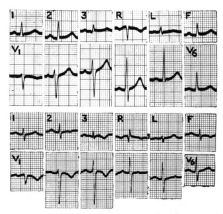

Figure 30.4. Acute cor pulmonale from pulmonary embolism. *Upper tracing*, taken 1 year before lower, within normal limits: note upright T waves in 2, 3 and aVF with normal shallowly inverted T in V_1; virtual absence of S waves in limb leads and in V_{5-6}. *Lower tracing* taken shortly after onset of symptoms: note simultaneous inversion of T waves in 2, 3 and aVF and V_{1-3}; development of significant S waves in all limb leads and in V_{5-6}.

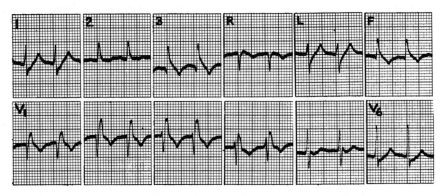

Figure 30.5 Acute cor pulmonale (from a patient with massive pulmonary embolism). Note simultaneous inversion of T waves in inferior (3, aVF) and anteroseptal (V_{1-4}) leads, and development of RBBB.

prominent over the left ventricle (indications of right ventricular dilation). The S wave in V_1 may become slurred and the R/S ratio decrease in two successive precordial leads.[47] Transient right bundle-branch block may appear. Many of these changes are to be seen in figures 30.4 and 30.5.

The differences between this pattern and that of inferior infarction may thus be summarized as follows:

1. Lead 2 tends to follow lead 1 rather than 3.
2. The changes may be fleeting and evolve and recede in a matter of hours or days rather than weeks or months.
3. ST-T deviations in limb leads are slight, whereas they may be major in inferior infarction; and in right precordial leads they resemble the anteroseptal rather than the inferior infarction pattern.

A helpful aphorism: If you find yourself diagnosing inferior infarction from the limb leads, and anteroseptal damage or infarction from the chest leads, think of pulmonary embolism.

Chronic Cor Pulmonale

In the presence of chronic lung disease, the four indications that the right ventricle is beginning to feel the strain are[19] rightward shift of the QRS axis by more than 30°; inverted, diphasic or flattened T waves in leads V_1-V_3; ST depression in leads 2, 3 and aVF; and right bundle-branch block.

Florid chronic cor pulmonale, most often seen in emphysema, is characterized by right axis deviation and sometimes the pattern of right ventricular hypertrophy and strain. Enlargement of the right atrium is manifested by the **P-pulmonale** pattern (fig. 30.6; also fig. 3.1, p. 15), consisting of a low P in lead 1 with tall, pointed P waves in 2, 3 and aVF. The single most characteristic electrocardiographic feature of diffuse lung disease is said to be a P-wave axis between +70° and +90°.[20] The P waves in right precordial leads are usually also pointed, or are diphasic with a distinct intrinsicoid deflection; and the P-terminal force is said to be often abnormally large.[66] Low voltage is not infrequently present, and T_1 is often of lower voltage than T_3.

Frequently, instead of the fullblown pattern of right ventricular hypertrophy and strain with tall R waves in V_1, an intermediate pattern is seen with deep S waves across the precordium from V_1 to V_6 (fig. 30.6). The Q-T interval in cor pulmonale, unlike that in other forms of heart failure, is not prolonged.[1] This may at times be a helpful differential point.

Salient Features of Chronic Cor Pulmonale

1. Right axis deviation
2. Right ventricular hypertrophy, or simply rS complexes across precordium
3. P-pulmonale pattern
4. Often low voltage QRS, and T_1 lower than T_3

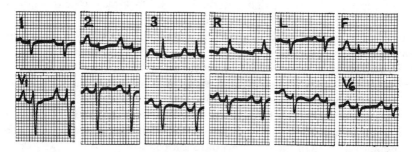

Figure 30.6. Chronic cor pulmonale. Note P-pulmonale pattern, marked right axis shift (+150°) and deep S waves across precordium with low R waves in left chest leads.

The five most typical findings in emphysema[28] have been grouped together into a "pentalogy": (1) prominent P waves in 2, 3 and aVF; (2) exaggerated T_P waves producing more than 1-mm depression of the ST segment in 2, 3 and aVF; (3) rightward shift of the QRS axis; (4) marked "clockwise rotation" in the precordial leads; and (5) low voltage of the QRS complexes, especially over the left precordium (V_{4-7}). The QRS axis in the frontal plane is surprisingly sometimes in the neighborhood of $-90°$, i.e. marked *left* axis deviation[24] (fig. 30.7). Thus the axis tends to be vertically down or up ($+90°$ or $-90°$) and is seldom inclined much to either side. This is because in emphysema the QRS is predominantly posterior (dominant S in V_{1-6}) and relatively little deviation up or down will swing the frontal axis through $180°$. Schaeffer[42] found that 15% of patients with chronic obstructive pulmonary disease had left axis deviation, while 9% had dominant S waves in the three standard limb leads ($S_1S_2S_3$ pattern). It is also not uncommon for Q waves simulating inferior infarction to develop in leads 2, 3 and aVF with simultaneous appearance of S waves in lead 1.

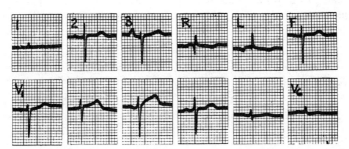

Figure 30.7. From a patient with chronic lung disease. Note marked *left* axis deviation ($-60°$).

Acute Pericarditis

In acute pericarditis, from whatever cause, the characteristic finding is an elevation of ST segments with upward *concavity* in many leads, including all three standard leads. The T wave remains upright at first, except in lead 3, where it may be inverted. Lead 3 is also often an exception in the shape of its ST segment, which may present an upward convexity. In most cases, the P-R segment is depressed in the limb leads and V_{2-6}[50]; in fact, P-R segment displacements were present in 28 (63%) of 44 consecutive cases.[8] These changes characterize the first or **ST stage** of acute pericarditis (fig. 30.8).

In a sizeable minority, the classical electrocardiographic constellation will not appear; out of the same 44 consecutive cases, 19 (43%) were atypical in some way. Eight had no ST elevation in the limb leads including three who showed no abnormalities of any kind; and in four, the *only* sign was P-R segment displacement.[8]

The second stage, or **T stage**, presents widespread T-wave inversion (fig. 30.9). At this stage the ST segments have returned to the isoelectric level. During both stages low voltage is a common finding. In the average case of acute pericarditis resolving in the course of 3 or 4 weeks, these stages each last for about 10 days to 2 weeks.

In mild cases, the ST stage may resolve with or without some T-wave flattening but without proceeding to the inverted T-wave stage.[52]

The changes in pericarditis are probably due to two causes:

1. Short circuiting of impulses by pericardial fluid or thickened pericardium causes the low voltage.
2. Spread of the inflammation to the immediately subjacent layer of myocardium (i.e., subepicardial myocarditis) accounts for the ST- and T-wave changes.

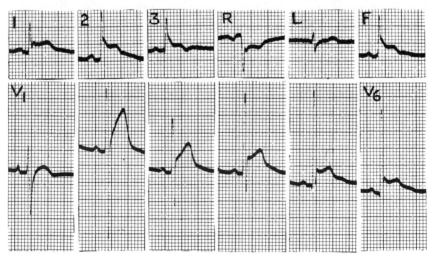

Figure 30.8.   Acute pericarditis (ST stage). Note widespread ST elevation, with upward concavity in 1, 2, aVF, and V_{4-6}.

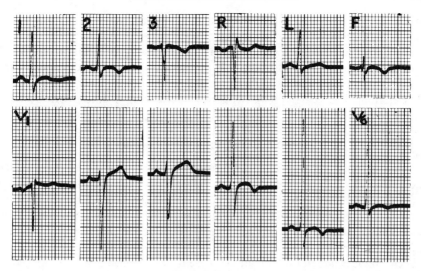

Figure 30.9. **Acute pericarditis** (T stage). Note T-wave inversions in 2, 3, aVF and V$_{4-6}$.

Table 30.1
Differentiation of Acute Pericarditis and Acute Infarction

	Acute Pericarditis	Acute Infarction
ST reciprocity (between 1 and 3)	Absent. Elevation in both 1 and 3	Present. Elevated in one, depressed in the other
ST shape	Concave upward	Convex upward
Q waves	Absent	Present
Period of evolution	Few weeks	Months

If the subepicardial involvement is localized rather than diffuse, ST-segment elevation may be restricted to a few leads with reciprocal depression elsewhere, closely imitating myocardial infarction; but, although R waves may be diminished, pathological Q waves usually do not develop.[9] Although Q waves are not expected in the absence of necrosis, in an occasional patient the subepicardial myocarditis may be severe enough to cause the temporary appearance of Q waves[60] thus enhancing the simulation of myocardial infarction.

The four most striking differences between acute pericarditis and acute infarction are tabulated in table 30.1.

Acute pericarditis must also be differentiated from the "early repolarization" syndrome. According to Spodick, pericarditis is more likely to present with ST elevation in both limb and precordial leads; an ST axis to the left of the T-wave axis, and ST *depression* in V$_1$ also favor the diagnosis of pericarditis. On the other hand, a vertical ST axis to the right of the T-wave axis and an isoelectric ST segment in V$_6$ favor early repolarization.[51] Exercise[2] and isoproterenol[34] may restore the elevated ST segments of early repolarization to the baseline— a palpably unlikely effect in acute pericarditis!

Another differentiating point, recently claimed to be of value, is the ST/T ratio in V_6.[65] Using the end of the P-R segment as baseline, if the apex of the T wave is more than 4 times higher than the onset of the S-T segment, it is said to be normal (i.e., "early repolarization"); if less than 4 times, pericarditis is suggested.

Chronic Constrictive Pericarditis

In the chronic constrictive or adhesive type of pericarditis, changes in the tracing are relatively fixed and nonprogressive. They are not unlike the findings in the T stage of the acute disease, two of the most characteristic features being low voltage and inverted T waves. Flat or inverted T waves are present in all cases, abnormal P waves in about three quarters of the cases and low voltage in over half.[12]

Such changes are found in all or at least many leads. It is of practical importance to note the degree of inversion of the T waves, for the depth of inversion is usually proportional to the degree of pericardial adherence to the myocardium[17]; deep T waves are associated with intimate adherence, which makes surgical stripping difficult or impossible, whereas flat or barely inverted T waves usually indicate a relatively easy surgical undertaking.

Atrial fibrillation is persistently present in over a third of the cases.[12]

One other characteristic which deserves passing mention is that the axis of the heart does not alter, as it does normally when the patient turns from one side to the other; for being bound by adhesions it is not free to swing from side to side with change in position. This electrocardiographic feature corresponds with the clinical finding of a fixed apex beat.

Pericardial Effusion

A triad that is virtually diagnostic of pericardial effusion is: low voltage, S-T segment elevation and electrical alternans (fig. 30.10). Total alternans, i.e., alternation of P waves as well as QRS, is almost pathognomonic of effusion due to malignancy.[4, 36]

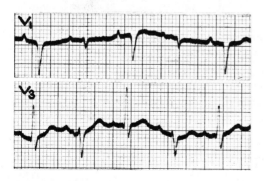

Figure 30.10. Malignant *pericardial effusion*. Note "total alternans" (i.e., alternation of P as well as QRS) in presence of regular sinus tachycardia, rate 118.

Salient Features of Chronic Pericarditis

1. Low voltage
2. Flat or inverted T waves
3. Fixed axis
4. Possible P-mitrale pattern or atrial fibrillation

Myxedema

The diagnosis of myxedema should certainly never depend upon electrocardiographic changes though it may be suspected when flattening or shallow inversion of many T waves is seen without comparable ST displacement (fig. 30.11). Its cardinal characteristics are three:

1. Low to inverted T waves in all or many leads
2. Low voltage
3. Sinus bradycardia (uncommon)

The QT interval is also always prolonged but, because of the low/flat T waves, its measurement is often difficult (58).

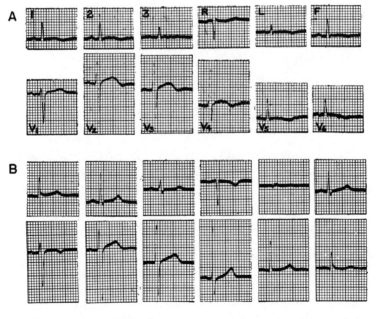

Figure 30.11. Myxedema. Tracing *A* was taken before treatment; note shallow inversion of T waves in many leads. *B* was taken after 10 weeks of treatment with thyroid extract; the previously inverted T waves are now upright.

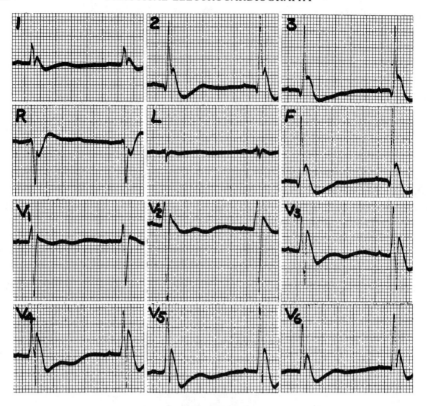

Figure 30.12. **Hypothermia.** Note marked elevation of the "J deflection" maximal in midprecordial leads.

Hypothermia

When the body temperature falls below 30°C, characteristic changes develop in the electrocardiogram (fig. 30.12). All intervals—R-R, P-R, QRS and Q-T—may lengthen, and elevated "J deflections" appear especially in left chest leads. Atrial fibrillation may develop at about 29°C.[16]

Hypokalemia

The electrocardiogram may be of great value in the diagnosis of this not uncommon and dangerous situation. A significant potassium deficit may be encountered in many metabolic disorders, including cirrhosis of the liver, diabetic coma after vigorous treatment, hypochloremic alkalosis from whatever cause (vomiting, diuresis, etc.) and in situations where excessive amounts of corticosteroids are being secreted (Cushing's syndrome, primary aldosteronism) or administered. The typical signs of potassium lack in the tracing may appear when the serum potassium is within normal limits, and conversely the tracing may be normal and show no evidence of potassium deficiency when hypokalemia is chemically proven. As the heart is most dangerously affected by too much or too little potassium, it may well be that the electrocardiogram is the most sensitive indicator of the immediate threat to life. Furthermore, an electrocardiogram can sometimes be taken when facilities for serum determinations are not available. It is therefore well worth while to know the electrocardiographic changes that a potassium deficit can initiate (figs. 30.13 and 30.14).

As the effect of potassium depletion progresses, there is gradual depression of the ST segment, lowering of the T wave and increase in the height of the U wave. As the potassium concentrations fluctuate, the T and U waves seesaw— as the T wave decreases in height, the U wave increases, and vice versa. When T and U are approximately equal, a "camelhump" effect (fig. 30.14*A*) is produced; when the U wave becomes taller than the T wave (figs. 30.13 and 30.14*B*), the plasma potassium is usually under 2.7 mEq per liter.[59]

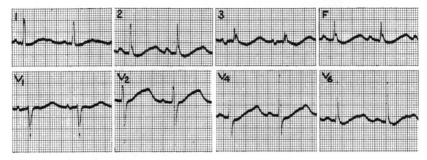

Figure 30.13. Hypokalemia. Note characteristic pattern with ST depression and extremely prominent U waves.

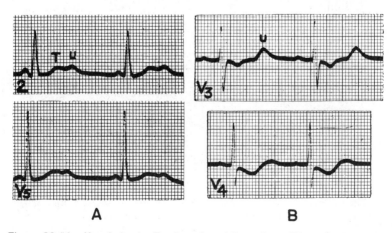

Figure 30.14. Hypokalemia. Tracings *A* and *B* are from different patients. *A* shows early changes of hypokalemia with prominent U wave merging to form continuous undulating wave with T wave. *B* shows changes of advanced hypokalemia (1.8 mEq per liter) in a patient with cirrhosis; note ST-T depression with very prominent U waves in V_3.

In hypokalemia the P wave becomes larger and wider and the P-R interval prolongs somewhat. In advanced stages, the QRS complex widens uniformly and the ST segment is markedly depressed with T-wave inversion. The fully developed pattern is seen in figure 30.14*B*. These changes rapidly revert to normal with administration of potassium salts.

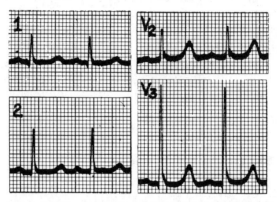

Figure 30.15. Hypocalcemia. Note the prolonged Q-T interval in an otherwise normal tracing. Q-T = 0.40 sec (upper limit of normal for this rate and sex is 0.35 sec). Patient's serum calcium was 7.0 mg per 100 ml, other electrolytes being normal.

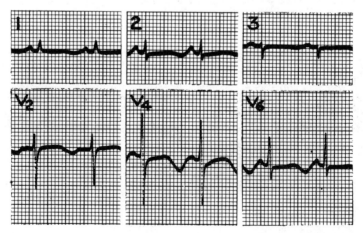

Figure 30.16. Hypocalcemia. Note prolonged ST and QT with late inversion of T waves. From a patient with serum calcium of 4.2 mg per 100 ml.

Hypocalcemia

Calcium deficiency produces a prolonged Q-T interval. This lengthening is effected through elongation of the ST segment, the T wave remaining relatively normal (fig. 30.15); terminal T-wave inversion, however, occurs in some leads in about a third of the cases (fig. 30.16).

Hyperkalemia

The earliest sign of potassium intoxication is the appearance of tall, thin T waves (fig. 30.17). Later the P-R interval becomes prolonged, the ST segment becomes depressed and the QRS interval lengthens. Finally the P waves

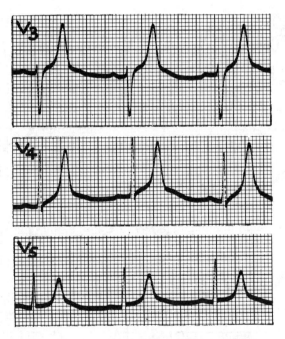

Figure 30.17. Hyperkalemia. Note tall, pointed, "pinchbottomed" T waves. (K = 6.1 mEq per liter.)

disappear and the QRS widens further (fig. 30.18) until ventricular fibrillation closes the picture. Disappearance of the P waves does not necessarily indicate a cessation of S-A node activity; despite atrial paralysis, sinus impulses may proceed to the A-V junction via specialized "internodal" conducting tracts without writing P waves, and thence onward to control the ventricles (**sinoventricular rhythm**).[46]

Hypercalcemia

The most striking change in the electrocardiogram is a shortening of the Q-T interval, but particularly of the distance from the beginning of the QRS to the *apex* of the T wave (Q-aT interval). This change gives the proximal limb of the T wave an abrupt slope to its peak that is most characteristic (fig. 30.19*A*). In some cases the P-R interval is prolonged.

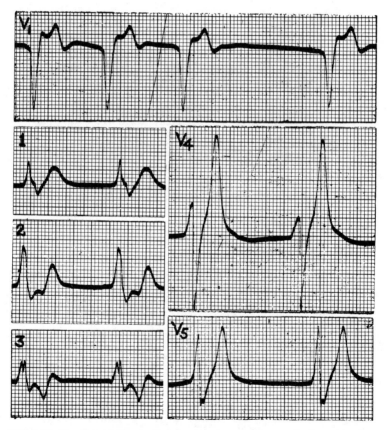

Figure 30.18.   Hyperkalemia. This tracing shows evidence of advanced potassium intoxication: tall peaked T waves, absent P waves, widened QRS complexes and irregular rhythm. From a patient with serum potassium level of 8.1 mEq per liter.

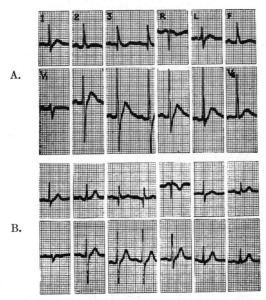

Figure 30.19. From a patient with **hyperparathyroidism.** (*A*) Before parathyroidectomy (serum calcium 15 mg.). Note virtual absence of ST segment, early peak of T wave and relatively gradual downslope of descending limb of T wave. (*B*) After parathyroidectomy (serum calcium 10.7 mg). Note normal contour of ST-T pattern. (Reproduced with permission from G. H. Beck and H. J. L. Marriott: The electrocardiogram in hyperparathyroidism. *American Journal of Cardiology*, 1959: **3,** 411.)

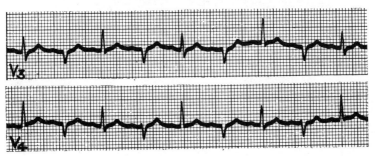

Figure 30.20. **Electrical alternans.** Note alternating direction of QRS complexes.

Electrical Alternans

This abnormality is readily recognized by the alternating amplitude of QRS complexes in any or all leads (fig. 30.20). It is much less common than, but has the same prognostic significance as, its mechanical counterpart, *pulsus alternans.* Electrical alternans is an important part of the pattern of pericardial effusion[31] (see p. 464).

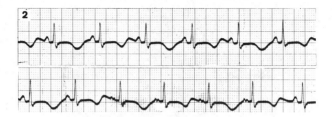

Figure 30.21. **Alternation of T-U** complex. Strips are continuous. Note shifting atrial pacemaker in *bottom strip.*

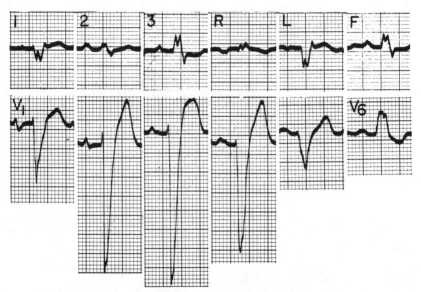

Figure 30.22. **Primary cardiomyopathy.** Note the atypical pattern of intraventricular block with notching and slurring of the QRS in limb leads. P waves are also wide and notched with evidence of left atrial enlargement.

Alternation may affect only the T wave,[27] only the U wave,[35] or both simultaneously (fig. 30.21); such alternation has been described in electrolyte disturbances and in terminal states.

Cardiomyopathy

Any electrocardiographic abnormality may accompany a cardiomyopathy,[30] and none is diagnostic, with the possible exception of the progressive pattern—from septal hypertrophy (see fig. 29.9) to generalized LVH—seen in the prolonged follow-up of hypertrophic cardiomyopathy.[6] There are, however, a few tendencies worth noting: a BBB pattern tends to be atypical and splintered (fig. 30.22); the association of the preexcitation syndrome with familial cardio-

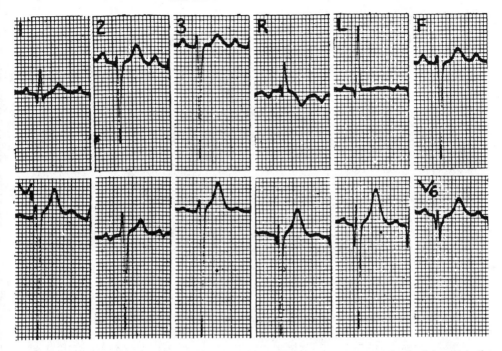

Figure 30.23. Hypertrophic cardiomyopathy. From a 29-year-old, asymptomatic physician. Note the marked left axis deviation ($-75°$) and prominent but narrow Q waves V$_{4-6}$.

myopathy, obstructive or nonobstructive; and the tendency to *right* ventricular hypertrophy and *right* BBB in endomyocardial fibrosis. The unusual combination of *left* bundle-branch block with *right* axis deviation, as in figure 30.22, may be uniquely characteristic of a primary cardiomyopathy.[68]

Hypertrophic cardiomyopathy (HCM) [*aliases*: muscular subaortic stenosis; idiopathic hypertrophic subaortic stenosis (IHSS); asymmetric septal hypertrophy (ASH); hypertrophic obstructive cardiomyopathy (HOCM)] has been given so many names that by 1981 a list containing no less than 46 terms could be compiled.[32] HCM can produce a variety of 12-lead patterns[3, 49]: more than 20% may be entirely normal[45]; many show the classical picture of left ventricular hypertrophy; others present with marked left axis deviation (fig. 30.23), presumably due to left anterior hemiblock; infants with HCM commonly present with a pattern of *right* ventricular hypertrophy.[67] The combination of *left* ventricular with right *atrial* hypertrophy is suspicious.[22] But perhaps the most suggestive clue of all is the finding of obviously pathological Q waves that just do not look like the Q waves of infarction—this broad hint is contained in both figure 30.23 and 29.9. Such "pseudoinfarction" Q waves are to be found in 20 to 25%.[33, 45] Subjects with HCM have an increased incidence of both supraventricular and ventricular arrhythmias.[64]

In cardiac amyloidosis[18] the diagnosis may be suspected from the combination of low voltage, marked left axis deviation and QS or tiny rS complexes from V_1 to V_3 or V_4 (fig. 30.24).

Glycogen storage disease tends to produce oversized QRS complexes in all leads in company with a short P-R interval.[41]

Intracranial Hemorrhage

Intracerebral or subarachnoid hemorrhage can produce dramatic changes in the electrocardiogram.[10, 25, 56] Precordial T waves become wide and prominent, usually inverted but sometimes upright, and are continuous with large U waves, giving the effect of a long drawn out T-U complex (fig. 30.25). Bradycardia frequently accompanies these changes.

Mysteriously, the development of a cerebrovascular accident has been reported to abruptly replace the deeply negative T waves of subendocardial infarction with normally upright T waves.[23]

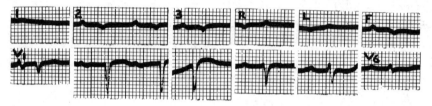

Figure 30.24. Primary amyloidosis. Note low voltage, marked left axis deviation (of what's left of the QRS), QS complexes V_{1-3}, abnormal P waves, and prolonged P-R. (Reproduced with permission from H. J. L. Marriott: Correlations of electrocardiographic and pathologic changes. In *Pathology of the Heart and Blood Vessels*, Charles C Thomas, Springfield, Ill., 1968.) Ed. 3, Chap. XX, edited by S. E. Gould.

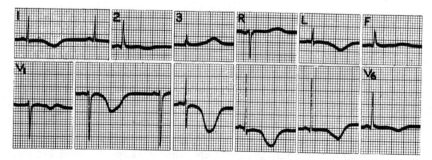

Figure 30.25. Intracerebral hemorrhage. Note bradycardia, large inverted precordial T and U waves.

Low Voltage with Inverted T Waves

It is opportune to review the several conditions which can cause low voltage QRS with inverted T waves in all or most leads:

1. Any diffuse myocardial involvement
   a. Diffuse ischemic disease
   b. Heart failure treated with digitalis
   c. Myxedema
   d. Cardiomyopathy
2. Pericarditis
   a. Acute ("T stage")
   b. Chronic constrictive

ST-T Depression

When ST segments are depressed and T waves flat to inverted in many leads, one should think of:

1. Digitalis effect
2. Diffuse ischemic disease
3. Left ventricular strain
4. Combined anterior and inferior infarction (antero-inferior infarction)
5. Subendocardial infarction
6. Hypokalemia

As well as the above causes of ST-segment and T-wave changes, the many factors that can influence these labile members of the electrocardiogram (pp. 413–417) should be constantly borne in mind.

REFERENCES

1. Alexander, J. K., et al.: The Q-T interval in chronic cor pulmonale. Circulation 1951: **3**, 733.
2. Alimurung, B.: The influence of early repolarization variant on the exercise electrocardiogram; a correlation with coronary arteriograms. Am. Heart J. 1980: **99**, 739.
3. Bahl, O. P., and Massie, E.: Electrocardiographic and vectorcardiographic patterns in cardiomyopathy. Cardiovasc. Clin. 1972: **4**,(1), 95.
4. Bashour, F. A., and Cochran, P. W.: The association of electrical alternans with pericardial effusion. Dis. Chest 1963: **44**, 146.
5. Bellet, S.: The electrocardiogram in electrolyte imbalance. Arch. Intern. Med. 1955: **96**, 618.
6. Braudo, M., et al.: A distinctive electrocardiogram in muscular subaortic stenosis due to septal hypertrophy. Am. J. Cardiol. 1964: **14**, 599.
7. Bronsky, D., et al.: Calcium and the electrocardiogram. I. The electrocardiographic manifestations of hypoparathyroidism. Am. J. Cardiol. 1961: **7**, 823. II. The electrocardiographic manifestations of hyperparathyroidism and of marked hypercalcemia from various other etiologies. Ibid.: **7**, 833.
8. Bruce, M. A., and Spodick, D. H.: Atypical electrocardiogram in acute pericarditis; characteristics and prevalence. J. Electrocardiol. 1980: **13**, 61.
9. Bullington, R. H., and Bullington, J. D.: "Pseudo-infarction" phenomenon of acute pericarditis. J.A.M.A. 1959: **171**, 2205.
10. Burch, G. E., et al.: A new electrocardiographic pattern observed in cerebrovascular accidents. Circulation 1954: **9**, 719.
11. Charles, M. A., et al.: Atrial injury current in pericarditis. Arch. Intern. Med. 1973: **131**, 657.

12. Dalton, J. C., Pearson, R. J., and White, P. D.: Constrictive pericarditis: a review and long term follow-up of 78 cases. Ann. Intern. Med. 1956: **45**, 445.
13. Demerdash, H., and Goodwin, J. F.: The cardiogram of mitral restenosis. Br. Heart J. 1963: **25**, 474.
14. Dreyfus, L. S., and Pick, A.: A clinical correlation study of the electrocardiogram in electrolyte imbalance. Circulation 1956: **14**, 815.
15. Eliaser, M., and Giansiracusa, F.: The electrocardiographic diagnosis of acute cor pulmonale. Am. Heart J. 1952: **43**, 533.
16. Emslie-Smith, D., et al.: The significance of changes in the electrocardiogram in hypothermia. Br. Heart J. 1959: **21**, 343.
17. Evans, W., and Jackson, F.: Constrictive pericarditis. Br. Heart J. 1952: **14**, 53.
18. Farrokh, A. et al.: Amyloid heart disease. Am. J. Cardiol. 1964: **13**, 750.
19. Ferrer, M. I.: Clinical and electrocardiographic correlations in pulmonary heart disease (cor pulmonale). Cardiovasc. Clin. 1977: **8**(3), 215.
20. Fowler, N. O., et al.: The electrocardiogram in cor pulmonale with and without emphysema. Am. J. Cardiol. 1965: **16**, 500.
21. Fraser, H. R. L., and Turner, R.: Electrocardiography in mitral valvular disease. Br. Heart J. 1955: **17**, 459.
22. Goodwin, J. F., et al.: Obstructive cardiomyopathy simulating aortic stenosis. Br. Heart J. 1960: **22**, 403.
23. Gould, L., et al.: Electrocardiographic normalization after cerebral vascular accident. J. Electrocardiol. 1981: **14**, 191.
24. Grant, R. P.: Left axis deviation. An electrocardiographic-pathologic correlation study. Circulation 1956: **14**, 233.
25. Hersch, C.: Electrocardiographic changes in subarachnoid haemorrhage, meningitis, and intracranial space-occupying lesions. Br. Heart J. 1964: **26**, 785.
26. Hull, E.: The electrocardiogram in pericarditis. Am. J. Cardiol. 1961: **7**, 21.
27. Kimura, E., and Yoshida, K.: A case showing electrical alternans of the T wave without change in the QRS complex. Am. Heart J. 1963: **65**, 391.
28. Littman, D.: The electrocardiographic findings in pulmonary emphysema. Am. J. Cardiol. 1960: **5**, 339.
29. Mack, I., Harris, R., and Katz, L. N.: Acute cor pulmonale in the absence of pulmonary embolism. Am. Heart J. 1950: **39**, 664.
30. Marriott, H. J. L.: Electrocardiographic abnormalities, conduction disorders and arrhythmias in primary myocardial disease. Prog. Cardiovasc. Dis. 1964: **7**, 99.
31. McGregor, M., and Baskind, E.: Electrical alternans in pericardial effusion. Circulation 1955: **11**, 837.
32. McKenna, W. J., and Goodwin, J. F.: The natural history of hypertrophic cardiomyopathy. Curr. Probl. Cardiol. 1981: **6**(4), 1.
33. McMartin, D. E., and Flowers, N. C.: Clinical-electrocardiographic correlations in diseases of the myocardium. Cardiovasc. Clin. 1977: **8**(3), 191.
34. Morace, G.: Effect of isoproterenol on the "early repolarization" syndrome. Am. Heart J. 1979: **97**, 343.
35. Mullican, W. S., and Fisch, C.: Postextrasystolic alternation of the U wave due to hypokalemia. Am. Heart J. 1964: **68**, 383.
36. Nizet, P. M., and Marriott, H. J. L.: The electrocardiogram and pericardial effusion. J.A.M.A. 1966: **198**, 169.
37. Phillips, E., and Levine, H. D.: A critical evaluation of extremity and precordial electrocardiography in acute cor pulmonale. Am. Heart J. 1950: **39**, 205.
38. Phillips, R. W.: The electrocardiogram in cor pulmonale secondary to pulmonary emphysema: a study of 18 cases proved by autopsy. Am. Heart J. 1958: **56**, 352.
39. Rios, J. C., and Goo, W.: Electrocardiographic correlates of rheumatic valvular disease. Cardiovasc. Clin. 1973: **5**(2), 247.
40. Rios, J. C., and Leet, C.: Electrocardiographic assessment of valvular heart disease. Cardiovasc. Clin. 1977: **8**(3), 161.
41. Ruttenberg, H. D., et al.: Glycogen-storage disease of the heart. Am. Heart J. 1964: **67**, 469.
42. Schaeffer, J., and Pryor, R.: Pseudo left axis deviation and the $S_1S_2S_3$ syndrome in chronic airway obstruction. Chest 1977: **71**, 453.

43. Scott, R. C.: The electrocardiogram in pulmonary emphysema and chronic cor pulmonale. Am. Heart J. 1961: **61**, 843.
44. Selvester, R. H., and Rubin, H. B.: New criteria for the electrocardiographic diagnosis of emphysema and cor pulmonale. Am. Heart J. 1965: **69**, 437.
45. Shah, P. M.: Clinical-electrocardiographic correlations: Aortic valve disease and hypertrophic subaortic stenosis. Cardiovasc. Clin. 1977: **8**(3), 151.
46. Sherf, L., and James, T. N.: A new electrocardiographic concept: synchronized sinoventricular conduction. Dis. Chest 1969: **55**, 127.
47. Smith, McK., and Ray, C. T.: Electrocardiographic signs of early right ventricular enlargement in acute pulmonary embolism. Chest 1970: **58**, 205.
48. Spodick, D. H.: Electrocardiographic studies in pulmonary disease. I. Electrocardiographic abnormalities in diffuse lung disease. Circulation 1959: **20**, 1067.
49. Spodick, D. H.: Hypertrophic obstructive cardiomyopathy of the left ventricle (idiopathic hypertrophic subaortic stenosis. Cardiovasc. Clin. 1972: **4**(1), 133.
50. Spodick, D. H.: Electrocardiogram in acute pericarditis. Distributions of morphologic and axial changes by stages. Am. J. Cardiol. 1974: **33**, 470.
51. Spodick, D. H.: Differential characteristics of the electrocardiogram in early repolarization and acute pericarditis. N. Engl. J. Med. 1976: **295**, 523.
52. Spodick, D. H.: Pathogenesis and clinical correlations of the electrocardiographic abnormalities of pericardial disease. Cardiovasc. Clin. 1977: **8**(3), 201.
53. Surawicz, B., and Lepeschkin, E.: The electrocardiographic pattern of hypopotassemia with and without hypocalcemia. Circulation 1963: **8**, 801.
54. Surawicz, B., et al.: Quantitative analysis of the electrocardiographic pattern of hypopotassemia. Circulation 1957: **16**, 750.
55. Surawicz, B.: Electrolytes and the electrocardiogram. Am. J. Cardiol. 1963: **12**, 656.
56. Surawicz, B.: Electrocardiographic pattern of cerebrovascular accident. J.A.M.A. 1966: **197**, 913.
57. Surawicz, B., and Lasseter, K. C.: Electrocardiogram in pericarditis. Am. J. Cardiol. 1970: **26**, 471.
58. Surawicz, B., and Mangiardi, M. L.: Electrocardiogram in endocrine and metabolic disorders. Cardiovasc. Clin. 1977: **8**(3), 243.
59. Surawicz, B.: The interrelationship of electrolyte abnormalities and arrhythmias, p. 83. In *Cardiac Arrhythmias: Their Mechanisms, Diagnosis and Management*, edited by W. J. Mandel. J. B. Lippincott, Philadelphia, 1980.
60. Tiefenbrunn, A. J., and Roberts, R.: Elevation of plasma MB creatine kinase and the development of new Q waves in association with pericarditis. Chest 1980: **77**, 438.
61. Wasserburger, R. H., et al.: The T-a wave of the adult electrocardiogram: an expression of pulmonary emphysema. Am. Heart J. 1957: **54**, 875.
62. Wasserburger, R. H., et al.: The electrocardiographic pentalogy of pulmonary emphysema. Circulation 1959: **20**, 831.
63. Weaver, W. F., and Burchell, H. B.: Serum potassium and the electrocardiogram in hypokalemia. Circulation 1960: **21**, 505.
64. Bjarnson, I.: Cardiac arrhythmias in hypertrophic cardiomyopathy. Br. Heart J. 1982: **48**, 198.
65. Ginzton, L. E., and Laks, M.M.: The differential diagnosis of acute pericarditis from the normal variant; new electrocardiographic criteria. Circulation 1982: 65, 1004.
66. Lynch, P., and Webb-Peploe, M.M.: The P terminal vector in lead V_1 of the electrocardiogram in cor pulmonale. J. Electrocardiol. 1982: **15**, 205.
67. Maron, B. J., et al.: Hypertrophic cardiomyopathy in infants: clinical features and natural history. Circulation 1982: **65**, 7.
68. Nikolic, G.: Personal communication, 1982.
69. Siegel, R. J., and Roberts, W. C.: Electrocardiographic observations in severe aortic valve stenosis. Am. Heart J. 1982: **103**, 210.

Review Tracings

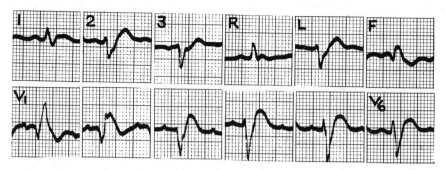

Review Tracing 30.1

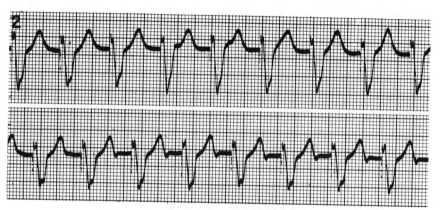

Review Tracing 30.2

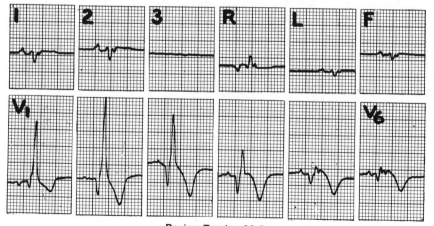

Review Tracing 30.3

For interpretation, see pages 485–486

Review Tracing

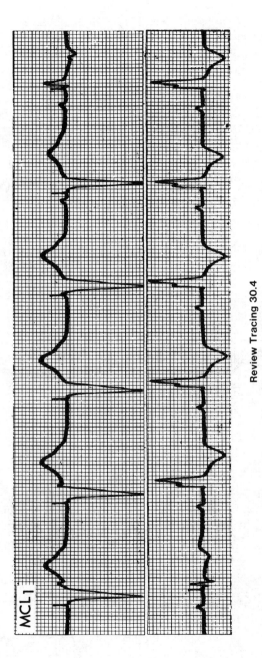

Review Tracing 30.4

For interpretation, see page 486

Review Tracing

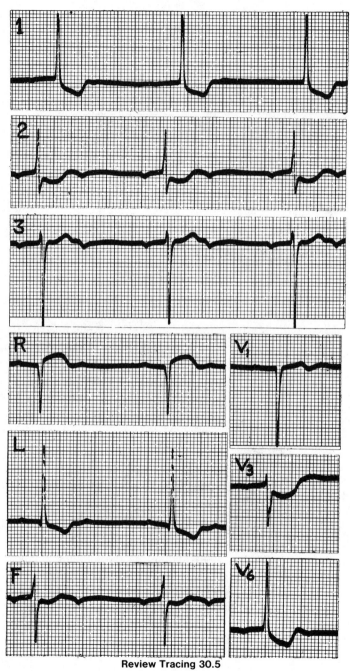

Review Tracing 30.5
For interpretation, see page 486

Review Tracing

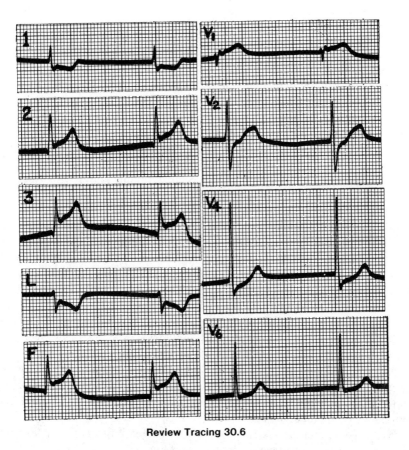

Review Tracing 30.6

For interpretation, see page 486

Review Tracings:
Interpretations

11.1, page 148: Left ventricular hypertrophy and strain. (From a 34-year-old man with coarctation of the aorta.)

11.2, page 148: (1) Right bundle-branch block. (2) The third beat in each lead is a ventricular premature beat. (3) Thanks to the respite of the long compensatory pause, the beat following the extrasystole is conducted with less block—incomplete RBBB—a manifestation of "critical rate."

12.1, page 167: The numbered beats are: sinus with RBBB (1), right ventricular extrasystole (2), and left ventricular extrasystole (3).

12.2, page 167: Right ventricular hypertrophy and strain with right atrial hypertrophy as well. From a patient with pulmonic stenosis and tricuspid insufficiency resulting from the malignant carcinoid syndrome.

13.1, page 179: Supraventricular tachycardia, probably "slow-fast" reciprocating tachycardia in the A-V junction. Sinus rhythm restored in the bottom strip.

13.2, page 180: (1) P-congenitale (right atrial hypertrophy). (2) Right ventricular hypertrophy and strain. Axis −160°. From a patient with pulmonic stenosis.

14.1, page 188: (1) Atrial flutter with varying A-V block (atrial rate about 330, ventricular about 102). (2) Right bundle-branch block, incomplete.

14.2, page 189: (1) Atrial fibrillation; at times (beginning of lead 2, end of lead aVF) atrial activity is regular enough to be called flutter; so rhythm might be called flutter-fibrillation. (2) Two ectopic ventricular beats. (3) Left ventricular hypertrophy and strain. From a patient with rheumatic heart disease with mitral and aortic involvement.

15.1, page 210: (1) Left ventricular hypertrophy and strain. (2) Intra-atrial block (presumable evidence of left atrial enlargement). (3) The left axis deviation (−40°) indicates the likelihood of left ventricular disease besides hypertrophy and incomplete left anterior hemiblock is probable.

15.2, page 210: LBBB with slight left axis deviation (−25°).

16.1, page 243: (1) Atrial fibrillation. (2) Right bundle-branch block with (3) primary T-wave changes (to which digitalis might be contributing). (4) Marked left axis deviation (close to −90°) presumably due to left anterior hemiblock.

16.2, page 243: (1) Numerous atrial premature beats with (2) prolonged P-R intervals and (3) varying patterns of RBBB and LBBB aberration.

17.1, page 255: (1) Atrial fibrillation with rapid ventricular response. (2) Incomplete RBBB aberration of two beats.

17.2, page 255: (1) Abnormally notched P waves (intra-atrial block). (2) Fourth beat in top strip is an atrial extrasystole with minor aberration. (3) Ventricular extrasystoles with retrograde conduction to atria.

18.1, page 275: (1) Fourth beat is an atrial extrasystole; this slightly lengthens the next cycle, enough to precipitate (2) ventricular bigeminy ("rule of bigeminy"). (3) Nonspecific ST-T changes.

18.2, page 275: Ventricular tachycardia: Note marked left axis deviation (−80°) and concordant negativity in chest leads.

18.3, page 276: (1) Atrial fibrillation, with slow to moderate ventricular response. (2) Left bundle-branch block.

19.1, page 288: After one sinus beat, these three simultaneous leads illustrate an atrial premature beat, conducted with a prolonged P-R interval, initiating reentry in the A-V junction which lasts for only two cycles. Note the deeply inverted, retrograde P waves in leads 2 and 3.

19.2, page 288: (1) Sinus tachycardia. (2) Wolff-Parkinson-White syndrome ("type A").

19.3, page 288: (1) Increased "P-terminal force" indicating left atrial enlargement. (2) Three left ventricular extrasystoles, in bigeminal rhythm, the second produces a fusion beat.

20.1, page 299: (1) Intra-atrial block (P-mitrale). (2) Shifting atrial pacemaker. (3) Ventricular extrasystoles with retrograde conduction to atria. (4) Junctional escape beats terminate the pauses following the extrasystoles. From a patient with severe mitral stenosis.

20.2, page 300: Right bundle-branch block

20.3, page 300: Accelerated junctional (or ectopic atrial) rhythm (rate 72/min).

21.1, page 313: (1) Sinus bradycardia, resulting in (2) A-V junctional escape and A-V dissociation. The third beat in bottom strip is a capture beat.

21.2, page 313: (1) Following the third sinus beat, there is a nonconducted atrial premature beat which, in turn, is followed by a junctional escape beat. (2) Digitalis effect.

21.3, page 314: Wolff-Parkinson-White syndrome ("type B").

22.1, page 320: (1) Sinus arrhythmia. (2) Accelerated idiojunctional rhythm at rate 90/min resulting in intermittent isorhythmic A-V dissociation. Note the slightly changed QRS morphology in the junctional beats (taller R and shallower S wave)—type B aberration.

22.2, page 321: Tachycardia-bradycardia syndrome consisting of (1) atrial fibrillation and (2) sinus arrest with junctional escape. The escape rhythm gradually accelerates until, in the bottom strip, the rhythm is "accelerated idiojunctional."

22.3, page 321: Wolff-Parkinson-White syndrome; note the unusual rSR′ imitation of RBBB in lead V_1.

23.1, page 338: (1) Type I A-V block with a 4:3 Wenckebach period. (2) Two junctional escape beats. (From an asymptomatic 6-year-old girl.)

23.2, page 339: (1) 3:2 A-V Wenckebach periods and 2:1 A-V block, presumably type I. (2) Right bundle-branch block. (*Note:* The "A-V" block *could* be due to simultaneous LBBB, i.e., type II.)

23.3, page 339: (1) Atrial tachycardia with varying A-V block, mostly 2:1. (2) One left ventricular extrasystole. (The block is presumably type I—prolonged P-R intervals and absence of BBB.)

23.4, page 339: (1) Abnormal non-specific ST-T pattern. (2) The third beat in each lead is a ventricular premature beat. (3) Following the premature beats retrograde conduction to the atria occurs (retrograde P waves deforming the ST segments). (4) Post-extrasystolic T-wave changes (increase in depth of T-wave inversion) are noted in the cycles following the premature beats. From a patient with severe hypertension.

24.1, page 351: (1) Atrial tachycardia, rate 224/min. (2) Wenckebach periods (5:4, 4:3, 3:2, etc.). (3) Abnormal axis deviation, probably left. The marked apparent variation in QRS morphology is entirely due to the varying relationship to large, positive P waves.

24.2, page 352: Shifting (wandering) pacemaker. Third P wave in each strip is an atrial fusion beat.

24.3, page 352: (1) Atrial fibrillation. (2) Complete A-V block with idioventricular rhythm at rate 38/min. (3) Multiform ventricular premature beats. This combination suggests digitalis intoxication.

24.4, page 352: (1) P-pulmonale (right atrial hypertrophy). (2) Low voltage of QRS with dominant S waves V_{3-6}. From a patient with severe emphysema.

25.1, page 371: (1) Partially ineffective right ventricular pacemaker. (2) Two right ventricular escape beats.

25.2, page 371: (1) Sinus tachycardia controlling atria. (2) Complete A-V block with idioventricular rhythm at rate 40/min. Note the shallowly inverted T_P waves following most of the P waves.

25.3, page 372: Type II A-V block. The P-R interval of the conducted beats is constant and normal (0.15 sec) and there is intraventricular block (QRS interval = 0.11 sec).

25.4, page 372: (1) Intra-atrial block. (2) First degree A-V block (P-R interval 0.22 to 0.24 sec). (3) Shifting atrial pacemaker. (4) Numerous atrial premature beats, in V_1 producing bigeminy. The third atrial premature beat in V_1 shows (5) aberrant ventricular conduction of RBBB type. (6) Left ventricular hypertrophy and strain (judging by the high voltage of the QRS and ST-T pattern).

26.1, page 399: Acute extensive anterior myocardial infarction.

26.2, page 399: (1) First degree A-V block (P-R = about 0.34 sec). (2) Acute inferior infarction.

26.3, page 399: (1) Sinus tachycardia, rate 102. (2) Nonconducted atrial premature beat every third beat. (3) Slight prolongation of the second P-R interval in each pair of sinus beats (indicates potential Wenckebach periodicity).

26.4, page 400: Atypical intermittent left intraventricular block, probably rate-related. Precordial leads show classical LBBB, but the block is not typical since there is a prominent Q wave in lead 1, which strongly suggests anteroseptal infarction. In aVR the block changes to an unblocked pattern that persists through aVL and aVF.

27.1, page 423: (1) A-V junctional rhythm with retrograde conduction. (2) Imcomplete RBBB. (3) Acute inferior myocardial infarction.

27.2, page 423: (1) Sick sinus, permitting (2) junctional escape with slow junctional rhythm at rate 31/min with retrograde conduction. (Note that the escaping junctional rhythm is not the *primary* diagnosis—the primary disturbance is in the sinus node and this allows the rescuing A-V pacemaker to take over.)

27.3, page 424: Early acute lateral infarction (early ST elevation in leads 1, aVL and V6 with reciprocal changes in 3, aVF and V_{1-3}).

27.4, page 424: (1) Right bundle-branch block. (2) Anteroseptal infarction. (3) Marked left axis deviation, presumably due to anterior hemiblock.

28.1, page 440: (1) Right bundle-branch block (with marked right axis deviation of about +120°, presumably due to left posterior hemiblock). (2) First degree A-V block. (3) Digitalis effect.

28.2, page 440: Type I A-V block with a 42:41 Wenckebach period. The dropped beats occur after the third beat at the beginning of the *top strip* and before the last beat in the *bottom strip.*

28.3, page 441: (1) Atrial fibrillation. (2) High grade A-V block; ventricular rhythm is completely regular (except for two beats referred to under (3) below) at rate 32—idionodal rhythm. (3) The fourth beat in V_3 and the third in V_5 have a somewhat different form from the dominant beats in their respective leads, have a shorter QRS interval and are slightly earlier than the next expected idioventricular beat; these then are presumably conducted supraventricular beats arising in the fibrillating atria. (4) Acute inferior infarction.

28.4, page 441: (1) Right bundle-branch block. (2) Inferior myocardial infarction.

29.1, page 454: Low voltage of QRS with flattened T waves, without much ST displacement. A nonspecific pattern but most suspicious of hypothyroidism. (From a patient with severe myxedema.)

29.2, page 455: (1) Sinus bradycardia with arrhythmia, rate 43 to 55. (2) Intra-atrial block (P-wave duration = 0.14 sec) with P-mitrale; note horizontal axis of P waves (+20°) with vertical axis of QRS (+90°)—this combination is highly suggestive of mitral stenosis. (From a patient with rheumatic heart disease.)

29.3, page 455: Abnormal nonspecific tracing because of ST-T abnormalities and inverted U waves (V_{5-6}). (From a 22-year-old man with rheumatic aortic and mitral regurgitation.)

30.1, page 478: (1) Acute anterior infarction. (2) RBBB. (3) Left anterior hemiblock.

30.2, page 478. Artificial pacemaker with dissociated atrial activity in the top strip; in bottom strip, 1:1 retrograde conduction (retrograde P waves produce sharp negative deformity at end of T-wave downstroke).

30.3, page 478: (1) RBBB. (2) Extensive anterior infarction of uncertain date, probably recent. (3) LA and RL electrodes reversed. (Whenever the tracing in a bipolar lead is a virtual straight line—as in lead 3—that lead is probably recording the potential difference between the two legs which is virtually nil; in this case the retaken limb leads—see below—reveal marked left axis deviation (−60°) indicating presumable left anterior hemiblock.)

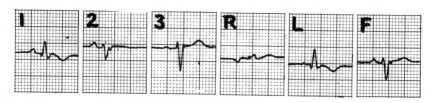

30.4, page 479: (1) Sinus bradycardia. (2) First degree A-V block. (3) Right bundle-branch block. (4) Right ventricular demand pacemaker, producing three fusion beats (last two beats in top strip and first in bottom strip.)

30.5, page 480: (1) P waves are inverted in 2, 3 and aVF, upright in aVR; this is therefore an ectopic atrial rhythm. (2) 2:1 A-V block (atrial rate 84, ventricular 42) with prolonged P-R in conducted beats, presumably type I block. (3) Left ventricular hypertrophy and strain. (4) Digitalis effect.

30.6, page 481: (1) Junctional rhythm. No P waves are visible preceding the QRS complexes; tiny notches are apparent at the very beginning of the ST segments in several of the leads—these are presumably retrograde P waves. (2) Acute inferior infarction.

Index

NOTE: All initial entries are nouns. Boldface page numbers refer to primary discussions.